Sheffield Hallam University
Learning and IT Services
Collegiate Learning Centre
Collegiate Crescent Campus
Sheffield    S10 2BP

NCE

# NE WEEK LOAN

Sheffield Hallam University
Learning and Information Services
Withdrawn From Stock

# Human performance:
# Cognition, stress and individual differences

**Gerald Matthews**

*University of Cincinnati, USA*

**D. Roy Davies, Stephen J. Westerman**

*Aston University, UK*

**Rob B. Stammers**

*University of Leicester, UK*

 **Psychology Press**
Taylor & Francis Group

HOVE AND NEW YORK

First published 2000 by Psychology Press
27 Church Road, Hove, East Sussex BN3 2FA

http://www.psypress.com

Simultaneously published in the USA and Canada
by Taylor & Francis
325 Chestnut Street, Suite 800, Philadelphia, PA 19106

Reprinted 2004 and 2008 by Psychology Press
27 Church Road, Hove, East Sussex BN3 2FA
270 Madison Avenue, New York, NY 10016

*Psychology Press is part of the Taylor & Francis Group, an Informa business*

© 2000 Gerald Matthews, D. Roy Davies, Stephen J. Westerman, Rob B. Stammers.

All rights reserved. No part of this book may be reprinted or
reproduced or utilised in any form or by any electronic,
mechanical, or other means, now known or hearafter invented,
including photocopying and recording, or in any information
storage or retrieval system, without permission in writing from
the publishers.

*British Library Cataloguing in Publication Data*
A catalogue record for this book is available from the British Library

*Library of Congress Cataloging in Publication Data*

ISBN 978–0–415–04407–3

Cover design by Jim Wilkie
Typeset in Hong Kong by Graphicraft Limited
Printed and bound in Great Britain by CPI Antony Rowe

This publication has been produced with paper
manufactured to strict environmental standards and with
pulp derived from sustainable forests.

SHEFFIELD HALLAM UNIVERSITY
WL
153
HU
COLLEGIATE LEARNING CENTRE

# Acknowledgements

We are grateful to Andy Bridges, Angus Craig, and Ann Taylor for their comments on various draft chapters. We also thank Bill Dember, Lisa Dorn, Ian Glendon, Dylan Jones, Raja Parasuraman and Joel Warm for their help in shaping our view of human performance, and for their valuable advice. Additionally, we are appreciative of the patience shown by Routledge and Taylor & Francis during the evolution of this book and are grateful for the helpful reviews of the material they solicited. Gerald Matthews would like to register special thanks to his graduate students, Sian Campbell, Paula Desmond, Shona Falconer, Lucy Joyner, and Abdalla Mohamed for their always insightful and sometimes provocative views on the subject. Roy Davies is indebted to Ruth Pickford for enabling him, many years ago, to embark on postgraduate work, and to Stephen Griew and the late Hywel Murrell for introducing him to the possibilities of human performance research.

# Contents

# List of tables

# List of figures

# Prologue

Performance is central to the lives of many of us, not only at work, but also when we drive a car, surf the internet or engage in sports. We are also dependent on the performance of others, as anyone who has endured a turbulent flight is aware. Psychology has had much to say about the central issues of performance, such as people's capabilities for succeeding with tasks, the roles of stress and emotion, and differences between individuals. However, the research literature has become increasingly scattered over the years. "Performance" variously identifies laboratory studies in the human experimental tradition, occupational performance and, as defined by *The Handbook of Human Performance* (Smith & Jones, 1992a), the effects of stress factors. None of these aspects of performance research fully reflects the diversity of the field, and we perceived a need for an introductory review of the area, balancing its different aspects.

In taking on this task, one of our inspirations was the work of Donald Broadbent, and his books on *Perception and communication* (1958) and *Decision and stress* (1971). Perhaps better than any subsequent researcher, Broadbent was able to demonstrate the interlinked support for psychological theory afforded by both laboratory and real-world studies, avoiding narrow "cognitivism". Especially in his later work, he also recognised the importance of stress and individual differences. However, performance research has changed dramatically since the times at which Broadbent wrote his two major books on the subject. Theoretical conceptions of performance have been invigorated by new developments such as cognitive neuropsychology, connectionism, and cognitive psychological research on emotion and individual differences. In applied psychology, there have been major developments in human factors, cognitive ergonomics and engineering psychology, encapsulated in Wickens' (1992) book on *Engineering psychology and human performance*. There is also increasing recognition of the contribution of performance concepts and data to other branches of applied psychology, such as clinical and health psychology.

In writing this book, we aimed both to maintain the Broadbentian tradition, and to accommodate, so far as possible, the many new developments in the field. To compile a compendium of relevant research would be an impossibly laborious task. The performance psychologist must be prepared to be something of a polymath with interests in several areas of psychology. Instead, we considered that the most useful resource for student and established researcher alike would be an outline of key empirical findings placed within an overall conceptual framework to bring some structure to the pandemonium of contemporary research. The framework we chose was contemporary cognitive science and, especially, the notion of multiple levels of explanation for cognitive phenomena.

Performance may be viewed variously as a biologically-based activity supported by neural systems, or as a consequence of information-processing "programs", or as the outcome of an intentionally-chosen strategy. In common with most researchers in the area, we place information-processing models at the centre of performance studies, but we aim also to signal the essential contributions of cognitive neuropsychology and conceptions of the performer as an active, intentional agent.

This book makes no claims towards comprehensive coverage of all research relevant to human performance. In particular, this book is a text neither of cognitive psychology nor of human factors. Instead, we have selected for review the topics related to cognition, stress and individual differences that we see as being at the core of performance psychology theory. Readers' understanding will be enriched by their knowledge of allied disciplines of cognition, neuroscience, emotional processes, differential psychology and applied psychology.

Following an introduction to performance psychology, the remainder of the book is organised as three sections. First, we review studies focusing on the cognitive basis for performance. We outline principles for constructing information-processing models of performance (Chapter 2), and their application to modelling some of the processing sub-systems of most interest to performance researchers (Chapter 3). The next three chapters review studies of attention, one of the central concepts in performance research. Chapter 4 looks at the problem of selection of information, whereas Chapter 5 is concerned with studies of divided attention, and what they reveal about the nature of capacity limitations on processing. Chapter 6 surveys research on sustained attention and the maintenance of vigilance during signal detection. Chapter 7 is concerned with models of skilled performance, and their application to cognitive and motor skills, and Chapter 8 with human error, especially as it relates to real-world environments. Second, we review effects of environmental stress factors on performance. An overview of theories of stress (Chapter 9) is followed by accounts of stress factors related to loud noise (Chapter 10), other physical stressors such as heat (Chapter 11), fatigue, circadian rhythms and sleep deprivation (Chapter 12), and aspects of lifestyle and health (Chapter 13). Third, we review individual and group differences in performance, focusing in turn on ability and intelligence (Chapter 14), personality and emotional state (Chapter 15), and the performance of the elderly (Chapter 16).

# 1

# Introduction

## 1.1 WHAT IS PERFORMANCE PSYCHOLOGY?

Human beings are born to perform. Many integral parts of our culture, such as education, work and sport, explicitly value successful performance. In a broader sense, we perform every time we engage in a goal-directed activity, from making a point in discussion with our friends to executing successfully the instructions on a cooking recipe. In contemporary Western society at least, the urge to perform successfully has been seen as a basic drive. The philosopher Marcuse (1955) dignified these strivings as "The Performance Principle", a drive similar to the pleasure principle of psychoanalysis. Similarly, motivation theorists have proposed a basic drive for behavioural competence, mastery over the environment, or need achievement, which may fuel our urges to perform (McClelland, 1961; Murray, 1938).

The psychology of performance seeks to understand the behaviours initiated by these strivings for competence, or even excellence. The primary aim is to understand the psychological processes that allow people to drive cars, pass examinations, carry out tasks at work and so forth. A focus on applications is more central to performance research than to many disciplines of psychology.

We wish to understand how people perform not only on contrived laboratory tasks, but also on the often complex tasks of the real world. Hence, a particular concern is the breakdown and failure of performance, illustrated most dramatically by the role of human error in car and plane crashes, and in industrial disasters such as Chernobyl. In addition, the accumulation of small inefficiencies in work performance may significantly influence national productivity and economic success. McClelland (1961) presented extensive evidence suggesting that the economic success of nations reflects the degree to which cultures value need achievement.

Performance psychology is directed towards real-life behaviour, but it is concerned with more than just a disconnected set of specific applications. As a branch of psychological science, it aims to understand the behaviour of people in the real world on the basis of rigorous, empirically testable psychological theory. The most useful theories have proved to be those of cognitive psychology, which describe how task performance depends on information processing. However, real-life performance depends not just on the task, but also on the influence of stress factors such as noise, heat and fatigue. Furthermore, individuals differ in their abilities and motivations when called upon to perform. Hence, performance psychology requires an integration of the formal models of cognitive psychology with an understanding of stress and individual difference factors.

Performance psychology overlaps to a considerable degree with both cognitive psychology and applied subjects such as ergonomics and human factors. However, it may also be seen as a distinct discipline. In this book, we envisage performance studies as supporting a distinct branch of psychological theory although, in many cases, it is theory with fairly direct application. The theory of human performance derives primarily from cognitive psychology, which is based on *the computational metaphor* for performance, discussed further in 1.3. The brain is considered to function like a computer, with groups of neurons performing logical operations or computations. Cognitive models use the computer metaphor to describe the encoding of incoming stimuli, the computations performed on the internal codes, and the eventual selection of a motor response. Modelling is fundamental to cognitive psychology, with the testing of models against empirical data providing the fundamental step in theory development. Performance psychologists often build and test such models. However, performance psychology may be distinguished from cognitive psychology in at least four respects: research aims, concern with "context", use of multiple levels of explanation, and applied relevance.

### 1.1.1 Aims of performance psychology

Both cognitive psychology and performance psychology investigate objective, measurable qualities of behaviour such as speed and accuracy of response. However, researchers have different motives for measuring reaction times and counting up errors in performance. For the cognitive psychologist, these indices of performance are a means to the end of understanding information processing, not an end in themselves. Speed and accuracy of response are relevant only in so far as they are informative about basic cognitive science questions such as the nature of mental representation or the relationship between language and thought. In contrast, the performance psychologist is interested in reaction time, for example, because speed of response is important in

everyday life—in working productively, in completing tests in a set time, and in reacting to hazards during driving. Of course, understanding the factors which control reaction time requires extensive laboratory work, and an understanding of cognitive models of response. The distinction between performance psychology and mainstream cognitive psychology is subtle and, in some respects, a matter of emphasis.

The difference in research aims relates to the distinction sometimes made between competence and performance. *Competence* refers to the fundamental capacity of the mind to perform some task or set of computations: cognitive psychology is concerned with what the mind *can* compute or, put differently, the limitations on processing (Pylyshyn, 1984). *Performance*, in this sense, refers to what the mind *does* compute in a given set of circumstances. Performance may fall short of competence if the person is tired or unmotivated, for example. Explaining performance requires both a model of competence (provided by cognitive psychology), *and* an understanding of how the expression of that competence in observable behaviour varies with factors such as stress and voluntary intentions.

### 1.1.2 Contextualisation of performance

Performance psychology is concerned especially with various "contextual" factors which may influence response. By contextual factors we mean factors additional to the task itself, which may be features of the external environment, or internal qualities of the person, such as their emotional state. In standard cognitive psychology, models are typically concerned with performance of specific tasks under laboratory conditions, but performance psychology requires a wider focus that takes in stress factors and individual differences. This approach entails more emphasis on emotional and motivational factors than is usual in cognitive psychology, to explain the effects of factors such as anxiety, fatigue and interest in the task. It may also be necessary to model biologically-based influences on performance, such as the caffeine, nicotine and alcohol that people consume in everyday life. Extending cognitive models in this way is challenging, as it is not always immediately obvious how the computer metaphor of cognitive psychology can be applied to real-world factors. One of the main themes of this book is that we need the wider perspective provided by contemporary cognitive science to organise our knowledge of influences on performance. A second theme is that the person is an active agent whose wishes and strategies shape their objective performance and subjective experience of task environments. Modelling voluntary control and strategy use is a further challenge for performance psychology, discussed further in 2.5.

### 1.1.3 Multiple levels of explanation

Performance psychology tends to place more emphasis on the use of several distinct levels of description or abstraction than does standard cognitive psychology, because of the requirement to understand contextual factors. Suppose we aim to understand why drivers commit errors. Cognitive psychology suggests that we should construct a model of how drivers encode stimuli such as traffic signs and other vehicles, and how they select steering and speed-control responses on the basis of this information. Such models can tell us which processes are error-prone in a given traffic situation, but they do not provide the full story. On the one hand, we may need to consider more abstract issues such as the driver's motivations to maintain safety, the extent to which "correct" driving is culturally valued, and so forth. Cognitions operate within a wider context, including the physical and social external environment, and intra-personal factors such as emotion, motivation and personality. On the other hand, we may need to understand the neural processes which support cognition; neuropsychological methods may provide a more fine-grained understanding of, say, attention to traffic signs or the stress imposed by the driving task. More generally, human performance psychology recognises that it is often valuable to investigate cognitive activity at more than one level of abstraction (Aleksander & Morton, 1993; Parasuraman, 1998a). Cognitive science provides a formal framework for distinguishing levels of description of cognitive phenomena, which we describe in section 1.3. Performance psychology often uses the "standard" information-processing models of cognitive psychology, but it seeks also to place these models within the larger perspective of real-world performance contexts.

### 1.1.4 Applied relevance

The wide scope of performance psychology lends itself to more direct practical application than much of cognitive psychology. Indeed, performance studies help to bridge the gap between the theoretical concerns of cognitive psychology and practical problems. Performance research overlaps with applied psychology, but here too there are significant differences in emphasis. Human performance psychology is not restricted to the study of applied settings, and draws evidence from both applied and laboratory-based studies. The search for basic principles that govern behaviour is central to the discipline, and human performance psychology considers applied evidence in parallel with controlled laboratory studies. Performance psychology can also be distinguished from the applied disciplines of human factors and ergonomics (see 1.4.1) because it maintains primary focus on the cognition of the individual, as opposed to the interface between the individual and technology.

In this chapter we first present a brief history of psychology as it relates to the study of human cognitive performance (1.2). We then introduce and evaluate the computer metaphor which provides the basis for cognitive psychology and cognitive science, and hence the theoretical basis for performance psychology (1.3). In section 1.4 we turn from theory to practice, and survey some of the applied disciplines to which performance psychology is allied. We conclude (1.5) by emphasising the multilevelled nature of performance psychology and outlining the topics covered by this book.

## 1.2 THE HISTORICAL ROOTS OF HUMAN PERFORMANCE PSYCHOLOGY

### 1.2.1 Pre-scientific conceptions of performance

Human performance psychology is not a new area of scientific enquiry. This section outlines its multidisciplinary heritage. The description of cognitive activity, including the development of models speculating covert cognitive processes, certainly dates back to ancient Greek times. For example, Hippocrates (460–377 BC) proposed physiological bases for personality and mental illness, involving the comparative predominance of four humours of the body (blood, black bile, yellow bile, and phlegm); Plato philosophised about the nature of knowledge and Aristotle (384–322 BC) developed hypothetical descriptions of many aspects of human cognitive activity, relating perception and understanding of the world to specific mental faculties. Although a rise in religiosity led to a decline in scientific thinking about cognitive processing during medieval times (Leahey, 1997), some continuation of the Aristotlean tradition persisted. The Persian physician and administrator, Avicenna (Ibn Sina) (980–1037), and St Thomas Aquinas (1225–1274) independently developed models of mental faculties, with Avicenna hypothesising a physiological basis for these faculties, believing (inaccurately) that they were housed in the ventricles of the brain.

In the late 17th century, Locke, the "father of empiricism", set the scene for the rise of behaviourism more than two centuries later, proposing that the human mind begins life as a "tabula rasa" and that knowledge is derived from experience. At this time, the philosophy of Descartes, although advocating the mind–body divide required by contemporary religious thinking, provided the basis for more mechanistic approaches to cognition. For example, Descartes' *representational theory of mind* proposed that we do not have direct access to reality but, instead, our understanding of the world depends on immaterial mental objects which the mind manipulates. This approach was extended by Hobbes' dictum that "all reasoning is but reckoning", that expressed the view that thought is a form of calculation. From the eighteenth century, notable advances were made with respect to models of human memory. Hartley (1705–1757), influenced by Newton's theory that nerve impulses were generated by the vibration of submicroscopic particles, proposed a theory akin to the notion of a "memory trace", suggesting that repeated sensory activation would lead to a stored copy

(of reduced magnitude) of the associated nerve impulse. Hume (1711–1776), influenced by Newtonian theories of attraction of objects (Leahey, 1997), proposed principles describing how ideas may become associated (see 2.3.1). "Lockean" empiricism and the concepts of association were extended successively by James Mill (1773–1836), and his son John Mill (1806–1873), with the latter proposing theories of the composition of ideas that resemble modern-day notions of automatic processing (see 3.3.1).

### 1.2.2 The origins of psychological science

Early in the 19th century, a more empirical approach was taken to the study of psychology. This change of direction was largely in response to scientific activity in other fields (e.g. physics, physiology), but later owed much to the development of university-based psychological laboratories, initially in Germany and subsequently in America. For example, Helmholtz (ca. 1850) designed techniques for assessing response time that allowed nerve conductance velocity to be determined, and proposed theories relating to the conservation of energy. Based on Helmholtz's work, F.C. Donders (1868) invented methods for the decomposition of cognition processes, using measures of reaction time. Weber, and subsequently Fechner, examined sensory discrimination at Leipzig University, and Weber's Law was developed, indicating that human cognition was concerned with relative rather than absolute sensory differences. In the latter part of the 19th century, the discipline of psychology became formally recognised with the establishment of the first psychological laboratory by Wundt, also at Leipzig. The brand of psychology pursued by Wundt and his students became known as the *structuralist* school, a term coined by one such student, E.B. Tichener. The structuralists aimed to discover elementary constituents of the mind through *introspection* of inner experiences. In America, structuralism was superseded by *functionalism*, in part due to the work of William James at Harvard, which was more concerned with action, and relationships between mental life and functioning in the outside world. Notable developments in experimental psychology towards the end of the 19th century included Herman Ebbinghaus' studies of memory and forgetting, using nonsense syllables, and Sir Francis Galton's studies of individual differences in ability to perform.

During the early part of the 20th century, especially in America, the behaviourist movement gathered momentum, becoming the dominant psychological paradigm. The behaviourists regarded the investigation of "mentalistic behaviour" as unnecessary and unscientific, taking the view that psychology should restrict itself to the study of observable patterns of stimulus and response (although as Leary (1990) points out, these are two of the most loosely interpreted terms in psychology). Introspection was replaced with rigorous experimental data, often from animal studies. Cognitive research continued to a limited degree: Bartlett's (1932) studies of memory showed that information is actively structured in the mind, for example.

Also important, during the early part of the 20th century, was the development of branches of applied psychology concerned with performance (Kanfer, Ackerman, Murtha, & Goff, 1995), and the application of scientific principles to the management of industrial workforces, notably by the industrial engineer, Fredrick Taylor (1856–1915). This eventually included the use of time-and-motion studies and psychometric testing of intelligence and job proficiencies, facilitated by large-scale military testing in the US during World War I. The use of psychometric testing became widespread, especially in the military, by the time of WWI. The war added its own impetus to psychology. Studies of individuals with localised brain damage caused by gunshot wounds facilitated the development of neuropsychology. The debilitating effects of "shell shock" highlighted the role of the emotional factors which would later be described as "stress", a term invented by Hans Selye in the 1930s.

Similarly, World War II provided a renewed impetus for the study of human cognition. It became apparent that some of the demands that were being placed on the human operator by complex new war technologies exceeded human capacities (Welford, 1968). Errors were being made in detecting U-boats on radar screens, flying aeroplanes, and so on, and it was important to find out why. It was apparent that behaviourist notions of learning had little to contribute. Many of these performance errors could not be attributed to motivational or training factors (Lachman, Lachman, & Butterfield, 1979). Researchers made progress by using the approach of modelling the user's activity in quasi-engineering terms, especially by identifying poor design. Lachman et al. (1979, pp. 56–57) give the example of a particular type of plane that often crashed when landing, because the braking lever was placed next to the lever that retracted the landing gear. At this time, K.J.W. Craik and F.C. Bartlett established the "Cambridge Cockpit" programme of laboratory studies at Cambridge University, that examined human performance under demanding conditions, representative of those experienced by war-time pilots (Sherwood, 1966). Studies of vigilance originated from the difficulties of radar operators in maintaining attention over time (Mackworth, 1948). Over the next decade, the disciplines of ergonomics and human factors were established, and the notions of the [hu-]man–machine system and human engineering came into being.

### 1.2.3 The cognitive revolution

Although cognitive research continued during the time of behaviourist dominance, the "cognitive revolution", a term attributed to William Dember, is usually dated to the 1950s. There was a growing recognition that behaviourist explanations of complex cognitive task performance were inadequate (Gardner, 1987; Hoffman, 1997). For example, with respect to language acquisition, Miller (1965, p. 19) pointed out that the application of punishment and reward as mechanisms by which language is acquired is "improbable and indirect" (p. 20), and therefore unlikely to promote learning in this context. At this time, interdisciplinary collaboration began to provide new ways of describing human cognitive behaviour. For example, links between psychology and engineering were strengthened, with engineering approaches to the description and quantification of information processing (Shannon & Weaver, 1949) being used as one method for describing the limits of human cognitive performance. The rapidly-developing discipline of computer science provided psychology with an enduring metaphor for describing cognitive behaviour, that of the digital computer. A 1956 symposium (at MIT) attended by Chomsky, Bruner, Newell, Simon and Miller was a key factor defining the application of the computer metaphor, and the rise of cognitive psychology (Gardner, 1987; Miller, 1985).

In the 1960s, formal analyses of cognition, such as Chomsky's language theory, and increasingly impressive demonstrations of artificial intelligence (AI) cemented the position of cognitive psychology as the dominant approach to explaining behaviour. This decade also saw a proliferation of information-processing models of various aspects of performance. Herbert Simon's work on emotion showed how cognitive processes might relate to domains traditionally considered "non-cognitive", including stress and individual differences (Matthews, 1997a). In the 1970s the discipline of "cognitive science" came into being (Aleksander & Morton, 1993; Anderson, 1993), combining philosophy, artificial intelligence, linguistics and psychology (Hoffman, 1997). More recently, connectionist approaches to the description of cognition have come to the forefront, based on parallel processing models. These models contrast with the serial processing models inspired by the computers of the 1950s, in which a single central processor perfomed a series of computations, one at a time.

## 1.3 THE COMPUTATIONAL METAPHOR FOR PERFORMANCE

### 1.3.1 Human information processing

There are many possible metaphors that describe human performance. For instance, K.J.W. Craik's writings include comparisons with valve amplifiers, petrol-driven compressors and telephone exchanges (Sherwood, 1966). However, perhaps the most fundamental metaphor in performance psychology is the description of human cognition in terms of information processing (Eysenck & Keane, 1995; Lachman et al., 1979). At its most basic, perhaps it is inaccurate to view this description as a metaphor (see Pylyshyn, 1984). It seems correct to say that human cognition *is* information process-

ing. Humans can be conceived as information-processing devices in the same way that a radio or a computer can be. However, within this broad framework there are many specific metaphors, and consequent specific models of performance.

We will come to the rather special example of the computer metaphor shortly. For the moment, let us consider information processing in a rather more generic sense, and take the example of a radio to illustrate some key elements of information processing descriptions. We may start by distinguishing between information content and the process by which it is transformed or transmitted. In the case of a radio, the information content might be the evening news or a drama series, but this content has no bearing on the process by which the information is transmitted. In either case, people speak into a microphone that transforms their voices into electrical signals, that can be relayed to a transmitter where the signals are transformed into radio waves, that are received by a radio set that transforms them into auditory information that we can hear. This example demonstrates two further important elements of the metaphor. First, human information processing can be described in terms of a number of stages during which information is transmitted or transformed. Second, the form in which information is represented may change during the process. In this example, information initially takes the form of variations in air pressure produced by the human voice. This information is then transformed into electrical signals, and conveyed through an electrical cable. It is then transformed into the radiowaves that are transmitted to your radio. At this stage it is transformed to its original acoustic form, i.e. variations in air pressure, that are emitted from the speaker of your radio for you to hear.

The information processing approach entails extending the behaviourists' "black box" approach to psychology, and describing cognition in terms of a number of stages through which information must pass, beginning with input (stimulus) and ending with output (response). At its simplest, information is received through the senses, transformed into an internal representation, and then transformed into a response. However, information processing descriptions of human performance can be considerably more complex, with several stages, or processes, hypothesised between input and output. The number and nature of intermediate stages depends on the particular theory; and as we will see, many have been proposed.

## 1.3.2 Application of the computational metaphor

In an extension of the information processing metaphor, extremely influential parallels have been drawn between human cognition and the way in which computers work. In pioneering work, Turing, a British mathematician, devised a theoretical "machine" that was capable of using binary symbols to calculate the answer to any problem that could be expressed in logically determinable fashion. Scientists rapidly began to realise the potential synergy that could be achieved through the combination of psychology and computer science (e.g. Craik, 1948). Many comparisons have been made, at this time and since, between the way in which computers process information and the way in which the human mind appears to do so.

To explore this metaphor further, we need to distinguish *software* and *hardware*. Software refers to the programs or sequences of instructions that the computer supports. The basis for software programming is symbol manipulation, i.e. the application of symbols to represent states of the world, and the specification of logical operations which act on symbols. For example, a business payroll program might define symbols ("variables") to represent employees' salaries. It then performs computations on the "salary" symbol, dividing it by twelve to find the monthly wage, deducting percentages for taxes and so forth. As Miller (1985, p. 3) has observed "... the ability to accept input symbols and generate output symbols, to store and erase them, to compare them and to branch according to the outcome of the comparison are the only kinds of building block required for the synthesis of intelligence ...". By analogy, the mind represents concepts by internal symbols, and performs stimulus analysis and response selection by performing computations on these symbols (Newell, 1990).

The software metaphor suggests a variety of constructs which may be used in models for human performance, such as codes, memory storage, search processes and other information structures and operations (Leahey, 1997). It also points to the importance of the internal structure of processing: what is the order in which processes operate and how do processes feed into one another? We can answer such questions for a computer program by drawing a flow-chart or some other representation of the sequence of processing. In the human case, we aim simultaneously to identify and discriminate different processing components, and to specify how they are inter-related within some larger "program". In doing so, we have to discover some of the larger design principles for mental software. For example, there is a long-running debate over whether the processing system carries out its computations in *series* or in *parallel*. Serial models assume that each operation is carried out a step at a time: the last operation must finish before the next one in the series commences, as happens in a conventional computer program. Parallel models, however, comprise multiple processors operating simultanously. There has also been considerable interest in whether a unified account of the general "software" principles can be formulated (e.g. Newell, 1990), or whether the programming is fundamentally untidy, with many special-purpose programs or "modules" patched together by natural selection on a somewhat ad hoc basis.

Descriptions of software need make no reference to the physical machine or *hardware*. Cognitive neuropsychologists wish to describe the neural systems that permit information processing. At the most fundamental level, brains resemble computers in their use of binary representations. The fundamental "machine code" of computers is expressed in binary (0s and 1s), and the neurons of the brain are either firing ("on") or resting ("off"). Baddeley (1997, p. 40) observed more general parallels between human and computer memories:

> "It did not ... escape the notice of two-process theorists that the architecture of computers typically involves two kinds of memory, a large-capacity long-term storage system, often using disk storage, and a

separate working memory system that has more rapid input and storage capabilities but which is much more limited in storage capacity, and this was used as further support for the plausibility of the two-component model of memory."

There are various techniques for investigating the neural bases for cognition, described further in 2.6, which may, in turn, feed back into understanding of information processing. Cognitive neuropsychology capitalises on the behavioural deficits of brain-damaged patients. Experiments may be devised to investigate how specific information-processing functions are affected by damage to the neurons in specific brain areas. For example, some patients show impaired long-term storage but normal short-term memory, whereas others show short-term memory impairment only, a *double dissociation* (Baddeley, 1986). Correlating type of impairment with the nature of the physical damage to the brain provides evidence on the localisation of memory functions in the brain. In addition, electrical recording techniques may be used to investigate brain activity during task performance: for example, brain imaging techniques might be used to see which brain areas are active as the person attempts to retrieve a memory (see Posner & Raichle, 1994).

In general, neuropsychological evidence suggests that the brain is similarly composed of a set of interconnected but distinct processing areas, performing specialised tasks. Brain areas for vision, hearing and certain language functions have been quite comprehensively mapped, though it is still controversial how higher-level cognitive functions such as thinking should be localised. This view of brain function is incompatible with early cognitive theories which assumed that most processing was performed by a single "central processor", akin to the first digital computers (Allport, 1989). Instead, the brain to some degree resembles contemporary computers, which have several independent processors or "chips"; there are separate chips which handle specialised tasks such as sending signals to the screen, or generating speech, for example. Martindale (1991) likens the brain to a large number of slow computers all operating in parallel, and each dedicated to a fairly specific task. Interest in parallel computing systems has stimulated interest in connectionist models that resemble neural networks (see 2.3.2). Hence, "neuropsychological plausibility" is a useful criterion for information-processing models to meet.

### 1.3.3 Limitations of the computer metaphor

As we will see in subsequent chapters, the computer metaphor has proved extremely useful in many areas of performance psychology. Nevertheless, the metaphor has attracted a variety of criticisms. First, there are a variety of philosophical issues (see Stillings et al., 1995, Chapter 8) which relate to traditional questions such as the mind–body problem. Further controversies concern relationships between information processing and brain states, the relationships between information-processing states and meaning, and the conscious experience of having mental states (*qualia*). Although these issues are important, they are removed from the immediate concerns of performance psychology.

Second, the metaphor may be broadly correct but unhelpful, because of the diversity of possible computational systems. Anderson (1990) has discussed the "identifiability problem": there may be a diversity of processing models, constructed on different principles, which will explain any given data set. There may be fundamental differences between the operation of the brain and the operation of even the most advanced parallel-processing computer. As Solso (1991, p. 26) has stated, "Unfortunately, what computers do well—perform high-speed mathematical functions, abide by rule-governed logic—humans do poorly, relatively speaking. And what humans do well—form generalisations, make inferences, understand complex patterns, and have emotions—computers do stupidly or not at all". The brain, of course, is an organ evolved through natural selection, and consequently its design principles may not be obvious. This criticism may be countered through development of neurologically-informed processing models, such as certain types of connectionist model (*computational neuroscience*).

Third, the computer metaphor may be appropriate to some psychological functions, but not to some of the essential attributes of humanity such as emotion, personality, creativity and intelligence (in the sense of adaptation to a complex and changing external world). We have already noted the difficulties of capturing conscious experience within computational models, and it is hard to see how a computer could experience emotions, or even how we would know if it did. Leaving these fundamental issues aside, cognitive models may have a surprising range of application. It is now well-established that emotional disorders are linked to particular styles of information processing, characterised by negative self-referent cognitions and irrational beliefs (Wells & Matthews, 1994). Oatley and Johnson-Laird (1987) have suggested that emotions constitute a primitive signalling system, working in conjunction with symbol-based processing. Personality too may relate to differences in the internal models people construct about themselves and their interactions with others (Hampson, 1988). Chapter 14 discusses how personality and mood appear to relate to information processing. In Chapters 8–12, we consider the effects of stress on objective performance; sometimes such effects reflect the person's cognitions of the task and its personal significance (Jones, 1984). Computers do not have feelings, but emotions and personality may nevertheless have a cognitive basis.

Fourth, the computer metaphor suggests undue passivity. Computers run programs instigated by an external agent, but people pursue goals actively and flexibly within complex environments. Neisser (1976) coined the term *perceptual cycle* to describe his dynamic view of cognition. A *schema* representing the person's beliefs about the external environment guides information-search and action, which in turn modifies the schema. In other words, control of behaviour resides in the dynamic interplay between person and environment, rather than in some fixed "program". This view resembles the ecological perspective usually attributed to J.J. Gibson. Information is structured by environmental "affordances": the opportunities and threats it provides. We should ask "not what is inside the head, but what the head is inside of" (Gibson, 1979). Our position here is that the computer metaphor should not be abandoned but,

especially in studies of real-world performance, internal processing should be seen as part of a broader cycle of interaction between person and environment (cf. Nelson, 1997).

None of these limitations should be seen as fundamental difficulties for the computer metaphor. The computational framework is useful for describing many aspects of human behaviour, and remains the only scientifically acceptable basis for conceptualising performance. However, we do need a certain sense of adventure in taking models beyond those suggested by the programs of a desktop PC. Maintaining the rigour of these wider-ranging models requires the formal framework for distinguishing levels of analysis provided by cognitive science, which we discuss next.

### 1.3.4 Levels of description of cognition

Cognition requires different levels of description. Rasmussen (1986), within the context of human–machine systems, suggests an "abstraction hierarchy" in which the highest levels describe the functional purpose of the system, while the lowest levels of abstraction are concerned with the physical structure of the system. If we take the example of the motor car, we can "view it from a distance", taking a generic overview, and see it as an object that carries people to their destination. Alternatively, we can "move closer" and describe it in terms of some of the processes it performs, e.g. we can concern ourselves with the fact that it requires petrol, that the steering wheel changes the direction of the road wheels, that the road wheels revolve, and so on. Finally, we could get even closer and look at the car at a "nuts and bolts" level and describe it in terms of the mechanical components that enable power to be delivered to the wheel. Choice of level of description depends on which qualities of cognition we wish to emphasise.

The so-called *classical theory* of cognitive science provides a formal account of three levels of description of cognition (Newell, 1982; Pylyshyn, 1984). There are three complementary ways in which we can describe any cognitive phenomenon, such as a person performing a task:

1. *The semantic or knowledge level*. This level is concerned with the guiding "intelligence"

of the system, and the meaning of behaviour. We can deal with these rather elusive qualities by focusing on the system's goals, its knowledge of how to achieve goals, and the principles through which goals influence the initiation and regulation of information processing. Subsequently, we will use Newell's (1983) term—knowledge —because it can signify the performer's knowledge of the personal significance of the task environment.

2. *The symbol level.* Computation requires symbolic representations which can be manipulated by explicit rules, such that applying the rule requires no insight into the purpose of the computation. A computer program expresses a computational routine of this kind. The models of information processing which are the cognitive psychologist's stock-in-trade are descriptions of symbol manipulation.

3. The *physical or biological level.* The "software" of the symbol level requires physical "hardware" for its operation which, in the case of humans, is the central nervous system.

Figure 1.1 illustrates Pylyshyn's (1984) levels in a little more detail. Conventional cognitive psy-

chological models are concerned with the intermediate, symbolic level. Pylyshyn subdivides this level into *algorithm* and *functional architecture*. The algorithm refers to the nature of the symbols and the logical operations capable of being performed on them: i.e. the data representations and instructions available for programming. For example, the different parts of speech in language might be represented by different types of symbol: attaching a verb to a noun would then be a computation performed using those symbols. By contrast, the functional architecture refers to the facilities available for carrying out computations in real time, such as, in speech comprehension, the memory space required to retain a sentence input while it is parsed and comprehended. In terms of the computer metaphor, consider the word-processing programs which are available for both PC and Macintosh computers. The algorithm is the same (barring trivial differences) in each case, because the program uses the same internal rules in responding to the user's commands on both machines. However, the functional architecture would be different because the Macintosh provides different real-time processing facilities. One might find that the program ran more quickly on one or other machine, or was prone to different kinds of errors ("bugs").

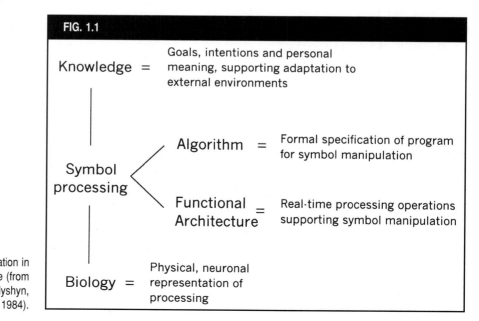

FIG. 1.1

Knowledge = Goals, intentions and personal meaning, supporting adaptation to external environments

Algorithm = Formal specification of program for symbol manipulation

Symbol processing

Functional Architecture = Real-time processing operations supporting symbol manipulation

Biology = Physical, neuronal representation of processing

Levels of explanation in cognitive science (from Newell, 1982; Pylyshyn, 1984).

Loosely, we can differentiate performance psychology from cognitive psychology (see 1.1) in terms of their concern with algorithm and functional architecture. Cognitive psychology is sometimes concerned with the algorithm alone. For example, models of language are often concerned with the formal nature of the computations performed on symbols representing verbal concepts: Chomsky's (1965) transformational grammar is a well-known example. Such algorithm-level issues may be investigated without reference to performance data, for example, by analysis of the properties of the grammars of different languages (although psycholinguists also use data from sources such as speech errors). By contrast, performance psychology is particularly concerned with computation in real-time, which requires understanding of both the algorithm and the functional architecture. Consequently, performance psychology often aims to model fairly simple tasks, so as to avoid some of the more complex algorithm-level questions, for example, by using single words or flashes of light as stimuli.

In this book, we take the view that a further key characteristic of performance psychology is its concern with the knowledge level as well as the symbol level: often, understanding real-world performance requires some insight into the person's aims and beliefs. The operator of a real-world system often has much more freedom of action than an experimental participant conforming to a precise protocol. In real life, performance frequently reflects the person's choice of goals and activities: drivers choose to break the speed-limit, factory workers choose not to over-exert themselves, emergency service personnel improvise new procedures to deal with crises, and so forth. These motivational factors require the perspective of the knowledge level. In laboratory work, we can often sideline the knowledge level by simply assuming that the person is motivated to perform the task set by the experimenter, so that performance variations tell us about the symbol level. However, in real-world contexts, the person's choice of goals, and means to achieve those goals, are important.

At the same time, performance cannot be conceptualised solely at the knowledge level. Motivational accounts tend to be over-general, and they have difficulty predicting objective indices of performance, such as reaction time, in detail. The behavioural consequences of pursuing a chosen course of action depend on the operation of information-processing routines, over which the person has only limited control. We can link the knowledge and symbol levels using the concept of *strategy* (Matthews, 1997a). At the knowledge level, strategy refers to the performer's choice concerning what goals to meet. There is considerable evidence suggesting that adoption of more ambitious goals tends to be associated with superior performance (e.g. Kanfer et al., 1994). Strategy choice is important for even the simplest tasks. Most laboratory tasks present the performer with decisions concerning whether to emphasise speed, at the cost of a greater likelihood of errors, or to focus on maintaining accuracy, even if response is relatively slow (the speed–error tradeoff: Pachella, 1974). As we shall see, more subtle strategic choices must be made also. At the symbol level, strategy choice refers to alternative "programs" (or attributes of programs) which can be run to perform a particular task. For example, the program controlling the behaviour of a cautious driver might contain routines for checking for certain hazards, routines perhaps missing from the program of a driver in a hurry.

The appropriate level of explanation depends on the particular research problem of interest. In devising a road safety advertising campaign, a knowledge level analysis of risky driving might be sufficient to indicate the motivations and attitudes which should be targeted. However, if the research aim is to investigate how risk-taking is expressed in specific behaviours such as neglect of peripheral information sources, we might need an information-processing analysis. We might also need the neural level of analysis, in that pathological risk-taking might be the consequence of some brain dysfunction feeding into maladaptive processing. In sum, we need to be able to look at performance from three distinct standpoints: the aims and goals of the performer, the formal rule-based processing which supports performance, and the neural hardware underlying symbolic computation.

## 1.4 APPLICATIONS OF PERFORMANCE PSYCHOLOGY

Thus far, we have focused mainly on the theoretical basis which cognitive science provides for performance psychology. However, as we saw in 1.2.2, in this century much of the impetus for studies of performance has been provided by practical problems, such as helping people to use complex equipment and information technology, to resist stress and fatigue and to make best use of their personal aptitudes and interests. In fact, despite differences in aims and emphases, performance psychology has enjoyed fruitful partnerships with both cognitive and applied psychology, which have enriched each area of study. Donald Broadbent, one of the dominant figures of all three fields, saw much of his theoretical work on cognition as initiated by problems in real-life settings, such as work. As Broadbent (1971, p. 4) stated, "The detection of faint stimuli is a function used by sonar operators and industrial inspectors; the forgetting of telephone numbers, through its impact on the amount of telephone switch-gear and other equipment tied up unproductively in wrong numbers, is a matter of some economic importance". Most often, interventions intended to enhance performance have derived from understanding processing constraints (cognitive architecture) or the operator's intentions, but there is currently increasing interest in biologically-based interventions. Parasuraman (1998b) has coined the term *neuroergonomics* to refer to direct ergonomic application of biocognitive research: Table 1.1 lists some examples.

Broadbent would have agreed that "nothing is so practical as a good theory": validated models of cognition enable the prediction of human performance in "real world" settings. The close link between theory and practice in the human performance field continues to be important. Whilst theory will still be developed and tested in an abstract form, there are also many examples where theory is put into practice in this field and, in turn, real world problems will continue to present problems for interpretation and solution. There is

### TABLE 1.1

**Examples of "neuroergonomic" research work (adapted from Parasuraman, 1998b).**

Using knowledge of brain mechanisms and neuro-chemical systems that control circadian rhythms to devise optimal schedules for shift work or to minimise circadian disruption due to travel across time zones.

Developing electroencephalographic or functional brain imaging measures of mental workload during complex, multi-task performance so as to optimise the design of human-machine systems.

Applying knowledge of brain and cognitive architectures to develop "neural chips" that could produce intelligent user interfaces with exceptionally fast computing systems. These could be used to develop "neuroergonomic aids" for the physically incapacitated.

Using new insights into the computational and neural basis of spatial navigation to develop improved virtual reality systems.

a healthy interchange between basic and applied research (Warr, 1996a). Good theories will help in solving problems, but may not be a complete answer. Thus shortcomings can be fed back into basic research for further study, and the reciprocal relationship of basic and applied research continues. As we will see in subsequent chapters, in many situations it is important to predict performance at both the overall "molar" level, and the more fine-grained "molecular" level of component processes.

In principle, performance psychology may contribute to many, diverse areas of applied psychology. Understanding the mechanics and capacities of human performance helps the clinical psychologist to understand disorders of cognition; it enables sports psychologists to advise sports people on optimal training regimes; and it helps educational psychologists in developing valid tests of academic learning. Historically, though, performance psychology has been applied most extensively to industrial and organisational psychology. Topics such as skill acquisition, human error, performance under stress and selection of high-performance individuals all have direct relevance to the workplace. In the remainder of this section, we indicate the practical relevance of performance psychology to three areas of organisational psychology (although this book does not aim to review applications in detail).

## 1.4.1 Ergonomics and human factors

The applied side of the subject contributes to the interdisciplinary field of *ergonomics*, which studies the interaction of technology and its human users. The objective is to promote the safe and efficient utilisation of technology. As well as psychology it also encompasses physiology and anatomy. One of the basic concepts of ergonomics is that of compatibility between person and system. The main use of the term was originally with reference to the response of a display, say the needle of a dial, moving in the "expected" direction, after operation of a control. Early studies showed this expected movement would be left-to-right for a clockwise movement. However, the concept of compatibility can now be broadened out from these expectations to include ideas such as:

(i) the compatibility of a computer screen display with the user's mental model of the activity being displayed;

(ii) the "fit" of an office chair to a user's body dimensions;

(iii) the compatibility of the force needed to operate a door handle with the person's physical strength;

(iv) the compatibility of an in-car navigation device with the driver's normal strategies for scanning the traffic environment.

A broad view needs to be taken of "technology" in this context, as it can range from the simple printed word or symbol and its interpretation, through to a highly complex machine such as an aircraft, and its safe and expeditious piloting. It is becoming clear that the possibilities for the use of technology will be limited by the extent to which human characteristics are catered for. In turn, the safety of any use of technology is also heavily influenced by the potential it contains for human error.

Application of our understanding of human performance can operate in two ways. One way is "fitting the job to the person", which focuses on designing the technology to fit human capacities as described above. This area of research is also known as *human factors* (Meister, 1989). In recent years, there has been considerable interest in the ways in which constraints on information processing limit the person's ability to work with machines and technology (e.g. Wickens, 1992). Research of this kind is described as *engineering psychology*. It is based on cognitive theory, but aims to use that theory in the design of technology by capitalising on the user's capabilities, and "working around" the user's limitations. As Stanton (1996) pointed out, in a special issue of *The Psychologist* on engineering psychology, the practical problems addressed by engineering psychology range from the trivial but aggravating, such as programming a video recorder, to those crucial for safety, such as the design of systems for nuclear power plants.

The second approach is "fitting the person to the job". Here, human performance findings can be used in a variety of ways. What we know about how people learn skills helps in the design of training programmes (Schneider, 1985). For example, the need for effective and safe practice environments has led to the development of simulators for training. Our knowledge of individual performance in tasks will help in the design of tests for selecting people for jobs—another form of compatibility. Sometimes those tests will indicate different learning needs that people have and training can be designed to take this into account (see Chapter 7).

Ergonomics and human factors are concerned with both the fine detail of people's work performance and broader aspects of the person's contribution to the organisation. An individual might be superb at task performance, but a liability to the organisation, if he or she is frequently absent or continually provokes conflicts with coworkers. Figure 1.2 illustrates Blumberg and Pringle's (1982) theory of work performance, which represents these wider concerns. Blumberg and Pringle identify three factors determining work

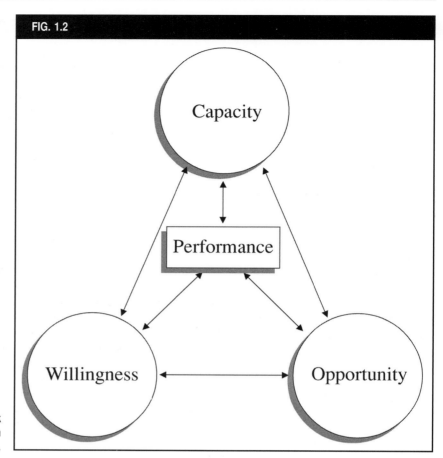

FIG. 1.2

Determinants of work performance (from Blumberg & Pringle, 1982).

performance. The first is *capacity* (C), which refers here to all the basic characteristics that promote good performance, such as intelligence, learned skills and physical fitness. This definition lumps together a variety of qualities which performance psychologists would normally wish to distinguish, but to which organisational psychologists must, necessarily, adopt a broad-brush approach for practical reasons. The second is *willingness* (W), referring to motivational and attitudinal factors which may allow the person to use their capacities to full advantage, or, alternatively, hinder them in fulfilling their potential. The third factor, *opportunity* (O), refers to the physical and social environment provided by the organisation: workers need the right tools and social support to give of their best. Performance reflects the interaction of these three factors, so the determinants of work performance can be expressed as follows:

$$\text{Performance} = f(O \times C \times W)$$

## 1.4.2 Stress and wellbeing

A second application of performance psychology concerns the relationship between stress and performance in the workplace. Stress is important as both a cause and a consequence of workplace performance. It is popularly supposed that stress impairs attention, memory and action, and extreme forms of stress such as "burnout" and clinical anxiety and depression are often detrimental to performance (e.g. Wells & Matthews, 1994). However, it is simplistic to view stress simply as a performance deficit factor, and experimental studies have played a major part in determining which forms of stress are most damaging.

Stress is commonplace at work. Survey data show that 67% of US workers report that their work is either moderately or very stressful— although the same survey also showed that 89% were at least somewhat satisfied with their work (Wirthlin Worldwide, 1999). As discussed in 7.4, stress may contribute to accident likelihood. Stress may also affect the "willingness" as well as the "capacity" aspect of work performance, through promoting resentment, loss of motivation and absenteeism. Wellbeing and performance may be degraded through stress-related health problems. Figure 1.3 shows data from the Second European Survey on Working Conditions (European Founda-

tion for the Improvement of Living and Working Conditions, 1996), based on questions put to a representative sample of 15,500 workers from all the European Union nations. Stress, and related problems such as fatigue, irritability and anxiety, are highly-ranked as health problems. The costs to industry of accidents, reduced productivity, workdays lost through illness and absenteeism and worker compensation are considerable. The International Labour Organization (1996) estimates that stress-related illness and absenteeism cost the United Kingdom economy the equivalent of 10% of GNP, i.e. approximately 100 billion dollars. Likewise, the annual costs in the US may be as high as several hundred billion dollars annually, although these estimates are very imprecise (Karasek & Theorell, 1989).

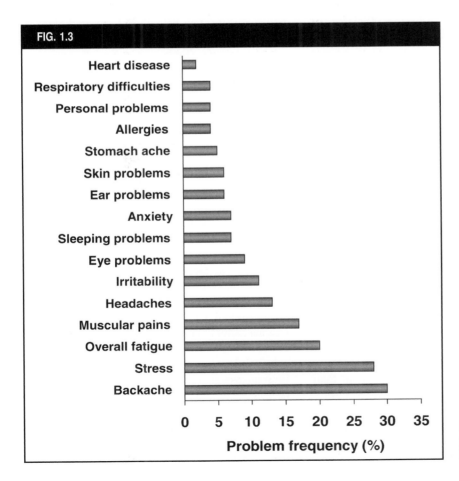

**FIG. 1.3**

Incidence of health problems at work in a European Union sample.

Stress is a rather nebulous term, which is used to refer to a variety of qualitatively different physiological, subjective and behavioural reactions. At the least, we must distinguish between external sources of stress (*stressors*) and the person's internal reactions. Some of these reactions may actually be beneficial. Stressors may have an arousing, energising effect, or they may be perceived as challenges to be overcome: some people may produce their best work under pressure. Stress is also difficult to conceptualise theoretically: accounts of stress refer to all three levels of explanation (see Chapter 9). At the neural level, stress may be seen as a set of biological responses to challenging stimuli. Acute stress reactions are reflected in central and autonomic system response, whereas over the longer term there may be changes in circulating hormones and immune system function. At the level of the cognitive architecture, stress may influence efficiency of information processing and, at the knowledge level, stress may be related to motivations and beliefs about the self. Transactional models of stress (Lazarus & Folkman, 1984) are expressed primarily at the knowledge level. They emphasise the person's active attempts to manage or cope with external demands, on the basis of their significance to the individual.

According to the transactional model (Lazarus & Folkman, 1984), performance and stress are dyamically interrelated. Stress reactions may impair or enhance performance, but performing demanding tasks is itself a source of stress. There is a large literature that shows that effects of stress factors on performance vary with the information-processing demands of the task (Hockey, 1984). Environmental stressors such as noise and heat may have differing effects on attentional and working memory tasks, for example. The nature of the stress response also controls performance change. Studies of test anxiety show that performance on examinations is more vulnerable to worry, a cognitive stress symptom, than to emotional aspects of anxiety such as tension (Zeidner, 1998). Hence, dealing with workplace stress as a practical problem requires a detailed understanding of how different aspects of stress influence different types of task.

Stress may also be a *consequence* of performance. Even short laboratory tasks may elicit substantial changes in subjective tension and energy (Matthews et al., 1999b). Prolonged excessive workloads may lead to the burnout syndrome of emotional exhaustion and cynicism (Maslach & Jackson, 1981), or even, according to Japanese studies (Tsuda et al., 1993), to health problems and the death of the employee. The combination of high workload and lack of control over work activities is particularly detrimental to wellbeing (Karasek & Theorell, 1989). Stress research shows that even relatively minor "daily hassles" may have adverse effects (Kohn, 1996), and the workplace is often a rich source of such hassles, ranging from equipment failures to arguments with coworkers and supervisors. Broadly, stress reactions may follow both from the demanding nature of the work itself and from the more general organisational climate. The potential of the workplace to cause stress is often expressed in terms of *person–environment fit* (French, Caplan, & Harrison, 1982): work activities should match the person's abilities and interests, without offending their values and principles. In sum, the enlightened employer aims for both high productivity and employee job satisfaction, and performance studies may contribute to both of these goals.

### 1.4.3 Individual differences: Selection and assessment

Any study of performance will reveal differences between individuals in speed and/or accuracy. People differ also in stylistic variables such as willingness to respond, and preference for speed over accuracy. In applied contexts too, it is often important to identify individuals who are unproductive or who are prone to make dangerous or costly errors. Individual differences are associated with various factors, including cognitive aptitudes such as general intelligence, personality and mood variables, and ageing (see Chapters 14–16). Organisations assess the performance of individuals so as to recruit able trainees, to track performance change during training, and to monitor the contributions of existing personnel. Performance psychology contributes to assessment in conjunction with other disciplines, notably *psychometrics*, the science of measuring human qualities reliably and validly (see Anastasi & Urbina, 1997, for a review). There is more to assessment than measuring task performance, because the process is concerned with both "capacity" and "willingness" factors: employees must be both able and willing to perform effectively.

A basic problem in developing valid assessment procedures is deciding what "work performance" actually means, i.e. what criterion or criteria of good performance to use (Guion, 1997). Campbell, McCloy, Oppler and Sager (1993) list eight separate factors which may contribute to good overall performance, shown (as modified by Guion, 1997) in Table 1.2, although not all factors are necessarily relevant to any individual job. These factors relate both to Blumberg and Pringle's (1982) capacities (e.g. task proficiencies) and to willingness (e.g. personal discipline). Performance psychology can thus make an important but incomplete contribution to assessment. Studies of performance can tell us how to assess proficiency on various tasks, and how measurements may be influenced by additional factors such as effort and stress. However, assessment of qualities such as teamwork and leadership must draw on other disciplines such as social psychology.

In fact, the contribution of performance psychology depends on the philosophy for selection and the various techniques used, most of which have at least some validity (see Anderson & Herriot, 1997). Assessment may be performed without direct reference to objective performance measurement at all, for example, through using interviews or

---

**TABLE 1.2**

**A taxonomy of higher order performance components in the workplace (adapted from Campbell et al., 1993; Guion, 1997).**

1. *Job-specific task proficiency*
   Proficiency in the performance of the job's central substantive or technical tasks.

2. *Non-job-specific task proficiency*
   Proficiency in general tasks performed by virtually everyone in an organization or in a group of related jobs within the organization.

3. *Written and oral communication task proficiency*
   Proficiency in tasks requiring use of language, whether formal oral or written presentations to a group or interpersonal communication.

4. *Demonstrating effort*
   Consistency of effort, expending extra effort as needed, and persistence in working even under adverse conditions.

5. *Maintaining personal discipline*
   Avoidance of negatively valued behaviour: alcohol and substance abuse at work, violating laws or rules, excessive absenteeism etc.

6. *Facilitating peer and team performance*
   Supporting and helping peers as a de facto trainer; facilitating group functioning by example, by keeping focus on goals.

7. *Supervision/leadership*
   Influencing subordinate performance by setting goals, teaching, being a good model, and appropriate use of reward and punishment.

8. *Management/administration*
   Management functions broader than direct supervision.

*biodata*, items of biographic information such as educational level and home ownership. It may also seek to assess relatively complex tasks considered representative of real work, most directly through *work sample tests* which require the applicant to perform an actual work task under standard conditions. Applicants may also be required to perform a variety of relevant tasks in *assessment centres*, over an extended period, perhaps of several days. This technique allows the person's motivations and resistance to stress to be observed, typically in a group setting. Techniques of this kind are somewhat removed from the central concerns of performance psychology because they make little or no reference to psychological theory, although they may capitalise on methodological advances arising from performance studies.

A further philosophy is to measure various stable characteristics of the person thought to be relevant to the job, such as intelligence, personality and integrity. In this case, performance studies are often of central importance. Ability testing uses objective tasks to assess various aptitudes including general intelligence, and more specialised aptitudes such as verbal, spatial and mechanical abilities. The objective test score may be used directly to select individuals who attain a given level of competence. Traditionally, such measures have been derived from paper-and-pencil tests, but there is growing use of computerised performance tests which measure specific, theoretically-derived cognitive functions. Aspects of personality and motivation related to work performance may be assessed using standard questionnaires (Matthews, 1997b), as further discussed in 14.5. Here, performance studies have a role to play, in that questionnaires should be validated in terms of their capacity to predict objective task performance under controlled conditions, although it is equally important to show that questionnaires predict other relevant criteria such as vocational choice and measures of global work performance (Furnham, 1992).

## 1.5  CONCLUSIONS

This chapter has described how performance psychology represents a distinct discipline at the intersection of theoretical cognitive psychology and the applied study of real-world tasks.

Performance theory aims to cover the whole spectrum of real and artificial tasks, and the various factors which influence task-related behaviours in real-world settings. Central topics in performance psychology are the development of information processing for simple and complex tasks, investigating the impact of stress factors on performance, and mapping individual and group differences. Cognitive science provides the main theoretical basis for the field, comprising not just standard information-processing models, but an appreciation of neural and "knowledge-level" levels of explanation.

Thus, we need a variety of approaches to the subject, including an understanding of how people's performances are shaped by their strategies and personal goals. Theory should delineate the information-processing circuitry that underpins performance, and the neural processes which support information-processing. The multilevelled nature of performance psychology is important at the practical level too. Knowledge of the operator's intentions and strategic goals assists design of technology (human factors), and individual differences in motivation are important for personnel selection and assessment. Workplace stress management techniques, such as training in coping skills, often aim to guide the person towards realistic goals which they can accomplish. Information-processing models are central to the engineering psychology, as a subdiscipline of human factors. Such models also inform assessment of work performance and cognitive techniques for combating stress. Neuroergonomic techniques based on understanding of the brain processes which support performance may become increasingly important.

## FURTHER READING

Posner's (1989) edited volume provides a good overview of contemporary cognitive science, including an introduction to the concept of levels of explanation (Pylyshyn, 1989). Applications of performance psychology to human factors are discussed in texts by Sanders and McCormick (1993) and Proctor and Van Zandt (1994). Hancock (1997) has written an engaging and provocative account of the social implications of new technology in the workplace. Broadbent's books on *Perception and communication* (1958) and *Decision and stress* (1971) were enormously influential in shaping human performance research, and demonstrate the interdependence of theoretical and applied research. Baddeley and Weiskrantz's (1993) edited book, which honours Broadbent's contribution to psychology, refers to several key areas of performance research.

# 2

# Modelling the cognitive architecture

## 2.1 COGNITIVE MODELS OF PERFORMANCE

Performance psychology is built on the foundation provided by theories of cognition and information processing. In this section of the book, we look at the explanations for performance which cognitive theory provides. One of the peculiarities of cognitive psychology is that it is a science of the unobservable. We can never directly read off the internal symbols or program steps of the mind in the way we can read the lines of a computer program. Hence, "explanation" in cognitive psychology is closely related to the development of *models* of cognition. The basic technique of cognitive psychology is to construct a model of the cognitive activities that supports performance on a given task or family of similar tasks. The model resembles a computer program in that it specifies in detail how information is processed. It must include a description of how cognitive processes, that cannot be directly observed, influence measurable performance variables such as reaction time and frequency of errors. We accept the model as an accurate account of cognition only if it successfully predicts how human participants will perform on the task or tasks concerned.

The purpose of modelling is not just to explain isolated pieces of data, but to discover general principles of the organisation of cognitive processes and, ultimately, a detailed description of the complete processing system. In this chapter, we outline principles of modelling, and discuss some of the organisational issues which models address. We begin with an account of methods for investigating cognition (section 2.1); then in 2.2, we discuss the components used to construct models of the internal programming, and ways in which these components may be "connected up" to control the flow of processing. Section 2.3 develops the theme of control of processing further, by describing parallel processing models in which there is no separate processor for handling control. In performance psychology, it is important to determine not just the formal logical structure of the internal software, but the constraints on its successful operation. As with computers, the functioning of software may be limited by the processing capacity and facilities provided by the hardware. In 2.4 we consider the problem of limited capacity, and the related issue of whether processing requires some kind of "energisation" to operate. In the final sections of this chapter we develop the point made in 1.3, that information-processing models may be necessary but insufficient to explain the full range of influences on performance, such as stress factors. Sometimes, we must accommodate the person's goals and intentions as influences: section 2.5 looks at how we can model voluntary control of performance and strategy. Section 2.6 briefly addresses questions relating to the neural hardware level by looking at some of the principles of cognitive neuropsychology and cognitive psychophysiology.

This chapter aims to introduce the principles of constructing cognitive models: in the next chapter we go on to discuss how these principles have been applied in developing models of processing systems central to performance, such as those controlling attention and memory. We emphasise that this chapter provides an outline account of cognitive theory only: the reader should refer to a cognitive psychology or cognitive science text for more background in this area.

### 2.1.1 Measuring cognitive processes

If we accept the premise that there are a number of *covert* cognitive processes that intervene between the input and output stages of the human information processing system, how are these to be measured? Historically, there has been extensive debate over the relative worth of subjective and objective assessment of cognition. As mentioned in 1.2.2, around the turn of the 20th century, structuralist psychologists (e.g. Wundt, Titchener) used the technique of *introspection* as the fundamental technique available to psychology. Trained observers reflected on the nature and course of their sensations, emotions and thoughts. It was thought that introspection provided a direct indication of the contents of conscious awareness, including motivations, and contextual factors which may influence cognition. However, introspection lacks the objective rigour required of experimental methods. First, it can be argued that people are not aware of all cognitive processing. It is hard to report processes with a time-scale of less than a second or two, which limits the use of

introspection in many areas of performance psychology. People also have little insight into motor processing; it is difficult to describe in detail how one rides a bicycle or even walks. Second, some mental events, such as experiencing a mental image, are accessible to consciousness but difficult to describe in words. Third, even recent events, such as a complex chain of thought, may be difficult to maintain in memory. Asking participants to report on their thoughts has been shown to disrupt problem-solving (Schooler, Ohlsson, & Brooks, 1993). Fourth, introspection may not be accurate, even though the person feels confident that they are reporting their thoughts accurately.

The problem of unconscious bias in self-report was demonstrated by Nisbett and Wilson (1977). They reviewed various studies in which objective data show that some external factor influenced behaviour, but participants denied being influenced by the external factor, and offered an alternative account. For example, when participants were presented with five essentially identical pairs of stockings laid out in a line, they tended to judge the right-most pair as being those of the best quality. However, virtually all participants denied that the spatial position of the stockings influenced their judgement; they were simply unaware of how their preferences originated. Nisbett and Wilson suggested that during introspection participants (unconsciously) construct a plausible explanation for their thoughts after the event, an explanation which does not necessarily describe the information processing that actually took place.

### 2.1.2 Modelling objective data

Given the difficulties of subjective accounts of cognition, most performance research attempts to develop information-processing models for objective data. The procedure is one of *reverse-engineering*. We assume there is a program "in the head" that controls performance on a given task, but we cannot observe the program instructions directly. The problem is then to work out a description of the program by taking objective measurements of the person's performance under different task conditions. We test our program description by showing that it predicts real, objective data. For example, Rumelhart and Norman

(1982) developed a simulation of touch-typing which fairly accurately reproduced the errors made by human typists. It is also highly desirable that models make novel predictions which can be tested experimentally; there is a danger that models may fit existing data not because they are correct, but because the researcher has been able to "tweak" model parameters to obtain good fit.

Models are often *chronometric* in nature, i.e. they predict how long it will take a real person to perform a particular task (see Posner, 1978). In the simplest case, models are intended to explain performance on variations of perhaps just one basic task, such as searching a display for a single-letter target, or memorising pictures of objects. However, one of the fundamental difficulties of cognitive modelling is that we can usually find several ways to explain performance on any given task, i.e. we can write alternative "programs" which produce the same outputs. Anderson (1990) refers to this as the *identification problem*. There is no simple solution to this problem, but it can be partially addressed by requiring the model to explain performance (usually measures of speed and accuracy) on several different versions of a task. For example, we might require a reaction time (RT) model to explain the increase in RT as the number of response alternatives increases.

In some cases, the model may be expressed mathematically, or it may be simulated as a computer program so the researcher can see exactly what predictions the model makes. The model can then be falsified by observed data, leading to rejection of models that fail to gain empirical support (Popper, 1959). Some cognitive researchers see this standard hypothesis-testing procedure as being unduly destructive (Newell, 1990). The underlying principles of the model might be correct, but it might fail due to a relatively minor misspecification of some part of the program. Newell (1990) believes that over-emphasis on falsification results in psychology moving from one dichotomy to another, e.g. serial vs parallel processing. Instead, he proposes "nurturing" of theories and models as a more constructive approach, in which models are "refined and reformulated, corrected and expanded" (p. 14) according to empirical evidence. Other approaches include setting up direct comparative tests of competing models, and attempting to derive new and unexpected predictions from models.

Models may be intended not just to explain data from particular tasks, but to investigate general principles of the internal programming. For example, traditional cognitive psychology is based on the symbol-processing level of description discussed in 1.3.4, leading to models that look very much like conventional computer programs, and which can be expressed as flow-charts describing the succession of computations performed on input data. In a conventional computer program, one instruction is executed at a time, and the next instruction executes only when the previous one has completed. *Serial stage* models of cognition follow this principle. We can also design *parallel processing* computers in which information passes freely between multiple processors. Similarly, human information processing may operate on the principle of parallel processing. Connectionism refers to a special case of parallel models in which each processor can perform only the very simple operation of transforming analogue inputs into an output according to some internal rule or algorithm, as discussed in 2.3.2. Connectionist models have been influential because simulations have demonstrated that these models can perform fairly complex cognitive operations without requiring a supervisory control process. In addition, increased recognition of the need for different levels of description of cognition has generated a variety of innovative models. Cognitive neuroscience models aim to describe the neural "hardware" as well as the processing "software" (see 2.6). Models of human error (e.g. Reason, 1988) are increasingly concerned with the person's intentions and motivations as a source of error. Error cannot be attributed solely to faulty software, but also to the person's adaptation to a wider context (see Chapter 8).

### 2.1.3 Applications of self-report

Despite the limitations of introspection, self-report methods are still used by psychologists to evaluate some aspects of cognitive performance. *Verbal protocols* are one such technique that requires an individual to give a constant verbal description of their current on-task performance. This method has been particularly successful in studies of problem-solving, in which it tends to be the person's qualitative insights into the problem that are critical, as opposed to the speed of execution of individual component processes (e.g. Newell & Simon, 1972). Verbal protocols are often used with the context of human-machine systems, and potentially provide an insight into the way in which the operator conceptualises the system. It has been suggested that this may be "the single most valuable usability engineering method" (Nielsen, 1993, p. 195), in that, whilst the results obtained are not readily quantifiable, they can provide a wealth of information relating to the strengths and weaknesses of particular system designs. A number of variations on this method have been developed, e.g. retrospective testing (the operator gives a verbal "walk-through" of performance previously recorded on video) and codiscovery (two operators "codiscover" a system, and data are gathered from the communication between the two).

Self-reports may also provide a valuable means of obtaining data from real-world situations, such as accidents in transportation and industry. Studies of human error (see Chapter 8) have used *diaries* to investigate mistakes in everyday life. *Questionnaire measures* are important in studies of stress and individual differences. For example, the Cognitive Failures Questionnaire (CFQ: Broadbent, Cooper, Fitzgerald, & Parkes, 1982) aims to identify people who are particularly prone to make errors in perception, memory and action, although, as discussed in Chapter 8, its validity is controversial. Constructs of personality, emotion and motivation are, of course, primarily assessed through self-report (see Chapter 15). Finally, it may be possible to measure some general aspects of cognition through self-report. *Workload*, the overall level of demand imposed by a task, is frequently measured through subjects' ratings of demands, effort, task-imposed stress etc. (e.g. Hart & Staveland, 1988), as discussed further in 5.4.

## 2.2 FUNDAMENTAL CONSTRUCTS OF COGNITIVE MODELS

Thus far, we have seen that the principal technique of cognitive psychology is the construction of models which can be tested against objective performance data. So, how do we build models? In this section, we aim to describe the basic building blocks or components of cognitive models, and the principles on which sets of processing components operate to enable performance. In doing so, we are working with the constructs of Pylyshyn's (1984) symbol processing level (and especially those of the algorithm sub-level: see 1.3.4). The aim of modelling is generally to describe the computations performed on internal symbols or codes as explicitly as possible. Modelling the time-course of computation in detail generally requires that we also model aspects of the functional architecture: the memory space, communication channels and so forth that allow the "program" to run in real time.

### 2.2.1 Processing codes

Models of symbol processing begin with the fundamental distinction between strings of symbols and the operations performed on those symbols. In other words, we must distinguish the internal program from the data on which it operates. A processing model begins with some input data, supplied by sensory or perceptual processing. Operations are then performed on those data, transforming them into new data. Eventually, some output, such as a response is produced. One of the fundamental concepts required for building and understanding models is the idea of *codes* for representing data. The stimuli which impinge on our senses are extremely rich, and a variety of different kinds of information may be extracted from them. Imagine that you are looking at an advertisement in a newspaper. From a superficial glance you might notice the colours used, the objects depicted, or the standard meanings of any words included. From more prolonged inspection you might pick up the quality of execution of the design, more subtle meanings and emotional connotations. The same stimuli may be encoded in different ways. Stimuli typically have multiple attributes or qualities, and the assumption of information-processing models is that there are different internal codes to represent different attributes, such as colour, meaning and so forth.

Inherent within models of human information processing is the concept of different processing codes. For example, if we think of the input to the cognitive system, we can draw a clear distinction between the form, or code, in which auditory information is presented and the form, or code, in which visual information is presented. On this basis, just in terms of our basic five senses, there are five different "input" codes that our cognitive processing systems must be able to interpret in order to function effectively. Similarly, we can think in terms of "output" codes. However, the situation is more complex than this. We can also think in terms of different "internal" processing codes. For example, a letter (e.g. "a") has a different physical form depending on whether we use the upper ("A") or lower ("a") case representation. However, the semantic content, or code, in both cases is equivalent; both mean the same. Posner (1978) developed a letter matching task for investigating these particular codes experimentally. Participants were required to press a key to indicate whether two letters were the same (e.g. A A) or different (e.g. A B). Posner showed that, when the letters were same, response was faster if they were the same case (A A) than if they were printed in different cases (A a). He suggested that detecting the letter match for the "A a" pair required formulation of letter name codes. This process was slower than the comparison of the visual codes generated by the pair of capital As. Further tests allow the operations taking place on the visual code of the letters to be isolated from those taking place on the phonological code.

Table 2.1 lists some of the codes commonly used in modelling cognition. Some of these codes are extracted by perceptual processing, such as visual codes for the shape and form of stimuli, and acoustic codes for properties of sound such as intensity and pitch. Such codes are often referred to as *physical* codes. Other codes, such as semantic codes for the meanings of stimuli, are harder to localise within the processing system. It is conventional to suppose that stimuli undergo a series of analyses during which ever more abstract codes are generated, so that meaning is a higher-order property extracted from visual and acoustic codes. However, aspects of meaning important for adaptation, such as the threat value of stimuli, may be extracted at an early stage of

---

**TABLE 2.1**

**Examples of processing codes.**

| Code | Description |
|------|-------------|
| Visual | Stimulus properties derived directly from visual perception: e.g. colour, brightness, shape, location. |
| Spatial | Stimulus properties relating to spatial relationship or configuration, such as those coding for geometric shapes. |
| Acoustic | Stimulus properties derived directly from auditory perception: e.g. pitch, intensity, direction of sound. |
| Phonological | Speech sounds. |
| Lexical | Word entry in an internal dictionary.[1] |
| Semantic | Stimulus meaning. |
| Graphemic | Letter code used in spelling and writing. |
| Motor | Code for instructions sent to muscles to produce response. |
| Articulatory | Code for instructions sent to larynx to produce speech. |

[1] Sometimes multiple dictionaries are distinguished: see Ellis (1993).

stimulus analysis (e.g. Kitayama, 1997). Issues relating to coding are central to selective attention, which we will discuss in Chapter 4. Because of the potential for information overload the system often selects one form of coding stimuli in preference to others. For example, in reading a report you have just written, you might choose either to attend to the individual letters of the words, if proof-reading it for spelling (graphemic code), or you might attend to the meanings of the words (semantic code) if you wanted to check that it conveyed your message successfully.

## 2.2.2 The cognitive architecture

The next step in modelling is to consider the computations performed on codes. It is assumed that such computations are carried out by processing units or component processes. A processing unit may be anything from a complex "central processor" performing a wide variety of operations, or a very simple neuron-like unit. In each case, codes are delivered to the unit, which then performs some computation on the code, according to some explicit rules, and then, typically, outputs a different code that may be sent to other processing units. A model of cognition requires a description of the various processing units that specifies how each unit transforms an input into an output, and

a description of connections between units, that allows the output of one unit to act as the input to other units. The description of this information-processing circuitry is the *cognitive architecture*. Research generally aims to model some sub-system of the architecture in sufficient detail to predict performance on some particular set of tasks. Note that the term "cognitive architecture" is broader than Pylyshyn's (1984) "functional architecture", described in 1.3.4: it refers to both algorithm and functional architecture.

Figure 2.1 shows an example architecture of historical importance in the development of cognitive psychology, proposed by Broadbent (1958) to explain data on short-term memory and selective attention. Stimuli are initially analysed for simple sensory properties, and the outputs of these analyses are placed in a sensory memory. It is now customary to distinguish an "echoic" auditory memory, persisting for a few seconds, from an "iconic" visual memory which decays within one second (Massaro & Loftus, 1996; Neisser, 1967). Sensory memory is essentially a relay station, that passes sensory codes to a selective attentional filter. This processing unit selects stimuli for further analysis on the basis of sensory properties such as, in the auditory case, pitch or the ear at which the stimulus arrives. Subsequent processing, includ-

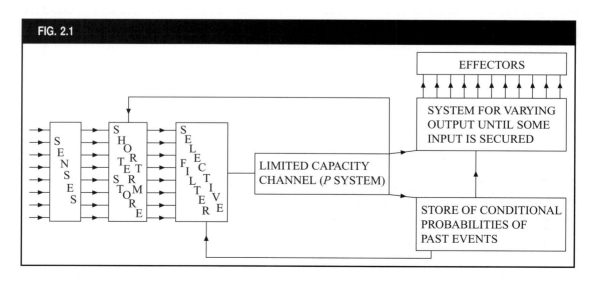

Broadbent's information-flow diagram for the organism (from Broadbent, 1958).

ing analysis of meaning and initiation of response, then takes place in a limited capacity channel which corresponds to primary or short-term memory (STM). A further processing structure is a store of conditional probabilities for past events, which corresponds to long-term memory (LTM). Information can be passed from STM into long-term storage, and STM can retrieve information from LTM when required for "on-line" processing.

Broadbent's (1958) model addresses one of the fundamental architectural issues: the extent to which processing is either *serial*, such that only one operation is executed at a time, or *parallel*, such that multiple operations take place simultaneously. The model suggests that different structures have different modes of operation. Prior to the attentional filter, processing is parallel. As already noted, sensory analysis takes place through the operation of multiple analysers which function simultaneously. However, STM operates in serial fashion, one step at a time. We shall see in Chapters 4 and 5 that Broadbent's (1958) model has been superseded by more recent work. However, the general idea that processing is parallel in its early stages, and has at least some tendency to seriality in later stages, remains influential. Certain types of response, such as speech, are necessarily serial in nature, whereas others, such as the complex motor adjustments made by a footballer running into position to receive a pass, take place in parallel.

### 2.2.3 Top-down and bottom-up control of processing

Another critical aspect of architecture is its *control structure*, the "programming" that controls when particular processors will operate. If we hypothesise a serial architecture, we can envisage a control structure similar to that of a standard computer program, in which instructions are executed one after another. The termination of one instruction (i.e. process) initiates the next instruction in the sequence. However, more complex architectures supporting parallel processing require other mechanisms for control (see Pylyshyn, 1989). We may need a system in which processing units can "capture" control from other units; and, rather than having a processor direct a code to a specified other processor, a processor may "broadcast" its output to a variety of other processors, in parallel. One of the major issues to be resolved is the respective roles of *bottom-up* and *top-down* processing. Bottom-up processing refers to stimulus analysis driven by the input data alone. For example, visual perception of objects may proceed through stages of extracting line and boundary information, using this information to discriminate the simple sub-objects of which the object is composed, such as the head, limbs and torso of a person and, finally, recognition of the whole object on the basis of the configuration of its constituent parts (Biederman, 1995).

*Context effects* demonstrate that not all processing can be of this form. Object recognition is facilitated by context: we expect to see animals in zoos, office equipment at work, and so forth. Experimental studies (e.g. Palmer, 1975) demonstrate that object recognition depends on the appropriateness of its visual context. A person would recognise a photocopier more rapidly in an office than in a zoo cage. As a further example, look at the stimulus shown in Fig. 2.2. You probably read two words—THE CAT—although the H and the A are physically identical. The other letters provide sufficient context to suggest what these characters should be. In other words, the relatively abstract information provided by the context feeds

**FIG. 2.2**

A demonstration of context. The same stimulus is perceived as an H or an A depending on the context (from Selfridge, 1955).

"downwards" within the architecture to influence the process which transforms the code for the physical appearance of the characters into codes for the individual letters. The same physical code is transformed into two different character codes. Similarly, in auditory perception of speech, we can replace occasional phonemes with a pure tone, and the person fills in the missing phoneme from the context provided by the surrounding phonemes (the phoneme-restoration effect: Samuel, 1996; Warren, 1970). The person does not intellectually work out what the missing phoneme should be: it is actually perceived as being present, indicating that top-down processing is sometimes unconscious.

Models of word recognition and reading illustrate the distinction between top-down and bottom-up processing. All such models begin with the assumption that early parallel stimulus processing identifies elementary features of letters, such as the horizontal and vertical line segments of a capital "T". Figure 2.3 shows two instances of bottom-up models for word detection discussed by Pollatsek and Rayner (1989). In the *direct word recognition* model, letter and word information are processed in parallel, so that words are identified directly from relatively primitive visual information such as features. Recognising a word does not require identification of the individual letters. In *serial letter processing* models, word recognition depends on information supplied by an earlier stage of letter detection. It is likely that there is more than one bottom-up route permitting

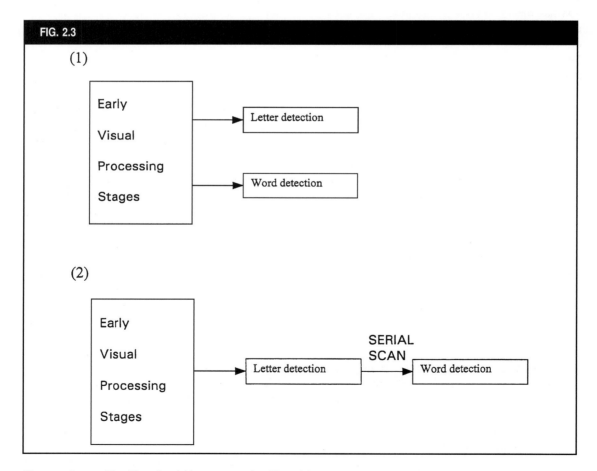

**FIG. 2.3**

(1)

Early Visual Processing Stages → Letter detection

→ Word detection

(2)

Early Visual Processing Stages → Letter detection → **SERIAL SCAN** → Word detection

Direct word recognition (1) and serial letter processing (2) models.

words to be identified from visual input. One of the more subtle routes is through "unitisation": recognition of the overall shape of a word, which allows the letter stage to be bypassed (Healy, 1994). For example, "the" in lower case has a hump in the middle, whereas "ran" appears rectangular. In applied settings where important information must be presented, such as road signs, use of lower-case letters capitalises on unitisation to facilitate reading.

All the bottom-up models are flawed by their inability to explain context effects. It is quite easy to read visually degraded words because we can use the context to guess what the word should be. To take an example from Lindsay and Norman (1977, p. 135), "wx cax drxp oxt exerx thxrd xetxer, xnd xou xtixl mxnaxe pxetxy wxll". Context has been investigated empirically by a variety of techniques, including the word superiority effect (Grainger & Jacobs, 1994; Reicher, 1969). Discrimination of a briefly presented letter is easier if the letter is embedded in a word. Participants appear to combine feature information about the specific letter with contextual information derived from the letters around it. Identifying the "K" in WORK is facilitated because there are only a few English words with the form WOR_. Of course, context is not enough on its own, as the letter might be D or M or N. A mixture of top-down and bottom-up processing is required.

## 2.3 PARALLEL PROCESSING MODELS

It is fairly straightforward to grasp the basic principles of the one-step-at-a-time serial architecture, but parallel processing models may be harder to understand intuitively, as it may not be immediately clear how the flow of information between processing units is controlled. In this section, therefore, we look in more detail at two of the most widely-used parallel architectures: spreading activation models of semantic memory, and connectionist models based on networks of very simple processing units. Parallel architectures have great promise but, so far, have found limited application in studies of human performance, so our treatment will be fairly brief.

### 2.3.1 Spreading activation

Spreading activation models were developed as a result of work on people's use of concepts for categorising stimuli, objects and events in making sense of the world. They are concerned with, first, the structure of long-term memory (LTM) and, second, the way in which information retrieved from LTM is used in making decisions about concepts, i.e. "central processing" and thought. These models bring together two general ideas about information representation which predate the modern era. First, information is represented as *traces* or *engrams* whose activation varies (see Estes, 1991). Remembering a concept involves increasing the activation of the trace to some threshold value at which it enters conscious awareness. Second, memory has an *associationist* structure. Concepts are linked in memory, so that retrieving one concept leads to retrieval of the other. Look at a picture of Stan Laurel, and probably Oliver Hardy will come to mind also. Three principles of association, dating back to the work of Aristotle (see Leahey, 1997), have been proposed:

1. *Contiguity*: two things become associated because they occurred together in time.
2. *Similarity*: two things become associated because they are alike.
3. *Contrast*: two things become associated because they are opposites.

Associationist principles apply not just to memory for concepts but memory in general. For example, an important event will be represented as interlinked traces for its main components (Anderson & Bower, 1981). If you think of an interview for a job or a university place, you might recall the rooms you went into, the people you met and so forth. Furthermore, activation of one component will tend to evoke the others: a picture of the interview room might elicit thoughts of the interviewers, the clothes you wore, and so on. Emotions may be similarly represented (Bower, 1981): recalling an interview might make you feel tense, and feeling tense might make it easier to recall details of the interview (see 15.4.2).

By way of illustration of the way in which theories of spreading activation have been developed to describe such processes, we will consider two types of experimental task: the *semantic verification* and *priming* paradigms. Studies of retrieval of information of events constitute a further important area of experimental research, beyond the scope of this book. The semantic verification task was developed to test a *spreading activation* network model of semantic memory (Collins & Loftus, 1975; Collins & Quillian, 1969). The model makes two types of statement. First, it describes the *structure* of associations between concepts in semantic memory. The assumption is that it has a hierarchic structure, as shown in Fig. 2.4, so that information is stored as economically as possible. Thus generic information about birds, such as "has feathers" is associated directly with the "bird" concept, but more specialised information about particular types of bird is stored lower down in the hierarchy, as represented in Fig. 2.4 by the associative links between "canary" and "can sing" and "is yellow".

The second type of statement refers to spreading activation. The basic idea is that each concept has an activation value, which is normally low or zero. Stimuli will tend to activate corresponding concepts, and activation will then spread to associated concepts, after which it decays over time. Presenting the word CANARY may evoke thoughts of birdsong, although activation of the associated birdsong concept may be insufficient to reach the threshold for conscious recognition. The rate of spread of activation reflects the strength of the associative link which, in turn, reflects factors such as the similarity of the concepts, and the amount of prior learning of the association. The sentence verification task (Collins & Quillian, 1969) tests the spreading activation model by requiring participants to answer "true" or "false" to questions such as "is a canary a bird?". Response time depends on how long it takes sufficient activation to spread from the canary concept to the bird concept. Collins and Quillian confirmed the simplest prediction from the model, that RT should increase with the number of associative links between concepts. It takes longer to confirm that a canary has skin (2 links) than to confirm that a canary can fly (1 link).

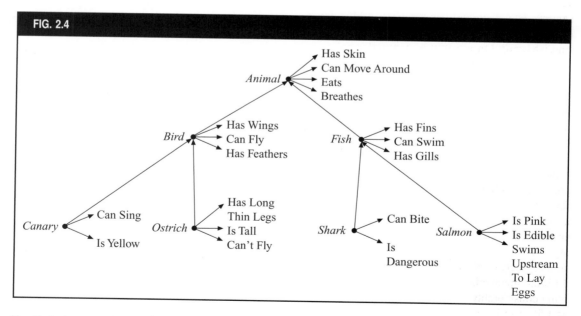

**FIG. 2.4**

Hypothetical memory structure for knowledge about animals. From Collins & Quillian, 1969. Reprinted with permission from Academic Press

Subsequent research has shown some deficiencies of the model. For example, response times reflect the typicality of concepts: sentences relating to *prototypical* birds such as robins are processed faster than those relating to penguins, vultures or peacocks (Rosch, 1973). It is also unlikely that knowledge is organised in neat hierarchies such as that shown in Fig. 2.4. Nevertheless the model successfully illustrates some important principles in the organisation and processing of concept knowledge (see Baddeley, 1997). Regarding architecture, it shows how information can be processed in parallel without any of the restrictions on information flow associated with serial stage models. If a person views a complex scene, a variety of concepts may be activated simultaneously, and there may several simultaneous flows of information between related concepts. However, like (simple) serial architectures, the control of processing is essentially bottom-up. Once a concept is activated, the subsequent spread of activation obeys simple mechanistic rules, and the model would have to be elaborated to accommodate strategies for voluntary search for information.

Spreading activation models may also be investigated through studies of semantic priming. The task most commonly used is *lexical decision* (Meyer & Schvaneveldt, 1972). The person must decide whether or not a string of letters is a valid English word. On positive trials (i.e. the string *is* a word), lexical decision is speeded by prior presentation of a semantically related prime. For example, the decision that DOCTOR is a word is faster if the person has previously been presented with the priming word NURSE. The explanation is that activation spreads from the "Nurse" concept to the "Doctor" concept. The latter is already somewhat activated when the word DOCTOR is presented, so that activation reaches the threshold for recognition more quickly. Semantic priming is a robust phenomenon, which has generated an enormous experimental literature, but the spreading activation model is over-simplified. For example, Neely (1991) suggests that there are several different mechanisms for priming effects. Simplifying considerably, the spreading activation model best fits priming when the time-lag between prime and target word is short (<300 ms) and when the non-words presented on negative trials do not resemble actual words (e.g. NXQTD). At longer time-lags, priming reflects voluntary search driven by expectancies. When non-words are easily confused with words (e.g. NIRSE), response times to words are influenced by a checking process operating after initial access to the word.

### 2.3.2 Connectionist models

*Connectionist models* (see Quinlan, 1991, for an introduction) resemble semantic network models in that they are based on parallel processing and activation spreading within a network, but they have the following distinctive features:

1. Semantic network models tend to be unclear about the way in which flow of activation through the network is controlled. In contrast, connectionist models explicitly reject the notion of a controlling executive system.
2. Connectionist models typically aim to use representations consistent with physiological reality, i.e. networks resembling interconnected neurones. Each *unit* or *node* in the net does no more than calculate an activation output from the various activation inputs it receives, according to a fixed set of rules or algorithm, rather as the integration of inputs to a neuron determines its rate of firing.
3. Semantic network models have a hierarchical structure. Units may be freely interlinked in connectionism, although constraints on different sets of units (*modules*) are sometimes imposed.
4. Many, though not all, connectionist models are explicitly concerned with learning appropriate responses to stimuli, by applying a simple algorithm to an initial unstructured network.
5. Connectionism aims to explain the full range of human cognitive phenomena, not just associative memory. However, demonstration of some psychological function through simulation is a common aim of connectionism, and models are often compared with detailed experimental data.

In the connectionist model, processing units can be conceived as neurons. Units are massively interconnected, with a single unit generally receiving input from, and giving input to, many other units. Each unit has an "activation" level, an associated level of energy, that can be transmitted to other units. The nature of this transmission depends, in part, on the type of connection between units. Connections have "weights" that can be either facilitatory, in which case high activation in the originating unit will tend to increase activation in the receiving unit, or inhibitory, in which case high activation in the originating unit will tend to decrease activation in the receiving unit. These weights can vary in size as well as direction. So, for example, if the connection between two units had a large positive weight, and if one of the units output a high level of activation, this would have a strongly excitatory effect on the receiving unit. If, however, the connection weight was weaker, the level of excitation transmitted from one unit to the other would be attenuated.

Further to this, there are a number of "rules" of the system. First, there is an activation rule that determines the way in which a unit deals with input from other units and determines its current state, i.e. how it adds up input, and how fast activation within the unit decays. Second, there is an output rule that determines what the unit will output to other units, given the current level of activation. If a unit only mirrored the activation it received to other connected units, the operations of the network would be limited. By using non-linear functions the potency of the network is increased. Finally, there is a learning rule that determines the way in which the "weights", associated with the connections between units, are changed. In this way associations can be formed. For example, Hebb (1949) suggested that high levels of activations co-occurring in two units will tend to strengthen the associative links between them. All these rules are "hardwired", i.e. they are contained within the physical properties of the system. "The behaviour of the network as a whole is a function of the initial state of activation of the units and of the weights on its connections, which serve as its only form of memory" (Fodor & Pylyshyn, 1988, p. 5).

Figure 2.5 shows a typical network (McClelland & Rumelhart, 1981), intended to simulate experimental data on word recognition, such as the word superiority effect discussed in 2.2.3 (it was not intended to simulate learning). The units are arranged in three levels, such that each level effectively codes for a different type of property. Incoming stimuli first activate the elementary feature units representing the line segments of the letters. Activation spreads from these units "upwards" to units representing individual letters: this is a bottom-up, parallel process. Note that features inhibit letter units that do not contain the feature, so that a central horizontal line activates the A unit but inhibits the N unit. Activation spreads from letter units to word units, so that eventually one of the word units becomes activated to a high enough level for conscious recognition and identification. At these levels, there is also top-down processing in that, as a word unit becomes activated, it tends to suppress units for letters that are not part of the word. That is, the downwards arrows represent context effects. For example, as the word "ABLE" becomes activated through bottom-up spread of activation, it tends to feed activation downwards to letter units such as that for "A", but inhibits units for letters such as "T".

The use of connectionism in performance psychology is in its infancy, but is likely to increase rapidly. We must be clear about what connectionism does and does not deliver. It offers a radically different way of explaining performance data to traditional, symbol-processing models. Connectionist models can be "sub-symbolic", in that symbols can be represented indirectly rather than directly, as patterns of activation across processing units. This aspect of connectionism has been criticised by Fodor and Pylyshyn (1988), who claim that connectionism fails to represent the formal structure of the interrelationships between mental states, and so connectionism lacks the explanatory power associated with symbolic approaches to cognition. However, in practice, connectionism has had considerable success in explaining a variety of cognitive phenomena, such as many aspects of the acquisition of language that elude behaviourist or symbolic approaches.

Consider the rules associated with generating the past tense of verbs (see McLeod, Plunkett,

FIG. 2.5

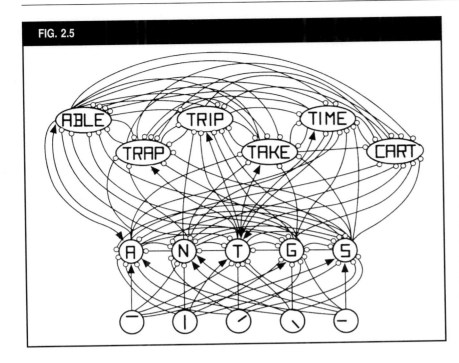

The McClelland and Rumelhart (1981) interactive activation model, illustrating excitatory (arrowheads) and inhibitory (rounded heads) connections between units at three levels. Copyright © 1981 by the American Psychological Association. Reprinted with permission.

& Rolls, 1998). Such rules are complex. The past tense of "I show" would be "I showed", although the past tense of "I go" would not be "I goed". This latter sentence contains an over-regularisation error, in that a rule that commonly applies has been used in an inappropriate context: fluent speakers do not, of course, make such errors. Symbolic descriptions of cognition explain this competence with reference to two types of cognitive activity, one concerning the processing of a rule and another the processing of a list of exceptions (occasions when the rule cannot be applied). However, the complexities that must be incorporated with such rules provide difficulties for this approach. A more parsimonious account is provided by connectionism. Plunkett and Marchman (1993, 1996) trained a multi-layered network to generate past tenses for verbs. Initially, (present tense) words were presented to the input units of the network, and errors generated by the output nodes formed the basis of changes to connection weights. Importantly, during the course of training, the network produced a pattern of errors very similar to those made by children during language

acquisition (see McLeod, Plunkett, & Rolls, 1998). Further, as with many instances of human performance, the network appeared capable of applying rules without being explicitly informed of the rule. Validatory evidence for the network was also derived from the fact that it was predictive of the relative speed of a number of other aspects of human language acquisition.

The central metaphor of activation may correspond to properties of neurons such as rate of firing. Hence, connectionism may allow us to represent the interface between biological and symbolic levels of description. However, although connectionist models are inspired by actual neural networks, they are not intended as direct models of neural processes, and often differ from real neural nets in important ways (Smolensky, 1988). Computational neuroscience models are explicitly intended to copy neural functioning (e.g. Banquet et al., 1997), but have limited application so far. Some authors (e.g. Anderson, 1990) have seen connectionist models as describing the computational machinery for symbol processing, rather than to the biological level as such. It is certainly the case that connectionism can be used to address the traditional modelling problems of the cognitive psychologist, without reference to biology. Nevertheless, connectionism takes us closer to being able to construct an unbroken chain of explanation from neural to cognitive architecture levels.

## 2.4 THE ENERGETICS OF COGNITION: CAPACITY, RESOURCES AND ATTENTION

So far, we have discussed architecture essentially as a question of determining the internal programming supporting cognitive functions. However, this approach may not capture *energetic* aspects of performance. Subjectively, we sometimes feel that cognition is effortful, especially when the task is difficult, or when we feel impaired, by fatigue or illness, for example. At an objective level, various *capacity* limitations may be demonstrated through experiments. People can attend efficiently only to a limited number of stimuli; they often have difficulty performing more than one task at a time (see Chapter 5); and the capacity of short-term memory is often said to be $7 \pm 2$ "chunks" of information (Miller, 1956). There are two ways of attempting to explain such capacity limitations. The first is to relate capacity to the individual component processes of the architecture. For example, if you download a file from the Internet, the rate of information transfer is limited by one of the components of your computer, the modem: transfer rate cannot exceed an upper limit (e.g. 56 kilobytes per second). Other components in your computer, such as memory, also have capacity limits. Human information processing is necessarily subject to similar limitations.

A second approach is to suppose that processing requires some metaphorical energy or fuel to operate successfully. With a battery-powered radio, there comes a point at which reception gets progressively poorer as the battery runs down. The failing battery imposes a constraint on performance over and above the capacity limitations of the individual components of the radio. *Attentional resource* theories (Norman & Bobrow, 1975) similarly suppose that some human information processing requires energisation. Resources may be insufficient for performance either because of task demands (running too many appliances off a single battery), or because the person's resources are reduced for some reason, such as fatigue (failing battery). Consistent with these two approaches to the description of capacity limitations on human performance, a distinction can be made between fixed resource models, in which resource availability is treated as constant, and variable resource models, in which availability varies with factors such as motivation and fatigue. Fixed models are more amenable to formal treatment but, of course, cannot explain loss of attention due to internal factors such as fatigue.

The resource concept is intuitively appealing in that we sometimes encounter situations in which it feels subjectively as though we just do not have enough "attention" to follow everything which is happening. Indeed, subjective workload has been related to the extent to which the person has sufficient resources for performance (see Wickens, 1992). Resource usage can be investigated formally in experiments that overload attention, through having the person perform demanding or multiple tasks (see Chapter 5). The concept is also useful in stress research, in that stress factors may have generally energising or de-energising effects on the person, such that one aspect of energisation for action is increased availability of resources (Matthews & Davies, 1998). Resource availability may have some physiological basis, so that it is sensitive to biological agents such as drugs. However, the idea has proved controversial: one view is that any capacity limitations relate to individual component processes, and there is no general resource supply (Allport, 1989).

In terms of cognitive theory, resources are a part of the functional architecture (see 1.4.3) that supports computation. Thus, we can treat resources as a processing-level construct, without referring in detail to their neural basis. In modelling performance, the issue is then how the computations performed by processing units are affected by resource availability. In principle, questions related to resource limitation are separate from those related to other aspects of the architecture. For example, both serial and parallel processing might be resource-limited (Townsend & Ashby, 1983). However, empirical studies have led to agreement among resource theorists that some processes are more affected than others by variation in the availability of resources. Early perceptual processes seem to be relatively less sensitive to capacity limitation than later processes, and some highly-practiced tasks also make few attentional demands. Performance of this kind is sometimes described as *automatic*, though the term has other connotations too (see 3.3.1). Resource theory is used most often in studies of attention. Attention has both *selective* and *intensive* aspects. Selection refers to choosing to act on some stimuli rather than others, whereas the intensive aspect refers to the general efficiency of performance on demanding tasks (*concentration*). Selection tends to be seen as dependent on the structure of information-flow within the architecture, as in the Broadbent (1958) model previously described, whereas intensive concentration may reflect either high resource usage, or efficient organisation of the specific processes contributing to performance.

Both aspects of attention may be investigated with the three main paradigms for investigating attention:

1. *Selective attention*: the participant must respond to some stimuli, or stimulus properties, whilst ignoring others.
2. *Divided attention*: the participant must perform two (or more) tasks simultaneously, which may lead to performance breakdown (*dual-task interference*).
3. *Sustained attention*: the participant must maintain the focus of attention over a relatively long time-period.

The evidence on what these paradigms reveal about selective and intensive aspects of attentions is reviewed in Chapters 4, 5 and 6. The broad question is whether or not we need to postulate general resource pools to explain data on performance break-down, and different researchers have arrived at different answers. We discuss the resource metaphor further in Chapter 5, and consider its application to stress research in Chapter 9.

## 2.5 VOLUNTARY CONTROL AND STRATEGY

### 2.5.1 Closed- and open-loop control

Achieving high levels of performance on demanding tasks requires effort. However, as discussed in 1.3.3, the computer metaphor tends to provide a rather passive view of performance. We need, therefore, rigorous ways of investigating how goals, motivations and the person's voluntary choice over processing and action influence performance. The architecture will support a variety of different programs between which the person must choose. We can, of course, simply ask people about their intentions but, as discussed in 2.1.1, self-reports are often misleading: people lack insight into how they process information. From the perspective of cognitive science, the issue is partly one of architecture; we can build control loops into information-processing models which mimic the processing associated with voluntary control. Such models may guide collection of data which establishes objective criteria for voluntary control. However, we also need the perspective of the knowledge or semantic level of description, that deals with people's motivations for controlling their own processing.

The theory of control, whether of cognitive or mechanical systems, is known as cybernetics (Ashby, 1956). A basic theoretical distinction is that between *open-loop* and *closed-loop* control. In open-loop control, the stimulus directly triggers a sequence of processing operations leading to a response. For example, there is a species of seagull in which the chick obtains food from the mother bird by pecking at the mother's beak, which has a distinctive marking on it (Tinbergen, 1953). Pecking behaviour is open-loop in that it is triggered specifically by the beak stimulus. The same behaviour can be elicited using a suitably painted cardboard beak: the chick's behaviour is unaffected by the lack of reward for its behaviour. Behavioural reflexes in humans, such as the proverbial knee-jerk, tend to be of little psychological interest, and people retain at least some flexibility of control over most behaviours. It is likely that only true instincts are rigorously open-loop but,

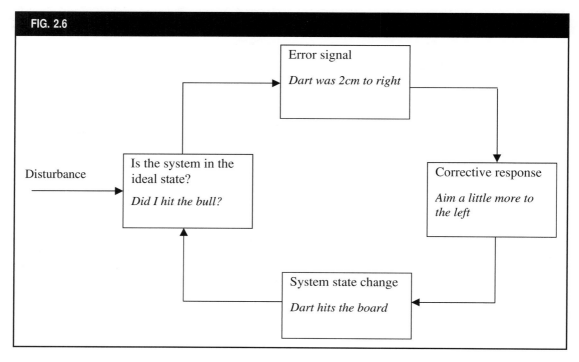

**FIG. 2.6**

How a simple closed-loop control system operates.

as we shall see in Chapter 7, highly skilled performance sometimes approximates to open-loop control. The impressive rapidity of performance of a skilled typist may owe something to open-loop control of key-press responses, with little need for voluntary selection of response.

The defining feature of open-loop control is its rigidity; the response to the stimulus is not immediately affected by feedback, indicating that it is not achieving its aim. Of course, over-learned behaviour is slowly altered by feedback. In contrast, closed-loop control is characterised by sensitivity to feedback signalling that an error has occurred. Figure 2.6 shows how a simple closed-loop control system operates. Seeking the "ideal state" is the system's goal. If the actual state deviates from the ideal, a feedback or error signal is produced. The error signal initiates corrective behaviour so as to reduce the deviation. The cycle continues until the system arrives at the end-point of homeostasis, at which the error signal is zero. For example, for a darts player, the ideal state might be to aim the dart at the target of the bulls-eye. The player might throw the first dart at the board and miss the target, perhaps deviating to the right. Processing feedback signals supports perception of the error. On the next throw the player would try to aim a little more to the left. If the dart still misses, feedback will generate a fresh correction, and so forth. The arrow marked "disturbance" indicates that homeostasis may be upset by external factors. Dartboards are stationary, but in clay-pigeon shooting the trajectory of the target would vary on each cycle.

The darts game requires a series of discrete responses, but the same principle applies to tasks in which continuous control is required, such as steering a car. If the driver is too close to the kerb, he or she will steer in the opposite direction to reduce the error. In driving, of course, the car is subject to external disturbances, such as curves in the road, so that homeostasis is achieved only transiently. Open- and closed-loop controls are ideals rarely encountered. In most real systems, such as vehicle driving, both modes of control coexist (Pew, 1974). The driver can use open-loop

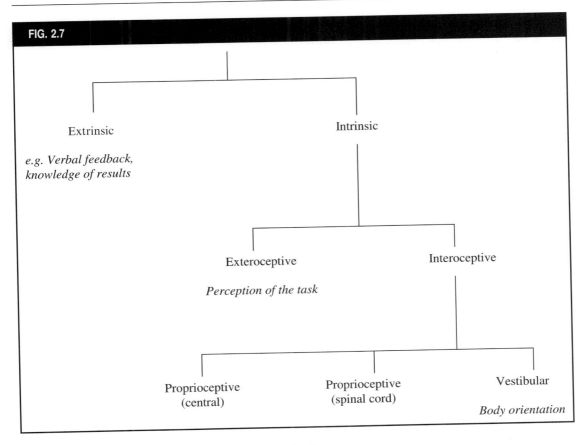

FIG. 2.7

Differing types of feedback that may be used for regulation of performance.

control to the extent that the road is familiar, and well-learned stimulus–response sequences may be applied. The capacity to preview the road ahead assists in the implementation of open-loop control. According to Pew (1974), people performing continuous control tasks used open-loop control where possible, supplemented with closed-loop compensatory corrections to deal with errors.

## 2.5.2 The role of feedback

As these examples might suggest, voluntary control seems to relate to closed-loop control, in that reaction to error feedback is goal-dependent. However, we cannot simply equate voluntary and closed-loop control, because of the differing types of feedback that may be used for regulation of performance, shown in Fig. 2.7. The first distinction is between intrinsic and extrinsic feed-

back (Winstein & Schmidt, 1989). Extrinsic (or "augmented") feedback is provided by some outside agency, such as the comments of a driving instructor. In studies of motivation, participants are often informed of their level of performance (knowledge of results). Intrinsic feedback results directly from the person's perceptions of task stimuli, and their variation with response, such as information about speed conveyed by the apparent motion of roadside objects when driving.

Intrinsic feedback may be further divided into exteroceptive, arriving through the external senses, and interoceptive, arriving through internal systems such as the proprioceptive (or kinaesthetic) sense of body position and movement, and the sense of balance and orientation provided by the vestibular system. Proprioceptive feedback operates both at the level of the central nervous system, where it may provide the principal error signal for closed-loop control of action (Adams, 1976), and at the level of the spinal chord (Summers, 1989). At the spinal level, proprioceptive feedback drives fast-acting, closed-loop regulation of muscle activity, providing fine but unconscious control over motor actions (Schmidt, 1982). We may also have little awareness of sensory (exteroceptive) feedback, as when we catch an object which someone has unexpectedly thrown towards us. Hence, some instances of closed-loop control are involuntary, in that the feedback processing required is not dependent on immediate goals. We can thus arrive at a working definition of voluntary control as that subset of closed-loop control in which feedback and corrective behaviours relate to goals and motivation. Thus, vehicle driving is voluntary to the extent that it is controlled by feedback regarding goals such as arriving at the desired destination and preserving personal safety. The open-eyed sleep-walker who successfully avoids furniture and other obstacles may be showing closed-loop control, but it is involuntary in that the person's locomotion has no explicit goal.

## 2.5.3 Implementing control through strategies

A strategy may be defined as a voluntarily-chosen style of performance, intended to meet specific goals. Strategy does not affect the cognitive architecture, but it does affect the way it is used by the performer, with respect to the person's encoding of task stimuli and their sequencing of processing operations. In experimental studies, we can manipulate strategies by changing the participant's goals through instruction. In reaction time studies, we can generate a speed–accuracy tradeoff function by emphasising the importance of either rapidity of response, or avoiding errors, so that the participant chooses either a risky or cautious strategy. Figure 2.8 shows a typical speed–accuracy tradeoff; each data point represents a different instructional set. Rabbitt (1989) reviews extensive data showing that people have a high degree of flexibility in exerting adaptive control over speeded responses, as we discuss further in 2.1.3.

We may require differing symbol-processing models for performance depending on strategy choice. For example, the picture–sentence verification task (Clark & Chase, 1972) uses stimuli such as those shown in Fig. 2.9. The subject must decide, as quickly as possible, whether the sentence matches the "picture", i.e. the star and plus symbols. Different types of items may be constructed, depending on whether the sentence is affirmative or negative and whether the description of the "picture" is true or false. MacLeod, Hunt and Mathews (1978) presented evidence that participants use one of two strategies for encoding and processing the stimuli. One strategy is linguistic, such that the person encodes both sentence and picture as verbal propositions, whose meanings may be compared. The other strategy is visual, in that the person compares mental images for sentence and picture. Critically, the strategy a

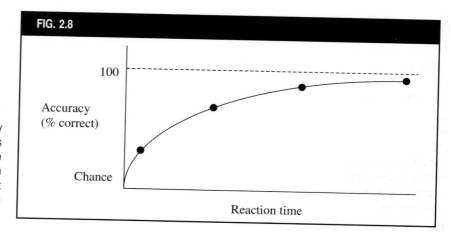

FIG. 2.8

100

Accuracy (% correct)

Chance

Reaction time

The speed–accuracy tradeoff. As instructions increasingly emphasise accuracy over speed, both percentage of correct responses and reaction time increase.

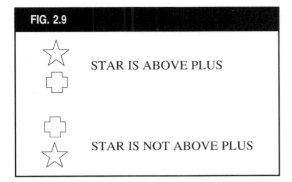

FIG. 2.9

STAR IS ABOVE PLUS

STAR IS NOT ABOVE PLUS

True and false items from the picture–sentence verification task (adapted from Clark & Chase, 1972).

person is using can usually be inferred from objective data. Use of the two strategies may be modelled in detail. The models predict the pattern of RTs across the different types of item: for example, processing of negative sentences tends to be slow when the linguistic strategy is used. Hunt and MacLeod (1977) showed that participants can voluntarily select either strategy, and that the pattern of RTs is consistent with the strategy chosen. Strategies influence the control of information flow through the architecture, rather than the architecture itself, which, by definition, is fixed. However, when strategies are radically different, descriptions of the processing structures involved will also differ.

A final comment on strategies is that the concept has both advantages and dangers. On the positive side, objective investigation of strategies through performance studies allow us to construct processing models that incorporate voluntary control (see 3.3). The facility for strategic intervention seems to be an important "design feature" of the architecture. Understanding strategy may help us to understand the energetics of performance: the effortful striving required for performance under demanding conditions is a particularly type of strategy. Conversely, stimulus-driven "automatic processing" seems effortless. Some authors have equated mental effort and resources (Kahneman, 1973), though this view is over-simplified. The relationship between voluntary control and attentional resources is further discussed in 3.3. Investigation of why people choose strategies allows us

to integrate knowledge level and cognitive architectural perspectives. Voluntary control is partly a question of the control structures discussed in 2.2.3, in that it is necessarily top-down (though not all top-down control is voluntary). However, such architectural accounts of control do not in themselves tell us how a strategy meets the person's needs within a particular external environment, for which understanding of intention and motivation is required.

On the negative side, it is easy to use the strategy concept in a post hoc, circular fashion. When data fail to match prediction, it is usually possible to think, after the event, of some strategy which might have generated the data observed. As in the MacLeod et al. (1978) study, we must have a clear rationale for predicting strategy use, and an independent test of which strategy is being used. Second, strategy selection may appear to be done by an "homunculus", a little man in the head (e.g. Allport, 1980), with all the powers of thought of the person. Even if we predict use of some strategy in advance, it may not explain in itself the empirical phenomena. The nemesis of homunculi is detail: we must model as fully as possible how the strategy is selected and how the strategy influences processing. As Baddeley (1996) indicates, the homunculus is often simply a recognition that we do not know how a system performs its various functions. It is increasingly possible to discriminate different strategic or "executive" functions (Gopher, 1996; Logan, 1985; Meyer & Kieras, 1997a), and, tentatively, to relate them to different brain areas (Shallice & Burgess, 1993).

## 2.6 BIOLOGICAL BASES FOR PERFORMANCE

### 2.6.1 The neural level of description

As we have seen, useful processing models can be constructed without any reference to the brain. However, a more complete explanation requires an understanding of the neural bases of the cognitive architecture. Furthermore, the concerns of performance psychology include the effects of biological agents. This section describes cognitive science principles for relating performance to neural functioning, and experimental and other methods for investigating biological agents.

The principal research issue is the neural basis for the cognitive architecture: which brain systems support processing constructs such as working memory and attentional capacity, and how do they do it? Much of this work is concerned with mapping processing functions onto brain structures. Cognitive neuropsychology is based on the premise that there are numerous modules in the brain that function relatively independently. Modules are believed to be anatomically distinct, so brain damage will often affect some modules while leaving others intact. Patients show selective impairments in psychological functions, such as long- and short-term memory (see Baddeley, 1993). If we know which parts of the brain are damaged, the function can be mapped onto a particular brain structure or system. Beyond establishing correspondences or mappings between processing and neurology, researchers are increasingly working on detailed models of neural support for cognition, using the connectionist or "neural net" approaches described previously.

The brain has evolved through natural selection to perform a collection of special-purpose functions which aid survival and reproductive success. Even the capacity to learn language in childhood may be programmed into the brain by the genes (Pinker, 1994). The brain has some ability to function as a general-purpose processor, but it should also be understood as hardware designed to support adaptive software (see Anderson, 1990, for a review of the adaptive character of thought). Thus, we have a further research question: how have brain circuits evolved to support adaptation to real-world environments? Evolutionary psychology is largely beyond the scope of this book. However, it is useful to preserve a sense of what the mind is "naturally" equipped to do. For example, in Chapter 6 we will see that people find it difficult to sustain over time a focus of attention on a succession of simple stimuli. If the stimuli have little immediate impact on well-being, it may well be maladaptive to focus attention on a single source of stimuli, to the neglect of sampling information from other sources.

## 2.6.2 Experimental methods for the psychobiology of performance

Work on the neural underpinnings of the cognitive architecture relies heavily on the "natural experiments" afforded by brain-damaged patients. Obviously, it is not possible to manipulate experimentally the biological bases of basic architectural properties, such as features of language. However, there are various stress factors, which may be manipulated experimentally, that may provoke temporary changes in architecture. The most obvious example is that of drugs such as caffeine, nicotine and alcohol, whose effects on performance may be compared with those of a placebo treatment. The physiology of drug action may be investigated through animal studies, allowing inferences about drug mechanisms in humans. Human studies show that nicotine enhances performance on various attentional tasks, whereas animal studies show that nicotine stimulates neurons using the neurotransmitter acetylcholine. Activity of cholinergic neural pathways ascending to the cortex may then support attention (Sarter & Bruno, 1997; Warburton, 1979).

Other factors with a clear biological basis for influencing performance include toxic chemicals, nutrients, infections and biological rhythms such as diurnal variation and the menstrual cycle. Stress responses, emotion and personality may also have biological bases (e.g. Zuckerman, 1991). Gray's (1982) animal model for anxiety describes in considerable detail how anti-anxiety drugs influence the animal's processing of stimuli related to punishment signals. Its application to human behaviour remains controversial (Matthews & Gilliland, 1999). There is a general problem that "biological" manipulations may also influence cognitive factors such as the person's appraisal of the task and choice of strategies. One view of menstrual cycle effects is that they are largely due to the woman's attributions of stress symptoms rather than to hormonal change per se. In the premenstrual phase, women may blame emotional distress caused by other factors on "PMT" (Asso, 1987; Veeninga & Kraaimaat, 1995). Even in "double-blind" drug studies, subjects form expectancies that may influence performance (Kirsch & Weixel, 1988; see 13.7). Nevertheless, biological factors exert pervasive influences, and in the chapters on stress (9–13) we will discuss relevant experimental studies of performance. Ageing and individual difference factors such as intelligence may also have biological bases, as discussed in Chapters 14–16.

### 2.6.3 Cognitive psychophysiology

The alternative to experimental manipulation of biological factors is to monitor brain function through psychophysiological recording. Traditionally, much of this work has been based on *arousal theory*—the idea that the brain varies in its overall level of activity, from states of deep sleep through normal wakefulness to extreme excitement. Arousal may be assessed through central nervous system measures (the electroencephalogram or EEG) and autonomic nervous system measures such as increased skin conductance and heart rate. Arousal theory is described further in Chapter 9. In this section, we highlight two more recent techniques which may be more informative about specific cognitive processes than the gross activity measures provided by arousal indices (see Jennings & Coles, 1991). Work on *event-related potentials* and on *brain imaging* seeks to establish close correspondences between psychophysiological indices and cognitive functions, so as to track processing in time and space (i.e. brain localisation).

*Event-related potentials* (ERPs) are recorded using electrodes on the scalp. However, as the name suggests, it requires the examination of activity in relation to a specific event. Following a stimulus or event, the EEG is recorded and subsequently computer averaged across perhaps 50 trials. The averaged record shows a characteristic pattern of peaks and troughs, representing changing electrical polarity (positive or negative). These ERP waves or components are labelled in terms of their polarity and the length of time that has expired since the initiating event: P300 is a positive component that occurs approximately 300 milliseconds after an event. Experimental manipulations of stimuli and cognitive demands show how the components may be linked to particular types of processing (Luck & Girelli, 1998). For example, early components (e.g. N100) are most sensitive to stimulus characteristics, implying that they index early perceptual processes. Conversely, later components such as the P300 are sensitive to more cognitive factors such as expectancies and task demands.

Two examples of how ERPs may be informative about processing are as follows. First, as discussed in Chapter 4, a basic issue in selective attention is whether selective analysis of incoming stimuli occurs early on, as part of perception, or later, as the person selects a response. ERP studies of selective attention have typically presented tone stimuli to the two ears. The participant is asked to attend to one ear or the other. Work of this kind shows that attention influences the ERP at an early stage of processing: stimuli presented to the attended ear generate a larger amplitude N100 (or N1) wave than do stimuli arriving at the unattended ear (Hillyard & Hansen, 1986). In some ways, this is a rather indirect way to look at selective attention but, taken with other evidence, it supports the hypothesis that people have a capacity for early selection (although other, later processes may also contribute to selection). As a second example, the P300 component may be promising for measuring work-load, in that its amplitude decreases with the cognitive demands of the task (Parasuraman, 1990).

*Brain imaging* (Posner & Raichle, 1997, p. 58) refers to a family of techniques that monitor activity of different regions of the brain. We illustrate them by describing positron emission tomography (PET). A PET camera is a doughnut-shaped set of radiation detectors that circles the participant's head. After the participant is positioned in the machine, the experimenter injects a vein in the participant's arm with a small amount of water labelled with the positron-emitting radioactive isotope oxygen-15. Over the next minute or so following the injection, the radioactive water accumulates in the brain in direct proportion to the local blood flow. The greater the blood flow, the more the radiation is recorded by PET, and the brighter the colour scale. PET scanning can be used to investigate cortical activity associated with the presentation of a particular stimulus or the performance of a particular task, and requires that cortical activity is measured in an experimental condition, where a stimulus is presented or a task is performed, and also in a control condition. The difference between experimental and control conditions is calculated, and averaged across individuals, to give an overall impression of the locations where activation occurs. The technique of subtracting control activity level from experimental activity resembles the "additive factors" performance-based technique, which we discuss in 3.2.2.

As an example of the use of PET to examine human performance, we will consider an investigation of the cognitive processes involved in visual word recognition (see Posner & Raichle, 1997, pp. 77–81). Previous PET studies had demonstrated increased cortical activity in the extrastriate cortex, and particularly the left hemisphere, when passive (no response required) viewing of a word was compared to viewing a fixation point. However, the question remained as to the specific cognitive processes responsible. In 2.2.1 we discussed the concept of processing codes and described, for example, how letters can be represented by both physical and semantic codes. Using an extension of this logic, Posner and Raichle hypothesised four processing codes that described a hierarchy of cognitive processing associated with visual word recognition (cf. 2.2.3). At the lowest level, it was proposed that the visual features, from which letters are constructed, are recognised (i.e. lines and dots). At the next level, specific patterns of these features are recognised as letters. Level three is concerned with orthographic recognition and relates to the application of certain rules of language, e.g. recognising the pattern

of consonants and vowels that must exist within a word. Finally, at the highest level, semantic content of the word is recognised.

Based on this decomposition, four types of visual stimuli were devised, each of which was designed to "map" to a different level of the processing code hierarchy (see Fig. 2.10). Strings of "false fonts" (patterns of lines similar to those found in letters but not describing any letter) were used to "map" to the process of visual feature recognition. Unpronounceable strings of letters were "mapped" to the process of letter recognition. Pseudo words (pronounceable non-words) were "mapped" to orthographic recognition. Finally, real words were "mapped" to the process of semantic recognition. Participants were instructed to observe these stimuli passively, while cortical activity was recorded. It was argued that, if the previously observed pattern of cortical activation was due to the visual features of the stimulus and nothing else, then all stimuli should produce the same response. If the pattern of activation was due to the letter code, then the activation should be produced only by letter strings, pseudowords and words. If the pattern of activation was due to the orthographic regularity of words, the results with words and pseudowords should be identical, and dissimilar from those obtained in the other two conditions. Finally, if the pattern of activation was due to the meaning of words, even during passive presentation, then words would produce a unique response.

In fact, although all four types of stimuli were associated with activity in visual areas outside the primary visual cortex, only pseudowords and

**FIG. 2.10**

| Words | Pseudowords | Letterstrings | False fonts |
|---|---|---|---|
| ANT | GEEL | USFFHT | ᴙᵁᴲ |
| RAZOR | IOB | TBBL | ᒐᕁᒐᴚ |
| DUST | RELD | TSTFS | ᴚᴐ?ᴙ |
| FURNACE | BLERCE | JBTT | ᖶᒐᴒᴎ |
| MOTHER | CHELDINABE | STB | ᴮᴙᴚᒐᴒ |
| FARM | ALDOBER | FFPW | ᴋᴙᴐᴮ |

Examples of the four types of visual stimuli used by Posner and Raichle (from Posner and Raichle 1997, p. 79).

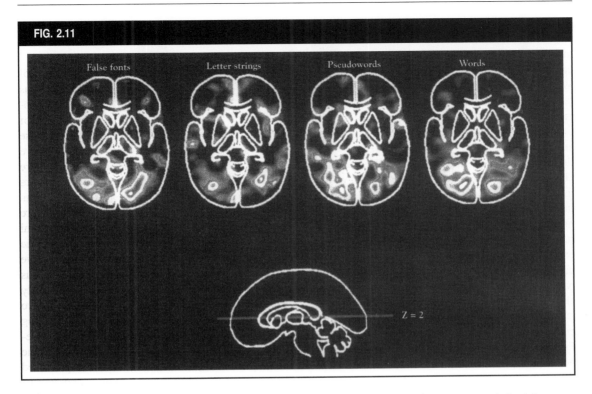

Blood flow responses in visual cortices to the visual stimuli (see Fig. 2.10). Note the prominent responses in the left hemisphere to pseudowords and words as compared to letter strings and false fonts (from Posner & Raichle, 1997, p. 80).

words produced the pattern of response originally observed with words alone. Figure 2.11 shows that all four stimulus types generate some response. However, posterior parts of the left hemisphere are more activated by words and pseudowords than they are by false fonts or letter strings. Thus, it can be argued that two levels of analysis occur in the visual system as we passively view words. At one level, the brain analyses the visual features of the stimuli regardless of their relationships to letters and words. At the second level, the brain analyses the visual word form, incorporating the orthographic rules of the English language.

One of the difficulties of PET is that it takes a comparatively long time (relative to the speed of human information processing) to gather data, and it is therefore not well suited to investigating the time-course of cognition. In contrast, ERP is capable of providing information with high temporal resolution but localisation of informa-

tion is problematic. Each of the cognitive psycho-physiological techniques that can examine brain activity directly has limitations along at least one of these dimensions. For this reason, recent empirical investigations often combine a technique that is capable of fine-grained localisation with one that can achieve high temporal resolution.

## 2.7 CONCLUSIONS

In this chapter, we have reviewed principles for modelling the cognitive architecture. Typically, information-processing models specify one or more processing units, the computations on processing codes performed by those units, and the flow of information between units. The predictions of the model can then be tested against empirical data. Modelling requires the researcher to consider the overall organisation of processing units. For example, to decide on the extent to which processing is serial or parallel, and the extent to which control of processing is bottom-up or top-down. We may contrast architectures based on serial processing by a central processor with those in which processing is parallel, and performed by an array of very simple units (connectionism). Some models are readily expressed as a flow-chart or simulation resembling a conventional computer program. However, especially in modelling the various influences on human performance, we need to introduce constructs unfamiliar in conventional programming. One such construct is attentional resources, a metaphorical reservoir of energy for processing, that may limit speed and accuracy under demanding conditions. It may also be important to model voluntary control and strategy choice; in this instance, we may need to understand the person's intentions as well as the different "programs" which support different strategies. Finally, variation in "hardware" functioning may be more important in human information processing than it is in the computer, and principles and techniques for linking processing constructs to neural function were discussed.

## FURTHER READING

There are many excellent cognitive psychology textbooks (e.g. Eysenck & Keane, 1995; Reisberg, 1997), although Anderson's (1995) text has better coverage of skilled performance than most. Quinlan (1991) and McLeod et al. (1998) have provided accessible introductions to connectionism. At a more advanced level, Posner's (1989) edited volume covers many of the key areas of cognitive psychology and cognitive science. Issues relating to the energetics of performance are covered in the Hockey, Gaillard and Coles (1986) volume. Posner and Raichle (1997) present a nicely-illustrated overview of cognitive neuropsychology.

# 3

# Key subsystems of the cognitive architecture

## 3.1 INTRODUCTION: DIVIDING THE ARCHITECTURE INTO SUBSYSTEMS

In their more ambitious moments, cognitive scientists hope for a complete model of mental function, i.e. a full account of the cognitive architecture. At present, this is a remote aspiration which current theory does not approach, due to the complexity of the processing system. Models are abstractions, which are necessarily specialised to some degree. Typically, researchers focus on *subsystems* of the architecture, such as short-term memory and selective attention. In empirical studies, tasks are designed in the hope that performance reflects only the sub-system of interest, and restricted but manageable models can then be developed. In this chapter we discuss how the general principles of modelling described in Chapter 2 have been applied to some of the key subsystems for performance research.

Before looking at models of these specialised functions, it is worth gaining a sense of how the processing system may be organised at a very general level. Various "general" models of the cognitive architecture have been proposed. The "SOAR" model described by Laird, Newell and Rosenbloom (1987) and Anderson's (1983) ACT* are two well-known examples. We discuss ACT* in Chapter 7. However, although these models attempt to describe general principles, in fact each one directly explains only a small part of the available data on cognition and performance. For purposes of organising the research data, a more suitable human information processing model is the one shown in Fig. 3.1 (Wickens, 1992). It has evolved from the Broadbent (1958) model discussed in 2.2.2, and expresses much of what performance psychologists tend to believe about the cognitive architecture and its component subsystems. It should not be taken literally as a "circuit diagram" of the mind. It does not really address the control structures of the architecture, and some authors would revise it drastically: for example, by eliminating attentional resources altogether (Allport, 1989), or by making the architecture more parallel in nature. It does not include self-regulative processes, such as appraisal and coping, which are critical to stress reactions (see Chapter 9). Nevertheless, it is useful as an overview. Our discussion of its components follows Wickens (1992, pp. 16–20).

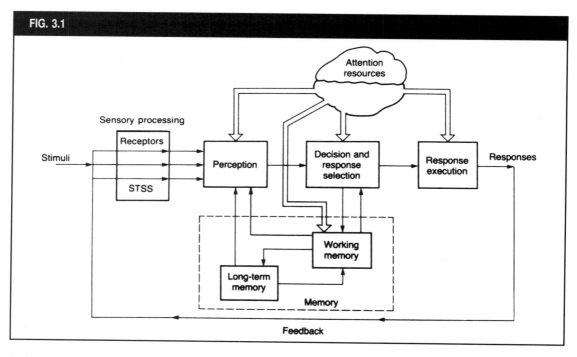

**FIG. 3.1**

A structure for information processing. From Wickens (1992). Reprinted by permission of Prentice Hall, Inc., Upper Saddle River, NJ.

The box labelled *sensory processing* represents initial perceptual processes that transform the neural outputs from the senses into abstract codes representing objects and their attributes such as (in vision) colour, size, distance and so forth. The neuropsychology of these processes is quite well understood; specialised nerve cells, operating in parallel, analyse stimulus input for its primitive "features" (see Table 2.2). Physical properties of stimuli are preserved in rapidly-decaying *short-term sensory stores* (STSS), referred to as *iconic* (for visual input) and *echoic* (auditory) memories. These memories maintain codes for basic perceptual properties of the stimulus for periods of a few hundred milliseconds (iconic memory) or a few seconds (echoic memory). *Psychophysics* concerns the relationship between the physical properties of stimuli (e.g. the frequency of a sound) and qualities of their initial representation in awareness (e.g. pitch). These topics are beyond the scope of this book.

Information from the STSS is passed to later stages of *perception*, at which the stimulus is identified or categorised in terms of its personal significance, which requires some analysis of its semantic properties as well as physical attributes. It is at this stage that stimuli may be represented as abstract codes as described in 2.2.1. Following recognition, information is passed to *decision and response selection* processes in which its implications for action are assessed, including choice of an overt response. These so-called *central processes* are intimately related to memory. Evaluation of the stimulus and its implications is guided by past experiences and knowledge represented in *long-term memory*. Central processing may also require the use of *working memory* as the person "thinks about" the stimulus; i.e. performs internal computations which may reveal further properties of the stimulus, or facilitate response selection. Eventually a response is selected, leading to execution of the response by the appropriate muscles. The system is in dynamic interaction with the external world, driven by feedback signals.

Energetic aspects of the system are represented by the irregular shape labelled *attentional resources* (cf. 2.4). The speed and accuracy of the component processes may depend on their being allocated sufficient resources. In Fig. 3.1, a variety of different types of process are energised by the same resource pool, so that performance is sensitive to the overall level of demands for resources. We will see in Chapter 5 that this view may be over-simplified.

In this chapter, we first review models of speeded response (3.2). On tasks such as choice reaction time, the issue is how to model the flow of information from sensory processing through perception and decision to response execution. As Fig. 3.1 suggests, one approach is to conceptualise processing as a series of stages, each performing a particular operation on the input data. However, this "sausage-factory" view of processing as a kind of computational production line neglects issues related to voluntary control. In 3.3 we examine levels of control theories which propose that a parallel processing system is overlaid by a supervisory control system that tends to operate more serially. These theories also address issues related to attentional resources and the energisation of performance. Section 3.4 examines different aspects of memory, and the architectural components which may support them. Finally, 3.6 focuses on models of working memory, a topic of particular importance for performance.

## 3.2 MODELS FOR RAPID RESPONSE

In many cases, performance requires a simple but rapid response to a single stimulus, such as braking for a red traffic light. While speed of muscular response contributes to speeded performance in such situations, the most important factors are often cognitive: the speed with which the stimulus can be analysed and a response selected. For example, a soccer goalkeeper facing a penalty must rapidly judge the flight of the ball, and decide whether to dive left or right, or to guard the centre of the goal (crudely, a three-choice task). Choice–reaction time tasks make the decision process explicit. In one such task, five-choice serial

reaction, the participant rests the fingers of one hand on five keys. Next to each key is a light and, when a light comes on, the participant must press the corresponding key as quickly as possible. Overall speed of reaction reflects both the speed with which the position of the light is encoded, and the speed with which the correct finger response is selected. The example suggests that we might model speeded response on the basis of a series of *stages* of processing. The first stage might be to form a code for the position of the light, followed by a second stage of accessing a code for the correct response, followed by a stage of transmission of the code to the muscles of the appropriate finger for actual response. In other words, we have a *serial processing* model in which, as in a conventional computer, a series of operations are performed on some input, one step at a time.

This section discusses various approaches to speeded response, but focuses especially on serial processing models and the concept of processing stages. As we shall see, these models may explain not just reaction time, but also other speeded but relatively simple tasks, such as searching short-term memory. We begin the section by taking a look at the precursors to stage models: information theory models of reaction time based on the metaphor of the telephone line rather than the computer. We then describe stage models and their limitations, which include their neglect of the person's voluntary, strategic control over response.

### 3.2.1 Information theory accounts of reaction time

Among the simplest tasks are those that require no more than rapid response to an important or "imperative" stimulus: the sprinter reacting to the starting-gun or the trainee driver performing an emergency stop. The most elementary reaction time (RT) measure, simple reaction time, requires a single response to a single stimulus, as in the initiation of a sprint race. In this case, the stimulus conveys no information about choice of response, only about the timing of response. Hence, information-theory models of simple RT are concerned with the accumulation of sensory evidence over the 150 ms or so time interval between stimulus and response. Response speed depends on rate of accumulation of evidence, although there may also be a further decision process required to evaluate when evidence is sufficient for response. Consistent with this underlying model, factors which speed the accumulation of evidence, such as increased stimulus intensity and stimulus predictability, also speed simple RT. The various models of the accumulation process are beyond the scope of this book (see Welford, 1976). However, we will reconsider the basic principle that decisions are made on the basis of accumulated sensory evidence in a different context, that of vigilance, in 6.1.

More typically, tasks require a choice between responses, and the more response options there are, the slower the response will be. Early models of choice reaction time were based on information theory (Shannon & Weaver, 1949), which seeks to quantify the capacity of communication channels such as telephone lines, i.e. how fast information passes from input to output or, in psychology, from stimulus to response. Calculation was made using "bits" (binary digits). A bit can assume a value of one or zero. Therefore, if we are given a task where we have to select between two equiprobable alternatives we require one bit to register this information. If we are required to select between four alternatives this requires only two bits, as the combination of ones and zeros for bits gives four alternatives (see Fig. 3.2). Arithmetically, the number of bits is the base 2 log of the number of choices, e.g. the base 2 log of four is two.

We can apply information theory to choice–reaction time as follows. Suppose that the person views a number of lights, each of which has a key associated with it. As soon as a light comes on, the person must decide which key to press as quickly as possible. The complexity of the decision reflects the number of bits of information, i.e. zero bits for simple RT, 1 bit for 2-choice RT, 2 bits for 4-choice RT, and 3 bits for 8-choice RT. The model predicts that RT should be linearly related to the number of bits of information transmitted. If we run experiments in which number of choices is varied and RT recorded, we find the predicted straight-line function (see Fig. 3.2). This is known as Hick's Law (Hick, 1952; Hyman, 1953). Arithmetically,

$$RT = a + b.\text{bits},$$

where $a$ and $b$ are constants, the intercept and slope of the straight line function. We could write the same expression as $RT = a + b.\log_2(N)$, where N is the number of choices. Information seems to be transmitted at a fixed rate, described as the *bandwith*, measured in bits/second.

Hick's Law describes the effects on RT of the number of stimulus choices. Fitts (1954) derived a similar expression for effects of response difficulty, known as Fitts' Law. His initial study investigated how long it took participants to tap a rectangular target with a stylus. Fitts found that movement time increased with movement length or "amplitude" (A), and decreased with the width of the target rectangle (W). The exact relationship is given by Fitts' Law, where $a$ and $b$ are intercept and slope constants:

$$\text{Movement time (MT)} = a + b.\log_2(2A/W)$$

Notice how this expression resembles the formula for Hick's Law, expressed in terms of number of choices. To make the comparison even more explicit, Fitts defined the term $\log_2(2A/W)$ as the *index of difficulty* (ID) of the response. Fitts' Law then can be rewritten as $MT = a + b.\text{ID}$, which resembles Hick's Law expressed in number of bits. Fitts' Law has been shown to apply to a variety of psychomotor tasks (see Wickens, 1992).

Other evidence suggests that information theory is over-simplified. Wickens (1992) discussed various factors whose effects on choice RT cannot be predicted from information theory, such as stimulus discriminability and the nature of the response. Choice RT is strongly affected by stimulus–response compatibility, the degree of intrinsic match between stimulus and response. Steering a small boat is problematic to the novice, because the tiller must be moved in the opposite direction to the change of course desired. In contrast, steering a car is more "intuitive", because S–R compatibility is greater. The S–R compatibility effect suggests that there may be a specific processing component concerned with response selection, in addition to any information-based limitation on information transmission. Comparable findings for

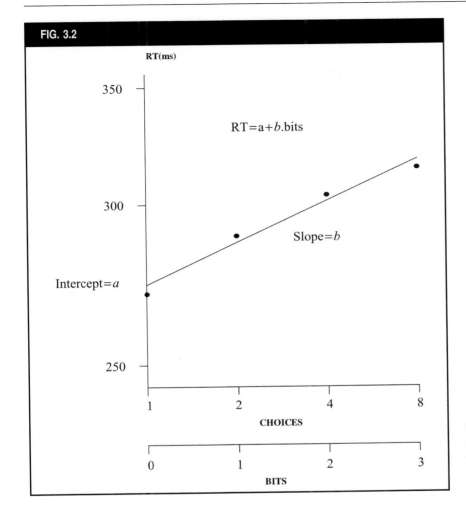

FIG. 3.2

$$RT=a+b.\text{bits}$$

Slope=$b$

Intercept=$a$

Hick's Law: The relationship between choice reaction time and complexity of decision (illustrative data).

other qualities of the task suggest that it may be necessary to distinguish several independent components to model choice RT data successfully. Furthermore, the ways in which task factors influence RT vary with training: S–R compatibility effects are reduced (but not eliminated) with practice (Dutta & Proctor, 1992).

### 3.2.2 Serial processing models and the additive factors method

Difficulties with information theory led to the replacement of the telephone wire metaphor with the information-processing metaphor. Reaction time was seen as the output of several distinct processes, so the challenge was to develop testable

models that specify the nature and architecture of these processes. Historically, the first attempt to develop a method for measuring processes contributing to RT was Donders' (1868) subtraction method (see 1.2.2). He reasoned that since choice RT is slower than simple RT, the difference between the two RTs measures the latency of the response–choice process. However, there are various difficulties with the subtractive method, which amount to uncertainty over whether or not subtraction isolates a single mental operation (Pachella, 1974).

In order to address some of the difficulties with the subtraction method, Sternberg (1969) developed a new approach to the decomposition

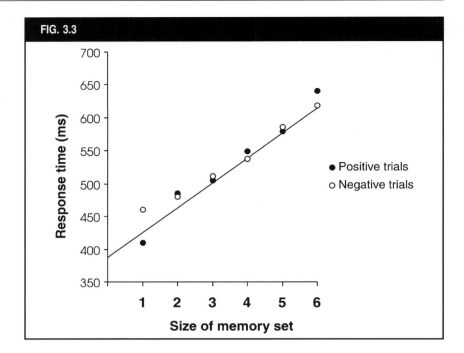

**FIG. 3.3**

Reaction time as a
function of memory
set size in a memory
scanning task
(from Sternberg, 1969).

of cognitive processes, using a *memory scanning* task. Imagine being given a series of numbers to remember. After a brief interval a single target number is presented and you are required to indicate, as quickly as possible, whether that number had been in the original list. Sternberg proposed that performance of this task comprises four serial stages: encoding, comparison, decision and response execution. First, the probe must be encoded. Second, a serial comparison is made between the probe and the items held in memory. Third, a binary decision is taken as to whether the probe was present in the memory set. Finally, this decision must be translated into a response which is executed.

This description of four stages of operations on input data constitutes an information-processing model. If the model is correct, it should be possible to isolate the different stages by examining the effects of variables that influence one stage only. For example, suppose we increase the number of items the person has to memorise initially, *the memory set size*. Sternberg assumed that the memory set size has no effect on time taken to

encode the probe, or on the decision and response stages. However, the time required for serial comparison of the internal code for the probe and the internal code for each memory set item should increase linearly with the number of comparisons to be made. The model makes a testable prediction: that if we measure RT with various memory set sizes, we should obtain a straight-line relationship between the two variables. Sternberg (1969) successfully confirmed the prediction: Fig. 3.3 shows that the time needed to perform this task increases linearly with the memory set size. The graph shows that each time another item is added to the memory set, RT increases by about 38 ms. If the model is correct, this time indicates how long it takes to compare the probe and memory set item codes.

The data are informative in other ways too. Note how Fig. 3.3 presents two sets of data: one for positive trials, in which the probe was matched to one of the items on the memorised list, and one for negative trials, in which the probe was not on the list. Both sets of data are described by the same straight line function. This finding implies an *exhaustive* search model: even if a match is found on positive trials, the comparison process continues through the rest of the comparisons before the decision stage operates. Positive and negative trials require the same number of decisions, so the RTs are the same for each. An alternative serial search model, the *self-terminating* model, supposes that when a match is detected, the next step is to feed a code for "positive match found" into the decision stage, without performing further comparison. In the self-terminating case, fewer comparisons will be required on positive than on negative trials to arrive at a decision, on average. With 2 memory set items, the decision will, on average, be made after 1.5 comparisons, with 3 items after 2 comparisons, and with $n$ items after $(n + 1)/2$ comparisons. It can be shown from the model that the slope of the RT–memory set size plot for positive trials should be half the slope for negative trials in this case, and plots of this kind are found in other search tasks (Shiffrin & Schneider, 1977).

We can distinguish rather more formally between the different stages by manipulating other factors experimentally. The length of the list influences only the second of the four serial stages: searching active memory via the comparison process. If the cognitive processing stages are independent it follows that manipulating any variable that affected a different stage would have the same effect on overall reaction time for all memory set sizes. In a second experiment, Sternberg (1969) examined the effects of degrading the probe (using a masking effect to make it more difficult to perceive the stimulus). Sternberg reasoned that, if the four identified stages were independent, this manipulation would only affect the first, encoding stage. The data (from the second of two experimental sessions) supported this hypothesis, with responses in the degraded condition taking approximately 100 ms longer, regardless of the size of the memorised list.

The technique here is known as *additive-factors*. Sternberg (1969) showed that higher memory load and masking both slow RT, but their combined effect is simply the sum of their individual effects. It is assumed that if two experimentally-manipulated factors have additive effects, they influence different stages. Conversely, Sternberg (1969) assumed that factors that tend to degrade a similar stage will have a non-linear or *interactive* effect. The combined effect of the two factors will be greater than the sum of their effects when applied individually. For example, suppose that we manipulated the brightness (luminance) of the stimuli as well as whether or not they were masked. We would expect both brightness and masking to affect the first encoding stage, so response to a dimmed, masked stimulus would be slower than would be expected from the effects of dimming and masking when looked at singly. By investigating the effects of different pairings of factors, it is possible to deduce the number of stages necessary for the model.

### 3.2.3 Serial stage models of choice-reaction time tasks

Additive factors methodology has been applied to choice–reaction time tasks by Sanders (1983, 1990). Figure 3.4 shows, in simplified form, a part of the Sanders model, which seeks to relate effects of both stressors and task parameters to specific stages (Sanders, 1983). At this level, the achitecture is entirely bottom-up and serial. The various stages are sensitive to both experimental variables such as stimulus intensity and stress factors such as drugs and sleep loss. Sanders (1983) developed the model by including biological and strategic factors. He discriminated three arousal mechanisms that influence different stages of processing: motor adjustment, for example, is affected by an activation mechanism. There is also an evaluation mechanism that responds to feedback on task performance, and which regulates the arousal mechanisms, aiming to maintain them at their optimal levels of activity. Unusually, therefore, strategic control of performance is effected through top-down control of biological mechanisms, rather than through direct effects on information processing.

Methods for distinguishing discrete stages are becoming increasingly sophisticated, and the additive factors approach has been quite successful in explaining choice RT data (Schweickert & Mounts, 1998). However, there are various problems associated with the approach. It is sometimes

**FIG. 3.4**

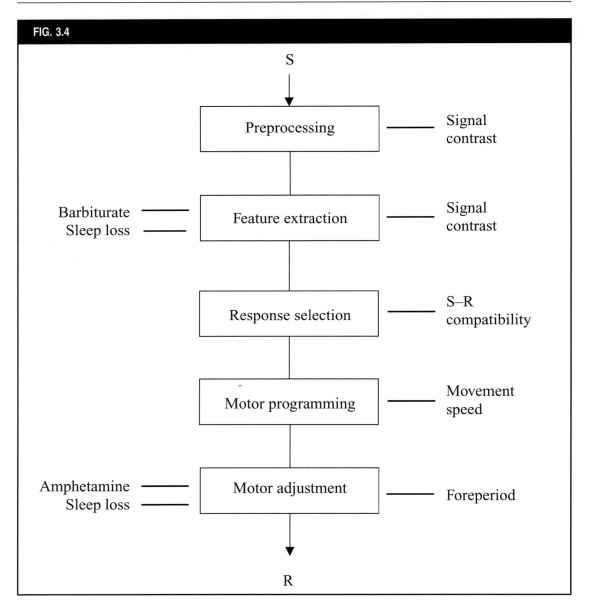

Sanders' stage model. Reprinted from ACTA PSYCHOLOGICA, Vol. 53, Sanders "Towards a Model of Stress and Human Performance" pages 61–97, 1983, with permission from Elsevier Science.

difficult to apply in practice because complex patterns of interaction may be found, which suggest that experimental manipulations may influence multiple stages. For example, probability interacts with both stimulus quality and stimulus discriminability, but the effects of stimulus qual-

ity and discriminability are additive (see Wickens, 1992). More seriously, the architectural assumptions may be incorrect. There are uncertainties over whether the representational codes at each stage are themselves discrete or continuous, whether processing at a particular stage takes place in a discrete, single-step manner or continuously, and whether information is transmitted from stage to stage continuously or discretely (Massaro & Cowan, 1993).

Continuous-flow models of processing (Coles et al., 1985; Miller, 1988) suggest that even if there are discrete stages, processing may not be strictly serial. Information may flow from one stage to the next, while processing is still taking place at the first stage. Sanders (1990) argues that additive factors methods may still be applied in this case, although he believes that there is limited evidence for continuous flow. It also seems dangerous to assume that combined effects of stressors on a single stage are necessarily non-linear. Nevertheless, additive factors analysis remains an important technique. According to Posner (1986), its assumptions often hold up but, even when they fail to do so, examination of the time course of information flow reveals much about the structure of internal mental processing.

### 3.2.4 Voluntary control of speeded response

The processing stage construct presents a rather passive view of speeded response; codes are fed from one stage to the next with little active involvement of the performer. Sanders' (1990) model, of course, attempts to relate voluntary control to arousal systems, but does not specify specific strategies in detail. Rabbitt (1989) argues that processing stage models are especially deficient in their scope for explaining control over speed–accuracy tradeoff. With multiple processing stages, it is plausible that each stage has its own speed–accuracy tradeoff characteristics, but it is highly unlikely that people have information about the speed and error probability for each stage. Thus, control must be exercised over speed and accuracy for the task as a whole. If the person aims to complete all the stages in a particular time, then an extension of processing at one stage must be compensated by curtailing processing at a later stage. That is, processing times for stages will not be independent, which violates a basic assumption of processing stage models. Hence, stage models may only be satisfactory when there is no time pressure, and the person can afford to

let the processing at each stage run to completion. A model of speeded response that cannot accommodate voluntary efforts to respond rapidly is evidently unsatisfactory.

Rabbitt's (1989) own extensive work on reaction time tasks emphasises adaptive control of response speed, which can be investigated by studying the speed–accuracy tradeoff described in 2.5.2. Performers discover through practice the likelihood of error for each speed of response, and choose a band of RTs appropriate for the point on the speed–accuracy tradeoff for which they are aiming. Instructions to experimental participants often stress both speed and accuracy, so typically participants aim to discover the band of RTs which is just too long for errors to be likely. Several lines of evidence support this adaptive view. First, in continuous RT tasks, in which response is rapidly followed by a new imperative stimulus, we can investigate the interdependence of speed and accuracy on a trial-by-trial basis (Rabbitt & Vyas, 1970). Figure 3.5 shows typical data (from Brewer & Smith, 1984). The sequence of responses is centred on an error response, labelled as "Error". The graph shows RTs for trials preceding and following the error. Characteristically, as the first part of the response sequence shows, relatively unpractised participants are prone to respond progressively faster, as long as no error is made. Error responses are typically rapid; the person has responded so fast that he or she is no longer within the "safe", low-error RT band. The person recognises the error and slows down markedly following it, and the process of testing the limits of the safe band continues.

A second line of evidence derives from studying not just the mean or median RT, but the distribution of RT across blocks of trials. For example, a fast response is more informative to the subject than a slow response, because only the fast response generates error feedback. Slow responses can only be regulated with respect to some internal clock of limited precision. Hence, RT distributions should show a sharp lower cut-off and a diffuse "tail" of slow responses. This "positive skew" is a familiar feature of RT distributions. Put differently, both the lower and upper ends of the distribution are under closed-loop control.

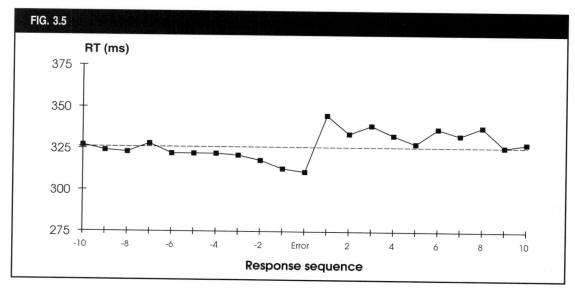

FIG. 3.5

RTs before and after commission of an error (from Brewer & Smith, 1984).

However, the error signal provided by inaccurate response allows for more precise control than the error signal provided by the internal clock used for time estimation. A third line of evidence derives from studies of performance changes with practice, as the person becomes more skilled in maintaining response within the desired RT band. Studies of RT distributions show that variation in RT across trials decreases with practice, as predicted, though processing efficiency also improves, in that the lower end of the distribution, marking the fastest error-free response possible, is reduced with practice (Rabbitt & Banerji, 1989).

Rabbitt's (1989) work has added a new dimension to understanding of speeded reaction, and there is little doubt that data from continuous RT paradigms support his adaptive model. It is something of an open question how important are adaptive control processes such as "tracking" of a critical RT band in other tasks. It is entirely conceivable that some of the factors that influence performance operate on the basic efficiency of processing, rather than on adaptive control. Rabbitt (1989) discusses evidence from other tasks, such as reaching out to press a switch, which suggests that it is common for subjects to learn how to coordinate different processes to optimise overall

performance. "We have to assume dynamic, active, adaptive control of a number of interlocked systems all of which, acting together, must adjust to any change in task characteristics" (Rabbitt, 1989, p. 168). Even if, say, a stress manipulation impairs processing efficiency, we must still take active adaptation into account. The stressor may also induce attempts to compensate for impairment, or it may impair detection of error and capacity to compensate. We will pursue these ideas further in two contexts in particular: the acquisition of skill (Chapter 7), and research on stress and performance (Chapters 9–13).

## 3.3 LEVELS OF CONTROL MODELS

The models reviewed so far have, in general, provided rather limited accounts of the architecture of control. Although evidence from studies of speeded response shows the importance of control processes (Rabbitt, 1989), formal models of response time, such as stage models, neglect control issues. Parallel processing models either evade the issue or, in the case of connectionism, assume explicitly that there is no need for any specialised architecture for implementing control (see Cohen, Dunbar, & McClelland, 1990). In this section, we describe a class of models that aims to integrate issues relating to control, architecture and energetics. They propose the architecture comprises independent subsystems for voluntary and involuntary control, and so they can be called levels of control models. The basic idea is that there are two levels of control of attention, variously described as *upper* and *lower* (Broadbent, 1977), *controlled* and *automatic* (Shiffrin & Schneider, 1977), or *conscious* and *automatic* (Posner & Snyder, 1975).

The lower, automatic level is reflexively triggered by incoming stimuli, requires few or no attentional resources, and is inaccessible to conscious awareness. It is widely accepted that early phases of processing, such as analysis of primitive stimulus features, possess these attributes. It is more controversial to suppose that later, more central, processes may become automatised. It is easy to think of complex tasks such as riding a bicycle, recognising a friend in a crowd or reading an undemanding piece of prose in which processing seems automatic. However, it is often difficult to demonstrate automaticity rigorously (cf. Broadbent, 1982). The upper level is associated with voluntary control of performance, and carries out specific executive functions that bias the operation of the lower level. Its operations are prone to be resource-demanding, and at least some of its aspects, such as the person's principal goals, are accessible to consciousness. Theories based on the distinction between levels attempt to show how resource-limitation of performance is constrained by the architecture of the system. Next we describe two prototypical examples.

### 3.3.1 Automatic and controlled processing

Shiffrin and Schneider's (1977; Schneider & Shiffrin, 1977) theory of automatic and controlled processing is noteworthy for its attempt to develop rigorous empirical techniques for discriminating the two types of process. Their studies were based on a search paradigm, in which the participant first memorises 1–4 target characters, and then searches a briefly-presented display for targets. The display may also contain up to four characters, including distracting non-targets. Searching a multi-character display for a single target is visual search; searching a single-character display for two or more targets is memory search. Shiffrin and Schneider compared performance in two qualitatively different conditions. In varied-mapping (VM) search, targets and distractors are drawn at random from the same pool of letters, so that the target for one trial might subsequently appear as a distractor, and vice versa. Under these conditions, Shiffrin and Schneider suggest, the person must carry out an effortful serial search that requires attentional resources and controlled processing. The Sternberg (1969) serial search model described in 3.2.2 appears as a special case of the more general model. In consistent-mapping (CM) conditions, targets and distractors belong to two distinct categories, digits and letters. A digit in the display searched is always a target, and a letter is always a distractor. Under these circumstances a target appears to "pop out" of the display effortlessly. CM search is said to take place through automatic parallel processing of the display stimuli, and requires no resources.

In their initial studies, Shiffrin and Schneider (1977) tested the effect of varying processing demands on CM and VM search, with the results shown in Fig. 3.6. The left panel shows visual search data, for both positive and negative trials (i.e. target present or absent). In VM conditions, RT shows a roughly linear increase with number of display items on both trial types: performance is sensitive to task demands as the serial search model predicts. In CM conditions, RT is hardly affected by number of items, consistent with the parallel search model. Similarly, as the right panel shows, in memory search RT is more sensitive to the memory load, the number of items memorised initially, in VM compared with CM search. The development of automaticity may be observed by training participants on two sets of characters, one set of targets and one set of distractors. Search slowly acquires the attributes of automaticity, most notably that, after extended practice, it is difficult to change the detection rule and respond to the distractor set rather than the target set. The overlearnt detection response appears to become

**FIG. 3.6**

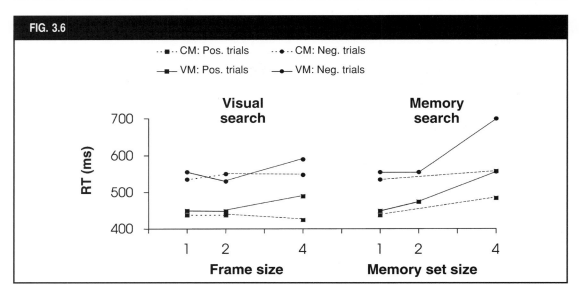

Effects of processing demands on response time (RT). From the Schneider and Shiffrin (1977) studies of visual and memory search (CM = consistent mapping; VM = varied mapping).

increasingly involuntary. Mechanisms for automatisation are discussed further in 7.3.

Further studies showed that VM search is more sensitive than CM search to dual-task interference (Schneider & Fisk, 1982), consistent with the hypothesis that only VM search is resource limited. Furthermore, results generalise to tasks requiring semantic rather than physical encoding. Fisk and Schneider (1983) demonstrated that distinctions between performance in VM and CM conditions are maintained when the person must search for category instance targets: searching for the target VEGETABLE requires the person to detect words such as CARROT and ONION. Schneider and Detweiler (1989) have developed a model of the two types of processing based on connectionist principles. The architecture comprises a number of independent processing networks or modules, operating with different internal codes (e.g. semantic, spatial, speech-based etc.) to translate specific inputs into outputs. Control structures act on the flow of information between modules, but when module outputs are highly activated, information flow bypasses control structures so that processing is

automatic. Consistent mapping allows inputs to activate outputs strongly enough for automatic processing to take place.

### 3.3.2 A schema activation model

Norman and Shallice (1986) proposed a somewhat similar model that aimed to discriminate levels of control of skilled performance. Their model (Fig. 3.7) focuses on real-world skills such as typewriting, and it tries to specify the processing routines supporting control in more detail than did the Shiffrin and Schneider (1977) model. It also has a neuropsychological basis in that supervisory control is located in frontal lobe structures (see also Shallice & Burgess, 1993). However, it lacks the detailed experimental support provided by the Shiffrin and Schneider search studies, and it has relatively little to say about learning.

The Norman and Shallice (1986) lower level comprises a set of special-purpose "schemas" or internal programmes for well-learnt thought and action. For familiar tasks, output from perceptual systems automatically triggers the appropriate schemas and actions. As in the Schneider and Detweiler (1988) model, the model is based on

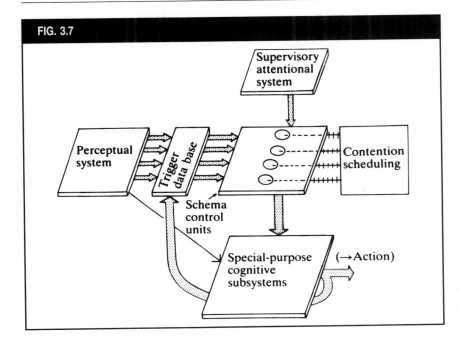

**FIG. 3.7**

The Shallice and Burgess (1993) schema activation model.

the activation metaphor; schemas operate when sufficiently activated. Any conflict or competition between schemas is also resolved automatically, through a "contention scheduling" mechanism that modulates schema activation. A further element of the model, the Supervisory Attentional System (SAS) effects voluntary control by biasing the activation of the lower level schemas upwards or downwards, a process which is resource-limited. The SAS is called into operation for tasks requiring planning or trouble-shooting, for novel or difficult tasks, and when a strong habitual response is to be overcome. Again, these task or situation attributes overlap with those for controlled processing in the Shiffrin and Schneider model. However, Shallice (1988) goes considerably further than Schneider and his colleagues in discriminating specific executive functions performed by the SAS. For example, developing novel plans and error correction may be distinct functions associated with different brain areas.

The primary source of evidence for the model derives from the cognitive neuropsychology of patients with damage to the prefrontal cortex and anterior cingulate, where the SAS is believed to

be localised (Shallice, 1988). Impaired executive control in frontal lobe patients has been demonstrated on various problem-solving tasks requiring advance planning. Shallice and Burgess (1993) suggest that the clinical phenomenon of "utilisation" represents stimulus-driven processing under the control of contention scheduling but not the SAS. Patients may spontaneously perform an action on an object, such as dealing out a pack of cards, for no obvious reason. More recently, neuroimaging techniques have been used to examine the function of the central executive. D'Esposito et al. (1995) used fMRI to investigate the separate and dual-task performance of two non-working memory tasks (a semantic judgement task and a spatial rotation task). Activity of the prefrontal cortex and anterior cingulate was identified that was only present in the dual-task condition. Further, this could not be accounted for by changes in task difficulty. Consistent with this result, Posner and Raichle (1994) examined PET scans in relation to performance of the Stroop task. Participants were presented with either conflicting (words and colour not the same) or non-conflicting (words and colours the same) stimuli. PET scan activity for the non-conflicting condition was subtracted from that for the conflicting condition, leaving activity relating to the process of dealing with the conflict between word and colour. Again, strong activity was found in the anterior cingulate. Posner and Raichle surmise that this might be associated with the inhibition of automatic processes. Neuroimaging studies of the effects of task practice are also supportive of the hypothesis that there exists a localised central executive that is responsible for controlled processing. It has been found that prefrontal activity, associated with task performance, declines following extended practice, presumably when automatic processing is in operation (Posner & Tudela, 1997; Toni, Krams, Turner, & Passingham, 1998).

### 3.3.3 Limitations of levels of control models

There is little doubt that, as Shallice and Burgess (1993) point out, the components of levels of control theories reflect a prevailing *zeitgeist*. There is broad agreement that attention and performance are controlled at different levels. However, both specific levels of control theories and the general constructs have attracted criticism. A basic difficulty is that criteria for automaticity may dissociate. Automaticity is said to be associated with three logically distinct properties: involuntary processing, resource-free processing and lack of conscious awareness. There are a number of demonstrations that these properties may dissociate. For example, perception of single letters is involuntary, but appears to require resources (Paap & Ogden, 1981). Recent work on controlled and automatic processing has tended to blur the sharp distinctions made in earlier theory (e.g. Shiffrin & Schneider, 1977). It has been claimed, for example, that there is a continuum of degrees of automaticity, such that processing may be partially automatised (Bargh, 1992). Such an idea is consistent with activation-based accounts of automaticity, which see the control of processing as jointly influenced by stimulus-driven and voluntarily-controlled activation (Cohen et al., 1990).

Neuropsychological evidence also suggests that the distinction is not clear-cut. Kramer, Schneider, Fisk and Donchin (1986) recorded ERPs during automatic and controlled memory search, using a measure of the N200-P300 waveform (see 2.6.3) to index mental demands. In fact, the amplitude of this measure was the same for both automatic and controlled processing, although both P300 and RT latencies were shorter for automatic processing. Shallice (1988) has discussed how the SAS may be fractionated into a variety of specific functions, associated with different brain regions. Consistent with this view, different performance tests of executive function seem to be uncorrelated (Lehto, 1996). This revision to theory calls into question the unitary nature of the SAS and its resource-limitations.

There are difficulties, too, with some of the architectural assumptions common to levels of control models, notably that early, "pre-attentive" stages of processing are entirely automatic. Logan (1992) turns the normal assumption on its head, arguing, in effect, that controlled processing is necessary for initial stimulus identification, which is followed by automatic retrieval of stimulus-related information held in memory. Schneider and Shiffrin's (1977) distinction between the seriality of controlled search and parallelism of automatic search has also proved difficult to sustain. As Townsend and Ashby (1983) have shown, there are generally both serial and parallel models that will explain any given set of search data, especially if parallel processing is permitted to be resource-limited.

Despite these difficulties, the basic distinction between levels has been enormously influential. In cognitive psychology, it has been applied to a wide variety of tasks. For example, semantic priming seems to have both automatic and controlled aspects (see 2.3.1; Neely, 1991). The levels hypothesis is also useful in understanding the qualitative changes in performance which ensue as people acquire cognitive skills, as described in Chapter 7. Performance becomes at least partially automatised as expertise grows. In stress research, controlled processing tends to be more sensitive to disruption than automatic processing. Similarly, individual and group difference factors such as age, personality and mood tend to have stronger effects on controlled processing (e.g. Matthews, Davies, & Lees, 1990). The theory of controlled and automatic processing provides a framework for linking ability dimensions such as general intelligence to individual differences in task performance (Ackerman, 1988). We will explore these applications in subsequent chapters.

## 3.4 MODELS OF MEMORY FOR PERFORMANCE RESEARCH

Memory is one of the main research topics of cognitive psychology. Much of this work is concerned with basic questions relating to the processes through which memories are encoded, maintained in storage and retrieved. Such issues are somewhat peripheral to human performance studies, and we do not attempt to present a comprehensive review of memory research in this book. Performance is, of course, highly dependent on both the operator's memory for how the task should be done, and their memory for the events of a particular performance episode. Obviously, a pilot's memory should contain representations of the various skills required to fly an aeroplane (which may or may not be accessible to consciousness). On a given flight, the pilot must keep an internal record of information related to that particular flight: where the aircraft is currently located, recent instructions from air traffic control, the next step in the flight plan, prevailing weather conditions, and so forth. In describing memory models for performance studies, we focus on three aspects of memory of special relevance to performance issues: *categories* or *varieties of memory, memories for skilled performance*, and *working memory*.

By "varieties of memory", we mean the different types of memory distinguished by researchers. These often come in pairs: short-term vs. long-term, semantic vs. episodic, implicit vs. explicit, and so forth. Different aspects of performance may depend on different aspects of memory. It is the pilot's long-term memory for procedures for flying aircraft that determines his or her basic competence (e.g. "what is the standard take-off procedure?") , but short-term memory which relates to the current flight operation (e.g. "which

runway should I take off from?"). In 3.4.1, we sketch some of the basic distinctions and related architectural issues. Memory research subsumes research on learning. If a person has learned some task or skill, we infer that there has been a change in processing structures which represents that learning, even if the person cannot report verbally exactly what they have learnt (c.f. 2.1.1). For example, a pilot cannot say exactly how controls such as the joystick are moved to keep the plane on course. In developing models of memories for skilled performance, we are concerned with the particular types of memory such as implicit memory and procedural memory that relate to the sometimes unconscious memories for "how to do things". We define these terms briefly in this section, and discuss in detail in Chapter 7 models for skill acquisition and retention.

The third aspect of memory we highlight is working memory, which refers to short-term storage of information in conjunction with active processing of information (Baddeley, 1986). A person holding a telephone number (i.e. a string of digits) in memory is using short-term memory: a person adding two three-digit numbers together is using working memory. Demanding tasks often tend to overload working memory: during landing, a pilot might be simultaneously implementing instructions from air traffic control, receiving new instructions and conversing with the co-pilot. Safety depends on the pilot's ability to combine the various processing and short-term storage operations involved. Because working memory is central to performance we will review models of working memory in detail, in section 3.5. In this section, we provide a brief overview of memory concepts encountered in performance studies. We begin by outlining the first attempts to develop cognitive models of memory, which focused on different memory stores. Next, we consider different functions of memory, and some of the architectural issues they raise. The final subsection concerns the role of consciousness, and the distinction between explicit and implicit memory.

### 3.4.1 Memory stores
Memories may be distinguished on the basis of how long they persist in the system. An influential

model of the 1960s, the *modal model* (Atkinson & Shiffrin, 1968), described three duration-based components in a multi-store model of memory. Sequential stages were proposed in which information is initially received into a sensory store. From here, a selective attention mechanism (see Chapter 4), transferred some information to a short-term store. This short-term store was of limited capacity, capable of holding only a small number of items of information, such as the digits of a phone number. Information was rapidly lost, unless the person engaged a process of active rehearsal, such as repeating back a phone number. Information was transferred from the short-term store into effectively unlimited long-term storage, whence it might be retrieved at a later time.

Allied to this conception of memory were various experimental techniques for investigating the different components. When a person reads and memorises a list of, say, 20 single words, and then recalls them immediately, the probability of recalling any given word depends on its position in the list. Recall is best for the first few words (the *primacy effect*) and the last few words (the *recency effect*), whereas words in the middle part of the list are recalled poorly. Studies (see Baddeley, 1990) showed that recall of the recency items (last part of the list) and "pre-recency" items (early and middle parts of the list) were sensitive to different experimental manipulations. If the rate at which the person was presented with the items was increased, recall of the pre-recency items was impaired, but the recency items were unaffected. Conversely, if, prior to recall, the person had to perform some other task for 30 seconds after the last word was presented, the recency effect was eliminated, but recall of the pre-recency items was unaffected. Results of this kind suggested that the recency effect was associated with a rather fragile, easily disrupted short-term store, whereas recall of pre-recency items depended on long-term storage.

Forgetting from short-term storage is a consequence of *displacement*: as each new stimulus arrives from sensory storage it displaces the oldest of the memories in the short-term store. In contrast, forgetting from long-term memory results primarily from *interference* and *retrieval failure*

(see Baddeley, 1990). New memories tend to be "written over" existing ones, making both the new memory and the older memory harder to access. Furthermore, even if there is a memory representation, it may be difficult to retrieve a specific memory. Retrieval is highly dependent on cues that somehow facilitate access to the correct "address" in memory. For example, in a spreading activation model, activation of the cue may spread from the cue representation to the representation of the memory the person is trying to retrieve. A traditional method for investigating retrieval processes was by comparing *recognition*, in which the person simply has to say whether or not the stimulus was presented during the learning phase of the study, and *recall*, in which the person is given no particular cue. It was assumed that recall involved some process of retrieval or search through long-term memory, whereas recognition short-circuited this process, and depended only on the quality of the memory trace.

A further aspect of memory models of the 1960s was the distinction of memories by processing code. Conrad (1964) showed that errors made in short-term recall were based on acoustic confusions; for example "B" might be recalled when the similar-sounding letter "V" had been presented. This finding implied STM was based on an acoustic or phonological code. Conversely, long-term memory appeared to be based on a semantic (meaning-based) code.

The 1960s conception of memory remains influential, but it is over-simplified, and detailed models based upon it (e.g. Atkinson & Shiffrin, 1968) have been shown to be incorrect. The modal model failed in various respects in experimental tests. For example, recency effects were demonstrated in long-term memory, calling into question evidence for a separate short-term store (Baddeley & Hitch, 1977). The assumption that long-term storage follows directly from holding information in the short-term store is also wrong. People have poor recall of familiar information that must often have occupied the short-term store, such as details of the designs appearing on coins (Nickerson & Adams, 1979). In experiments, simple rehearsal of material does not lead to better LTM, although more active, elaborative processing does (Tulving, 1966). Both recall and recognition are more complex than once thought. It remains plausible that recall is more dependent than recognition than memory search. However, "recognising" an item is not just a simple identification, because it is influenced by various factors, such as familiarity and contextual information (Johnston, Hashtroudi, & Lindsay, 1993) which imply a more complex decision process. The modal model has also faded from prominence for two more general reasons. First, as discussed in the next section, there may be multiple short-term storage functions, based upon differing processing codes. For example, storage of verbal and spatial information may relate to different processes and/or memory stores, and vary with different factors. Short-term memory is not exclusively phonological. Second, the modal model neglects the integration of storage and processing functions. Current research emphasises an integrated working memory, which may comprise multiple systems.

### 3.4.2 Functions of memory

The traditional view of memory centres on the organisation of record-keeping. To use an office metaphor, how should records be allocated to different stores such as desktop, filing cabinet and archives in the cellar? A rather different approach is to consider the functions of memory: perhaps memories are distinguished by the types of processing problem for which they are needed. An office might have different sets of files for accounting and personnel, for example. A basic distinction is between memories for various types of abstracted information, and memories bound up with action and response. Remembering "facts" may be rather different to remembering how to do something. Anderson (1983) distinguishes *declarative memory* for consciously reportable items of information, from *procedural memory*, which represents skills for interacting with the outside world. As discussed below, it is often maintained that procedural memory is unconscious: people cannot say exactly how they ride bicycles or solve complex problems. Declarative memory may be further subdivided into *episodic* and *semantic* memory. Episodic memory refers to recall of spe-

cific events ("what did you have for breakfast?"), whereas semantic memory refers to general knowledge of the world ("what are typical breakfast foods?"), which may be represented in the network forms described in 2.3. Procedural memory is rarely formally subdivided, but it is worth distinguishing cognitive and motor aspects. It is likely that cognitive skills such as playing chess are differently represented from motor skills such as delivering a service in tennis. Another action-oriented memory function is *prospective memory*: remembering to do something, such as phoning a colleague at 11 am on Tuesday.

These various forms of memory are not models but problems to be solved, by specifying an architecture that explains the observed data. Debates over memory models are beyond the scope of this book, but we highlight briefly three key issues: the *modularity* of memory, the *organisation* of memory, and the *voluntary control* of memory. "Modularity" refers to whether there are separate representational systems for different types of memory, such as semantic and episodic memory. One approach is to suggest that both semantic and episodic information is represented within a single parallel-processing mechanism. For example, concepts may become associated with information about specific instances of those concepts (Anderson & Bower, 1973). Other researchers (e.g. Tulving, 1993) argue for separate systems: for example, some amnesics are unable to form episodic memories, but they are able to acquire new factual information. Another long-running modularity debate concerns imagery. Paivio (1969) proposed a dual-coding hypothesis that information may be represented as separate visual and verbal codes, whereas Pylyshyn (1984) claims that imagery is actually represented as language-like propositions.

A second architectural issue is the extent to which memory is organised. On a simple associationist model, we might suppose that connections between concepts and/or representations of events are simply an arbitrary consequence of the person's life history, following the principles of association listed in 2.3.1. Memory would then be a tangled web of associations with no particular structure. However, experimental evidence suggests that memory may be organised as schemas, structured representations of generic concepts and events. The term *script* is sometimes used for more action-oriented generic information, such as how to behave in a restaurant (Schank & Abelson, 1977). Schemas and scripts guide encoding of information, and its subsequent retrieval. Bartlett's (1932) classic studies of recall of a native American folk-tale showed that when material was difficult to relate to a pre-existing schema, it became progressively distorted as time elapsed. Conversely, supplying a schema for otherwise confusing material tends to enhance both comprehension and recall.

The third issue is the role of voluntary control. At one level, intention is clearly important. People spontaneously reorganise material, perhaps on the basis of a schema. For example, if you watch a movie, where the action periodically cuts to "flashbacks" of prior events, you will probably try to reorganise your memories around a schema for events developing in chronological order. However, intention to learn does not always seem to help memory. A theory of the 1970s, *levels of processing* theory (Craik & Lockhart, 1972), presented evidence suggesting that intention to learn was irrelevant. What seemed to determine subsequent recall was the type of processing performed. "Deeper" semantic processing seemed to improve recall irrespective of intention, whereas shallower processing of phonemic and visual properties of stimuli led to relatively poor recall. The idea that processing varies in depth has been discarded. The critical factor appears to be the qualitative nature of processing. The advantage of semantic processing is due to the *elaboration* it tends to elicit: subjects spontaneously generate new propositions about the material which facilitate subsequent recall (Anderson & Reder, 1979). Some mnemonic techniques aim to bring such *rehearsal strategies* under voluntary control in order to enhance memory.

### 3.4.3 Consciousness and memory

The traditional memory study requires participants to respond by reporting their conscious awareness of a memory item. Memory may also be inferred from behaviour, in the absence of conscious awareness. As previously described, unconscious memories make an important contribution to skill acquisition and procedural knowledge. However, such effects may also be demonstrated in experiments using simple stimulus materials. The most dramatic examples come from studies of brain-damaged patients. Graf, Squire and Mandler (1984) gave amnesics word lists to learn, and confirmed their performance was very poor (<10% recall). The patients were also given a task in which they were asked to complete a three-letter word stem, such as JAC-, so as to form a complete word. The stems belonged to words they had previously seen (e.g. JACKET). Patients performed as well on this task as normal controls did (>50% correct), showing that they had memories for some of the words they had previously seen, even though they were usually unable to access them consciously. The patients were *primed* to respond on the stem-completion task. Priming effects on stem-completion and other tasks can also be demonstrated in normal subjects, leading to a theoretical distinction between *explicit* or conscious memory, and *implicit* or unconscious memory (Schacter, 1987).

Research on implicit memory has mushroomed in recent years, and a wide variety of tasks have been used (see Dienes & Berry, 1997, for a review). For example, people seem able to learn particular sequences of stimuli and rules for classifying stimuli, with little or no awareness of stimulus structure (Reber, 1989). People are also able to learn how to control dynamic complex systems without being able to express the rules involved (Berry & Broadbent, 1988). Dienes and Berry (1997) list three features that distinguish implicit learning from explicit learning:

1. *Limited transfer of knowledge to related tasks.* Implicit knowledge transfers less to tasks with a similar logical structure than explicit knowledge does.
2. *Learning tends to be associated with a focus on particular items rather than on underlying rules.* Implicit knowledge relates to memory for specific items or sequences of information, rather than insight into general principles.

3. *Robustness of learning and knowledge.* Implicit learning tends to be resistant to psychological and organic disorder, age and so forth. It has been claimed that storage and retrieval of implicit knowledge is insensitive to the attentional demands of secondary tasks, but in this case the evidence is mixed. Implicit learning may be attentionally demanding in some circumstances (e.g. Curran & Keele, 1993).

There has been considerable debate over implicit memory and learning, much of which is concerned with technical issues related to specific paradigms, which need not concern us here. The more general issue relates to the difficulties of using consciousness, a non-computational construct, to distinguish between two types of processing. Within a connectionist model, both explicit and implicit learning might be expressed as changes in connection strengths or resting levels of activation: it is irrelevant to the model whether or not there is conscious awareness of changes in these network properties. Implicit knowledge may simply be difficult to bring into consciousness, rather than being qualitatively different from explicit knowledge (Shanks & St. John, 1994). Turning the argument around, one might suppose that explicit rather than implicit knowledge raises conceptual difficulties: why should conscious awareness be linked to using information insightfully? The solution to these difficulties is to try to express the difference between explicit and implicit memories in terms of the cognitive architecture. Schacter (1993) suggests that there may be a separate perceptual representation system, distinct from semantic memory, which supports many priming effects. It is, of course, a rather large assumption to suppose that either implicit or explicit memory relates to a distinct system: different instances of implicit memory may relate to different systems.

## 3.5 WORKING MEMORY

Many tasks require a period of internal computation or "thought", requiring the recycling of codes.

These high-level aspects of central processing are explored in studies of decision-making, problem-solving and logical reasoning. Work in this area tends to be mostly concerned with the algorithms used for handling specific types of problem, such as the "heuristics" used to simplify decision-making, rather than real-time performance. Our treatment of these topics is selective (see cognitive psychology texts such as Reisberg, 1997, for general accounts). Subsequently, we review general principles of the acquisition of complex cognitive skill (Chapter 7), and the use of mental models in operational decision-making (8.1.2). In this section, we address the issue of the architecture necessary to support prolonged internal computation through the topic of working memory. As we have seen, traditional models of short-term memory tended to neglect processing issues, which have been rediscovered within the working memory construct. In this section, we describe some of the different approaches to modelling working memory.

### 3.5.1 Activation and blackboard models

There are three broad approaches to conceptualising the architecture of working memory, which might be termed activation, blackboard and multistore models. The basic assumption of activation models is that short-term memory is simply the activated parts of long-term memory (LTM), an idea that may be simulated directly by connectionist models of STM (e.g. Brown, Hulme, & Dalloz, 1996). Cowan (1988, 1995) has attempted to use the activation metaphor as the basis for a working memory model which integrates retention and attention. According to Cowan's model, activation does not necessarily imply conscious recognition, which requires focused attention. Only a subset of activated LTM items are within the focus of attention, whose direction is dependent on both bottom-up and top-down processing. Novel stimuli attract attention automatically, until they become habituated following repeated presentation. However, there is also a central executive system that exerts voluntary, top-down control over both the focus of attention and controlled actions. Cowan's model deals with the multiple function issue by stating that LTM may comprise a number of different subsystems or modules, whose activation might be governed by different principles, or which might tend to initiate different top-down strategies. Working memory is defined by Cowan (1995, p. 99) as "information in the activated portions of long-term memory, in the service of the focus of attention as applied by the central executive to the solution of a specific problem."

Blackboard models of processing and memory are especially concerned with control processes. The central idea is that processing is controlled by independent modules that send information to a central "blackboard" which registers these processing outputs. Processing modules read the information on the blackboard and process any information relevant to their own specific processing functions. Short-term memory is simply the content of the blackboard, which is over-written (interference) or which decays with time. This general idea has been particularly influential in skill theory, as we will see in Chapter 7. As with

activation theories, retention is something of a by-product of information processing, rather than being dependent on specific stores.

Jones (1993) has developed a blackboard model of memory in which discrete objects are activated on the blackboard, interlinked and organised as separate streams. It differs from activation models in that the essential problem for working memory is not maintaining activation of individual items, but keeping track of links between them. Furthermore, contents of memory share a common representation, rather than being segregated by processing code. Like Cowan's model, it does not suppose that multiple functions require multiple stores. Jones, Farrand, Stuart and Morris (1995) present evidence that interference between concurrent memory tasks depends not so much on coding (i.e. verbal or spatial), but on whether both tasks contain serial order information. Such information is used for rehearsing the two streams corresponding to the two tasks, so rehearsal is disrupted if both streams are serially ordered.

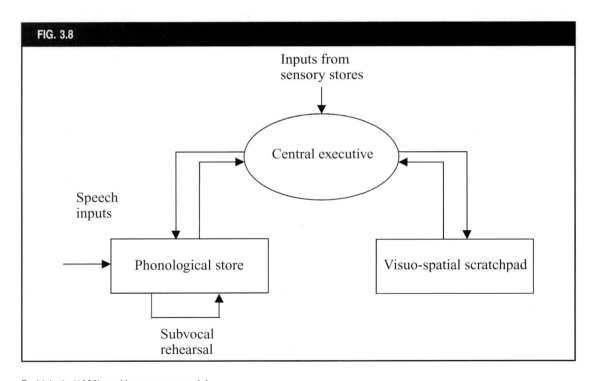

**FIG. 3.8**

Inputs from sensory stores

Central executive

Speech inputs

Phonological store

Visuo-spatial scratchpad

Subvocal rehearsal

Baddeley's (1986) working memory model.

## 3.5.2 A multi-store model

Baddeley's (1986; Baddeley & Hitch, 1974) working memory model differs from those reviewed in that it proposes a variety of different stores. Figure 3.8 shows the architecture of the model. Top-down control of processing is implemented by the central executive, a general-purpose processor, which performs a variety of specific functions. These include control of short-term retention of information supplied from early stages of processing (it is unclear whether the executive itself contributes directly to memory). Baddeley (1986) relates the central executive to the Norman and Shallice (1986) supervisory attentional system discussed above. It has at its disposal two special-purpose "slave" systems that allow it to implement short-term storage of information. The phonological or articulatory loop holds information as a code in a phonological store. This phonological representation tends to decay, so it is maintained through sub-vocal rehearsal, i.e. through translation into an articulatory code, which is then retranslated to the original phonological code. Voluntary rehearsal, under the control of the executive, allows a variety of types of information to be coded in this way. Speech inputs enter the phonological store directly. The second system is the visuo-spatial sketchpad, which may be used for storage of information such as geometric figures. Like the phonological loop, retention may depend on retranslation processes (not shown in Fig. 3.8): Logie (1995) refers to an "inner scribe" which maintains information in a visual store. Logie notes that conceptualising the slave systems as holding decaying information, which must be periodically refreshed, brings the working memory model somewhat closer to activation-based accounts of memory.

Baddeley and others have made considerable progress in relating working memory functions to complex tasks and activities. The central executive may be closely linked to general intelligence (Kyllonen & Christal, 1990), as we shall see in 14.3. The phonological loop appears to contribute to aspects of language which include comprehension, vocabulary acquisition, and learning to read (Gathercole & Baddeley, 1993). Indeed, verbal components of working memory may have evolved at least partially, so as to facilitate language. Visuo-spatial memory may be important for the control of movement (Logie, 1995). As in other areas of performance, we cannot deal with working memory at the symbol processing level alone. At one level, the debate over different working memory models reduces to the question of which special-purpose memory functions evolution has equipped us with. Evolution may have been remiss in failing to provide us with the memory we need for contemporary tasks such as solving complex mathematics problems. Anderson (1990) suggests that we have failed to evolve a separate short-term store, and so we use such strategies as we can learn to compensate. Finally, we may note that there is increasing evidence on the cognitive neuroscience of memory: both Baddeley (1986) and Cowan (1995) discuss possible neural underpinnings of their models.

## 3.6 CONCLUSIONS

The cognitive architecture is far too complex for any complete, detailed model to be developed in the near future. Instead, researchers adopt the strategy of dividing it into subsystems that can be modelled more readily (at the possible cost of losing sight of how the system works as a whole). In this chapter, we reviewed models of some of the subsystems of most interest to performance researchers, which illustrate some of the general principles discussed in Chapter 2. First, we looked at speeded response, a field dominated by serial stage models of performance. Such models have been successful in explaining how task and other factors influence response time, but have difficulties in accommodating the influence of voluntary control and strategy.

Next, we considered in more detail how different levels of control of performance may be modelled. There may be separate levels of the architecture concerned with implementing voluntary and "automatic", stimulus-driven control of processing, although this approach has its critics. Multilevel models of control have been especially influential in studies of attention. Finally, we reviewed models of memory for performance research. There are various aspects of memory, and many more models of memory than a book of this kind can describe. We focused especially on the "working memory" which directly supports human performance, and contrasted activation-based and multi-store models of this function.

## FURTHER READING

Recommended texts for the topics of this chapter include Proctor and Dutta (1995) and Wickens (1992) for speeded reaction, Shallice (1988) for discussion of levels of control and their neuro-psychological basis, and Baddeley (1990) for an overview of memory. The papers by Schneider and Shiffrin (1977; Shiffrin & Schneider, 1977) had a rapid impact on performance studies: a special issue of *American Journal of Psychology* (1992) provides various thoughtful commentaries on the levels of control issues raised by the Schneider and Shiffrin research. Cowan's (1995) book is interesting as an attempt to integrate attention and memory research.

# 4

# Selective attention

## 4.1 BASIC ISSUES

For more than a century, there has been explicit
recognition that human cognitive performance involves a process of attentional selectivity. William
James (1890, pp. 403–404) famously defined attention as ". . . the taking possession by the mind,
in clear and vivid form, of one out of what seems
several simultaneously possible objects or trains
of thought". Similarly, Titchener (1910) described
an attentional dichotomy in his "law of two levels";
an upper level of "clearness", or attention, and a
lower level of "obscurity", or inattention. The common theme running through these, and more recent, characterisations of attention is that a process
of selection occurs from the enormous number
of stimuli to which we could attend, at any given
moment, such that only a proportion are subject
to intensive cognitive processing.

### 4.1.1 The bottleneck concept

Important empirical and theoretical precursors
to the subsequent study of selective attention
occurred in the late 1940s when the notion of
a "bottleneck" within the human information
processing system began to surface. Craik (1948)
noted that, during the performance of a psychomotor tracking task, corrections were not made

continuously but only every .5 sec. He suggested
that this may have been due to the effects of a
neurological refractory period (see also Telford,
1931) that resulted in central processing limitations. Although this mechanism was soon recognised as implausible, the fundamental concept was
extended in the 1950s by Welford (1952), who
used the term "*psychological* refractory period"
(PRP). The most direct experimental studies of
the PRP (e.g. Elithorn & Lawrence, 1955; Marill,
1957) presented participants with two stimuli in
quick succession, and required them to make
a timed response to each. The interval between
the presentation of the stimuli (stimulus onset
asynchrony: SOA) was manipulated. Response
times to the second stimulus were found to be
dependent on SOA. Reducing SOA so that the
second stimulus was presented before the response
to the first stimulus was executed resulted in increased response times to the second stimulus. It
appeared that there was a bottleneck in cognitive
processing between stimulus perception and response. Research using variations of the additive
factors method, as described in 3.2.2, has localised the bottleneck to what may be termed "central processing" (see Pashler & Johnston, 1998 for
a review). Figure 4.1 illustrates how processing
of the second stimulus (S2) must wait for completion of processing the first stimulus (S1).

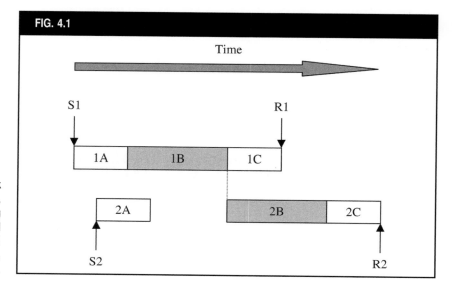

**FIG. 4.1**

The response bottleneck (Pashler & Johnston, 1998, p. 166). Processing of S2 is postponed until response selection of S1 (stage 1B) is completed. Reprinted with permission.

The concept of a "bottleneck" in attentional processing provided a basis for much work, dating from the early 1950s, devoted to uncovering the nature of cognitive limitations as they relate to the process of selective attention. This research focused, almost exclusively, on attentional selection between competing *external* stimuli, i.e. those stimuli acquired through our senses, rather than *internal* stimuli, i.e. relating to thoughts and knowledge (Johnston & Dark, 1986), perhaps because the former are more readily subject to experimental manipulation (Eysenck & Keane, 1995). The key point of contention was, and to some extent still is, the level of semantic analysis of incoming stimuli required before selection for attention. Some models (e.g. Broadbent, 1958) suggest that the bottleneck occurs at an early stage, and operates principally on the basis of the physical characteristics of stimuli. Other models (e.g. Deutsch & Deutsch, 1963) suggest that semantic processing is required for all stimuli before a response can be chosen. Further models (e.g. Treisman, 1964) suggest a compromise position, in which limited ("attenuated") semantic information is processed before selection. Important differences between these models can be identified with respect to the distinction between top-down and bottom-up processing, as discussed in 2.2.3.

Early filter models of selective attention view the selective process as "data-driven", in that selection is made, in a primarily bottom-up fashion, on the basis of the characteristics of the stimuli. Late filter models, in contrast, allow for increased top-down processing, with the semantic contents of the stimuli being related to the contents of long-term memory, and in this respect can be regarded as "conceptually-driven" (Norman & Bobrow, 1975).

## 4.1.2 Dynamics of selection: Attentional channels

The bottleneck metaphor assumes a static view of selection in which stimuli, or stimulus properties, are clearly divided into those to be attended and those to be ignored. In real life, however, we habitually switch the focus of attention between sources of stimuli. At different times, a driver might select the road ahead, pedestrians by the roadside, mirrors and the instrument panel. The concept of *channels of attention* has provided a useful framework for this broader view of selective attention. It has proved convenient to divide the physical environment into a set of separate channels, such that each is a distinct source of stimuli (Moray, 1986). For instance, the attentional demands placed on a pilot may be characterised as the receipt of information through a large number of visual channels, with each cockpit instrument defining a channel, and a smaller number of auditory channels, such as radio messages, utterances of a co-pilot, and auditory signals and alarms. In experimental settings, the number of channels is usually restricted, perhaps to a single channel only. However, in real life, as in the example of the pilot, we have to sample many channels, shifting the focus of attention from channel to channel to maintain adequate performance. This sampling process requires a sampling strategy, which determines the sequencing of attention shifts. Sampling strategy is, in turn, based on the individual's expectations regarding the frequency and importance of events on the different channels available. Ideally, sampling strategies should be adaptive in that they optimise the uptake of important information. Hence, people tend to sample channels on which events take place frequently more often than channels with low event rates. However, maintaining a mental representation of channel properties requires memory, which is prone to overload, so that sampling strategy may be less than optimal, for example, like a motorist who runs out of fuel through failure to sample the fuel gauge.

In applied contexts, training on tasks such flying an aeroplane or controlling complex industrial processes involves acquisition of an adaptive model of the task. The practical issue is how to ensure that the cognitive representation acquired by the operator, of event frequencies and importances, promotes use of optimal or near-optimal sampling strategies. People may simply forget to sample channels of low priority (e.g. the fuel gauge). Bellenkes, Wickens and Kramer (1997) recorded visual scanning patterns in samples of novice and expert pilots. The experts were found to scan across most instruments more rapidly and flexibly. They also seemed to apply a better mental model to controlling the aircraft. Data of this kind are useful in pilot training. Another promising approach is to develop the theory of how actions and mental operations are scheduled and sequenced. Scheduling theories may be used to discover optimal strategies, and to assess the quality of the strategies actually used by the operator (Dessouky, Moray, & Kijowksi, 1995).

In addition, the operator's task may be eased by providing a preview of scheduled events, which allows advance development of sampling strategy (Sanderson, 1989). Meyer and Kieras (1997a) have proposed a model that assigns control of scheduling to an executive system, within a levels of control model similar to those discussed in 3.3.

### 4.1.3 Theoretical issues in selective attention research

Currently, there is a proliferation of detailed theories of selective attention: Schneider (1995) discusses 12 major visual selection theories, for example. The aim of this chapter is not to review these theories in detail, but to try to identify some of the main conceptual issues currently exercising attention theorists. The disadvantage of this broad-brush approach is that important technical details of the theories are neglected, and it is recommended that the reader refers to the original reports for adequate understanding of specific theories. Selective attention research can be confusing because theorists disagree not just about architectures for selection, but on the basic questions to be addressed in research.

The first set of issues relates to the functions of attention: what is attention for? Schneider (1995) distinguishes two functions of visual attention: "selection-for-object-recognition" and "selection-for-action". Object selection is the problem addressed especially by the early selection theories of the 1950s and 1960s. If there is some limit on the capacity of the system to recognise multiple objects in the visual field, how does the system select a small subset of objects for full analysis? The output of the function is an internal representation or code, perhaps in working memory. Action selection is the problem of selecting the information needed by motor systems to perform actions such as reaching for a mug of coffee (Tipper, Lortie, & Baylis, 1992), so that the output of the function is a motor response. Action selection resembles the response selection process of 1960s late selection theories (e.g. Deutsch & Deutsch, 1963). The two functions correspond to two potential adaptive challenges: perceptual overload, and response incoherence due to simultaneous activation of incompatible response tendencies

(Kahneman & Treisman, 1984). Tipper and Weaver (1998) describe an integrative position, such that attention may flexibly support different functions, accessing different forms of internal representation according to behavioural goals.

A second type of issue concerns whether there are actually any selection mechanisms at all. The conventional view, associated especially with early selection theories, is that overload of processing requires, as a component of the architecture, a special-purpose selection mechanism which imposes a bottleneck and filters out irrelevant stimuli: attention operates as a "cause" (Johnston & Dark, 1986). Alternatively, attention may be an "effect": an observed phenomenon which does not in fact result from a dedicated selection mechanism. For example, within parallel processing models, priming effects may lead to prioritisation of information without there being any overt selection stage of processing. This view is compatible with a strand of contemporary thought that supposes that the processing "capacity" of the system is sufficiently high that information overload does not present a problem. This view is supported by demonstrations of "negative priming": apparently disregarded distractor items may in fact be inhibited on subsequent trials (Fox, 1995), as further discussed in 4.4.2. Van der Heijden (1992) argues that the sole adaptive function of the visual system is to control action, through two types of selection. First, there is an "intention" mechanism that chooses which action or skill is to be implemented. Evidently, it relates to the person's strategies and goals, and to Pylyshyn's (1984) semantic level of analysis. The second mechanism, the one addressed by most experimental studies, is "attention", in the sense of selecting the stimulus information that will control the intended action. Van der Heijden (1992) discusses an architecture for attention that implements these mechanisms. Interestingly, the attention mechanism works through selection at an early stage of visual processing, although it differs from typical early selection models in that there is no capacity limit on stimulus processing anywhere in the system. There is increasing neuropsychological evidence for top-down control of the response of brain areas related to early visual processing stages (Schneider, 1995).

We can perhaps address only the third type of issue, the details of the architecture, when the functional and causal aspects of attention are understood. The traditional debate between early and late selection theorists may have failed to reach a clear-cut resolution because it largely neglected this wider perspective. In contemporary work, there remains a divide between two camps. The first perspective is to continue to characterise attention as "selection-for-object-recognition", and to develop models of the selection process. Alternatively, attention may be seen as the output of multiple mechanisms operating within a parallel processing system, a view compatible with cognitive neuroscience (Duncan, 1996). As Allport (1989) has stated: ". . . to pursue a general 'theory of attention', without first specifying the computational functions that the theory is to account for, would appear to be a likely recipe for disaster." In other words, attentional theory should deal with specific cognitive operations, and the computations that lead to prioritisation effects.

In this chapter, we begin with the basic problems of channel selection and establishing an attentional focus addressed by early and late selection theories. One of the fundamental issues here is the processing of "unattended" information. Is information delivered on unattended channels discarded at an early stage, or is it in fact analysed in detail but disconnected from response? We continue by reviewing contemporary selection theories relating to object-based selection, spatial location-based selection, and mechanisms identified through cognitive neuroscience. The chapter is concluded with a look at the priming-based processes that may permit selection in the absence of a discrete selection mechanism.

## 4.2 EARLY VS. LATE SELECTION

In this area of study, the dominant empirical theme of the 1950s was the examination of mechanisms of *auditory* selective attention. This was possibly because auditory stimuli provided a more tractable experimental paradigm than visual stimuli, in that the focus of attention is easier to control

(Broadbent, 1971). Studies often used the two ears as channels, and tested whether the person could attend to one ear exclusively. Data from such paradigms were used to support early or late selection positions, and in this section we review the evidence from these classic studies of attention, and outline contemporary perspectives.

## 4.2.1 The case for early selection: Filter theory

Early studies concerned themselves with the "cocktail party effect"; that is, the extent to which it is possible to listen to a message conveyed by one voice while other voices are simultaneously audible. Typically, experimental designs (e.g. Broadbent, 1952a; Cherry, 1953) were based around dichotic listening tasks, in which participants were presented with two auditory messages via headphones, one to each ear, and were instructed to "shadow" one message (to repeat aloud each word in the message as soon as it has been presented) and to ignore the other channel. Various experimental manipulations of the characteristics (both physical and semantic) of the messages were examined. Results emphasised the importance of physical, rather than semantic, characteristics of stimuli to the process of selective attention. For instance, it was demonstrably easier to distinguish between voices if they were spatially (Broadbent, 1952a; Poulton, 1953), temporally (Treisman & Riley, 1969), or tonally (Broadbent, 1952b; Egan, Carterette, & Thwing, 1954) distinct.

Further, it was apparent that participants gained very little information from the unattended channel (Cherry, 1953), and generally failed to notice, for example, that the language had changed from English to French, or that the message consisted of speech played backwards. Similarly, Moray (1959) had participants "shadow" one message while a short list of words was presented 35 times in the unattended channel. Participants had no recollection (when tested 30 sec after task completion) of the contents of the unattended channel. In a recent replication of Cherry's work, Wood and Cowan (1995, Experiment 1) found that only about 14% of participants could report any content from the unattended message. However, rather higher percentages (29–67%), depending on the length of shadowing prior to onset, noticed reversed speech contained within the message.

On the basis of experimental results such as these, Broadbent (1958) proposed an "early filter" theory of selective attention, in which an attentional "bottleneck" occurred prior to semantic processing. Broadbent viewed this selective process as adaptive, in protecting the cognitive system from overload. Broadbent's model has been presented in Fig. 2.1 (page 26): information transferred from primary (short-term) memory to subsequent processing is selected on the basis of physical *features*, i.e. elementary stimulus properties such as the ear at which an auditory stimulus arrives, or the colour of a visually-presented stimulus (see Table 4.1).

Further support for this model from a visual paradigm was provided by Sperling's (1960) classic demonstration of the properties of iconic memory (a term coined by Neisser, 1967).

| **TABLE 4.1** | | | |
|---|---|---|---|
| **Examples of basic sensory features.** | | | |
| **Auditory** | | **Visual** | |
| **Feature** | **Example** | **Feature** | **Example** |
| Ear | left vs right | Colour | red vs green stimuli |
| Pitch | high vs low | Orientation | horizontal vs vertical line segments |
| Timbre | violin vs clarinet | Motion | upward-moving vs stationary stimuli |
| Intensity | loud vs quiet[1] | Position in depth | close vs near stimuli |
| [1] Provided loud stimulus does not mask quiet one. | | | |

Initially (see Fig. 4.2), Sperling empirically determined that when participants were briefly (50 ms) presented with arrays of 12 letters (3 rows of 4 letters) they were able to recall only approximately 5 items ("whole report" condition). However, participants reported that during presentations they could "see" the whole array. Sperling hypothesised that information was being lost from a sensory store before oral report could take place. This was tested by presenting participants with a tone (immediately after the display of letters). The pitch of the tone (low, mid, high) indicated (cued) a row of letters (bottom, middle or top) that participants were required to recall. Performance in this "partial report" condition was considerably improved (see Fig. 4.3). Participants were able

to consistently report approximately three of the four letters in the cued row. Subsequently, Sperling examined the consequences of introducing increasing delay between the array presentation and the tone that cued report. Accuracy of recall indicated that the contents of iconic memory are available for approximately 500 ms. Beyond this point there was no performance advantage for the "partial report" condition.

### 4.2.2 Difficulties for the early selection model

Many experimental results were difficult to reconcile with an early filter account of selective attention, in that some processing of unattended stimuli was apparent. For instance, Lawson (1966) conducted an experiment in which participants

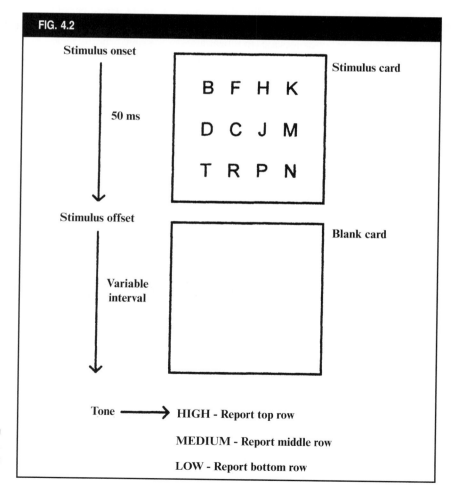

FIG. 4.2

Stimulus onset

50 ms

Stimulus offset

Variable interval

Tone ⟶ HIGH - Report top row

MEDIUM - Report middle row

LOW - Report bottom row

Stimulus card

B F H K

D C J M

T R P N

Blank card

Sperling—display (from Styles, 1997, p. 36). Reprinted by permission of Psychology Press.

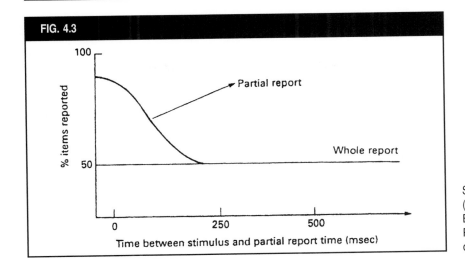

**FIG. 4.3**

% items reported (vertical axis)

100

Partial report

Whole report

50

0    250    500

Time between stimulus and partial report time (msec)

Sperling—graph of results (from Humphreys & Bruce, 1989, p. 120). Reprinted by permission of Psychology Press.

performed a dichotic listening task during which brief tones were presented, on either the attended or the unattended channel, that required a manual response. Although responses were faster and more accurate on the attended channel, there were still some hits on the unattended channel, indicating some awareness of content. Similarly, in an imaginative study that examined "primed" galvanic skin response (GSR) to unattended words, Corteen and Wood (1972; Corteen & Dunn, 1973) found evidence of unattended semantic processing. During the first phase of this experiment, participants were conditioned with mild electric shocks to specific words, to the point where presentation of these words produced measurable changes in GSR. These words were then presented to the unattended ear during a dichotic listening experiment. Corteen and colleagues found that these words still evoked a change in GSR.

It appears that intrusions or "breakthrough" from the unattended message are more probable when the information concerned has semantic relevance. For example, participants are quite likely to notice the occurrence of their own name (Moray, 1959) in a non-shadowed channel. Treisman (1960) demonstrated this more formally using an experimental design in which one message was connected prose, and the other a sequence of unrelated words. Initially the prose was presented to the attended ear but, periodically, the messages

were switched across ears so that the unrelated words were presented to the attended ear and the prose to the unattended ear. Broadbent's filter theory predicts that the person should continue to follow the message presented to the initially attended ear, and so report the unrelated words as if they were part of the message to be shadowed. In fact, Treisman found that participants sometimes spontaneously switched from the initially attended ear in order to follow the sense of the prose. They can do this only if the meaning of words arriving at the unattended ear is processed prior to selection, contrary to predictions made by filter theory.

A similar effect was found by Gray and Wedderburn (1960) using a "split span" technique in which participants were presented with three pairs of words, one word from each pair being presented to each ear. In an earlier experiment, using a similar design, Broadbent (1954) found that participants preferred to report digit stimuli "ear by ear", rather than by sequence of presentation. This result is consistent with an early filter model in which selection is based on physical characteristics of stimuli. However, in contrast, Gray and Wedderburn (1960) found that when semantic context would be maintained by switching between ears during report, e.g. presenting "mice, two, cheese" to one ear and "eight, eat, five" to the other, participants tended to report "mice eat cheese" and "eight, two, five", indicating some degree of semantic processing.

### 4.2.3 Late selection theory

In order to address the apparent unattended processing of semantic information, Deutsch and Deutsch (1963), Norman (1968) and others have proposed late selection models, in which all stimuli are fully analysed and selection takes place only for purposes of response. In such models, no feature-based filtering takes place. Instead, incoming stimuli are "cross-referenced" with the semantic contents of long-term memory and, on the basis of this assessment of importance, are selected for response. One of the main reasons for suggesting an early filter is that information can readily be ignored if it is on an unattended channel. However, such performance could still be consistent with a late selection model if, at the time of perception, information was "tagged" with physical characteristics, such as its source (Welford, 1968). In support of the central role of long-term memory within the selection process, Norman (1969, p. 85) pointed out that, for example, "the somewhat arbitrary visual and sound patterns of speech and writing must be stored in permanent memory". He presented evidence that memory of the contents of a non-shadowed channel is possible if recall of material is immediate, in contrast to earlier studies (e.g. Moray, 1959), in which recall was delayed. However, these results may have been influenced by the fact that Norman's participants knew that they would be tested on the material and were well practised on the task. Contrary results are provided by MacKay (1973), who found that participants were generally unable to report the contents of the unattended channel even though report was immediate and the information presented on the unattended channel comprised a single word.

Although the evidence for semantic analysis of unattended auditory material is persuasive, there are difficulties with late selection models of attention. For example, given the large number of stimuli, how is it possible to compare every one with the contents of memory and with each other before making a selection decision? Furthermore, late selection implies a view of early processing as

no more than passive registration of information. Broadbent (1971, p. 147) dismissed late selection on these grounds, arguing that the nervous system must behave ". . . not as a tape recorder but as a much more complicated recognizing device". A counter-argument is that connectionist models may provide a means for both the simultaneous registration and analysis of multiple stimuli. Broadbent (1971) also argued that late selection seems inefficient, in that complete analysis of neglected messages negates the whole point of a selection system, to produce an economy in processing. Further, if selection occurs at a late stage, why is it that so little information from unattended sources is available to us? For example, Treisman showed that breakthrough of the unattended channel happens only very infrequently (6% of trials).

It would seem that both early and late filter accounts of selective attention are incomplete (Lachman et al., 1979). Early filter theories struggle to deal with intrusions from unattended channels that have been observed using several different experimental paradigms. There is also evidence from visual search studies to show that people can often identify not just features but individual letters in parallel (Pashler, 1998a) although, according to Broadbent (1958, 1971), categorisation of this kind should operate serially, after filtering. However, late selection theories fail to recognise the potential adaptive significance of early selection, i.e. the reduction of processing load. They also cannot account for the ease with which channels can be selected using physical criteria, or the relative infrequency of intrusions from unattended channels. Pashler (1998a) points out that evidence for analysis of distractor stimuli is reduced as the processing demands of distractors increase, implying that early perceptual processing imposes a processing load, as early selection assumes. More recent work has explored possible compromise positions.

### 4.2.4 The attenuated filter model

An alternative account of selective attention, in which some semantic information is processed before selection, was proposed by Treisman (1964), and later supported by Broadbent (1971). This involves a filter that "attenuates" rather than excludes information, and a cognitive "dictionary" that determines the semantic importance of stimuli (see Fig. 4.4). If the physical properties of stimuli are inappropriate for attentive processing (e.g. a dissimilar voice to one currently being attended to), this information is attenuated within, rather than excluded from, the cognitive system by an initial filter. All sensory information is then received by a cognitive "dictionary" that uses principles of activation and thresholds, in a manner somewhat analogous to the spreading activation and connectionist models described in 2.3.1, to determine the most important stimuli for further processing, based on semantic content.

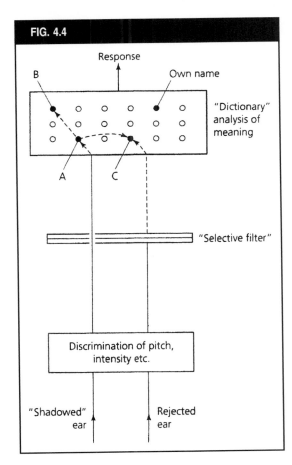

**FIG. 4.4**

Treisman's model of selective attention (from Treisman, 1960). Reprinted by permission of the Experimental Psychology Society.

This model can deal with the results that were anomalous for the early filter model. For example, breakthrough of familiar material (e.g. one's own name) on an unattended channel can be explained by supposing that the thresholds required for attention to such material are lower than for less-familiar stimuli. Similarly, because this model recognises the importance of semantic context, it can explain the results of Treisman's dichotic listening studies, in which the shadowed message swapped ear of presentation. However, Treisman's theory proved problematic because the nature of the attenuation process was never precisely specified, and models of this type have evolved into priming-based models in which there is no dedicated "attentional selector" mechanism at all. Selective attention is an "effect" generated by priming, rather than a separate mechanism (see Johnston & Dark, 1986). We return to these conceptions of selective attention in 4.4.

### 4.2.5 Neuropsychological studies of early vs. late selection

Over the last 20 years, a number of studies have used evoked potential reponses (ERPs) as a method for the study of selective attention (see Luck, 1998; Luck & Girelli, 1998, for reviews). The work of Hillyard has been particularly influential in determining the time-course of neurological activity as it relates to the dichotic listening, selective attention, tasks described above (e.g. Hillyard, Hink, Schwent, & Picton, 1973; Woldorff & Hillyard, 1991). Studies have compared ERP components for attended and unattended stimuli. Hillyard and colleagues reasoned that, if selection occurs at an early stage in cognitive processing of a stimuli, differences in the ERP traces produced by attended and unattended stimuli should be apparent shortly after stimulus presentation, with attended stimuli being associated with comparatively greater activation. In contrast, models of late attentional selection would be supported by no differences between early ERP components, and differences becoming apparent later in the trace.

The basic experimental paradigm, developed by Hillyard et al. (1973), involved dichotically presenting participants with a series of tones. Target tones were presented at a different pitch to distractor tones, and could occur on either channel. Participants were required to attend to just one of the channels (that varied across blocks of trials). The pattern of results supported the occurrence of early selection, with differences between attended and unattended stimuli being particularly apparent in the N1 component of the ERP trace (occurring earlier than 100 ms post-stimulus). However, if perceptual load was high, differences in the ERP trace were found after shorter time intervals (Woldorff, Hansen, & Hillyard, 1987; Woldorff & Hillyard, 1991). Confidence in this pattern of results is increased by similar findings (changes in P1 and N1 components) for visual selective attention tasks (e.g. Mangun, Hillyard, & Luck, 1993; van Voorhis & Hillyard, 1977) and visual search tasks (Luck et al., 1993).

## 4.2.6. Conclusions on early vs late selection

The debate continues (e.g. Cowan, 1988; Pashler, 1998a) as to where, within the processing system, selection of stimuli occurs. The "breakthrough" evidence, as presented above, would seem damaging for the early selection model, but the neuropsychological evidence indicates the presence of early selection. However, one possibility that we have not yet addressed is that, in the experimental paradigms described, a process of attention switching occurs between nominally attended and unattended channels (Holender, 1986; Pashler, 1998a). If this were the case, it would be possible to account for many, if not all, of these results. In support of such a hypothesis, Wood and Cowan (1995) present results from a series of dichotic listening experiments that indicate diversion of attention to the non-shadowed message, although they suggest that this only occurs once automatic detection of unusual stimuli (e.g. reversed speech) has already occured; and, in another dichotic listening experiment, Dawson and Schell (1982) found that, by shadowing in bursts, participants were able to maintain accuracy while also attending to the other channel.

It is possible, of course, that the stage of selecting for attention varies according to task parameters. Using a dichotic listening task, Johnston and Heinz (1978) demonstrated that the processing demands associated with selection using semantic criteria were greater than those associated with selection using physical criteria. In addition to shadowing a message that was differentiated by either physical or semantic properties, participants performed a probe reaction time task (see 5.3.3) as a measure of task demand. Responses to probes were slower when semantic selection was required than when physical selection was required, suggesting that participants found this condition more demanding. In an extension of this position, Lavie (1995) examined selective processes under different levels of perceptual load and concluded that early selection only occurred if processing load was high. Earlier experiments may have favoured a late processing solution by virtue of using low processing loads, and so, as a consequence, support for early selection has been reduced. However, such results appear to favour a flexible model of selective attention such as Treisman's attenuated filter.

## 4.3 CONTEMPORARY SELECTION THEORIES

Although the whole basis for selective attention as a "cause" has been questioned, many theorists are still concerned with the traditional question of selection-for-object-recognition. Duncan (1984) makes a useful distinction between space-based and object-based conceptual approaches. The former supposes that the area of space to which the observer can attend is limited, whereas the latter supposes that there are limits on the number of objects to which an observer can direct attention. In this section, we review these two types of theory, together with the neuropsychological approach of Posner and his colleagues.

### 4.3.1 Space-based theories of selection

A common metaphor for space-based theories is the idea of a mental spotlight, which "illuminates" or activates information from a certain region of space (LaBerge, 1983). There are several techniques for directing a subject's attention to a spatial location, and testing information processing at various distances from the attentional focus. Results of such studies suggest various spotlight characteristics, summarised in Table 4.2 which is based on a review by Johnston and Dark (1986). In many respects, the spotlight appears to function like a zoom lens which can be adjusted to attend to a variable area of space, but whose resolving power (processing efficiency) deteriorates as the size of the area is increased (Eriksen & Yeh, 1985). There is late selection within the spotlight, but only limited analysis of stimuli outside the spotlight. However, the mechanisms underlying the spotlight analogy appear to be adapted to function best in natural circumstances: processing is impaired if the spotlight fails to follow eye-movements, or if the beam is split and diverted to two or more separate locations.

The spotlight concept is a general analogy rather than a detailed theory. A more detailed model of this kind has been proposed by Treisman (1988, 1993, 1998), whose original filter amplitude model (Treisman, 1964) has undergone a series of evolutionary changes. She uses the spotlight analogy to the extent that she sees attention as a "moving window" on sensory information. However, although the model is space-based (see Duncan, 1984), Treisman has also been influenced by evidence that the visual system is adapted to perceive objects, specifically, rather than any arbitrary configuration of elementary visual properties. It is widely accepted that "preattentive" processes operate on Gestalt grouping principles to segment or divide up the visual world into separate "objects" at an early stage of analysis: processing of global features precedes the processing of local detail (Navon, 1991). In Treisman's model, preattentive segmentation influences the area of space attended. The model supposes parallel processing of elementary features across the visual field, to produce "maps" of where specific features are located. For example, one of the colour maps shows positions of redness, and one of the orientation maps represents straight line segments. Attention uses a "master map" that shows feature locations (but not which feature is located where) to bind or glue together the features to construct an object representation, which enters an "object file" in short-term memory.

Treisman's feature integration model has been tested in visual search tasks that require the location of a target item from an array. In *feature search* tasks, targets differ from non-target items in terms of a single feature, such as colour or shape, while in *conjunction search* tasks targets differ from non-targets in terms of a combination of features, for example, searching for a particular letter in an array of letters. In both feature and conjunction search tasks, target items are presented on some proportion of trials, typically 50%, and the response requirement is to indicate the presence or absence of a target by depressing a response key. One of the basic predictions of the feature integration model is that search for a single feature (e.g. any blue letter) takes place in parallel, whereas search for an "object" defined by a conjunction of features, such as a blue T, requires a serial search, with attention moving from location to location until the stimulus target is found. Many studies support this prediction (e.g. Treisman & Gelade, 1980): speed of feature search (assessed

| TABLE 4.2 | | |
|---|---|---|
| **Characteristics of the attentional spotlight (see Johnston & Dark, 1986).** | | |
| Size | Minimum constriction of about .5 degree | |
| | No clear maximum—but loss of attentional efficiency as size increased | |
| Shape | Functions most effectively when approximately circular—but can take on other shapes | |
| Divisibility | Functions most effectively when there is a single spotlight—but can split across two locations | |
| Link with eye fixation | Functions most effectively when coincides with the fovea—but spotlight and fixation can dissociate | |

by "target present" and "target absent" response times) is often independent of display size (the total number of items in the display), whereas speed of conjuction search increases linearly with the number of items searched. In the latter case, "target absent" response times increase much more steeply than do "target present" response times, suggesting that on "target absent" trials the search process is exhaustive, every item in the display being processed, while on "target present" trials the search process can be terminated once the target has been located. However, the prediction has not always been confirmed and there is considerable technical debate over the reasons for exceptions to the general rule (e.g. Wolfe, 1994, 1998). Treisman's model also successfully predicts that occasionally observers will make "illusory conjunction" errors, due to binding together features from different objects. For example, an observer might perceive a red T if the visual field contained both red letters and Ts, even if none of the Ts was actually red.

One of the weaknesses of Treisman's feature integration theory is that it neglects mechanisms for top-down control over early preattentive processing: the person uses either parallel feature search or serial conjunction search. Cave and Wolfe (1990) and Wolfe (1994) have developed a modification of Treisman's model, illustrated in Fig. 4.5. As in Treisman's model, preattentive processes generate feature maps of, for example, colour and orientation. Feature maps activate an activation map, similar to Treisman's master map, which essentially quantifies how interesting each location in space is, i.e. how likely a target is to be found there. The later, limited-capacity stage of processing is guided by the peaks of the activation map, so that the most interesting locations are searched first. In feature search, bottom-up processing will often ensure that the limited capacity stage is directed to the target location first, so that response is rapid. With targets defined by conjuctions of features, there will be several activation peaks, and search time will be prolonged. Voluntary attention is modelled by top-down activation of feature maps, which would allow for the implementation of a search strategy. The model has been represented as a (non-

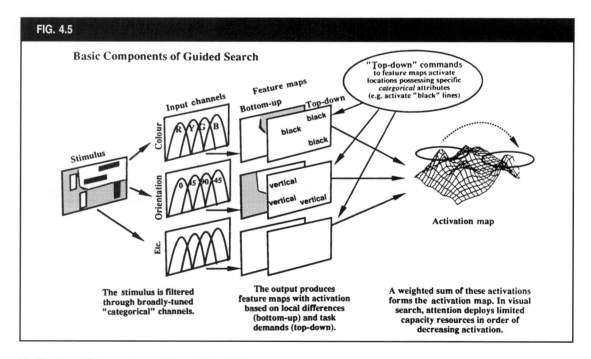

**FIG. 4.5**

**Basic Components of Guided Search**

Input channels

Feature maps

Bottom-up    Top-down

"Top-down" commands to feature maps activate locations possessing specific *categorical* attributes (e.g. activate "black" lines)

Stimulus

Colour    R  Y  G  B

black
black
black

Orientation    0  45  90  45

vertical
vertical  vertical

Etc.

Activation map

The stimulus is filtered through broadly-tuned "categorical" channels.

The output produces feature maps with activation based on local differences (bottom-up) and task demands (top-down).

A weighted sum of these activations forms the activation map. In visual search, attention deploys limited capacity resources in order of decreasing activation.

Modification of Treisman's model (from Wolfe, 1994).

connectionist) simulation (Wolfe, 1994) that reproduces an extensive body of visual search data.

A potential weakness of models of this kind may be their reliance on elementary features. Nakayama and Joseph (1998) identify problems resulting from a proliferation of possible features, and lack of evidence that visual search actually accesses feature-level representations. For example, Suzuki and Cavanagh (1995) found that it was difficult to search for features presented as part of face stimuli. Nakayama and Joseph suggest that search operates on higher-level representations, an idea consistent with the next approach discussed: object-based theories of selection.

### 4.3.2 Object-based theories of selection

The main alternatives to space-based theories are object-based theories (Kramer & Watson, 1996; Tipper & Weaver, 1998). The importance of "objectness" is shown by studies of attention to overlapping objects. On the one hand, people can select efficiently one of two overlapping objects, even though it is presumably difficult for preattentive processing to segregate the stimulus elements. A dramatic example is provided in a study in which two films were presented on the same screen, one showing a ball-throwing game, the other a hand-waving game (Neisser & Becklen, 1975). Participants efficiently attended to one film sequence only, despite the complexity of the visual input, but found it difficult to attend to both simultaneously. Participants' ability to select between overlapping scenes of this complexity probably depends on top-down processing. Neisser (1976) argues that selection is guided by a schema that actively interrogates the external environment. Schemas operate within a perceptual cycle, such that the information selected may modify the schema, and hence subsequent selection. Various studies confirm that there is a processing cost attached to attending to two objects simultaneously. For example, Baylis and Driver (1993) had participants make perceptual discriminations on ambiguous figures that might be seen as either one or two objects. Although the input features were controlled, participants found the task more difficult when the display was perceived as two objects rather than one.

Duncan and Humphreys (1989, 1992) have developed a detailed object-based model of selection: attentional engagement theory. It follows the traditional two-stage architecture. The first stage, perceptual description, produces a detailed representation of visual input, including codes for meaning and so the theory is one of late selection. Segmentation of the visual field structures the representation in terms of object-like units. Selection controls access of the input to a visual short term memory (VSTM), where it serves as the focus for action. Object representations compete for access to the VSTM, on the basis of activation levels. Activation is affected primarily by top-down control, which specifies a description or template of the target information. Hence, search efficiency is impaired as targets and distractors become more similar to one another.

Selection is also influenced by perceptual grouping effects. For example, similar units tend to lose or gain activation together. Searching for a target surrounded by distractors is easier when the distractors are similar to one another, because suppression of one distractor tends to lead to suppression of the others. Hence, in contrast to Treisman (1988), Duncan and Humphreys propose that there is no qualitative difference between feature and conjunction search. Instead, there is a continuum of search difficulty, which reflects both target–distractor similarity and distractor–distractor distinctiveness.

Studies of patients also demonstrate object-based selection. Driver and Halligan (1991) studied "unilateral visual neglect" patients, who ignore one half of the visual field. They showed that neglect was associated with the left or right side of objects rather than area of the visual field per se. Such findings are persuasive, although Stark, Grafman and Fertig (1997) have described a patient whose attentional deficit appears to relate to stimulus size, suggesting an impairment of the spotlight. Lavie and Driver (1996) showed that selection was object-based, even when elements of the object were spatially far apart. However, they also found that when participants were cued to expect target stimulus elements within a small area of space, object effects were eliminated, implying that object selection may only operate within a space-based spotlight. In addition, contrary to the Duncan and Humphreys (1989) model, object-based selection may be early rather than late. Neuropsychological evidence from monkey studies suggests that object-based attention is associated with enhancement of neural firing in area V1 of the visual cortex, which supports early preattentive visual processing (Roelfsema, Lamme, & Spekreijse, 1998). In general, it seems that object-based theories have some advantages over space-based theories, but at times, selection may operate within both frames of reference (Tipper & Weaver, 1998).

### 4.3.3 Cognitive neuroscience: Multiple brain mechanisms for selection

Another approach to identifying specific attentional mechanisms is through cognitive neuroscience (Cohen, 1993). Attentional processes may be localised by studying effects of brain lesions on performance, and by using brain scanning techniques such as PET (Positron Emission Tomography: see 2.6.3) to identify the brain areas active when the person is attending to stimuli. By combining these techniques with the experimental methods of cognitive psychology, we can make inferences about the brain structures that control specific processes (as opposed to gross features of performance). Some of the most impressive work of this kind has been carried out in a programme of research conducted by Michael Posner. Posner and Rothbart (1991) identify three neural networks that contribute to selective attention. The first is called the *posterior system*, after its location in posterior brain structures such as the parietal lobes. The posterior system controls aspects of spatial attention, such as orienting to stimuli, i.e. directing attention to spatial locations where something potentially important has happened. The system may be further broken down into components controlling highly-specific attentional functions such as the engagement, disengagement and shifting of spatial attention (Posner, Inhoff, Friedrich, & Cohen, 1987). These components may be studied through spatial cueing tasks, in which a cue—which may or may not be valid—indicates where the participant should direct the focus of attention (e.g. Maylor, 1985). The com-

ponents of the system may also be distinguished through studies of patients with parietal cortex damage, which can lead to deficits in switching spatial attention appropriately. The most dramatic instance is the unilateral neglect syndrome previously described, in which patients simply ignore one side of the body.

A second, *anterior* network controls the detection of events. It is active during performance of all tasks in which visual targets must be detected, whether targets are defined by colour, form, motion or word meaning. PET scans show that the brain structures concerned tend to be more active when the task is more demanding or complex. Activity of the brain system is reduced with practice. Loosely, the anterior system may relate to processing constructs such as controlled processing and working memory. A third system associated with sub-cortical innervation of the right frontal lobe controls *alertness* or *vigilance* in the absence of stimuli. It is thought to be implicated in variable-foreperiod reaction time tasks. The participant receives a warning that the critical stimulus to which they must respond is about to be presented, but the time lag to the critical stimulus varies, so that alertness must be maintained. It is uncertain whether this vigilance over no more than a few seconds is related to vigilance over longer time periods of an hour or so (see Chapter 6). The three systems may relate to different adaptive challenges: (1) deciding *what* an object is (anterior); (2) deciding *where* in space it is, so appropriate action may be initiated (posterior); and (3) handling temporal uncertainty (vigilance).

## 4.4 PRIMING AND SELECTION

Selective attention may be a consequence of priming mechanisms, rather than some special-purpose selection mechanism. We have discussed the concept of priming already in 2.3.1. Processing is dependent on activation of network nodes, which may represent either complex concepts such as "bird" (Collins & Quillian, 1969), or neuron-like processing units, as in connectionist models. Within such models, selection is a competitive process. If multiple stimuli are presented, the one which is "attended" is the one which generates the most activation. Priming effects can be shown within traditional selective attention paradigms. MacKay (1973) required participants to shadow ambiguous sentences (e.g. "they threw stones toward the bank yesterday"), while a disambiguating word was presented on the unattended channel (e.g. either "river" or "money"). When subsequently questioned about the meaning of the sentence, participants were found to be biased according to the word presented in the unattended ear, even though they could not recall the content of this message.

The priming approach lends itself to an action-oriented view of selection. Within a connectionist model, we can build in units representing responses. If the person has to press one of two keys, the model might include both a "left hand" and a "right hand" unit. Response selection then depends on which unit reaches some activation threshold first. In this section, we review

(1) the application of priming studies to selection problems,
(2) the role of inhibitory processes, and
(3) the contribution of connectionist models.

### 4.4.1 Studies of priming

Priming studies assume that selective attention is a competitive process, in which incoming stimuli activate streams of processing, and responses, in parallel. The stimulus that is 'attended' is the one that activates a response most strongly. One technique for linking attention to priming is to show that providing a prior cue towards the stimulus to be attended enhances the speed of response. An alternative strategy is to impair performance by priming distracting stimuli, which interfere with response to the stimulus to which the person is instructed to attend. Interference effects seem to be controlled primarily by the anterior attentional system discussed in 4.3.3 (see Posner & DiGirolamo, 1998, for a review). The role of interference in selection is demonstrated by the well-known Stroop effect. The task is simple—merely to name the ink colour in which printed words are written, as fast as possible. Stroop (1935) discovered that response is slowed considerably

when the word itself is a colour name; e.g. the word "RED" written in blue ink. Although the person is instructed to ignore the word, the meaning of the word is nevertheless selected for analysis, and interferes with the correct response. Most accounts of Stroop interference (see MacLeod, 1991, for a review) assume some involuntary selection of word meaning, which generates a competing response to the correct one. Next, we describe, first, facilitative priming effects, which enhance selection, and second, interference-based effects.

Facilitative priming was explored in a series of studies reported by Eriksen (e.g. Eriksen & Collins, 1969). In these studies, the participant is presented with displays showing a number of letters arranged in a circle, and must name a target letter. The target letter is designated by a visual cue, such as a black bar adjacent to the position of the letter in the circle, which was presented prior to the circle of letters. Eriksen varied the SOA between onset of the cue and the onset of the letter display, and found that "precueing" the letter led to better speed and accuracy of performance, compared to conditions where the cue was presented simultaneously with the letter circle. This basic result is unsurprising, in that the cue allows spatial attention to be directed towards the correct letter. As previously described, Michael Posner has investigated spatial cueing processes in considerable detail. Eriksen showed that maximum enhancement due to the cue was obtained at SOAs of 250 ms or greater, implying that it takes this length of time to orient attention in space. However, Eriksen also showed that performance tended to deteriorate as the number of letters in the display increased. This is surprising because, given an SOA of sufficient length, the participant knows exactly where to look. Eriksen (e.g. 1995) eventually decided that these effects are due to response competition. Participants in his studies sometimes named the wrong letter, implying that the irrelevant distractor letter primed the vocal response.

Eriksen also investigated interference effects. In the Stroop task, both meaning and colour are part of the same perceptual object (i.e. the word). However, the mechanisms generating interference effects are more easily studied by presenting distracting information as a separate stimulus. Hence, Eriksen studied response competition effects using a task known as the "flankers" task (Eriksen & Hoffman, 1973). Here, letter stimuli are divided into two sets. The participant might have to press one key if the letter is A or M, a second key if the letter is U or H. The letter is always presented in the same spatial position, so there is no spatial uncertainty. This central target letter may presented together with "flankers", distractor letters on each side of it. If the distractors are targets from the alternate set, response is slowed, for example, if the person must respond to the U in a display resembling A U A, where the As are the distractors. Various experiments (e.g. Eriksen & Eriksen, 1979) showed that interference due to the distractors depended not on the overall complexity of the stimulus, but on the similarity between the distractors and alternate targets. Hence, interference was not due to perceptual difficulties in distinguishing distractor and target, but due to response competition. Further evidence came from psychophysiological studies (e.g. Coles et al., 1985). Competing response distractors were associated with muscle activity in the hand used for the alternate response. Simplifying somewhat, Eriksen's continuous flow model supposes that activation of perceptual representations continuously feeds into activation of the possible responses, in parallel: interfering distractors prime the "wrong" response. It should be noted that these effects are seen as operating within the "zoom lens" of spatial attention (Eriksen & Yeh, 1985) previously described: there seems to be little interference outside the area of focal attention.

Eriksen's work seems to assume that priming is involuntary, but other paradigms provide a basis for distinguishing involuntary and voluntary priming effects. Posner and Snyder (1975) conducted studies of a letter matching task, in which participants had to decide whether pairs of capital letters were the same (AA) or different (AB). When the letters are the same, speed of response tends to be enhanced by cueing the letter, i.e. when A precedes AA. A conflicting letter (e.g. B) tends to slow response, to a lesser degree. Posner and Snyder distinguished two priming mechanisms, on the basis that cueing effects vary with both the probability that the prime matches the letter pair (which determines conscious expectancy), and with the SOA between cue and letter pair. The first mechanism was termed automatic activation: presenting the letter A primes the processing pathway associated with the letter. It operates over the first 300 ms or so after the prime is presented, and is insensitive to expectancy. It is entirely facilitative: presenting the letter B has no effect on the pathway for A. The second mechanism represents the person's voluntary conscious attention, driven by expectancy, and operates only when there is a high probability that the cue letter matches the letter pair. It produces both facilitation of response, when the letter pair matches expectation, and impairment, when the expectancy is not confirmed. It seems a slower process, operating at SOAs of 300 ms or more.

Neely (e.g. 1991) has demonstrated effects very similar to those of Posner and Snyder (1975) using semantic priming. It gives us a general picture of selection as a conflict between stimulus-driven and expectancy-driven priming effects (Maxfield, 1997). As discussed in 3.3.1, the distinction between automatic and conscious or controlled attention has been widely accepted, and applied to paradigms such as visual search (Shiffrin & Schneider, 1977) and skilled performance (Norman & Shallice, 1986). Specification of priming mechanisms avoids the problem of having controlled processing operate as an homunculus. Yantis (1998) discusses how interacting stimulus-driven ("automatic") and goal-driven ("controlled") processes may influence a variety of aspects of selection such as spatial attention, attentional shifts and attentional capture. For example, it is well established that rapid visual onsets (a light flashing on) have a distracting effect (attentional capture), presumably because they prime processing which interferes with task processing, possibly at some relatively early stage (Yantis & Jonides, 1990). However, if the person expects the distractor stimulus, its effects can be overridden. Within this general framework, detailed models are required of the architecture that allows integration of different priming mechanisms. The nature of such models remains controversial. Eriksen (1995) argues that some priming effects on stimulus matching tasks such as the Posner and Snyder (1975) task may reflect response competition effects, although it is unlikely that all priming operates on response selection.

### 4.4.2 Inhibition and negative priming

A final aspect of research concerns *negative priming* effects, which demonstrate longer-lasting inhibitory effects than those shown in conventional priming studies. Broadly, negative priming is defined by slow responses to stimuli, or properties of stimuli, that have previously been ignored (Milliken, Joordens, Merikle, & Seifert, 1998). The first demonstrations of negative priming (Dalrymple-Alford & Budayr, 1966; Neill, 1977) were based on the well-known Stroop effect. Suppose a person has to state the colour of the word "RED" written in blue ink (i.e. correct response is "blue"). Response is slowed because the person has to inhibit the competing response activated by the colour name. If, on the next trial, the person has to name the colour of a word written in red ink, response is also slowed, over and above any standard Stroop interference effect. The suppression of the "red" response on the first trial seems to carry over to the next trial, even though "red" is the correct response. This is a negative priming effect. Studies by Tipper (e.g. 1985) showed that negative priming could operate on a semantic basis also. In typical studies, participants have to respond to picture stimuli: one picture is attended and a second picture is ignored. If the person ignores a picture of, say, a cat on one trial, they will be slower to process a cat picture as target on the next trial. They will also be slower to process semantically-related stimuli such as a picture of a dog. A wide variety of negative priming effects have now been demonstrated (see Fox, 1995; Milliken et al., 1998 for reviews).

The theoretical significance of negative priming studies is that they suggest that selection is not just a question of the activation of attended stimuli, but also requires the active ignoring or suppression of distracting material, which persists from trial to trial in the experimental studies. According to Tipper and Cranston (1985), the rep-

resentation of the distracting material remains activated, but its capacity to activate response mechanisms is blocked. Negative priming seems to be at least partially voluntary, because it is sensitive to current behavioural goals (Tipper, Weaver, & Houghton, 1994). The inhibition account is consistent with late selection, in that it is an object representation which is inhibited. However, there are alternative explanations for the evidence. The best known is Neill, Valdes, Terry and Gorfein's (1992) episodic retrieval hypothesis. Their hypothesis is based on Logan's (1988) instance theory, which proposes that during performance of a task, memories of stimuli or "episodes" are stored together with information about how they were processed. It is best known for proposing that automatisation of performance is a consequence of storing response information in the episodic memory trace. Neill et al. (1992) propose that when a distractor is presented, "non-response" information is encoded, leading to slower response on subsequent trials. The experimental literature on negative priming is now extensive: Fox's (1995) thorough review of the evidence concludes that all the current theories can explain some findings but not others. Negative priming seems to represent some fundamental attentional mechanism, but it is unclear whether or not it is based on inhibition.

### 4.4.3 Connectionism and selective attention

Possibly, theoretical issues may be resolved by connectionist models (Houghton & Tipper, 1998). There are a variety of models relating to aspects of selective attention, such as interference effects (Phaf, Van der Heijden, & Hudson, 1990), visual search (Humphreys & Mueller, 1993) and negative priming (Houghton & Tipper, 1994). We illustrate these models with reference to Cohen, Dunbar and McClelland's (1990) model of Stroop effect. Figure 4.6 shows the network they used to simulate the Stroop effect: the weights attached to the connections result from training the network to respond appropriately to colour and word stimuli. The task stimuli activate the input units, from which activation spreads to the intermediate, "hidden" units, and thence to the output or response units. A response is produced when the

**FIG. 4.6**

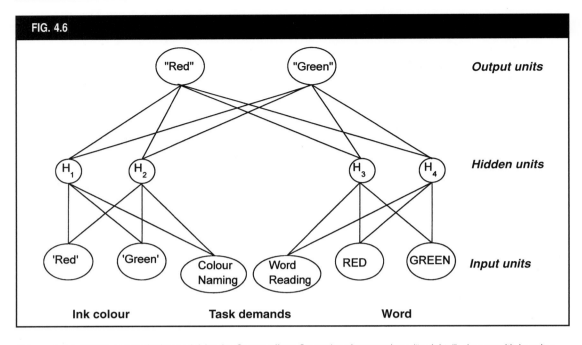

Cohen et al.'s (1990) connectionist model for the Stroop effect: Strengths of connections ("weights") change with learning.

output unit is sufficiently activated. Voluntary attention is simulated through task demand units, whose activation depends on task instructions and the participant's intentions. For example, during word reading, activation of the Word Reading task demand unit tends to sensitise the pathways connecting the word input units to response, so that response is more dependent on the word than the colour. Architecturally, the task demand units permit top-down control over parallel, bottom-up processing. The explanation for the Stroop effect is essentially adaptive; i.e. it refers to the person's "knowledge" of the real world rather than to intrinsic characteristics of processing. Cohen et al. (1990) point out that word reading is more highly practised than colour naming. In simulation studies of this kind, the network receives several hundred training trials during which it learns to associate inputs with outputs. To arrive at the network shown, Cohen et al. exposed the network to ten times more learning trials on reading words than on naming colours. In consequence, pathways connecting word inputs to response are stronger than those for colour inputs. Hence, the network tends to be distracted by word inputs during colour naming but not, as in real data, by colour inputs presented during word reading.

The important point in the present context is that the selection process by which word meaning tends to be prioritised over colour is highly specialised and contingent upon learning history. We might be able to use the connectionist approach to model other aspects of attention, but other selection processes might operate on entirely different principles. Note also that there is no specific attentional mechanism within the Cohen et al. (1990) model: selection is almost an incidental by-product of the way in which the network functions. The model offers a partial explanation for voluntary control, which is said to influence activation of the task demand units. However, the computations involved are beyond the scope of the model. Cohen, Servan-Schreiber and McClelland (1992) have discussed how connectionist approaches may resolve some of the difficulties with levels of control models discussed in 3.3.3. Automaticity, for example, may be a continuum reflecting the relative contributions of data-driven activation feeding through from input units, and activation delivered from top-down sources such as task demands units.

Researchers are beginning to integrate neuroscience approaches with connectionism. For example, Cohen and Servan-Schreiber (1992) have applied the network model for the Stroop test described above to explaining attentional deficits in schizophrenia. They suggest that a reduction in dopamine activity in prefrontal cortex may disturb network functioning, a disturbance which may be simulated by adjusting one of the parameters controlling network response to input.

## 4.5 CONCLUSIONS

Conceptions of the underlying architecture for selective attention have become ever more complex. The increase in complexity is perhaps inevitable. Studies of visual perception, for which neuropsychological evidence is more easily obtained, have distinguished around 30 distinct modules, with more than 300 interconnections (Felleman & Van Essen, 1991). At one level, performance theory has little choice but to engage with this complexity. Nevertheless, some more general themes may be identified. Perhaps the most important of these is the distinction between stimulus-driven and voluntary control of attention made by the levels of control theories discussed in 3.3 (Yantis, 1998). In selective attention, we have seen that the focus of attention may be guided both by involuntary, pre-attentive processing, and by search strategies (e.g. Wolfe, 1994). Activation-based models provide a means of integrating the two types of control: conflicts may be resolved by the relative strengths of the two types of influence on activation. Despite the plethora of research, various fundamental architectural issues remain

to be resolved, including the traditional early vs. late selection question, the respective roles of objects and areas of visual space, and the role of inhibitory processes. It is plausible, too, that selection operates on a flexible basis, using different representations and frames of reference as required by circumstances (Tipper & Weaver, 1998).

A second theme is the functional significance of selection. There may be different attentional systems with different adaptive goals, including localisation of stimuli in space, object recognition and control of action. Selection processes cannot be entirely divorced from the person's motivations and other "knowledge-level" constructs. As we shall see in 15.3.2, emotional influences on selective attention may indicate the role of schemas in selection on the basis of motivationally significant stimulus attributes, such as threat content. Finally, we have seen that the cognitive neuroscience of attention (e.g. Duncan, 1996; Posner & Rothbart, 1991) is increasingly successful in discriminating multiple mechanisms for attention, though detailed mappings between neural and cognitive architectures remain to be established.

## FURTHER READING

Pashler's (1998a) recent book presents a widely-acclaimed synthesis of the selective attention literature. Other integrative accounts may be found in various edited volumes (Kramer & Coles, 1996; Parasuraman & Davies, 1984; Pashler, 1998b). Visual attention is addressed by Wright (1998) and Bundesen and Shibuya's (1995) collection of articles from *Visual Cognition*. Cognitive neuropsychological work is covered in Parasuraman's (1998a) edited book, and in Desimone and Duncan's (1995) review.

# 5

# Divided attention and workload

## 5.1 INTRODUCTION

In the previous chapter, we reviewed research and theory in the field of selective attention, examining the basis on which the focus of attention is determined. In this chapter, we examine *divided attention*: the person's ability to perform two or more tasks simultaneously. Divided attention studies are closely linked to the theoretical issue of *attentional capacity*, i.e. limits on the quantity of attention applied to a task or tasks. The idea of capacity stems most straightforwardly from studies of *overload* of attention, in which performance deteriorates seemingly because the processing system cannot handle all the information presented to it.

Although attention may become overloaded during performance of a single task, capacity limits are most readily investigated during dual-task performance, for methodological reasons discussed subsequently. Divided attention studies are thus seen as addressing "intensive" aspects of attention, i.e. the person's ability to concentrate under high levels of task demand. However, attentional capacity can also be regarded as "the other side of the coin" to selective attention. Potentially, there is a tradeoff between the need for selection, on the one hand, and availability of attentional capacity, on the other. For example, one of the rationales underlying Broadbent's (1958) filter theory of selective attention was a perceived need to protect the central information processing system from overload; and models of selective attention have been proposed in which the degree of semantic processing that stimuli receive varies according to the availability of attentional capacity (Johnston & Heinz, 1978).

As we saw in 2.4, the nature of capacity limitations is controversial. Attentional resource theories propose that attention is somehow distinct from the individual processes supporting task performance, i.e. that attention must be allocated to processing. Capacity then refers to the total quantity of attention available for processing. This view of attention implies that task demands can be characterised similarly, in terms of the total quantity of resources required. The concept of *mental workload*, analogous to physical workload, has been developed to refer to the attentional demands experienced during the performance of cognitive tasks (O'Donnell & Eggemeier, 1986). Performance deficit may ensue when workload exceeds available resources. Workload also refers to people's experiences of cognitive task performance as effortful and fatiguing (Mulder, 1986), which may index task demands or attentional overload. Various measures of workload, including questionnaire and psychophysiological assessments, have been developed to assess workload. However, the measurement of workload is a complex problem and, although several new research methodologies have been developed, many issues remain to be resolved (Hex, 1988).

The alternative point of view is that all capacity limits are localised within the cognitive architecture, i.e. that there is no separate pool of resources. The simplest model of this type is *single-channel theory* (Welford, 1980), which proposes a single, serial-processing channel, limited by its capacity for throughput of information. Contemporary models generally envisage a network of independent processors functioning in parallel (Allport, 1989). Each individual processing component has its own operating capacity and, additionally, constraints may develop from interactions between processors. In this case, investigating capacity limits is subsumed under the more general problem of investigating the architecture, and overall workload has no particular significance.

The capacity problem interweaves many difficult conceptual issues: the validity of "resources" as something separate from individual processes; the measurement of capacity; the relationship between subjective experience and processing; and the amount of detail required to obtain a useful description of the architecture. At one extreme, resources, attention, workload, effort and subjective energy are used almost interchangeably as the key constraint on performance. At the other, these constructs are meaningless or irrelevant; all that is required is a valid computational model of the individual processing units. To some degree, too, approaches to the capacity problem vary with research background. Laboratory-based psychologists often reject the workload concept as too crude, and stress the importance of carefully designing simple tasks to investigate capacity issues (see Pashler, 1998a). On the other hand, measurement of overall capacity, if valid, has considerable utility to human factors practitioners. For example, being able to forecast whether the task-related demands placed on operators of a nuclear power plant control room are within their attentional capacity would be of critical importance

in determining the design of the work environment. High workload may also be a stress factor, leading to problems such as absenteeism and turnover.

In this chapter, we examine explanations for dual-task interference, focusing especially on the resource theories of attentional capacity introduced in 2.4. We review the main constraints on dual-task performance revealed by empirical studies, the explanations offered by resource theory, and alternatives to resource theory. The central issue is whether the evidence supports some resource or resources that may be allocated to qualitatively different tasks. The alternative point of view is that dual-task interference has many sources, depending on a variety of different interactions between specific processing operations. Two tasks may require a common processing structure, such as a short-term memory store, leading to *structural interference* (Kahneman, 1973). Research provides many examples of interference effects of this kind (see Pashler, 1998a), so the task for proponents of resource theory is to show that there are resource limitations on performance over and above processing-specific sources of interference.

## 5.2 CONSTRAINTS ON DUAL-TASK PERFORMANCE

Intuitively it seems possible simultaneously to perform more than one task. Apparently, people can walk and chew gum at the same time; people can drive and simultaneously conduct a conversation with a passenger in the car. However, studies often show performance deficits (dual-task interference) when people attempt to perform multiple tasks simultaneously. For example, using a mobile phone while driving is associated with a higher risk of crashing, even with "hands-free" equipment (Redelmeier & Tibshirani, 1997). In experimental studies, there are two rather separate areas of research on divided attention. The first, inspired initially by single-channel theory, investigates simple, "discrete-trial" tasks. For example, we can present two stimuli within a reaction-time paradigm, and test the extent to which response to one stimulus is slowed by the presence of the other. Simplicity of stimuli and responses, and knowledge of the exact time-course of events, facilitates investigating the architecture controlling any interference effects (Pashler, 1998a). The second approach is to investigate interference between more complex tasks, often involving continuous performance, which may be more representative of real-world tasks such as driving. However, it is hard to make inferences about architecture from these studies, because of uncertainties over how the person may be interleaving or switching between different task components.

### 5.2.1  Discrete-trial tasks

Welford's (1980) "single channel model" proposed that, following stimulus selection, further processing can only be performed serially. Performing two tasks concurrently would then depend on a process of task switching. This conception of capacity limits is supported by the studies of the psychological refractory period (PRP) discussed in 4.1.1, which show that processing a given stimulus may slow response to a second stimulus. There appears to be a "bottleneck" in cognitive processing between perception and response, at which point tasks can only be performed serially (see Broadbent, 1958; Pashler, 1994; Welford, 1980).

There are many persuasive aspects of PRP studies. The PRP effect has been replicated many times, and demonstrated to be reliable at different levels of practice and with different degrees of task similarity (Pashler, 1998a). However, the implications of PRP studies are important but limited. First, the single-channel model cannot explain all constraints on cognitive processing. For example, shifting visual attention does not appear to be constrained in this way, nor does the storage of information in visual short-term memory, although retrieval from long-term memory may require the response bottleneck (Pashler, 1998a). There appear to be distinct "perceptual capacity limits" in processing complex sensory inputs (Pashler, 1998a), demonstrated by performance deficits in detecting multiple targets (Duncan, 1980) or when targets and distractors are highly confusable (Kleiss & Lane, 1986). Such effects appear to be independent of the response bottleneck. Second, even within those areas of cognitive

processing that theoretically are subject to the PRP bottleneck, the results of some studies are difficult to explain within this paradigm. For example:

(i) sometimes reducing the inter-stimulus interval (ISI) does not produce an equivalent increase in RT2;

(ii) when the ISI is extremely short, often responses to both tasks are made together (grouped); and

(iii) manipulations of ISI have been shown to influence RT1 as well as RT2 (see Heuer, 1996).

Neumann (1996) cites work described in Koch's (1993) doctoral thesis that indicates the PRP effect may be due to:

(i) cognitive costs associated with the requirement for a specific sequence of responses to the two tasks;

(ii) the fact that the responses to the second task are less well prepared than would be those of a single task; and

(iii) interference between response channels (e.g. using both hands).

Meyer and Kieras (1997b) claim that modelling executive processes that control lower-level processing components flexibly gives a better fit to PRP and other RT data. It would seem, then, that although persuasive, bottleneck models of information processing do not provide a comprehensive account of human capacity for cognitive task performance. Resource theory represents an attempt to reintroduce the notion of a general capacity limit, without being committed to the architectural assumptions of single channel theory.

### 5.2.2  Continuous performance tasks

Studies of more complex tasks have used a wide variety of task types (see Wickens, 1980, 1992; Damos, 1991, for reviews). One task often used in combination with others is the "tracking" task. In a typical tracking task, an erratically-moving point of light is presented on a screen, and the observer must follow it with a cursor controlled by a joystick or mouse. Real-world tasks such as driving and flying have a central tracking component. It is assumed that monitoring the target stimulus and controlling the tracking device impose a more-or-less continuous demand on attention, although, in dual-task situations, uncertainties over timesharing remain. Other tasks commonly used include signal detection and short-term memory tasks. Results from these studies are complex but, in general, successful dual-task performances seem to be constrained by four main factors:

1. *Task difficulty.* Dual-task interference is most common when each component task is demanding. As in the case of telephoning while driving, interference is found even when tasks are qualitatively different, a finding that suggests limitation of performance by a common resource. For example, several studies have combined memory storage with tracking tasks (see Wickens, 1980). Wickens cited two studies showing that as tracking is made more difficult memory is impaired, and two studies showing that as memory load is increased tracking deteriorates.

2. *Skill.* Even with highly demanding tasks, skilled performers often show remarkably little dual-task interference. For example, skilled pianists can sight-read unfamiliar music while concurrently shadowing English prose at a rate of 150 words/minute (Allport, Antonis, & Reynolds, 1972), and Japanese abacus operators can answer general knowledge questions without any impairment of concurrent calculations on the abacus (Hatano, Miyake, & Binks, 1977). Hirst et al. (1980) investigated skill acquisition effects on interference. The participants in this study were required to combine reading for comprehension with taking dictation, copying auditorily presented words or sentences. Initially, participants showed considerable interference but, with extensive practice, attained high levels of dual-task performance. Allport (1980) interprets these findings as fatal for resource theory, in that simultaneous performance of dual tasks should lead to a considerable resource deficit. The alternative view is that, as discussed in 3.3.1, automatisation of performance progressively reduces the need for resources.

3. *Task similarity.* Although dissimilar tasks may interfere, the extent of interference increases with task similarity: the extent to which stimuli, processing operations and/or responses are similar. For example (see Wickens, 1984b), it is often harder to perform two tasks in which both sets of stimuli are presented in the same sensory modality (e.g. both visual or both auditory) than to perform a "cross-modal" task combination (one task visual, one task auditory). Similarly, responses to verbal stimuli presented during the performance of a tracking task are more efficient when the response is made vocally rather than manually (McLeod, 1977). Participants in this study used one hand for the tracking task, and the other for additional manual response, to minimise structural interference between the motor programmes for the two kinds of response. Nevertheless, similarity of responses (i.e. both manual) appeared to increase interference. These studies tend to challenge resource theory, in that they imply that it is the nature of structural interference between similar processes which is critical.

4. *Emergent properties.* It is easy to pat yourself on the head. It is also easy to rub your stomach in a circular motion. However, if you try to perform the two actions simultaneously, you will probably experience massive dual-task interference. There is something about the timings of the motions that makes them incompatible with one another. Duncan (1979) describes such effects as emergent properties of dual tasks. Such properties are especially important in divided attention because they moderate the effects of task similarity on interference. In particular, multiple stimuli differ in the ease with which they can be perceptually integrated according to their emergent properties (Wickens, 1992). For example, a display like that in Fig. 5.1, informing a pilot of the spatial attitude of an aircraft, has emergent features that are easier for the pilot to assimilate than, say, the same information presented in numerical form. One of the

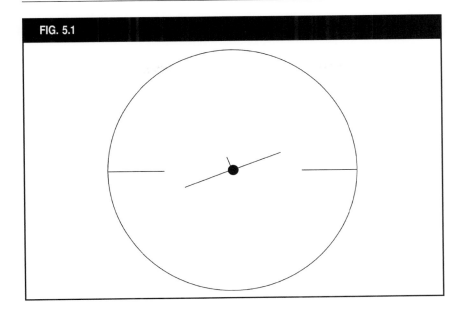

**FIG. 5.1**

Informing a pilot of the spatial attitude of an aircraft.

emergent features of the display is its "objectness", which is compatible with the way the pilot thinks of the aircraft; that is, as an object, rather than as a set of disconnected attributes.

## 5.3 RESOURCE THEORIES

Resource theory aims to explain dual-task interference in terms of insufficiency of some metaphorical "energy" for processing. However, the effects of similarity and emergent properties on dual-task performance show that resource theory cannot provide a complete account of processing limitations. All resource theorists recognise that resource limitations coexist with constraints associated with specific processing operations, such as the response bottleneck, and constraints related to specific task combinations, such as emergent features. The more difficult issue is whether resource theory is required at all: perhaps all instances of dual-task interference reflect structural interference, and the resource construct is redundant (Navon, 1984). In order to show that resource theory adds to the "structural interference" explanation, it is necessary to describe explicitly

what "resources" mean, and to develop methods for rigorous investigation of resource usage. In this section, we describe conceptualisations of resources and methods for testing resource theory. The most powerful methods test the dependence of dual-task interference on task demands.

### 5.3.1 Conceptualising resources

Broadly, resource theories (e.g. Kahneman, 1973; Moray, 1967) suppose that attentional resources can be flexibly allocated to more than one task at a time, up to the point that all attention has been allocated. Figure 5.2 illustrates Kahneman's model. Concurrent performance of more than one task is easily represented in such models. A "pool" of attentional resources is hypothesised that can be flexibly allocated to more than one task at a time, up to the point that all attentional resources have been allocated. The "fuel" needed to perform each task is taken from this central reservoir. The effort that an individual invests in task performance equates to the level of resources allocated to the task. Generally, if people try harder they will perform to a higher standard, but task performance will require comparatively more fuel. Equally, the more difficult a task is to perform, the more fuel, or resources, it will require.

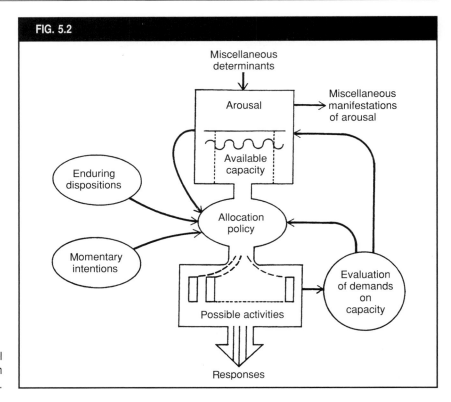

**FIG. 5.2**

A capacity model for attention. From Kahneman (1973).

These fundamental principles, underlying such attentional resource models, can be expressed, albeit rather loosely, in terms of the formula: $P = R / D$ (Wickens, 1991). This describes, in broad terms, the association between performance (P), resource allocation (R), and task demand (D). It is not intended to be a precise statistical description, but gives a general indication of the association between these components. If more resources are allocated to a task (increased effort), and task difficulty remains constant, levels of performance increase. If task difficulty is increased and resource allocation remains constant, then performance declines. There are restrictions, however, on the circumstances to which this formula can be applied. An important distinction can be made between between *data limited* and *resource limited* processing (Norman & Bobrow, 1975). It may be, for example, that a task is so simple, such as calculating $2 + 2$, that allocation of additional resources beyond a minimal requirement will produce no improvement in performance.

Equally, it may be that characteristics of the task, such as the differentiation of signal from noise when searching for faint targets on a "noisy" radar screen, are beyond human physiological capacities and, again, allocation of additional resources will not improve performance. In these circumstances, performance can be said to be "data limited". Data limits may also derive from the quality of information in memory.

In contrast, the PRD formula does apply when the allocation of additional resources results in an increase in performance. In these circumstances, performance can be said to be "resource limited". The association between resource allocation and levels of performance can be represented graphically as a "performance–resource function" (PRF: Norman & Bobrow, 1975). Figure 5.3 presents PRFs for a relatively easier and a relatively more difficult task. For the easier task, there is a region of resource limited performance, for which allocation of additional resources results in increased levels of performance. There is also a point

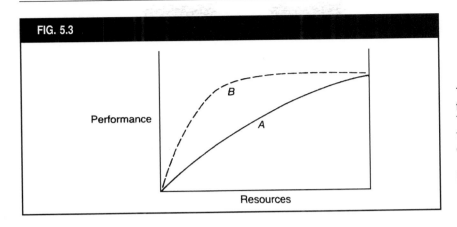

**FIG. 5.3**

The performance resource function and practice. Task B: practised or easy; task A: unpractised or difficult (from Wickens, 1992, p. 371). Reprinted by permission of Prentice-Hall, Inc., Upper Saddle River, NJ.

beyond which performance becomes data limited, and further allocation of resources produces no performance improvement. For the more difficult task, a linear trend is apparent, with all levels of performance being resource limited.

If concurrently performed tasks "compete" for a limited attentional capacity, then resources allocated to the performance of one task cannot be simultaneously allocated to the performance of another task. So, if the demands of two concurrently performed tasks do not exceed attentional capacity, these models indicate that perfect time-sharing would be possible. If combined demands exceed this quantity then performance on one or both tasks must suffer. On this basis, predictions can be made about the effects of manipulating task difficulty within the context of multiple task performance. "Difficulty–sensitivity" can be hypothesised, with a resource-dependent *tradeoff* between performance levels on the two tasks. On the assumption that there are insufficient resources for perfect timesharing, performance gains on one task may only be achieved at the cost of performance deterioration on the other.

The central difficulty with resource theory is that the construct is hypothetical, and the theory outlined above does not specify any direct means of assessment. We need to infer the allocation of resources to processing, while avoiding "circularity", i.e. assuming that performance deficit reflects lack of resources, and lack of resource is expressed as performance deficit. If we assume the person has a fixed quantity of resources available,

the problem becomes one of *workload* assessment, determining the extent to which the person has sufficient resources to deal with task demands. Next, we introduce single- and dual-task procedures for inferring resource usage from performance data. In the following section, we survey attempts to measure workload from physiological measures and from self-report.

## 5.3.2 Resource limits on single-task performance

Resource theories are typically tested within dual-task paradigms, but this section considers the possibilities for measuring resource usage and workload when a task is performed in isolation. Although it seems reasonable to assume that levels of performance on a single task will give an indication of workload, the situation is not this simple. What we do not know is how much spare attentional capacity the person performing the task has available. It may be that they find task performance easy and well within their capabilities; or it is possible that they find the task highly demanding and have no spare attentional capacity. It is often important to be able to make this distinction. For example, consider a pilot flying an aircraft. It may be that, under normal circumstances, all required tasks are performed adequately and the pilot has plenty of spare attentional capacity to deal with any emergency requirements as they might arise, such as interpreting the significance of a sudden warning light. In contrast, it may be that the pilot, although performing perfectly well under normal circumstances, is close to the limits of their attentional capacity and would be unable to deal with additional demands relating to a sudden emergency. Assessing task performance levels under normal flying conditions would not provide an indication of spare capacity, i.e. the safety margin.

One technique that can be used to gain more information from primary task performance involves the manipulation of task difficulty. Decrements in levels of performance with increments in task difficulty can provide an indication of capacity limitations. However, there are several instances (see O'Donnell & Eggemeier, 1986) where difficulty manipulations have failed to produce changes in task performance. Such situations can be explained if it is assumed that participants protect their levels of performance by devoting greater effort (more resources) to the task. Obviously, there are limits to the extent that performance levels can be maintained in this way, and the use of multiple measures of task performance (usually speed and accuracy) can facilitate detection of strategy changes in performance. Nevertheless, we can see that primary task measures of workload are not particularly sensitive to changes in resource allocation. Further, primary task measures of workload are highly task-specific, and do not provide information that can be generalised to other tasks.

### 5.3.3 Dual task techniques for assessing resource-allocation

Knowles (1963) was one of the first to realise the limitations of examining levels of single-task performance alone. Following this line of reasoning, many laboratory studies subsequently have assessed attentional capacity demands using a dual-task paradigm, in which performances of a primary and a secondary task are examined together. The participant is told that the principal goal is to maintain performance on the task designated as "primary", so that performance on the secondary task provides an index of the remaining spare capacity. A difficulty with this method is that there may be structural interference between primary and secondary tasks, which is sometimes called the *cost of concurrence*. In

a more sophisticated test for the *difficulty-sensitivity* of secondary task performance, it is often possible to vary difficulty so that the task remains qualitatively similar. For example, the perceptual discriminability of stimuli might be varied in a detection task. The test made is to vary the difficulty of the primary task, and to assess performance change on the secondary task. It is assumed that increasing primary task difficulty increases the amount of resources the first task requires, which in turn reduces the quantity of "spare" resources that can be allocated to the second task. Hence, the resource model predicts secondary task performance deterioration as primary task difficulty increases.

Figure 5.4 represents levels of performance of primary tasks with two different levels of difficulty. In this figure the dotted line represents the total amount of resources available. We can see that, when the primary task is performed, although in both instances task demands are well within attentional capacity, there are different amounts of spare resources. As indicated above, examining single task performance in this circumstance would tell us little about task demands. In contrast, from an appraisal of levels of performance of a secondary task, we can infer the amount of remaining capacity. Variations are possible but the general principles are as follows. First we assess participants' levels of performance on the secondary task when it is performed on its own. This provides a baseline. Then participants are instructed to maintain levels of performance on the primary task while simultaneously performing the secondary task. Given the assumptions of difficulty sensitivity, described above, the decrement in secondary task performance levels between single- and dual-task conditions provides an index of remaining attentional capacity when the single task is performed alone. It should be noted that this dual-task methodology will not be successful if sufficient resources are available to make perfect timesharing possible, or if varying task difficulty leads to qualitative differences in the way task stimuli are processed.

Many different secondary tasks have been used in experimental paradigms such as the one described, including tracking, random number

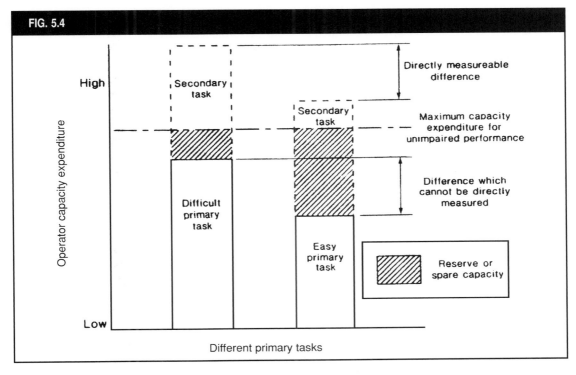

FIG. 5.4

Representation for use of the secondary task to measure operator reserve processing capacity (from O'Donnell & Eggemeier, 1986, p. 42-25). Reprinted by permission of John Wiley & Sons Inc.

generation, and probe reaction time. For secondary random number generation tasks participants are required to generate concurrently a series of random single-digit numbers; as processing demands of the primary task increase the numbers generated tend to become less random (Baddeley, 1986). One of the most common approaches to secondary task assessment involves the use of probe reaction time measures (Posner & Boies, 1971). In addition to a primary task, participants are presented with occasional tones or visual stimuli at unpredictable intervals and required to make a speeded response. The length of time taken to respond is taken to be an index of remaining attentional capacity after performing the primary task. From his position as a proponent of single-channel descriptions of human information processing, Pashler (1994) argues that probe RT tends to be elevated at approximately the time when response selection for the main task is in progress. Consequently, slowing of probe RT may

reflect not lack of resources, but postponement of the response to the probe at the response selection bottleneck.

### 5.3.4 The Performance Operating Characteristic

An extension of the secondary task technique investigates the tradeoff between two tasks explicitly, by constructing a graph of performance interdependence known as the Performance Operating Characteristic (POC: Navon & Gopher, 1979). It tests for a resource-dependent *tradeoff* between performance levels on the two tasks. On the assumption that there are insufficient resources for perfect timesharing, performance gains on one task may only be achieved at the cost of performance deterioration on the other.

Description of the POC here is based on the account given by Wickens (1992). Although slight variations in procedure are possible, constructing a POC generally requires participants to perform the same two tasks (say, A and B) several times over. On each set of trials, the priority afforded to the two tasks is manipulated by instructions. In one condition, participants might be told that task A is relatively more important than task B, an instruction that should lead them to direct the majority of their attentional resources to task A. In other conditions, task B is the one prioritised, or the tasks are designated as being equally important. The POC is constructed by plotting levels of performance on task A against levels of performance on task B, as shown in Fig. 5.5. Each

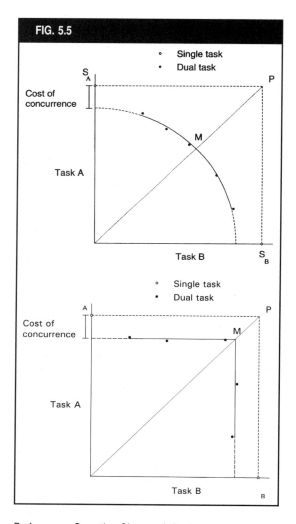

FIG. 5.5

Performance Operating Characteristics for resource limited (upper panel) or data limited (lower panel) performance.

data point (the filled circles) represents levels of performance under a particular set of priority instructions. A POC may be plotted either for individual participants or for a sample, to show a group trend. The upper panel shows a resource-limited POC. There is a smooth tradeoff such that as performance of one task improves, performance on the other deteriorates. It is assumed that the tradeoff reflects the performer's ability to allocate and reallocate resources freely across the two tasks. The box-like POC in the lower panel of Fig. 5.5 is indicative of data limitation, such that performance changes on the two tasks are independent of one another. For example, the horizontal segment of the POC indicates changes in task B with performance on A remaining constant.

The POC also illustrates other attributes of performance. By extrapolating the POC as shown by the broken lines in Fig. 5.5, so that it meets the axes of the graph, we can estimate what dual-task performance would be like if the participant was attending actively to one task only, that is, allocating 100% of resources to that task. We can then compare these points with single-task performance to estimate the cost of concurrence, the loss of performance efficiency due solely to the demands associated with concurrent processing. Single task performance is represented by the open circles labelled $S_A$ and $S_B$ in Fig. 5.5. It is often assumed in dual-task studies, such as those used to test difficulty–insensitivity, that participants obey instructions to prioritise tasks equally. However, the possibility that participants may, in fact, allocate their resources unequally across tasks is one of the problems inherent in this type of study. The POC allows us to consider explicitly the observer's allocation of resources. The mid-point M of the POC indicates a 50–50% division of resources across the two tasks. We can then assess the allocation bias of a given priority condition, in terms of its distance from the mid-point. For example, the condition nearest to M in Fig. 5.5 is a little off-centre, indicating a bias towards task A. To assess overall efficiency of performance, we can use single-task data to locate point P, which represents optimal dual-task performance; that is, no interference at all. The distance M–P indicates the extent of dual-task interference, taking into account both cost of concurrence, and any resource limitation.

## 5.4 WORKLOAD ASSESSMENT

### 5.4.1 Physiological measures

The appraisal of energetic systems within the human body takes many different forms. For our purposes, an important distinction can be made between assessing activity of the central nervous system and that of the autonomic nervous system (see Kramer, 1991). The rationale for an association between cortical activity and cognitive performance may be seen more readily. It is consistent with our discussion, in 2.3, of the concept of activation in relation to connectionist models of cognition and models of human memory. However, the rationale underlying an association between activity of the autonomic nervous system and cognitive performance is more problematic. A number of theories have been developed that propose such an association (see Hockey, Gaillard, & Coles, 1986; Robbins, 1997, for summaries), and the general position is consistent with our initial conception of mental workload, i.e. that there is a physiological "cost" associated with the performance of cognitively-demanding tasks. However, it is improbable that this "cost" arises only from the physiological "energy demands of mental work" that "continue to be a trivial factor in the organism's overall energy economy" (Brener, 1986, p. 113). Perhaps it is unsurprising, then, that initial efforts to use measures of physiological arousal as an index of mental workload produced mixed results, at best. Two particular difficulties were apparent. First, these measures are often poorly correlated with one another (Eysenck, 1982); and second, they are subject to a range of other environmental influences (Lacey, 1967). Although these problems have not been solved, some promising physiological indicators of mental workload now have been identified. Here we briefly describe two: pupil diameter and event related potentials (ERPs).

Kahneman (1973) was one of the strongest advocates of pupil diameter as an index of mental workload and, although not all studies have obtained the same results (Kramer, 1991), empirical evidence favours such an association (Beatty, 1982). Pupil diameter generally has proved to be sensitive to differences in task difficulty and to individual differences in task-related effort. This association with resource allocation does not appear to be influenced by anxiety or muscular strain. However, levels of illumination and demands of depth perception, factors that may be unrelated to the task, produce larger changes in pupil dilation than manipulations of task load (Kramer, 1991).

As described in 2.6.3, ERPs are an averaged recording of electro-cortical activity following a discrete stimulus or response. ERP components can take the form of relatively brief peaks (negative) or troughs (positive), or more prolonged tendencies for activity (slow waves). The more temporally proximate to the stimulus, the more the ERP component tends to reflect involuntary ("exogenous") activity, whereas the more temporally distant the ERP component is from the stimulus, the more it reflects voluntary ("endogenous") activity.

Different ERP components have been found to be sensitive to different aspects of cognitive task performance. Early (shorter than 250 ms) negative components appear to be sensitive to perceptual demands associated with task performance (Kramer, 1991). The P300 component (a positive component that occurs approximately 300 ms after the stimulus) has been found to be particularly sensitive to both perceptual and central processing demands, but insensitive to response processing demands. This frequently-studied component is associated with endogenous (voluntary) factors, such as variation in the effort allocated to task performance. Many studies have found that P300s for a secondary task tend to decrease if primary task difficulty is increased, suggesting that the P300 is sensitive to the attentional capacity allocated to task performance (Kramer, 1991). There is also evidence, although slightly less compelling, that the slow negative wave (a prolonged negative drift) is also sensitive to manipulations of task difficulty, as it has been found to increase in size with increased task demand, or increased investment of effort, across a range of tasks (Kramer, 1991; Rosler, Heil, & Roder, 1997).

### 5.4.2 Self-report measures

Another, more simple, approach to determining demands on attentional capacity is simply to ask the person performing the task to report the level of workload they are experiencing. This method has the advantage that it is easy to collect data. Unlike secondary task or physiological approaches to workload measurement, it is minimally intrusive. It is perhaps reasonable to suppose that, regardless of other indices, if a person reports experiencing high workload, then that is the reality of the situation. However, dissociations between self-report measures and performance measures have been reported. In comparison with performance measures of workload, it would seem that self-report measures are relatively more sensitive to the number of tasks performed, and relatively less sensitive to resource competition (Aretz, Johannsen, & Obser, 1996; Yeh & Wickens, 1988).

Several different workload scales have been developed to provide more comprehensive measurement. One of the most widely used, the NASA Task Load Index (NASA TLX: Hart & Staveland, 1988) is shown in Fig. 5.6. The respondent is required to assess the level of workload that they experienced during task performance on six scales. Following this, a series of pairwise comparisons of scales is made, in which the respondent has to indicate the relative importance that they ascribe to each of the six dimensions of workload. The final estimate of workload is calculated by combining the initial ratings with the subsequent weightings for each dimension, to give a single figure.

Measures of self-report workload have proved valuable in many instances. For example, Eggemeier, Crabtree and LaPointe (1983) presented participants with three letters of the alphabet in 20 item sequences (e.g. a, b, a, c, c, a, . . . ), and required them to retain a running count of the number of times each letter occurred. Task demand was manipulated by the interval between letter presentations (1, 2 or 3 seconds). As Fig. 5.7 shows, although task performance was not affected by this experimental manipulation of task diffi-

| **FIG. 5.6** | | |
| --- | --- | --- |
| **Title** | **Endpoints** | **Descriptions** |
| Mental Demand | *Low/High* | How much mental and perceptual activity was required (e.g. thinking, deciding, calculating, remembering, looking, searching, etc)? Was the task easy or demanding, simple or complex, exacting or forgiving? |
| Physical Demand | *Low/High* | How much physical activity was required (e.g. pushing, pulling, turning, controlling, activating, etc)? Was the task easy or demanding, slow or brisk, slack or strenuous, restful or laborious? |
| Temporal Demand | *Low/High* | How much time pressure did you feel due to the rate or pace at which the tasks or task elements occurred? Was the pace slow and leisurely or rapid and frantic? |
| Performance | *Good/Poor* | How successful do you think you were in accomplishing the goals of the task set by the experimenter (or yourself)? How satisfied were you with your performance in accomplishing these goals? |
| Effort | *Low/High* | How hard did you have to work (mentally and physically) to accomplish your level of performance? |
| Frustration Level | *Low/High* | How insecure, discouraged, irritated, stressed and annoyed versus secure, gratified, content, relaxed and complacent did you feel during the task? |

Scales of the NASA Task Load Index (from Hart & Staveland, 1988, p. 168).

| TABLE 5.1 | |
|---|---|
| **Criteria for workload indices (based on O'Donnell & Eggemeier, 1986; Wickens, 1992).** | |
| Sensitivity | The index should be sensitive to changes in demands for resources |
| Diagnosticity | The index should discriminate sources of demand (e.g. multiple resources) |
| Selectivity | The index should be sensitive to demands on information processing, but not to extraneous factors such as emotional state |
| Obtrusiveness | Assessment should not disrupt task performance |
| Reliability | The index should be reliable, but sensitive to changes in demand over time |

culty, self-report workload increased as the length of time between stimuli was reduced. It would appear from this that participants were able to maintain levels of primary task performance in the more difficult conditions, but only by investing more effort (resources), and this was reflected in their self-report of workload.

### 5.4.3 Criteria for selecting a workload assessment methodology

In selecting a technique for workload assessment there are a number of criteria to be considered (see Table 5.1). Perhaps the most important of these is that the technique is sensitive to changes in levels of workload. As mentioned above, single-task measures perform comparatively poorly in this respect. The application of both secondary task techniques and, to a lesser extent, physiological measures of workload, in "real world" settings is severely restricted by their implementation requirements. In the case of secondary task techniques, in many situations there would be associated safety implications. For instance, if an airline required a measure of pilot workload, using secondary tasks during a real flight to place the pilot in an "overload" situation might not be too popular with the passengers on the plane. Fortunately, the availability of realistic flight simulators means

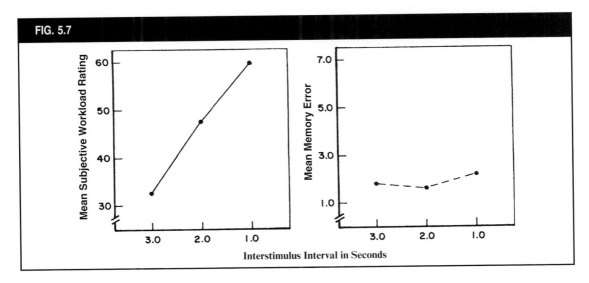

Mean subjective workload ratings and mean memory task errors as a function of interstimulus interval (from Eggemeier et al., 1983, p. 44).

that this method can still be applied. However, a further important issue regarding the use of secondary tasks concerns task performance strategy. It is possible that primary task performance strategy changes to adapt to the presence of a secondary task.

A key criterion, that we have touched on in the preceding sections, concerns the ability of the various workload measurement techniques to discriminate different types of workload (sometimes referred to as the "quality of diagnosticity"). So far, resources have been considered as unitary, i.e. a single pool from which all tasks draw. The importance of diagnosticity will become apparent as we now turn to consider more complex possibilities.

## 5.5  TASK SIMILARITY AND DUAL-TASK INTERFERENCE

Studies using the performance-based techniques described in 5.5 (see e.g. Damos, 1991; Wickens, 1992) provide many instances in which the concept of a single pool of attentional resources is supported by difficulty–sensitivity of performance or tradeoffs in performance between dual tasks. Similarly, workload measures often vary with task demands as resource theory would predict (Warm & Dember, 1998). In terms of the four determinants of dual-task interference listed in 5.2, resource theory provides a satisfactory explanation for task difficulty effects. The automatisation hypothesis discussed in 3.3.1 explains the role of skill in reducing interference effects. However, task similarity effects and emergent features remain a problem. One possibility is simply to suggest that structural interference effects, which are presumably stronger for more similar tasks, are overlaid on top of any general resource limitation. Another possible explanation for similarity effects is that there is not a single pool of attentional resources, from which task performance is fed, but there are multiple pools and each of these tasks draws on different resources (Navon & Gopher, 1979). A final possibility is that the resource metaphor is misconceived, and more

attention to sources of task-specific interference within the cognitive architecture is required.

### 5.5.1  Multiple resource theory

Following a substantial review of dual task studies, Wickens (1980) concluded that, contrary to a single-pool model of attentional capacity, for some dual-task combinations: (i) difficulty–sensitivity tradeoffs did not (or rarely) occur; and, (ii) performance on one task could be improved by simply changing the response format for the other task (structural alteration effects). For example, if a tracking task is paired with a tone detection task, dual-task performance is improved if the response to the detection task is vocal rather than manual. For these reasons, Wickens (1980, 1984a, 1991) hypothesised that human attentional capacity should be conceived as multiple resource pools, with dual-task interference being greatest when tasks compete for similar processing resources and least (or non-existent) when tasks draw from different resource pools.

Wickens' (1984a) model identified dichotomies along each of three orthogonal attentional resource dimensions (see Fig. 5.8). A distinction was made with respect to processing stages. Tasks requiring early and central processing were held to draw from a different pool of resources than tasks requiring response selection/execution. As discussed in Chapter 2, it is incorrect to view information processing as being strictly serial. However, as a macro-level description, in addition to the dual-task evidence considered by Wickens, support for a distinction between processing stages can be found in Sternberg's (1969) additive factors analysis of information processing (see 3.2.2), and the cognitive–energetic model of attention developed by Sanders (1983, see 3.2.3). Further, the dichotomy identified by Wickens bears comparison with the point in the information processing chain at which the PRP bottleneck is thought to occur.

A further dichotomy was identified with respect to processing codes. Spatial and verbal processing were held to draw from different resource pools. Parallels can be drawn with Baddeley's (1986) identification of an articulatory loop and a visuospatial sketchpad in his model

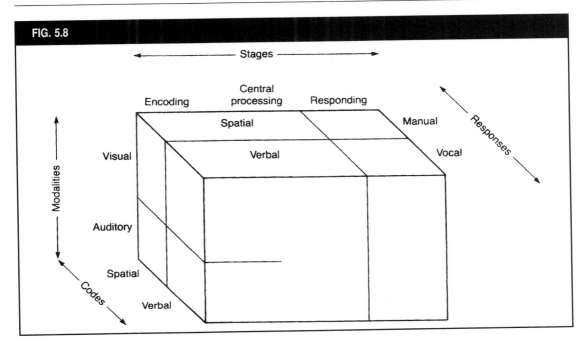

The proposed structure of multiple processing resources (from Wickens, 1984b, p. 375).

of working memory (see 3.5.2). Wickens (1984a) suggests that there may be a neurophysiological basis for spatial and verbal processing codes, with the right hemisphere predominantly processing spatial information and the left hemisphere predominantly processing verbal information. This is discussed further below.

Finally, a distinction was made with respect to processing modality. Auditory tasks were held to draw from a different resource pool than visual tasks. Initially, Wickens (1980) also included the manual vs. vocal response dichotomy as part of the modality dimension, although later versions of the model placed these elements within the processing code dimension. Subsequent studies have challenged the resource-like properties of this dimension, and Wickens (1991) regards the evidence for a modality dichotomy as being the weakest of the three. For instance, it appears that interference between two visual tasks is often due to the requirement to shift fixations between task stimuli, a source of structural interference. When visual scanning is controlled, there is often no difference between performance of two visual

tasks ("intra-modal" performance) and a visual plus an auditory task ("cross-modal" performance) (Wickens & Liu, 1988). Wickens (1991) suggests that it is too soon to make a final judgement, but that the differences between modalities appear to be mainly structural rather than concerned with energetical systems.

## 5.5.2 Resources or outcome conflict?

The multiple resource model has proved extremely influential, perhaps particularly within the human factors research community. A problem for Wickens' theory of multiple resources arises from empirical studies that have demonstrated an association betweeen dual-task interference and the semantic similarity of the dual tasks. Hirst and Kalmar (1987) used dichotic listening tasks, in which participants were required to detect errors in both channels, to show that increased between-task similarity of processing or semantic content increased interference. Consistent with this position, Navon and Miller (1987) report experiments in which participants performed dual visual search tasks. Response times were slower if nontargets in one task were used as targets for the other. One explanation for these findings is that dual-task performance is better described in terms of the effects of "crosstalk" between tasks rather than by competition for resource pools (Navon, 1984; Navon & Miller, 1987). It is possible that ". . . the processing of a task may produce outputs, throughputs, or side effects that are harmful to the processing of the other task in that they change the state of some alterant that is relevant to the performance of the concurrent task" (Navon, 1984, p. 220). In other words, processing of dual tasks may result in "outcome conflict" between two streams of processing that should be independent of one another (Navon & Miller, 1987). This view of processing also elucidates the effects of skill acquisition on dual-task performance: people may learn how to segregate streams of processing (Hirst, 1986). The Stroop test provides an example of outcome conflict, in that the "irrelevant" word meaning stimulus tends to activate a colour-naming response that interferes with activation of the correct response. Cohen et al.'s (1990) connectionist simulation of Stroop interference, discussed in 4.4.3, shows how this process might operate computationally.

It remains an open question whether *all* instances of interference may be attributed to such mechanisms, or whether resource theory provides a more parsimonious account of a portion of the interference data. Pashler (1998a) points out that demonstrations of outcome conflict use rather extreme manipulations of similarity, as in the Stroop test. Similarity effects on discrete-trial tasks are otherwise rather limited. According to Pashler (1998a), stronger similarity effects observed on continuous-performance tasks are a consequence of task switching. Performing one task may overwrite the memory stores used by the other task, disrupting performance when attention is switched.

### 5.5.3 Processing similarity vs. semantic similarity

From the examples presented so far, it would appear that crosstalk increases with the functional similarity of paired tasks. However, the position is more complex than this. There is evidence to indicate that increases in task similarity can

also result in reduced dual-task interference. For example, Heuer (1996) describes a number of situations in which increasing the similarity of two concurrently performed, or prepared, responses produces reduced competition. He concludes that "coupling of, or mutual association between, concurrent movements seems to exist at least with respect to timing, phasing, forces, and muscle groups involved. Most conspicuous is the tendency toward certain temporal relations between concurrent movements" (p. 140). As with the studies of semantic similarity described above, it should be noted that the dimensions along which task similarity has been manipulated do not map onto Wickens' MRT. In 7.5.2, we describe how motor skill theories emphasise the importance of ease of coordination of muscle groups, irrespective of attentional factors.

Fracker and Wickens (1989) attempted to explain how manipulations of task similarity can produce such disparate effects. They generated a "compatibility-of-proximity" hypothesis, in which the relative "psychological proximity" of tasks at different stages of processing (perceptual, central and response) was held to determine the degree of dual-task interference. If the output of one stage was not compatible with the required input for the next stage a "mapping" process must be engaged, resulting in performance decrement. In order to test this, participants were required to perform a two-dimensional tracking task, with each of these dimensions representing a task. Compatibility of tasks was manipulated for perceptual processing through stimulus integrity (whether there was a separate or combined cursor for each tracking dimension), for central processing through tracking control dynamics, and for response processing through response integrity (using single- or dual-response mechanisms). Contrary to their hypothesis, although results suggested that compatibility-of-proximity for perceptual and response stages may account for some variance, resource demand and outcome conflict also appeared predictive of tracking performance. The "proximity compatibility" principle has been applied to designing displays, in that integrated displays are easier for operators to use (Bennett & Flach, 1992).

How, then, can the apparently conflicting results of increasing task similarity be reconciled? More recently, Wickens (1991, p. 27) has suggested that a "reasonable hypothesis, which awaits further empirical validation, depends on a distinction between processing similarity and representational similarity. When processing routines of two tasks are made more similar (stimulus–response mapping, control dynamics, response timing) dual-task performance is seen to benefit through cooperation. But when the semantic or physical representation of material is made more similar, confusion will result".

## 5.6  THE FUTURE OF RESOURCE THEORY

It remains to be seen whether better understanding of the cognitive architecture and its neurological foundations will revive or kill off resource theory. In this section, we look at some current views of capacity and resources likely to be influential in future research. On the one hand, all instances of dual-task interference may be attributed to interactions between specific processes, or specific neural systems. On the other hand, advances in neuropsychology and in our understanding of executive control processes may provide stronger support for the resource construct.

### 5.6.1  Alternatives to resource theory

Several authors (e.g. Allport, 1980, 1989; Navon, 1984) have voiced fundamental objections to the resource concept, beginning with methodological difficulties in studies of resources. Navon (1984) argues that criteria for resource limitation, such as tradeoffs shown on the POC, may be a consequence of "demand characteristics", i.e. participants behaving in accord with the experimenter's preconceptions, although he offers little direct evidence for this view. Different criteria for resource limitation may disagree. Matthews, Sparkes and Bygrave (1996) had participants perform an auditory version of the picture-sentence verification task (see 2.5.3) concurrently with simulated driving at two levels of difficulty. They showed that dual-task interference was greater when driv-

ing was more difficult, but POCs showed no tradeoff between task versions. Multiple resource theory raises additional problems. Allport (1980) points out that the POC loses diagnosticity when resources may be multiple. The "box-like" POC shown in Fig. 5.5 may indicate either data limitation, or that the two tasks use different multiple resources. There is uncertainty over how many dimensions of resources should be distinguished, and when a "resource" is better conceptualised as a specific process. Boles and Law (1998, p. 206) suggest that the number of resource pools is constrained only by "the number of orthogonal processes by which information can be processed". They report a series of dual-task studies, in which resource independence is demonstrated between tasks identified as orthogonal using factor analytic methods. They draw the conclusion that Wickens' multiple resource theory may be incomplete and that there may be many more dimensions of task similarity that bear on the outcome of dual-task performance. However, such an approach is open to the criticism that multiple resource descriptions of attention are insufficiently specific with respect to the number and type of resource pools, in that the number of resource pools can be expanded or amended to fit any empirical data (Hirst & Kalmar, 1987; Navon, 1984; see also Sanders, 1997). Navon's (1984) view is that resources are a "soupstone", a component of theory added for essentially superstitious reasons, rather than because it has an real explanatory value.

Allport (1980) develops an architectural argument that the assumption of serial processing often made by resource theorists is incompatible with the parallelism of brain function shown by cognitive neuropsychology. Compatible with this view is evidence from animal studies that neurons responding to attended stimuli inhibit neuronal response to unattended stimuli (Braun, 1998). Desimone and Duncan (1995) propose that attention is limited as a side effect of inhibition between the neurons representing feature maps (see 4.3.1). Braun (1998) relates such interactions to the classic lateral inhibition effects in the visual cortex: "attention" might allow a neuron in the attended receptive field to inhibit response to surrounding receptive fields, without itself being inhibited by its neighbours. Of course, this mechanism might apply better to "perceptual capacity limits" (Pashler, 1998a) than to constraints on central processing.

There are two counter-arguments to Allport's (1980) critique. First, "software" and "hardware" issues refer to different levels of explanation, so that processing may operate serially even if hardware components function in parallel. Second, the questions of the seriality and resource limitation of processing are logically distinct (Townsend & Ashby, 1983). Resource-based, parallel processing, models of human information processing have proved valuable in accounting for empirical evidence (see Neumann, 1996; Pashler, 1998a). A related issue is that resource models may provide only a coarse-grained account of performance that fails to represent processing operations adequately, such as the task-switching process proposed by Welford (1980). However, if intertask switching is sufficiently rapid, then making this distinction may not be achievable or helpful and processing may "for all intents and purposes, be labeled as shared resources" (Wickens, 1984b, p. 87).

## 5.6.2 Neurological structures and attentional resources

We have seen that some neurological evidence suggests that dual-task interference may reflect local interneuronal interactions rather than resource shortfalls. However, other evidence appears more supportive. One possibility is that resource availability relates to subcortical afferent pathways, which innervate cortical areas extensively, including the cortical attention systems identified by Posner, and discussed in 4.3.3. Drug studies may be used to investigate the effects of specific neurotransmitters, as further discussed in Chapter 13. Dopaminergic, cholinergic and noradrenergic pathways have all been implicated in variation in attentional efficiency, associated with changes in signal-to-noise-ratio at the cellular level (Marrocco & Davidson, 1998; Parasuraman, Warm, & See, 1998). A subcortical origin for resources is an attractive hypothesis in that it shows how cortical cell assemblies operating in parallel may be subject to a common influence. The hypothesis fits well with some of the stressor effects discussed

later in this book. However, explaining dual-task interference would require some further central coordination of the "resources" afforded by subcortical innervation, which remains conjectural. Such an explanation would also require an explanation of how resources, as a "software" construct, were affected by variation in neural functioning. For example, Cohen and Servan-Schreiber (1992) developed a connectionist model to show how dopamine depletion might be linked to attentional impairments in schizophrenics.

Other work has focused on the cortex, and the role of the two hemispheres in divided attention. Wickens (1991) suggested that the distinction made, in multiple resource theory, between spatial and verbal processing codes may operate at this level, with spatial processing (in right-handed individuals) tending to rely on the right hemisphere and verbal processing tending to rely on the left hemisphere. However, this description of hemispheric localisation of function may be too simplistic and inflexible. Kinsbourne and Hicks (1978) proposed the concept of a cognitive workspace, in which the functional distance between areas of the brain engaged in task performance determines the level of interference between tasks or task components. In this regard, hemispheric differences in function may be adaptive, in so far as they facilitate separation of cortical activity. However, Kinsbourne and Hicks point out that, although different regions of the brain may be involved in task performance, at some point this activity must be coordinated. On this view, it would be wrong to view functional distinctions between hemispheres as being rigid. A series of studies by Friedman, Polson, Dafoe and Gaskill (1982; Friedman, Polson, & Dafoe, 1988; Polson & Friedman, 1988) extended this area of investigation. They used a working memory "loading" task that was paired with various other "target" tasks which were presented separately to left and right hemispheres. Task priorities were manipulated (see 5.3.4), and performance tradeoffs between loading and target tasks were assessed. Although a cost of concurrence was apparent for all dual-task performance, task priority tradeoffs only occurred when there was hemispheric competition. This was interpreted as indicating that each hemisphere constitutes a separate pool of resources, but the allocation of these resources within hemispheres is more flexible than suggested by distinctions between spatial/verbal or local/ global processing.

More recent experimental work has provided qualified support for allocation of activity between hemispheres being determined, in part, by the overall level of resource demand and, in part, by the need to avoid interference between tasks or task elements (Liederman, 1998; although see Pashler & O'Brien, 1993). For example, Banich (1998) reported a series of studies which used target-matching tasks with stimuli presented within or across hemispheres. Results showed that division of processing between hemispheres is particularly beneficial when the cognitive demands associated with task performance are high. However, Banich suggests that there may also be a cost associated with the division of cognitive performance between hemispheres that relates to increased difficulty in coordinating action. In high complexity situations, then, the costs of coordination are overtaken by the advantages of hemispheric task division, whereas in simple tasks they are not.

### 5.6.3  A hierarchy of resources?

A further difficulty for Wickens' model of multiple resources comes from studies that demonstrate dual-task performance costs associated with tasks that do not share common "cells" within the model shown in Fig. 5.8, i.e. task combinations that should not produce interference (see Wickens, 1984b). One possible explanation for this is that inefficient strategy selection or a shortfall of resources leads individuals to perform tasks using resources of an inappropriate type. So, for example, a spatial task might be performed using a verbal strategy and hence verbal processing resources. Navon and Gopher (1979) recognise this possibility and distinguish between fixed proportion and variable proportion functions. Variable performance functions allow resources of different types to be substituted. Alternatively, these findings can be accommodated if resource pools are conceptualised as hierarchical, similar to "g" factor models of human intelligence discussed

in Chapter 14 (see Heuer, 1985, 1996), with a non-specific pool of resources available to, and demanded by, all tasks at the highest level of the hierarchy. For example, Wickens (1984b) suggests that the modality distinction might form the lowest level of the hierarchy, processing codes the next level, processing stages the next level, with undifferentiated resources being at the top of the hierarchy. A difficulty with such models concerns the correct hierarchical ordering of resource pools. Empirical data, it seems, are available to contradict any possible fixed ordering (Neumann, 1996, p. 407; Wickens, 1984b). This led Wickens (1984b) to suggest a more flexible system, based on shared task features, as one possible solution.

The concept of undifferentiated resources at the highest level of a hierarchy is consistent with several models of cognitive performance that propose a high level mechanism of supervisory control. For example, Norman and Shallice (1986) propose a Supervisory Attentional System (SAS) that regulates the process of contention scheduling, as described in 3.3.2; Baddeley (1986) incorporates a central executive as a controlling component within his model of working memory (see 3.5.2); and Broadbent (1971) hypothesised upper and lower mechanisms, based on different arousal systems, with the upper level exercising regulatory control over the lower level. As discussed in 3.3.2, there is neuropsychological evidence for such an executive system. Such executive control is generally thought to be attention demanding. Within Schneider and Shiffrin's (1977) terms, it is controlled rather than automatic processing. However, as skill is acquired for a given task and processing becomes more automatic, an executive function may still be required to coordinate action between tasks and to determine strategy (Gopher, 1996). For example, executive processing might be required to allocate processing functions to the two hemispheres, as previously discussed. It remains unclear whether overload of executive processing reflects some resource limitation, or whether two apparently dissimilar tasks may compete for the same specific executive process, which would be an instance of structural interference. In general, though, capacity limits on executive processing are worth further investigation as a possible source of dual-task interference.

## 5.7 CONCLUSIONS

The attentional resource theory of capacity has proved to be intuitively appealing but controversial. It has inspired development of workload measures that are widely used in human factors applications. However, dual-task studies have indicated that "single pool" resource theories (Moray, 1967; Kahneman, 1973) do not describe performance data sufficiently well, and consequently multiple resource theories have been developed. We have examined Wickens' (1984a, 1991) theory, being the most prominent example, in some detail, and identified a number of difficulties. These include the general criticisms that resource theories are underspecified, so that new resource pools can be included or old resource pools excluded to suit any pattern of performance data; and the more specific criticism that Wickens' theory requires revision of the resource structure in order to cope with some patterns of dual-task interference. Multiple resource theories provide an approximate account of performance deficits in some dual-task paradigms, which is useful in applied contexts but are obviously not the whole story. How best can further progress be made? One approach, proposed by Allport (1992), is to accept that the disparate pattern of results produced to date reflect a complex and diverse set of attentional mechanisms and that these are best pursued individually within a modular architecture. These mechanisms include perceptual capacity limits, the response bottleneck (Pashler, 1994) and "outcome conflict" between processing streams operating on similar codes. On the other hand, others are convinced that a more unified description of attentional performance is still possible. Developing resource theory requires better understanding of the difficult issue of task-similarity effects on interference, constraints on executive control of processing, and the neuropsychological underpinnings of resources.

## FURTHER READING

Pashler's (1998a) book covers "discrete-trial" studies of divided attention in detail. Wickens (1992) provides a good textbook account of multiple resource theory and its application to explaining patterns of dual-task performance. Of earlier works, Kahneman (1973) is recommended for its attempt to link resources to other related constructs such as effort, and Norman and Bobrow (1975) set out explicitly the assumptions on which most versions of resource theory depend. Parasuraman and Davies' (1984) edited volume includes several contributions relating to divided attention. Cognitive neuropsychological work is discussed in the Parasuraman (1998a) volume. Navon's (1984) "soupstone" critique of resource theory has probably been the most influential challenge to the concept.

# 6

# Vigilance and sustained attention

In the two previous chapters, we reviewed research and theory in the fields of selective and divided attention respectively. In this chapter, we consider a further distinct variety of attention, namely sustained attention or "long-term attentive behaviour" (Adams, 1963). Sustained attention involves the maintenance of a focus of attention over a relatively long period of time, as in industrial inspection, military target spotting, air traffic control and medical monitoring. Impairments of sustained attention are a feature of many clinical and neurological disorders, such as schizophrenia (Nestor et al., 1990; Pigache, 1996), epilepsy (Fedio & Mirsky, 1969; Goldstein, Rosenbaum, & Taylor, 1997), closed head injury (Parasuraman, Mutter, & Molloy, 1991) and unilateral neglect (Robertson et al., 1995). Tests involving sustained attention have also been used as aids in the diagnosis of brain damage (for example, Robertson et al., 1997; Rosvold et al., 1956) and attention-deficit/hyperactivity disorders in both children (Losier, McGrath, & Klein, 1996) and adults (Seidman et al., 1998). Further, a growing body of research is concerned with the assessment of sustained attention in animals (Bushnell, 1998; McGaughy & Sarter, 1995; Robbins, 1998).

It is very difficult for human observers to focus attention on one source of information exclusively for very long. More than a century ago, William James observed that *"there is no such thing as voluntary attention sustained for more than a few seconds at a time"* (James, 1890, p. 420, italics in original) and that "no-one can possibly attend continuously to an object that does not change" (p. 421). Experiments carried out by Billings (1914) also suggested that the amount of time for which attention could be focussed on a single object or idea was extremely limited, a matter of a few seconds. Studies conducted in industry by the Industrial Fatigue Research Board between the two World Wars further emphasised the difficulties of maintaining attention over prolonged periods. For example, Wyatt and Langdon (1932) conducted an investigation of the performance of cartridge-case inspectors and reported that there was a sharp decline in the number of cartridge cases that were rejected as being faulty after about 30–45 minutes of work. Laboratory research on sustained attention began in earnest during World War II, as an attempt to solve a serious practical problem. Operational reports indicated a relatively high incidence of failures to detect military targets, particularly by airborne radar operators searching radar displays for German submarines. A research team at the Applied Psychology Unit in Cambridge was already examining fatigue in aircrew, and one of its members, Norman Mackworth, was commissioned by the Royal Air Force (RAF) to determine the optimal length of watch for airborne radar operators. The operators' task involved detecting small spots of light, about 1 mm in diameter, which appeared only for a few seconds. Detecting such targets proved to be problematic because they occurred extremely infrequently, and the radar screen also displayed quite a lot of random information or "visual noise". The RAF established that detection efficiency markedly declined after about 30 minutes or so, even though the operators were highly motivated to detect targets. Moreover, "false alarms" were quite common, since fishing vessels could easily be mistaken for submarines until visual contact was established.

Mackworth (1950) reported a series of laboratory studies of the performance of experienced and trainee radar and sonar operators on various simulated radar and sonar tasks (see Table 6.1). One of the main tasks devised by Mackworth was the "Clock Test", in which observers were instructed to monitor a black pointer, moving in discrete steps around a white clock face. The pointer made one movement, or "jump", every second but very occasionally, about 12 times every 30 minutes, it moved through twice the usual distance, making a "double jump". This double jump of the pointer, which occurred at irregular intervals, was the signal or target that the observer was required to detect. Mackworth found that, as with operational radar monitoring, detection efficiency deteriorated after about half an hour of work. He was also able to demonstrate that this performance decrement could be abolished by rest periods, by the provision of feedback or "knowledge of results", and by the prior administration of a small dose of the stimulant drug amphetamine sulphate, or "benzedrine".

Mackworth referred to the decline in detection efficiency observed in the Clock Test and other simulated radar tasks as a breakdown of "vigilance" (for example, Mackworth, 1948). The term was borrowed from the neurologist Henry Head, who used it to refer to a state of maximum physiological efficiency (Head, 1923). Subsequently "vigilance" has been used in a more restricted sense to denote a state of "readiness" (Mackworth, 1957), thought to underlie performance at certain kinds of task known as "vigilance tasks", of which the Clock Test is an example. Vigilance tasks have

| TABLE 6.1 | | | | | | |
|---|---|---|---|---|---|---|
| The principal results obtained by N.H. Mackworth (1950) with four different task situations. | | | | | | |
| Task | | Participants | Percentage of correct detections in half-hour periods of task | | | |
| | | | 1 | 2 | 3 | 4 |
| Clock test I | | 25 RAF cadets | 84.3 | 74.2 | 73.2 | 72.0 |
| | | 25 Naval ratings | 82.3 | 72.7 | 72.7 | 72.7 |
| Synthetic radar task | Bright echo[a] | 17 Naval ratings, 5 RAF cadets, 3 wireless operators | 94.0 | 91.8 | 84.3 | 88.5 |
| | Dim echo | 23 RAF cadets | 72.0 | 62.2 | 61.2 | 60.1 |
| Main listening task | | 22 RAF aircrews, 3 Naval ratings | 80.4 | 71.6 | 70.6 | 64.0 |
| [a] Average of two runs about one week apart. | | | | | | |

In Davis, D.R. & Parasuraman, R. The Psychology of Vigilance. Academic Press. Reprinted with permission.

come to be regarded as providing "the fundamental paradigm for defining sustained attention as
a behavioral category" (Jerison, 1977). Such tasks
require the unbroken direction of attention to one
or more sources of information in order to detect
and respond to infrequent changes in the nature
of the information being presented (see Davies &
Parasuraman, 1982; Warm, 1984). In sensory vigilance tasks, these changes are generally difficult
to discriminate and are often presented at near-
threshold levels: for example, a faint tone embedded in a noise burst, or a small increment in the
brightness of a flash of light. In cognitive vigilance tasks, on the other hand, alphanumeric
stimuli (letters or digits) are presented to the
observer at above threshold levels. The observer's
task typically is to detect and report a specified
sequence of digits or letters; for example, three
consecutive odd digits that are all different, or the
occurrence of a particular letter or digit, such as
the letter "X". In most studies of vigilance and
sustained attention, task durations tend to be relatively long, ranging from 30 minutes to several
hours (Davies & Parasuraman, 1982; Krueger,
1989). However, investigators using relatively short
sustained attention tasks, lasting for 10 minutes
or less, have reported that performance is essentially similar to that observed in longer tasks
(Craig, Davies, & Matthews, 1987; Matthews,
Davies, & Lees, 1990; Nuechterlein, Parasuraman,
& Jiang, 1983). Task duration does not therefore
seem to be a critical factor in the assessment of
sustained attention.

The temporal decline in the performance of
vigilance tasks, seen in Table 6.1, has become
known as the "vigilance decrement", and much
research on vigilance has investigated the task
factors and other influences that may reverse or
enhance the decline in detection efficiency with
time on task. A performance decrement occurs in
most, but not all, vigilance tasks. It is less likely
to be observed in multi-source monitoring tasks,
in which several displays have to be inspected,
rather than just one (for example, Broadbent, 1950;
Jerison & Wallis, 1957) or in tasks with complex
signals (Moray, Haudegond, & Delange, 1999).
In laboratory tasks where only one signal is presented, significantly fewer observers detect the
signal if it is presented towards the end of the
task, rather than towards the beginning (Loeb &
Binford, 1970; Parasuraman & Molloy, 1996).
Such tasks are more similar to real-life monitoring tasks, which generally have very low signal
rates (see Mackie, 1987). When it occurs, a vigilance decrement is usually apparent after about
half an hour of work. However, fine-grained analyses of detection efficiency (for example, Jerison,
1959), in which the proportion of observers
detecting each signal is calculated, indicate
that performance may begin to decline from the
presentation of the first signal. Figure 6.1 shows
Jerison's comparison of fine- and coarse-grained
analyses of the performance of 36 observers on a
version of the Clock Test. It can be seen that the
decline within the first period of the task (each
period lasted for approximately 27 minutes) was
quite steep, while that between the first and subsequent time periods was much less marked.
Coarse-grained analyses of the decrement may
thus provide a somewhat conservative picture of
the frequency with which a vigilance decrement
occurs (Teichner, 1974). Even when signals are
clearly visible, so that almost all signals are detected, significant increases in reporting times may

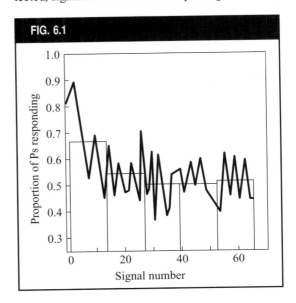

Fine-grained analysis of the probability of making a correct
detection on a version of the Clock Test as a function of
time at work (from Jerison, 1959). In Davis, D.R. &
Parasuraman, R. The Psychology of Vigilance. Academic
Press. Reprinted with permission.

be apparent (Boulter & Adams, 1963), as shown in Fig. 6.2. Boulter and Adams compared the effects of three presentation schedules, involving respectively high, moderate and no temporal uncertainty, on performance at a three-hour vigilance task in which 99.5% of signals were detected. Nonetheless, the time taken to report the presence of a signal became progressively longer with time on task in all conditions, as Fig. 6.2 indicates. Although theories of vigilance have been primarily concerned with attempting to explain the vigilance decrement, it is also worth noting that overall levels of detection efficiency in vigilance situations can sometimes be quite low, whether or not performance deteriorates with time at work. For example, overall detection rates for faulty items in industrial inspection tasks range from 90% for the detection of flaws in rubber seals (Astley & Fox, 1975) to 20% for the detection of faults in electronic equipment (Harris, 1968).

We begin this chapter by considering various measures of performance in vigilance situations in more detail. We then outline the principal task factors affecting vigilance performance. The chapter concludes with a discussion of the major theories of vigilance.

## 6.1 THE ASSESSMENT OF PERFORMANCE IN VIGILANCE SITUATIONS

Detection efficiency in vigilance situations is typically assessed by the number of correct target detections (or "hits"), and by target detection latencies (the time required to identify a target correctly). A further measure of vigilance performance is the number of occasions on which a non-target event is incorrectly identified as a target. Such "false detections" are generally termed "false alarms" or "commission errors". Thus the principal measures of performance in vigilance situations are the correct detection and false alarm rates, together with correct detection latencies. All three measures are necessary for the understanding of the way in which detection efficiency varies with time on task and across different experimental conditions. However, in early studies of vigilance, from which many of the major theories of vigilance performance were derived, investigators tended to report only correct detections and detection latencies, and largely ignored false alarm rates. The main reason for this was that there appeared to be no satisfactory way of

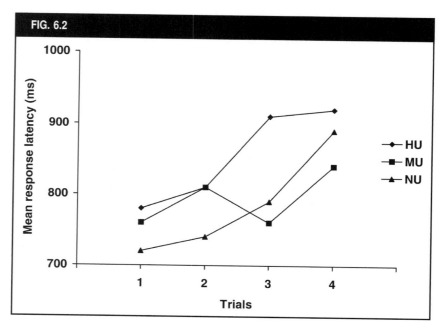

**FIG. 6.2**

Mean response latency as a function of time on task (blocks of trials) in a three-hour visual vigilance task under conditions of high (HU), medium (MU), and no (NU) uncertainty (from Boulter & Adams, 1963). In Davis, D.R. & Parasuraman, R. The Psychology of Vigilance. Academic Press. Reprinted with permission.

combining correct detections, detection latencies and false alarms into a common metric. False alarms were commonly regarded as the consequence of "random guessing" under conditions of uncertainty (see Broadbent, 1971). But it became increasingly apparent that broadly similar detection rates could be associated with both high and low false alarm rates. Furthermore, declines in detection rate with time on task were sometimes accompanied by a decline in the false alarm rate, while sometimes they were not.

Howland (1958) was the first to suggest that the reduction in the detection rate with time on task might be attributable either to a progressive increase in the observer's degree of caution in responding, or to a genuine decline in the ability to distinguish targets from non-target events. A parallel decline in both correct detections and false alarms during a vigil is suggestive of an increase in the criterion to be exceeded before a detection response is made to a potential target. In contrast, a decline in correct detections, accompanied by either a stable or an increasing false alarm rate, is suggestive of a reduction in the discriminatory power of the observer's perceptual system. The subsequent application of the theory of signal detectability (frequently referred to as signal detection theory or SDT) to vigilance situations in the early 1960s (Broadbent & Gregory, 1963; Egan, Greenberg, & Schulman, 1961) represented a major advance in the assessment of detection efficiency. SDT (Green & Swets, 1966; Swets, 1977, 1984; Tanner & Swets, 1954) provides a metric for combining both correct detection and false alarm data to produce indices of response criterion placement (reflecting the observer's willingness to respond affirmatively) and perceptual sensitivity (reflecting the efficiency of the observer's perceptual system).

## 6.1.1 Signal detection theory and vigilance

SDT proposes that sensory evidence about actual or potential signals is received by a noisy nervous system, and that a separate decision process acts upon such evidence to determine whether or not a detection response should be made. Signal detection responses are thus the joint outcome of the operation of sensory and decision processes.

An observation is made of the sensory events occurring during a particular time interval, and the observer then decides on the basis of this observation whether the interval contained only random background activity (noise) or the signal as well (signal + noise). The probability that the observation derived from noise alone is represented by a normal distribution, as is the probability that the observation derived from the addition of the signal to the noise (the signal + noise distribution; see Fig. 6.3). For data from vigilance situations the assumption of normality for the two distributions seems broadly justified (Craig, 1987, 1988). The abscissa in Fig. 6.3 can be thought of as representing the strength of the sensory evidence or the magnitude of the sensory impression received by the observer. Since in the majority of vigilance situations it is difficult to discriminate signals from noise, there is a considerable area of overlap between the noise and signal + noise distributions, as Fig. 6.3 indicates. In the region of the overlap, it is virtually impossible to determine whether the strength of the sensory evidence is indicative of the presence of a signal or is simply attributable to noise. Observers are assumed to resolve this dilemma by setting a criterion level for the strength of the sensory evidence they receive, and to report the presence of a signal only if they judge that this level has been exceeded.

Figure 6.3 illustrates the distinction between sensory and decision processes suggested by SDT. The detectability of a signal depends on the difference between the means of the noise and signal + noise distributions, and is indexed by $d'$ (d prime). The greater the overlap between the two distributions, the lower the value of $d'$, and the more difficult it becomes for the observer to discriminate signals from background noise. The same index, $d'$, is also used to refer to the observer's (perceptual) sensitivity. Readiness to respond relates to the value of the response criterion, which is designated as $\beta$ (beta). Figure 6.3 shows two possible values for $\beta$: $\beta_1$ and $\beta_2$. $\beta_2$ represents a high, or conservative, response criterion: that is, the observer will respond only if the strength of the sensory evidence that a signal is present is judged to be relatively high. If $\beta$ is high, the observer will be more likely to miss signals,

**FIG. 6.3**

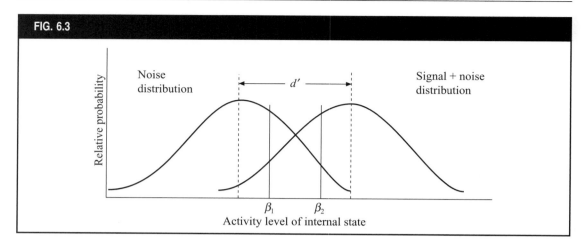

Probability density functions of the 'sensory' evidence given stimulus events classified either as 'signal' or as 'noise'. The detectability of the signal, the difference between the means of the 'noise' and 'signal + noise' distributions, is indexed by $d'$. The placement of the response criterion, $\beta$, determines whether a 'yes' (signal) or a 'no' (noise) response is made to a stimulus event, and hence the correct detection and false alarm probabilities. $\beta_2$ represents a more conservative criterion than does $\beta_1$. In Davis, D.R. & Parasuraman, R. The Psychology of Vigilance. Academic Press. Reprinted with permission.

but will be less likely to make false alarms, and will generally respond extremely cautiously. Conversely, if $\beta$ is low, as with $\beta_1$ in Fig. 6.3, the observer will be more easily persuaded that the strength of the sensory evidence arising from an observation is sufficient to justify a detection response being made. Errors will tend to take the form of false alarms rather than missed signals, and responding will appear to be somewhat impulsive.

Response latencies in vigilance situations can also be accommodated within an SDT framework (Davies & Parasuraman, 1977; Parasuraman & Davies, 1976). Parasuraman and Davies (1976) instructed observers to respond to each stimulus event that was presented in a 45-minute sustained attention task, which required the detection of an increase in the intensity of a flash of light. They reported that latencies associated with correct and incorrect affirmative responses (correct detections and false alarms) increased with time at work, while latencies associated with correct and incorrect negative responses (correct rejections and misses) either decreased or remained stable (see Fig. 6.4). These results suggest that response latency in sustained attention situations is inversely related to the strength of the evidence received

by the observer relative to the criterion level of evidence differentiating affirmative from negative responses. This conclusion is supported by the further finding that correlations between response latencies and log $\beta$ tended to be significantly positive for correct detections and false alarms and significantly negative for correct rejections and misses.

As will be seen below, in most vigilance studies utilising SDT indices the typical reduction in detection efficiency in vigilance situations appears to be associated with a progressively more stringent response criterion, so that $\beta$ increases with time on task. In a significant minority of sustained attention situations, however, the reduction can be attributed to a decline in the observer's perceptual sensitivity, so that $d'$ decreases with time at work, while $\beta$ either increases or remains stable. Considerable research effort has been devoted to the attempt to specify the conditions under which there is a genuine decline in perceptual sensitivity (See, Howe, Warm, & Dember, 1995). Thus there seem to be at least two qualitatively different sustained attention phenomena, the criterion increment and the sensitivity decrement, which may reflect the operation of different mechanisms.

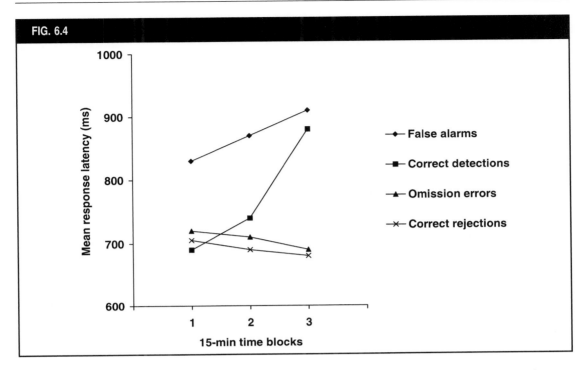

**FIG. 6.4**

Mean latencies of positive (correct detections and false alarms) and negative (correct rejections and omission errors) responses in consecutive 15-minute time blocks of a 45-minute visual vigilance task. After Parasuraman & Davies (1976). In Davis, D.R. & Parasuraman, R. The Psychology of Vigilance. Academic Press. Reprinted with permission.

To conclude this brief outline of SDT, it is worth noting that there has been some debate over alternative indices of both perceptual sensitivity and response bias (see Davies & Parasuraman, 1982; MacMillan & Creelman, 1996; See, Warm, & Dember, 1997). In some studies of vigilance and sustained attention non-parametric measures of sensitivity and bias have been used, thus avoiding the SDT assumptions of normality and homogeneity of variance with respect to the noise and the signal + noise distributions. But many researchers are content to accept standard SDT assumptions, and to use the parametric indices of sensitivity and bias, $d'$ and $\beta$.

## 6.2 TASK FACTORS AFFECTING VIGILANCE PERFORMANCE

Vigilance tasks have often been considered to be unstimulating tasks, in which observers have little to do. However, evidence from studies employing measures of perceived mental workload, such as the NASA Task Load Index or TLX (Hart & Staveland, 1988), suggest that vigilance tasks are rated as highly demanding tasks, at the upper end of the TLX scale in terms of overall workload. Vigilance tasks involve higher mental workload levels than do a wide range of other tasks, such as memory search, choice reaction time, mental arithmetic, time estimation, simple tracking, and grammatical reasoning (see Warm, 1993, for review). Typical vigilance tasks thus seem to impose high mental workload levels, which can be augmented by manipulations of task factors.

Vigilance performance is clearly affected by the manipulation of what Dember and Warm (1979) have described as "first order psychophysical factors", in which some physical parameter of the signal is altered. As might be expected, if signals are made more conspicuous by increasing their intensity, duration or predictability, then detection efficiency improves, because increased signal conspicuity tends to enhance perceptual sensitivity. Increasing the rate at which events are presented for inspection, the event presentation rate, tends to reduce perceptual sensitivity, and thus detection efficiency is impaired. Other characteristics of the signal may not be immediately apparent to observers, but must be inferred from their experience of the task. Such "second order psychophysical factors" include the frequency or probability of signal occurrence (Dember & Warm, 1979). Increases in signal probability (the probability, given a stimulus event, that it will be a signal) improve detection efficiency through their effects upon the response criterion, rather than by affecting perceptual sensitivity. Both first and second order psychophysical factors therefore affect the overall level of performance in sustained attention situations as well as, in most cases, affecting the maintenance of performance over time. As will be seen below, the overall level of perceptual sensitivity, which can be considered to provide an index of the level of difficulty of a sustained attention task (See et al., 1995), is a good predictor of the extent of the sensitivity decrement. But, in many cases, low overall levels of detection efficiency are attributable to observers adopting extremely conservative response criteria that are appropriate to the low signal probabilities they experience in the majority of sustained attention tasks (see Craig & Davies, 1991).

### 6.2.1 Factors affecting criterion placement

Manipulations of signal probability thus affect criterion placement (Baddeley & Colquhoun, 1969; Parasuraman & Davies, 1976). Increases in signal probability generally increase both correct detections and false alarms, indicating the adoption of a more relaxed criterion. Decreases in signal probability have the reverse effect; observers tend to adopt more stringent response criteria, so that fewer affirmative responses (correct detections and false alarms) are emitted. Criterion increments with time on task are more likely to be observed in vigilance tasks where the signal probability is low (for example, less than .05) than in high signal probability tasks (Williges, 1973). Moreover, signal probability appears to be the major task factor affecting criterion shifts over a vigilance session. For example, Williges (1973) showed that the typical criterion increment observed in low signal probability tasks can be eliminated if signal probability is markedly increased half way through the task, as shown in Fig. 6.5. Such findings broadly suggest that the readiness to make an

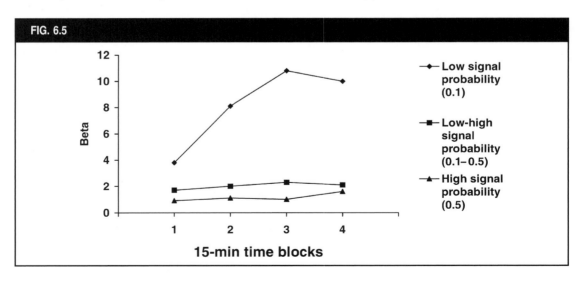

**FIG. 6.5**

Changes in criterion (ß) over time on task under low (0.1) and high (0.5) signal probability conditions, and under a condition in which signal probability changed from low to high (0.1–0.5) during the task. From Williges (1973). In Davis, D.R. & Parasuraman, R. The Psychology of Vigilance. Academic Press. Reprinted with permission.

affirmative response is related to the observer's expectancies concerning the frequency of signal occurrence, as is further discussed in 6.3.3 below. Criterion placement is also influenced by the instructions given to observers (for example, Colquhoun, 1967) and by the respective costs and payoffs associated with making affirmative and negative responses (for example, Sostek, 1978).

## 6.2.2 Factors affecting the sensitivity decrement

Although signal probability is the principal influence on criterion placement, whether or not a perceptual sensitivity decrement occurs appears to depend on the information processing requirements of the vigilance task being performed. Parasuraman and Davies (1977) attempted to identify the task factors conducive to a sensitivity decrement through a taxonomic analysis of 27 published studies. This analysis suggested that two task factors appeared to be important in producing a sensitivity decrement: the event presentation rate and the type of signal–non-signal discrimination to be made, whether simultaneous or successive. Sensitivity decrements were found to occur only in successive discrimination tasks with high event presentation rates, more than 24 events per minute. Presentation modality, whether auditory or visual, appeared to be unimportant, as was the number of displays to be monitored. In simultaneous discrimination vigilance tasks each individual trial or event provides the observer with sufficient information to determine whether or not the event constitutes a signal. For example, the observer might have to detect a difference in hue of one of a number of simultaneously presented coloured disks, or a difference in length of two parallel lines presented at the same time. In successive discrimination tasks the information required to identify an event as a signal has to be integrated across successive trials, and the observer has therefore to rely on information held in working memory. An example of a successive discrimination task would be the discrimination of an occasional brighter flash from a series of light flashes (Davies, Lang, & Shackleton, 1973) or the detection of specified sequences of digits from a series in which only one digit is presented

on each trial (Bakan, 1959). Parasuraman and Davies (1977) therefore concluded from their taxonomic analysis that the combination of a high event presentation rate with a successive discrimination requirement was a critical determinant of the sensitivity decrement (see also Davies & Parasuraman, 1982; Parasuraman, 1979). In vigilance tasks lacking this combination of task characteristics—for example, low and high event rate simultaneous discrimination tasks or low event rate successive discrimination tasks—a sensitivity decrement would be unlikely to occur and any decline in detection efficiency would be likely to result from a criterion increment alone.

Further tests of this taxonomy, however, indicated that sensitivity decrements could also be observed in high event rate simultaneous tasks, under certain conditions. For example, Nuechterlein et al. (1983), using a brief duration visual vigilance task, required observers to detect occurrences of a target digit in a sequence of digits, presented singly. They found that at high event rates (60 digits per minute) a sensitivity decrement occurred very rapidly—within five minutes or so—when stimulus events were degraded, through blurring in conjunction with a visual mask. Three levels of stimulus degradation were employed, but a reliable sensitivity decrement was only obtained in the most degraded condition. Similar findings have been reported in a computerised version of the Nuechterlein task, in which stimulus degradation is achieved by reversing the polarity of a random 30% of the pixels constituting each digit (Craig et al., 1987; Matthews, Davies, & Lees, 1990; Matthews, Davies, & Holley, 1990). The overall level of task demands, rather than any specific task requirement such as an increase in working memory load, may thus be the key factor in determining whether or not a perceptual sensitivity decrement occurs (Parasuraman, Warm, & Dember, 1987). Certainly task factors that adversely affect detection efficiency in vigilance situations generally combine in their effects on performance. For example, Parasuraman and Mouloua (1987), using a line length discrimination task with three levels of discriminability (high, moderate and low), found that in a successive version of the task, reliable sensitivity decrements occurred for all three discriminability levels. In a simultaneous version of the same task, a reliable sensitivity decrement was obtained only for the low level of discriminability. Other task factors adversely affecting detection efficiency have also been shown to exert greater effects on performance at successive, rather than at simultaneous vigilance tasks (Craig & Davies, 1991; Parasuraman et al., 1987). Examples include increasing event presentation rate, increasing the temporal irregularity of signal occurrence, or increasing the uncertainty about where a signal will appear on a visual display.

See et al. (1995) conducted a meta-analysis of the data from 42 vigilance studies comprising 138 different conditions, examining both the frequency with which the sensitivity decrement occurred and its magnitude. The magnitude of the decrement (the "effect size") was assessed in each study, and effect sizes were then related to various task factors. See et al. found that in their sample of studies a sensitivity decrement was a relatively frequent occurrence; moreover, in the majority of cases where a decrement was observed, it was moderate to large in magnitude. Their meta-analysis indicated that, in general, effect sizes were larger for high event rate tasks, and for tasks

requiring a successive discrimination. They also showed that task difficulty, indexed by the mean level of perceptual sensitivity for the task, influenced the sensitivity decrement independently of other factors: the more difficult the task, the greater the sensitivity decrement. However, using a multiple regression model, See et al. found that the predicted effects of event rate and of the information-processing requirements of the task interacted rather differently, depending on whether the task was a sensory or a cognitive vigilance task (see Figs 6.6 and 6.7). As Figs 6.6 and 6.7 indicate, for simultaneous discrimination tasks, the effect of increasing event presentation rate in a sensory vigilance task is to reduce the magnitude of the sensitivity decrement, while for cognitive vigilance tasks increasing event rate increases the magnitude of the decrement. For successive discrimination tasks, on the other hand, increasing event rate exerts a considerable effect on the magnitude of the decrement in sensory vigilance tasks, while for cognitive tasks increasing event rate slightly reduces the extent of the sensitivity decrement. Further, as Figs 6.6 and 6.7 also show, the magnitude of the decrement is generally greater for sensory than for cognitive vigilance tasks, except at very high event rates.

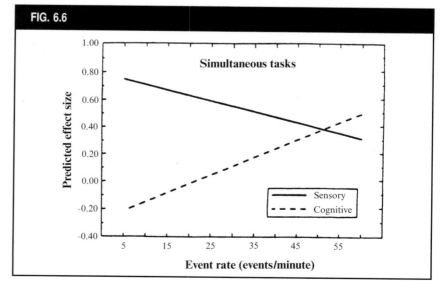

Predicted effect size as a function of event rate for sensory and cognitive simultaneous-discrimination tasks (larger effects are associated with larger decrements in sensitivity). From See, Howe, Warm, & Dember (1995). Copyright © 1995 by the American Psychological Association. Reprinted with permission.

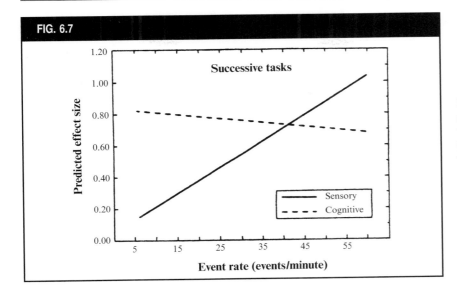

**FIG. 6.7**

Predicted effect size as a function of event rate for sensory and cognitive successive discrimination tasks (larger effects are associated with larger decrements in sensitivity). From See, Howe, Warm, & Dember (1995). Copyright © 1995 by the American Psychological Association. Reprinted with permission.

## 6.3 THEORIES OF VIGILANCE

Low overall levels of performance in vigilance situations can thus result from manipulations of both first and second order psychophysical factors. Theories of vigilance attempt to explain both overall levels of performance and the vigilance decrement which, as noted above, sometimes appears to be associated with a criterion increment and sometimes with a decline in perceptual sensitivity. Probably only the latter can be regarded as a genuine "breakdown" or loss of vigilance, as originally described by Mackworth (1948) since, unlike the criterion increment, the sensitivity decrement does not appear to be amenable to training effects (Davies & Parasuraman, 1982). Some theories of vigilance attempt only to explain variations in detection rate, since they were developed before the application of SDT to vigilance data became widespread. Others specifically address the criterion increment and/or the sensitivity decrement. Four of the main theories of vigilance, together with some related approaches are now outlined, beginning with Mackworth's original inhibition theory, together with related developments, based on habituation processes.

### 6.3.1 Inhibition and habituation

Mackworth (1950) regarded the vigilance decrement as analogous to the extinction of a conditioned response when that response is no longer reinforced. The decline in detection rate was therefore attributed to the accumulation of inhibition, a fatigue-like construct, which eventually results in a failure to produce the detection response, usually a key-press, when a signal is presented. Support for inhibition theory was provided by Mackworth's own findings that both knowledge of results (KR) and the introduction of rest pauses during task performance abolished the decrement. The provision of KR was considered to be a reinstatement of the reinforcing agent present during practice sessions, but usually absent during test sessions. Rest pauses enabled the dissipation of inhibition to take place; this is the phenomenon of "spontaneous recovery" observed by Pavlov (1927) in his experiments on classical conditioning. Similar findings were obtained by McCormack (1962) in a task that required observers to respond as quickly as possible to an unpredictable, but clearly visible, light signal. Observers invariably detected the onset of the light, but the normal increase in detection latencies with time on task was abolished by feedback relating to the speed of responding and by rest pauses. McCormack also interpreted his findings in terms of an inhibition–reinforcement theory, similar to that put forward by Mackworth.

Mackworth's inhibition theory is solely concerned with the vigilance decrement, and does not attempt to provide an explanation of the low overall levels of performance seen in some vigilance situations. But the main objection to inhibition theory as an explanation of the decrement in vigilance has been that increases in the frequency with which signals are presented should increase the decline in detection efficiency with time at work. Increases in signal frequency will produce an increase in the number of non-reinforced detection responses, and thus accelerate the accumulation of inhibition. In fact, contrary to the predictions derivable from inhibition theory, increases in signal frequency tend to reduce the decrement (see Davies & Parasuraman, 1982). Mackworth's theory also implicates the output stages of the information-processing sequence in the vigilance decrement, since it is the key-pressing response to a potential target that is held to undergo extinction. A rather different approach, though still within an inhibitory framework, is to regard the attentional or observing responses to the non-target events in the Clock Test (the single jumps of the pointer) as liable to extinction (for example, Broadbent, 1958). This extinction can then be regarded as generalising to the attentional responses to target events. Posner (1978) also suggested that inhibition may affect input stages of information processing, specifically psychological pathways, described as sets of internal codes and their interconnections that are automatically activated by sensory stimuli specific to that pathway. Thus the visual pathway is automatically activated by visual stimuli, the auditory pathway by auditory stimuli, and so on. Posner argued that repeated stimulation of the same pathway eventually produces pathway inhibition, which results in a decline of central processing efficiency and a decrease in the detection rate. High event presentation rates accelerate the accumulation of inhibition and increase the vigilance decrement. It is possible, therefore, that the accumulation of specific pathway inhibition could be prevented by alternating

the sensory modality to which stimulus events are presented during task performance (Galinsky et al., 1990). Sensory alternation might thus markedly reduce, if not abolish, the effects of event presentation rate on both the overall level of detection efficiency and the vigilance decrement. Galinsky et al. compared performance on continuous 50-minute auditory and visual vigilance tasks with performance on a combined auditory/visual vigilance task, in which presentation modality was alternated at five-minute intervals. They used two event presentation rates, high (40 events per minute) and low (5 events per minute). Galinsky et al. found that although the usual effects of event rate on detection efficiency were observed during both continuous vigilance tasks, in the combined auditory/visual task the event rate effect was eliminated. However, a vigilance decrement was obtained in all three tasks, as Fig. 6.8 shows. While Posner's pathway inhibition hypothesis thus provides a possible explanation of the effect of event rate on the overall level of detection efficiency, like Mackworth's original inhibition theory it fails to provide a satisfactory explanation of the vigilance decrement.

A broadly similar approach to inhibition theory was put forward in the late 1960s by Jane Mackworth (Mackworth, 1968, 1969). Her theory suggested that the performance decrements, including the perceptual sensitivity decrement, found in vigilance and other monotonous tasks may be due to habituation processes. Habituation is the substantial reduction or elimination of neural responses following repeated presentations of the same stimulus event or one that is closely related to it (see Groves & Thompson, 1970). Examples of such neural responses include the alerting response seen in the electroencephalogram or EEG record, as well as in several components of the cortical evoked potential, such as N100. Habituation theory proposed that due to the habituation of neural responses to non-target events, the observer becomes progressively less able to discriminate targets from non-targets, resulting in a sensitivity ($d'$) decrement. It also suggested that increasing event presentation rate enhances the decrement, because it speeds up the habituation process. In a test of the habituation hypothesis, Parasuraman

**FIG. 6.8**

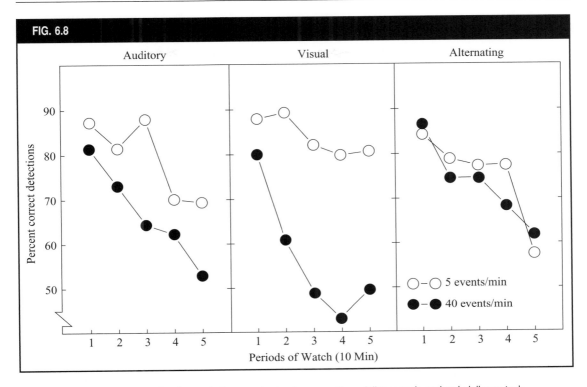

Percentages of signals detected at fast and slow event rates for an auditory vigilance task, a visual vigilance task, and a condition in which auditory and visual stimuli were alternated. From Galinsky et al. (1990). Reprinted with permission from *Human Factors*, Vol. 32, No. 6, 1990. Copyright 1990 by the Human Factors and Ergonomics Society. All rights reserved.

(1985) examined both decrements in detection efficiency and the rate of habituation of the N100 component of the cortical evoked potential in a vigilance task in which events were presented at low and high rates. He found that the vigilance decrement was greater in the high event rate condition, as anticipated, but that the event rate manipulation exerted no effect on the rate of habituation of the N100 response. Behavioural evidence also fails to provide strong support for habituation theory (Krulewitz, Warm, & Wohl, 1975).

## 6.3.2 Filter theory and observing response approaches

According to Broadbent's (1958) filter theory (see Chapters 2 and 4) attending to the same information source for long periods of time, as in a typical vigilance situation, is liable to intermittent interruptions, or "internal blinks", that tend to increase with time on task. This is because the hypothetical mechanism that selects information from the environment for further processing, the filter, is biased towards the selection of novel information. Since the novelty of performing a vigilance task soon palls, the filter will be progressively more likely to select information from non-task sources. Filter theory thus attributes the vigilance decrement to periodic failures to select task-relevant information, which become more frequent with time at work. Filter theory predicts that vigilance tasks in which signals are present only for a brief period will yield a more pronounced decrement than tasks in which signals are present for longer periods, which is consistent with the results obtained by Baker (1963a). Increasing event presentation rate enhances the decrement (for example, Jerison & Pickett, 1964; Parasuraman & Davies, 1976) because more events are presented within a given time interval and hence are more likely to escape notice when attention is diverted from the task. Filter theory also predicts that the decrement in self-paced vigilance tasks, where observers work at their own pace, should be less marked than in tasks where observers work at a rate that is externally imposed. In self-paced tasks, observers can stop the task if they consider they are not paying sufficient attention to it, thereby minimising the likelihood of a performance decrement. However, studies of performance in self-paced vigilance situations have observed significant decrements in detection rate, frequently accompanied by a progressively faster rate of responding, implying that observers are making a speed/accuracy "trade-off" (Colquhoun, 1962; Craig et al., 1987; Wilkinson, 1961).

Some vigilance studies have elicited overt observing responses, requiring observers to press one key to illuminate a display on which a signal might or might not be present, and to press another key to make a detection response to a possible signal. The results of such studies indicate that observing responses tend to increase with time at work, even while detection responses are declining (Broadbent, 1963a; Guralnick, 1972). Moreover, making an observing response is no guarantee that a signal will be detected. For example, in Broadbent's (1963a) study, observers made several observing responses before finally reporting the signal that had been presented. Such delayed detection responses tended to increase with time on task, as did the number of signals to which no detection response was made following the emission of an observing response. Furthermore, increasing signal frequency which, as noted earlier, improves detection efficiency, has no appreciable effect on observing responses (Blair & Kaufman, 1959). Observing responses, at least as indexed by illumination responses, do not therefore appear to be strongly related to detection responses.

Jerison (1970) suggested that there were three different categories of observing responses, ranging from "alert" (optimal observing) through "blurred" (sub-optimal observing), to "distracted" (effectively non-observing). He suggested that the vigilance decrement resulted from a progressive increase in the amount of time spent in distracted observing, resulting in part from the increased attentional costs associated with alert observing. While this approach could account for a decline in detection rate, it is less satisfactory as an explanation of the sensitivity decrement (see Davies & Parasuraman, 1982).

### 6.3.3 Expectancy theories

An influential approach to the explanation of vigilance performance has been the general idea that observers keep track of past signal occurrences in order to predict future ones, which leads to the formulation of expectancies about signal occurrences. The development of appropriate expectancies can be considerably assisted by particular characteristics of the task situation. For instance, if signals are presented frequently and on regular schedules, or if KR concerning the accuracy of signal detection is provided, expectancies will be more accurate and detection efficiency will improve. Deese (1955) suggested that signal frequency was a major influence on the formulation of expectancies. If average signal frequencies are low, expectancy levels will remain low. If signal frequency increases, then expectancy levels will rise. Baker (1959, 1963b), emphasised the temporal distribution of signal presentations. He argued that observers perform a continuous averaging process on the time intervals between previous signal presentations in order to predict the occurrence of future signals. Expectancy is maximal at the average inter-signal interval, and declines thereafter. Presenting signals at regular time intervals facilitates the averaging process, and results in a higher level of detection efficiency and an attenuated vigilance decrement, compared to irregular signal presentation schedules (Baker, 1959). Similarly, providing knowledge of results enables observers to extrapolate future signal occurrences from a more accurate cognitive representation of past signal occurrences, and thus improves detection efficiency (Baker, 1962). However, time interval estimations by human observers tend to be rather imprecise and, in any case, appear to be unrelated to detection efficiency in vigilance situations (McGrath & O'Hanlon, 1967). More recent versions of expectancy theory have focussed on signal probability as a determinant of expectancies, and have examined its effects on criterion placement (Craig, 1978, 1987; Craig & Colquhoun, 1975; Vickers & Leary, 1983; Vickers, Leary, & Barnes, 1977; Williges, 1969, 1973).

Versions of expectancy theory emphasising signal probability propose that the observer's expectancy level determines criterion placement and that the strongest influence on expectancy level is the probability of signal occurrence. Observers' initial criterion settings in vigilance situations are largely determined by the signal probabilities they experience in the practice sessions that generally precede test sessions (Colquhoun & Baddeley, 1964, 1967; Williges, 1969). For example, Colquhoun & Baddeley (1967) showed that $\beta$ was higher after a practice session in which signal probability was high (0.18) than after one in which the signal probability was low (.02), regardless of whether the signal probability in the vigil itself was high or low. Observers given practice sessions in which signal probabilities are higher than they are in the subsequent test session also tend to show greater criterion increases with time on task. But even when signal probabilities in practice and test sessions are equated, and observers are given additional practice to stabilise their response criteria, criterion increments are still found (Baddeley & Colquhoun, 1969; Parasuraman & Davies, 1976; Williges, 1973).

Increases in the response criterion with time on task have been interpreted as reflecting cumulative changes in observers' subjective estimates of signal probability. When observers first encounter a vigilance task, they often over-report the occurrence of signals (Craig, 1978), suggesting that the objective signal probability (which is usually less than 0.50) is being overestimated. Initially, therefore, criterion placement is fairly lax. As observers gain more experience of the task, they learn that the signal probability is much lower than they originally supposed (McGrath & O'Hanlon, 1967). In accordance with this reduction in the subjective estimate of signal probability, the criterion becomes more conservative. This produces a decrease in affirmative responses, a further reduction in the subjective estimate of signal probability, and another upward revision of

the criterion. This cycle continues until the vigil terminates. The increase in the response criterion during a vigilance task can thus be explained in terms of progressively lowered expectancies concerning the probability of signal occurrence. Conversely, when signal probability exceeds 0.50, the criterion either decreases with time on task, or remains stable (Williges, 1969, 1973), which is consistent with expectancy theory. However, the criterion also decreases when signal probability is lowered during a vigil. Vickers et al. (1977) progressively lowered signal probability from 0.50 to 0.05 in six successive time blocks of 100 trials and obtained a progressive, though non-significant, reduction in the response criterion ($\beta$). Following the first block of trials, in which signal probability was 0.50, observers responded in subsequent blocks as if they were trying to minimise the discrepancy between the current signal probability in a particular block and the cumulative signal probability for the task as a whole up to that point. Similarly, Vickers and Leary (1983) began with a signal probability of 0.50 for the first 20% of the task, gradually reduced signal probability to 0.06 over the next 20%, and maintained it at this level for the remaining 60% of the vigil. Again, during the period when signal probability was gradually declining, the response criterion decreased rather than increased, and there was no significant change in the criterion during the final phase of the testing session. Observers thus seem to be adjusting their response rates to the average experienced signal probability, in an attempt to match current response rates with overall signal rates. Evidence for such "probability matching", particularly towards the end of a period of continuous vigilance, has been reviewed by Craig (1978, 1983, 1987).

### 6.3.4 Resource theory

As discussed in 6.2.2, perceptual sensitivity decrement seems to be controlled by overall task demands (See et al., 1995). Specific psychophysical parameters such as high event rate, use of a successive task, and degraded stimuli increase the likelihood of decrement, but no single parameter seems to be either necessary or sufficient to induce decrement. Overall workload seems to be the major factor that controls the vigilance decrement (Warm, 1993). This observation suggests a resource theory of vigilance (Parasuraman et al., 1987). Prolonged performance on detection tasks may deplete the pool of resources as the person becomes fatigued. If so, more demanding tasks should be most sensitive to resource loss, giving rise to workload-dependent decrements, as actually observed. The resource hypothesis gains credibility from the generalisation of the decrement across qualitatively different tasks, such as those requiring sensory or cognitive discriminations.

Three other lines of evidence support the resource interpretation. First, as noted in 6.2, although vigilance tasks are often considered rather undemanding, studies using the NASA-TLX workload measure (Hart & Staveland, 1988; see 5.4.2) consistently show that vigilance tasks impose a high workload (Warm, Dember, & Hancock, 1996; Warm & Dember, 1998). Rated mental demands and frustration are the most salient sources of workload in these studies. As task demands are increased by experimental manipulation, both NASA-TLX workload and the extent of the sensitivity decrement increase (Temple et al., in press). Second, a small number of dual-task studies show interference patterns consistent with resource theory (Davies, Matthews, & Westerman, submitted), although much more work remains to be done in this area. Parasuraman (1985) compared performance on high and low event rate versions of a digit detection task. Subjects were also required to respond to secondary auditory stimuli. On the low event rate task, both sensitivity and probe RT showed little change over time. However, with a high event rate, sensitivity declined and RT increased towards the end of the vigil, suggesting resource depletion (subject to the limitations of secondary RT studies discussed in 5.3.3). Third, perceptual sensitivity during vigilance may be linked to use of controlled processing, which tends to be resource-demanding. Controlled processing is more vulnerable to sensitivity decrement than automatic processing (Fisk & Schneider, 1981), and sensitivity on high event-rate vigilance tasks correlates with performance of controlled visual search (Matthews, Davies, & Holley, 1993).

At the same time, there are difficulties for the resource theory of vigilance to overcome. As with resource theory generally (cf. Chapter 5), it is unclear whether there may be specific processing components that control the decrement as opposed to a general resource. The workload hypothesis (Warm & Dember, 1998) suggests a unitary resource, although this work has mostly used visual tasks, with a sensory discrimination. The taxonomic approach to vigilance (Davies & Parasuraman, 1982) envisages successive tasks as imposing a higher workload than simultaneous tasks. However, there may also be qualitative differences between simultaneous and successive tasks, which are often poorly correlated (Davies & Parasuraman, 1982). Becker et al. (1994) showed that (with knowledge of results), training on a simultaneous task transferred to a simultaneous task but not a successive task. Similarly, training on a successive task generalised only to subsequent successive performance. This finding suggests that it might be the differential processing requirements of successive and simultaneous tasks rather than workload differences that are responsible for their differential sensitivity to decrement. For example, the working memory component of successive task performance might be especially sensitive to decrement (Parasuraman, 1979). A more precise account of the decrement may eventually be obtained by discriminating various processing functions independently sensitive to fatigue (Matthews, 1996).

It is also unclear exactly how resource depletion operates. The account of resource theory here suggests that more demanding tasks are more sensitive to loss of resources. However, it is unclear whether higher workload also leads to a faster depletion of resources over time. It is uncertain too whether there is some overall loss of resources, or whether the observer is simply less inclined to allocate resources to the task, a possibility suggested by motivational effects on vigilance. Scerbo (1998) reviews studies suggesting that the sensitivity decrement is related to boredom. If so, observers may simply withdraw effort and resources from the task, even though they are potentially available for performance. Similar effects are found in fatigue studies (see 12.2), where performance effects often seem to relate to strategy rather than to loss of resource availability. The interrelationship of workload and motivational effects on vigilance decrement remains to be investigated.

### 6.3.5 Arousal theories

The final theoretical approach to be considered is the idea that prolonged task performance leads to a lowering of central nervous system arousal or activation, which in turn results in performance deterioration (for example, Duffy, 1962). This view is certainly plausible, in that observers do indeed show psychophysiological indications of lowered arousal during vigilance performance (see Davies & Parasuraman, 1982; Parasuraman, 1984; Parasuraman et al., 1998). They also report feelings of boredom (see Davies, Shackleton, & Parasuraman, 1983; Sawin & Scerbo, 1995), fatigue (see Craig & Cooper, 1992; Galinsky, Rosa, Warm, & Dember, 1993) and become more restless (Galinsky et al., 1993). Furthermore, as Mackworth (1950) demonstrated, the vigilance decrement can be reduced by arousing agents, such as the stimulant drug, amphetamine. Conversely, de-arousing manipulations, such as sleep deprivation, enhance the decrement (Horne, Anderson, & Wilkinson, 1983; Wilkinson, 1960, 1964). Studies using psychophysiological indices of arousal (for example, Munro, Dawson, Schell, & Sakai, 1987) have found little effect of arousal on criterion placement. Arousal may therefore affect perceptual sensitivity, but not the response criterion.

Numerous studies have examined the relationship between vigilance performance and the level of cortical arousal, using both EEG and event related potential (ERP) measures. The EEG frequency tends to fall during the course of a vigil, and the slowing of the EEG appears to be related to the reduction in the detection rate (Davies & Krkovic, 1965; Gale, 1977; Makeig & Inlow, 1993). With time on task, theta activity (4–7 Hz) rather than alpha activity (8–13 Hz) tends to predominate in the EEG record, and there is a negative relation between the presence of theta activity and detection efficiency (O'Hanlon & Beatty, 1977). Missed signals also tend to be preceded by higher levels of theta activity than are detected signals (Horvath, Frantik, Kopriva, & Meissner, 1975).

Evoked potential studies of vigilance have examined whether the vigilance decrement is associated with a general reduction of ERP activity, which would indicate lowered cortical arousal, or only with changes in specific ERP components. Missed signals, but not detected signals, are preceded by reductions in the amplitude of some early ERP components (Haider, Spong, & Lindsley, 1964; Wilkinson, Morlock, & Williams, 1966) and there are reductions in the amplitude of both early and late ERP components during the course of a vigil (Davies & Parasuraman, 1977). Both these findings could be interpreted as providing support for arousal theory. Davies and Parasuraman recorded four ERP components —N100, P200, N250 and P300—during the performance of a 45-minute visual vigilance task in which responses were made to all stimulus events. ERP amplitudes could thus be related to both correct and incorrect affirmative (correct detections and false alarms) and negative responses (correct rejections and misses). Detection latencies were also recorded. For both correct detections and detection latencies, significant correlations were only obtained for the amplitudes of the late ERP components N250 and P300, positive in the case of correct detections and negative in the case of detection latencies. Since there were very few false alarms, correlations with ERP amplitude were not computed for this performance measure. However, no significant correlations between late ERP component amplitudes and either the accuracy or speed of correct rejection and miss responses were obtained. The amplitudes of late ERP components were thus significantly correlated only with correct detections and detection latencies, suggesting that they are specifically related to detection efficiency. Davies and Parasuraman (1977) concluded that the amplitude of late ERP components reflected decision processes in vigilance, rather than changes in a general state of arousal. More recent studies have also indicated that only the amplitudes of late ERP components are closely related to performance measures in vigilance situations (Koelega et al., 1992; Rohrbaugh et al., 1987).

Although the level of cortical arousal falls during a vigilance task, it does not appear that a reduction in arousal level is a necessary condition for the occurrence of a vigilance decrement. As Parasuraman (1984) has pointed out, arousal level declines during task performance whether or not a decrement is obtained, and it also declines during the performance of tasks that are not monitoring tasks. Arousal level even declines if an individual does not perform any task for half an hour or so. It seems likely, therefore, that the vigilance decrement is primarily influenced by factors other than a progressive reduction in the level of cortical arousal.

## 6.4 CONCLUSIONS

In this chapter we have focussed on the assessment of vigilance performance, emphasising the usefulness of SDT measures, and on task factors affecting the vigilance decrement. Sketches of the main theoretical approaches to the explanation of vigilance performance have also been included. In addition to the topics covered here, it should be pointed out that there are a large number of studies investigating individual and group differences in vigilance (see Davies, 1985; Eysenck, 1989). In addition, there has been much research on the effects of noise and other environmental factors on detection efficiency (see Chapters 10–13). There is also an extensive literature on brain mechanisms and vigilance (see Parasuraman et al., 1998). There are two main conclusions to be drawn from the evidence reviewed above. First, performance decrements occur fairly frequently in monitoring situations, though they are less common in complex tasks. Second, such decrements tend to be associated either with an increase in the response criterion or with a decline in per-

ceptual sensitivity. The characteristics of the task being performed strongly influence the nature of the performance decrement that is observed. Criterion increments tend to occur in simultaneous or successive discrimination tasks in which the event presentation rate is low. Sensitivity decrements tend to occur in successive discrimination tasks in which the event presentation rate is high, or in high event rate simultaneous discrimination tasks in which signals are difficult to discriminate from non-signal events. The sensitivity decrement thus seems to reflect the overall level of task demands. The criterion increment appears to be best explained by expectancy theory, but a satisfactory explanation for the sensitivity decrement has not yet been formulated. However, given that task demands exert a strong effect on the sensitivity decrement, a possible approach would utilise resource theory. As is further discussed in 15.4.1, a number of studies employing a self-report arousal measure suggest that arousal may be related to resource availability, especially in vigilance situations in which task demands are high (Matthews & Davies, 1998).

## FURTHER READING

The topic of vigilance is reviewed in detail in books by Davies and Parasuraman (1982) and Warm (1984). Applications of vigilance research to the contemporary problem of automated systems are included in Parasuraman and Mouloua's (1996) edited book. Parasuraman et al. (1998) review the limited literature on neurological bases for vigilance. For more detailed accounts of signal detection theory and its applications, a useful introduction can be found in McNicol (1972), while a more advanced treatment is provided by MacMillan and Creelman (1991).

# 7

# Skilled performance

## 7.1 THE LEARNING OF SKILLS

The problem for any theory of skill learning is to explain the changes that occur as people learn a new skill. These changes can be accounted for subjectively and qualitatively experienced by the skilled performer as a feeling of growing competency and more "free capacity". Alternatively, they can be accounted for in terms of measurable performance changes in tasks directly, as in time and errors, or indirectly in terms of secondary task performance or ratings of task demands. Even something as simple as a reaction time task will show changes due to practice. By the same token, whilst there are tasks that many people can master, such as driving a car, there will remain those tasks, and levels of performance in them, that will be beyond the capacities of all but an elite few. An example of the latter would be piloting a high performance aircraft. This chapter is concerned with the general characteristics of skill learning in humans, but we return to individual differences in learning and performance in Chapter 14.

### 7.1.1 Quantitative aspects of skill acquisition: The power law of practice

When someone is acquiring a skill, performance changes both quantitatively and qualitatively.

Naturally, the overall efficiency of performance tends to improve, but so too does the style of performance. Figure 7.1 (a) shows a typical learning curve for skill acquisition, taken from a study of learning how to generate mathematical proofs (Neves & Anderson, 1981). The graph shows how the time taken to reach the solution decreases as the person's experience (number of problems solved) increases. Each data point represents a single trial. Neves and Anderson (1981) found that in the early stages of learning, performance speeds up rapidly but, as the person becomes more practiced, "diminishing returns" set in, and the rate of improvement progressively decreases. A smooth curve has been drawn through the data points in Fig. 7.1 (a) to illustrate this effect. After solving 80 problems, the gain in speed from trial to trial is hardly noticeable, although performance continues to improve slowly.

The curve shown in Fig. 7.1 (a) can be represented by an arithmetical expression: the *power law of practice* (Newell & Rosenbloom, 1981). If $T$ is the time taken to perform a task (e.g. solving a problem), and $P$ is the amount of practice (number of trials), the power law states that:

$$T = aP^{-b}$$

Here $a$ and $b$ are constants, which relate to initial level of performance and rate of improvement

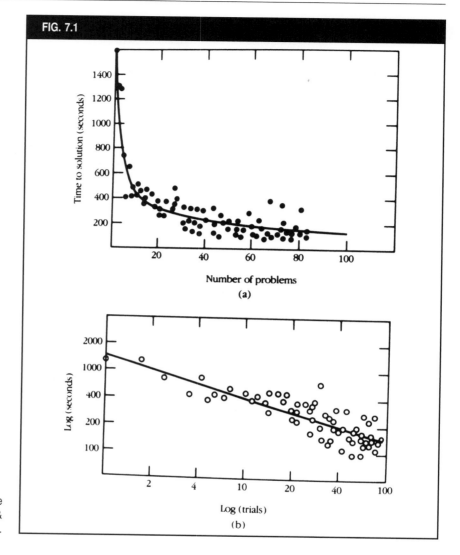

**FIG. 7.1**

Time to solution (seconds)

1400
1200
1000
800
600
400
200

20    40    60    80    100

**Number of problems**

**(a)**

Log (seconds)

2000
1000
400
200
100

2    4    10    20    40    100

**Log (trials)**

**(b)**

The power law of practice (Anderson, 1990; Neves & Anderson, 1981).

respectively. A wide variety of skills show learning curves described by the power law expression, but the values of *a* and *b* vary according to the difficulty of the task (and the measurement units used).

The power law can be expressed slightly differently, by thinking in terms of logarithms. Figure 7.1 (b) shows the Neves and Anderson (1981) data graphed as log (time) versus log (practice). Transforming the data in this way gives a linear function, which can be expressed as follows:

$$\log(T) = A - b \log(P)$$

This formula is equivalent to the power law (the constant *A* equals log *a*). It is remarkable that quantitative improvement in learning many different skills is described by this simple linear expression.

### 7.1.2 Qualitative aspects of skill acquisition

It is clear that when faced with the same task demands, the skilled person performs and experiences the task in a very different way to the unskilled. The contrast is between the overload of new information flowing to individuals as they begin to perform the task and the effortlessness of the skilled performer dealing with those same demands. Annett and Kay (1956) characterised this observation as the skilled performer being able to exploit the redundancy in sequences and being able, through consistent responses, to generate a much more stable and thereby predictable "display" of events. Skill in being able to steer a car brings with it a much more stable set of road scenes, whereas the learner's jerky set of corrections to moves in the wrong direction leads to further unpredictable events in the form of a rapidly changing set of views through the windscreen as the vehicle swerves. Theories of skill need to explain not just performance improvement, but also the transition from the hesitancy of the novice to the fluency of the expert.

It is likely too that the type of errors committed by the skilled person will be different to those committed by the novice. Thus, "skilled errors" are more likely to be based on the selection of the wrong "sub-routine" rather than on errors of sequencing and/or timing as likely to be committed by the learner, as further discussed in Chapter 8. A complete account of skill also requires understanding of various contextual factors that affect skill acquisition and performance. Models of skill learning should account for the more informal aspects of learning, in that skills are sometimes learned outside of direct training. Learning may result from self practice, non-intentional "incidental learning" and in a range of recreational settings, e.g., learning the words of a song from one or more hearings of it. Learning and performance may also be impaired by the stress factors discussed in the next section. In sports psychology, there is a particular concern with the conditions under which sports professionals achieve peak performance or go "off-form".

It is perhaps best to start by examining the conditions that bring about these changes, and then move on to focus on possible mechanisms. Taking firstly the case of formal instruction, from the learner's point of view two things happen. Firstly, there is a phase of *instruction*: this can come from a trainer, from self-instruction media, or from the observation of others carrying out the task. Secondly, there is a phase of *practice* at the task. Practice may proceed for greater or lesser amounts of time but, until the appropriate amount of practice occurs, the characteristics of skilled performance—smooth, seemingly effortless, accurate—will not be seen. The instruction phase for a reaction time task will be short and simple. Practice may then continue, in a laboratory context, for several hundred trials before performance levels off. On the other hand, the instruction phase for driving a car will be fairly lengthy. Information for the learner will come from a variety of sources and the practice phase will continue for weeks, even months.

There is of course no guarantee of permanence and skilled performance can suffer from retention loss as can any other stored acquisition. Because of its importance in a number of applied areas, skill retention has been studied to determine the nature of any skill loss and its possible amelioration. The bad news is that skill loss can be considerable when first measured (Glendon et al., 1988, Hagman & Rose, 1983). The good news, however, is that such losses can be made up quickly with practice. The best preventative measure is overpractice initially and frequent rehearsal training.

### 7.1.3 Cognitive vs. motor skills

Before moving on to theories of skill, it is worth pausing to consider whether it is worthwhile making a distinction between physical (or perceptual-motor) skills and cognitive skills. Such a distinction is often made on the basis of the type of task demands that are being dealt with. Thus, solving a geometry problem would be seen as a cognitive skill, whereas carrying out a gymnastics manoeuvre can be seen as a perceptual-motor skill. However, they can both be seen as problem solving in that an objective is set by external events, and some activity must be planned to tackle those events. Early cognitive modelling envisaged generally applicable planning characteristics such as this (Miller, Galanter & Pribram, 1960). Similarly, there must be some form of motor output in any activity, even if it is as simple as writing on a page or pressing a button. Thus, a distinction can only be made in terms of the predominant mode of activity and a judgement on the level of skill will be made on the basis of the judged quality of the solution to the problem.

As an example, a soccer goalkeeper in training will become skilled at catching or deflecting balls kicked at the goal. A combination of cognitive decision-making and planning will be supported by the motor skills inherent in leaping, diving and hand movements. These motor skills will attain a level of consistency that, when seen in isolation, can be judged to be skilled, coordinated sequences of action. However, if in a game situation the goalkeeper carries out a smoothly, highly coordinated dive to the right, and the opposing player kicks the ball to the goalkeeper's left, the lack of skill in anticipation of direction will be all too apparent. Better a clumsy scramble that saves a goal, than a balletic movement that allows the opposing team to win. Thus all skills are cognitive in that an objective is set and performance must be organised, but all involve some form of motor output. It is the relative influence of these two classes of activity in relation to achieving the task's objective that best determines whether the label "cognitive" or "motor" is used.

## 7.2 THEORIES OF SKILL ACQUISITION

### 7.2.1 Phases of skill acquisition

Fitts (1962) gave an early description of the phases of skill acquisition. He derived his view from the results of experimental research, and from discussions with sports coaches and pilot trainers. A description of his theory also allows us to examine the conditions that can bring about skill learning. These "conditions" are idealised. As mentioned above, skills can be learnt in a variety of ways, not all them open to easy scrutiny. For instance, it is possible to find a garden implement never encountered before and in a few hours become skilled in its use. This would be mainly on the basis of previous experience of similar objects, general knowledge about the world and the "affordances" (Norman, 1988) of the object

that make certain modes of use apparent. However, it is equally possible that an already experienced user could give a few words of advice on principles of good usage, and could thereby prevent a bad working posture being developed and give tips on the device's efficient use.

Fitts (1962) describes a first *cognitive* phase, where in a typical instruction session a way of carrying out a task is provided for the learner. This could be based on description—written, verbal, or pictorial. Attempts are then made at carrying out the task. Typically errors or inefficiencies will occur. In a formal training session, feedback will be given to learners on the basis of their performance (cf. 2.5.2). Many studies show that such feedback is a very potent learning variable, although it may be difficult to distinguish benefits on learning, which will benefit subsequent performance from more transient benefits on immediate performance (Salmoni, Schmidt, & Walter, 1984). Feedback may have motivational and/or arousing effects. It is also possible to prevent mistakes occurring by the use of guidance and prompting. However, it is important not to rely on such techniques too much as they may produce distortions of what is required eventually in the real task. The feedback mentioned above must also be tailored to the task demands, i.e. be timely and relevant (Patrick, 1992).

Given that the learner progresses, Fitts then describes a transition to a second *associative* phase. During this stage of learning, the correct patterns of activity are practised until they are error-free and have appropriate timing characteristics. Feedback may still be given early in the phase, but learners should come to rely increasingly on self-monitoring of activity in order to assess their performance. Larger and larger chunks of activity will be put together to form smoothly-executed sequences. It also becomes possible to carry out other tasks at the same time as the main task, leading to better dual-task performance (see 5.1.3). Performance may become increasingly flexible to changing task demands and extra processing capabilities may become incorporated into the main task performance. This phase is the one that many people will remain at for many skills. The key to the movement to the next phase is practice; as the proverb says, "practice makes perfect".

The final phase should lead to what for some is the essence of what is meant by skilled performance, the *autonomous* or *automation* phase. Activity at this stage of learning has been variously described as "automatic", "unconscious" or "instinctive". None of these descriptions stands up to close scrutiny, given difficulties in defining automaticity (3.3.3), but they do convey the idea of performance that is carried out in a very different way to that described for the earlier stages. With increasing practice, there is increasing resistance to distractions from other sources of information and stressors (Hartley et al., 1989). There is an increasing ability to handle other, simultaneous or at least concurrently performed tasks (e.g. Bahrick & Shelly, 1958). One the best examples of the changing nature of skilled performance as a result of practice was provided by Pew's (1966) study. In this experiment, participants learned to keep a spot of light centred on a screen by means of rapid alternation between keys under the right and left index fingers. High levels of performance were initially achieved by rapid alternation between the keys, followed by periodic corrections. Even higher levels of performance were found when participants altered the pattern of responding such that one key became more active than another. The strategy used changed from making individual responses in a closed-loop mode with feedback on each individual response being used, to an open loop mode of responding, characterised by rapid alternation followed by single corrective movements. Eventually, feedback control was regained, but for patterning of actions and no longer for individual actions.

Fitts' theory was couched in very descriptive terms and there were limited experimental data from long-term skill acquisition studies (Blackburn, 1936). One classic study, often cited as evidence of long-term skill learning (Crossman, 1959) is, in fact, a cross-sectional study of factory workers making cigars, showing faster cycle times for those with longer service. These workers would have performed many millions of task cycles. Indeed, this continued increase in skill with practice was commented on by Fitts as a characteristic

of skill—a lack of asymptotic performance. Thus, only the physical limitations of the task (as in Crossman's study) or a decline in capabilities with ageing (see Chapter 16) are the limiting factors. Experimental data are limited but, anecdotally, the idea of increased experience of a task leading to higher levels of professionalism is the common assumption. An example would be in soccer where the average age of goalkeepers is higher than that of other players. It would appear that exposure to the trajectories of balls aimed at the goal mouth is important, rather than physical fitness of the long-term endurance kind. Stars of other sports for which physical demands are moderate, such as golf and snooker, may also compete at the top level into their forties, or even beyond.

### 7.2.2 Anderson's (1982) ACT* theory

Fitts' theory was very much in the perceptual-motor performance context, although early on the ideas were never seen as exclusively applicable to this area (e.g. Fitts, 1964; Fitts & Posner, 1967). More recently, the ideas have been revived in a "cognitive" skills context by Anderson (1982, 1983, 1995) in the developments of his ACT* theory although, conversely, Anderson uses examples from perceptual-motor skills for illustration. Anderson's theory draws on Fitts' ideas, but puts them in line with a basic idea from the philosophy of mind, of a distinction between "knowing that" and "knowing how". In psychological terms the former kind of knowledge is termed "declarative" and the latter is "procedural". The fundamental principle is that as a skill is learned there is a change in the type of knowledge that underpins its performance. The early stages are marked by a reliance on declarative forms of knowledge. These would be based on the explicit rules for carrying out a task, e.g. how to carry out an arithmetical calculation. The information is gained by the learner and used to carry out the task. This knowledge can be judged to be present from performance of the task, or by reporting on behalf of the learner. The parallel here would be with Fitts' cognitive stage. Anderson, however, is clearer about the change that takes place in the way that knowledge is represented as a result of practice. A process of *knowledge compilation* is deemed to take place as the task is practised. As a result of practice, the declarative knowledge is "compiled" into procedural knowledge and is thus stored in a different form. The analogy here is with a high level of computer language where the code of the language is translated into the machine code of a particular computer. This different form of knowledge representation then supports skilled performance through the use of *productions*.

Procedural knowledge can only be instantiated as performance of the task and requires the learner to have possession of the appropriate declarative knowledge and to have had the necessary amount of practice. Possession of procedural knowledge is equivalent, for all or part of a skill, to Fitts' phase of automation. The process of compilation is probably equivalent to Fitts' associative stage. Anderson (1982) elaborates on the effects of practice on procedural knowledge: a process of *tuning* allows for the *generalisation* of procedures to other contexts, their restriction of application to certain situations only through *discrimination* and their *strengthening* whereby less successful procedures are eliminated at the expense of more successful ones.

It is possible both to be able to carry out the task as a procedure and report on the declarative knowledge that it was based on. However, it is a feature of well-practiced skills that this declarative knowledge is often no longer available in its original form—the task can be done but its underpinning knowledge may not be accessible in the short term. The example given by Anderson (1980) is that of showing someone how to change gear when driving a car with a manually-operated gearbox. It was found that the teacher needed to move to the driving seat and work through the task, in slow motion, and recreate the declarative rules of sequence and timing in order to communicate them to the learner. This is supported by the established wisdom in training practice (Stammers & Patrick, 1975; Patrick, 1992) that a skilled job incumbent is not necessarily the best person to teach a task. It is better to base training on a formal analysis of task demands and a translation of this into a form of *instruction* for the task that communicates the task information (declarative knowledge), and allows for *practice*, as a different

but integrated training activity that will allow for the development of declarative knowledge (Stammers, 1996).

### 7.2.3 Language and action in skill learning

As with any theory that attempts a global solution, problems appear when specific cases are put to it. Fitts' ideas and a simplified view of Anderson's ideas work well at a descriptive level, but certain phenomena do not fit well and, if taken too far, Fitts' ideas can be seen as oversimplification, although it is unlikely that the theory was ever seen as a global one. The model suggested by Annett (1991) seeks to account for a wider range of phenomena, and it can be suggested that it does not supplant the "stages to automatisation" theory but extends the ideas into a broader perspective. Fitts' and Anderson's views seem very much influenced by a formal training model of skill acquisition whereas Annett's model is more influenced by a less verbally-based view of instruction and puts equal emphasis on perceptual demonstrations of skills. It is clear that infants learn motor skill before language, indeed they must learn to speak before they can demonstrate their learning of a language in terms of its grammatical rules, etc.

Annett's model has two input processes, followed by two interlinked but separate paths of input to output, or external events leading to motor output activity. A verbally-based system comprises a subsystem for representing the task information (perceptual process) and a separate one for initiating and controlling actions. The usual output from this subsystem would be speech. In parallel with this there is an action-based system, which also has a representational system but in this case for holding the results of physical demonstrations of tasks or simply the observation of other task performers. It also has a motor output system. There is also an interaction between the verbal and the motor systems, the "action–language bridge", which will be described below.

The complexities of Annett's model are to account for phenomena that the simple "stages to automatisation" model does not deal with. Firstly, implicit in earlier models there is the idea of a single mechanism for the representation of learned skills and for initiating their activity, whether this activity be based on declarative or procedural knowledge. Adams (1971, see also Schmidt, 1975) had pointed to the illogicality of a single mechanism for both storage and action initiation and control. Adams suggests the need for a *memory trace* of a movement to store the representation of the movement. However, once a movement is initiated, a separate mechanism was needed, the *perceptual trace*, to control the movement to its termination. This idea is taken up in Annett's pairs of subsystems.

A second feature of Annett's model is the presence of two subsystems, an action and a verbal one. As mentioned above, any model based on a formal training task paradigm, where verbal instruction is followed by practice, is an oversimplification. Annett points to several examples of human activity where perceptual demonstrations are very powerful. The learning of social behaviour would be one example where observational behaviour is held to be paramount (Bandura, 1986). Another example which leads him to suggest that there is a specialised mechanism for gathering representations of action is work by Johansson (1973). In the latter studies, participants were able to give accurate descriptions of the nature of movements made by an "actor", of whom all that was visible was a set of light sources attached to clothing. When the actor was stationary, only a random collection of lights would be perceived. When the actor moved, even with a much reduced set of "normal" clues, accurate descriptions of movements could be reported. Moving to specific skill studies there are examples of where imagery of interpolated movements has been shown to distort the memory of simple linear movements in the same way that actual interpolated movements will (P. Johnson, 1982). Studies by Annett himself (1983) have demonstrated the difficulty of giving verbal descriptions of skilled activities. Whilst superficially this might be held to be a result of "automatisation", the fact that verbal description becomes easier when simultaneous movement is allowed suggests a storage of movements in action terms.

This last point brings to attention the action–language bridge. Annett (1993) reviews evidence

from a number of cognitive and neuropsychological studies that point to the importance of interplay between these systems. The previously-mentioned characteristic of making hand movements when giving verbal descriptions of task activity is one example.

## 7.3 MODELLING SKILL ACQUISITION USING PRODUCTION SYSTEMS

### 7.3.1 Production systems in ACT*

So far, ACT* has been described in broad outline only. However, ACT* is recognised as one of the most successful general theories of skill because it specifies detailed principles for modelling skilled performance. ACT* represents a cognitive architecture for skill acquisition, developed and tested using the modelling principles discussed in Chapter 2. The processing units in ACT* are *productions*, which are IF . . . THEN . . . rules, specifying that IF some input condition is true, THEN some action is to be executed. For example, a simple production for braking at a traffic light might be:

> IF light is red
> THEN bring car to a halt

At this level, productions resemble the simple S–R associations of behaviourism, but there is more to them than this. First, productions can include quite complex logical expressions in the IF part. Second, the condition typically includes not just stimuli that trigger the production, but also statements of *goals* that specify when the production should be applied. Inclusion of goals gives the person the flexibility of action and intentional control missing from classical behaviourism. For example, in the case of a reckless driver, the traffic light production might be:

> IF light is red AND there is no traffic visible
>     AND I am in a hurry
> THEN continue

The first two parts of the condition refer to stimuli, and the third to a goal. Third, the action is often not an overt response, but another production. Sets of productions may be linked together to form a *production system*, permitting extensive "central processing" of information. Productions are usually arranged in a hierarchy, so that top-level productions express general goals, intermediate-level productions express subgoals needed to achieve the overall goal, and lower-level productions execute the actions required to meet the subgoals. For example, a top-level "start car" production might look something like this:

> IF seated in car AND goal is to drive
> THEN 1. call "start engine" subroutine
>       2. call "select gear" subroutine
>       3. call "depress accelerator" subroutine
>       4. etc.

The "start engine" subroutine might then specify the muscle movements required to insert the key in the ignition and turn it to the correct position. Implicit in the production system concept is the idea that productions can specify recoding of data. Lower-level productions take as inputs codes for abstract descriptions of actions (e.g. "turn key") and output motor codes for delivery to actual muscles.

### 7.3.2 Explaining skill acquisition with production system models

The production system model explains various features of the empirical data on skill acquisition, and the changes in style of performance consequent upon expertise. In the early, "cognitive" stage of skill learning, Anderson (1987) suggests that performance is controlled by "weak-method" productions. These are general-purpose productions that are highly flexible but often operate ineffectively. Such productions might include following instructions or, in problem-solving, trying to work back from the solution. Hence, at the cognitive stage, the person typically runs the most appropriate weak-method production, but makes frequent errors because the production does not specify in detail the action to be performed. A novice driver obeying a "brake" instruction might not apply the correct pressure to the pedal. At this stage, processing tends to be verbally coded, which may lead to particular difficulties in translating verbal instructions into muscle movements. Anderson (1982) also points out that at this stage the

trigger conditions for productions must be held in working memory, leading to errors due to overload of memory if instructions are complicated. Feedback from errors initiates the knowledge compilation process, and leads to the acquisition of special-purpose procedures for controlling the various components of the skill.

Different levels of skill acquisition are sometimes referred to as *strategic* and *tactical* learning. Strategic learning refers to deciding on the general approach to a problem, as represented by initial choice of weak-method production, for example. It has been demonstrated in studies of the verbal protocols produced by novices and experts solving physics problems (Chi et al., 1981). Novices tend to think about superficial features of the problem, such as whether it involves a spring or a pulley. Experts, however, organise their thinking around abstract principles such as conservation of energy or momentum, leading to more efficient problem solving. Strategic learning is thus associated with the higher levels of production which set the person's overall goals. Tactical learning, in contrast, refers to more specialised knowledge about how to achieve a particular subgoal, such as calculating the kinetic energy of a moving body, and so refers to the acquisition of lower-level productions.

As the person reaches the later "associative" and "autonomous" stages of skill learning, components of the skill become proceduralised, i.e. controlled by special-purpose productions which operate smoothly and quickly. In the expert, these productions incorporate rules covering all the inputs that the person is likely to encounter, so that action is appropriate whatever the circumstances. The tuning process continues to refine the operation of productions with further practice, subject to the diminishing returns expressed by the power law of practice. As discussed in 3.3.1, automatisation (proceduralisation) depends on the task having consistent mappings between stimuli and responses (Schneider, 1985). If the appropriate response to a given stimulus is always context-dependent (varied mapping), no specialised rule or production can be acquired. In fact, performance of varied-mapped tasks often does improve with practice (Ackerman, 1987), but probably due to strategic rather than tactical learning. The person learns an overall strategy for handling the task, but does not acquire fixed routines for handling individual stimuli or patterns of stimuli.

This view of skilled performance as controlled by a large number of special-purpose productions gives us a view of expert performance as *pattern-recognition*. This idea has been developed in empirical studies of expert (grand master) chess players, who have remarkable abilities to recognise significant configurations of chess pieces. In a classic study, de Groot (1965) presented chess masters with various pieces on a chessboard for 5 seconds, and then had them reconstruct the positions from memory. He found that they could accurately reproduce the positions of more than 20 pieces, whereas weak chess players could only reconstruct positions of 4 or 5 pieces. Further work (e.g. Chase & Simon, 1973) showed that chess masters "chunk" meaningful patterns of pieces. Simon and Gilmartin (1973) estimated that, as a result of years of practice, chess masters can distinguish around 50,000 different patterns. Presumably chess masters maintain this information in procedural form, which specifies not just the input pattern but its implications for their next move. In skilled performance generally, then, the expert can rely on these highly-detailed, elaborated memories, in the form of procedural knowledge, whereas the novice must decide on actions from scratch, using the very limited guidance provided by general-purpose, weak-method productions.

### 7.3.3 Production systems for human–computer interaction

One of the forerunners, and most influential examples of a production rule system, is the GOMS (Goals, Operators, Methods, & Selection) model of Card, Moran and Newell (1983). This was developed primarily to describe the processes of human–computer interaction, and does so in terms of a hierarchy of goals, and a description of the broad methods by which each goal and subgoal may be achieved. Sometimes several methods are possible, and a selection rule is used to choose between them. Finally, perceptual, cognitive or motor "operators" which actually implement the methods are specified. GOMS was developed as a means for *task analysis*, in applied settings, and it has been widely used in the development of displays and human–machine interfaces.

A number of variations of GOMS have been developed. A comparatively recent example is Cognitive Complexity Theory (CCT: Bovair, Kieras, & Polson, 1990; Kieras & Polson, 1985). The central component of CCT is a representation of the working memory demands imposed by task performance. Upon this basis, an examination of the complexity and consistency of the task is possible. This information is computable, and elements of cognitive processing may therefore be simulated in a manner which enables estimations to be generated of task execution times and training demands.

CCT uses production systems of the form IF (condition) THEN (action) in order to describe the cognitive demands associated with task performance. The condition element of production rules relates to either the contents of working memory or environmental factors (e.g. screen display). The action component relates to manipulations of either the environment (e.g. keypresses) or the contents of working memory (e.g. deleting current goals). The clauses contained within the "condition" component are combined using logical AND. If the pattern of goals, notes and external information in working memory matches the condition clauses the rule is said to "fire" and the action operators are executed. Current goals and variables must be stored in working memory, and it is upon this basis that task demands are estimated. Once added to working memory by a production, GOALS and NOTES must be retained in working memory until deleted by later productions. A number of production systems may be generated in order to describe complete task performance. The sequence in which these productions are performed may depend upon selection rules that define different methods of achieving the current task goals (cf. Card et al., 1983). It is therefore possible to represent individual differences in task performance strategies.

Execution time can be predicted using the following formula:

Execution time =
   NCYCLES * a + WMIN * b + i

Where NCYCLES is the number of cycles required to complete the task, a is the activation time per cycle, WMIN is the total number of add-goal and add-note actions, b is the time taken for add-action, and i is the intercept parameter (assumed to be 0). a, b, and i are estimated using multiple regression techniques.

Training time is assumed to be a function of the number of new rules a user must learn in order to perform the task:

Predicted training time = t * n + c

Where t is the training time per production, n is the number of new rules to be learned, and c is the time required to complete the parts of the task not involving the acquisition of new rules (e.g. the criterion run). Both t and c are estimated from the data and assumed to be constant over tasks and serial positions in a training sequence. The model has been successfully applied to predicting times taken to learn, perform and transfer text editing skills (Bovair et al., 1990; Payne, Squibb, & Howes, 1990).

## 7.4 MOTOR AND COGNITIVE–MOTOR SKILLS

### 7.4.1 Motor programs

As we have discussed, cognitive and motor skills may be governed by the same general principles. At the same time, motor skills are differentiated by the inaccessibility of the processes involved. One of the difficulties in learning how to ride a bicycle or execute a golf swing is that it is hard to describe exactly how it should be done. Neurological evidence shows that motor behaviour is controlled by dedicated brain structures, such as the sensorimotor cortex, basal ganglia and cerebellum. Brain motor systems presumably omit to send sufficient feedback signals on their operation to the neocortical systems which support verbal representation. As Annett (1993) proposes, there must be an "action system" guided by non-verbal feedback.

One of the main issues in motor skills research is the nature of the "memory trace" (Adams, 1971) or "motor program" which preserves acquired skills. At one time, the motor program was held to be stored sets of motor instructions, capable of being triggered by a decision and then being used to initiate and execute a movement in open-loop fashion without conscious control (Keele, 1968). There are several lines of evidence which suggest the existence of some form of internal program, all of which amount to demonstrations that complex movements may sometimes be produced without sensory feedback (see Summers, 1989). First, there is the phenomenon of *deafferented movement*. It seems that, normally, movement is controlled by proprioceptive feedback loops that send signals from the muscles through afferent neurons to the spinal cord or motor centres of the brain. In some patients these afferents are destroyed, by gunshot wounds, for example. However, Lashley (1917) reported a case of a patient able to move his limbs without proprioceptive feedback, implying that the movement is controlled by some preexisting program.

Second, the rapidity with which actions may be performed implies an internal program. It is difficult for a cricketer or baseball player to modify the movement of the bat during the short time the ball is in flight (c. 500 ms in baseball). Swinging the bat is perhaps more a matter of selecting and then "launching" a preprogrammed or "ballistic" action than trying to adjust to the feedback cues provided by swinging at a fast-moving ball. There is an extensive literature on the time course of sensory feedback and various perceptual, motor and proprioceptive processes beyond the scope of this book (see Schmidt & Lee, 1999, for a review). It seems that responses to visual feedback may sometimes be generated very rapidly, e.g. adjusting the bat during the last 100–150 ms of ball flight in the case of expert table tennis players (Bootsma & van Wieringen, 1990). However, it is difficult to use feedback effectively over such short time intervals. In fact, baseball batters take about 100–150 ms to decide on response, a further 150 ms or so to initiate the swing, and a further 150 ms to execute the swing so as to intercept the trajectory of the ball (Schmidt & Lee, 1999).

Movements of this kind may be controlled by some pre-existing program which is executed automatically once triggered, leading to the embarrassment of "swinging and missing" if the initial decision is faulty, or if the ball moves unpredictably in flight. Third, animal evidence suggests the existence of *central pattern generators*: electrical stimulation of motor centres may elicit complex, naturalistic movements such as walking.

There is clearly some pre-existing representation of motor procedures, but Keele's (1968) motor program concept seems to be insufficiently flexible in response to changing motor demands. The key observation here is that generically similar actions may involve very different muscle contractions. One may sign one's name with implements such as pens and spraycans, which vary in weight and the way in which they are held. Signatures may be large or small, and written on horizontal or vertical surfaces. The motor program hypothesis implies that different programs are required for different circumstances, which seems implausible. The difficulties of the concept are also supported by more detailed study of phenomena such as deafferented and electrically-elicited movements, which seem to differ in some respects from normal movement (Summers, 1989).

Finally, the motor program concept is difficult to apply to motor learning, i.e. the problem of how novel actions are developed from existing skills. A novice practising a golf swing or tennis serve may produce a long sequence of movements which are similar but differing in detail from one another and, over time, showing systematic change. It is hard to believe that there is a motor program for each individual movement, and hard to see how new programs are developed during learning (see Schmidt & Lee, 1999). Traditionally, in fact, motor learning theorists emphasised the closed-loop aspects of skill acquisition, the shaping of response through error feedback. Adams' (1971) closed-loop theory (see also 7.2.3) supposed that comparison of perceptual and memory trace on each trial allows the person to progressively reduce the discrepancy between them. Initially, comparison is under verbal-cognitive control, guided by knowledge of results. With growing expertise, proprioceptive feedback is used

for comparison, affording a lower-level closed loop control (Fig. 7.2). However, Adams' theory fails to recognise the role of open-loop control, demonstrated by deafferented movements.

### 7.4.2 Motor schemas and learning

Theories of cognitive skill emphasise the control of behaviour by mental structures, and the shift of control from high-level decision-making structures to more specialised routines during skill acquisition. A similar perspective is often applied to motor skills: Keele (1986) suggested that complex skills are acquired by integrating motor programs for simple movements into a more complex, integrated program, much as knowledge compilation operates for cognitive skills. Although this

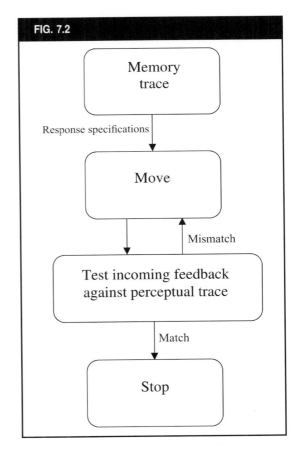

Closed-loop control by proprioceptive feedback in Adams' (1971) model of motor skill.

view is plausible, the control processes are not well understood, perhaps because researchers cannot obtain verbal protocols as they can for cognitive skill acquisition. Much of the research in this area is concerned with representation of the procedural knowledge required for executing movements and processing feedback.

Schmidt (1975, 1976) put forward his motor schema theory to accommodate the roles of both closed-loop and open-loop mechanisms in performance and learning. The theory incorporates the idea of the motor program as part of the response process, but envisages a more flexible, generalised system based on "schematic" representations (as in other memory theories) capable of being used to put together varying patterns of response to changing circumstances, some under feedback control, others not. The generalised program for signing one's name would describe the lines and loops which comprise the signature as an abstract code. The actual motor instructions are then obtained by adding "local parameters" such as shape and weight of writing implement to the information encoded within the program. Handwriting analysis supports this view, in that, as Lashley (1942) observed, individuals show characteristic invariant features of letter writing, such as dotting an "i" with an open circle, irrespective of the way in which the letters are produced by different muscle groups. The main local parameters identified by research are the duration (i.e. speed) of the action, the force applied, and the particular muscles selected (Schmidt & Lee, 1999).

The theory also predicts *invariant relative timing*. The sequencing and phasing of the subcomponents of an action should be constant, and the proportion of total duration of the action occupied by each subcomponent should remain the same, irrespective of how quickly or slowly the action is executed. Shapiro (1977) confirmed this prediction in a study in which subjects practised a sequence of wrist-twist movements, and then were required to speed up the action. Subsequent studies have found exceptions to the principle, perhaps because of variability in peripheral muscle actions (see Schmidt & Lee, 1999). In general, though, ". . . a given overall sequence [of

movements] can be sped up or slowed down as a unit while the constant phasing in the sequence is maintained" (Schmidt & Lee, 1999, p. 163).

So far as learning is concerned, Schmidt (1975) proposed that information about a particular type of motor skill is stored in two schemas (see 3.4.2) whose development and strengthening support skill acquisition. The *recall schema* is a model of how movement outcome depends jointly on (a) local parameters of the generalised motor programme, such as force, and (b) initial environmental conditions, such as the weight of a manipulated object and the person's own body position. The recall schema controls the motor program used for rapid, largely open-loop movements. The *recognition schema* describes how movement outcome depends jointly on initial conditions together with the sensory consequences of the movement, e.g. how it looks and feels to perform an action in a given context. Hence, the recognition schema is used to evaluate the movement-produced feedback. Slow positioning movements may be guided by a simple closed-loop whereby the person reduces to zero the discrepancy between actual sensory feedback and the sensory consequences specified by the recognition schema. Schmidt and Lee (1999) provide an evaluation of the theory, noting both predictive successes in studies of motor learning, and its limitations, such as vagueness about the learning process.

Implicit in much work on motor programs is the idea of some kind of central executive control of selection of programs, especially for unpractised actions. A radical alternative is the *dynamic pattern approach* (Kelso, 1995), which is concerned with how skills may arise from the dynamic interaction of body parts and objects in the external world, without central involvement. In 5.2.2, we saw that combining motor actions such as patting one's head and rubbing one's stomach simultaneously may have "emergent features" which generate dual-task interference. Researchers within the dynamic pattern approach are concerned with these problems of coordinating different actions. It is argued that practice leads to the spontaneous emergence of low-level "coordinative structures" comprised of muscle groups and joints working together as defined by their mechanical characteristics (Zanone & Kelso, 1992). This "self-organisation" of patterns of coordination may be described by nonlinear equations. The dynamic pattern perspective is surely correct in highlighting the role of biological and physical constraints on action, but the cognitive psychologist may find the lack of specification of voluntary control of action unsatisfactory.

### 7.4.3 Cognitive–motor skills

In real-world settings, many skills are "cognitive–motor", in that the operator must perform nontrivial computations on incoming data, and execute some relatively complex motor response. Driving, playing most sports and operating machinery fall into this category. In today's workplace, an important set of cognitive–motor skills is that relating to input devices for computers, such as keyboards and mice. In this subsection, we look briefly at the cognitive–motor skill of copytyping, i.e. the more traditional skill of using a keyboard to type a passage of text. Studies of typing provide a further perspective on how cognitive and motor processes may be integrated, and illustrate some of the general principles of skill theory previously described.

As with skills generally, novice typists show both quantitative and qualitative changes in performance with practice. Overall speed of performance, assessed in words per minute (wpm), increases, and error rate drops. In studies of typing (Salthouse, 1986), response speed is assessed as the median elapsed time or *interkey interval* between successive keystrokes as the person types a standard sentence. This measure may average as little as 100 ms in an expert typist (depending on the particular keystroke); remarkably fast, given that simple RT to a stimulus such as a starter's pistol is rarely less than about 150 ms. As previously discussed, the rapidity of successive movements (keypresses) is evidence for preprogramming of motor responses. Naturally, inexpert typists tend to be slower. However experts and novices also differ qualitatively, in that performance is generally more variable in the unskilled typist, with some very slow responses on the more unusual letters such as "x" and "z". Novice typ-

ists (at the Fitts cognitive stage) are said to use a "hunt-and-peck" strategy of processing each letter in a series, i.e. completing the keypress before starting to process the next letter in the sequence. Unskilled typists also show greater variability in typing the same keystroke on different occasions. Skilled typists continue to show variability in interkey interval across letters, but the effect is less marked. Processing here is presumably more "automatised" and more parallel in character (Fitts' autonomous stage).

Typing is an interesting example of skill because the task is sufficiently constrained that detailed models of the task can be developed. Models focus on the component processes of typing, which are linked together within an overall architecture. The best known model is Rumelhart and Norman's (1982) schema activation model (see Fig. 7.3), which distinguishes the following component processes:

(i) *Perceptual processes*. Text input is perceived, and coded as individual *word schemas*;

(ii) *Parsing*. Codes are computed and activated for each letter in the words.

(iii) *Keypress schemata* are activated by the parser. For example, a word containing the letter "f" activates a schema representing "keypress f" (left hand, index finger, "home" row of keys);

(iv) *Response activation*. Keypress schemata activate appropriate finger and hand muscles, taking into account the physical characteristics of the keyboard.

The Rumelhart and Norman model focuses on the response selection aspects of typing, which is modelled in more detail than earlier processing stages. They programmed a simulation which specified in detail how activation was transmitted between the different "schemata" (i.e. processing units). For example, the most activated keypress schema tends to inhibit other activated schemata, so the person does not attempt to press several keys at once. Once a key is actually pressed, the schema is deactivated, so that the schema for the next key in the sequence is disinhibited and can take over control of response. The keypress

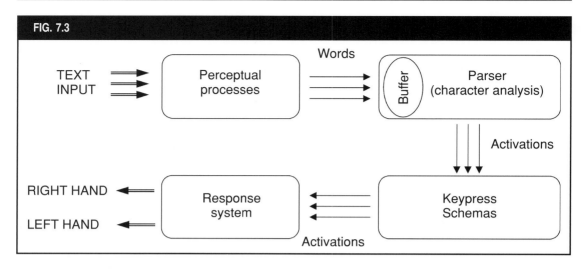

**FIG. 7.3**

A model of transcription typing (adapted from Rumelhart & Norman, 1982).

schemata and response units operate in parallel, so this part of the model functions rather like the connectionist models discussed in 2.3.2. Rumelhart and Norman accept that the model is incomplete, but they showed that it predicted various features of the speed and accuracy of real-life typing, such as the interkey intervals associated with typing particular pairs of letters. For example, interkey intervals are shorter when the two keypresses are made with different hands, rather than the same hand.

Rumelhart and Norman (1982) were concerned with modelling expert performance, rather than the acquisition of typing skill. However, we can obtain some insights into skill acquisition by considering component processes of the type described by their model. In general, it seems that processing becomes more parallel in character as the typist gains expertise. A good example is provided by *eye–hand span*. Broadly, typists look ahead in the text, so that as the keypress for a given letter is being selected and executed, words and letters further on in the text are being perceived and parsed, so that the response system is already prepared for moving onto the next letter in sequence. The number of characters the person is looking ahead is the eye–hand span. Take the phrase "the quick brown fox". When the finger is

pressing the "q" key, the eye may be encoding the letter "w". This letter is 9 characters ahead of the "q" (counting the space), so the eye–hand span is said to be 9. This value is typical of expert typists.

Eye–hand span can be measured either by monitoring eye movements and keypresses simultaneously, or by experimental studies of *preview*. In these studies, the number of letters the typist may look ahead is controlled artificially by presenting the text to be copied on a VDU. With a preview of five, only the next five characters in the text are visible. As each character is typed, the next character in sequence appears. Eye–hand span is measured by reducing preview to the point at which performance is slowed. For example, if eye–hand span is 9 characters, performance will be the same irrespective of whether 20, 15 or 10 characters may be previewed. However, once the number of characters drops below 10, median interkey interval will slow. Salthouse (1986) showed that eye–hand span is quite substantially correlated with overall performance. It seems that one component skill acquired by expert typists is the ability to look further ahead in the text so that reliance on parallel processing is increased. In terms of ACT* (Anderson, 1982), we might imagine that the person is acquiring specialised productions for encoding text. Component skills related to response processes also seem to be acquired, such as the ability to coordinate pairs of finger movements (Grudin, 1983). Such skills allow the person to start executing a keypress while the previous key is being pressed.

## 7.5 CONCLUSIONS

Understanding skilled performance is difficult, because of the complexity of skilled action, but also critical for application of performance psychology to real-world situations. In this chapter, we have described how performance becomes more efficient, more flexible and more fluent as the person acquires expertise at a given skill. Broadly, the person learns many special-purpose routines for encoding and responding to task stimuli, which replace verbal "declarative knowledge" with nonverbal "procedural knowledge". Some skills are simply too complex to capture with a manageable model, although we may be able to model critical elements of them. However, modelling relatively simple skills such as solving certain kinds of problem, or copytyping allows us to explore general principles of skill acquisition and expert performance. Anderson's (1982, 1983) ACT* model describes a production system architecture that allows complex skills to be built up from the building-blocks provided by simple, explicit IF–THEN rules. Principles of ACT* are especially useful in understanding cognitive skills such as problem-solving.

The principles described by cognitive skill theory have also been applied to understanding motor skills, although cognitive and motor pro-cesses may be controlled by two separate, but interacting, subsystems. Motor skill acquisition is often seen as a process of assembling a "motor program" for some novel skill from pre-existing programs, under some form of central control. The control structures supporting motor learning are not well understood although, as in Adams' (1971) closed-loop theory, it is often supposed that the motor program ("memory trace") is shaped by comparison with a feedback representation ("perceptual trace") which specifies the nature of feedback from zero-error performance. Schmidt's (1975) motor schema theory attempts to reconcile the roles of closed-loop performance with the open-loop control seen in rapid movements. An alternative approach to the control problem, the dynamic pattern approach, emphasises the role of self-organisation of low-level coordinative structures. Many real-world tasks have both cognitive and motor aspects, and research on typewriting illustrates the cognitive control of action, with cognitive and motor schemata operating in parallel during skilled performance.

## FURTHER READING

At the textbook level, Proctor and Dutta's (1995) book, focusing mainly on cognitive skill, is the most comprehensive. Schmidt and Lee's (1999) text offers excellent coverage of the motor skills area. Anderson's (1983) book on skill acquisition and cognition is a classic work in the field. The volume edited by Holding (1989) has contributions from many of the leading researchers on human skill. Patrick (1992) reviews the contribution of skill research to training issues.

# 8

# Human error

## 8.1 INTRODUCTION

Skilled performance is achieved through extensive practice, guided by training and feedback, as indicated in the previous chapter. Most skills continue to improve even after considerable amounts of practice, eventually becoming largely automatic. The acquisition of skill requires the progressive elimination of errors because, unless they are rapidly corrected, errors made in the early stages of learning tend to become ingrained (see Welford, 1968). Nevertheless, even highly-skilled individuals performing familiar tasks make errors which, depending upon the task and the environment in which it is being carried out, can have serious, and sometimes disastrous, consequences; the nuclear power plant accidents at Three Mile Island in 1979 and at Chernobyl in 1986, the pesticide plant disaster at Bhopal in 1984, the capsize of the passenger and freight ferry *The Herald of Free Enterprise* at Zeebrugge in 1987, and the fire at Kings Cross underground station in 1987, are frequently cited examples of disasters involving human error (see Reason, 1990). As will be seen in 8.4 below, human error has been regarded as the most important contributory factor in the great majority of accidents, in a variety of contexts ranging from aviation to medicine. From a practical point of view, therefore, the study of human error may help to prevent accidents and disasters in the operation of complex systems, and lead to better system design and more effective system maintenance procedures. While, in absolute terms, the number of errors is small compared to the number of correct actions that are successfully completed, the investigation of human error can lead to a more complete understanding of human performance, since it examines the different ways in which performance can fail to achieve its objectives. We begin this chapter by outlining the role of the human operator in human–machine systems, the human–machine interface, and emphasise the importance of the concepts of "mental models" and "situation awareness" in the operation of complex, dynamic systems. Next, the kinds of errors that occur in complex human–machine systems are described, together with some of the principal taxonomies of human error. The relation between errors and accidents is then considered and the chapter concludes with a discussion of individual differences in error proneness and accident liability.

## 8.2 THE HUMAN–MACHINE INTERFACE

An important consideration in the design of human–machine systems is to make optimal use of the abilities and skills of the individuals who are expected to operate them. System tasks can be allocated either to system operators or to the system's software and hardware on the basis of the respective capabilities of humans and non-human system components for speed, power, consistency of operation and flexibility. The relative economic costs are also an important consideration. In order for human operators to function effectively within a system, information must be exchanged between the operator and the non-human components of the system. The system sends information to the operator via a display, or more usually a series of displays, which permits the state of the system to be monitored and enables the operator to take corrective action as and when it is thought to be necessary. Broadly, displays are of three main types: *qualitative* (for example, a warning light or an alarm bell), *quantitative* (for example, a linear scale or a counter) and *representational*, whereby the operator is provided with a "working model" of the process being monitored. After a decision has been taken about what action is required on the basis of information provided by the display, the operator must convey this information to the system in the most efficient way possible. This is achieved by activating a control, such as a switch or a keyboard. The

changed state of the display then provides feedback to the operator as to whether the action taken was appropriate, although information of this kind can sometimes also be supplemented by the "feel" of the control. Thus the display–control loop, shown in Fig. 8.1, is the basic element of the human–machine system.

## 8.2.1 Automated systems

Automation can be defined as "the execution by a machine agent (usually a computer) of a function that was previously carried out by a human" (Parasuraman & Riley, 1997, p. 231). It has been widely implemented in human-machine systems, as some system functions are thought to be more accurately, more reliably and more safely performed by automated system components than by human operators. In many such systems, automation has assumed control of routine physical activities, which can be tedious and time-consuming for human operators to perform and, through the development of artificial intelligence and expert systems, it is likely to be increasingly applied to higher-level cognitive tasks, such as decision making. But it is less clear whether automation has led to a significant reduction in mental workload (see Chapter 5), which was expected to be one of its major benefits, at least from the perspective

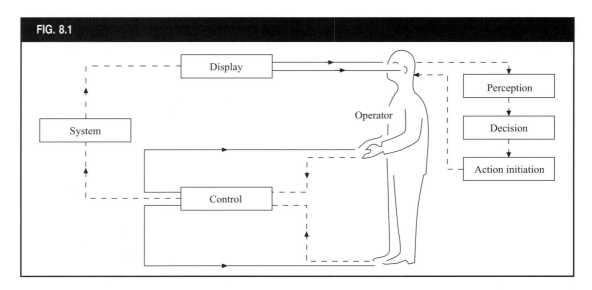

FIG. 8.1

Information flow between the human operator and a system. From Stammers (1979).

of the human operator. For example, in a series of studies of the attitudes of pilots to cockpit automation, Wiener reported that only a minority agreed that automation reduced mental workload, while a number of pilots believed that automation actually increased workload, especially in the highly demanding situations of take-off and landing, where often the automated system would require reprogramming in order to accommodate changing conditions or flight instructions (Wiener, 1985, 1989; Wiener & Curry, 1980). Later studies have obtained similar findings (see Parasuraman & Riley, 1997).

Human-machine systems vary in the degree to which they are automated (see Fig. 8.2). At one extreme, the operator has full manual control of the system, with no system function being carried out by a computer or other non-human system component. At the other, all system functions, including system monitoring, are controlled by system components, with only the outputs of the system being visible to the human operator who, in some systems at least, is unable to override system decisions. As Fig. 8.2 indicates, intermediate stages can range from automated decision support, where operators receive recommendations from the system which they may accept or reject, to automatic implementation of decisions, where the system determines and implements actions

unless these are vetoed by the operator (see Endsley & Kiris, 1995; Parasuraman & Riley, 1997). The greater the degree of automation, the more the operator's principal task becomes one of supervisory control, monitoring the state of the system and intervening only when system goals (or system tolerances) are perceived to be threatened.

Automation therefore increases the "psychological distance" between the operator and system events, because the level of interaction and the degree of familiarity with the state of the system are reduced. The operator is pushed out of the inner loop directly connecting him or her to the system through the display–control loop shown in Fig. 8.1, into an outer loop, where the connection between the operator and the system is mediated by a computer, thereby creating what has been described as the "out-of-the-loop performance problem" (Endsley & Kiris, 1995; Wickens, 1992). When faced with system failure, operators working with automated systems appear to be less efficient both at reporting system errors and in carrying out system tasks manually. Endsley and Kiris suggested that these difficulties are attributable to the loss of manual skills resulting from disuse, and to a reduction in "situation awareness", a concept which is outlined briefly in 8.2.2 below.

**FIG. 8.2**

| Level of automation | | Roles | |
| --- | --- | --- | --- |
| | | Human | System |
| None | 1 | Decide, act | ———— |
| Decision support | 2 | Decide, act | Suggest |
| Consensual AI | 3 | Concur | Decide, act |
| Monitored AI | 4 | Veto | Decide, act |
| Full automation | 5 | ———— | Decide, act |

Levels of control in automation (from Endsley & Kiris, 1995). Reprinted with permission from *Human Factors*, Vol. 37, issue no. 2, 1995. Copyright 1995 by the Human Factors and Ergonomics Society. All rights reserved.

Although there are exceptions, it is usual for the human operator in an automated system to have some discretion regarding the extent to which automated system components are utilised. The determinants of the decision either to use or not to use automation have been reviewed by Parasuraman and Riley (1997). They observed that operators can *misuse*, *disuse*, or *abuse* automated systems. Automation is misused when operators over-rely on an automated system, monitor the system's state ineffectively and, in consequence, fail to revert to manual control when it is appropriate to do so. Automation is disused when operators do not use it when they should, for example, when automated alarms or warning systems are deliberately disabled, perhaps because of a high false alarm rate. Finally, automation is abused when it is applied and implemented by designers and managers without due consideration of the operator's role in system performance. An implicit assumption frequently made by system designers is that the introduction of automation into a human–machine system reduces human error although, as Parasuraman and Riley (1997) pointed out, making a system less vulnerable to operator error through the application of automation may possibly make it more vulnerable to designer error, thus substituting one kind of human error for another.

Operators' use of automation is influenced by a number of factors, perhaps the most important being the perception of the advantages and disadvantages of using automation. This will be based on the demands of the situation (such as the current level of mental workload and the cognitive "costs" or "overhead" of automation utilisation) and on the operator's previous experience of automation (for example, whether automated systems have been observed to function reliably, thereby creating a high degree of trust between the operator and the system). Muir (1994) has argued that individuals learn to trust automated systems in much the same way as they learn to trust people; just as they come to trust particular people because they find them to be reliable and honest, so they come to trust particular machines on the same basis. On the other hand, individuals tend to lose trust in another person when they feel let down

or betrayed, and it may take some time for the trust to redevelop. Other factors that may affect the decision to use automation include operators' levels of confidence in their cognitive skills, the degree of risk they are prepared to tolerate, how tired they feel, the complexity of the task to be performed and the ease with which the state of the automated system can be determined (see Parasuraman & Riley, 1997). A model of the possible interactions among these various factors is shown in Fig. 8.3.

## 8.2.2 Mental models and situational awareness

The experience of operating complex, dynamic human-machine systems results in the accumulation of knowledge about how a particular system works, together with the development of cognitive strategies that facilitate the performance of system tasks. System knowledge is generally thought to be encapsulated in some form of mental representation of the system and its environment, variously described as a "mental picture" (Bainbridge, 1978), a "mental model" (Wilson & Rutherford, 1989) or, more recently, as "situation awareness" (Endsley, 1995a, 1995b). Air traffic controllers, for example, receive information from a variety of sources, such as radar and radio systems, which they use to build up a mental picture of air traffic in the sector for which they are responsible. The maintenance of an accurate mental picture of the current air traffic situation is regarded by controllers as essential for effective air traffic control or ATC (Mogford, 1997). While there is some debate about how a mental model should be defined, partly because human factors specialists and cognitive psychologists hold somewhat different views (Wilson & Rutherford, 1989), the air traffic controller's mental model of the ATC system can be thought of as an underlying knowledge base that develops depth and stability relatively slowly over time, gradually enabling the controller to understand and predict system behaviour, and providing a basis for the mental picture of the ongoing situation (Mogford, 1997). Mogford suggested that the mental models of air traffic controllers comprise two components, both of which are essential for the successful performance of the

**FIG. 8.3**

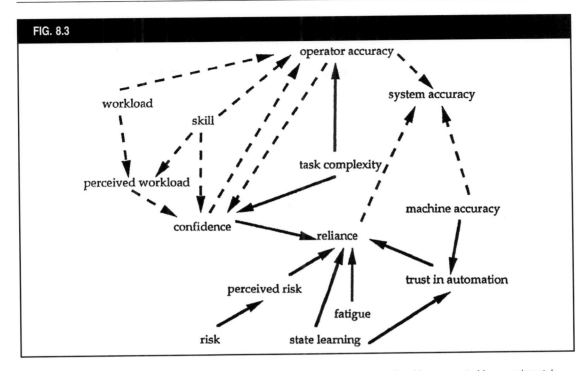

Interactions between factors influencing automation use. Solid arrows represent relationships supported by experimental data, dotted lines are hypothesised relationships or relationships that depend on the system in question. From Parasuraman & Riley (1997). Reprinted with permission from *Human Factors*, Vol. 39, issue no. 2, 1997. Copyright 1997 by the Human Factors and Ergonomics Society. All rights reserved.

controller's task of separating and guiding aircraft: a *domain* model, encompassing the airspace and the aircraft which controllers regulate and the ATC procedures that enable them to do so; and a *device* model, which represents their understanding of the various electronic and computerised systems that support the ATC function. Similarly, in process control, where operators may be regulating a wide variety of industrial processes, ranging from blast furnaces, paper mills, the distillation of gas and the distribution of electrical and nuclear power, successful performance in part depends on an adequate mental model of the dynamics of the process, as well as on an accurate mental representation of its current state (see Wickens, 1992). But the formation of an adequate mental model of the dynamics of a system may become extremely difficult if the number of variables is large, and the interactions among them complex. For instance, in a commercial aircraft cockpit,

pilots may have to acknowledge and interpret information presented by up to 400 different displays (Adams, Tenney, & Pew, 1995), while in nuclear power plant control rooms there may be more than 3000 different displays and controls (Wickens, 1992).

An adequate mental model can be regarded as a prerequisite of situation awareness (Sarter & Woods, 1991), which has been defined as "the perception of the elements in the environment within a volume of time and space, the comprehension of their meaning, and the projection of their status in the future" (Endsley, 1995a, p. 36). Endsley distinguishes three levels of situation awareness (see Fig. 8.4): *Level 1*, the operator's attention to and perception of current situational events; *Level 2*, the operator's integration of information concerning the current process state into an overall understanding of the current situation and its relation to system goals; and *Level 3*,

**FIG. 8.4**

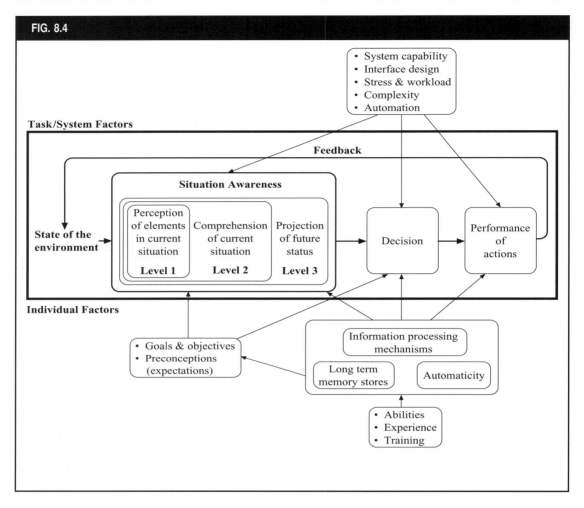

Model of situation awareness in dynamic decision making. From Endsley (1995a). Reprinted with permission from *Human Factors*, Vol. 37, issue no. 1, 1995. Copyright 1995 by the Human Factors and Ergonomics Society. All rights reserved.

the operator's extrapolation of information from Levels 1 and 2 to project the current process state into the near future, and to compare it with the desired process state. Endsley's (1995a) discussion emphasised that situational awareness involves attentional, perceptual and comprehension processes to a greater extent than decision-making and response selection processes.

Loss of situation awareness has been considered to be a significant causal factor in aviation accidents, particularly those involving highly-automated aircraft, with failures to observe or monitor sources of information sometimes accounting for just over

a third of all situation awareness errors (Endsley, 1996; Hardy & Parasuraman, 1997; Jones & Endsley, 1995). Gugerty (1997) suggested that poor situation awareness may also be implicated in driving accidents. In-depth studies of accident causation have highlighted attentional and perceptual errors as important direct causes of road accidents (for example, Shinar, 1978). While the concept of situational awareness has been applied most frequently to the task of flying military and commercial aircraft, and to a lesser extent to the task of vehicle drivers, it has also been discussed in relation to anaesthesiology (Gaba & Howard,

1995) and process control (Hogg, Folleso, Strand-Volden, & Torralba, 1995).

Situation awareness, like mental workload, has been assessed by a variety of different procedures, ranging from physiological measures (specifically evoked potentials such as P300 and other electro-cortical measures) to the collection and analysis of task performance data of various kinds. Embedded task measures, subjective ratings and post-task questionnaires have also been employed in the assessment of situation awareness. The advantages and disadvantages of these different procedures have been reviewed by Endsley (1995b). One of the most direct ways of assessing situation awareness is the use of simulated operational tasks which are "frozen" at some randomly chosen point in time, whereupon observers are asked to provide as full an account as possible of their current level of situation awareness. Using this technique, which appears to be largely non-intrusive, Endsley (1995b) reported that observers were able to preserve relatively accurate levels of situation awareness without apparent memory decay for several minutes. Hogg et al. (1995) have developed similar procedures for assessing situation awareness in process control tasks.

## 8.3 APPROACHES TO HUMAN ERROR

As Reason (1995) has observed, human error is not confined to the human operator of a system, such as the driver of a car, the pilot of an aircraft, or the supervisory controller of a nuclear power plant control room. In addition, system errors can also result from poor system design, inadequate system maintenance, and inappropriate system management practices. However, in one or more of its forms, human error accounts for a relatively high proportion of system failures; one estimate, cited by Van Cott (1994), suggested that the incidence of system failures attributable to human error is 90% in air traffic control systems, 85% in cars, 70% in US nuclear power plants, 65% in worldwide jet cargo transport, 31% in petrochemical plants, and 19% in the petroleum industry. The average across all systems was estimated to be around 60%, with the remaining 40% being

attributable to failures of system hardware, such as electrical, mechanical and material failures. But system hardware failures may stem from errors made by maintenance engineers or equipment inspectors. Hsu (1991) emphasised the pervasiveness of maintenance errors, citing studies conducted by Griffin-Fouco and Ghertman (1987), whose analysis of human error data in nuclear power plants found that 60% of such errors occurred during maintenance work, and by Sears (1986), whose examination of airline accident records over the period 1959–1983 indicated that 12% of these accidents were due to faulty maintenance and inspection procedures.

### 8.3.1 Definitions of human error

From a systems perspective, an error can be defined as an action that violates one or more system tolerance limits, and such limits vary from system to system. The same action can thus constitute an error in one system, but not in another. For example, turning the steering wheel sharply to the right when travelling at about 20 miles an hour may make little or no difference to vehicle handling in an estate car, but may cause a jeep to topple over. From a psychological perspective, an error can be defined as an unintended action or an undesirable one (see Senders & Moray, 1991) and errors arise from a transaction between system requirements and operator actions (Fuller, 1990). The concept of "intention" is thus central to human error. Errors can result from a discrepancy between a planned and an executed action; that is, operators did not do what they intended to do, either due to a failure of response execution, which has been called a "slip", or to a failure of memory, which has been called a "lapse". Errors can also result from a discrepancy between the plan that should have been formulated to achieve the desired task outcome or system goal, and the plan that was actually formulated; that is, the operator made an error of planning or judgement, termed a "mistake" (see Reason, 1990). These distinctions are discussed below.

### 8.3.2 Taxonomies of human error

Errors have been classified in a variety of ways and at number of different levels. The simplest is the phenomenological level, where errors are described essentially as they are observed. For example, errors can be divided into the following five categories (Miller & Swain, 1987; Swain & Guttman, 1983).

1. *Errors of omission*, where an action that should have been performed is not carried out; for instance, a pilot attempts to land an aircraft without first ensuring that the landing gear is down and locked in position.
2. *Errors of commission*, where an action that should not have been performed is, in fact, executed; for instance, an industrial inspector passes a faulty electronic component as perfect when it should have been rejected. Errors of commission can be further subdivided into:
3. *Extraneous acts*, where an action is performed that is likely to hinder or prevent the attainment of system goals; for instance, a driver uses a mobile phone while attempting to locate the correct exit on an unfamiliar roundabout.
4. *Sequential errors*, where a particular task element is performed out of sequence; for instance, a driver puts a car in gear and then turns the ignition key.
5. *Time errors*, where the correct action is performed too early, too late or not within the permitted time; for instance, a driver returns to a car park to find that the parking ticket has expired, resulting in a fine.

Other approaches to error classification seek to specify, usually in fairly general terms, the information-processing systems or the cognitive mechanisms that may underlie different types of errors, and also to identify the contexts in which particular errors may occur. The main distinction made by information processing approaches to human error is that between slips and lapses on the one hand, and mistakes on the other (Norman, 1981, 1988; Reason, 1984, 1990).

As noted above, slips are errors of commission, where the intended action is wrongly executed, commonly because a frequent and habitual action takes over from the intended one. Such errors have been termed "capture" errors (e.g. Norman, 1981). Norman (1988) quoted as an example of a

capture error playing a piece of music which is reasonably familiar, without paying much attention to it, then suddenly realising that the piece has turned into a similar, but much more familiar, tune. Capture errors may also be triggered by factors in the external environment, or by ongoing mental preoccupations. "Mode errors" are a second type of slip, in which the current situation is misconstrued or misclassified. Norman (1981) observed that the term derives from experience with computerised text editors that require the computer to be in one mode (text mode) when text is being entered, but in another (command mode) when commands are being given. Failure to identify the current mode can result, for instance, in attempts to enter text when the computer is in command mode, which may lead to the text being lost.

Sarter and Woods (1995) pointed out that mode errors may occur more frequently in modern aircraft cockpits with highly-automated flight management systems. These can assume a much greater number of modes than previous automated systems, and require pilots to have much greater knowledge of system operations, since they have to select the most appropriate mode for a particular flight situation as well as monitoring which mode the system is in. This is because the system can change modes automatically in response to environmental inputs or for protection purposes, without the necessity for pilot intervention. There is also greater interaction across modes, which can create increased delays between pilot input to the flight management system and feedback about system response; this makes the pilot's task of keeping track of which system mode is active even more difficult, and adds considerably to pilot workload. As an example of the potential importance of mode errors in aviation, Sarter and Woods (1995) discussed the role of mode errors in the 1990 Bangalore air crash, as well as in a series of studies based on experienced pilots' descriptions of the problems they had encountered with highly-automated flight management systems. They concluded that most of the difficulties pilots encountered with cockpit automation "were related to lack of mode awareness and to gaps in mental models of how the various automated modes work and interact" (p. 11).

Lapses are errors of omission, a deviation from an intended action, where the action was not in fact carried out, either because of a failure of memory or a failure of attention. A lapse of memory, when the operator forgets to perform an intended action, can result from distraction; Wickens (1992, p. 428) quotes an example of an air crash in the Detroit area, where pilots working their way through a routine take-off checklist were interrupted by air traffic control who requested a change of runway. When the checklist was resumed, a critical step had been omitted (setting the flaps), with the result that the aircraft crashed while attempting to take off. A lapse of attention occurs when, for example, radar or sonar operators fail to detect a target for which they are looking or listening, as noted in Chapter 6. Lapses, especially lapses of memory, have been referred to as "loss-of-activation errors" (Norman, 1988).

Rasmussen's distinction (e.g. 1983, 1986) between *skill-*, *rule-* and *knowledge-based* behaviour has also been extensively utilised in taxonomies of human error. In Rasmussen's framework (see Chapter 1), skill-based behaviour is sensory–motor performance, guided by an intention, which proceeds smoothly and in a highly integrated fashion while being minimally under the control of conscious attention. Since slips of action are particularly likely to occur when actions have become automated and no longer require conscious control (e.g. Heckhausen & Beckmann, 1990), errors at the skill-based level will be predominantly either slips or lapses (see Reason, 1990). In contrast to skill-based errors, errors made at either the rule- or knowledge-based levels are classified as mistakes, errors of planning or judgement. Rule-based behaviour is guided by rules and procedures that are either stored in memory or made available through explicit instructions or protocols. Rule-based mistakes may arise through failures of interpretation or comprehension of the situation with which the operator is confronted. Operators may believe that they understand the situation and develop a plan of action for dealing with it, using an "if–then" strategy. But if the nature of the situation has been misperceived, the implementation of the plan may well be inappropriate. Rule-based mistakes may also occur if the plan itself is poorly

conceived or misapplied. Such mistakes, however, are generally made with a high degree of confidence. Knowledge-based behaviour is based on the operator's knowledge of how the system works and of its current state, and on the decisions made in the light of this knowledge. Knowledge-based mistakes may arise because the operator's knowledge of system capabilities and dynamics is inaccurate or incomplete, or because he or she is overwhelmed by the complexity of the information available, perhaps through inexperience, or as a result of excessive workload. Such mistakes are made with a lower degree of confidence than are rule-based mistakes.

One of the main differences between slips and mistakes is the ease with which they can be detected (Wickens, 1992). Slips can be detected relatively easily: skilled typists, performing a highly-practiced sensorimotor skill, can detect any errors they may make extremely rapidly and with virtually perfect accuracy (Rabbitt, 1978). Similarly, studies of relatively simple sensorimotor tasks, such as choice reaction time (see 3.2.4), indicate that observers can successfully detect and correct response execution errors, with error-correction responses usually being made more quickly than correct responses (Rabbitt, 1966). Observers thus appear to detect their execution errors, which result from faulty response selection, by monitoring response feedback and comparing it with an internal model of the correct response. Some errors in perceptual-motor tasks, however, result from misperceptions of the stimulus to which a response is required, rather than from faulty response selection. Most perceptual errors tend to be omission rather than commission errors, and can also be relatively easily detected and corrected (Rabbitt, Cumming, & Vyas, 1978). In contrast, operators are often unaware that they have made a mistake and, in consequence, detection rates for mistakes are relatively low. Woods (1984), for example, in an analysis of simulated nuclear power plant incidents, reported that overall operators detected 38% of the errors they had made. However, when these errors were categorised as slips or mistakes, it was found that while about half the slips were detected, none of the mistakes were. Reason (1990, p. 166) compared error frequencies and error detection rates for skill-based errors (slips and lapses), and rule- and knowledge-based mistakes in three different published studies. Averaging over the three studies, he found that skill-based errors accounted for 61% of the total number of errors, rule-based mistakes for 27%, and knowledge-based mistakes for 11%. The corresponding overall detection rates were 86% for skill-based errors, 73% for rule-based mistakes, and 70.5% for knowledge-based mistakes. In general, then, most errors are detected by their perpetrators, but slips and lapses are more easily detected than are mistakes.

Other taxonomic approaches to human error have categorised errors in terms of where they occur in a hypothetical sequence of information processing stages. For example, Nagel (1988), focussing on aircraft cockpit errors, suggested that most such errors could be assigned to one of three processing stages: "information", "decision", and "action". The first stage (information) involves the acquisition of information, for example, from cockpit displays, as well as processing it and communicating it to others; the second (decision)

involves planning a course of action, and the third (action) involves carrying out the selected action. A broadly similar classification was made by Gerbert and Kemmler (1986), in an analysis of over 1400 "near misses" reported by German air force pilots. Slips, lapses, mode errors and mistakes can also be mapped onto a sequential model of information processing stages (Wickens, 1992), as shown in Fig. 8.5.

## 8.4 ERRORS AND ACCIDENTS

Accidents are generally unplanned (Arbous & Kerrich, 1951), and an accident can be defined as "an error with sad consequences' (Cherns, 1962). However, as Senders and Moray (1991) have pointed out, errors and accidents are not synonymous, and accidents often happen when no error has in fact been made. Nevertheless, accident researchers have attempted to use taxonomies of human error to provide a basis for classifying the

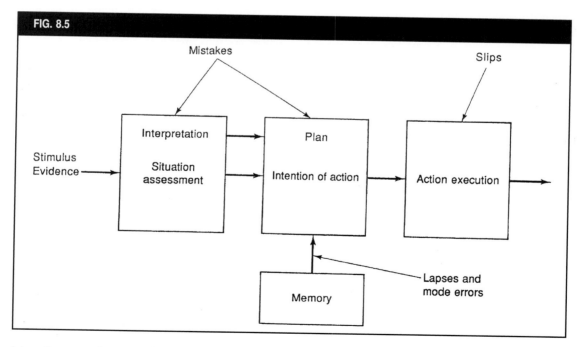

Information processing context for representing human error. From Wickens (1992). Reprinted by permission of Prentice-Hall, Inc., Upper Saddle River, NJ.

causes of accidents in a variety of contexts, and some of these attempts are described below.

Reason (1995) argued that organisational accidents can arise from either "active failures", which are unsafe acts perpetrated by system operators, or from "latent failures", which result from organisational decisions or practices that create an organisational climate or "safety culture" characterised by high workload levels, excessive time pressure and low morale, serving to undermine the system's "defences", and hence increase the likelihood of accidents (see Fig. 8.6). The concept of a "safety culture" includes the norms and rules for dealing with hazardous situations, attitudes to safety, and the regular monitoring of safety procedures (see Lucas, 1992; Pidgeon, 1991, for further discussion).

Unsafe acts include not only skill-based, rule-based and knowledge-based errors, but also *violations*. Violations represent a wilful, and therefore intended, departure from those practices deemed necessary to preserve system safety and the safety of others using the system, such as, in the driving context, other road users. They can be further subdivided into *routine violations*, which tend to be habitual, and which may be encouraged (or at least not prevented) by an organisation's safety culture, and *exceptional violations,* which tend to be isolated, atypical departures from safe practices. The relation between slips, mistakes and violations is depicted in Fig. 8.7.

### 8.4.1 Error taxonomies and accident data

Reason et al. (1990) classified drivers' self-reported driving failures into three categories: violations, dangerous errors, and lapses. As indicated above, driving violations represent "deliberate deviations from safe driving practice", and are therefore intentional actions, while errors are regarded as "driving mistakes or omissions" (see Parker, Reason, Manstead, & Stradling, 1995). Examples of driving errors would include forgetting to check the rear mirror before pulling out, or attempting to drive away in the wrong gear. Violations, in contrast, would include drunk driving, breaking the speed limit, or running a red light. Reason et al. (1990) suggested that violations may be attributable to social and motivational factors, and there seems to be a relation between the tendency to commit violations and the tendency to make other kinds of "social deviations" (e.g. West, French, Kemp, & Elander, 1993). Errors, on the other hand, are attributable to deficiencies in information processing. Using a 50-item Driver

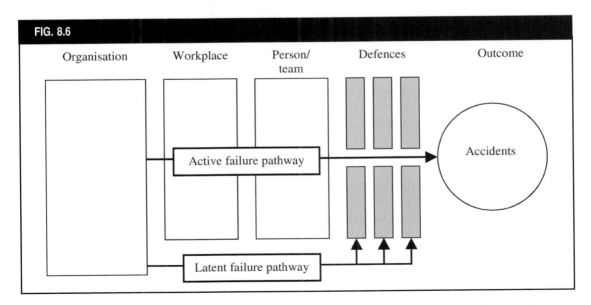

FIG. 8.6

The distinction between active and latent failure pathways. From Reason (1995). *Ergonomics*, Vol. 38. Reprinted with permission. Routledge.

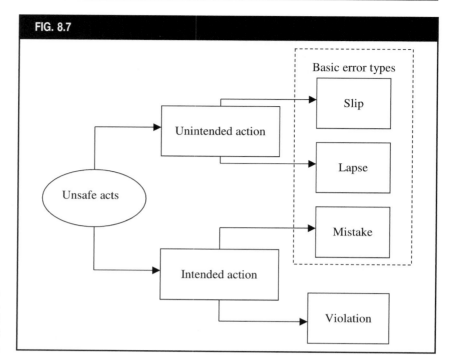

**FIG. 8.7**

Basic error types

Slip

Lapse

Mistake

Unintended action

Unsafe acts

Intended action

Violation

A model for unsafe acts.
From Reason (1990).
Reprinted by permission
of Cambridge
University Press.

Behaviour Questionnaire (DBQ), requiring drivers to report how often they committed violations, or were aware of making errors or lapses, Reason et al. found that men, especially young men, reported a higher violation rate than did women, while women reported a greater number of relatively harmless lapses. Violations tended to decline with age, while errors did not. Moreover, violations, rather than errors or lapses, have been found to predict self-reported accident involvement and appear to be related to specific types of accidents, with high violators being involved in more active loss-of-control and passive right-of-way accidents (see Parker et al., 1995). High violators also report a greater number of speeding convictions (Blockley & Hartley, 1995).

Various attempts have also been made to classify accidents in terms of the sort of errors thought to be associated with them. These rely mainly on hypothetical sequences of information processing stages, for example, those of Nagel (1988) and Wickens (1992), mentioned earlier, or on error classification systems derived from Rasmussen's (i.e. 1983) skill-, rule-, and knowledge-based hier-

archy, and Reason's (1990) taxonomy of unsafe acts (see Fig. 8.7). For example, O'Hare, Wiggins, Batt and Morrison (1994) compiled a database of accidents and incidents involving New Zealand civil aircraft for the period 1983–1989, coding accident reports into one of Nagel's (1988) three error stages (information, decision and action) referred to above. From a total of 284 aviation accidents and incidents involving fixed-wing aircraft, 71% were associated with some form of human error. Of these, 22% were coded as information errors, 35% as decision errors, and 43% as action errors. O'Hare et al. then compared the 34 fatal or serious injury accidents with the 169 cases of minor/non-serious injury accidents and found that 62.5% of the former but only 30.5% of the latter involved decision errors, a difference that proved to be highly significant. Minor accidents tended to result predominantly from action errors. It thus appears that more serious accidents are likely to be associated with decision errors.

Subsequently, O'Hare et al. (1994) investigated the same database, extended to 1991, using a taxonomic algorithm of cognitive errors based on

Rasmussen's (1983) hierarchy. The six cognitive errors were: information errors, diagnostic errors, goal errors, strategy errors, procedure errors, and execution errors. Of the 373 accidents and incidents analysed, 70% could be coded into one of the six cognitive error categories, with procedural errors (failures to execute procedures consistent with the strategy selected), being the most frequent, associated with 26% of the total number of accidents or incidents. Accidents were divided, as before, into serious and minor accidents. Goal errors (failures to select a reasonable goal given the circumstances) and diagnosis errors (failures to diagnose accurately the state of the system on the basis of the information available) were much more likely to be associated with serious accidents than with minor ones. In contrast, minor accidents tended to be associated with procedural errors.

In a similar study, Wiegmann and Shappell (1997) utilised a classification framework derived from an information processing approach (Wickens & Flach, 1988), O'Hare et al.'s (1994) taxonomic algorithm based on Rasmussen's hierarchy, described above, and Reason's (1990) taxonomy of unsafe acts, to reorganise the human factors database of US Navy and Marine Corps aviation accidents occurring between 1977 and 1992. They found that all three approaches were able to accommodate well over 80% of the accidents directly attributed to pilot-causal factors by the original accident investigators. Processing errors associated with the information processing approach were subdivided into sensory errors, pattern recognition errors, attention errors, decision/response selection errors and response execution errors. About 75% of the errors made by pilots in accidents for which they were adjudged responsible were either response execution errors (45%) or decision/response selection errors (30%), with response execution errors being more frequently associated with minor accidents, and decision or response selection errors being more frequently associated with major accidents. Using Rasmussen's (1983) framework, as extended by O'Hare et al. (1994), procedural errors were also found to occur with the highest frequency, in

about 39% of cases, and such errors were more strongly associated with minor accidents than with major ones. Both of these results confirm those of O'Hare et al. (1994).

In terms of Reason's (1990) unsafe acts taxonomy, mistakes occurred with the highest frequency (58%), followed by violations (17%), slips (14%), and lapses (11%). Violations were more frequently associated with major accidents than with minor ones, while minor accidents tended to be associated more with slips, lapses and mistakes than with violations. For both major and minor accidents, however, mistakes were the single most important cause, being well over 50% for both types of accident. Taken together, the findings of O'Hare et al. (1994) and Wiegmann and Shappell (1997) suggest that different types of human error contribute to major aviation accidents (which may involve fatalities, serious injuries or permanent disabilities as well as extensive aircraft damage), compared to minor ones (where no injuries of any consequence are sustained and aircraft damage is negligible). Major aviation accidents appear to result mainly from judgement errors (errors in decision making, goal setting and strategy selection, as well as intended violations of safe aviation practice). Minor accidents are principally due to procedural and response execution errors.

Error taxonomies, especially Rasmussen's skill-rule-knowledge hierarchy, have also been applied to occupational accidents. For example, Williamson and Feyer (1990), in an investigation of fatal occupational accidents in Australia, attributed around 55% of accidents to skill-based errors, and about 14% to rule-based and knowledge-based errors respectively. Salminen and Tallberg (1996) examined 178 fatal occupational accidents in Finland over the period 1985–1990 and 99 serious occupational accidents in southern Finland in 1988 and 1989. In broad agreement with the findings of Williamson and Feyer (1990), Salminen and Tallberg reported that 66% of fatal accidents were associated with skill-based errors, compared to 46% of serious accidents, while 33% of serious accidents were associated with rule-based errors. Only 10% of fatal accidents and

5% of serious accidents were associated with knowledge-based errors. The remaining accidents, of both types, were associated with technical faults rather than with errors made by the individual involved. In a further study of Australian occupational accidents, covering all fatal accidents over the period 1982–1984, Feyer, Williamson and Cairns (1997) examined the relation between skill-based errors (slips), rule- and knowledge-based errors and work practices involving unsafe operating procedures, which could originate with management or with the individual worker. These procedures were considered with respect to three kinds of equipment: general job-related equipment, personal protective equipment, and safety equipment. Unsafe procedures were most common, occurring in 54% of cases, with the majority originating with management; for instance, failures to provide safety equipment or personal protective equipment. These management-originated unsafe procedures were quite strongly related to knowledge-based errors, while individual worker unsafe procedures tended to be associated with slips. Unsafe acts, unsafe conditions and unsafe supervisory practices have been used by Shappell and Wiegmann (1997) in the development of a taxonomy of unsafe operations, which aims to provide accident investigators with a method for identifying causal factors in accident situations.

Edkins and Pollock (1997) investigated railway accidents and incidents in an Australian public railway authority, analysing 112 train accidents and "near misses" over a three-year period, using Reason's (1990) error classification framework. As in the New Zealand and American aviation accident analyses described above, Edkins and Pollock reported that the majority of train accidents (59%) were associated with errors at the skill-based level, with 34% of accidents being associated with errors at the rule-based level. Errors at the knowledge-based level were associated with fewer than 1% of accidents, and violations accounted for around 6% of all recorded incidents. The most frequent accident- or incident-related occurrence was a SPAD, a signal passed at danger, comprising 39% of cases, followed by a train running through junction points, which accounted for 33%. Attentional factors, implicated in 70%

of the total number of accidents and incidents and 73% of SPADs, were the most significant psychological precursors of unsafe acts in Edkins and Pollock's study, confirming the results of a number of earlier investigations of railway accidents (for example, Davis, 1958, 1966; Haga, 1984; Hildebrandt, Rohmert, & Rutenfrantz, 1975a; Smiley, 1990). The second most significant precursor of unsafe acts comprised latent organisational failures, which were implicated in 15% of cases. The most frequently-occurring latent organisational failure was associated with "staff attitude", accounting for 31% of latent failures. Included in this category were such factors as low morale, complacency and poor motivation, which reflect the "safety culture" of an organisation.

A number of significant industrial disasters, such as Three-Mile Island, Chernobyl and Bhopal, occurred at night, and accidents tend to occur more frequently during the night shift than at other times, as might be expected from the variations in performance with time of day, discussed in Chapter 12.4. Folkard (1997) reviewed the relation between transport accident risk and time of day, and noted that road accidents peaked between 2 and 3 am (see Fig. 8.8). Although accidents attributable to drivers falling asleep at the wheel increase markedly between midnight and 8 am (see Brown, 1994), Folkard's detailed analysis of circadian rhythms in sleep propensity suggests that these rhythms cannot fully account for the circadian variation in road accident risk. A broadly similar trend to that seen in Fig. 8.8, though with a peak about four hours later, was observed for ship collisions. Industrial accidents also appear to be highest during the night shift (Smith, Folkard, & Poole, 1994). Smith et al. analysed all reported accidents resulting in injury in a large production engineering company over a one-year period. Workers operated on a rotating three-shift system where the *a priori* accident risk appeared to be constant. Smith et al. found that accidents were approximately 25% higher on the night shift, followed by the afternoon shift, with the morning shift being associated with the lowest frequency of accidents. Thus there are consistent temporal variations in accident risk over a 24-hour period.

**FIG. 8.8**

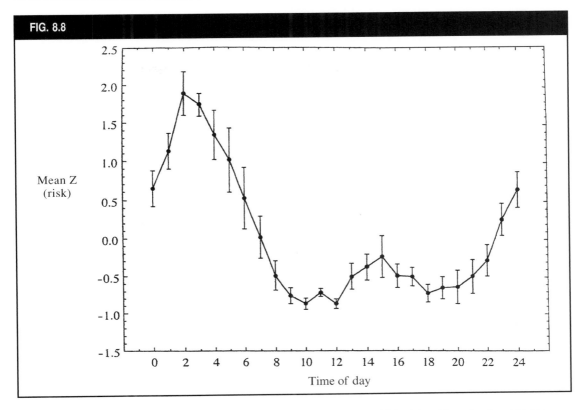

The mean trend in road traffic accident risk over the 24-hour day, derived from published data. The value for midnight is plotted at both 0 and 24 hours to emphasise the cyclic nature of the trend. From Folkard (1997) *Accident Analysis and Prevention*, Vol. 29. Reprinted by permission of Elsevier Science.

## 8.5 INDIVIDUAL DIFFERENCES IN ERROR PRONENESS AND ACCIDENT LIABILITY

Individuals may differ with respect to "error proneness", so that some people consistently make more errors than do others. People who make one kind of error, for example, an attentional error, may also be more likely to make other kinds of error, for example, a memory error. There may thus be general characteristics such as "cognitive failure" (Broadbent et al., 1982), which are positively related to the tendency to make cognitive errors. If people differ with respect to error proneness, they may also differ with respect to their accident liability, and much research has been carried out on "accident proneness" and on possible personality, cognitive and attitudinal correlates of accident liability (see Hale & Glendon, 1987; Hansen, 1988; Lawton & Parker, 1998; McKenna, 1983; Porter, 1989 for reviews). Not surprisingly, most investigators of individual differences in accident liability have employed retrospective designs, rather than the more expensive and time-consuming prospective, or longitudinal, designs. The use of retrospective designs severely limits the causal inferences that can be drawn from the results. Many such studies have examined correlations between accident involvement and some individual differences variable, although in both retrospective and prospective studies these correlations seldom exceed .40, and often account for less than 10% of the variation in accident rates. Nevertheless, the practical implications of even such small effects, provided that they can be replicated, should not be underestimated (Lawton & Parker, 1998). The evidence for individual differences in error proneness and, in particular, in accident liability, is now briefly outlined.

## 8.5.1 Accident proneness and differential accident involvement

Probably one of the best-known hypotheses concerning the causation of accidents is the notion of "accident proneness", stemming from some of the earliest work on industrial accidents carried out by the Industrial Fatigue Research Board in Britain during the First World War (Greenwood & Woods, 1918; Vernon, 1919). These researchers put forward three hypotheses concerning the distribution of accidents in a population exposed to equal risk: first, that the distribution was purely random; second, that having had one accident altered the probability of having a second, either increasing or decreasing it; and third, that some individuals are initially more likely to have accidents than others. The latter became known as the "accident proneness" hypothesis. It was further argued that, given certain assumptions, these three hypotheses could be portrayed by different statistical distributions which could be fitted to observed accident data. A number of studies of accident rate distributions were carried out, many of which provided some support for the accident proneness hypothesis, so that accident proneness gradually came to be regarded as a stable, unmodifiable characteristic of the individual (see McKenna, 1983; Porter, 1989).

The popularity of the accident proneness hypothesis has waxed and waned over the years. It is a truism that over any given period a few individuals will have many accidents, while many others working in the same job will have only a few, or none at all (see Cameron, 1975). Yet there has been considerable argument over the extent to which individuals in many studies of accident proneness can be regarded as being exposed to an equal risk of accident involvement. It is quite common in many industries for more experienced workers, who also tend to be older, to be assigned to more dangerous and hence higher risk jobs (see Davies, Matthews, & Wong, 1991). Moreover, as Hale and Glendon (1987) have pointed

out, there can be large and consistent differences in exposure to different types of risk even among individuals with the same job title. Relatively few studies of accident proneness conducted over long periods have been able to control adequately for both risk exposure and job experience. But some of those studies that have able to do so provide clear evidence for stable individual differences in accident liability, and hence for a form of "accident proneness" (for example, Boyle, 1980; Shaw & Sichel, 1971). The results of other well-conducted studies, however, are somewhat more equivocal (for example, Cresswell & Froggatt, 1963). Furthermore, as Hale and Glendon (1987) also observe, the evidence for the transfer of accident liability differences across different work tasks or different working environments is quite weak, so that accident proneness would appear to be largely task specific. A similar point has been made by Porter (1989), who suggested that accident proneness is not an enduring characteristic of an individual, but arises from the temporary conjunction of personal predispositions, current circumstances and task demands. In view of the difficulties with the traditional concept of accident proneness, McKenna (1983) suggested that it should be replaced by the less historically loaded term "differential accident involvement".

Porter (1989; Porter & Corlett, 1989) developed a questionnaire (the Accident Proneness Questionnaire or APQ), to assess individual differences in the propensity for making motor slips and errors, thought to be related to differential accident involvement. The test–retest reliability of the APQ was very high ($r = 0.90$) over an 18-month period, suggesting that over this period at least "accident proneness" is a stable characteristic. Using the APQ, Porter and Corlett (1989) compared the performance of accident-prone and non-accident-prone individuals in a dual-task situation involving a computerised pursuit tracking task, paired with a blind reach task requiring the manual location of one of eight possible targets in response to a tone that had to be "decoded" to determine target location. Porter and Corlett found that the level of performance of accident-prone individuals on the tracking task was significantly worse than that of non-accident-prone individuals, both when the task was performed alone and in combination with the blind reach decoding task. In the dual-task situation, accident-prone individuals were also slightly slower on the decoding task, although they showed no impairment in accuracy.

## 8.5.2 Personality characteristics and accident involvement

Since it appears that some individuals are more likely to be involved in accidents than others, many attempts have been made to relate various personality characteristics to accident involvement, particularly traffic and occupational accidents (see Hansen, 1989 for a review). These include locus of control, extraversion, aggression, general social maladjustment, anxiety and neuroticism, and impulsivity (see Chapter 15 for a more extended discussion of personality and performance). Hansen concluded that there is ample evidence that locus of control is significantly related to accident involvement, with those individuals having an external, rather than an internal, locus of control incurring higher accident rates. In a meta-analysis of vehicular accident involvement, Arthur, Barrett and Alexander (1991) obtained a mean overall r of 0.20 for the locus of control/accident involvement relationship, although all the primary studies used in their meta-analysis used retrospective rather than prospective designs. In a subsequent study, Arthur and Doverspike (1992) used both a retrospective and a prospective design to assess the relation between locus of control and accident involvement. Although locus of control predicted "not-at-fault accidents", albeit modestly, (r = 0.16), it was a much less successful predictor of "at-fault" accidents and of the total number of accidents than was a measure of selective attention. Similarly, extraversion, aggression, impulsivity and social maladjustment have been consistently related to accident liability, although the interaction of these personality factors with situational factors is undoubtedly important in determining accident involvement (e.g. Mayer & Treat, 1977). Fewer studies have been conducted on anxiety and neuroticism in relation to accidents, but here too there are some indications of a relationship, with highly anxious or neurotic individuals being somewhat more likely to have higher accident rates.

However, Furnham and Saipe (1993) found that British drivers convicted of speeding or reckless driving had lower levels of neuroticism than did non-convicted drivers. But neuroticism does appear to be a stronger predictor of driver stress than does extraversion (Matthews, Dorn, & Glendon, 1991). Both Furnham and Saipe (1993) and Trimpop and Kircaldy (1997), in a study of young Canadian drivers, reported that convictions for moving violations and accident rates were significantly and positively related. However, in both studies, convictions and accident rates were predicted by different personality characteristics; sensation seeking, in particular, significantly predicted convictions but not accidents.

Lardent (1991) investigated differences between groups of US fighter pilots who had crashed, and those who had not and who were thus deemed to be "safe". He also examined the personality profiles of civil airline pilots and military (predominantly fighter) pilots, relative to the general population, using Cattell's 16 Personality Factor questionnaire (Cattell, Eber, & Tatsuoka, 1970). Lardent found that pilots in general are substantially different from the general population in terms of personality structure, with civil airline pilots also differing markedly from military pilots. He also reported that pilots who crashed were much more conscientious, substantially more trusting, naive and self-sufficient, and slightly more relaxed than those who did not. These five personality factors together accounted for 27% of the variance in "crashing".

While acknowledging that these results were somewhat unexpected, especially in the case of conscientiousness, Lardent suggested a possible interpretation. If conscientiousness is carried to extremes, perhaps because standards are set at an unrealistically high level, this may result in a lack of flexibility, and a failure to change a course of action when it would be appropriate, or even necessary, to do so. In contrast, however, a study of driving accident involvement in relation to conscientiousness, assessed by Costa and McCrae's five-factor measure of personality (Costa & McCrae, 1992), indicated that conscientiousness and accident involvement were inversely related (Arthur & Graziano, 1996), as might be intuitively expected.

Lardent also pointed out that fighter pilots see themselves as "loners" who belong to an elite group. They are fiercely loyal to other members of the group and very careful not to undermine group cohesion while remaining, at the individual level, extremely competitive, self-assured and achievement-oriented. Group norms foster co-operation, while individual characteristics engender competition, thereby creating conflict; pilots who crash may be more likely to emphasise individual characteristics over group norms.

### 8.5.3 Cognitive failure and accident involvement

Several studies have reported that measures of information processing and perceptual and cognitive functioning, especially measures of selective attention, are predictive of accident involvement (for example, Arthur, Barrett, & Alexander, 1991; Arthur, Barrett, & Doverspike, 1990; Kahneman, Ben-Ishai, & Lotan, 1973; Mihal & Barrett, 1976; North & Gopher, 1976; Owsley et al., 1991). Attempts have been made to develop self-report measures of information processing abilities, of which probably the best known is the 25-item Cognitive Failures Questionnaire or CFQ (Broadbent et al., 1982), which seems to be only weakly related to standard measures of intelligence and personality. Table 8.1 summarises some example items, relating to different types of error.

The CFQ has been held to index the efficiency of distributing attention over multiple inputs under stressful conditions (for example, Reason, 1988), so that high CFQ scorers may be relatively incapable of flexible attentional deployment in response to changing environmental demands. However, as Larson, Alderton, Neideffer and Underhill (1997) have pointed out, it is somewhat unclear whether the CFQ is assessing several different aspects of cognitive functioning, or whether there is a single dimension of cognitive failure. On the basis of a principal components analysis of the CFQ scores of 387 college students, Pollina, Greene, Tunick and Puckett (1992) concluded that the CFQ measured five different factors, labelled respectively as distractibility, misdirected actions, spatial/kinaesthetic memory, interpersonal intelligence, and memory for names. Matthews, Coyle

| TABLE 8.1 | |
|---|---|
| **Examples of cognitive failures on the CFQ (Broadbent et al., 1982).** | |
| **CFQ item** | **Type of failure** |
| Failure to notice signposts on the road | Perceptual |
| Failure to notice people speaking to you | Perceptual |
| Forgetting appointments | Memory |
| Forgetting where you put a book | Memory |
| Dropping things | Action |
| Bumping into people | Action |

Reprinted with permission from the *British Journal of Clinical Psychology*. © The British Psychological Society.

and Craig (1990) used four different procedures for determining the number of factors to be extracted from the CFQ responses of 475 students. They obtained four different outcomes, ranging from a one-factor to a nine-factor solution, though none of these solutions corresponds to that of Pollina et al. (1992). Matthews et al. (1990) concluded that the CFQ contains too few items to measure more than two clearly-defined factors, one being a general cognitive failure factor, while the other is a less important factor tapping the specific failure to remember people's names following an introduction. Finally, in the largest sample yet studied, Larson et al. (1997) conducted a principal components analysis of the CFQ responses of 2949 US Navy personnel and extracted three factors, although one was ill-defined and accounted for little variance. The remaining two factors were similar to those obtained by Matthews et al. (1990), a general cognitive failure factor and a factor concerned with the processing of people's names. What the CFQ would appear to be assessing, therefore, is a substantial general cognitive failure factor and a minor one related to memory for people's names.

A number of studies have also been carried out to examine the objective correlates of cognitive failure. While the relationship between cognitive failure scores and performance measures appears to be quite weak (see Reason, 1988; Wells & Matthews, 1994), workload measures suggest that the mental workload associated with task performance is perceived as greater for individuals obtaining high than for those obtaining low CFQ scores, even though performance scores may be much the same for the two groups (Grubb et al., 1994). High CFQ individuals would therefore seem to perceive themselves as expending more cognitive effort to achieve the same performance outcome.

There are also some indications that high CFQ individuals are more vulnerable to the effects of stress (see Reason, 1988). The CFQ relates more reliably to various measures of stress vulnerability and symptoms than to objective performance (Broadbent et al., 1982; Broadbent, Broadbent, & Jones, 1986). As further discussed in 15.3.2, the CFQ may to some degree index negative beliefs about the self, rather than objective vulnerability to error. Studies of related instruments, such as self-report memory questionnaires, also show poor validity (Herrman, 1982), which may demonstrate various limitations in people's ability to judge their cognitive efficiency and proneness to error (Rabbitt & Abson, 1990).

In a study of the relation between CFQ scores and driving accident involvement, Larson and Merritt (1991) asked US Navy recruits to indicate how often they had been cited for moving violations as well as the number of traffic accidents they had incurred. The results were highly consistent with objective data contained in US Navy personnel files. When extreme cases were excluded from the data analysis, Larson and Merritt found that those individuals who had been cited for causing traffic accidents had significantly higher CFQ scores than those who had not, although there was no reliable difference between high and low CFQ scorers in terms of the frequency with which they had been cited for moving violations. These findings were also replicated in a second study. Subsequently, in a later and more extensive study involving almost 3000 US Navy recruits (see above), Larson et al. (1997) reported that high CFQ scorers had a significantly higher incidence of composite mishaps, a category comprising one or more of the following three types of mishap: the number of citations for traffic accidents, the number of injury-caused hospitalisations, and the number of serious falls. Larson et al. also confirmed the relationship between handedness and accident rates hypothesized by Coren and Halpern (1991; but see Harris, 1993), with left-handers being significantly more likely to be involved in an accident. Larson et al. (1997) found that left-handers also obtained significantly higher CFQ scores than did mixed- or right-handers, and suggested that cognitive failure might mediate the relationship between handedness and accident involvement.

## 8.6 CONCLUSIONS

Automation is being employed increasingly in complex systems, probably adding to mental workload, or at least not reducing it, and probably also expanding the opportunities for human error. The successful operation of such systems requires the formation of adequate mental models of system dynamics, and a high level of situation awareness. Taxonomies of human error have been derived from information-processing approaches to human performance, as well as from Rasmussen's (1983) distinction between skill- rule-, and knowledge-based behaviour. In most jobs, skill-based errors (slips and lapses) are the most common, although in some highly-skilled occupations, such as anaesthesiology, knowledge-based errors may predominate. Skill-based errors occur in highly familiar routine tasks, offer little time for correction or recovery, and can occur at any time. Rule- or knowledge-based errors are categorised as mistakes, and largely comprise errors of planning or judgement. Reason's (1990) taxonomy of unsafe acts, in addition to slips, lapses and mistakes, also includes "violations", a category of deliberately unsafe actions which are probably linked to social and motivational factors. Aviation accidents, both major and minor, seem to be most frequently associated with mistakes, particularly decision or judgement errors, though violations are more likely to be associated with serious accidents than with minor ones. Violations also predict self-reported road accident involvement. Reason (1995) has also distinguished between active failures, which are errors or violations made by system operators, and latent failures, which are due to an organisation's safety culture.

Accident risk varies with time of day, and there have also been a number of attempts to link personality and cognitive factors to accident involvement. The traditional notion of "accident proneness" has almost certainly outlived its usefulness, although there do appear to be reliable individual differences in accident liability. However, such differences are likely to be specific to a particular job or work environment, and do not seem to transfer to different work situations. A variety of both personality and cognitive factors, such as locus of control and cognitive failure,

have been shown to predict accident involvement, though at a modest level. Further studies investigating the relation between personality and situational factors in accident involvement would seem to be required.

## FURTHER READING

Reason's (1990) book, *Human error*, provides the most comprehensive account of human error. Norman's (1981) article on the categorisation of action slips has been influential, while his 1988 book, *The psychology of everyday things*, puts models of error into the context of everyday events. Rasmussen's error taxonomy is widely used in human factors research and practice. A special edition of the journal *Human Factors* (March, 1995) provides a critical evaluation of the situation awareness construct.

# 9

# Stress, arousal and performance: An introduction

## 9.1 INTRODUCTION

Stress is experienced in many different ways: as negative emotion, as disruption of behaviour and as ill-health, for example. Sometimes, stress may even be challenging and energising. Stress is also experienced over different timescales, ranging from transient reactions to noxious stimuli to the chronic stress reactions associated with persisting life difficulties such as unemployment. All these various aspects of stress are potentially relevant to performance, but experimental psychologists have tended to focus on acute stress induced by manipulations such as noise and sleep deprivation. Much of the research derives from a simple "stressor-strain" model in which an external stressor such as noise is imposed on the person. Performance under stress is compared with performance in a control condition (e.g. quiet), and any deficit is seen as an indicator of "strain" or suboptimal functioning. We will see that this conceptualisation is over-simplified. Furthermore, in real-world settings, outcomes of chronic stress such as ill health and absenteeism may be equally, or more important.

In this section of the book, we describe how states of stress influence performance. Like many psychological terms which have passed into everyday usage, "stress" is a vague and complex concept. Before looking at performance studies in detail, we consider definitions of stress, and theories that aim to provide a general account of stress effects on performance. Historically, interest in stress derived from studies of the relationship between subjective emotion and physiological systems, and in the first section of this chapter we trace the development of the stress concept from this starting point. In the next section, we introduce the concept of "arousal", which has been an important bridge between physiology and performance. We also consider various shortcomings of arousal theory, and discuss alternative approaches derived from cognitive psychology. Such approaches emphasise that a variety of different processing functions may be sensitive to stress. Studies of motivation and performance demonstrate the role of the person's active attempts to strive effortfully for successful performance. Recent work on stress also takes into account the person's strategies for coping with adverse effects of stress-inducing agents.

## 9.2 STRESS AND AROUSAL

### 9.2.1 Psychobiological approaches

It has been recognised since antiquity that there is a close relationship between physiological and emotional reactions. We are all familiar with the physical sensations that often accompany states of high anxiety, such as racing heart, perspiration, muscle tension and gastric disturbances. There are two traditional approaches to explaining the correlation between physiology and emotion. The *centralist* approach, shown in Fig. 9.1 (a), is to suppose that both types of reaction are expressions of central brain systems. Walter B. Cannon (1927) proposed that the thalamus was the key brain structure that simultaneously caused both emotion and physiological response, although contemporary research does not assign any special significance to the thalamus. The term "stress" was popularised by Hans Selye (1976) who described a series of stages of physiological and concurrent reactions to noxious events that might be prolonged over periods of months or years. Selye suggested a "hypothalamic–pituitary axis" was the key brain system for these long-term reactions. Contemporary psychobiologists, such as Gray (1987) and LeDoux (1996), have described a variety of brain systems that may drive emotional experience. Gray (1987) differentiates several functional systems, each of which controls a particular type of behaviour and generates particular emotions. For example, the "Behavioural Inhibition System" is responsible for reorienting attention to novel or potentially threatening stimuli, and generates anxiety as one of its outputs.

The traditional alternatives to centralist theories are described as *peripheralist*, and are more "psychological" in character. William James proposed that the immediate consequence of emotionally significant stimulation is to initiate somatic and muscular responses. Subjective emotion results from perception of these responses—see Fig. 9.1 (b). Thus, turning everyday logic on its head, we feel sad because we perceive ourselves crying, rather than crying because we feel sad. More recently, the role of cognitive processing of peripheral responses was demonstrated by Schachter and Singer (1962). They injected volunteers with adrenaline, causing physiological symptoms such as increased heart rate, but showed that emotional change depended on the person's use of cues provided by the testing environment to "decide" which emotion was appropriate to the situation.

### 9.2.2 Transactional stress theory

Neither the peripheralist nor the centralist view has proved entirely satisfactory. There is still a thriving area of research on central bases for emotion, exemplified by recent animal work suggesting that the amygdala may operate as an "emotional computer" (LeDoux, 1996). Work also continues on the cognitive attributions people attach to physiological excitation (Winton, 1990), although there have been difficulties replicating and generalising the original Schachter and Singer study (e.g. Marshall & Zimbardo, 1979). However, it is difficult to explain the full range of human emotional response in terms of either animal models or cognitions of physiological symptoms. Contemporary cognitive models of stress tend to reject the traditional approaches to emotion as being over-simplistic (Matthews, 2000a). Instead, emotional disturbance and other symptoms of stress are seen as the outcome of an interaction or transaction between person and environment which develops and unfolds over time (Cox & Ferguson, 1991; Lazarus & Folkman, 1984; Lazarus, 1991). Specifically, stress reactions depend on the person's appraisals of environmental demands, and of their own competence in coping with those demands. A stressor is only stressful to the individual if it is appraised as likely to tax or exceed the person's coping skills (Lazarus & Folkman, 1984). Hence, stress is not a property of external stimuli, because appraisals of stimuli will vary across people and contexts. Likewise, stress is not simply a response, because it reflects a dynamic interaction between the person and environmental pressures. This view does not imply that emotion is necessarily the result of prolonged, conscious deliberation. It is likely that at least some of the appraisal processes involved are unconscious, and there may be several distinct processing systems involved. Van Reekum and Scherer (1997) describe how both automatic and

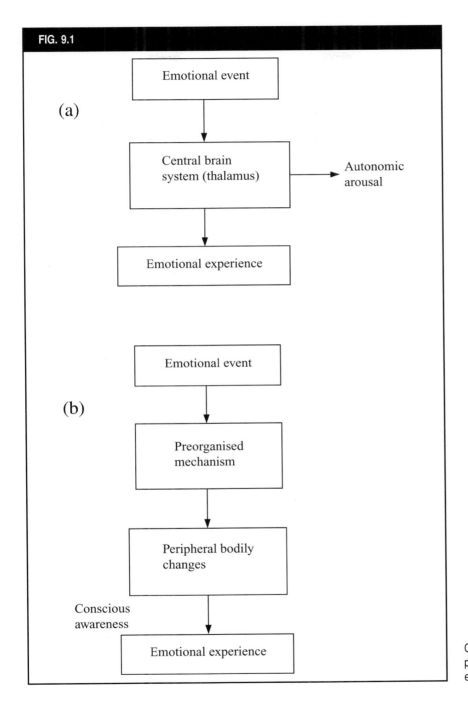

FIG. 9.1

(a)

Emotional event

Central brain
system (thalamus)

Autonomic
arousal

Emotional experience

(b)

Emotional event

Preorganised
mechanism

Peripheral bodily
changes

Conscious
awareness

Emotional experience

Centralist (a) and
peripheralist (b) views of
emotion.

controlled processing of inputs may contribute to emotional states.

## 9.3 AROUSAL THEORY AND THE YERKES-DODSON LAW

Traditionally, research on stress and performance has used a relatively simple version of centralism, *arousal theory*, as the basis for explaining performance change. Broadly, arousal refers to the person's overall state or level of activity. The activity continuum can be defined in various ways (see Fig. 9.2), including:

1. gross behavioural states such as sleep and wakefulness;
2. subjective emotion and alertness;
3. the changing pattern of waveforms evident in the electroencephalogram (EEG) as behavioural state changes; and
4. indicators of peripheral nervous system activity such as heart rate and skin conductance.

Brain circuits linking the cerebral cortex to structures in the brain-stem, such as the reticular formation, are seen as the primary influence on these various manifestations of arousal level.

The arousal theory of performance (Duffy, 1962), sometimes referred to as the Yerkes-Dodson

**FIG. 9.2**

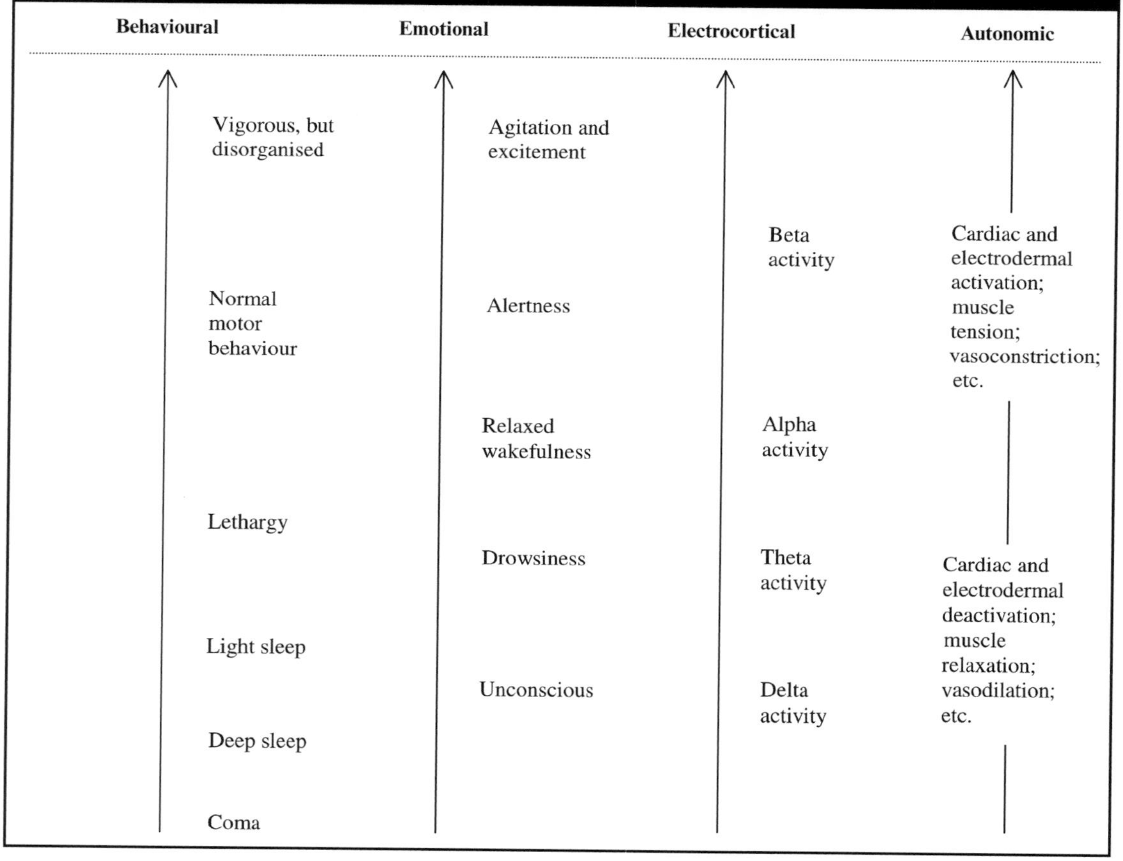

| Behavioural | Emotional | Electrocortical | Autonomic |
|---|---|---|---|
| Vigorous, but disorganised | Agitation and excitement | | |
| | | Beta activity | Cardiac and electrodermal activation; muscle tension; vasoconstriction; etc. |
| Normal motor behaviour | Alertness | | |
| | Relaxed wakefulness | Alpha activity | |
| Lethargy | | | |
| | Drowsiness | Theta activity | Cardiac and electrodermal deactivation; muscle relaxation; vasodilation; etc. |
| Light sleep | | | |
| | Unconscious | Delta activity | |
| Deep sleep | | | |
| Coma | | | |

Four ways of defining the arousal continuum.

Law (Broadhurst, 1957; Yerkes & Dodson, 1908), makes two principal statements. First, as shown in Fig. 9.3, the relationship between arousal level and performance may be expressed as an inverted-U curve. The cortex functions most efficiently at moderate levels of arousal, when the person is alert and wakeful, but not highly excited or agitated. The level of arousal at which performance is maximal is the *optimal level* of arousal for performance. Second, the optimal level of arousal for performance is inversely related to task difficulty. The more difficult the task, the lower the ideal arousal level for performance. It may be assumed that stress influences arousal, which in turn influences performance. Stress-inducing agents, or stressors, which raise arousal may then be grouped together as having similar effects. Commonly-used arousing agents include noise,

incentive and stimulant drugs such as nicotine and caffeine. Although performing under incentive, for example, is not necessarily unpleasant or "stressful", it is conventional to refer to all such influences as stressors. Similarly, dearousing stressors such as sleep deprivation and sedative drugs should have similar effects on performance.

### 9.3.1 Developing arousal theory: Methods and explanations

The simplicity of the Yerkes-Dodson Law belies a chequered history. In its original form, it concerned motivation ("drive") rather than arousal per se. Yerkes and Dodson (1908) demonstrated inverted-U relationships between strength of electric shock (a motivating factor) and speed of learning. In more recent times, the continuum of electrocortical states apparent in the EEG was seen

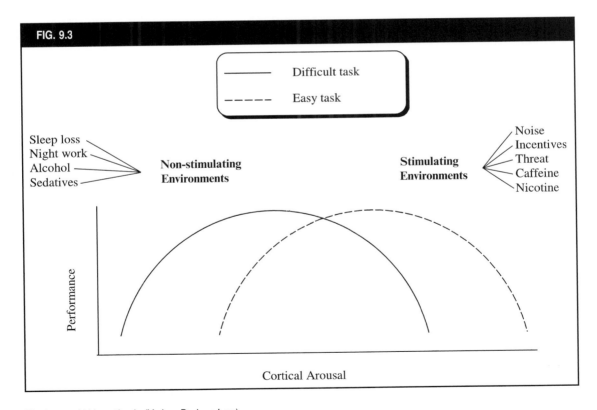

The inverted-U hypothesis (Yerkes-Dodson Law).

as the primary expression of arousal (e.g. Duffy, 1962). Subsequently, however, many performance psychologists became disillusioned by difficulties in measuring arousal reliably and validly using psychophysiological techniques, and sought a purely behavioural definition of arousal.

Broadbent (1971) rejected what has been called the "albatross of psychophysiology" (Davies & Parasuraman, 1982), and suggested arousal effects might best be investigated through studying the interactions between stressors. The simplest application of the method is to test whether two noxious agents impair performance in additive or interactive fashion when combined. Broadbent (1971) states that if the combined effect of the two agents is simply the sum of their effects when applied in isolation, it is likely that they influence separate mechanisms. However, if the combined effect is greater than the sum of the individual effects, it may be inferred that both agents impair the same underlying mechanism. Such an inter-active effect arises because the mechanism or processing function affected is likely to have a "safety margin" which provides some protection against performance impairment. The safety margin tends to reduce the impact of a single agent, but has no further protective effect when a second agent is applied. The method has been generalised to tests for interactions between any two stressors which might have facilitative as well as detrimental effects on performance.

The interaction technique has also been applied to testing the Yerkes-Dodson Law. Figure 9.4 illustrates Broadbent's explanation for interactive effects of noise and sleep deprivation on rate of errors committed during a continous reaction time task (Wilkinson, 1963). At first sight, the data are puzzling, in that noise is harmful to performance in control participants, undeprived of sleep, but beneficial to sleep-deprived participants. However, if the data are fitted to an inverted-U curve, the interaction may be explained. People deprived of sleep are under-aroused, so that subjecting them to noise, an arousing stressor, raises arousal to a level nearer to the optimum. Control participants are already close to the optimum, so the addition of noise to the testing environment makes them over-aroused, and performance deteriorates.

## 9.3.2 Attentional selectivity: An explanation for the inverted-U curve?

The Yerkes-Dodson Law is no more than a de-scription of the relationship between arousal and performance, and provides no explanation for *why* states of low and high arousal should im-pair performance. The most successful general explanation for the inverted-U curve has been Easterbrook's (1959) hypothesis that arousal is related to attentional selectivity. In Chapter 4, we saw that the focus of attention has been likened to a searchlight. In effect, the Easterbrook hypo-thesis states that the breadth of the searchlight decreases as level of arousal increases. When the person is low in arousal, the searchlight is broad, so that the person attends both to task stimuli and to additional, task-irrelevant stimuli such as the surrounding environment. As arousal increases, the focus of attention narrows so that task stimuli are still processed fully, but task-irrelevant stimuli are rejected, leading to optimal performance at moderate arousal levels. With further increases in arousal, the attentional focus becomes so narrow that some task-relevant stimuli are excluded from full attention, leading to performance impairment in states of high arousal. The Easterbrook (1959) hypothesis also explains the role of task diffi-culty in the Yerkes-Dodson Law, if it is assumed that difficult tasks require the person to attend to a wider range of stimuli or stimulus attributes. If so, difficult tasks require a broader focus of attention than easier tasks, and the focus of attention will narrow to the point of excluding task-relevant stimulus elements at a lower level of arousal when the task is difficult.

The Easterbrook (1959) hypothesis has been extensively tested using dual-task methods. Typic-ally, one task—the primary task—is designated as being the more important, and the other—the secondary task—as being less important. Other things being equal, the prediction is that arousal should improve performance of the primary task, but impair performance of the secondary task. Unfortunately, other things are not equal, in that some stressors have broadly facilitative effects on attentional task performance, whereas others tend to impair performance. However, reviews of re-search of this kind (Eysenck, 1982; Hockey, 1984)

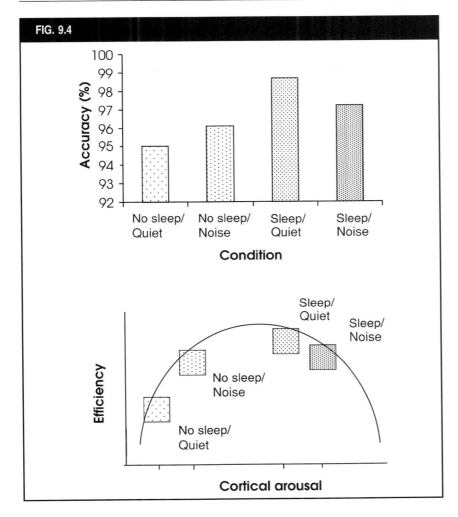

**FIG. 9.4**

Arousal theory explanation for an interactive effect of sleep deprivation and noise on performance.

show that arousing stressors typically have a *relatively* more facilitative effect on primary than on secondary task performance. In the case of incentive, performance effects are typically facilitative, so that incentive tends to improve primary task performance but, across studies, has rather inconsistent effects on secondary task performance. Conversely, anxiety tends to impair dual-task performance, so anxiety often degrades secondary task performance without having much effect on primary task performance. In addition, some studies have indicated that dearousing stressors, such as sleep deprivation, may be associated with increased breadth of attention, as the Easterbrook (1959) hypothesis predicts (Hockey, 1970).

Empirically, then, there is reasonable evidence that changes in arousal often, though not always, influence attentional selectivity. The more difficult question is whether this mechanism adequately explains the inverted-U curve. One problem is that the Easterbrook (1959) hypothesis, which predates the "cognitive revolution" of the 1960s and 1970s, is very vaguely specified by contemporary standards. As Eysenck (1982) points out, it is unclear whether arousal automatically influences the priorities assigned to processing the various impinging stimuli, or whether attentional narrowing is a voluntary strategy. In the case of anxiety, for example, it seems plausible that the person might cope with potential performance impairment by deliberately focusing attention on the most important components of a task. A second problem is that it is unlikely that all tasks are affected by variation in attentional selectivity as Easterbrook (1959) assumes. For example, the processes that influence working memory operate after attentional selection has taken place, so that it is difficult for the Easterbrook hypothesis to explain stressor effects on tasks of this kind. Hence, the Easterbrook hypothesis is at best only a partial explanation for stressor effects on performance.

### 9.3.3 Shortcomings of the Yerkes-Dodson Law

The Yerkes-Dodson Law has been subjected to a sustained barrage of criticism for 20 years or more; an example, perhaps, of the transience of "Laws" in human experimental psychology. Matthews and Amelang (1993) identify four distinct types of criticism: psychometric, methodological, conceptual and empirical.

Psychometric criticisms concern failures to demonstrate that arousal may be measured reliably and validly. Several well-conducted studies show that the traditional indices of arousal, such as heart rate and skin conductance, often fail to correlate with one another (e.g. Fahrenberg, 1987). The simplest interpretation of the data is that there is no single underlying dimension of "arousal" to which they relate. However, the proponent of arousal theory can argue that the concept of arousal is satisfactory, but measures such as heart rate lack validity. It was considerations of this kind that led Broadbent (1971) to reject direct measurement of arousal in favour of purely behavioural studies, though it is questionable whether a theory in which the central construct cannot be measured is really satisfactory.

However, investigating arousal through stressor interactions as Broadbent (1971) advocated introduces various methodological problems. One such problem is the difficulty of falsifying the Yerkes-Dodson Law. As Hockey (1984) has demonstrated, it is relatively easy to fit typical interaction data to the inverted-U curve post hoc. A second problem is deciding whether or not a stressor is arousing (Matthews, 1985). For example, anxiety

is traditionally seen as an arousing agent but, empirically, relationships between anxiety scales and psychophysiological indices of cortical and autonomic arousal are inconsistent or altogether absent (Naveteur & Freixa i Baque, 1987; Zuckerman, 1991). Uncertainty about the status of stressors compounds the falsification problem, for obvious reasons. A further difficulty is that stressors may influence performance through mechanisms other than arousal. Näätänen (1973) suggests that many of the detrimental effects of stressors on performance should be attributed not to over-arousal, but to physical discomfort, which has a distracting effect.

A third source of difficulty is the conceptual status of arousal. It has become increasingly apparent that there a variety of somewhat independent brain systems that influence the visible signs of a person's arousal level. For example, both nicotine and amphetamine are associated with increased arousal, measured psychophysiologically. However, the two stimulant drugs influence different neurotransmitter systems; nicotine is a cholinergic agonist, whereas the arousing effects of amphetamine are due mainly to activity in dopamine pathways. The various systems sensitive to stimulants differ in their effects on behaviour and performance (Robbins, 1986). There have been several attempts to develop multi-dimensional arousal models (e.g. Vanderwolf & Robinson, 1981), but there is currently no consensus on which dimensions should be discriminated. In addition, there is often little basis for deciding which specific brain systems are affected by particular stressors. Even when we can relate a drug to a particular system, it may have additional effects on other systems, or the system most strongly affected may interact with others. Broadbent (1971) and Sanders (1990) have attempted to use the interaction method to discriminate multiple arousal systems from performance data. However, the complexity of the relevant data has tended to discourage general acceptance of such theories.

The final source of difficulty is empirical in that, despite its predictive weakness, there are a variety of instances of data inconsistent with the Yerkes-Dodson Law (e.g. Neiss, 1988). A general difficulty is that effects of extremes of arousal are often weaker than expected. Idzikowski and Baddeley's (1983) review of the highly-arousing effects of fear and dangerous environments on performance shows that effects are elusive and inconsistent. At the other extreme, sleep deprivation may have little effect on performance, even on complex tasks, if the person is sufficiently motivated and interested (Johnson, 1982). Similar problems occur when arousal is measured directly. Matthews and Amelang (1993) tested the relationship between cortical arousal measured by the EEG and performance of a battery of tasks, and found that effects were weak and task-specific. There have also been difficulties arising from the stressor interaction method. For example, both noise and heat interact with time spent working on the task, but fail to interact with each other (Hancock & Pierce, 1985), implying that the assumptions on which the interaction method is based may not be valid.

## 9.4 PERSPECTIVES FROM COGNITIVE PSYCHOLOGY

The problems described have led a number of cognitive psychologists to reject the Yerkes-Dodson Law as the main basis for explaining stressor effects on performance (Eysenck, 1982; Hockey, 1984; Matthews, 1985). There are various cognitive theories of stress (see Wells & Matthews, 1994), but their common element is their differentiation of multiple processes contributing to stress reactions. For example, noise may simultaneously induce physiological arousal, impose distracting stimuli and change the person's perceptions of the task. Cognitive theorists seek to identify mechanisms of this kind, and to specify their basis in information processing. This section reviews two perspectives of this kind that respectively describe how stressor effects on subjective response and on objective performance depend on patterns of change of cognitive functions.

### 9.4.1 Patterns of subjective response

Cognitive models of stress (Lazarus & Folkman, 1984) state that stress reactions should be differentiated according to the nature of the challenge the person faces. According to Lazarus (1991), the personal meaning of the situation determines both the emotion experienced and tendencies towards action. This idea inspired a series of studies reported by Matthews et al. (1999b), using the Dundee Stress State Questionnaire (DSSQ) to sample emotional, motivational and cognitive responses. Stress might be experienced as negative emotion (e.g. tension), or as loss of motivation, or as disturbances of conscious cognition (e.g. intrusive thoughts). Factor analyses of the DSSQ discriminated ten dimensions of subjective stress, grouped together into three broader syndromes, summarised in Table 9.1. In states of low task disengagement, stress is experienced as tiredness, demotivation and poor concentration. Conversely, distress relates to negative emotion and cognitions of lack of personal control, and worry to intrusive thoughts ("cognitive interference"), self-consciousness and negative self-beliefs.

Experimental studies showed that the change in stress state induced by performing tasks varied with task demands. Performance of brief working memory tasks under time pressure produced

| TABLE 9.1 | | |
| --- | --- | --- |
| Three clusters of stress state symptoms (Matthews et al., 1999b). | | |
| **Task disengagement** | **Distress** | **Worry** |
| Lack of energy | Tense arousal | Self-focus of attention |
| Lack of motivation | Unhappiness | Low self-esteem |
| Poor concentration | Low confidence and control | Intrusive thoughts (task-related) Intrusive thoughts (personal concerns) |

not just distress, but also decreased worry and increased task engagement (Matthews et al., 1999b): the person seems to respond positively to the challenge. Conversely, vigilance tasks, which tend to be rather monotonous, provoke decreased task engagement. Prolonged driving elicits both distress and loss of task engagement, a finding that elucidates the nature of driver fatigue (Matthews et al., 1999a). Repeated failure on a simulated driving task elicited signs of both distress and worry. Matthews (2000a) proposes that, consistent with the transactional model, subjective response depends on the person's cognitions of task and environmental demands. Tasks appraised as overloading cognition provoke distress, whereas challenging tasks elicit task engagement. Worry seems to reflect the extent to which the task provokes evaluation of the self and personal goals.

These studies of subjective response conflict with traditional conceptions of stressor effects in several respects. First, subjective responses cannot be reduced to a single arousal dimension, although they may, in part, reflect brain systems (Thayer, 1989). Second, the individual's cognitions of the performance environment may often be critically important in determining stress response. Third, stress and performance are reciprocally linked. For example, performing a vigilance task leads to disengagement symptoms, such as tiredness, but disengagement seems to feed back into performance impairment (Matthews & Davies, 1998).

## 9.4.2 Patterns of performance change

Hockey's (1984) account of stress and cognition begins with a detailed critique of arousal theory.

He points out that, traditionally, researchers have used a narrow-band research strategy. That is, effects of a range of stressors are tested on a single task, such as the serial choice reaction time task used by Wilkinson (1963). The weakness of this approach is that the stressor effects observed may simply be a function of the somewhat arbitrary choice of task. The possibility that stressor effects vary across different tasks may be tested by adopting a broad-band approach, in which several tasks are selected for investigation. To counter the lack of explanatory power of arousal theory, it is important that each task represents a key aspect of information processing, so that the mechanisms for stressor effects may be identified. Research of this kind typically demonstrates a patterning of change resulting from stress manipulations. Some aspects of performance may improve whereas others deteriorate or are unaffected.

Figure 9.5 shows a part of Hockey's (1984) summary of stressor effects on four key performance indicators; the first column indicates whether the stressor is considered to be arousing. Each row indicates the cognitive patterning associated with a given stressor; the differences in patterning between each nominally arousing stressor are striking. Each column indicates how the various stressors affect a given performance indicator. Inspection of the columns shows that whether a stressor is arousing or de-arousing is a fair indication of its effects on attentional selectivity (especially for arousing stressors). However, other aspects of performance change, such as STM, do not seem to relate to arousal at all. In general, the data suggest that each stressor provokes a

| | | | Fast Responding | | |
|---|---|---|---|---|---|
| **FIG. 9.5** | **General Alertness** | **Attentional Selectivity** | **Speed** | **Accuracy** | **STM Capacity** |
| Noise | + | + | 0 | − | − |
| Amphetamine | + | + | + | − | ? |
| Incentive | + | + | + | − | + |
| Alcohol | − | +? | − | + | − |
| Sleeplessness | − | − | − | − | 0 |
| Prolonged work | − | +? | − | − | − |

A part of Hockey's (1984) summary of stressor effects on performance indicators (+ = positive effect; 0 = no effect; − = negative effect).

complex set of changes in several information-processing functions, and it is unlikely that any single "mega-theory" purporting to explain all effects is likely to be successful. It is better to adopt the more modest research aim of attempting to develop adequate theories of individual stressors, whose effects are likely to be sufficiently complex to test the researcher's powers of theory-building.

Hockey's (1984) review of the data provides a salutary warning against over-ambitious theories. However, cognitive approaches risk losing all theoretical content in a welter of ever-accumulating data. It can easily be argued that Hockey's classification of stressors and tasks is too coarse-grained to capture the empirical findings adequately. For example, Hockey (1984) treats "noise" as a single category but, as we shall see in Chapter 10, the cognitive patterning of noise effects may vary with qualities of the noise such as its predictability and informational content. Similarly, as Chapter 11 discusses, heat effects vary with the extent of disturbance of thermoregulation (Hancock, 1986). If the number of stressors may be multiplied indefinitely, so too may the number of task variables. Some categories of performance, and their associated theoretical constructs, such as dual-task performance and resource availability, are omitted altogether from Hockey's (1984) taxonomy. Other categories, notably STM, subsume a wide variety of specific processes (e.g. Baddeley, 1986) which may be differentially sensitive to stress. It is easy to see that the endpoint of the cognitive critique might be an exceptionally detailed description of stressor effects completely resistant to any attempt at explanation.

Fortunately, despite the complexity of the data, we need not abandon all attempts at theorising. A reasonable strategy is to attempt to identify cognitive mechanisms that contribute to a substantial number of the observed empirical effects. No single mechanism will explain all or even most of the effects, but we may be able to show that a mechanism contributes to the effects of a variety of stressors, and so is of some general significance. As previously discussed, most (but not all) stressors appear to influence attentional selectivity. A second example is overload of attentional capacity. This hypothesis is best known from anxiety research. Sarason, Sarason and Pierce (1990) propose that anxiety is associated with diversion of attentional resources from the task at hand to the processing of worries and intrusive thoughts, leading to performance impairment when the task is attentionally demanding. Resource depletion has also been used to explain detrimental effects of noise (Fisher, 1984a) and of breakdown in thermal regulation (Hancock, 1986). Of course, as in the case of attentional selectivity, there may be a variety of possible explanations for the stressor effects concerned, and careful experimental design is necessary to test resource hypotheses rigorously (see discussion of methodological problems of resource theory in 5.6.1). It may also be possible to group stressors on the basis of the subjective responses they induce. We might expect that stressors that increased distress or decreased task engagement would have common effects on performance (Matthews, 2000a).

## 9.5 MOTIVATION AND STRESS

### 9.5.1 Incentives and performance

As previously described, the Yerkes-Dodson Law was derived from studies of motivation in animals. However, the view of arousal as a general state that subsequently developed has rather obscured the role of motivation in stressor effects on performance. Conceptually, we can distinguish arousal from motivation with respect to the intensity and direction of behaviour. Arousal might be seen as amplifying the vigour of behaviour (Gray, 1987) without influencing the person's choice of activities. The two constructs are sometimes loosely compared to the accelerator and steering wheel of a car. In specific experiments, however, the distinction rapidly becomes blurred, as we shall see.

Perhaps the most clear-cut way to manipulate motivation is through providing people with rewards or incentives for performing well, such as a monetary payment. Motivation of this kind is sometimes referred to as "extrinsic motivation" to distinguish it from "intrinsic motivation" derived from interest in the task (Deci, 1975). Ensuring that monetary incentives are in fact motivating is not entirely straightforward (see Geen, 1995). The subject must have some expectancy that they can attain performance goals on the task: impossible tasks are demotivating irrespective of the rewards for success. Very high incentives may create anxiety and impair performance—the phenomenon of "choking under pressure" (Baumeister, 1984). There are also considerable individual differences in motivational response. People high in achievement motivation are generally more likely to be motivated when performing demanding tasks, so people low in achievement are actually more sensitive to external rewards (Harackiewicz & Manderlink, 1984). Personality factors such as extraversion–introversion may also influence susceptibility to incentives: several studies suggest extraverts learn better when rewarded for success, but introverts learn better when punished for failure (see Corr, Pickering, & Gray, 1995a).

Like any other stressor, incentives can be characterised in terms of a patterning of performance change (Hockey, 1984). Some of the key findings for effects of moderate incentives on typical laboratory tasks have been reviewed by Eysenck (1983). In fact, incentive effects are frequently beneficial, for both attentional and memory tasks, as we might expect if subjects simply apply more effort to the task. It has been claimed that incentives may increase attentional capacity (Fowler & Wilding, 1979). However, in dual-task performance, incentives have a more reliable facilitative effect on primary task performance than on secondary task performance, implying that incentives lead to greater selectivity of performance. Incentives may also impair certain types of problem-solving; the extrinsically motivated subject tends to be inflexible and lacking in insight (Condry, 1977). Intrinsic motivation may have more general benefits on performance (Condry, 1977).

Although incentives are normally motivating, they also tend to increase psychophysiological arousal. Broadbent (1971) conceptualised incentives as working through arousal, on the basis of interactions between incentives and other stressors. Increased attentional selectivity under incentive is also consistent with arousal theory, although it is possible that subjects appraise focusing on

the primary task as the strategy most likely to maximise reward. However, the case is not particularly compelling. Incentives do not just change arousal, but also change the way in which the person views the task, and their choice of strategy (see Eysenck, 1983). For example, under some circumstances incentives may suggest to the person that they are being controlled by the experimenter, with demotivating effects (Harackiewicz & Manderlink, 1984). So far, studies of incentives have not distinguished clearly between their consequences for arousal, and their consequences for cognitions about the task. There are also important differences between incentive effects and those of other arousing agents. For example, many arousers reliably reduce the vigilance decrement (see 6.3.4), but effects of external rewards on vigilance are unimpressive (Davies & Parasuraman, 1982).

### 9.5.2 Feedback and knowledge of results

Another manipulation commonly used in performance studies is knowledge of results (KR): feedback concerning the level of performance attained. At first sight, this might seem an informational rather than a motivational manipulation. In terms of the control theory conceptualisation of performance outlined in 2.5, adding extrinsic feedback to whatever intrinsic feedback cues are naturally present should enhance closed-loop control. Feedback assists the person in estimating the discrepancy between desired and actual performance. However, although feedback is likely to produce informational effects of this kind, studies of vigilance show that even false KR unrelated to actual performance often has beneficial effects on detection (Davies & Parasuraman, 1982; Warm, 1993). False KR is somewhat less effective than true KR, suggesting that the latter has both informational and motivational components. By analogy with incentive, it is sometimes suggested that KR may have arousing effects, but the evidence is circumstantial.

Feedback effects on vigilance are reasonably clearcut. However, as a recent review and meta-analysis shows, data from other tasks provides mixed results (Kluger & DeNisi, 1996). Their meta-analysis of 470 comparisons between feedback and no-feedback conditions from a large number of studies indicated that the average feedback intervention enhanced performance by about .4 standard deviations, but in 32% of cases feedback actually impaired performance. However, they included studies in which the feedback message was designed to be discouraging which, not surprisingly, tended to have a slight detrimental effect on performance. The meta-analysis shows also that feedback effects vary with task characteristics; memory tasks, for instance, seem particularly sensitive to feedback facilitation. Feedback effects were more beneficial for simple tasks than for complex tasks, in line with the suggestion that processing feedback signals when the task is novel and complex may divert resources away from the task (Kanfer & Ackerman, 1989).

### 9.5.3 Cognitive bases of motivation

Arousal may play a part in the effects of motivating manipulations, but contemporary motivational theory is largely cognitive in orientation. In the performance context, motivation is an intervening construct. We would like a theory of motivation to tell us how experimental manipulations, in conjunction with contextual and individual difference factors, influence motivation. We would also like the theory to specify how motivation influences performance. Motivation theorists have been primarily concerned with the first of these issues, and have tended to neglect how motivation effects may vary with information-processing demands of the task, the critical issue identified by Hockey's (1984) analysis of stress.

A detailed exposition of motivation theory is beyond the scope of this book (see Weiner, 1985, and Geen, 1995, for reviews). There is also a substantial literature on motivation and performance in occupational settings (see Kanfer, 1990, for a review). Here, picking up one of the themes of the transactional model of stress, we highlight the evaluations of personal *control* as a critical antecedent of motivation. It is often supposed that people have an innate need to master and manipulate their environments (White, 1959). Control also brings instrumental benefits, in that it permits the person to satisfy other motivations. The importance of control is demonstrated by the development of "learned helplessness" when the person's control is withdrawn experimentally (Seligman, 1975). Perceptions of control of outcomes may also elevate the intrinsic motivation of a task (Deci & Ryan, 1985). Control has emotional as well as motivational consequences. Experimental studies demonstrate that people experience unpleasant events such as electric shocks as less stressful when they can exert control over some aspects of the event, such as when it happens (Fisher, 1986). Control has been integrated into motivational theory through several additional cognitive constructs:

*Expectancy of success.* Beliefs that a goal is attainable tend to increase motivation. Bandura (1989) has developed the construct of *self-efficacy* (the person's beliefs that they can exert control over their surroundings), which is linked to more effective and more persistent performance (e.g. Cervone, 1989). Lack of perceived self-efficacy tends to generate negative cognitions and emotions that may interfere with successful performance (Bandura, 1989).

*Value of success.* Traditional motivational theories see motivation as the product of expectancy of success and the value placed upon success (e.g. Atkinson, 1974), although expectancy-value theory is now seen as somewhat simplistic (Geen, 1995). Incentive manipulations influence the value of success directly. More subtly, people may value tasks that tell the person about their capabilities for controlling the environment; people high in achievement motivation may especially prefer tasks (typically of moderate difficulty) which are diagnostic of their abilities (Trope, 1975).

*Causal attributions.* Contemporary learned helplessness theory emphasises the importance of the person's causal explanations for the outcomes of events. Depression results when people attribute negative events to internal, stable and global causes such as a basic lack of self-worth (Peterson & Seligman, 1984). Achievement motivation may also be related to causal attributions, such as attributing success to personal ability rather than to luck (Weiner, 1985).

*Goal-setting.* Choosing a difficult, but attainable, goal seems to be motivating. There is considerable evidence from both laboratory and occupational studies that performance is enhanced when people are given difficult but specific goals (Latham & Locke, 1991). Beneficial effects of incentives may operate both through people setting themselves higher goals and through greater commitment to meeting those goals.

### 9.5.4 Information-processing mechanisms for motivational effects

Task motivation may be the outcome of quite complex cognitive processes. Arousal may play some role, but possibly an indirect one. For example, perceptions of arousal, through awareness of heart rate and so forth, may reduce self-efficacy (Felz & Mugno, 1983). The second issue identified above is the relationship between motivation and performance. Common sense suggests that motivation is likely to be beneficial, but a satisfactory theory requires specification of the mechanisms that link motivational constructs to information processing. Neglect of this issue has limited the impact of motivational research on performance psychology, but some progress has been made in recent years. An important construct is the level of effort applied to the task. Effort may be seen as a transient state of goal commitment which entails tolerance of discomfort in striving to attain the goal the person has set. However, the interface between this knowledge-level construct and information processing is far from clear. Attempts to identify effort with arousal and resource availability (e.g. Kahneman, 1973) are over-simplified. Broadly, effort may have two qualitatively different effects: (1) general enhancement of at least some types of processing, and (2) more effective use of strategies: "working smarter" as opposed to working harder.

Kluger and DeNisi (1996), in their review of feedback effects, distinguish three possible mechanisms generally relevant to incentive and motivation studies:

1. *Task-motivation processes*. Homeostatic processes may operate to determine the level of effort the person deems necessary to attain success, provided that increased effort is perceived as influencing performance.

2. *Task-learning processes*. The person may actively search for new task strategies, especially when simple effort-regulation fails to maintain performance to the desired standard. The performance consequences depend on the novelty and duration of the task. For example, experimenting with new strategies for a well-learned task may disrupt existing proceduralised knowledge.

3. *Meta-task processes*. Theories of self-regulation (e.g. Carver & Scheier, 1990; Wells & Matthews, 1994) propose that people monitor their attainment of goals such as maintaining self-esteem, a process that requires the engagement of specific processes and attentional resources. Motivational signals may divert attention from the task to these meta-task processes, as the person evaluates the self-relevance of their performance and its context (as also discussed by the transactional model of stress). This process tends to be detrimental, especially when the task is demanding, as a resource hypothesis would predict. We shall return to processes of this kind in the context of anxiety (see 14.3) although, as Kluger and DeNisi point out, even positive feedback may impair demanding tasks if it engages self-focused processing.

## 9.6 STRESS AND THE ACTIVE CONTROL OF PERFORMANCE

Implicit in much cognitive research is a model of processing as comprising a collection of independent processing functions. A given stressor may be seen as affecting the efficiency of operation of a subset of these functions. However, studies of motivation present a much more active picture of the performer, as someone who evaluates the task and its personal significance, sets goals for performance and, if goal-committed, strives to attain them through effort and strategy. Active control is also important for performance change under unpleasant stressors. Control processes are demonstrated by evidence from three rather different research areas: the psychobiology of stress reactions, "transactional" models of stress, and cognitive psychological theoretical analyses of stress and performance.

Mulder (1986) reviews a variety of physiological indices of compensatory control: increased muscle tension, suppression of certain components of cardiac output, and release into the bloodstream of catecholamines, such as adrenaline. These physiological changes accompany efforts to compensate for potentially detrimental stress states through increased activity or effort. For example, secretion of adrenaline appears to be associated with better performance in stressful conditions (Frankenhaeuser, 1986). It appears that central brain systems may provide a biological substrate for adaptive cognitive responses to stress.

### 9.6.1 Coping strategies and performance

The transactional models of stress introduced in 9.2.2 discriminate various styles of coping with environmental demands (Endler & Parker, 1990). Coping may involve active efforts to regulate the external situation (problem- or task-focused coping) or somewhat less effortful responses such as rethinking one's attitude to the potential stressor (emotion-focused coping) or trying to avoid it altogether. In performance contexts, coping style may influence efficiency and style of response, with problem-focused coping tending to have more beneficial effects (Matthews & Wells, 1996). For example, loud uncontrollable noise has after-effects, in that quality of performance is impaired even after the noise is switched off (see 10.4). People also show less persistence on difficult problems, implying that noise exposure reduces use of effortful, task-focused strategies (Cohen, 1980). Similarly, using a vigilance task, Griffin, Warm and Dember (1986) showed that depressed individuals appear to be reluctant to modify strategy in response to probability information, a particular instance of a more general passivity (Johnson & Magaro, 1987). Use of active coping strategies may be accompanied by the physiological changes described above (Steptoe, 1991), although there is some debate over whether physiological or cognitive mechanisms are of primary causal importance (Wells & Matthews, 1994). Active coping also relates to the subjective task engagement response (Matthews, 2000a).

Emotion-focused coping may influence performance both directly and indirectly (Matthews & Wells, 1996). It is also linked to subjective distress (Matthews, 2000a). Hockey (1997) describes how stressed individuals may lower their standards for adequate performance, so that a lowered level of performance is judged acceptable: strategy change is a direct outcome of choice of coping. Strategies of this kind may also be described as "avoidance", such that the person deals with the problem by mentally withdrawing from it. Matthews and Campbell (1998) showed that avoidance related to poorer performance on a rapid information processing task, requiring detection of digit sequences, and in simulated driving. In addition, emotion-focused coping may generate worries or self-focused processing which interfere with processing of task stimuli more indirectly (see 15.3). Inducing the emotion-focused strategy of evaluating one's own performance experimentally leads to reduced performance efficiency and persistence (Kanfer & Stevenson, 1985).

### 9.6.2 Modes of compensatory control

Another approach to compensatory control is provided by cognitive theories which have developed Broadbent's (1971) idea that the processing system has some capacity to protect itself against performance decrement. Hockey (1986) proposes that information processing may operate in a variety of control modes which determine both performance and subjective state. In "appropriate" mode the person is able to compensate for any threats to performance through effort and active control. However, if demands are particularly high, so that compensation is no longer sufficient, the person will perform in "overload" mode, characterised by performance impairment and feelings of pressure and panic. In "fatigue" mode, the person may fail to apply much compensatory effort at all, leading to passivity and performance decrement, as discussed further in 12.2. These modes might be linked to distress and task disengagement, respectively (Matthews et al., 1999b). Hockey distinguishes various other modes in terms of the level and direction of effort. One of the consequences of active control is that stressor effects on performance of single tasks may be relatively weak.

More sensitive indices of stressor effects may include psychophysiological and subjective symptoms of compensatory effort, strategy change, and after-effects of performance under stress (Hockey, 1997). Similarly, Hancock and Warm (1989) propose that the person is often able to compensate adaptively for environmental stress and variation in processing demands, but adaptation may break down under conditions of both overload and "underload", as in a vigilance task in which events are rare. Psychological adaptation is more vulnerable to disruption than physiological adaptation.

Hence, stressors are unlikely to produce the same pattern of performance change in all individuals and in all testing contexts. It is important to take into account the person's appraisals of the task, and their strategies for dealing with the task and with sources of environmental stress. In the chapters which follow, we will encounter various instances of stressor effects on strategy which are likely to result from these active control processes.

## 9.7 CONCLUSIONS

We have seen that research on stress and performance has progressed considerably from its roots in centralist, psychobiological theories of emotional distress. The Yerkes-Dodson Law, which stimulated so much of the research in the 1950s and 1960s has fallen into some disfavour, though some researchers (e.g. Anderson, 1990) continue to see it as a useful unifying principle for interrelating different areas of psychology. At best, the Yerkes-Dodson Law provides a rough empirical guide to likely stressor effects. Extremes of arousal are, perhaps, statistically more likely to be associated with performance decrement than are intermediate levels of arousal. Difficult tasks may be somewhat more prone to detrimental effects of arousing stressors than are easy tasks, a prediction also made by resource theories of stressors such as anxiety and noise. There is general agreement that, irrespective of the descriptive value of the Yerkes-Dodson Law, it is necessary to distinguish between (1) different stressors, and (2) different processing functions. The complexity of the data does not favour development of general theories of stress and performance. However, a number of cognitive mechanisms which may generalise across several stressors and tasks have been identified, including changes in attentional selectivity, availability of attentional resources, and use of effortful coping strategies.

Within the general framework for cognitive science described in Chapter 1, all three levels of analysis are relevant to explaining stressor effects. Some "stressors", such as drugs, operate through affecting neural processes and, consequently, information processing. Arousal theory represents an attempt to explain *all* stressor effects through a mechanism of this kind. However, some stressor effects are best understood at the information processing level, through their effects on constructs such as resource availability and working memory capacity. In addition, the stimuli associated with the stressor may change the nature of the task. For example, noise entails extra, potentially distracting stimuli, which must be processed and may overload working memory or attention. Finally, recent work on motivation and coping emphasises the importance of the knowledge level: the person's goals in the performance context, and the strategies implemented to fulfill those goals. Often stressors may have effects best conceptualised at two or more levels. Effects of active control may be overlaid on more passive performance changes induced by biological mechanisms or informational input.

## FURTHER READING

The best sources for further reading are various edited books. Hockey (1983) and Smith and Jones (1992a) review the literature on a stressor-by-stressor basis: the latter book is the more comprehensive. Hockey et al. (1986) and Hancock and Desmond (2000) focus more on energetic issues, interrelating stress, fatigue and workload.

# 10

# Noise and irrelevant speech

## 10.1 INTRODUCTION

In this chapter we are primarily concerned with the effects of noise, especially loud noise, on human performance. Investigations of the effects of noise on behaviour have been conducted for several decades, beginning during the First World War, and there is now a substantial literature on noise effects both in laboratory situations, and in field settings such as the classroom and the workplace. Noise may be detrimental to performance for several reasons. First, it disrupts auditory perception. Exposure to high noise levels can impair hearing and make spoken communication difficult, if not impossible, to achieve (Ainsworth, 1985; Davies & Jones, 1982; Tempest, 1985). Second, the irrelevant information delivered by noisy environments may affect post-perceptual processing, perhaps reducing attentional resource availability or forcing greater selectivity of attention. Research conducted in the past 20 years or so shows that irrelevant speech of normal intensities influences performance of certain tasks (see Jones & Morris, 1992). Such distraction effects appear to have considerable practical and theoretical importance. Third, noise may have stress-related effects that are distinct from the more direct effects of noise on auditory information

processing. Noise may produce feelings of irritation and annoyance (Langdon, 1985), although there are marked individual differences in annoyance to specific noise sources (see Jones & Davies, 1984), and bring about changes in physiological state (Davies, 1968a, 1976). Noise is often defined as "unwanted sound", a definition that emphasises the role of emotional factors in response to noise.

The study of noise effects on performance is deceptively difficult. Noise can affect the efficiency of task performance, usually for the worse but occasionally for the better (Davies & Jones, 1985; Jones & Broadbent, 1987; Smith, 1989). However, measures of task performance under noise conditions, assessments of noise annoyance, and indices of physiological activity in noise, frequently show little or no agreement with one another. Individuals may not find a particular level of noise annoying, but their task performance may nevertheless be impaired. Conversely, they may find a particular noise level extremely annoying and yet their task performance may be unaffected. Similarly, noise may not influence performance but may alter physiological state, and performance may deteriorate in noise even though there are few detectable physiological changes.

There are also marked individual differences in response to noise. As discussed further in 10.3, this response varies with perceptions of noise, beliefs and attitudes towards noise, and the perceived degree of control over the noise source. These factors often appear to be more important determinants of annoyance than do the physical parameters of the noise. For example, it has often been reported that noise intensity may only account for about 25% of the variance in noise annoyance among individuals, whereas psychological factors, beliefs about and attitudes toward noise, may well account for about 50% of the variance (see Smith & Jones, 1992b). In the face of such difficulties one approach is to look for particularly sensitive tasks or performance measures, for which noise effects on performance broadly generalise across individuals. In the first part of this chapter a general overview of noise effects in laboratory and applied studies is given. Next, the evidence for specific mechanisms revealed by laboratory studies is discussed. In subsequent sections two of the factors which complicate interpretation of noise studies are discussed: after-effects of noise, and individual differences in susceptibility to noise. The final section of the chapter is concerned with the effects of irrelevant speech, a type of distraction that is frequently encountered in the working environment and which, as noted above, can disrupt performance considerably. Before considering the effects of noise on performance, the nature and measurement of noise stimuli are examined.

### 10.1.1 The measurement of noise

Sound is propagated by a pressure wave, moving outward from a vibrating object, through an elastic medium such as air. A simple sound wave, such as that arising from a tuning fork, can be represented by a sinusoidal or cyclical variation in pressure around ambient air pressure. It is generally described in terms of its frequency, amplitude and phase (the portion of the cycle through which the wave has progressed relative to some fixed starting point). Frequency refers to the number of complete variations or cycles that occur in one second, expressed in hertz (Hz), which gives rise to the sensation of pitch, while the amplitude of the wave corresponds to the intensity of the sound and gives rise to the sensation of loudness. The range of frequencies to which the ear is sensitive is known as the audible spectrum

and encompasses frequencies from approximately 20–20,000 Hz. But the human ear is differentially sensitive to sounds of different frequencies, as Fig. 10.1 shows. At very low frequencies, towards the lower end of the audible spectrum, sounds have to be perceived as much louder in order to be heard at all; that is, to reach the auditory threshold. At higher frequencies, however, auditory thresholds are much lower. Similarly, the range of intensities to which the human ear is sensitive is considerable. The ratio of the intensity of the loudest sound we can hear (the terminal threshold) to the intensity of the faintest sound we can detect (the absolute threshold) is enormous (of the order of several thousand billion to one). Sound intensity is therefore measured on a logarithmic scale, using the decibel (db) as the unit of measurement. The decibel scale represents the intensity or power ratio of a given sound relative to a reference level, usually bearing a strong relationship to the absolute threshold. The reference level is often expressed in terms of the pressure of the rms (root mean square) sound wave (most commonly 20 micropascals), so that intensity levels are expressed in terms of the sound pressure level (SPL), for example, 80 db (SPL). Each increase in intensity of 10 db, for example, an increase from 60–70 db (SPL), approximately doubles the subjective loudness of a sound.

The sounds which are typically heard in everyday life consist of pressure variations at a number of different frequencies. Because the ear is differentially sensitive to different frequencies, sound level meters used to measure noise intensities generally contain weighting networks that attempt to simulate the response of the human ear to sounds of different frequencies presented at different intensities. The A-weighted network simulates the response of the ear at low intensities, from 20 up to about 55 db (SPL), the B-weighted network simulates the response of the ear at moderate to high intensities, from 50 up to about 85 db (SPL), and the C-weighted network simulates the response of the ear at levels beyond 85 db (SPL). Of the three, the A-weighted network has been the most successful, in terms of the fidelity of simulation, and is the most frequently used (see Tempest, 1985). Table 10.1 gives the intensities

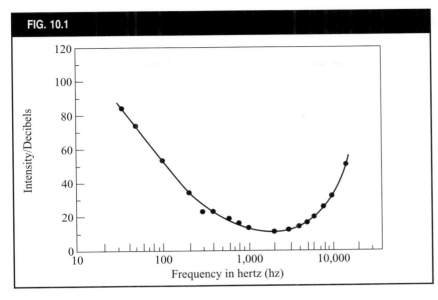

**FIG. 10.1**

The audibility threshold for a tone presented at different frequencies (modified from Wever, 1949).

| **TABLE 10.1** | |
|---|---|
| **Typical sound intensities for some commonly encountered sounds.** | |
| **Noise** | **Intensity (dbA)** |
| Large jet airliner | 140 |
| Large piston-engined airliner | 130 |
| Riveting on steel plate | 130 |
| Train on a steel bridge | 110 |
| Weaving shed | 100 |
| Pneumatic road drill at 30 m distance | 90 |
| Heavy road traffic at kerbside | 85 |
| Dining room | 80 |
| Male speech at 1 m distance | 75 |
| Typing office with acoustic ceiling | 75 |
| Light road traffic at kerbside | 55 |

of some commonly encountered noises in terms of dbA. Noises can vary in duration, as well as in intensity. They can be continuous or intermittent and intermittent noises may be repeated quickly or slowly at regular (periodic) or irregular (aperiodic) intervals. Very brief noises, such as a single gunshot, or the repeated "thuds" made by a mechanical hammer, are referred to as impulsive or impact noise. Intense noise of any kind can impair hearing, either temporarily or permanently.

Permanent hearing loss can result from repeated exposure during the working day to high noise levels (85 dbA and above) over a period of several years, or from a single very brief exposure if the noise level is sufficiently high (see Tempest, 1985). Prolonged exposure to loud noise can produce irreversible damage to the hair cells in the cochlea, the sensory receptors for hearing, while very loud sounds can rupture the eardrum. Occupational hearing loss follows a predictable sequence: there is initially a small loss in the frequency range of 3000–6000 Hz, followed by a greater loss peaking at around 4000 Hz, which interferes with the comprehension of speech. Hearing loss is also associated with the ageing process (see Chapter 16), a condition known as presbycusis, and presbycusis correction factors have sometimes been employed to assess hearing impairments attributable to noise exposure (see, for example, Corso, 1980). In the attempt to mitigate the effects of occupational noise exposure, various national standards with respect to noise exposure limits have been established (Hay, 1975; Shaikh, 1999).

## 10.2 NOISE AND PERFORMANCE

### 10.2.1 An overview of noise effects

As Hockey (1984) has observed, it is now fairly simple to demonstrate that noise can affect task performance. Yet up until the early 1950s there was considerable doubt as to whether noise exerted any significant effect on performance at all, as early American reviews of the effects of noise on behaviour attest (see, for example, Berrien, 1946; Kryter, 1950). The most common view of the influence of noise on behaviour around 1950 was that even loud noise had not been shown to exert any effect on work performance of any practical significance. But by the end of the Second World War new tasks, which psychologists had not previously considered, had become available for the investigation of human performance. Many such tasks simulated actual military activities, for example, the job of the aircraft pilot or the airborne radar operator. During the 1950s performance at several of these tasks under conditions of loud noise was investigated by psychologists working in both civilian and military settings. The main features of these tasks were that they involved sustained attention, performance without a break, and lasted for a relatively long time, usually at least half an hour. Examples are vigilance, tracking and serial reaction tasks.

Noise was assumed to act as a distracting agent which increased the number of "internal blinks", whereby attention was diverted away from the task being performed (Broadbent, 1958). The internal blink was seen as a brief failure of the selective filter, described in 2.2.2. The incidence of internal blinks was presumed to increase as a function of time at work. Hence noise would only affect the overall level of performance in tasks of long duration, due to poorer performance towards the end of the task resulting from the accumulation of fatigue. Broadbent's interpretation of the effects of noise in terms of distraction was later challenged by Poulton (1978, 1979), who suggested that loud noise impaired performance by masking helpful cues from the task being performed, which provided feedback concerning the accuracy

of performance. These approaches are further discussed below.

During the 1960s a number of studies, mainly using vigilance and serial reaction tasks, made detailed comparisons of the effects on performance of noise and other stressors. In 9.3, we described how the "arousal theory of stress" (Broadbent, 1963, 1971), based on the Yerkes-Dodson Law, was developed from studies of this kind. One of the basic predictions is that noise should tend to impair performance in the presence of arousing agents such as environmental warmth or incentives, but should act to offset the detrimental influence of dearousing factors such as sleep deprivation. White noise, as a continuous stimulus, has been seen as a relatively pure arousing agent, without the potential for distraction of intermittent noise bursts. However, because interactions between noise and other agents are not entirely consistent with arousal theory (see Hockey & Hamilton, 1983), the uni-dimensional arousal model has been to some extent supplanted by the multi-dimensional "variable state" approach proposed by Hockey (1984), discussed in 9.4. Noise has been one of the major foci for attempts to develop detailed maps of the patterns of state change associated with specific stressors, by examining performance change in a wide range of task situations. Mapping the noise state entails investigating the nature of information processing in conditions of loud noise and the kinds of strategies adopted by observers to counteract the influence of noise (see, for example, Jones, 1984; Smith & Jones, 1992b).

Noise also affects task strategy. In perceptual-motor tasks, such as serial responding, speeded classification (where cards bearing different symbols have to be sorted into different piles) or proofreading, noise alters the speed–accuracy trade-off in favour of speed. People work faster but make more errors. This effect is sometimes attributed to an increase in arousal level and, indeed, is sometimes more apparent in the afternoon or evening, when arousal levels tend to be higher (see Colquhoun, 1971). Equally, however, it might reflect the disruption of control processes for regulating speed–accuracy trade-off (see Jones, 1984; Rabbitt, 1979). Noise may also affect strategies for allocating attention across multiple tasks and for retaining information in short-term memory (Eysenck, 1982). Finally, noise not only affects performance while it is present, but also after it has ceased, and there is a sizeable literature concerned with the after-effects of working in loud noise, stimulated by the original studies of Glass and Singer (1972). Possible explanations for such after-effects have been reviewed by Cohen (1980) and Cohen & Spacapan (1978).

## 10.2.2 Effects of noise in the workplace

Many of the early studies of the effects of noise on performance were conducted in the workplace, although a major disadvantage of industrial studies of noise is the lack of control over other features of the working environment which may also influence accident rates or productivity. For example, factory departments in which noise levels are high are more likely to contain potentially dangerous machinery than are departments where noise levels are lower. Any variation in accident rates between noisy and quiet factory departments could thus be attributed as much to differences in the type of machinery as to differences in the noise levels they emit. Moreover, intervention studies, in which prevailing noise levels are altered and performance is examined before and after the change, may also raise morale, leading to improvements in productivity.

A number of early studies in the weaving industry demonstrated that the effects of noise on productivity could be quite substantial. Weston and Adams (1932, 1935) compared productivity levels over a six-month period when workers were wearing ear defenders and when they were not, ear defenders being worn on alternate weeks. Ear defenders attenuated noise levels by 15 db (SPL) and productivity was around 12% higher when they were worn. Moreover, this improvement in productivity was not attributable to workers" beliefs about the efficacy of ear protection devices since output improved significantly among workers who did not like wearing ear defenders and considered them to be of little value in protecting hearing.

In a similar study, Broadbent and Little (1960) examined the effects of reducing noise levels, from 98 db (SPL) to 88 db (SPL), on productivity in workers engaged on the perforation of cinefilm. The factory had embarked on a noise reduction programme and it was possible to compare the rate of work and the incidence of errors in the same workers at work stations which had been acoustically treated to reduce noise levels and at those which had not. Care was taken to ensure that workers were moved in a systematic fashion from one work station to another. Broadbent and Little found that work rates were much the same at both noise levels, but that errors, such as broken rolls of film or equipment shutdowns, were more likely to occur at the higher noise level. Noweir (1984), in a study of the work behaviour of over 2000 Egyptian textile workers in three different textile mills, also found that noise levels in excess of 90 db reduced the quality of work, with workers operating in high noise levels damaging material more often than workers operating at low noise levels. Compared to noise levels of below 90 db, Noweir also found that noise levels above 90 db were associated with a higher frequency of disciplinary actions for material damage, with reductions in productivity and with increases in absenteeism.

The finding that loud noise increases errors is supported by retrospective studies of accident statistics in the workplace. Kerr (1950) showed that the average ambient noise level in a factory department was the second most powerful of around 40 work-related factors in predicting accident frequency among employees in an electronics company, although noise level was a less powerful predictor of accident severity. Cohen (1974) found that people who worked in high noise areas (at or above 95 dbA) of a factory manufacturing boilers experienced more accidents than did those working in low noise areas (80 dbA or below). Among workers in the high noise group, 35% incurred 15 or more injuries over the five-year period of the study, while only 5% of the low noise group had a comparable injury rate. Young and inexperienced workers had the highest accident rates in the high noise areas and, to a lesser extent, in the low noise areas too. Cohen (1976) also conducted an intervention study of the effects of noise on accidents, the results of which are shown in Fig. 10.2.

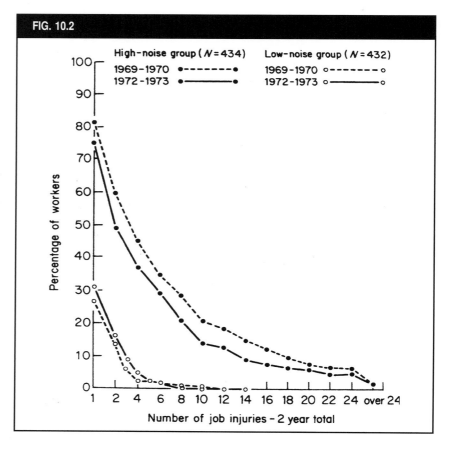

**FIG. 10.2**

Cumulative percentage frequency distribution for high and low noise exposure in two sampling periods (1969–1970 and 1972–1973). The points represent the proportions of workers who had received injuries in excess of the value given by the abscissa. From Cohen (1976). In A.P. Smith & D.M. Jones (Eds.), Handbook of human performance. Volume 1: The physical environment. Academic Press. Reprinted with permission.

Figure 10.2 shows injury rate data for over 400 workers in high noise areas for two-year periods both before and after the introduction of a hearing conservation programme. As Fig. 10.2 indicates, there was a significant reduction in injury rates for workers in high noise areas following the adoption of hearing protectors, but no change occurred for workers in low noise areas. But since similar improvements were observed both in workers who used hearing protectors regularly and in those who did not, it seems likely that other factors than noise reduction may have been implicated in the decrease in injury rates.

Noise effects on performance in the workplace appear to vary with the type of task being performed. Levy-Leboyer (1989) compared the performance of similar groups of car workers engaged on assembling either a carburettor, a task which involved 19 separate parts and took about three minutes to complete, or an air conditioner, a task which involved 10 parts and took about 80 seconds. Different groups of workers completed either one job or the other in noisy (90 dbA) or quiet (62 dbA) conditions. He found that noise increased the speed with which the air conditioner was assembled, but reduced speed of work on the carburettor assembly. Analyses of the two tasks indicated that the two tasks required different skills. Noise tended to increase error rates associated with a high cognitive load or with a high degree of control precision, to reduce errors associated with physical strength, and to have no effect on errors associated with manual dexterity.

## 10.2.3 Effects of noise in the classroom

The development of reading in schoolchildren living in relatively noisy homes, such as apartment blocks close to railtracks or major highways, may sometimes be delayed, probably due to the adverse effects of noise on auditory discrimination (Bronzaft & McCarthy, 1975; Cohen, Glass, & Singer, 1973). As well as interfering with speech intelligibility in classroom settings, noise can also exert detrimental effects on attention and learning and, more generally, on children's health and wellbeing (see Hetu, Truchon-Gagnon, & Bilodeau, 1990). Cohen, Evans, Krantz and Stokols (1980) examined the effects of aircraft noise on the performance of children attending schools near a busy airport. The measures used by Cohen et al. included not only tests of academic attainment but also tests assessing attentional strategies, persistence at problem solving, and cognitive performance, which were relatively free from classroom influences. Testing was conducted in a soundproofed laboratory rather than in the noise-exposed classrooms. Children were tested on two occasions a year apart, which enabled the investigators to determine whether any adaptation to noise had occurred during the intervening period. Cohen et al. found that, compared to children attending schools in less noisy areas, the noise-exposed children were less able to resist auditory distraction and were less persistent in solving problems. They also had higher blood pressure. Although the effects of noise were fairly modest, they showed no evidence of adaptation over the one-year interval.

## 10.3 MECHANISMS FOR NOISE EFFECTS ON PERFORMANCE

### 10.3.1 Serial reaction

Many early studies of the effects of noise on task performance in the laboratory (see Davies & Jones, 1985; Kryter, 1994, for reviews) sampled a wide range of noise intensities, with the result that the "noise" condition used in one study may be the "quiet" condition in another. Hence, interpretation of results is somewhat problematic. Nevertheless, there does appear to be general agreement that noise exerts little or no effect on the basic components of performance from which more complex skills are assembled (see Smith &

Jones 1992b). For example, sensory functions such as visual acuity, contrast sensitivity, dark adaptation and accommodation show minimal effects of noise. Similarly, motor skills are rarely impaired by noise unless vestibular functions are involved. In general the effects of noise on the speed of performance in discrete RT situations are fairly slight, although there may be lengthening of simple reaction times (see, for example, Theologus, Wheaton, & Fleishman, 1974), and of the psychological refractory period, discussed in 3.2.3 (Goolkasian & Edwards, 1977).

As indicated in 10.2, noise produces brief periods of inefficiency in relatively simple RT tasks requiring continuous or serial responding, where performance is maintained for several minutes without a break. The most widely studied task of this kind is the five-choice serial reaction task, which typically lasts for at least half an hour. The task consists of five small light bulbs, each adjacent to a metal disc. When a bulb is illuminated it can be extinguished once a metal disc (not necessarily the correct one) is tapped by a metal stylus, whereupon another bulb is illuminated. Three measures of performance can be derived from the five-choice serial reaction task: first, the number of correct responses; second, the number of errors; and third, the number of long response times, or "gaps", defined as response times of 1.5 sec or longer. As Table 10.2 shows, noise presented at a level of 90 dbC, relative to a control condition of 60 dbC, increases error rates in serial reaction performance (Jones, 1983). Errors increase with time at work, especially at the higher noise level,

---

**TABLE 10.2**

Mean number of errors in the four 10-minute periods of a 40-minute serial reaction task under conditions of loud (90 dbC) and soft (60 dbC) noise. The noise was switched off in the final 10-minute task period. Adapted from Jones (1983).

| Noise | Ten-minute periods of task | | | |
|---|---|---|---|---|
| | 1 | 2 | 3 | 4 |
| Loud (90 dbC) | 14.9 | 20.5 | 27.2 | 30.3 |
| Soft (60 dbC) | 13.8 | 14.5 | 15.8 | 18.5 |

and continue to increase even when the noise is switched off. Loud noise sometimes increases the number of gaps as well, though the number of correct responses is unaffected by noise (see Davies & Jones, 1985 for review). The accuracy of performance in serial reaction tasks is thus impaired by loud noise, but the speed of working is much the same in noise as in quiet. In this task noise affects the balance, or trade-off, between the speed and accuracy of performance. In noise, individuals performing the task try to maintain their normal pace of working, but this can only be achieved at the cost of making more mistakes. Both errors and, to some extent, gaps tend to increase with time on task, being more frequent towards the end of the task.

Four main explanations have been advanced to account for the observed increases in errors and, less frequently, in long response times under conditions of loud noise. As noted in 10.2 above, Broadbent (1958) proposed that noise acted as a distractor, interfering either with the selection of task-relevant information, or the selection of an appropriate response, or both. Broadbent suggested that noise increased the number of involuntary interruptions in the intake of task information, resulting in brief periods of perceptual inefficiency which increased the chances of making an error and of taking a long time to complete a response. A second possibility is that noise functions as an arousing agent, increasing arousal level and eventually producing a state of overarousal, in which efficiency is impaired, with errors and long response times becoming more apparent (Broadbent, 1971). One problem with this explanation is the increase in errors with time at work. Prolonged work is usually assumed to lower arousal levels (see Davies & Parasuraman, 1982) while noise is assumed to increase arousal (see, for example, Davies, 1968a). But it is difficult to see how a state of overarousal could result from working in noise for a period of about 30 minutes, since the dearousing effects of prolonged work would presumably cancel out any arousing effects of loud noise, producing a state of moderate, rather than heightened, arousal.

A third, and more recent, suggestion has been that noise acts as a mask (Poulton, 1977). Noise is said to impair performance by masking task-relevant acoustic cues that provide helpful feedback to individuals performing the task, informing them, for example, whether the metal disc has been correctly "tapped" by the stylus. Feedback of this kind is thought to help maintain the speed and accuracy of responding; if it is removed or degraded through being masked by loud noise, performance is liable to be impaired and more errors will be made. However, when acoustic cues are eliminated from the serial RT task altogether, by using a silent keyboard, noise has been shown to affect performance in exactly the same way as in the normal version of the task, when these cues are present. Jones (1983) found that loud noise significantly increased both error rates and long response times in the modified version of the serial RT task. It seems, therefore, that masking is unlikely to provide a satisfactory explanation of the effects of noise on serial responding.

A fourth interpretation of the effects of noise on performance at the five-choice serial reaction task is that noise impairs the speed–accuracy trade-off function, discussed in 2.5.3 (Rabbitt, 1979). In order to perform the five-choice task efficiently, response speed has to be maintained at a level below that at which errors are likely to increase, but above that at which long response times will occur more frequently. The balance between accuracy and speed has to be fairly precise and there is little margin for error. If noise affects the control processes responsible for keeping this balance, then both errors and long response times will be likely to become more apparent, although the average speed of responding will be little affected.

## 10.3.2 Signal detection

In general, loud noise exerts little or no consistent effect on detection efficiency in single-source sensory vigilance tasks, in which observers typically respond to changes in the brightness or duration of a light (Koelega & Brinkman, 1986). However, noise does seem to have a variety of more subtle effects. Becker, Warm, Dember and Hancock (1995) showed that jet engine noise greatly reduces the beneficial effects of knowledge of results (KR) on vigilance. They suggest that noise reduces attentional resource availability, and so makes it difficult for subjects to make use of the information provided by the KR signals. Noise also affects the confidence with which detection responses are made—the proportion of confident responses rises while the proportion of doubtful responses falls. Observers working in noise are thus more confident in their judgement that a target either has or has not been presented (Broadbent & Gregory, 1963; Poulton & Edwards, 1974). Depending on the type of vigilance task being performed, this increased confidence could influence either the number of false alarms or the number of omissions (see Davies & Parasuraman, 1982). In monitoring displays for the presence of faint and infrequent targets, noise seems to bias the weighing of evidence in some way, perhaps by affecting the costs and payoffs associated with correct detections and false alarms.

In cognitive vigilance tasks, where observers are required to detect and respond to specified sequences of letters or digits, quite low levels of noise, around 80 dB, can increase omissions (Benignus, Otto, & Knelson, 1975; Jones, Smith, & Broadbent, 1979). It is unclear why noise should impair performance to a greater extent in cognitive vigilance tasks than in sensory ones. A tentative possibility is that cognitive vigilance tasks are more dependent on the development of a task strategy, a process that may be impaired by noise (Miles, Auburn, & Jones, 1984). Finally, varied noise, such as music, can reduce the vigilance decrement, the decline in correct detections as a function of time at work (Davies, Lang, & Shackleton, 1973; McGrath, 1963). This may be an arousal effect, as varied noise may act as a stimulant that may offset the dearousal induced by prolonged performance.

### 10.3.3 Dual-task performance
Several studies suggest that dual-task performance may be more sensitive to noise than is single-task performance, but it is not entirely clear whether such effects result from loss of functional attentional resources, or from strategy shifts. Noise may impair some aspects of multi-source monitoring for targets defined by physical properties, as demonstrated by Broadbent (e.g. 1954), using the 20-dials and 20-lights tasks. To the extent that multi-source monitoring is more difficult than single-source monitoring, such results might be

seen as supporting the Yerkes-Dodson Law, which suggests that more difficult tasks have a lower optimal level of arousal, and so noise-induced overarousal is more likely than for easier tasks. However, Broadbent also found that noise-induced impairment on the 20-lights task was restricted to more peripheral parts of the display. Noise may have been associated with a focusing of attention on the centre of the display, in line with the attentional selectivity hypothesis described in 9.3.2, rather than with a general loss of attentional efficiency.

If two perceptual–motor tasks are performed concurrently, for instance when a tracking task is performed at the same time as a simple multi-source monitoring task, noise affects attentional selectivity (Hockey, 1970a). As Fig. 10.3 shows, in Hockey's (1970a) study, 100 dbA noise actually improved performance on the tracking task, designated by instructions as the primary task, while impairing the detection of peripheral targets in the monitoring task, the secondary task. The difference between performance levels in the primary and secondary tasks was much less marked in the control condition. The distribution of attention thus appears to be different in noise and quiet, with attention becoming more selective in noise, so that more attention is devoted to the primary task and less to the secondary task.

The results discussed so far suggest that the primary effect of noise on dual-task performance is strategic. The alternative view is that the primary effect is on attentional resources. Evidence for this hypothesis is provided by dual-task studies which show that detrimental effects of noise are accentuated as task demands increase. For example, Finkelman and Glass (1970) compared the effects of predictable and unpredictable noise bursts, reasoning that the latter make more attentional demands. They showed that only the unpredictable bursts impaired secondary task performance. Boggs and Simon (1968) paired a primary reaction-time task with a secondary target detection task, and varied the complexity of the primary task (simple or complex RT). Noise was found to impair secondary task performance only when the primary task was complex. Both Eysenck (1982) and Fisher (1984b) interpreted these results as suggesting that noise drains attentional resources, and

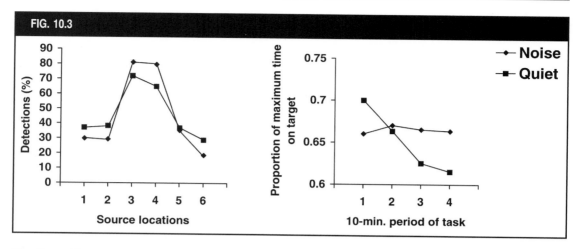

The effects of loud noise on dual-task performance, one task (above left) requiring the detection of the onset of lights placed at different locations, and the other (above right) involving pursuit tracking. From Hockey (1970a). In A.P. Smith & D.M. Jones (Eds.), Handbook of human performance. Volume 1: The physical environment. Academic Press. Reprinted with permission.

so performance is impaired only when the overall level of task demands is sufficiently high. The resource hypothesis explains why noise deficits in secondary task performance are much more prevalent than is noise facilitation of primary task performance (Eysenck, 1982). It also explains why noise-induced errors in serial reaction become more frequent as time progresses: fatigue may deplete resources (see Chapter 12). Attentional selectivity may be a strategic consequence of loss of resources, as individuals attempt to preserve the most important components of the task (Eysenck, 1982). Thus data from dual-task studies are open to differing interpretations. It is, of course, possible that the intermittent noise bursts used by Boggs and Simon (1968) and Finkelman and Glass (1970) were more likely to divert attentional resources from the tasks at hand than is the continuous white noise used in the majority of studies. Next, we consider evidence from other paradigms that is more clearly supportive of a primary effect of noise on strategy.

### 10.3.4 Memory and choice of strategy

Noise has somewhat complex effects on memory. Early studies of paired-associate learning suggested that noise impairs STM but enhances long-term recall (e.g. Berlyne, Borsa, Hamacher, & Koenig, 1966). Arousal is often believed to exert this general effect through enhancing the consolidation of information in long-term memory (e.g. Revelle & Loftus, 1992). However, research inspired by information-processing models has shown that noise effects on short-term recall cannot be conceptualised simply as a loss of capacity. For example, noise actually improves the retention of very recently presented items at the expense of earlier ones: the noise state appears to facilitate rapid throughput of information at the expense of holding material in short-term storage (Hockey, Maclean, & Hamilton, 1981). Increased selectivity in noise has also been reported in memory situations (Smith, 1982). Smith found that noise benefited performance on whichever of two memory tasks, recalling words or recalling the locations in which the words were presented, was given priority in the instructions.

The effects of noise on both the speed–accuracy trade-off in serial responding and the distribution of attention in dual-task situations can be regarded as strategic changes, and strategic effects are also apparent in memory situations. Several studies suggest that individuals performing memory tasks in loud noise are more likely to use maintenance rehearsal (for example, repeating to-be-remembered items over and over again) and less likely to use elaborative rehearsal (for example, generating verbal or pictorial associations to the to-be-remembered material) (Wilding & Mohindra, 1980). In other words, noise leads to "parroting back" of material (Dornic, 1975). Consistent with this hypothesis, the retention of order information, which is preserved by maintenance rehearsal, seems to be improved in noise (Davies & Jones, 1975; Hockey & Hamilton, 1970). The improvement persists when the requirement for item retention is either reduced to a minimum by using already familiar items (Wilding & Mohindra, 1980) or dispensed with altogether by supplying the original items contained in the list with the instruction to place them in their original order (Daee & Wilding, 1977).

Why do people "parrot back" in noise? The most straightforward explanation is that people may prefer to use less effortful strategies in noise, because resisting distraction in noise is likely to require effort. Wilding and Mohindra (1980) showed that noise improves the retention of phonemically related material (for example, lists of words that sound alike), but impairs the retention of semantically related material (for example, lists of words that have similar meanings). This finding suggests that in noise less attention is devoted to the semantic properties of the to-be-remembered material and hence that noise discourages "deeper", more elaborate levels of processing verbal information, favouring instead "shallower", less effortful processing. An effort-reduction hypothesis also explains why noise appears to reduce category clustering (the tendency to recall items from the same semantic category together) in free recall without affecting the total number of words correctly recalled, thus affecting the organisation of memory (Daee & Wilding, 1977; Smith, Jones, & Broadbent, 1981). Category clustering is an index of the individual's attempts actively to reorganise material in memory.

An alternative possibility is suggested by studies conducted by Wilding, Mohindra and Breen-Lewis (1982). They confirmed that individuals spontaneously tend to adopt maintenance rehearsal as a strategy when working in noise. However, their first study included recall of words from a semantically associated list, a task at which performance would be facilitated by use of a "deeper" semantic strategy. In one condition, participants were simply asked to recall the words, and noise impaired recall slightly, perhaps due to increased use of maintenance rehearsal at the expense of semantic processing and elaboration. In a second condition, participants were oriented towards a semantic processing strategy by having them make judgements on the pleasantness of the words. Under these circumstances, noise actually enhanced recall, suggesting *increased* semantic processing in noise, contrary to the maintenance rehearsal hypothesis. Wilding et al. (1982) concluded that noise tends to enhance the use of the dominant strategy, with maintenance rehearsal being the normal dominant strategy in the absence of a specific orienting task. Smith and Jones (1992b) have arrived at a similar conclusion. A possible interpretation of these results is that noise does not so much elicit strategies that reduce effort, but strategies that minimise the executive processing required to determine how effort should be allocated. Perhaps people spontaneously use maintenance rehearsal in noise because there is only one way to parrot back material, but there are multiple ways of elaborating meaning, requiring greater executive involvement in choosing a particular strategy.

## 10.4 CONTEXTUAL AND SITUATIONAL EFFECTS

Impairments of task performance by loud noise can persist after the noise has stopped; these effects on performance are referred to as "after-effects" of noise (see Cohen, 1980). Such after-effects were first reported by Glass and Singer (1972). In a series of laboratory studies, Glass and Singer investigated the effect of giving individuals a greater or lesser degree of mastery or "perceived control" over the noise to which they were exposed while performing a proofreading task lasting for about 25 minutes. The type of noise employed in these studies was "conglomerate" noise, consisting of the superimposed sounds of two people speaking Spanish, a desk calculator, a typewriter and a mimeograph machine. It was presented in bursts, on regular or irregular time schedules, at levels of either 108 dbA or 56 dbA, termed "loud" and "soft" respectively. Glass and Singer found that noise intensity did not affect proofreading performance, but once the noise had ceased and individuals were required to continue working on a different series of tasks, generally concerned with problem solving, the effects of noise became apparent. Those individuals who had performed the proofreading task in loud noise showed markedly less persistence in problem solving, although those who had previously worked in soft noise were unaffected. But this after-effect of working in loud noise could be considerably reduced, and even abolished, by giving "perceived control" over the noise while performing the proof-reading task. Individuals working in noise were told that they could terminate the noise at any time by pressing a key. Only those people who did not exercise this option were included in the final data analysis, that is, people who perceived themselves to have had control over the noise stimulus but who did not use it. The performance of the perceived control group in the problem-solving situation was found to be much the same as that of the group who had been exposed to soft noise while performing the proofreading task. Perceived control thus largely eliminated the after-effects of working in loud noise.

Several attempts have been made to extend Glass and Singer's findings both to other kinds of noise (Jones, Auburn, & Chapman, 1982; Percival & Loeb, 1980) and to other kinds of behaviour (Donnerstein & Wilson, 1976; Sherrod & Downs, 1974). These studies indicate that some kinds of noise, particularly conglomerate noise, loud speech and combinations of aircraft noise peaks, are more likely to produce after-effects than are other kinds of noise. Further, after-effects are not confined to persistence at problem solving but can encompass changes in aggression and helping behaviour. The generally accepted explanation of noise after-effects is a version of the adaptive-cost hypothesis, originally advanced by Glass and Singer (1972), which emphasises both the psychological and physiological costs involved in the adaptation to a stressor (see Cohen, 1980, for discussion). A possible physiological explanation for noise

after-effects, involving activation of the endogenous opioid system, has also been explored by Davidson, Hagmann and Baum (1990), in a replication of Glass and Singer's original study.

The instructions given to task participants have also been shown to moderate the effects of noise, though instructional effects are not particularly consistent. Early studies, such as that of Mech (1953), gave participants different information concerning the probable effects of noise on performance. He found that, initially at least, performance was altered in the direction suggested by the information provided, despite the presence of noise. However, the effects on performance of different types of information were short-lived and noise effects soon became more important. Gawron (1982) was only able to replicate Mech's results with limited success, but did confirm the finding that at least in some task situations observers worked better in noise when they were informed that noise facilitated performance. Although instructional effects are neither particularly strong nor very long-lasting, they indicate that the effects of noise on performance are not solely dependent upon the acoustic properties of the noise. The way that people perceive general features of the setting in which the noise is presented exerts some effect upon the likelihood that noise will affect performance. Not surprisingly, the performance of some individuals is more susceptible to the effects of noise than is that of others.

## 10.5 SUSCEPTIBILITY TO THE EFFECTS OF NOISE

Much of the research concerned with examining individual differences in susceptibility to noise effects has focussed upon personality dimensions such as extraversion–introversion and neuroticism or anxiety. The dependence of response to noise on extraversion has been demonstrated using measures of both performance and preference. The vigilance performance of extraverts is more likely to benefit from higher levels of broadband noise (85–95 dbA), which tend to impair the performance of introverts. Conversely, lower levels of noise benefit the performance of introverts somewhat but slightly impairs the performance of extraverts (see, for example, Davies & Hockey, 1966; Geen, McCown, & Broyles, 1985). On the basis of self-report scales, extraverts are less sensitive to noise than are introverts (Campbell, 1992; Dornic & Ekehammar, 1990). Behavioural validation of the self-reports has been established in studies in which individuals are able to choose either the preferred intensity of noise or the amount of varied noise in which to work. Extraverts choose higher noise levels and greater amounts of varied noise than do introverts (Davies, Hockey, & Taylor, 1969; Geen, 1984). Compared to introverts, extraverts seem to require higher levels of noise stimulation to reach the same level of psycho-physiological arousal, and working at the preferred noise intensity was found to exert a beneficial effect on performance at a paired-associate learning task, for both introverts and extraverts (Geen, 1984). As further discussed in 15.2, findings of this kind have been interpreted as support for the hypothesis that extraverts tend to be lower in cortical arousability than introverts (Eysenck & Eysenck, 1985).

Neuroticism, a second major personality dimension, appears to relate to vulnerability to noise-induced performance impairment. Retention of a prose passage learned in noise but recalled in silence was found to be disrupted to a significantly greater extent in anxious and "neurotic" individuals than in stable and non-anxious ones (Nurmi & von Wright, 1983). Neuroticism also seems to increase vulnerability to impairment on a semantic memory task (von Wright & Vauras, 1980). As we discuss in 15.3, there is general agreement that neuroticism relates to reduced availability of attentional resources or working memory, due to diversion of attention to processing internal worries (e.g. Sarason, 1989). Hence, neurotic individuals may be susceptible to overload of attention in noisy environments. The closely-related personality traits of neuroticism and anxiety are often grouped together as "negative affectivity", defined as the disposition to experience aversive emotional states (Watson & Clark, 1984). Stansfeld (1992) has proposed that indi-

vidual differences in annoyance and dissatisfaction with environmental noise relate to negative affectivity, as well as to the cognitive constructs of perceived threat, and lack of perceived control. Personality characteristics such as anxiety and general annoyance, which are strongly linked to negative affectivity, may moderate noise annoyance in a wide variety of situations. Moreover, Stansfeld's findings indicate that there may be a relation between noise dissatisfaction on the one hand, and physiological arousal and psychological distress attributable to noise sources on the other, with noise sensitive individuals being both more highly aroused and more severely distressed. Exposure to noise can thus have implications for both physical and mental health (see Smith, 1989).

Age and sex differences in performance seem to be little affected by noise, although relatively few studies have been conducted and their results are not particularly consistent. Davies and Davies (1975) found that in a visual checking task the rate of work of older individuals (aged 65–72 years) was significantly improved by noise, although that of younger individuals (aged 18–31 years) was not. Accuracy was unaffected. Lahtela, Niemi, Kuusela and Hypen (1986), however, found that the choice-reaction time of older individuals was significantly more impaired by noise than was that of younger individuals. Gulian and Thomas (1986) found that women's speed of work was significantly reduced by noise while that of men was unaffected. While some studies suggest that time of day may moderate the effects of noise on sex differences in performance (for example, Baker & Holding, 1993; Loeb, Holding, & Baker, 1982), others find no evidence that time of day, noise and sex interact in their effects on performance (Smith & Miles, 1987).

## 10.6 IRRELEVANT SPEECH

Noise is a feature of many office environments, especially open-plan offices, and can impair performance on clerical and other typical office tasks (Loewen & Suedfeld, 1992; Sundstrom, Town, Rice, & Osborn, 1994), as well as reducing job satisfaction (Sundstrom et al., 1994). Of the components of office noise, conversation, in the form of irrelevant speech, is likely to be a much more important contributor to performance decrements than other forms of noise, such as footsteps, telephones, keyboards, or traffic noise. As mentioned in 4.1.1, Treisman's (1960) shadowing studies showed that even unattended speech is analysed for semantic content. It has been suggested that automatic processing of speech may make it impossible to ignore (Loewen & Suedfeld, 1992). However, people do habituate to irrelevant speech, so this view may be over-simplified (Morris & Jones, 1990).

In recent years there have been a number of studies concerned with the effects of irrelevant speech on performance, and their results have, for the most part, been remarkably consistent (see Jones, 1995; Jones & Morris, 1992, for review). These studies have demonstrated that performance is impaired if irrelevant speech is present during the learning and retention of verbal materials,

though the amount of impairment is reduced as the number of voices increases, particularly if it is difficult to localise individual voices (Jones & Macken, 1995). White noise, in contrast, produces little or no impairment on the tasks used in these studies. However, the semantic characteristics of irrelevant speech seem to be unimportant, since impairments can be obtained with languages other than English, with nonsense materials, and with speech played backwards (see Fig. 10.4). Perhaps more importantly, from a practical point of view, the effect of irrelevant speech on performance is independent of its intensity, at least within the range 55–95 dbA. The magnitude of the irrelevant speech effect is quite substantial; the serial recall of visually presented materials can be reduced by about 30% if irrelevant speech is present. Irrelevant speech appears to affect memory rather than perceptual encoding. In terms of the working memory model discussed in 3.5.2, speech may interfere with the phonological store, because its disruptive effects appear to depend on the extent

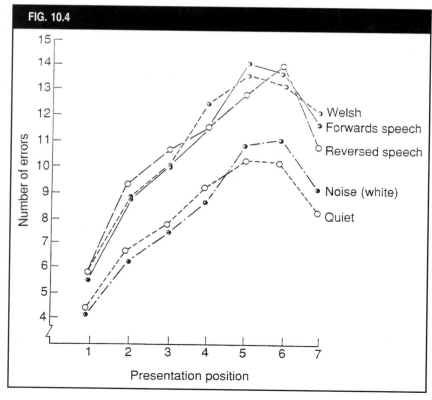

The effects of five different types of sound (English, reversed English, Welsh, loud noise at 70 dbA, and quiet, approximately 45 dbA) on the number of errors in serial recall in a short-term memory task. From Jones et al. (1990). In A.P. Smith & D.M. Jones (Eds.), Handbook of human performance. Volume 1: The physical environment. Academic Press. Reprinted with permission.

to which the task requires phonological coding (Jones & Morris, 1992). Hence reading, which relies on phonological working memory, may also be impaired (Jones & Morris, 1992).

More recently, Jones (e.g. 1993) has developed the blackboard model of memory discussed in 3.5.1 as an explanation for irrelevant speech effects. The "changing state" hypothesis (Jones, 1994) suggests that a critical component of the irrelevant speech effect is the "changing state" of the irrelevant auditory material; that is, successively presented sounds have to exhibit change from one sound to the next for the effect to be observed. Thus, the irrelevant speech effect is not found with single repeated utterances, for example "a a a a a", but does occur with irrelevant non-speech sounds such as tones or segmented glissandi (pitch-glides). However, state-change disruption is reduced by stereophonic presentation, implying that the attentional systems involved function relatively well when stimulus sequences are organised as discrete "streams". According to the blackboard model, state changes segment auditory input as discrete "auditory objects" organised in streams, such as those associated with the two ears. The stream generated by irrelevant speech is distracting when it cannot be successfully segregated from the internal streams generated by processing task stimuli, so that it is difficult to keep track of which object belongs to which stream. This idea resembles Hirst's (1986) view that learning to perform tasks in combination depends on skills for segregating the processing sequences involved (see 5.5.2).

Originally, the irrelevant speech effect was thought to be confined to serial recall, where items must be recalled in the order in which they were presented. This finding is consistent with the position of the blackboard model in that it is the links between objects that are sensitive to disruption, rather than the objects themselves (Jones, 1993). However, LeCompte (1994) found that irrelevant speech also impaired free recall to a significantly greater extent than white noise, even when the speech was presented after the items to be recalled, an effect previously obtained only for serial recall. LeCompte found that list length moderated the irrelevant speech effect on free recall,

in that no effect was observed with 16-item lists. But impairment of performance by irrelevant speech was also found with recognition memory and with a cued recall task that discouraged serial rehearsal of the to-be-remembered items. The extent of the irrelevant speech effect on performance in memory tasks other than serial recall is thus somewhat uncertain and requires further clarification.

## 10.7 CONCLUSIONS

Noise effects are often subtle, but they are reasonably reliable within carefully-designed paradigms. There are several competing explanations for performance change in noise, but there is no accepted general theory, so that is difficult to predict noise effects on tasks other than the standard ones. The majority of the effects of noise on performance examined in this chapter can be regarded as strategic, and it is probable that working in noise modifies an individual's style of task performance. While noise may lead to the choice of certain strategies over others and may even reinforce the use of the particular dominant strategy with which a task is typically performed (see Smith & Jones, 1992b), the evidence is neither as abundant nor as consistent as might be desired. The effects of noise in changing an individual's general approach to task performance are most clearly demonstrated in the after-effect studies.

Noise may also influence specific information-processing mechanisms, as shown most clearly by the studies of irrelevant speech and other sounds, in which impairment depends on the precise acoustic properties of the stimuli. There seems little doubt that noise, like fatigue and some other stressors, makes task performance more effortful; perceived mental workload increases (Becker et al., 1995) and frustration tolerance is reduced (Glass & Singer, 1972). It seems plausible that under such circumstances more attentional resources need to be deployed to ensure successful task performance, although it is unclear whether resources are diverted primarily to processing the noise stimuli, or to coping with subjective discomfort. Noise may impair performance when task demands are particularly high, or when resources are depleted due to other factors, such as fatigue or anxiety. The decline in accuracy of serial reaction as time progresses is perhaps the most reliable of this category of noise effects. Finally, the psychobiological level of explanation exemplified by arousal theory has fallen into disfavour, but the effects of noise on arousal level are still of some importance.

## FURTHER READING

Smith and Jones (1992b: Vol. 1) includes chapters on noise and irrelevant speech effects. Kryter's (1994) book provides a comprehensive review of the various psychological effects of noise. The volume edited by Jones and Chapman (1984) remains a useful source, as does the handbook edited by Tempest (1985).

# 11

# Thermal stress and other physical stressors

## 11.1 INTRODUCTION

Noise stress, reviewed in the previous chapter, is just one example of a physical stressor. By a physical stressor, we mean a stressor associated with the external environment defined by its objective physical properties. Some physical stressors may be *psychophysically* defined: they are potentially disturbing because of their stimulus properties, such as the intensity of a bright light. Other physical stressors are more insidious, in that they operate primarily through physiological change rather than through the senses. Certain chemical toxins may affect brain functioning without the person necessarily being aware of their influence. Some stressors exert both types of influence. As we shall see, heat generates thermal discomfort, in relation to its psychophysical intensity, but may also influence the brain through changes in thermoregulation.

Physical stressors may be contrasted with more psychological stressors, such as major "life events", whose most important feature is their motivational and emotional significance. Most people's lifestyles are directed towards minimis-

ing the impact of physical stressors. We prefer our homes, offices and cars to be comfortable and pleasantly warm, for example. Nevertheless, people do sometimes live and work under various types of physical stress, often in combination. Pilots and astronauts may have to deal with extremes of temperature, lack of oxygen and vibration. Mountaineers encounter a somewhat similar cocktail of cold and hypoxia, and firefighters are confronted by heat, smoke and toxic fumes. Experience of physical stressors may be laced with the rather more psychological stressor of fear. Physical stressors are also common in the workplace, as illustrated in Fig. 11.1 which shows survey data from the European Foundation for the Improvement of Living and Working Conditions. The acceptability of physical stressors is likely to depend on cultural factors. Physical stressors may become an increasing problem as people become more health conscious, and more disposed to hold employers accountable for poor working conditions.

As the examples indicate, physical stressors may be life threatening. Knowledge of how people perform under such conditions is thus of critical importance. However, threats to life cannot be

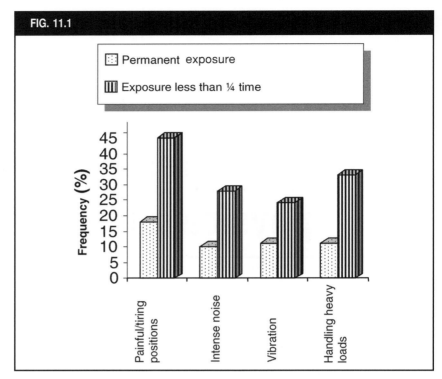

**FIG. 11.1**

Exposure to physical stressors in EU workers (European Foundation for the Improvement of Living and Working Conditions, 1996).

reproduced in the laboratory, and so experimental psychological research is concerned with lower levels of stress which may correspond to occupational sources of stress. Understanding performance under severe physical threat is based on case studies of specific incidents, such as accident reports, and on extrapolation from laboratory data. An important strand of ergonomics is concerned with simulation of real-life events that may be thermally challenging. For example, there are studies of how protective clothing used by firefighters and military personnel may affect performance in heat (e.g. Fine & Kobrick, 1987). Volunteers for such studies need a certain dedication to science: Bakkevig and Nielsen (1994) had their participants sit in wet underwear for an hour in their investigation of thermal discomfort. In this chapter, however, we will emphasise laboratory studies of ambient temperature. Normally, such studies are conducted in a climatically-controlled chamber, although techniques have also been developed for heating or cooling specific body parts, such as the head.

The previous chapter shows in some detail how we can map out the psychological consequences of a particular stressor or class of stressors. For any given stressor, controlled experimentation will indicate its effects on physiological functioning, on subjective stress, on information processing and on strategy selection. A theory of the impact of the stressor may be synthesised with these building blocks. This chapter does not attempt to review work of this kind in detail (see Smith & Jones, 1992a). Instead, we look first at thermal stress (heat and cold) as further examples of the research process, followed by a brief review of some of the other physical stressors which may be important in the workplace.

## 11.2 HEAT AND PERFORMANCE

### 11.2.1 The nature of thermal stress

Assessment of thermal stress is not simply a matter of recording the ambient temperature. There are various routes for heat transfer between the body and the external environment and, as warm-blooded creatures, our physiology actively regulates temperature, aiming for thermal equilibrium at a temperature of around 37°C. Table 11.1 lists the physical factors that affect equilibrium. Thermal regulation is effected most directly through shivering to increase temperature, and sweating which leads to evaporative cooling. In addition, people use voluntary strategies such as choosing clothing, exposure to sunlight and muscular activity. Chronic exposure to thermal stress, as when a European moves to a tropical country, for example, also leads to acclimatisation at a physiological level.

It is normally impracticable to assess the various physical factors. The thermal state of the person may be assessed by taking their temperature although, as discussed below, it may be important to monitor temperature over time to assess the dynamic state of thermoregulation. To assess the potential for stress of an environment, specialised indices have been developed which take into account physical factors other than the dry air temperature measured by a standard thermometer (Mairiaux & Malchaire, 1995). Effective Temperature (ET) is an index based on the standard "dry bulb" temperature, together with humidity and air velocity (wind). Hence, ET would be particularly high in a humid tropical environment, and particularly low in a windy Arctic environment, accommodating the windchill effect. A second, widely-used index is wet bulb globe temperature (WBGT). It is calculated from measures taken from a dry bulb thermometer, and two more specialised thermometers: a wet bulb thermometer sensitive to evaporation effects, and a globe thermometer sensitive to radiant heat from the environment. These indices are somewhat approximate, but they provide a better indication of the degree of thermal discomfort imposed by an environment than standard temperature readings.

## 11.2.2 Heat and psychomotor performance

Recent reviews of heat and performance have been provided by Ramsey (1983, 1995), Enander and Hygge (1990), and Hygge (1992). Earlier reviews (Grether, 1973; Ramsey & Morrissey, 1978) also contain much useful information. In the next two sections, we discuss the main empirical findings from studies of psychomotor performance, and of more cognitive tasks.

Reviews of heat effects on reaction time and on simple motor performance have been published by Grether (1973) and Ramsey and Morrissey (1978). Simple reaction time is relatively insensitive to heat, and may even improve (Ramsey & Morrissey, 1978). Enhancement of RT has been linked to the intriguing hypothesis, originally put forward by Hoagland (1933), that heat may increase the rate of a chemical clock such that time appears to run faster. However, evidence for this hypothesis is mixed, and it is unlikely that there is any simple, linear relationship between body temperature and time perception (Hygge, 1992). In contrast, choice reaction time tasks tend to show performance decrements, particularly after some time on the task although, as Hygge (1992) points

| TABLE 11.1 | | |
|---|---|---|
| **Factors influencing heat exchange with the environment.** | | |
| **Factor** | **Gain (+) or loss (−)** | **Notes** |
| Metabolism | + | |
| Physical work | + | Includes shivering |
| Conduction | ± | Usually a minor influence only |
| Radiation | + | Significant in direct sunlight |
| Convection | ± | Usually a heat loss factor |
| Evaporation | − | Mechanism for cooling by perspiration |

out, there is considerable variation in findings from study to study. Curiously, direct warming of the head seems to facilitate choice reaction time (Holt & Brainerd, 1976).

More complex psychomotor tasks also show heat-induced decrements. Both pursuit and compensatory tracking show performance impairments in heat; pursuit tracking is perhaps more reliably affected. Heat effects on tracking increase only slightly with time on task. Although physical strength appears to be minimally affected by temperature, perceptual-motor tasks requiring muscular exertion may also be detrimentally affected by heat (Ramsey, 1983). However, heat does not seem to impair eye-hand co-ordination. Ramsey and Morrissey (1978) reviewed 11 studies from their laboratory of effects of heat on two eye-hand coordination tasks: maze tracing and tweezer

manipulation. Two studies showed an improvement in heat, the remainder no significant effect.

Heat stress affects a significant minority of workers, especially in industries such as steel and mining, and in restaurants; around 17% of French workers complain of frequent heat exposure (Meyer & Rapp, 1995). Hence, it is important that heat effects found in the laboratory seem seem to generalise fairly well to applied settings. For example, steering a motor vehicle is a real-life example of pursuit tracking. Mackie and O'Hanlon (1977) had subjects drive for 600 km (with a rest-break half way through) at an ambient temperature of either 67°F (20°C) or 90°F (32.2°C) WBGT. They measured the frequency of large steering wheel movements (>10 degrees) as an index of degradation of performance. Figure 11.2 shows the results. In the later part of the drive,

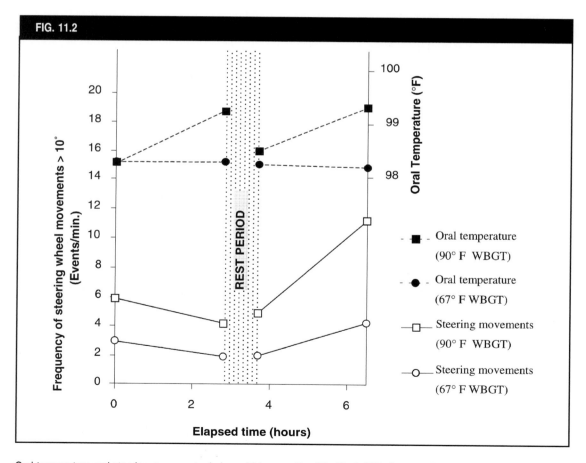

**FIG. 11.2**

Oral temperature and steering movements during vehicle operation (Mackie & O'Hanlon, 1977).

there was a general trend for steering to become impaired with increasing time on task. However, this trend was accentuated at the higher temperature. Figure 11.2 also shows that body temperature tended to increase in both parts of the drive, so performance change did not directly correspond to temperature change. Possibly heat impairs driving only when the driver is somewhat fatigued by prolonged driving. Heat-induced impairment of performance has also been observed in flight simulator operation, during the more complex flight operations, but not during routine, straight and level flight (Iampietro et al., 1972). In real-world environments, detrimental effects of heat are often exacerbated by the protective clothing worn by operators such as firefighters and military personnel (Caldwell, Caldwell, & Salter, 1997; Reardon, Fraser, & Omer, 1998).

Beneficial effects of heat have been observed in a study in which tasks included simulated factory tasks requiring manual skills, such as moving screws and nuts from one plate to another and simulated spot-welding (Meese, Lewis, Wyon, & Kok, 1984). However, in this study (of acclimatised South Africans), there tended to be a curvilinear relationship between temperature and manual performance. Performance improved between 20° and 32°C, but then deteriorated as temperature increased to high values of up to 38°C.

## 11.2.3 Heat, attention and cognitive function

Several studies suggest that there is a curvilinear relationship between heat and vigilance. An early study, using the Mackworth clock, showed that signal detection increased from 21° to 26°C ET, but then deteriorated at temperatures of 31° and 36°C ET (Mackworth, 1950). Several reviewers (e.g. Ramsey, 1983) have suggested that there is an optimum temperature range of around 27°–32°C for vigilance. A factor contributing to vigilance effects may be loss of sensory acuity. Temperatures of up to 50°C appear to reduce visual acuity and high frequency contrast sensitivity (Hohnsbein, Piekarski, & Kampmann, 1983; Hohnsbein, Piekarski, & Noack, 1984).

Results from studies using more complex attentional tasks are mixed. Figure 11.3 shows results from a study by Carlson (1961), who varied the number of sources of stimuli to be monitored (i.e.

complexity of the display). Heat produced a strong impairment on the most complex display only, implying that tasks which are particularly attentionally demanding may be most sensitive to heat. This hypothesis is partly substantiated by studies of dual-task performance. Several studies do show that secondary, but not primary tasks, are impaired by heat. For example, Bell (1978) had people performing a pursuit-rotor (tracking) task as the primary task, while also detecting numerical targets as the secondary task. Secondary task performance was worse at 35°C ET than at 22° or 29°C ET. However, as Hygge (1992) indicates, it is unclear that it is specifically dual-task performance which is impaired: the secondary tasks may also be sensitive to heat when performed as single tasks. In a real-world study of attention during driving (Wyon, Wyon, & Norin, 1996), drivers responded to pre-programmed signals such as unusual changes in car instrument readings. Speed and accuracy of response was substantially worse at 27°C than at 21°C, especially in the second half of the one-hour drive. Heat effects were also stronger when driving in city traffic, as opposed to the open road, implying that, as in laboratory studies, heat is more detrimental as task load increases.

More complex cognitive tasks are often insensitive to heat. Several studies have failed to show heat effects on tasks such as dominoes, intelligence tests and anagram solution. Ramsey and Morrissey (1978) review four studies of heat and short-term memory: two studies show no heat effect, one shows an improvement, and one a decrement with increased temperature. Mental arithmetic is fairly reliably impaired by heat (Poulton, 1970), although raising head temperature by one degree by means of a helmet improves mental arithmetic (Hancock, 1983). Coding tasks performed in a realistic military context also show heat-related impairment (Fine & Kobrick, 1978). Classroom learning may be impaired by heat: Wyon (1970) reviews studies showing impairment of learning in a language laboratory, reading and comprehension at 27°C compared to 20°C. However, other studies of learning and memory have shown curvilinear trends: somewhat surprisingly, Pepler and Warner (1968) showed that speed of learning was poorest at the intermediate temperature of 26.7°C, and

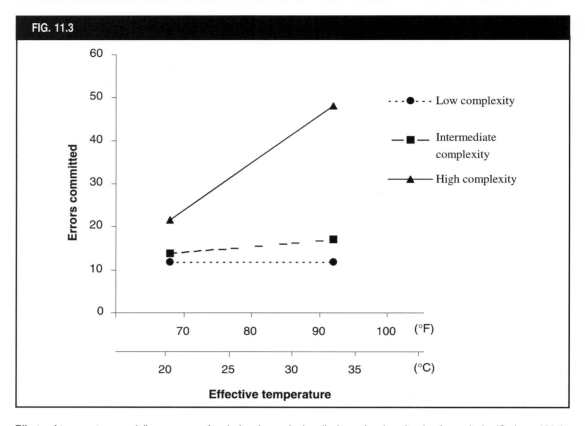

Effects of temperature on vigilance errors of omission, in monitoring displays of various levels of complexity (Carlson, 1961).

superior at colder and hotter temperatures, although data were complicated by speed–accuracy tradeoffs. Effects of heat on more complex tasks appear to be particularly sensitive to the exact nature of the task.

### 11.2.4 Theories of heat effects

The inverted-U relationship between temperature and vigilance is suggestive of the Yerkes-Dodson Law. Furthermore, heat tends to raise autonomic arousal. Hence, performance improvements under moderate thermal stress have been attributed to heat raising arousal towards the optimum (Poulton, 1977). Decrements in performance at higher temperatures might be attributed to overarousal. However, there are difficulties for such an arousal theory explanation. The subjective effects of heat include anxiety, irritability, fatigue, drowsiness and loss of motivation (e.g. Gafafer, 1964), so it does

not seem to act as a straightforward stimulant. Interactions between heat and other stressors consistent with arousal theory are occasionally reported (e.g. Hygge, 1991), but there are also failures to confirm predictions. Heat and noise often have additive rather than interactive effects, for example (Bell, 1978; Hancock & Pierce, 1985). The tendency for heat to be more detrimental after some time at work is also puzzling: the arousing effects of heat would be expected to offset the dearousing effects of prolonged performance. It is possible that, when feelings of lassitude predominate, heat is associated with cortical underarousal. However, as Hancock (1986) points out, such arguments are post hoc and have no practical or predictive utility.

Hancock's (1986) review of the vigilance literature makes two essential points. First, there may be different mechanisms for different types of thermal stress effects. Second, attentional mechanisms may have more explanatory power than arousal theory. It appears that the body's state of thermal homeostasis is more important than temperature per se. Hancock suggests that effects of heat on vigilance depend on whether heat (1) has no effect on body temperature, (2) induces static hyperthermia, or (3) induces dynamic changes in deep body temperature. If heat fails to affect body temperature, then sustained attention is unaffected, for temperatures of up to about 34°C. If the participant's body temperature can be stabilised at an elevated level (static hyperthermia), sustained attention improves. For example, Wilkinson et al. (1964) maintained people in a stable hyperthermic state by circulating heated air through a suit worn by participants. With body temperature elevated by 2°C, responses on an auditory vigilance task were both faster and more accurate. Finally, the environmental thermal load may be sufficient to induce dynamic, noncompensable changes in body temperature, which may increase without attaining a steady state. Under these conditions, efficiency of sustained attention appears to deteriorate. Hancock (1986) suggests that such disturbances of thermal equilibrium are common at heat exposures above about 29°C.

Hancock (1986) develops an attentional theory of performance impairment associated with non-compensable temperature change. He suggests that this form of physiological stress drains attentional resources. Performance on demanding attentional tasks is then impaired although, in dual-task situations, the person may be able to preserve primary task performance at the expense of single-task performance. This hypothesis fits the data reviewed fairly well, with the literature providing some clear demonstrations of increasingly detrimental heat effects as attentional demands increase (e.g. Carlson, 1961). As Hancock points out, it also explains why skilled performers are resistant to detrimental effects of heat, because automatisation of skill may reduce the requirement for resources. Figure 11.4 shows how operator skill mitigated the detrimental effect of heat on telegraphic reception in an early study (Mackworth, 1946).

The main source of difficulty for the resource hypothesis is the variation of heat effects with the nature of the task. This observation forces us to make unsatisfactory post hoc assumptions about which tasks are sensitive to resource availability, and which are not. There is also some doubt over the general validity of resource theory as a basis for characterising performance change; Hancock and Warm (1989) draw attention to the weaknesses of resource theory. It remains to be seen how well Hancock's analysis applies to tasks other than vigilance. There are some promising signs. Consistent with the thermoregulation hypothesis, Razmjou and Kjellberg (1992) showed that performance impairment in choice–reaction time was related to rate of change of core body temperature, but not to temperature itself. Pepler and Warner's (1968) study of learning, discussed above, provides evidence for the hypothesis that stress tends to generate compensatory effort. They found a U-shaped relationship between body temperature and effort, such that both relatively cold and warm conditions elicited more effort. Effort appeared to relate to faster, although also more error-prone, performance.

## 11.3 COLD AND PERFORMANCE

Effects of cold on performance have been less extensively investigated than those of heat, but there is nevertheless a substantial research literature, reviewed by Ramsey (1983) and Brooke and Ellis (1992). Tasks with a pronounced motor component, such as manual dexterity and manipulative tasks, are reliably impaired by cold (Ramsey, 1983). Such effects may be attributed primarily to loss of tactual sensitivity resulting from lowered hand skin temperature (Dusek, 1957). More complex motor tasks such as tracking (Enander & Hygge, 1990) also show decrements. In such cases it is unclear whether it is a motor or an attentional component of the task which is affected. It is also unclear whether cold should be conceptualised as an arousing agent. Some results are suggestive of raised arousal: people who immersed their forearms in ice-cold water (Patil, Apfelbaum, & Zacny, 1995) reported higher blood pressure and critical flicker fusion (a perceptual index of alertness).

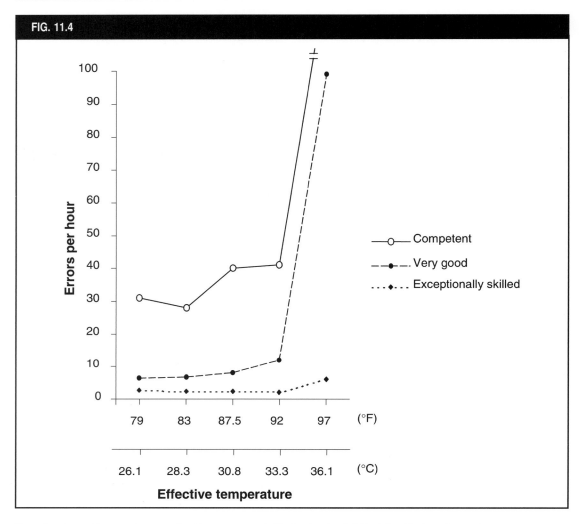

**FIG. 11.4**

Errors in telegraphic reception committed by operators of differing levels of ability (after Mackworth, 1946).

Several studies suggest that sustained attention is impaired by temperatures close to freezing point (e.g. Poulton, Hitchings, & Brooke, 1965). More moderate levels of cold tend to have little effect, although Enander (1987) reports that effects of moderate cold on vigilance are obtained if the task is made sufficiently demanding. Hancock (1986) suggests that, as with heat, cold-induced decrements in sustained attention depend on dynamic perturbation of deep body temperature. However, in the absence of studies comparing the effects of noncompensable declines in body temperature with those of static hypothermia, this hypothesis remains speculative. There is also one contrary finding: Enander (1987) reports impairments at 5.5°C on vigilance and digit classification when deep body temperature remained stable.

Simple reaction time is relatively insensitive to cold (Teichner, 1958), although there are occasional reports of moderate cold reducing response time on simple tasks (Brooke & Ellis, 1992). It has been suggested that arousal associated with moderate cold may increase rate of transmission of information in the CNS (Brooke & Ellis, 1992). Cold is associated with increased error rate in serial choice reaction, but only if participants are rapidly cooled (Ellis, Wilcock, & Zaman, 1985). Figure 11.5, adapted from Ellis et al. (1985), shows that loss of accuracy was greater for the more demanding, 8-choice task used. Sensitivity to task demands is consistent with an attentional resource mechanism, but there are difficulties with such

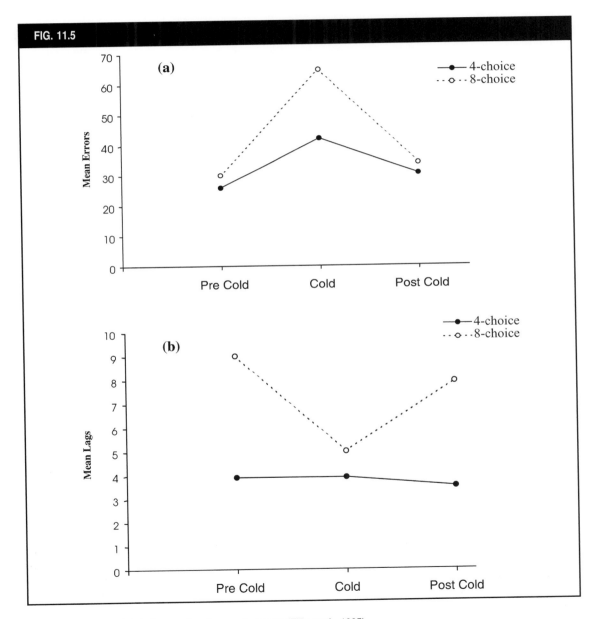

FIG. 11.5

Effects of cold on serial choice reaction time performance (Ellis et al., 1985).

an interpretation. Figure 11.5 also shows cold effects on "lags" (unusually slow responses). With respect to this indicator, cold actually improves performance. Furthermore, the cold manipulation influenced skin temperature but not body core temperature, implying there was no disruption of thermoregulation. Brooke and Ellis (1992) state that subjective discomfort is not a reliable guide to performance decrement, implying that decrement is not a consequence of distraction by feeling cold. They argue instead that cold effects are due to increased arousal induced by rapid skin cooling. However, evidence for a causal effect of arousal seems somewhat circumstantial, in the absence of evidence from direct measures of arousal. Also problematic for the arousal hypothesis is the tendency for noise (an arouser) to increase rather than decrease lags (10.3.1). Effects on more complex cognitive and memory tasks seem somewhat task-specific, with several studies showing no effects of cold on tasks requiring higher cognitive functions, such as verbal reasoning, navigation and symbol substitution (Ellis, 1982).

A recent study supported by the US Navy shows how cold may affect real-life operational performance of cognitive demanding tasks. Van Orden, Benoit and Osga (1996) required navy personnel to perform on a simulated "command and control" warfare task. They managed a military engagement through subtasks such as monitoring a complex display showing the movements of ships and aircraft, seeking further information, and firing missiles. Across the task as a whole, participants performing in cold (4°C) performed at a similar level to participants performing at a comfortable 22°C. However, effects of cold were evident on specific sub-tasks, especially when hostilities had commenced and operators had to make their own decisions on the actions to be taken. Under these conditions, cold participants were less responsive to explicit commands, and more likely to fire missiles without being prompted. Van Orden et al. (1996) suggest that cold may impair short-term memory, and perhaps also affect decision criterion. They showed also that cold was associated with elevated heart rate, and increased secretion of two catecholaminergic hormones associated with stress, adrenaline and noradrenaline. This particular type of arousal response may be implicated in effects of cold on performance.

## 11.4 PERILS OF THE WORKPLACE: OTHER PHYSICAL STRESSORS

### 11.4.1 Glare and visual discomfort

Stress originating from lighting conditions is important in factory, office and transportation contexts. The most obvious form of visual discomfort is glare (see Megaw, 1992). Disability glare is typically caused by a bright light close to the person's line of sight, such as sunlight passing through a window or the headlights of an oncoming car, which produces scattering of light in the eye. The experience may be disturbing, but the most obvious source of performance impairment is the ensuing loss of contrast for visual stimuli. Discomfort glare is more subtle, in that it is caused by a light source or sources further from the line of sight. Alferdinck (1996) reports a typical study in which a simulated headlamp was switched on while the participant performed a tracking task using a steering wheel. The glare source was located at angles varying from 1.7° to 6.8°. Discomfort was rated on a nine-point scale, ranging from 1 = unbearable to 9 = inappreciable. Not surprisingly, discomfort due to glare increased with the intensity of the headlamp, and decreased with the angle of glare. The practical contribution of the study was to show that the size of the headlamp had a minor effect only on discomfort.

There is a considerable literature on the effects of ambient lighting on visual performance (see Megaw, 1992; Wilkins, 1995), but these may be largely attributable to perceptual effects, such as loss of contrast sensitivity, rather than to discomfort or stress. Some studies address the ergonomics of lighting in the workplace. Hedge, Sims and Becker (1995) showed that the more diffuse light provided by uplighting was associated with more visual comfort and greater self-reported productivity in office workers, compared with parabolic downlighting. Knez (1995) found that indoor lighting colours, which enhanced mood, also improved performance on long term memory and problem solving tasks. However, there were gender differences in optimal lighting, with women preferring 'warmer' lighting than men. A subsequent study (Knez & Enmarker, 1998) failed to find any performance effects of lighting, but it did confirm a gender difference in the effects of lighting on mood. Arousing effects of bright light may occasionally enhance performance: Kozena, Frantik, and Dvorak (1996) report that a 20-minute light exposure delayed vigilance decrement on a subsequent task. Flicker may also be a source of discomfort (Grandjean, 1987; Kueller & Laike, 1998). Fluctuating light sources such as VDUs and fluorescent lighting may cause headaches and eye strain even if flicker is not perceived (Wilkins, 1995). As with noise, there are individual differences in sensitivity to visual discomfort; Lindner and Kropf (1993) showed that females aged 20–30 are most vulnerable to discomfort induced by fluorescent lighting.

Unlike many stressors, glare is not particularly damaging to more difficult tasks. Dugas Garcia and Wierwille (1985) found that glare slowed reading time for easy passages, but speeded reading of difficult passages. There has been occasional interest in interactive effects of lighting and non-visual factors in influencing performance and discomfort. Arousal theory would suggest that glare, as a form of additional stimulation, would tend to especially impair performance in the presence of arousing stressors. However, although interactions are sometimes found, they appear to be task-specific and do not support any particular theoretical conclusions (see Megaw, 1992).

Special factors pertain to use of VDUs, including glare associated with screen reflections and, under some circumstances, musculoskeletal discomfort (see Tattersall, 1992, for a review of work with VDUs). Prolonged VDU use is popularly seen as a source of stress, but the evidence is equivocal. Tattersall (1992) concludes that although VDU use may sometimes be related to eye strain, stress symptoms may reflect non-visual aspects of VDU work, such as lack of perceived control and delays in feedback. For example, Johansson and Aronsson (1984) found that computer use in an insurance company produced feel-

ings of lack of control and anxiety, in part because the computer work was prone to be interrupted by system breakdowns. As Tattersall points out, it seems likely that reported "VDU stress" can be reduced or eliminated through attention to the visual ergonomics of VDUs and, as for any job, providing adequate operator support and training. Use of a VDU may be associated with substantial deficits in reading time. Gould and Grischkowsky (1986), for example, found a 20–30% slowing of proofreading but, again, such decrements are probably attributable mainly to visual factors rather than to stress. The extent to which visual discomfort leads directly to performance deficits in VDU use is unknown, although it is plausible that the more severe symptoms, such as headaches, would have a distracting effect. Another potential source of impairment is the computer anxiety which some individuals experience. Anxiety effects are discussed in Chapter 15.

### 11.4.2 Vibration

Bouncing around in a bus on a rough road is not a pleasant experience. Excessive vibration of the body as a result of its placement on an oscillating surface is a particular problem in transportation contexts. The passenger may experience discomfort, but there are safety concerns over the performance of drivers of buses and trucks, and of pilots of light or military aircraft. In such circumstances, both the person and the machine operated are in motion. In laboratory studies, however, we can distinguish between vibration of the person and vibration of an external system such as a display. Research on the consequences of vibration has focused mainly on its direct physical effects, with rather little attention paid to psychological reactions associated with discomfort and distress.

Many of the consequences for performance of vibration may be attributed to two causes: disturbance of manual control, and disturbance of visual fixation (see Griffin, 1992, 1997 for reviews). The body's transmission of vibration leads to disruption of manual tasks such as tracking, writing and even speech, due to its effects on airflow through the larynx. Vibration, especially at high frequencies, may also interfere with neuromuscular processes (Ribot, Roll, & Gauthier, 1986). Griffin (1992) discusses how the magnitude of disruption varies, sometimes rather subtly, with qualities of the vibration and of the task. Vibration also causes the position of images on the retina to vary; the reason why it is difficult to read in a car. The person has some ability to compensate for difficulties in visual fixation, through eye movements, for example, although this type of compensation becomes increasingly ineffective as vibration magnitude and frequency increase (O'Hanlon & Griffin, 1991). People are also able to compensate behaviourally through motor response when the task provides good visual feedback (McLeod & Griffin, 1995).

As Griffin (1992) points out, the literature on cognition and vibration is sparse and difficult to summarise. It is often difficult to assess whether performance effects reflect anything more than the disruptions of motor control and vision just described. Sherwood and Griffin (1990) conducted a study using a version of the Sternberg memory scanning tasks, whose results suggested that vibration-induced impairments in speed and accuracy were due to a cognitive rather than visual impairment. It is unclear whether such "central" effects of vibration are due to arousal, to distraction by the sensations of vibration, or to motivational changes. Vibration is of practical importance, and there is a considerable ergonomic literature on the design of systems to minimise its effects. However, it is not particularly promising as a technique for investigating cognitive effects of physical stress.

### 11.4.3 Chemical and electromagnetic factors

Naturally, poisoning people or depriving them of oxygen impairs performance. Hypoxia, for example, is associated with slowing of response on a variety of information-processing tasks. Application of the additive factors approach, discussed in 3.2.2, suggests that hypoxia mainly affects early stages of visual processing, such as preprocessing (Lindeis, Nathoo, & Fowler, 1996). Research has also focused on relatively subtle effects which might sometimes be encountered in working environments. Low levels of carbon monoxide (<10%) have been reported to impair some psychomotor and cognitive tasks, although findings are incon-

sistent (Horvath & Drechsler-Parks, 1992). Other pollutants produced by car exhausts, such as ozone, may also have damaging effects (Horvath & Drechsler-Parks, 1992). Low level exposure to organic solvents is relatively common in industry. Epidemiological evidence suggests that individuals such as painters exposed to solvents in poorly-ventilated conditions have increased risk for senile dementia and psychiatric disorders (e.g. van Vliet et al., 1989). Stollery (1992a) reviews evidence that solvents may impair various performance on various tasks, including reaction time, short-term memory and manual dexterity. He cautions that acute and chronic effects are often poorly distinguished, and the CNS basis for impairment is unclear. Recent work in this area has focused on neuropsychological assessment for loss of cognitive function; for example, dichotic listening (see 4.2.1) appears to be especially sensitive to solvent-induced impairment (Varney, Kubu, & Morrow, 1998).

Study of the possible psychological dangers associated with electromagnetism comes dangerously close to fringe science. In recent years the UK has seen various popular scares over sources of radiation such as microwave ovens, power lines and mobile phones. Conversely, machines for producing negative ions are marketed on the basis of increased wellbeing. Work on the extremely low frequency (ELF) fields generated by electrical power equipment has been reviewed by Stollery (1992b). Studies conducted in the Soviet Union in the 1960s and 1970s suggested that exposure to fields was associated with various symptoms of malaise and stress, but subsequent studies have either failed to substantiate these claims or have suffered from methodological weaknesses. Experimental studies suggest some rather inconclusive effects of ELFs on performance, and rather stronger, though complex, effects on evoked potentials.

Finally, what of negative ions? Machinery such as air-conditioning equipment or electric heaters may deplete negative ions in the workplace. Ion concentrations may also be affected by the weather. Adverse effects of negative ion depletion on health, such as increased asthma and headaches, seem to be fairly well substantiated (Farmer, 1992). However, Farmer's (1992) review also concludes that effects on mood and performance appear weak and inconsistent, although there is some evidence for simple RT being decreased by negative ions but increased by positive ions. There seems to be little evidence for beneficial effects of increasing ion concentrations beyond natural levels, as a negative ion machine does.

## 11.5 CONCLUSIONS

The physical environment is a rich source of potential stressors. It is clear that intense stimuli of various kinds often affect performance, and extremes of temperature seem to be a particularly potent stressor. The extent to which performance is vulnerable to significant impairment in typical working environments is less clear. Thermal stress has been fairly extensively investigated, but data on other sources of stress, such as those associated with information technology, are patchy and inconclusive. Where effects are observed, they may be explained at several different levels. There is good evidence for biologically-based effects of a variety of stressors, including heat-induced breakdown of thermoregulation, and temporary or permananent damaging of CNS functioning induced by pollutants and toxins. Physical stressors often influence arousal, but there is little evidence on whether arousal change actually mediates the stressor effect on performance, or whether changes in arousal and cognitive functioning are independent of one another. Arousal theory often seems to be more a ritual invocation than a satisfactory explanation in this area of research.

Other performance effects seem to be due to the processing of the specific stimuli associated with the stressor. Glare effects, for example, appear to be primarily perceptual, and vibration directly disrupts both visual fixation and muscular activity. In other words, such influences act through changing the nature of the task, and they should probably not be attributed to "stress" in the transactional sense discussed in 9.2.2. The importance of information-processing analyses is also demonstrated by the task-dependence of stressor effects, although the exact nature of task-dependence is often unclear from the data available.

Finally, performance change may also reflect the impact of the stressor at the knowledge level, in influencing strategy and appraisals of the personal significance of the task. This level of analysis has been neglected in studies of physical stressors, though its relevance seems clear. For example, the effects on a painter of a headache are likely to depend on whether it is appraised as a minor cold symptom or as a sign of solvent poisoning. In the area of VDU use especially, it seems that the operator's beliefs about personal competence in using information technology are likely to impact on stress and performance.

If arousal theory explanations are often vague, so too is the alternative hypothesis that stress effects are due to "distraction". The present analysis indicates that two senses of distraction should be distinguished. First, there is distraction in the sense of additional information to be processed, with no particular personal or affective significance. Second, there is distraction operating at the knowledge level, in the sense that the focus of attention is diverted towards processing of the personal significance of stimuli (as discussed further in 15.3.4). Indeed, distraction in this sense may operate in the absence of any distraction at the symbol processing level, if the person is worried about a stressor such as radiation from VDUs, which does not impact directly on processing. As described above, several studies suggest that effects of stressors on discomfort are dissociated from their effects on performance. Discomfort does not necessarily induce performance deficit, perhaps because of the person's ability to compensate for any processing-level distraction (Hancock & Warm, 1989). However, a discomfort rating may not adequately represent the person's success in coping with stressors. Distance runners routinely ignore high levels of discomfort because it is understood to be an integral part of the experience. Conversely, even minor physical symptoms may be highly stressful for hypochondriacs.

At a practical level, there is sufficient evidence to suggest that physical stressors may be a significant problem in some real-world environments. Ergonomists have made significant advances in minimising these problems. For example, controls in vehicles may be designed to be insensitive to vibration, lighting can be designed to minimise glare and flicker, and the person may be shielded from thermal environments by suitable clothing. The role of the individual's appraisal of the stressor has been neglected, and requires the application of the methods of differential psychology discussed in Chapters 14 and 15.

## FURTHER READING

Much of the literature in this area must be obtained from rather specialist journals, such as *Aviation,* *Space, and Environmental Medicine*. Furthermore, the level of research activity on specific stressors tends to wax and wane over the years, and, in some cases, the clearest demonstrations of performance effects are to be found in papers published in the 1950s and 1960s, or even earlier. However, the impact of various physical stressors on performance is well covered by Smith and Jones (1992a: Vol. 1). Ramsey (1983) provides an accessible account of thermal stress. Hancock's (1986) analysis of heat effects is considered a classic paper in the field.

# 12

# Fatigue and the energetics of performance

## 12.1 INTRODUCTION: FATIGUE AND ENERGETICS

The idea that processing requires some form of energisation was introduced in 2.4. We discussed the concept of "resources" as a metaphorical reservoir of energy or fuel for processing. We have seen also that studies of vigilance (Chapter 6) suggest that the reservoir of attentional resources may become depleted as a result of prolonged demanding work, leading to deterioration in performance efficiency over time. In this chapter, we consider in more detail the circumstances under which the person may have difficulty energising performance adequately.

Fatigue refers to feelings of tiredness and bodily discomfort associated with prolonged activity. Table 12.1 shows some symptoms of fatigue identified in a factor analysis of questionnaire responses (Matthews & Desmond, 1998). The boredom factor here overlaps considerably with the "task disengagement" stress factor discussed in 9.4.1. Fatigue may cause errors and accidents. For example, truck drivers seem to be more prone to accidents when the drive is very long (>14 hours),

or when it takes place at night (McDonald, 1984). Fatigue is also a concern in various work environments, such as hospitals where junior doctors are expected to work long hours (Spurgeon & Harrington, 1989). It is often difficult to pinpoint the exact role of fatigue in accidents and performance impairment. Apart from sleep itself, fatigue may influence various information-processing functions in the wakeful operator. Furthermore, it may be important to distinguish different sources of fatigue. Prolonged concentration, loss of sleep and working at night may all cause subjective tiredness, but differ in their effects on performance. Hence, well-controlled laboratory studies are essential for investigating fatigue effects. Such studies also control for extraneous factors such as absence of daylight which may influence real-world data.

Studies of fatigue are not simply studies of depletion of attentional resources. As we saw in 5.3, resources can be defined and investigated purely in terms of variation in the quality of performance as task demands are varied. Resources can be studied without making any reference to the performer's state of mind, or to states of subjective fatigue. However, people often feel that

**TABLE 12.1**

Four types of fatigue symptom identified by factor analysis (Matthews & Desmond, 1998).

| Visual fatigue | Boredom | Malaise | Muscular fatigue |
|---|---|---|---|
| Eye strain | Task monotonous | Nausea | Physical tiredness |
| Blurred vision | Apathy | Headache | Limb tremors |
| Flickering sensations | Task aversion | Auditory problems | Stiffness |

performance is vulnerable to impairment when they are tired or sleepy, so it is important to assess whether fatigue relates to the cognitive energisation mechanisms previously discussed, or to other mechanisms entirely.

In this chapter, we assess the psychological impact of three distinct influences on fatigue and energisation: prolonged task performance, sleep deprivation and time of day. Two themes of the chapter should be highlighted. First, as with stressors generally, fatiguing agents influence a variety of processing functions, including strategy selection and adaptive control of performance. Equating fatigue with reduced resource availability at best explains only a part of the empirical data. Second, psychobiological approaches have been particularly important for investigating this class of stressor. For example, it has been tempting to attribute fatigue-related impairment to under-arousal, as specified by the Yerkes-Dodson Law. We shall see that, although more specific physiological mechanisms may be important, arousal theory does not provide an adequate explanation for either the psychological or physiological correlates of fatigue.

## 12.2 TASK-INDUCED FATIGUE

We are all familiar with the fatigue that results from prolonged mental activity but, psychologically, there are two distinct senses in which we can conceptualise fatigue (see Holding, 1983). First, the fatigue may be task-specific; loosely, the person is tired *of* performing a particular task, so that fatigue may be alleviated by doing some different activity. Alternatively, the fatigue may be generalised; the person is in a state of tiredness, and switching to another task will not help recovery. In reviewing fatigue, we first describe components of the fatigue state, and then assess the consequences for performance of the two senses of fatigue. Reviews by Holding (1983), Krueger (1989) and Craig and Cooper (1992) are recommended for further reading on task-induced fatigue effects.

### 12.2.1 Physiological and subjective components

It has been recognised from the first systematic analyses of fatigue (Bartley & Chute, 1947; Bills, 1934) that the fatigue state may have several distinct components. Bills (1934) distinguished physiological fatigue, subjective fatigue and objective fatigue, evident in measures of performance. Physiological fatigue symptoms have generally been seen as of marginal relevance to performance studies (see Craig & Cooper, 1992). Craig and Cooper (1992) make two essential points. First, physiological changes during performance are not directly related to the brain's consumption of energy during performance; the brain does not simply runs out of fuel (i.e. blood glucose), except under rather unusual circumstances such as hypoglycaemia (see 13.3.3). Second, concomitants of fatigue such as increased muscle tension often reflect secondary consequences of the person's compensatory effort. Intense physical activity may evoke rather more substantial physiological changes, but physical fatigue is beyond the scope of this chapter.

Assessment of subjective fatigue symptoms is straightforward, and there are a variety of fatigue indices in use (e.g. Yoshitake, 1978): Table 12.1

lists some typical subjective fatigue symptoms grouped into clusters on the basis of a factor analysis of symptom reports (Matthews & Desmond, 1998). These clusters themselves intercorrelate to define a general fatigue factor. Depending on the context, we may wish to treat fatigue as a single construct, or focus on one or more of its components. As we saw in 11.4.1, there is a specialised literature on visual fatigue, for example (Chi & Lin, 1998; Wilkins, 1995).

Subjective fatigue symptoms also relate to other forms of subjective distress. Matthews & Desmond (1998) found that fatigue symptoms are substantially correlated with tension and unhappiness, implying a degree of overlap between subjective fatigue and other stress states. As Galinsky et al. (1993) have shown, maintaining concentration on a tedious or difficult task over time may itself be a source of stress. In addition, the conflict between the requirement to perform the task and the person's perceived incapacity to perform successfully is likely to be stressful. The potential complexity of fatigue states is illustrated by the work-induced "burnout" syndrome in which tiredness may be accompanied by feelings of anger, anxiety and tension (Maslach & Jackson, 1981). Subjective fatigue symptoms (like physiological fatigue measures) show a mixture of indications of raised and depressed arousal. Fatigue also changes the way the person thinks about the task. The perceived exertion felt in performing a task of constant workload rises with prolonged performance (Ryman, Naitoh, & Englund, 1989).

## 12.2.2 Studies of task-specific fatigue

It is relatively straightforward to investigate task-specific fatigue by monitoring performance levels during a protracted period of work on some task. In fact, deterioration in overall performance efficiency is relatively unusual, particularly when the task is complex or skilled (Holding, 1983). Studies of vigilance (see Chapter 6) demonstrate that on certain tasks it may be difficult to maintain performance over time, but even in this case, loss of perceptual sensitivity (as opposed to changes in response criterion), depends on the nature of the task. The most demanding vigilance tasks, with features such as high event rates, memory loads

and degraded stimuli show sensitivity decrement most reliably (See et al., 1995). Broadly, it seems that the task must be both uninteresting and mentally demanding for reliable fatigue effects on performance efficiency to be found. In real-world settings, social factors may also be important. Performance in groups may be more fatigue-sensitive because fatigued individuals engage in 'social loafing', i.e. leaving tasks for others to perform (Hoeksema-van Orden, Gaillard, & Buunk, 1998).

On tasks other than vigilance, fatigue may be most evident in measures of response variability, and occasional very slow responses (Craig & Cooper, 1992). On continuous performance tasks, fatigue leads to occasional pauses or failures of attention. Bertelson and Joffe (1963) showed on a continuous four-choice reaction time task that slow responses are preceded by a short period of relatively slow, inaccurate responding, which may reflect either an accumulation of fatigue or a progressive breakdown of voluntary control of performance (Craig & Cooper, 1992).

Fatigue effects more subtle than simple loss of performance efficiency are also evident in skilled performance. The pioneering work in this area was conducted by Drew (1940) and Bartlett (1943), using a device known as the Cambridge Cockpit, a crude simulation of controlling an aircraft in response to information presented on a number of displays. The detailed observations of the researchers have rarely been surpassed in subsequent studies (see Rolfe, 1996). Several kinds of performance impairment were found, including failure to execute otherwise correct actions at the appropriate time, periodic lapses of attention, and a tendency to focus attention on the most important displays such as the compass, while neglecting secondary displays such as the fuel gauge. Bartlett (1943) characterised these changes as resulting from a progressive loss of coordination of the various components of the task. More recent studies of extended flight have provided similar results, although fatigued pilots normally avoid major incidents (Krueger, 1989). In terms of contemporary theory, the data are suggestive of impairment of the supervisory executive attentional functions described in 3.3.2. Loss of executive control may also explain why effects of other stressors on performance, such as noise and sleep deprivation, become more pronounced as the period of work is extended (Broadbent, 1971).

More recent work on skill has focused on fatigue in transportation. Survey data suggest that 7% of motor vehicle accidents may be attributed to fatigue, a figure rising to 15% for motorway (freeway) accidents (Maycock, 1997). Similarly, pilot fatigue may be implicated in upwards of 20% of near-accidents in aviation (Stokes & Kite, 1994). Heightened accident risk is partly due to sleepiness and night-time impairment of performance, factors discussed further below. However, there is a considerable literature on vehicle operation that has investigated time on task effects in daytime driving. Results are somewhat inconsistent (McDonald, 1984), but a number of studies (e.g. Brookhuis & De Waard, 1993) have shown impairment of lateral tracking (i.e. maintaining lane position). Vigilance decrement occurs infrequently (Parasuraman & Nestor, 1991), although some studies showed slowing of response to secondary target stimuli (Lisper & Eriksson, 1980). These studies tend to neglect the coordination of task components identified as critical by Bartlett (1943). Some evidence has been found for loss of active control of performance, such as increased frequency of large steering movements, which may compensate for major lapses of attention (Mackie & Miller, 1978). Performance also tends to become more variable as time progresses (Haworth, 1996), and manoeuvres become more risky (Brown, Tickner, & Simmonds, 1970). It is plausible, but unconfirmed, that the driver loses his or her overall grasp of the task environment (sometimes termed "situation awareness", see 8.2.2).

### 12.2.3  After-effects of prolonged work

The second sense in which a person may be fatigued is that a general fatigue state is produced, which is associated with performance decrement or change across tasks other than that used to produce fatigue. If such a state is induced, it should be possible to demonstrate fatigue *after-effects*. For example, Welford, Brown and Gabb (1950) required flight crew to perform an electrical problem-solving task following a long flight. The effect of exposure to the flight was to increase the number of resistance readings taken with a meter during problem solution; crew members tended to forget readings previously taken when fatigued. However, the evidence for after-effects obtained by this study is unusual; as Holding (1983) points out in his review of the area, most studies fail to show after-effects, even after strong fatigue inductions. Chiles (1955; cited in Craig & Cooper, 1992) failed to show any deterioration on a tracking task performed during breaks from an aircraft simulator task on which subjects performed for durations as long as 56 hours. Some became so fatigued they were unable to walk, but still performed at normal levels on the tracking task! In fact, after-effects may even be positive. Hogervorst et al. (1996) found that performance on cognitive and psychomotor tasks was enhanced by prior strenuous exercise on a bicycle ergometer, effects attributed to arousal and/or expectancies. Their choice of physically fit participants —competitive cyclists and triathletes—may also have contributed to the finding.

After-effects may be more evident on more subtle performance measures. Shingledecker and Holding (1974) designed an electrical fault-finding task, known as COPE (choice of probability/effort), to investigate people's willingness to invest effort to improve performance. Participants were forced to choose between three stategies for problem-solving which differed in required effort and likelihood of success: the less the effort, the lower the probability of finding the faulty component in the circuit. After practice, non-fatigued participants choose the most effort-demanding, high probability alternative about 50% of the time. However, when participants were fatigued by 24–32 hours' work on a battery of information-processing tasks, they tended to opt for easy but less successful strategies, choosing the high probability option on only about 25% of occasions. As in the case of task-specific fatigue, there may be increasing reluctance or inability to exert voluntary control over performance.

Desmond and Matthews (1997) developed a simulated driving paradigm, in which fatigue was induced by a dual-task manipulation, having participants perform a perceptually and cognitively demanding signal detection task concurrently with driving. The demands of the driving task itself were varied by having participants drive on both straight and curved road sections. The lower part of Fig. 12.1 shows performance data from the fatigue condition of the Desmond and Matthews study, whereas the upper part shows subjective fatigue scores (obtained from Fairclough & Ward's, 1996, PASS measure), collected during a subsequent, similar study (Desmond, 1997). Driving performance was assessed with a measure of "heading error"; higher values indicate poorer control of lateral position. After a period of single-task driving, fatigue was induced during four

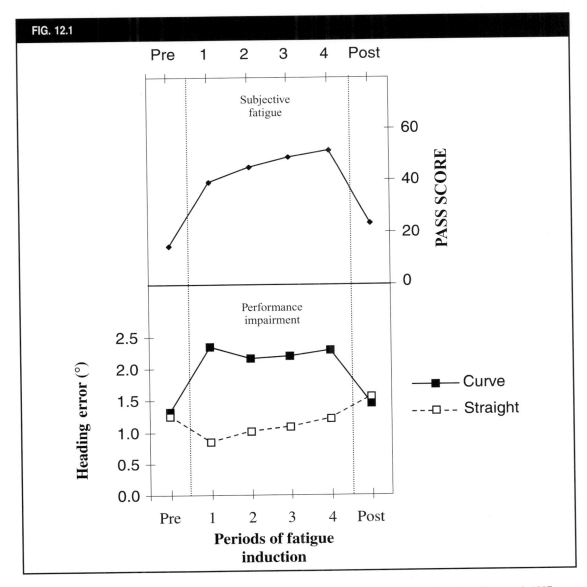

**FIG. 12.1**

Driving performance (heading error) and subjective fatigue before, during and after a fatigue induction (Desmond, 1997; Desmond & Matthews, 1997).

successive periods of dual-task driving, which imposed a high workload and subjective fatigue. After-effects were assessed in a post-induction phase of single-task driving.

One possibility is that prolonged, demanding driving depletes resources. If so, fatigue effects should increase as the driving task becomes more demanding. In fact, impairments were found on straight but not on curved road sections, i.e. when task demands were relatively low. Figure 12.1 shows that, during fatigue induction, the driver's heading error (a measure of impaired vehicle control) increased progressively during straight road driving, continuing to increase even when workload was decreased, in the post-induction phase. Dual-task interference was evident during curve driving, but there was no progressive performance deterioration, and performance recovered following the fatigue induction. Hence, the fatigue effect did not appear to be mediated by loss of attentional resources. Instead, Desmond and Matthews (1997) suggest that drivers become reluctant to apply effort to the task when it is appraised as undemanding. They reported reduced motivation and efforts at active coping, consistent with this hypothesis, together with fatigue symptoms of the kind listed in Table 12.1. However, Fig. 12.1 also shows dissociation between subjective fatigue and objective performance change, implying that it may be the driver's ability to cope with fatigue symptoms, as much as the symptoms themselves, which is critical. Survey data from airline pilots also suggest that choice of coping strategy is important for maintaining alertness in operational settings (Petrie & Dawson, 1997).

## 12.3 SLEEP DEPRIVATION

Sleep is something of a curiosity. If forced by circumstances to stay awake all night, we feel the lack of sleep acutely. However, the function of sleep remains obscure. Webb (1979, 1982a) identifies two broad possibilities. First, sleep may have a restorative effect, allowing the brain to restore its function after the waking period, although there is little direct evidence of the nature of the physi-ological processes involved, and there is no consistent evidence for a chemical indicator of need for sleep (Borbely & Tobler, 1989). Second, sleep may be a biological rhythm, with the adaptive function of keeping the person inactive during the night.

Sleep actually comprises a variety of states. The electroencephalogram (EEG) of a person in "normal" sleep typically shows signs of cortical inactivity; the waveforms have a lower frequency and higher amplitude than those of an EEG taken during wakefulness. Sleepers also experience so-called REM sleep, characterised by high frequency, low amplitude EEG waveforms and rapid eye movements (REMs). REM sleep is also associated with dreaming. Within normal, non-REM sleep, a series of stages, from Stage 1–4, may be distinguished from the EEG. Stage 1 is the lightest sleep; Stage 4 the deepest. For example, Bonnet, Johnson and Webb (1978) reported a study in which, on average, a 70 db tone was sufficient to wake a Stage 2 sleeper, but a 92 db tone was necessary for a Stage 4 sleeper. Deep sleep occurs mainly during the early part of the night; light sleep and REM sleep later in the night, as shown in Fig. 12.2. Thus, when a person stays awake and fails to sleep, there may be more than one distinct deprivation effect, associated with the different types of sleep.

### 12.3.1 The investigation of sleep loss effects

The simplest design for a total sleep deprivation experiment involves monitoring performance during a period of wakefulness lasting at least 24 hours. People must, of course, be prevented from falling asleep during this time although, with increasing levels of sleep deprivation, it becomes impossible to prevent the person taking brief "microsleeps" (Dement, 1974). Performance may be measured before and after sleep deprivation and, ideally, compared with performance in control participants not subjected to sleep deprivation. In some studies, performance is also measured after the sleep-deprived participants have recovered from their ordeal by catching up on the sleep lost. Measurement of performance after recovery provides a degree of control for effects of practice or repeated exposure to the tasks

FIG. 12.2

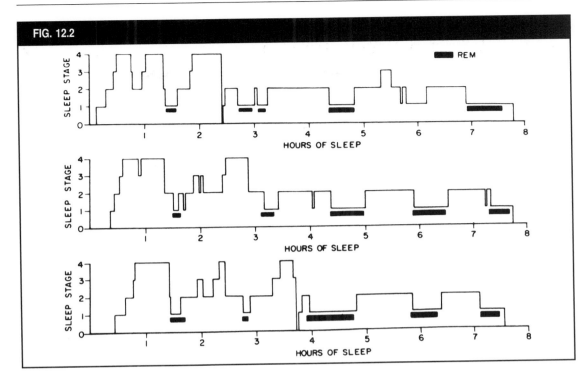

Structure of sleep stages during the night (Webb, 1982).

performed. It is also important to control for the time of day in such studies; hence, the performance of sleep-deprived volunteers is normally tested during the day rather than during the night, for comparison with normal, non-sleep deprived performance levels. Testing over several days of sleep deprivation allows its accumulating effects to be distinguished from the cyclic changes in performance driven by circadian rhythms (Babkoff, Caspy, & Mikulincer, 1991).

Sleep deprivation has quite a variety of subjective effects, including tiredness, boredom and irritability (e.g. Mertens & Collins, 1986). Use of self-report arousal measures suggests sleepiness is primarily dearousing in that it strongly reduces subjective energy and vigour although, to a lesser degree, it also increases feelings of tension (Matthews, Jones, & Chamberlain, 1990). Physiological changes are generally minor, and the traditional autonomic nervous system (a.n.s.) indicators of arousal such as heart rate and skin conductance are often little affected. EEG record-

ings, however, are indicative of reduced cortical arousal; the EEGs of sleep-deprived individuals are similar to those of people in the process of falling asleep (Tilley & Brown, 1992). Broadbent (1971) suggests that effects on the a.n.s. depend on task demands, with lowered arousal when the task is easy but increased arousal when the task is demanding. For example, Wilkinson (1962) showed that during sleep deprivation mental arithmetic performance was maintained more effectively in those participants who showed the largest muscle tension increases. Muscle tension in this context may be an indication of compensatory effort.

## 12.3.2 Performance decrements

Performance decrements associated with total sleep deprivation are frequently observed (see Johnson, 1982, Pilcher & Huffcut, 1996 and Tilley & Brown, 1992, for reviews). A variety of processing functions may be impaired including visual perception (Quant, 1992), serial reaction and sustained attention (Davies & Parasuraman, 1982), short-term (Polzella, 1975) and long-term recall (Idzikowski, 1984), implicit learning (Heuer et al., 1998), and psychomotor tasks such as tracking (Mertens & Collins, 1986). More complex information-processing tasks showing deficits include logical reasoning and mental arithmetic (Angus, Heslegrave, & Myles, 1985) simulated driving (Lenne, Triggs, & Redman, 1998; Fairclough & Graham, 1999), and simulated flight (Morris & Miller, 1996). However, performance is not always impaired by sleep loss, and some tasks appear more sensitive than others. Complex intellectual tasks such as reading comprehension, decision-making and intelligence test performance show relatively weak sleep deprivation effects (Horne, 1988); possibly such tasks are more engaging for the subject than information-processing tasks such as memory search. Johnson (1982) and Caldwell and Ramspott (1998) identify a number of variables that moderate the impact of sleep deprivation on performance, including task difficulty and complexity, and participant interest and motivation. Various manipulations of task difficulty seem to accentuate performance decrement. For example, decrement effects are stronger on tasks of long duration, with vigilance tasks being particularly sensitive to performance impairment (see Davies & Parasuraman, 1982). Wilkinson (1964) showed that 10-choice card sorting was more strongly impaired by sleep deprivation than 4-choice card sorting. Similarly, sleep deprivation effects on memory search increase as memory load increases (Babkoff et al., 1988).

The importance of motivation was demonstrated by Wilkinson (1964), who had sailors perform two complex, serial decision tasks simulating aspects of naval warfare. One was relatively realistic and was popular with the sailors, whereas the other was more abstract. Performance of the better-liked task was preserved across 50 hours of sleep deprivation, but performance of the other task declined rapidly and severely. Games such as darts and table tennis were also unaffected. Caldwell and Ramspott (1998) point out that task complexity may decrease the sensitivity of the task to sleep deprivation effects through increasing motivation, but complexity may also increase sensitivity if it is associated with higher task de-

mands. Spurgeon and Harrington (1989), in reviewing the rather inconsistent evidence on sleep deprivation effects in junior doctors, suggest that motivation helps them to maintain performance, at least at relatively moderate levels of deprivation. Hockey, Wastell, and Sauer (1998) found no generally detrimental effects of sleep deprivation on a process control task, although participants showed slower re-sponse to secondary probe stimuli and strategy changes when the task was machine- rather than human-controlled. They found that compensatory effort appeared to protect performance. External manipulations of motivation, such as incentives for performance, also tend to reduce detrimental effects of sleep deprivation (e.g. Horne & Pettitt, 1985).

### 12.3.3 Theories of sleep deprivation effects

One explanation for sleep deprivation effects is that performance is impaired due to the low arousal evident at a subjective level. The arousal hypothesis receives some support from studies showing that arousing stressors such as noise and stimulant drugs tend to reduce performance decrement (Broadbent, 1971; Johnson, 1982). For example, in military helicopter pilots flying during 40-hour sleep deprivation periods, dextroamphetamine reduces subjective fatigue, increases arousal as indexed by EEG measures, and enhances performance of turning manoeuvres (Caldwell & Caldwell, 1997). If sleep-deprived people are underaroused, they should show reduced attentional selectivity. The evidence on this issue from studies of dual-task performance is conflicting: Hockey (1970b) found that sleep deprivation impaired primary task performance only, consistent with arousal theory. However, Sanders and Reitsma (1982) obtained the opposite result, with sleep deprivation slowing response times more to peripheral than to central stimuli. The tendency for sleep deprivation to have more adverse effects on more difficult tasks is strongly inconsistent with arousal theory; the Yerkes-Dodson Law states that optimal performance should be achieved at low levels of arousal when the task is difficult.

The most-widely accepted alternative theory is the *lapse hypothesis*. This hypothesis states that sleep loss does not actually lead to a tonic

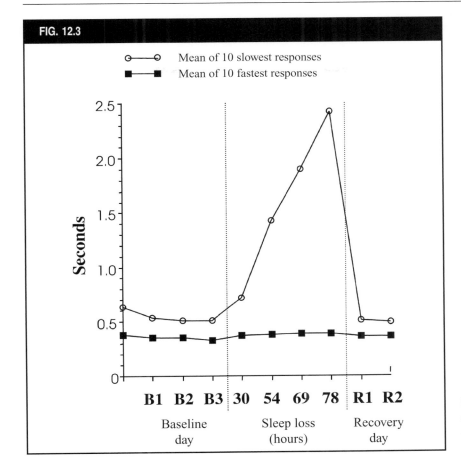

**FIG. 12.3**

○——○ Mean of 10 slowest responses
■——■ Mean of 10 fastest responses

B1  B2  B3  30  54  69  78  R1  R2

Baseline       Sleep loss       Recovery
day           (hours)          day

Lapses in attention during choice reaction time, in a sleep loss study (Williams et al., 1959).

impairment of processing efficiency. Instead, the person becomes increasingly prone to lapses of attention lasting for two seconds or so, which may coincide with "microsleeps". Broadbent (1955, p. 2) compared the sleep-deprived individual to "... a motor which after much use misfires, runs normally for a while, then falters again and so on". Figure 12.3 shows data from a study of 2-choice reaction time (Williams, Lubin, & Goodnow, 1959) which support the lapse hypothesis. For each set of trials (72 in total), Williams et al. (1959) picked out each participant's 10 fastest and 10 slowest responses, and computed mean RT for each type of response. Figure 12.3 shows that the mean for the fastest times was essentially unchanged during sleep loss, but the mean for the slowest times increases dramatically with increas-

ing sleep loss. In other words, the processing system is at times capable of functioning as well as it does when the person has slept normally. Sleep deprivation acts to interrupt normal functioning with short periods of inefficiency. It follows from the lapse hypothesis that sleep deprivation is only likely to lead to errors if stimuli are briefly presented, such that if a lapse coincides with stimulus presentation it will not be attended at all. Errors are thus more likely on externally-paced tasks, in which the participant lacks control over the presentation of important stimuli (Koslowsky & Babkoff, 1992). For example, the sleep-deprived motorist might not notice that a car in front is braking until too late to avoid an accident. The main weakness of the lapse hypothesis is that it is essentially a re-description of the data, and does not explain the nature of attentional lapses in detail (Eysenck, 1982). Furthermore, a recent study (Monk & Carrier, 1997) showed that sleep deprivation affected processing time on a logical reasoning task separately from microsleeps, psychomotor slowing and inattention. Sleep deprivation may not be restricted to lapse effects.

### 12.3.4 Sleep disturbance studies

There are a variety of other ways in which sleep may be disrupted, other than total sleep deprivation. In *partial sleep deprivation* studies, the person is permitted a certain number of hours sleep per night before being woken. Minor loss of sleep, curtailing sleep duration to five or six hours per night, does not always affect performance, but there is a cumulative effect. Dinges et al. (1997) restricted sleep to five hours per night for seven nights and tested participants on a short battery of measures three times each day. Participants became progressively sleepier across the days of the study. Their performance on a psychomotor task also deteriorated. They appeared to develop a progressively larger sleep "debt" with each night of limited sleep. Data of this kind are disturbing because comparable, relatively minor levels of sleep deprivation have been linked to loss of alertness in real world operators such as long-haul truck drivers (Mitler et al., 1997). Gilberg, Kecklund, Axelsson and Akerstedt (1996) showed that a 30-minute daytime nap was effective in eliminating sleepiness and loss of vigilance induced by restricting sleep to four hours only.

More severe deprivation (three hours or less of sleep per night) leads to decrements which may be as large as those of total sleep deprivation (Tilley & Brown, 1992). Sleep disorders such as insomnia and narcolepsy (involuntary daytime sleeping) also appear to be associated with disturbances in psychological function (e.g. Bonnet & Rosa, 1987). Wilkinson, Edwards, and Haines (1966) suggest that performance may be especially impaired by loss of deep (Stage 4) sleep. Because deep sleep is concentrated in the early part of the night, a person sleeping for four or five hours may obtain close to the normal quantity of this type of sleep. When people are asked to sleep for *longer* than usual performance may

also be impaired. On the basis of this "Rip van Winkle" effect, Taub and Berger (1976) suggest that any disruption of normal sleep patterns tends to degrade performance. However, other work shows benefits from moderate sleep extension, implying that normal sleep durations of 7–8 hours are actually insufficient (Carskadon & Roth, 1991).

Sleep deprivation causes lack of both normal, non-REM sleep and REM sleep. It is possible selectively to deprive the person of REM sleep by monitoring the sleeper's EEG and eye movements, and waking the person whenever a period of REM sleep begins. Pearlman (1982) concludes from a review of the relevant literature that REM sleep deprivation most strongly affects learning and long-term retention when the task is complex or challenging. For example, Tilley and Empson (1978) compared people selectively deprived of either REM sleep or Stage 4 sleep. The REM-sleep deprived group showed poorer retention of two short stories. Findings of this kind suggest that REM sleep (and perhaps dreams) facilitate the consolidation of meaningful events in long term memory, although it may have other functions also (Pearlman, 1982).

## 12.4 TIME OF DAY AND CIRCADIAN RHYTHMS

### 12.4.1 Early studies: Synchrony of performance and body temperature rhythms?

Research on the effects of time of day on performance has quite a long history, beginning in the later years of the last century (see Folkard, 1983). Early studies comparing performance at times during the morning, afternoon and evening provided rather inconsistent results, due to somewhat arbitrary selection of tasks (see Freeman & Hovland, 1934). Modern research owes much to work by Kleitman (1963), who noticed that time of day had similar effects on both body temperature and RT. Figure 12.4 shows illustrative data from a single participant, graphed with faster RTs at the top to show the parallelism between the two measures. Early in the morning, the body was relatively cool, and RTs long. During the day

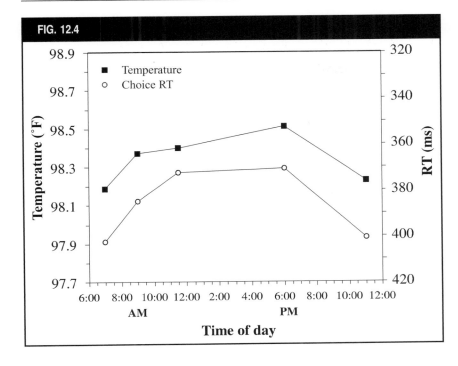

**FIG. 12.4**

Parallelism of diurnal rhythms in body temperature and RT (Kleitman, 1963).

the body temperature increased, and RTs became shorter, up until the late afternoon or early evening, after which the person became cooler and slower to respond again. Changes of this kind in physiological or psychological functioning are often called diurnal or circadian rhythms. Kleitman also noted that some indices of a.n.s. activity showed somewhat similar diurnal trends to body temperature. Kleitman (1963) proposed that body temperature is an index of metabolic activity, which directly influences performance.

Three findings obtained in subsequent research showed that Kleitman (1963) committed the error of inferring causality from correlation. First, Rutenfranz, Aschoff and Mann (1972) measured choice RT and body temperature at various times of day, and correlated RT and temperature at each of the times. The correlations were non-significant, implying that there was no direct relationship between the two variables. Second, in the early afternoon there is a "post-lunch dip" in performance, but not in body temperature (Colquhoun, 1971), showing that time of day effects on performance and temperature are not as

similar as Kleitman (1963) supposed. The post-lunch dip is discussed further in 13.4.1. Third, not all tasks show peak performance late in the day: as Kleitman (1963) himself recognised, short-term memory tasks and card-sorting tasks are performed best in the morning or around midday.

### 12.4.2 The arousal hypothesis for time of day effects

Blake (1967) and Colquhoun (1971) attempted to remedy some of the deficiencies of Kleitman's (1963) hypothesis by proposing an arousal theory of time of day effects. Like Broadbent (1971) they de-emphasised the direct measurement of arousal, in favour of experimental evidence taken from studies of the interaction of time of day with other stressors. Colquhoun (1971) proposed that, as the circadian rhythm in body temperature rhythm would tend to suggest, people are more aroused in the evening than in the morning. However, body temperature is not a direct index of arousal; people also tend to be dearoused during the post-lunch dip, despite the lack of a dip in temperature at this time. The differing circadian rhythms in

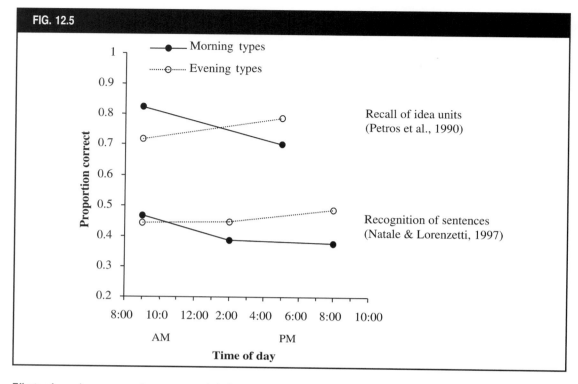

**FIG. 12.5**

Effects of morningness–eveningness on verbal short-term memory, in two studies.

performance shown by different tasks result from variation in task difficulty, as specified by the Yerkes-Dodson Law. Tasks such as reaction time, which show an evening peak, are relatively simple and so benefit from high arousal. Other tasks, such as those requiring STM, are more difficult, so the person is overaroused for performance in the evening, and morning performance is better. Blake (1967) and Colquhoun (1971) discuss interactions between time of day and stressors such as noise and sleep deprivation which appear to support the arousal hypothesis.

The arousal theory of time of day effects has encountered three types of difficulties. First, it is uncertain whether arousal is actually highest in the evening, as other indices attain peak levels at other times. Unlike body temperature, adrenaline excretion and subjective energy reach a peak at about midday. Second, it has transpired that time of day has a variety of quite subtle effects on performance, such as change in task strategy. The Yerkes-Dodson

Law seems inadequate to explain these effects, as we shall see when we consider the performance data in more detail in the next section.

Third, people show pronounced individual differences in preferred time of day. Several questionnaires discriminate individuals who feel at their best in the morning (morning types or "larks") from those who prefer to be active in the evening (evening types or "night owls"), as well as intermediate types without marked preference (Smith, Reilly, & Midkiff, 1989). Matthews (1988) confirmed that morning types were higher in subjective arousal in the morning than in the evening, but subjective arousal was higher in the evening for evening types. Figure 12.5 plots data from two studies of immediate memory for verbal material, which obtained results consistent with expectation, such that morning types tend to show better recall and recognition in the morning, whereas evening types do better in the evening. However, it is not clear that these effects are

**TABLE 12.2**

Examples of tasks differing in time of peak performance.

| Peak time | Task |
| --- | --- |
| Early morning | Immediate memory for prose (Folkard & Monk, 1980) |
| Midday | Logical reasoning (Folkard, 1975)<br>Ordered digit recall (Blake, 1967)<br>Motor performance (Monk & Leng, 1982) |
| Afternoon or evening | Serial reaction time (Elsass et al., 1981)<br>Serial visual search (Monk, 1979)<br>Retrieval from semantic memory (Tilley & Warren, 1983) |

mediated by individual differences in arousal, as circadian rhythms in performance and arousal in these groups do not seem to coincide (Eysenck, 1982), and morningness–eveningness effects seem to vary with the processing demands of the task (Natale & Lorenzetti, 1997).

Fourth, the pattern of interaction between time of day and other stressors is not fully consistent with arousal theory. Smith (1992a) describes a number of failures to find interaction between time of day and noise. In addition, interactions between time of day and arousing stressors are different in individuals of extravert and introvert personality. Although Blake (1967) attempted to incorporate these effects into arousal theory, subsequent research has identified a number of difficulties in doing so (e.g. Eysenck & Folkard, 1980), as we shall see when we look at personality effects on performance in Chapter 15.

### 12.4.3 Circadian rhythms in performance

Experimental studies show that tasks differ in the time of day at which performance is best (see Monk, 1994, for a review of performance studies). Table 12.2 summarises some of the evidence. A critical issue is whether time of day influences the basic efficiency of certain information processing, or whether effects are mediated by strategy and executive control of performance. It is reasonable to suppose that there is some circadian variation in the efficiency of processing function. Folkard (1983) characterises cognitive tasks performed best at midday as those that require work-

ing memory, whose capacity may vary during the day. However, recent research has tended to emphasise the importance of strategy change, which will be discussed next.

The first potential strategic influence is speed–accuracy tradeoff. There is some evidence that people tend to show faster but more error-prone patterns of response later in the day (e.g. Monk & Leng, 1982). Studies of vigilance show that time of day influences response criterion ($\beta$) more reliably than it does $d'$. People appear ready to respond on the basis of less perceptual evidence later in the day (Craig et al., 1987). However, not all studies show evidence for speed–accuracy tradeoff. For example, Testu (1986) used a version of the Schneider and Shiffrin (1977) controlled visual search task discussed in 3.3.1 to show that both speed and accuracy of visual search were maximal in the early evening. Neither efficiency nor speed–accuracy tradeoff were affected when an automatic search task was used.

The strongest evidence for time of day effects on strategy use is provided by studies of memory. Folkard (1979) has proposed an influential hypothesis that people tend to rehearse material through subvocal articulation in the morning, but through semantic elaboration in the afternoon. Subvocal maintenance rehearsal is likely to benefit STM rather than LTM, with semantic elaboration having the opposite effect. Hence, the morning advantage for STM and the afternoon advantage for LTM shown in Table 12.2 may result from strategic preferences, rather than from changes in the efficiency of memory-related processing. Consistent with the hypothesis, Folkard (1979) demonstrated that when participants were prevented from using subvocal rehearsal experimentally, by repeating a nonsense phrase aloud, immediate free recall was impaired in the morning but not in the afternoon. Similarly, Oakhill (1986) has reported several studies of text recall which suggest that people tend to rely on verbatim memory in the morning, but greater elaboration and integration of the central themes of the text in the afternoon. Such strategic effects might account for the afternoon superiority for classroom learning of verbal material demonstrated by Davis (1987). However, it remains somewhat unclear *why* these strategic changes occur.

### 12.4.4 Multi-oscillator models of circadian rhythms

Contemporary theories of circadian rhythms in performance are based on the assumption that periodicity depends on both internal and external factors. There appear to be internal "clocks" within the brain which are predisposed to drive circadian rhythms at a fixed temporal period. However, unlike a wristwatch, the timekeeping of internal clocks is also influenced by external cues which indicate the time. In daily life, we are surrounded by obvious time cues such as clocks and the amount of daylight, and more subtle cues related to the timing of daily activities. For example, traffic jams on a road leading into a city centre suggest that the time may be around 0800. Such cues are collectively known as *zeitgebers*. When a person travels between time zones, zeitgebers influence the internal clock to reset its time to the new time zone, though it may take some time to do so. Technically, this process is known as *forced oscillation*; the time taken for the internal clock to complete a full cycle depends on both its natural, intrinsic cycle time, and the periodicity of external cues. Normally, of course, circadian rhythms in metabolic rate and performance are synchronised around the 24-hour day–night cycle, so that their natural periodicity is not apparent.

Investigation of internal clocks or *oscillators* requires rather specialised methods. Typically, experimental participants are required to spend several days or weeks in an underground bunker, in which the experimenters have complete control over time cues. In one type of experiment, there are no zeitgebers at all. Over time, the periodicity of internal clocks should then settle down at its natural, "free-running" cycle time. Studies of this kind (Campbell, 1992; Wever, 1979) show that, surprisingly perhaps, indices of psychological and physiological functioning do not usually show a 24-hour period. Body temperature, for example, adopts a 25-hour cycle.

A further technique is to provide false zeitgebers; a clock, set to run slow or fast, is provided so that the person's day is artificially lengthened or shortened. Under these conditions, different rhythms may become desynchronised, and adopt differing periods. For example, Folkard, Wever and Wildgruber (1983) showed that, after some days, working memory performance followed a 21-hour cycle. The false zeitberger technique (or *fractional desynchronisation*) can also be used to investigate the "strength" of internal oscillators; how willing the oscillator is to adopt the period of the external cues. Body temperature is a strong rhythm, in that its period never deviates by very much from its natural 25-hour cycle. In contrast, the wake–sleep cycle is more malleable, such that participants in temporal isolation studies may eventually adopt "days" ranging in duration from 12 hours to as much as 65 hours (Wever, 1985). Wever (1979, 1985) distinguishes a strong Type I oscillator controlling body temperature and performance on certain simple processing tasks from a weak Type II oscillator controlling the wake–sleep cycle, although both oscillators may influence any given rhythm to some degree. The strong oscillator produces marked "endogenous" rhythms, whereas the weak oscillator is more susceptible to "exogenous" influences.

In summary, multiple oscillators have potentially important implications for understanding circadian rhythms in performance. However, as yet, multi-oscillator theory does not account for the performance data reviewed in detail, and there are some anomalies. For example, serial search performance is normally better late in the day (Monk & Leng, 1982), and roughly parallels the body temperature rhythm. However, in temporal isolation, the serial search and temperature cycles become dissociated, the former peaking over five hours earlier (Folkard et al., 1985), implying that the two indices are not controlled by a common oscillator. It is also unclear whether strategy shifts during the day should be attributed to oscillators or to learning unrelated to oscillator function. Campbell (1992) points out that sample sizes in studies of performance oscillation are frequently small, and so conclusions drawn from such studies should be treated with extreme caution.

### 12.4.5 Applying multi-oscillator theory: Shift work and jet lag

Multi-oscillator theory has applications to the real-world problems of shift work and jet lag (Folkard, 1996; Monk & Folkard, 1985). Working during the night on a temporary or permanent basis often causes sleepiness and fatigue. There are concerns too about gastrointestinal and other physical health problems; it is estimated that about 20% of shift workers have to give it up after a short time because of physical and mental disturbance (Costa, 1996). Shift work is becoming increasingly prevalent worldwide, so it is important to investigate the causes of stress related to shift work, its consequences for performance, and practical interventions. For example, Luna (1997) expresses concerns about shift systems for air traffic controllers in the USA, which lead them to carry an acute sleep debt onto the night shift.

The majority of shift workers work nights on a rotating basis; permanent transition to a nocturnal existence is rare. Hence, one of the factors underlying development of stress symptoms is the speed with which circadian rhythms can adjust to shifts in activity. In the case of the person working rotating shifts, in which periods of day and night work are alternated, psychological disturbance may result from the process of adjustment of circadian rhythms to the new shift. It may take the "strong" body temperature rhythm up to two weeks or so to resynchronise (e.g. Monk, Knauth, Folkard, & Rutenfranz, 1978), leading to disruption of circadian rhythms. Reinberg et al. (1984) showed that poor tolerance of shift work was associated with desynchronisation of the body temperature and sleep–wake cycles. One consequence

of desynchronisation may be sleep disruption: night workers often experience difficulty sleeping during the day, and may build up an increasing sleep deficit (Akerstadt, 1988). Folkard (1996) points out that shift work tends to flatten out the body temperature cycle, rather than to induce clear phase shifts. He infers from studies modelling the cycle that shift work tends to affect the weak rather than the strong oscillator, assuming that both influence body temperature.

Folkard (1996) and Scott (1994) review the performance consequences of shift work. Night shifts are associated with reduced productivity and, as previously discussed, increased risk of industrial accidents and injury (see also 8.4.4), with worst performance at around 3am. In part, accidents happen at night because people fall asleep inadvertently, but performance efficiency on some tasks may be affected in the wakeful operator also as experimental studies simulating shiftwork conditions have shown (Monk & Folkard, 1983). Performance deficit may have a variety of sources. In addition to sleepiness, endogenous rhythms controlling performance may affect efficiency: tasks with high memory loads appear to show faster adjustment than those with low memory loads. The strong, slow-adjusting oscillator which drives body temperature may influence low memory load search tasks, but not more cognitive tasks with a high memory load.

As with most sources of "stress", the practical difficulties of shift work may be addressed at different levels. One strategy is to try to manipulate the underlying biology of the oscillators directly. We can reset a forced oscillation by delivering a "push" to the system at the appropriate part of its periodic cycle. Exposure to bright light of approximately 10,000 lux at times that phase-delay circadian rhythms has been beneficial for NASA personnel working on the space shuttle (Stewart, Hayes, & Eastman, 1995). Circadian rhythms appear to be controlled biochemically through melatonin secretion. Appropriately-timed administration of melatonin may be beneficial, although one recent study shows greater performance enhancement from bright light (Dawson, Encel, & Lushington, 1995). Alternatively, we can focus on the cognitive architecture, and try to develop shift work schedules that minimise loss of processing efficiency, i.e. through setting the timing and duration of shifts. The preferred schedule may depend on the information-processing demands of the task. Folkard (1996) argues that rapidly-rotating shifts may be more effective than long-term shifts for preserving performance on high-memory load tasks. Thirdly, the individual may be assisted in adjusting their lifestyle to shift work, by capitalising on the opportunities for daytime leisure, without sacrificing needed social interaction. There has been some interest in enhancement of coping strategies through effective temporal scheduling, although this approach is in its infancy (see Penn & Bootzin, 1990). Workers with an internal locus of control, with respect to shift work, report fewer problems of adjustment, perhaps because they apply greater effort to coping with difficulties (Smith, Spelten, & Norman, 1995). Bobko, Karpenko, Gerasimov and Chernyuk (1998) report that professionally adapted power plant shift workers are normally able to maintain a fairly constant level of performance, but performance is more variable under unfavourable working conditions. Alarmingly, they investigated the notorious Chernobyl nuclear power plant and found unfavourable working conditions and relatively high variability of performance.

Similarly, fatigue associated with jet lag may be the consequence of the several days it takes for oscillators to resynchronise to a change of time of day (Redfern, Minors, & Waterhouse, 1994). Because of the natural 25-hour period of the body temperature rhythm it should be easier to resynchronise to a backward time shift (i.e. later rising time) than to a forward shift (earlier rising time). Thus, adjustment to westbound travel may be more rapid than adjustment to eastbound travel (Klein, Wegmann, & Hunt, 1972). Time-scheduled melatonin supplements and bright light may assist adjustment.

## 12.5  THEORIES OF FATIGUE REVISITED

The research reviewed shows that there is no simple explanation for fatigue effects on performance. It is important to look at sources of fatigue in detail, and to distinguish different levels of explanation. In this section, we reconsider the theoretical questions raised earlier.

### 12.5.1  Fatigue as a general state

Attempts to develop explanations for fatigue in terms of a general, possibly physiologically-based state raise two questions. First, is there a "general fatigue state", with clear-cut consequences for performance? Second, if so, can this state be identified with low arousal? At a subjective level, we can indeed define and assess a general state of fatigue (Desmond & Matthews, 1997). Performance data are inconclusive, but this state may be associated with loss of vigilance, a tendency to lapses in attention, and reluctance to apply effort to the task in a variety of contexts. However, a state theory cannot explain the full range of performance consequences of the different sources of fatigue (prolonged work, sleep loss, circadian rhythms), such as the task-specific circadian rhythms illustrated in Fig. 12.5. In addition, subjective and objective measures of fatigue often dissociate. For example, people feel sleepy and tired first thing in the morning, but perform well on immediate memory tasks. We might suspect that people are often able to compensate for impairment associated with subjective feelings of fatigue, except, perhaps, when the task places particular demands on active regulation of effort (Desmond & Matthews, 1997).

Let us suppose, then, that there is a general fatigue state which may relate to some but not all of the observed performance decrements. Can we identify this state with general arousal? In some cases, stressor interactions are supportive of arousal theory, in that adverse effects of sleep deprivation and early time of day may be counteracted by arousing agents such as incentive (Blake, 1967; Broadbent, 1971). However, other arousing stressors, such as noise, often fail to offset performance decrement as expected, though stressor interactions are perhaps more consistent with arousal theory for sleep deprivation (see Broadbent, 1971) than for time of day (see Smith, 1992a). There is also some evidence for mutual interaction between prolonged work, time of day and sleep deprivation (e.g. Johnson, 1982), which implies that at least some of their effects may be mediated by a common fatigue mechanism. Other evidence suggests that fatigue should be distinguished from low arousal. Fatigue states do not appear to be related to physiological and subjective indices of arousal in any simple way (Craig & Cooper, 1992). Also, task-induced fatigue and time of day do not seem to relate reliably to attentional selectivity, although selectivity changes are perhaps the most reliable behavioural index of arousal change (Hockey, 1984).

## 12.5.2 Fatigue and resource availability

It seems plain that fatigue manipulations may induce a variety of performance changes, relating to several independent mechanisms. Resource theory is not a complete explanation for fatigue effects, but is it useful as a partial explanation? In fact, the role of resources appears to be different for each of the three manipulations which have been reviewed. Resource theory does not appear to be adequate in characterising many of the subtle performance effects associated with task-induced fatigue, although, as discussed in 5.2.3, it may be useful for explaining performance decrements on demanding sustained attention tasks. In Chapter 15, we discuss evidence that individual differences in subjective tiredness are associated with resources for demanding attentional tasks (Matthews & Davies, 1998). Much of the sleep deprivation data are broadly consistent with loss of resources, although it is unclear that lapses of attention are associated with reduced resources. Resource theory explains the particular sensitivity of demanding tasks to performance decrements. However, the effects on performance of moderating factors such as subject interest in the task indicate that there is more to sleep deprivation than a simple loss of resources. In the case of time of day effects, a multiple resource framework might be more appropriate. The data might be characterised as showing a circadian rhythm in availability of resources for working memory, peaking at around midday, although further experimentation using the dual-task methods described in 5.1.1 is required. Performance of purely attentional tasks is optimal later in the day, with Testu's (1986) study of controlled visual search providing evidence for variation in resource avail-

ability. Again, though, resource theory provides only a partial explanation for performance change, and much remains to be done in differentiating changes in performance efficiency from changes in strategy. Where changes in resource availability are established empirically, it may be reasonable to attribute them to psychobiological mechanisms, such as the influence of oscillators in the case of time of day effects.

## 12.5.3 Adaptation to fatigue and strategy change

Adaptive models of stress and performance are, in principle, well suited to explaining strategic changes, such as the reduced willingness to exert effort sometimes found in task-induced fatigue and sleep deprivation studies. Again, failure to exert sufficient active control in response to task demands may provide only a partial explanation for effects on performance; lapses in attention resulting from sleep deprivation appear to be involuntary in nature, for example. Some performance changes may be due to involuntary biological adaptations directly dependent on neural mechanisms, whereas others are generated by the subject's strategy for coping with the perceived demands associated with fatigue states.

Time of day has well-documented effects on strategy use but, so far, adaptive explanations have not been forthcoming. There are several possible explanations for the propensity to use maintenance rehearsal in the morning, for example. Possibly, people are unwilling to exert much effort at this time, and the strategy is perceived as a relatively low effort one. Alternatively, the strategy might be seen as compensating for other processing deficiencies, or capitalising on processing functions efficient during the morning. So far, there has been little attempt to distinguish such explanations. A further problem is that it is unclear whether change in speed–accuracy tradeoff is genuinely strategic in nature (see Smith, 1992a). More generally, Hockey (1986) has linked fatigue states to a control mode characterised by aversion to effort, and consequent performance impairment. This hypothesis is plausible, but much more work is required before adaptive hypotheses of this kind are capable of explaining the performance data in detail.

## 12.6 CONCLUSIONS

Prolonged work, performance at certain times of day and sleep deprivation all generate subjective fatigue symptoms, but differ in their consequences for performance. Explaining these effects requires the differentiation of multiple mechanisms. At the psychobiological level, it is difficult to sustain arousal theory as a general explanation, although, especially in sleep-deprived persons, loss of arousal may play some part. Current work emphasises more specialised biological mechanisms, notably the internal oscillators that may drive circadian rhythms in both psychophysiological response and performance. As ever in stress research, fatigue effects vary with the information-processing demands of the task. Some of these effects may be characterised in terms of components of the cognitive architecture. Sleep deprivation may lead to loss of attentional resources, and we can track different circadian rhythms for tasks with different processing requirements. Other fatigue effects on performance require analysis in terms of adaptation and the person's knowledge of the task environment. Perhaps the most general effect of fatigue is aversion to effort (Hockey, 1986), as the participant trades off personal comfort against (perceived) success on the task. Such variation of effort-regulation may lead to both strategy shifts and loss of performance efficiency on tasks that require sustained active control.

## FURTHER READING

Fatigue and sleep deprivation effects are reviewed in Volume 3 of the Smith and Jones (1992) book. Hockey et al.'s (1986) edited book covers many of the theoretical and conceptual issues raised by research in this area. Hancock and Desmond (2000) also gives good coverage of fatigue. McDonald's (1984) review of the driving literature illustrates the practical application of fatigue research. More detailed accounts of the sleep and circadian rhythm literatures have been provided by Monk (1994), Pressman and Orr (1997) and Webb (1982b).

# 13

# Lifestyle and performance: Health, diet and drugs

In our review of "stress" effects, the factors discussed so far relate mainly to the nature of the task, or to the external environment in which the task is performed. The existence of endogenous circadian rhythms demonstrates that performance is sensitive to the internal, physiological environment also. Further influences of this kind relate to "lifestyle", including the person's physical health, the nutrition they receive from their diet, and the effects of socially approved drugs such as nicotine, alcohol and caffeine. In considering these factors, we shall revisit some of the main themes of stress research already considered. All the influences listed affect brain functioning, and there are psychobiological explanations for their effects on performance. However, people also have beliefs and expectancies which may influence performance independently, or in interaction with psychobiological mechanisms. Stimulant drugs are often taken specifically to enhance performance, for example. It is generally believed that strong coffee improves functioning late at night. Hence, one general question to be addressed is the extent to which lifestyle influences depend on physiology, expectancy or both.

A second theme is the specification of performance effects in terms of information-processing mechanisms. If coffee improves performance, we wish to specify the cognitive functions concerned, and to assess also whether benefits of coffee on certain types of processing are balanced by impairments in other processes. The psychopharmacology of performance is a relatively mature area of research, and questions of this kind are a central part of the research agenda. Work on health and on diet is more recent, and we are limited to describing a few example studies which point the way for future research.

## 13.1 ILLNESS AND PERFORMANCE

Nobody feels at their best when ill, and it is unsurprising that ill-health might be linked to performance impairment. As discussed in 1.4.2, stress-related illness in the workplace is a burden on industry. Self-rated health tends to relate to better performance, although the associations are generally small in magnitude (e.g. Hultsch, Hammer,

& Small, 1993). Of rather more interest are attempts to delineate the particular patterns of impairment associated with specific diseases, and to identify causal effects. There are a variety of ways in which illness might be linked to impairment:

*Impairment of neural functioning.* Some diseases directly influence neural functioning (see Cohen, 1993). For example, in Alzheimer's disease, a dementia found mainly in the elderly, examination of the brain shows loss of cells and other signs of neuronal deterioration. Similarly, multiple sclerosis is a disease in which the myelin encasing neurons is damaged, and patients often show cognitive impairments of varying degrees of severity. Performance may also be affected by the changes in immune system function which constitute the body's defence against disease and which influence neural functioning, such as release of interferon (Smith, 1992b).

*Impairment of cerebral blood flow.* Performance tends to be impaired by various diseases that impair the flow of blood to the brain and so reduce its ability to metabolise glucose and oxygen (Deary, 1992; Jagust et al., 1997). Cardiovascular disease tends to be associated with poor circulation of the blood, and is quite reliably associated with impairments on various cognitive tasks (Holland & Rabbitt, 1991). Abnormally high blood pressure (hypertension) is similarly associated with performance deficit (e.g. Elias, Elias, & Elias, 1990). There may also be indirect effects of diseases which reduce physical activity and hence general metabolic efficiency (Holland & Rabbitt, 1991). We discuss diabetes below, as an instance of a disease that disrupts glucose metabolism.

*Symptom effects.* Diseases may have indirect effects via symptoms of which the patient is conscious. For example, ill-health tends to be accompanied by unpleasant mood states such as anxiety and tiredness, which may be associated with performance impairment (see Chapter 15). Physical symptoms of disease may be distracting. A pain or headache may divert attention away from the task at hand, for example. Clinical data show that the attention of panic disorder patients may become so strongly focused on physical symptoms

such as a racing heart that they are unable to function normally (Wells & Matthews, 1994).

*Health behaviours.* Illness is associated with a variety of active attempts to manage and cope with the illness which may have implications for performance. Commonly-used medications such as the antihistamines used to treat hayfever, and minor tranquillisers may have side-effects which include performance impairment (Hartley, 1992). Medication is, of course, a potential confound in investigating direct effects of illness. Performance when ill may also be influenced by more psychological factors such as expectations, although such factors have been little researched. Plausibly, people believe they should avoid intensive effort when ill, or they may be less motivated to succeed. People also make active efforts to maintain a healthy state. Exercise is usually seen as benefical to physical health, and moderate levels of exercise may produce short-term performance enhancement, especially in individuals who are already physically fit (Tomporowski & Ellis, 1986). Health-promoting behaviours do not necessarily improve performance. A low cholesterol diet is advocated to reduce heart disease but, in women, low cholesterol may be associated with slowed decision and movement times in choice reaction (Benton, 1995). In laboratory studies, we can control for some of these factors, such as use of medication, but it is harder to take into account possible effects on motivation and expectancy.

In reviewing research on illness, we distinguish acute and chronic conditions. An acute illness, such as a cold, may be treated as a discrete episode during which performance may be impaired. Typically, symptoms will be salient in the person's conscious awareness, and are likely to drive various health behaviours. Some chronic illnesses may have little direct effect on psychological functioning for much of the time, so the person is aware of being ill but is not much troubled by specific symptoms. This relatively benign state is then punctuated by episodes of acute illness. Performance impairment is possible in both dormant and active stages of illness, though it would be expected to be more severe during acute episodes.

## 13.2 ACUTE ILLNESSES: COLDS AND INFLUENZA

Respiratory diseases are a frequent cause of absence from work, leading to a considerable loss of productivity. Such diseases are caused by continually evolving viruses. At a symptomatic level both colds and influenza (flu) may be associated with respiratory symptoms such as nasal discharge and sore throat, but flu is distinguished by rather more severe symptoms such as fever, headache and myalgia. Smith (1992b) has reviewed work on the consequences of colds and influenza for performance. Much of this work was carried out at the British Medical Research Council Common Cold Unit (sadly, the unit is now defunct). Volunteers were injected with a specific cold or influenza virus, and monitored for several days subsequently for presence of the virus and cold symptoms. Typically, rather less than half of the initial sample developed a significant cold. Performance tests could then be administered during the period of the cold. The studies reviewed by Smith (1992b) were designed to follow Hockey's (1984) broad-band research strategy, by investigating a variety of different aspects of performance.

Smith et al. (1987) compared influenza and cold effects on the same three tasks: tracking, simple reaction time and a digit detection task. Performance effects for the two viral conditions were strikingly different: simple RT and detection were impaired by flu but not by the cold, whereas tracking was disrupted by the cold but not by flu. Very broadly, influenza seems to affect attentionally demanding tasks, whereas colds affect those requiring hand-eye coordination (the RT task was demanding to the extent that it had a variable foreperiod). Further studies reviewed by Smith (1992b) show that influenza affects visual search tasks, in which target location is uncertain, but not the maintenance of attention on a single location. A further hand-eye coordination task, the pegboard task, was sensitive to colds but not flu. Performance on the widely-used five-choice serial RT task is also slower in those infected

with a cold. Hall and Smith (1996) demonstrated effects of colds on tracking, but, in contrast to Smith et al. (1987), also found effects on simple RT and attentional tasks. Working memory and semantic memory were unaffected by colds. However, colds have some effects on semantic processing. Smith (1992b) reports cold-related deficits in learning and recalling information presented in a story, an effect attributed to difficulties in following the overall theme. The mechanisms for these effects are unclear, though support for a direct biological mechanism is provided by evidence for performance impairments in subjects who are infected by the virus but have few overt symptoms. Lowered arousal may also contribute to effects of colds. Smith, Thomas, Perry and Whitney (1997) found that caffeinated coffee eliminated loss of alertness and slower psychomotor performance in people suffering from colds, although decaffeinated coffee also produced improvements.

## 13.3 CHRONIC DISEASES

### 13.3.1 HIV

Work on HIV infection and AIDS (reviewed by Egan & Goodwin, 1992) illustrates the role of direct biological effects in disease. It is believed that the HIV virus attacks brain cells early in infection. Price and Brew (1988) distinguish four stages of the AIDS dementia complex (ADC) that may result. The later, more severe stages are characterised by memory loss, difficulties in thinking, motor retardation and slowed information-processing speed. These impairments are attributed primarily to damage to sub-cortical structures such as the basal ganglia (Navia, Cho, Petito, & Price, 1986). It is sometimes claimed that cognitive impairment may precede medical symptoms, becoming progressively worse as AIDS develops (Stern, Silva, Chaisson, & Evans, 1996), but the data are conflicting. Most studies have failed to find impairment in HIV-positive individuals without symptoms (including absence of dementia), even when the immune system is impaired (Selnes et al., 1995). However, Sahakian, Elliott, Low and Mehta (1995) found that asymptomatic

HIV-positive persons showed an impairment on a test of of executive function, and Stout et al. (1995) report that these individuals show a deficit in working memory which becomes more severe as symptoms develop. There is also some evidence for a slowing of early ERPs in asymptomatic subjects (Bungener, le Houezec, Pierson, & Jouvent, 1996). Early effects on performance may be most prevalent in individuals of low intelligence and education level (Stern et al., 1996).

AIDS-related impairments have been demonstrated on a wide variety of different psychomotor, attentional and memory tasks and, in general, the extent of impairment is probably more strongly related to the severity of the disease than to the information-processing demands of the task (see Stern et al., 1996). Disturbingly, rational decision-making about treatment options becomes progressively impaired as the severity of dementia symptoms increases. Longitudinal data suggest that rapid decline in executive, language and attentional test performance is associated with earlier death (Stern et al., 1995). However, there are some reports of selectivity of deficit. Martin et al. (1995) found that HIV-positive participants were especially impaired on controlled processing and divided attention. Memory tasks are often sensitive: for example, Stout et al. (1995) found deficits in working memory, but not in information-processing speed, although other studies have found speed of processing deficits (Llorente et al., 1998). White et al. (1997) found that episodic memory deficits were considerably more severe than semantic memory deficits in dementing patients. Psychomotor speed also seems especially sensitive to deficit, as a result of damage to sensory nerves (Selnes et al., 1995).

In the case of HIV, there is little doubt that its primary effects on performance are biologically mediated. However, other factors may also contribute. Recreational drug use is common in HIV-positive individuals and may potentiate performance impairment (Claypoole et al., 1993). A diagnosis of being HIV-positive is generally followed by an adjustment reaction associated with various negative emotions, fatigue and hypochondria (Miller & Riccio, 1990), which may be long-lasting in some individuals. Indeed, clinical depression is generally prevalent in individuals with life-threatening illness (Van Servellen, Sarna, Padilla, & Brecht, 1996). Such a reaction, and its consequences for health behaviours, might affect performance on certain tasks, although the major cognitive impairments associated with AIDS are distinct from depression effects (Egan & Goodwin, 1992). However, self-reports of performance in HIV infection frequently conflict with objective data: progression of the disease may be associated with reduced awareness of deterioration (Hinkin et al., 1996).

### 13.3.2 Chronic Fatigue Syndrome

Chronic Fatigue Syndrome (CFS) is a condition or conditions characterised by severe, disabling muscle and mental fatigue. It is sometimes called myalgic encephalomyelitis (ME) or post-viral fatigue syndrome, although these labels presuppose aetiological factors which may not apply to all patients. For example, some, but not all, CFS sufferers show evidence of chronic viral infection, and other physiological symptoms such as muscle damage and immune system abnormalities. In addition, people with CFS often show psychiatric symptoms which frequently resemble those of depression. Hence, CFS research is challenging, in that it is unclear whether behavioural correlates of the condition derive from some physical aetiological factor, such as a virus, from the fatigue itself, or from some more complex mechanism.

Smith (1992c) reviews a variety of studies showing performance deficits. An American study reported by Daugherty et al. (1991) showed that patients were impaired on each one of a battery of cognitive function tests, with the largest deficits being those for psychometric intelligence, attention and verbal memory. In several studies, Smith has compared performance on information-processing tasks. The most reliable deficits have been obtained in attentional, semantic processing, and RT tasks and with the pegboard task assessing motor function. Effects on memory are more task-dependent, or at least less consistent across studies. Digit span is consistently unaffected by CFS, and results obtained with free recall and recognition tasks vary from study to study, although deficits for both kind of task have been reported. Recent studies have tended to confirm the conclusions of Smith's (1992c) review. For example, Michiels, Cluydts and Fischler (1998) concluded that demanding attentional and working memory tasks were those most sensitive to CFS, whereas focused attention and retrieval from memory did not seem to show deficits. However, Michiels et al. (1996) point out that the pattern of deficit varies considerably across individual patients, so it is hard to generalise results. Effects of CFS are not a simple consequence of under-arousal, as loud noise actually induces deficits in CFS patients, implying, instead, a difficulty in coping with environmental stressors (Beh, Connelly & Charles, 1997).

There has been some interest in how CFS effects relate to those of other clinical conditions associated with fatigue, such as depression. Most of the evidence suggests that CFS and depression are associated with similar deficits in attention, memory and response speed (Marshall et al., 1997; Vollmer-Conna et al., 1997). However, performance deficits are found in CFS patients without concurrent psychiatric disorders, so impairments cannot be attributed solely to depression (DeLuca, Johnson, Ellis, & Natelson, 1997). Figure 13.1 presents data taken from Smith (1992c), showing that CFS impairment on various tasks is fairly similar to that found in influenza patients (see 13.2). Viral infection is implicated in some CFS patients, and it may be that both illnesses are associated with similar neurological dysfunctions. Smith also points to similarities between CFS

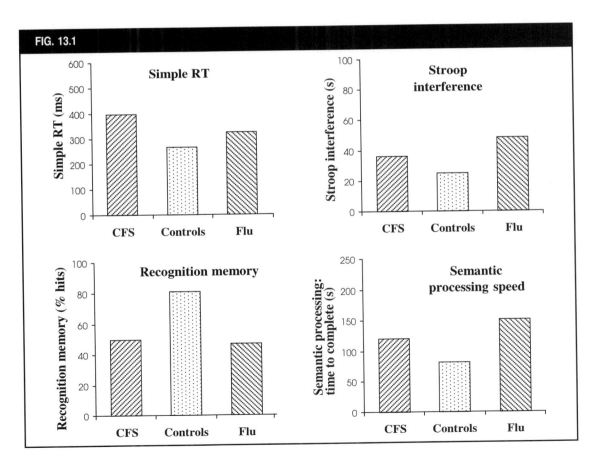

FIG. 13.1

Comparison of performance of CFS, influenza and control groups on several tasks (Smith, 1992c).

and AIDS patients in performance. However, Joyce, Blumenthal and Wessely (1996) established differences between CFS patients and those with dementia or amnesia. The CFS group showed normal performance on several memory taks, but appeared to have difficulties on effortful tasks requiring planned generation of responses from memory, a pattern of deficit rather speculatively attributed to reduced attentional capacity.

In general, CFS tends to produce stronger impairments than those obtained in laboratory studies of task-induced fatigue, reviewed in the previous chapter. A recent review (Tiersky et al., 1997) concluded that general intellectual abilities and higher level cognitive skills remain intact, and that complex information-processing speed was most subject to impairment. However, the cognitive patterning of deficits remains somewhat unclear. It is sometimes believed that CFS patients are merely malingering or over-sensitive, but the behavioural data help to establish that the condition is genuinely disabling, whatever its cause or causes.

### 13.3.3 Insulin-dependent diabetes

Diabetes mellitus results from lack of insulin, leading to disruptions of glucose metabolism with excess glucose in the blood and too little within cells. In general, the condition can be self-managed through diet and through insulin injection. Diabetes is associated with risk of various chronic health problems, and with hypoglycaemia (low blood glucose) due to insulin overdosage. That is, the risk of acute illness derives from the health management behaviour of insulin injection. Deary (1992, 1995) has reviewed studies of performance during hypoglycaemic episodes, which show deficits on a variety of tasks, especially when glucose depletion is more severe. Performance deficit reflects the brain's reliance on glucose as an energy source. Smid et al. (1997) report an ERP study using a hybrid selective-attention/ response choice task. Changes in ERPs during an episode of hypoglycaemia were interpreted as showing that hypoglycaemia delays both stimulus and response selection, although the stimulus selection process recovered more quickly after restoration of normal glucose.

The time course of cognitive deficit is of practical importance, because the patient's awareness of warning symptoms, such as impairment of attention, allows them to take precautions to manage the episode. In non-diabetic individuals, subjected to hypoglycaemia experimentally, hormone release and autonomic arousal appear to precede cognitive impairment (Mitrakou et al., 1991). However, it is unclear if diabetics experience similar warning signs before impairment (e.g. Hoffman et al., 1989). There is evidence too that reactions may remain slow 40 minutes after the conclusion of the hypoglycaemic episode, implying that diabetics should exercise caution in returning to performing tasks such as driving following an attack (Blackman et al., 1990). Finally, acute and chronic cognitive impairment may be interrelated: Deary (1995) reviews evidence that patients with a history of severe hypoglycaemia show deficits in performance on IQ tests and information-processing tasks such as choice RT and rapid visual information processing.

## 13.4 NUTRITION

Eating has both positive and negative connotations for subsequent performance. Breakfast cereals are promoted on the basis of their supposedly energising properties (somewhat at variance with bleary-eyed reality). A well-known brand of chocolate bar "helps you work, rest and play", according to its slogan. In contrast, the lethargy induced by a heavy meal is a familiar experience. Woods (1991) proposes the intriguing view that eating is something of a necessary evil, associated with a variety of disruptive physiological effects. Effects of meals can be studied experimentally, and work in this area has focused on both the size of the meal, in terms of calories of energy, and on nutrient composition. There are several mechanisms through which food may influence performance (Spring, Chiodo, & Bowen, 1987). First, some nutrients found in food are precursors of brain neurotransmitters, so it is conceivable that food influences neurotransmitter function. Of course, the body has various mechanisms for influencing neurotransmitter synthesis and metabolism so, if diet is generally adequate, there is not necessarily any direct link between nutrient intake and neurotransmitter function. Second, the energy content of food may influence blood glucose levels. As just discussed, work on diabetes shows that lack of glucose may influence performance (Deary, 1992). Third, there may be psychological mechanisms for food effects, such as the expectancies encouraged by advertising, although Spring et al. (1987) point out that there is little evidence for such effects.

### 13.4.1 The post-lunch dip

A basic difficulty in conducting research in this area is the role of circadian rhythms. People are accustomed to eating meals at particular times during the day, and post-meal effects may simply reflect circadian changes. For example, there is fairly good evidence for a "post-lunch" dip in performance on some but not all tasks. Real-world examples include train drivers' ability to detect warning signals, and speed of answering a switchboard (Monk & Folkard, 1985). People also tend to feel somewhat tired and drowsy after lunch. However, these effects might simply reflect a decline in the activity produced by internal oscillators, as discussed in 12.4, so that eating lunch has no direct effect on mood and performance. Wever's (1985) studies of "free-running" circadian rhythms showed a midcycle dip in performance linked to the body temperature rhythm but not to meals. The role of lunch may be investigated by comparing performance in people given or deprived of lunch, and then tested at the same time in the early afternoon. Such studies may not give conclusive results because somatic reactions may become conditioned to cues indicating the time of day, so the body prepares to digest food even though no food is actually ingested. Nevertheless, they are an important source of evidence.

Early studies, reviewed by Smith and Kendrick (1992), showed little effect of lunch, implying that the post-lunch dip reflects either circadian variation or a strongly conditioned somatic reaction. However, more recent research (e.g. Craig, Baer, & Diekmann, 1981; Smith & Miles, 1986) has shown some deficits directly attributable to eating lunch, especially on sustained attention tasks. Furthermore, an unusually large lunch seems to produce a relatively large performance decrement (Craig, 1986). Postprandial depression of activity following meals is well-established in animals, to the extent that activity and eating are largely exclusive activities (Woods, 1991). Smith and Kendrick conclude that the nature of the task determines the sensitivity of performance to meals and circadian rhythms, with sustained attention especially sensitive to food intake. Different meals (e.g. breakfast vs. supper) may also have differing consequences for performance (Smith, Maben, & Brockman, 1994).

### 13.4.2 The role of neurotransmitters: The tryptophan hypothesis

One line of research is concerned with the amino acid tryptophan, a nutrient obtained from dietary protein. Spring et al. (1987) describe the rationale. Tryptophan is a precursor of the neurotransmitter serotonin, and availability of tryptophan appears to affect serotonin synthesis. Serotonergic activity is implicated in several types of response potentially relevant to performance, including sleep and depression. Tryptophan appears to reduce onset time of sleep, and has inconsistent but sometimes beneficial effects on clinical depression. In fact, release of brain serotonin depends on the balance between carbohydrate and protein in the meal ingested: serotonin is elevated when the meal is rich in carbohydrates but low in protein. The reason is as follows. Dietary protein contains rather little tryptophan, so that such tryptophan that is present tends to be hindered in crossing the blood-brain barrier by other, more prevalent, amino acids. Conversely, the insulin released by carbohydrate ingestion causes most of the other amino acids to be taken up by muscles, enhancing access of tryptophan to the brain.

The hypothesis suggests that the psychological impact of meals should depend on the effects of carbohydrate–protein balance on serotonergic activity. Consistent with the hypothesis, several studies, reviewed by Spring et al., show that, like tryptophan, carbohydrate-rich/protein-poor meals tend to induce drowsiness. There is rather more limited evidence that such meals generate a pleasant, calm mood. In performance studies, it has usually been assumed that the adverse effects of drowsiness predominate over benefits of calmness. Spring et al. summarise the performance data as showing that carbohydrate meals tend to have adverse effects on tasks requiring sustained attention or speeded response, although data are not entirely consistent. Sensorimotor functions appear insensitive to the nutrients concerned. Hence, at a practical level, it may be sensible to ensure that meals taken before attentionally-demanding activities, such as driving, contain some protein.

### 13.4.3 Stimulant and depressant effects of meals

Given that both the post-lunch dip and "serotonergic" meals are associated with drowsiness, might performance decrement result from de-arousal? We can test this hypothesis by manipulating arousal experimentally. It would be expected that arousing agents should reduce post-lunch dip, but dearousing factors should accentuate it. There is indeed some evidence that increasing arousal through noise or caffeine may largely eliminate the post-lunch dip, at least on certain tasks (Smith & Kendrick, 1992). Studies in which arousal is lowered experimentally produce more complex results, although the post-lunch dip is accentuated by sleep deprivation (Hildebrandt, Rohmert, & Rutenfranz, 1975b). Changes in arousal may be linked to glucose metabolism. It is unlikely that normal individuals experience the hypoglycaemic states seen in diabetes research (Spring et al., 1987), but the initial release of glucose may be associated with increased autonomic arousal, reduced cortical arousal and greater subjective lassitude (Christie & McBrearty, 1979).

According to popular wisdom, sugar (sucrose) has an activating effect, sometimes blamed for hyperactivity in children who consume too many sugary snacks or drinks. Experimentally, eating a sugary candy bar produces a short-term increase in energy, followed about an hour later by feelings of fatigue and tension (Thayer, 1987). Studies of children show correlations between activity and carbohydrate intake, but experimental studies provide little support for direct effects of sugar

(Spring et al., 1987). However, these studies do not seem to have taken into account the time course of response to sugar. Recent work in adults shows that glucose drinks may enhance word recall and speed of reaction (Benton & Owens, 1993; Owens & Benton, 1994). In assessing the effects of sugar ingestion in real life, we must also take into account habitual diet. For example, there is evidence from animal studies that chronic high carbohydrate intake may increase vulnerability to hypoglycaemia (Spring et al., 1987). Chronically elevated glucose is associated with performance impairment on neuropsychological tests (Woods, 1991). A sugar-free diet may have mood-enhancing effects (Christensen, 1993). On the other hand, dieters show performance deficits which may relate to working memory impairment (Green, Elliman, & Rogers, 1997). Since moderate food deprivation in itself does not degrade performance, Green et al. (1997) attribute this result to the distracting effects of task-irrelevant cognitions about food. In sum, links between sugar consumption, arousal and performance are elusive, and require more fine-grained analysis of sugar effects than has so far been possible, taking into account possible moderating factors such as habitual diet. It is possible that there are short-term facilitative effects on energy and performance of some tasks, mediated by glucose.

## 13.5 DRUGS AND PERFORMANCE

Use of socially-approved drugs is an integral part of Western culture, although the boundaries of social acceptability are prone to change. Western values are ambivalent about alcohol use, for example, as attempts at prohibition demonstrate. Nevertheless, for many people ingestion of alcohol, caffeinated beverages such as coffee and tea, and cigarette smoking are a normal part of everyday life. These activities are not valued solely for their effects on conscious awareness and behaviour. A person may enjoy a cup of tea or glass of wine without expecting much change in psychological state. However, there are pronounced cultural beliefs about the impact of these substances on everyday functioning and, in the case of stimulants such as caffeine and nicotine, performance enhancement may be one of the goals of taking the substance. Illegal drugs are frequently damaging to both neural function and performance, and recreational drug use seems to be a general risk factor for impairment on neuropsychological tests (Claypoole et al., 1993).

Pharmacological mechanisms for alcohol, caffeine and nicotine effects are fairly well understood, at least in outline. These substances may be investigated as we would investigate any other drug, using double-blind designs in which neither subject nor experimenter knows whether the drug or a placebo has been taken. As we shall see, standard pharmacological research methods allow us to map out effects on performance. Limitations of these methods are three-fold. First, inferring mechanisms for psychological effects of drugs is far from straightforward, even when the neurotransmitters they influence are known. Neurons using any given neurotransmitter participate in a variety of different brain systems which interact in complex ways with other systems. For example, there are distinct "dorsal" and "ventral" noradrenergic pathways in the brain, whose impact on behaviour may be moderated by activity of dopaminergic systems (Robbins & Everitt, 1982). Hence, drugs are a blunt instrument for investigating brain function, and establishing physiological mechanisms for drug action is a difficult and arduous process.

A second problem is that in real-life situations people have expectancies which may influence performance. Hence, the double-blind design may not accurately indicate drug effects in real life. Furthermore, double-blind studies do not provide full control over expectancies: participants are likely to form beliefs and hypotheses about what is happening to them in the study. Below, we discuss a study of coffee drinking which shows that participants' beliefs are influenced by the conduct of the experiment, and affect subjective and objective response (Kirsch & Weixel, 1988). Thirdly, we should note that there are various methodological difficulties in controlling administration of substances (see, e.g. Finnigan & Hammersley, 1992). Factors such as body weight

influence absorption of ingested substances. In caffeine studies, it is difficult to ensure comparability of amount of caffeine absorbed across studies using pills and natural drinks such as coffee. Drug effects also vary over time, and the rates at which the drug becomes available in the body, and is then metabolised, depend on a host of physiological factors. Next, we consider alcohol, a CNS depressant, and two stimulants, caffeine and nicotine.

## 13.6 ALCOHOL AND PERFORMANCE

Alcohol acts primarily as a general CNS depressant, although small dosages may be stimulating. It is unclear whether alcohol necessarily leads to reduced cortical arousal in performance studies. A procedure often used in pharmacological research is the critical flicker fusion (CFF) task, which tests the person's threshold for detecting that a light source is flickering rapidly. It has quite good validity as a measure of cortical arousal (Corr, Pickering, & Gray, 1995b), but alcohol effects on CFF are inconsistent (Finnigan & Hammersley, 1992; Hindmarch, 1982). Subjective effects are variable and, depending on the context, may include both drowsiness, elation and calmness: tension reduction appears to be one of the main motivations for drinking (Cappell, 1987). There is extensive research on alcohol effects, and most reviews suggest that even moderate dosages of alcohol are detrimental to performance (Collins & Chiles, 1980; Finnigan & Hammersley, 1992). The British legal limit for driving of 80 mg alcohol/100 ml of blood might be seen as a "moderate dosage".

There are scattered reports of alcohol-related enhancement of performance. For example, Maylor, Rabbitt, Sahgal and Wright (1987) reported that a small dose of alcohol (29 mg/100 ml) increased accuracy of visual search. Intriguingly, in memory studies, alcohol given after exposure to the material learned may enhance recall, perhaps because it reduces retroactive interference from events between learning and recall (Mueller, Lisman, & Spear, 1983). In general, though, Finnigan and Hammersley (1992) conclude that alcohol tends to impair tracking, vigilance, memory and decision-making, although they point out various methodological difficulties in the studies concerned. They report that in recent published studies around 70% of tasks show alcohol impairment.

There is particular interest in effects of alcohol on driving and other real-world skills, given the need for psychologically-informed legislation. Motor vehicle accident investigations show that accident risk increases progressively with alcohol dosage, but the mechanisms for the loss of safety are unclear. One factor may be impairment of divided attention, which has been demonstrated in several driving simulator studies (e.g. Brewer & Sandow, 1980; Landauer & Howat, 1983). Visuo-spatial processing may also be impaired, as Stokes, Belger, Banich and Bernadine (1994) have shown, using a cognitive maze tracing task which requires no manual control. Slowed reaction time is probably of lesser importance.

### 13.6.1 Studies of information processing

As with many stressors whose effects are primarily detrimental, there is something of a trend towards stronger alcohol effects on more demanding tasks. This is the opposite effect expected to that predicted by the Yerkes-Dodson Law, implying that traditional arousal theory is not useful here. However, dearousal may well play some role; it is claimed that alcohol has similar effects to sleep deprivation in impairing psychomotor performance (Dawson & Reid, 1997). Hockey et al. (1981) investigated alcohol effects on a letter transformation task, requiring a number to be "added" to a letter sequence. For example, CWGE + 2 is transformed to EYIG. (The task is useful to stress researchers because memory load may be manipulated by varying the length of the letter sequence.) Hockey et al. showed that, with a low memory load, the alcohol-induced deficit in speed of response increased as a linear function of transformation difficulty. Early studies of vigilance produced inconclusive results (Davies & Parasuraman, 1982). Rohrbaugh et al. (1987), however, used the degraded digit detection task which is known to be particularly demanding (see 6.2.2). They showed that loss of perceptual sensitivity under alcohol increased with time on task, and with dosage of alcohol, as shown in Fig. 13.2. Alcohol also tended to slow speed of response. As we saw in 6.2.2, loss of sensitivity on this task can plausibly be attributed to depletion of attentional resources, so alcohol may reduce resource

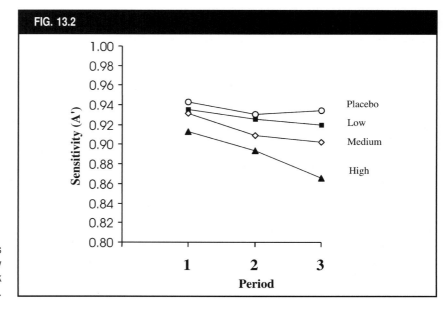

**FIG. 13.2**

Effects of various doses of alcohol on sensitivity on a vigilance task (Rohrbaugh et al., 1987).

availability. Rohrbaugh et al. also showed alcohol effects on evoked potentials which may relate to attention and processing capacity.

Other data are less supportive of a resource interpretation of alcohol deficits. Maylor and Rabbitt (1988) investigated alcohol effects on consistent- and varied-mapping word categorisation and visual search tasks, across several days of practice. As discussed in 3.3.1, these two types of task are thought to promote automatic and controlled processing respectively. Because controlled processing requires more resources, we would expect that, as the tasks are practised and the consistent-mapped task becomes automatised, the alcohol deficit should become restricted to the varied-mapping task. In fact, although alcohol impaired performance, the effect was similar early and late in practice, and in consistent- and varied-mapping conditions. Resource theory also predicts that alcohol should have particularly detrimental effects on divided attention. Maylor, Rabbitt, James and Kerr (1990) report a study in which participants detected tones during tracking, and also performed each task on its own. Alcohol affected RT to the tones rather than tracking, especially during dual-task performance. This result appears compatible with resource theory, but further analysis of the data showed that the costs of performing in the dual-task rather than the single-task condition were unaffected by alcohol. As in other studies conducted by Maylor and Rabbitt, alcohol deficits were unaffected by practice.

An alternative hypothesis is that alcohol simply reduces rate of processing irrespective of resource requirements: more complex tasks are more sensitive to variation in rate of processing because they depend on more constituent processes. Maylor and Rabbitt (1993) report a meta-analysis of alcohol studies. For both reaction time and recognition memory studies, performance under alcohol may be expressed as a linear function of normal function. For example, RT under alcohol is about 10–15% slower than normal RT across a range of tasks of varying difficulty. The authors propose that slowing is a consequence of loss of resources, but resource models used in alcohol research need more detailed specification.

### 13.6.2 Placebo and compensation effects

Alcohol researchers have used the "balanced" placebo design to investigate the role of expectancies. In this design, participants are told explicitly what substance is consumed, but the information may or may not be accurate. Expectancies and alcohol dosage are manipulated independently, so that their effects may be discriminated (Rohsenow & Marlatt, 1981). One possible outcome is a placebo effect, so that participants told they have been given alcohol, but actually given a placebo, show impairment. Alternatively, there may be compensation effects, such that alcohol deficit is reduced when people are aware that they have been given alcohol. Compensation may take place both through conditioning of physiological compensatory mechanisms to alcohol-related cues, and through voluntary, strategic efforts to compensate.

The evidence on performance, reviewed by Finnigan and Hammersley (1992), is somewhat patchy. There is rather little evidence for placebo-induced impairment, although alcohol-dependent individuals may show such effects (Laberg & Löberg, 1986), but there is rather more evidence for compensation effects. For example, Ross and Pihl (1988) had people check the spelling of a series of words. Those who were told they had received alcohol showed faster RT, irrespective of the actual amount of alcohol consumed. Although there is some evidence for conditioned compensatory physiological responses, it is plausible that effects of this kind are motivational. Young and Pihl (1982) showed that people given alcohol performed better on a visual RT task when they were motivated to behave as though sober. In a driving simulator study, McMillen and Wells-Parker (1987) showed that risk-taking behaviours such as overtaking were most prevalent in participants told they had been given a moderate dosage of alcohol, though actual dosage had no effects. It is likely that risk-taking effects are strongly moderated by context. Under different circumstances, one might imagine that a drunk driver would be motivated to show off to a passenger or to drive slowly to try to maintain safety.

Finally, a topic of concern to alcohol users is whether anything can be done to compensate for its adverse effects in real life. Folk wisdom receives some support from empirical studies. Eating prior to drinking reduces blood alcohol, and reduces alcohol-related performance impairments somewhat (Finnigan, Hammersley, & Millar, 1998). There is a tendency for caffeine and nicotine to reduce alcohol-related impairment on psychomotor and cognitive tasks, although outcomes are somewhat inconsistent and may be dose-dependent (Kerr & Hindmarch, 1998; White, 1994). It would certainly be unwise to suppose that drinking coffee permits one to drink and drive. Sedative drugs can interact with alcohol to produce strong performance impairments (Kerr & Hindmarch, 1998). In general, it is difficult to compensate for alcohol ingestion after the event.

## 13.7 STIMULANTS: CAFFEINE AND NICOTINE

### 13.7.1 Caffeine

The stimulant caffeine is found not only in coffee and tea, but also in soft drinks, chocolate and medications such as preparations for colds. The caffeine content of a typical cup of "real" coffee is around 100 mg, with other drinks containing rather less, although caffeine content varies considerably with the method of preparation. Hence, in experimental studies, dosages of up to 200 mg or so might be seen as representative of people's real life caffeine consumption, whereas the higher dosages of c. 500 mg sometimes used would be attained in a single consumption episode only by unusually dedicated drinkers of strong coffee. Caffeine produces stimulant effects through blocking brain receptors for a substance called adenosine. Adenosine is involved in the inhibition of a host of important neurotransmitters, including those related to arousal such as noradrenaline, dopamine and acetylcholine. Hence, caffeine increases activity in neurotransmitters related to arousal, and increases rate of cerebral glucose utilisation, but its effects cannot easily be localised with respect to any particular brain system (see Daly, 1993; Nehlig, Daval, & Debry, 1992 for reviews). Caffeine often produces increased arousal as assessed by the EEG, as well as increased subjective arousal and alertness, but relatively large doses may also produce anxiety (Loke, 1988).

Caffeine effects on performance have been extensively studied, most often using caffeine administered in tablet form. In reviewing this literature, Lieberman (1992) concludes that the most reliable beneficial effects of caffeine are found with reaction time tasks, and especially with vigilance tasks. One of the more caffeine-sensitive tasks requires the subject to detect an occasional change in duration of tones presented at a rate of one every two seconds. Lieberman's own work shows that on this task beneficial effects of caffeine may be found at dosages as low as 32 mg, as shown in Fig. 13.3. This amount of caffeine might be obtained from well-brewed tea or a 12 oz cola drink. Some other relatively simple information-processing tasks show caffeine-related benefits, but more complex cognitive tasks tend to be insensitive to caffeine (e.g. Loke, 1988), as do memory tasks (e.g. Roache & Griffiths, 1987). There is rather little research which indicates the precise information processing or attentional mechanisms sensitive to caffeine. Lorist, Snel, and Kok (1994) conducted a processing stage analysis (see 2.1.2) of caffeine effects on choice RT in sleep-deprived subjects. Caffeine tended to counteract sleep deprivation by enhancing processing at encoding and response activation stages, but not at the response selection stage. Somewhat similarly, Lorist and Snel (1997) found that caffeine speeded target localisation and response preparation in visual selective attention to letter targets. Caffeine has been found to enhance dual-task performance (e.g. Kerr, Sherwood, & Hindmarch, 1991), but there is little evidence to suggest any systematic differences in its effects on focused and divided attention. Beneficial effects of caffeine may generalise to real-world skills: Regina, Smith, Keiper and McKelvey (1974) showed that 200 mg of caffeine improved several aspects of simulated driving performance.

There is fairly good evidence for arousal-mediation of caffeine effects. As just described, caffeine tends to reduce performance deficits associated with sleep deprivation (Lorist et al., 1994). Caffeine may useful to night workers, with several studies showing it enhances overnight

**FIG. 13.3**

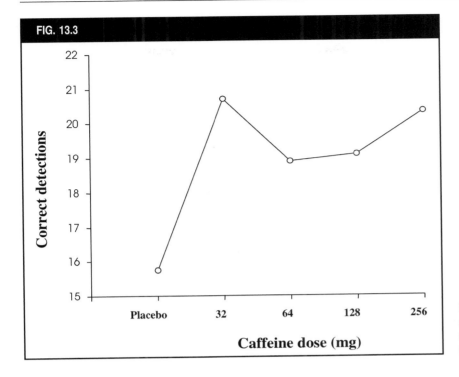

Effects of various doses of caffeine on correct detections on a vigilance task (Lieberman, 1992).

work performance and reduces sleepiness (e.g. Muehlbach & Walsh, 1995). It also counteracts the loss of subjective alertness and reduced vigilance associated with the post-lunch dip (Smith et al., 1990). Caffeine also tends to antagonise sedative effects of minor tranquillisers (benzodiazepines: White, 1994). A cautionary note is sounded by Kerr et al. (1991) who found beneficial effects of caffeine on performance, although it failed to influence the CFF index of cortical arousal. It seems that a dose of at least 500 mg caffeine is necessary to influence CFF (Corr et al., 1995b). Kerr et al. suggested that caffeine effects may derive from specific changes in information processing. Consistent with this hypothesis, there is evidence that caffeine effects on performance may precede effects on subjective alertness (Frewer & Lader, 1991). Temple et al. (in press) found that caffeine enhanced vigilance, but failed to influence subjective arousal (though other indices might have proved more sensitive).

As with other substances, caffeine effects may be influenced by various factors important in real life. Various factors such as oral contraceptive use

and cigarette smoking influence the rate at which it is metabolised (Lieberman, 1992). There has been some debate over whether caffeine use leads to tolerance, and withdrawal symptoms when users are deprived of caffeine (e.g. Phillips-Bute & Lane, 1997). Cessation of caffeine ingestion after heavy chronic use seems to lead to withdrawal symptoms such as headache and fatigue. Jarvis (1993) conducted a unique study in which 9003 volunteers completed a battery of tasks. Higher coffee and, to a lesser extent, tea consumption were associated with more efficient performance, implying that tolerance effects are weak or nonexistent. Expectancies may be important in real-world settings, given that most people expect stimulant effects. Kirsch and Weixel (1988) report a study in which participants were given decaffeinated coffee, but marked placebo effects were obtained, including heightened subjective alertness and blood pressure. The size of these effects varied with the experimental procedure, and tended to track participants' estimates. It was found also that performance on several tasks related to participants' beliefs about whether or not caffeine would enhance performance. Such expectancies also predict tracking performance when caffeinated coffee is used (Fillmore & Vogel-Sprott, 1994).

### 13.7.2 Nicotine

Nicotine is a stimulant which is rapidly absorbed into the bloodstream when a cigarette is smoked. Snuff and chewing tobacco also deliver nicotine fairly quickly, through mucosal membranes. Nicotine pills and chewing gum are less efficient. Nicotine releases the cholinergic neurotransmitter acetylcholine in the CNS, leading to increased cortical arousal. The physiological pathways involved are relatively well-understood (see Rusted & Warburton, 1995). Subjectively, nicotine tends both to increase alertness and arousal, and to improve mood generally (Thayer, 1989). Although nicotine effects are primarily pharmacological, there is also evidence for expectancy effects: Netter, Hennig, Huwe and Olbrich (1998) showed that performance tended to be better when people were given accurate information about whether or not a cigarette contained nicotine, compared with performance when given false information.

The basic design for nicotine studies is to compare performance levels in smokers who have taken nicotine with a control group of smokers not given nicotine. The study might compare effects of nicotine and placebo tablets, or of real cigarettes with nicotine-free cigarettes. Wesnes and Parrott (1992) review the fairly extensive research of this kind which has been reported. It is usual to deprive participants of nicotine for 10 or so hours prior to the study, so results are unaffected by smoking prior to the study. Short, relatively simple information-processing tasks frequently show nicotine benefits. For example, Snyder and Henningfield (1989) showed that nicotine gum enhanced performance on search, arithmetic, logical reasoning and digit recall tasks. Some of their results are shown in Fig. 13.4. Vigilance and sustained attention tasks also show fairly consistent beneficial effects of nicotine. Nicotine may improve certain aspects of real-world performance: Sherwood (1995) reports positive effects of smoking on tracking and brake reaction times on a driving simulator.

Wesnes and Parrott (1992) describe a series of studies that investigated the puff-by-puff effects of smoking, using a paradigm described as rapid visual information processing (RVIP). The task is a version of the Bakan (1959) vigilance task described in 3.3.3, with a very rapid event rate. Every minute, 100 digit stimuli are presented visually and the subject must detect three consecutive odd numbers or three consecutive even numbers. As Wesnes and Parrott discuss, puff-by-puff enhancement of performance relative to a control condition has been detected. Wesnes and Parrott also point out that there has been relatively little work on selective and divided attention, and it is unclear how sensitive nicotine effects are to level of task demands. Studies of memory show more complex nicotine effects, with several studies showing impairment of learning in free recall, nonsense syllable learning and paired-associate learning paradigms (see Wesnes & Parrott, 1992). There are occasional reports of memory facilitation, which Wesnes and Parrott attribute to enhanced attention to the experimental materials. Consistent with this hypothesis, Grobe, Perkins, Goettler-Good and Wilson (1998) showed that nicotine enhanced performance on the Sternberg (1969) memory scanning task only when distracting auditory stimuli were presented concurrently.

Arousal explanations are fairly well-established. Nicotine seems to counter de-arousal, induced by sleep deprivation, for example (Parkin et al., 1998). Nicotine-induced increases in cortical arousal during performance have been demonstrated using EEG measures (Warburton & Wesnes, 1979) and CFF: three puffs of a cigarette appear to be sufficient to lower CFF for 20 minutes (Waller & Levander, 1980). The cholinergic hypothesis for effects on attention is supported by studies showing that the cholinergic receptor blocker scopolamine impairs tasks facilitated by nicotine. Nicotine also reduces scopolamine-induced deficits on the RVIP task, implying that the two drugs tend to operate antagonistically (Wesnes & Revell, 1984). Beatty (1986) discusses neuropsychological evidence that cholinergic activity in brain pathways related to perception and attention is associated with improved signal-to-noise ratios at the cellular level.

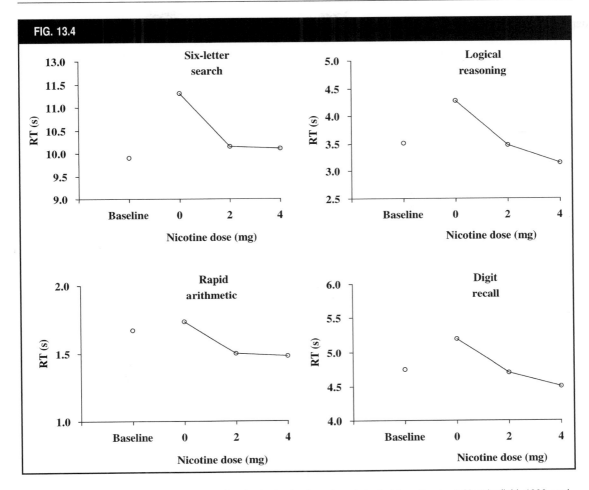

**FIG. 13.4**

Effects of various doses of nicotine on several tasks, in deprived smokers (adapted from Snyder & Henningfield, 1989, and Wesnes & Parrott, 1992).

Some puzzles remain. Smokers report having different motivations for smoking, with some people choosing to smoke to increase arousal, and others seeking relaxation (O'Connor, 1985). It is unclear whether differing motivations moderate performance consequences. Wesnes and Parrott (1992) discuss evidence from some studies that suggests an inverted-U relationship between nicotine dosage and performance on attentional tasks (though some studies show a simple linear relationship). There are two possible explanations. First, smokers may become accustomed to a certain intake of nicotine, so that excess nicotine leads to impairment. Second, high dosages may

induce the performance deficit due to over-arousal described by the Yerkes-Dodson Law. A further observation is that smokers given nicotine rarely out-perform non-smokers. It has been suggested that because smokers are deprived of nicotine prior to experimental study, they are impaired due to deprivation, and nicotine simply raises performance to a "normal" level. Deprivation effects are shown in Fig. 13.4. In the study concerned (Snyder & Henningfield, 1989), smokers were deprived of tobacco for 12 hours. The subjects given no nicotine showed performance deficits compared to a non-deprivation baseline condition. Furthermore, non-deprived smokers showed superior vigilance to deprived smokers (Wesnes & Warburton, 1983). Deprivation may not fully account for nicotine-induced performance enhancement. For example, Fig. 13.4 suggests that nicotine may enhance speed of arithmetic performance over baseline. Wesnes, Warburton and Matz (1983) found that nicotine tablets reduced the vigilance decrement on the Mackworth clock test, and the effect was similar in both nicotine-deprived smokers and non-smokers. Finally, Turner and Spilich (1997) reviewed 91 papers, and found that scientists acknowledging financial support from the tobacco industry were more likely to report positive effects on performance than scientists who did not. As the authors conclude, one can only speculate on possible reasons for this apparent bias.

## 13.8 CONCLUSIONS

The data reviewed show that performance is influenced by a variety of factors reflecting the person's lifestyle. Some of these factors, such as the more severe illnesses and alcohol consumption, tend to produce rather general impairments in information processing and performance. Even in these cases, some tasks are more sensitive to decrement than others, and there is scope for developing more detailed accounts of information-processing impairment. Of the other factors reviewed, colds, influenza, meals, caffeine and nicotine produce task-dependent performance changes. Sustained attention tasks appear to be particularly sensitive to food- and drug-induced performance change. It is likely that future research will amplify the specific information-processing changes produced by these agents. In part, these performance effects reflect brain mechanisms, but cognitive factors are also implicated. In the cases of caffeine and alcohol in particular, there is good evidence for expectancy effects on performance, and investigating the interplay between psychology and physiology is a considerable challenge for the future.

At a more applied level, some of these factors, such as nutrition and drugs, may be used as deliberate strategies for performance enhancement. Caffeine especially seems beneficial in some circumstances, and moderate use appears to carry few health risks (Lieberman, 1992). A degree of caution is necessary, however. For example, caffeine appears to benefit simulated driving, but further work is needed to show that any enhancement of real driving is not countered by more subtle performance deficits. Recommending caffeine use when the person is fatigued or sleep-deprived is also problematic. A safer option is for the person to refrain from potentially dangerous activities such as driving or operating machinery. In the case of nicotine, few would claim that the health risks justify the moderate improvements to attention demonstrated empirically, especially if performance enhancement partially reflects a deprivation effect. However, deeper understanding of the person's appraisals of performance change under nicotine may contribute to developing more effective techniques for cessation of smoking. Work on primarily detrimental factors is also of applied significance. Research on colds and flu may help to identify real-world tasks on which people may be significantly impaired, although there is currently a considerable gap between the laboratory tasks and applications. Alcohol studies confirm anecdotal evidence that drinking and performance rarely combine well.

## FURTHER READING

The studies reviewed in this chapter are somewhat scattered, and the best source for further reading is Volume 2 of Smith and Jones (1992). Some areas of health research, such as HIV/AIDS effects on performance, are progressing so rapidly that there is no substitute for reading recent research reports, such as those cited here. A recent volume edited by Snel & Lorist (1998) covers research on alcohol, caffeine, and nicotine use.

# 14

# Individual differences in ability and performance

## 14.1 INVESTIGATING INDIVIDUAL DIFFERENCES

On any task, some people perform better than others, even when the amount of practice is controlled. Individuals differ in their *ability* or basic aptitude for performing the task concerned. This chapter addresses the nature and practical significance of individual differences in ability. Research on ability and performance brings together several rather different research traditions. These include psychometric research focused on detailed statistical modelling of ability, applied research geared to predicting real-world performance, and cognitive psychological research concerned with individual differences in information processing. Hence, the chapter focuses on the interrelation of three types of construct:

1. Psychometric ability factors such as general intelligence or *g*, such as those measured by conventional IQ tests. Ability tests aim to abstract some general quality which may relate to individual differences in performance on a variety of tasks.

2. Measures of laboratory and real-world task performance (molar measures). Ability research is concerned with the prediction and understanding of individual differences in performance.

3. Elementary information-processing constructs, with a basis in theory (molecular measures). Researchers often wish to explain individual differences in performance on more complex tasks in terms of specific processes.

### 14.1.1 Theory and practice in ability research

The first step in ability research is to describe and characterise the major dimensions of ability. In the intelligence field, for example, there has been much debate between researchers who favour a single overarching ability (*g*), and those who posit multiple, independent "intelligences", such as separate abilities for logical, verbal, musical and other types of skill (Brody, 1997; Gardner, Kornhaber, & Wake, 1996). Next, we need to explore how the relatively pure measures of ability provided by psychometric tests relate to specific tasks. Real-world tasks often relate to a variety of abilities. For example, a pilot needs skills in attention, psychomotor response and communication with others (Stokes & Kite, 1994). Finally, cognitive psychologists seek to understand the underpinnings of ability in elementary processes which can be described computationally. Unfortunately, there is a conflict of cultures between psychometrically- and cognitively-oriented researchers. Psychometrics is driven by differences between people, cognitive psychology by differences between tasks. The psychometrician tends to seek broad, descriptive constructs, whereas the cognitive psychologist focuses on specific computational operations and their interrelationship within the cognitive architecture. Constructs of the two types, such as general intelligence and specific attentional processes, may not be interrelated in any simple way. Attempts to resolve these differences in research philosophy define one of the major themes of this chapter. Prediction of individual differences in performance requires understanding of both tasks and people.

The aims of the practitioner are rather different, and focus on proficiency or aptitude for specific real-world skills. Proficiency refers to present ability to perform representative tasks. Practical tests of this kind assess office skills such as typing and word-processing, or industrial skills such as lathe and grinder operation (Super & Crites, 1962). Aptitude is the individual's potential for learning some specific skilled task, prior to training. Proficiency and aptitude testing are often performed on an "actuarial" basis—i.e. from empirical data alone (as an insurance company might calculate risk). The aim is to measure or predict skills accurately, regardless of the psychological basis for the association between test scores and skilled performance. Anastasi and Urbina (1997) and Cronbach (1990) provide good reviews of such research. The actuarial approach is useful in some circumstances, but an injection of theory is required to derive general principles applicable to a variety of different contexts.

We begin the chapter by examining theories of abilities. First, we discuss psychometric research on broad ability dimensions or factors, including attempts to identify factors related to cognitive theory. Next, we consider how these rather general,

high-level constructs relate to individual differences in cognitive functions. Then we turn to the issue of how individual differences in learning and skill acquisition may be characterised psychometrically, and in terms of processing. The later parts of the chapter address practical issues: the prediction of proficiency and aptitude from ability measures, and the difficult problem of predicting how individuals will fare under different instructional regimes.

## 14.1.2 Reliability and validity of ability tests

Both theoretical and applied research into individual differences in performance require the application of psychometrics to ensure accuracy of measurement. Even if the aim is merely to predict some specific skill actuarially, it is essential to measure that skill accurately. If measurement of either the ability or the criterion is unreliable, then high correlations between skill and other measures cannot be expected, on purely statistical grounds (Cronbach, 1990). Problems of unreliability are particularly acute in applied research, where ratings or judgements of performance are often used. However, ratings are susceptible to a number of biases and are often unsatisfactory (Anastasi & Urbina, 1997). A meta-analysis showed that correlations between supervisor ratings and objective measures of job performance may be as little as .2 or .3 (Heneman, 1986). There are various other statistical difficulties that will tend to lower ability: performance correlations, such as restriction of range (i.e. reduced variation in ability and/or performance scores), and curvilinear relationships. Various techniques for correcting for these artifacts have been developed, with attendant statistical controversies and argument (see Cronbach, 1990).

No matter how reliable the measures, they must also be valid, in the sense of measuring a meaningful construct. A supervisor's rating of a worker may be both unreliable, in that it varies from day to day according to personal whim, and invalid, in that the supervisor focuses on attributes of the worker irrelevant to the task, such as personal appearance, rather than on the actual quality of the work performed. Palm-reading and graphology ( handwriting analysis) appear to be reliable, but their validity is highly questionable. A distinction is often made between criterion and construct validity. *Criterion validity* simply refers to the ability of a test or measure to predict some other intrinsically interesting measure. For example, a psychometric test of mechanical knowledge should predict performance in designing pulley systems, fixing cars and so forth. The correlation between an ability measure and some criterion, such as job performance, is known as the validity coefficient. In occupational contexts, a further validity issue is to ensure that performance measures actually relate to the organisation's goals, especially making a profit.

*Construct validity* refers to whether the ability measure actually assesses a meaningful theoretical construct. It is generally accepted that psychometric intelligence tests (IQ tests) are reliable and predict criteria such as job performance. However, there has been much debate over whether IQ tests measure "intelligence" or something else, such as quality of education. Establishing construct validity is a never-ending process because of the fallibility of theory. We cannot say that IQ tests measure "intelligence" in the absence of a scientific theory of what it means to be intelligent. Theories of ability may be expressed at the different levels of explanation discussed in Chapter 1. At the biological level, intelligence may relate to the efficiency of neural function or brain properties such as the connectivity of neurons (Jensen, 1998). Biological explanations gain credibility from the partial heritability of intelligence, and from correlations between intelligence and psychophysiological indices such as evoked potentials (Deary & Caryl, 1997). Information-processing theories seek properties of the cognitive architecture that relate to molar intellectual performance, such as the speed of execution of molecular components (Sternberg, 1977). This chapter is mainly directed towards this cognitive level of analysis. Knowledge-based accounts pose the question of what intelligence is actually for: i.e. how does intelligence help people to attain important real-world objectives? (Matthews, 1997c). Such "practical intelligence" may be distinct from psychometric intelligence, although, broadly, *g* may relate especially to the ability to handle complex and novel situations (Sternberg, 1985).

## 14.2 DIMENSIONS OF INDIVIDUAL DIFFERENCES IN PERFORMANCE

The traditional approach to the identification and assessment of individual differences in performance derives from the intelligence-testing movement pioneered by Binet (1903) and Spearman (1927), among others. The general approach is to construct batteries of tasks, and to identify the principal dimensions underlying individual differences from the set of correlations between the various measures of performance. Early work, conducted in an educational context, focused primarily on tasks requiring reasoning or problem-solving, but it is straightforward also to devise test batteries tapping other faculties such as memory or motor performance. After a century or so of work of this kind the construct of *g* is thriving, although a host of more specific abilities have also been identified.

The key method of analysis is the multivariate statistical technique of factor analysis (Comrey & Lee, 1992). Factor analysis seeks to identify the main dimensions underlying a set of correlations between variables. An adequate account of factor analysis is beyond the scope of this book (see Kline, 1994, for an introduction), but the general principle may be illustrated, very roughly, as follows. Suppose we have people perform one set of tasks requiring reasoning, and a second set requiring brute physical strength. We would probably find that indices of performance on the reasoning tasks intercorrelated: individuals performing well on one task tend also to perform better than others on the remaining tasks. Similarly, performance levels on the strength tasks intercorrelate with one another. Correlations within each of the two types of task are stronger than those between reasoning and strength tasks. Factor analysis then identifies two underlying dimensions relating to reasoning and to physical strength, and it tells us precisely how performance on each task relates to both dimensions. Formally, a factor is identified by the set of tasks which correlate with it, or "load" on it. In this contrived example, inspection of the correlations would most likely indicate the two dimensions. With real data, however, the dimensions are often far from obvious, and the sophisticated statistical procedures used in factor analysis are necessary. Factor analysis requires a number of difficult statistical decisions to be made, and papers on individual differences are liberally spiced with arguments over the validity of specific techniques or assumptions made in the context of specific problems.

Intelligence studies may be criticised because the initial stages of factor identification are often somewhat ad hoc and lack a fine-grained theoretical analysis (Sternberg, 1985). In recent years, the success of cognitive psychology has led to attempts to identify individual difference dimensions that relate directly to cognitive constructs such as working memory or time-sharing. In reviewing the contribution of psychometric research, we consider first the more traditional research on abilities, and then work on individual differences in attention driven by cognitive theory.

### 14.2.1 Psychometric models of ability

Historically, studies of individual differences in ability have been dominated by debate over the relative importances of $g$ and of more specific primary abilities such as verbal and spatial ability. There is now a reasonable consensus among psychometricians that mental abilities may be described as a hierarchy of at least three levels of successively more specialised abilities, with $g$ as the highest-level ability (Carroll, 1993; Haernqvist, Gustafsson, Muthen, & Nelson, 1994). At least so far as cognitive abilities are concerned, the data are inconsistent with Gardner et al.'s (1996) view that there are several entirely independent abilities (see Carroll, 1993, pp. 641–642). $g$ correlates with performance of a very wide range of simple and complex tasks, but these correlations are often modest in magnitude. For accurate prediction of performance, knowledge of more specific abilities is also necessary.

Carroll's (1993) book on human cognitive abilities presents a magisterial survey of factor-analytic studies. Figure 14.1 indicates how Carroll

organises the structure of abilities in terms of three levels or strata. Below $g$ is the level of broad or group factors. Some of these factors, such as processing speed, are easily understood as representing some basic psychological function. The first two factors, fluid intelligence ($g_f$) and crystallised intelligence ($g_c$), require a little more explanation (see Cattell, 1971). Fluid intelligence relates to the person's basic ability to perform intellectual functions requiring little learning or formal instruction, whereas crystallised intelligence represents intellectual abilities more dependent on the interaction of $g_f$ with learning and culture, such as reading ability. Each broad factor is defined by a set of lower-level primary abilities associated with speed or accuracy on particular sets of tasks. In addition to these mental abilities, there may also be broad factors associated with psychomotor and physical proficiency tasks (Fleishman & Quaintance, 1984). Again, the list of primary factors is long: Fleishman and Quaintance (1984) list 19 psychomotor and physical factors, such as static strength, multilimb coordination, manual dexterity and arm–head steadiness. It is unclear how these factors might be arranged in some more complex hierarchical structure.

### 14.2.2 Individual differences in attention

In traditional studies of ability the selection of tasks tends to reduce the role of attention in individual differences: tasks are typically performed singly, without distraction, and temporal change in performance is not assessed. Given the role of attention in skilled performance, this neglect of individual differences in attention may limit the capacity of orthodox ability tests to predict performance. There is only limited research on the structure of attentional abilities. There have been various factor analytic studies of attention (see Davies, Jones, & Taylor, 1984; Stankov, 1988) but little consensus on the main factors. These studies often have shortcomings, such as use of paper-and-pencil tests which may not discriminate different attentional functions, and limited sampling of measures.

The various aspects of attention described in Chapters 4–6 seem to be associated with several individual difference dimensions. For example,

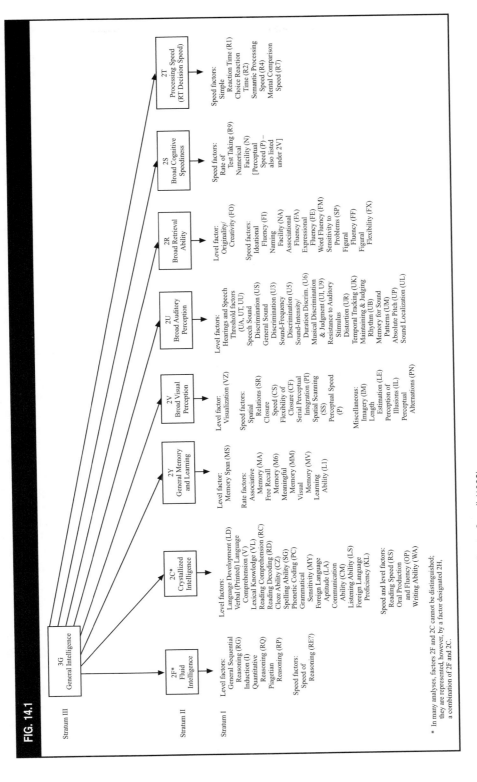

**FIG. 14.1**

The dimensional structure of abilities, according to Carroll (1993).

Davies and Parasuraman (1982) describe patterns of correlations between vigilance tasks suggestive of separate abilities for (1) "simultaneous" tasks, requiring detection of a stimulus element within a more complex display, and (2) "successive" tasks, requiring comparison of stimuli across trials. Modality-specific vigilance abilities appear to make a fairly minor contribution to performance: similar auditory and visual tasks correlate quite highly. Matthews, Davies and Holley (1993) found that successive tasks were more strongly correlated with controlled visual search speed than were simultaneous tasks. Controlled visual search and successive task performance may require a common attentional resource (see also 4.2.3). Similarly, a factor-analytic study of selective attention (Sack & Rice, 1974) suggested three separate abilities associated with selectivity: establishing a focus of attention, resisting distraction (i.e. maintaining that focus), and shifting attention from one focus to another.

The psychometrics of divided attention poses special problems. The basic question is whether there is an ability specifically associated with concurrent performance of two or more tasks. Are there some people who are particularly good at multiple-task performance, even though their single-task performance is unexceptional? If so, the performance decrement associated with pairing two tasks should predict the performance decrements associated with other pairings of tasks of different content to the first two. A number of investigators have assessed the intercorrelations of dual-task decrements associated with appropriately sampled sets of task pairings. The majority of studies fail to find any systematic correlation between decrements on unrelated task pairs (Ackerman, Schneider, & Wickens, 1984). There is no general ability to divide attention or to "timeshare" performance of concurrent tasks. Often, it appears that the best predictor of dual-task performance is single-task performance.

There may be more specific abilities of divided attention, time-sharing or coordination of multiple task components for particular types of task. Studies of tracking show that dual-task decrements associated with tracking across dual axes (Braune & Wickens, 1986) or tracking with different orders of control (Siering & Stone, 1986) are associated with a distinct tracking time-sharing ability. However, such abilities do not necessarily relate to $g$ (Brookings, 1990; Yee, Laden, & Hunt, 1994). There may also be an "attentional flexibility" ability, i.e. facility in rapid switching between tasks. Flexibility measures are among the best predictors of motor vehicle accident involvement (Arthur et al., 1991), but there is conflicting psychometric evidence on whether flexibility constitutes a distinct ability (Braune & Wickens, 1986; Keele & Hawkins, 1982). In addition, studies of flight performance suggest that multiple-task measures are more predictive of performance than single-task measures (Damos, 1993). For example, O'Hare (1997) showed that elite glider pilots performed particularly well on a test called WOMBAT, which required integration of performance on set of tasks involving tracking, pattern recognition, mental rotation and working memory. O'Hare sees WOMBAT as a test of "situation awareness", i.e. maintaining awareness of a complex, dynamic environment (see 8.2.2.). As O'Hare discusses, there are currently conflicting views on how much such abilities overlap with $g$.

In summary, there seems to be no general dual-tasking ability, but there are abilities related to more specialised dual-task paradigms, including the capacity to keep track of the rapidly-changing visual environments encountered by pilots. It is difficult to relate such abilities to general intelligence in the absence of a satisfactory factor model for multiple-task abilities. If attention is a bundle of discrete functions (Allport, 1989) a multiplicity of attention factors is expected. Conversely, flexibility and attention management tasks may index some more general executive control ability related to $g$ (Duncan et al., 1996).

## 14.3 COGNITIVE FOUNDATIONS OF ABILITY

### 14.3.1 Cognitive correlates of ability

Researchers have used two broad strategies for relating ability measures to cognitive constructs. The cognitive correlates approach (Hunt, 1978) seeks to identify specific processing functions that

FIG. 14.2

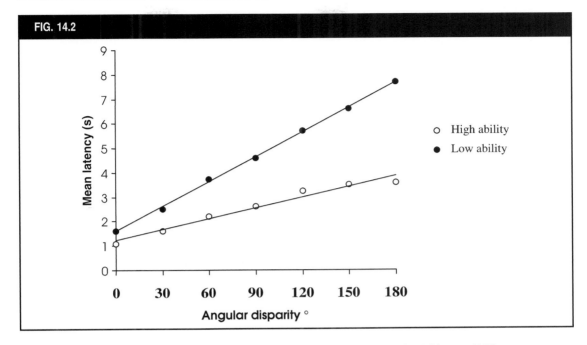

Response latencies for mental rotation in groups high and low in spatial ability (Pellegrino & Mumaw, 1980).

relate to psychometric ability factors. For example, Hunt showed that verbal ability related to performance on various information-processing tasks such as speed of letter-matching. Similarly, spatial ability appears to correlate with speed of processes such as rotation of a mental image (Pellegrino & Kail, 1982). On a typical mental rotation task, the participant must decide whether a rotated letter is the same as a second, upright letter. Response time is a linear function of the angle through which the first letter has been rotated ("angular disparity"), suggesting that the participant forms a mental image of the letter, and rotates it back to its normal orientation, allowing comparison with the upright letter. Figure 14.2 shows data from a rotation study (Pellegrino & Mumaw, 1980), comparing response latencies for the participant groups who scored in the top 25% and bottom 25% on a psychometric test of spatial ability. With an angular disparity of 0° (i.e. both letters upright), the lower spatial-ability group was only a little slower than the higher spatial-ability group. However, the difference between the groups increased sharply as angular disparity increased,

implying that it may have taken longer for the lower-ability group to rotate the mental image through a given angle.

Identification of cognitive correlates may allow extension of hierarchical models of ability (such as that shown in Fig. 14.1) downwards a further level, so that each ability can be related to a set of processing functions. In practice, it has proved difficult to achieve this goal, possibly because there is no simple set of mappings between processing functions and abilities.

However, cognitive correlates research has made two notable contributions. The first has been to identify some very simple information-processing correlates of general intelligence. Jensen (1987) averaged data from a variety to studies to demonstrate a correlation of −.18 between $g$ and simple RT, and a slightly larger correlation of −.23 between $g$ and choice RT. In 3.2.1, we discussed Hick's Law, which states that choice RT relates to the log of the number of "bits" of information required for the choice. The constant relating RT to log (bits) is lower in more intelligent individuals (the slope of the plot is flatter). That is, high $g$

becomes more advantageous as the task becomes more complex (although the magnitude of the effect is small). Rabbitt and Maylor (1991) suggest that intelligence operates as a simple scaling factor for response times. We can, for example, work out a constant that will allow us to predict how fast a person of a given IQ will react, given that we know the RT of a person of average IQ on a particular task. However, Rabbitt (1996a) cautions that although an individual's RT can be predicted from IQ with a fair degree of accuracy, it does not follow that RT on a particular task is simply a function of $g$. Individual differences in RT may also relate to functioning of specific processing units, or to individuals' strategies for controlling speed–accuracy tradeoff.

Intelligence also relates to certain perceptual tasks which appear to make even fewer intellectual demands. In the inspection time task, the person must simply say which one of two briefly-presented masked lines is longer. The accuracy with which this simple discrimination may be made at short presentation intervals correlates at about .3 with $g$ (Kranzler & Jensen, 1989). It has been suggested that intelligence may not relate to processing in these paradigms, but to strategy. In fact, tests of this hypothesis show that strategy does not seem to account for the relationship (e.g. Egan & Deary, 1992; Neubauer, 1997). Intelligence relates to elementary processing functions which most people would not describe as "intelligent", as well as to abstract problem-solving and reasoning. Some researchers have argued that "mental speed" is fundamental to intelligence (Neubauer, 1997), but others have argued for the contrary view that intelligence cannot be reduced to processing speed alone (Stankov & Roberts, 1997).

The cognitive correlates approach also shows how intelligence relates to more complex attentional and cognitive processes. Spearman (1923) saw $g$ as a kind of intellectual energy, an idea which prefigured resource theories of performance. A series of studies conducted by Stankov, Spilsbury and others have investigated this idea, by comparing relationships between $g$ and single and dual-task performance. These studies showed that $g$ is more strongly correlated with dual-task performance, as a resource explanation might predict. Roberts, Beh and Stankov (1988) related speed on a card-sorting task to performance on Raven's matrices, a standard "fluid" intelligence test. The correlation between speed and intelligence was higher when card sorting was performed concurrently with a word categorisation task. However, further studies argued against a resource interpretation. Sullivan and Stankov (1990) measured resource availability by having people detect target words while also performing the shadowing task described in 4.2.1. Intelligence predicted shadowing accuracy, but not speed of target detection. Spilsbury (1992) concludes that correlations between intelligence and performance do not depend on task difficulty in any simple way. Instead, the magnitude of the correlation depends on task complexity so that, in dual-task performance, intelligence may relate to the executive processes which implement the person's strategy for combining the two tasks. Carpenter, Just and Schell (1990) have provided a more detailed account of how $g$ may relate to strategy use on Raven's matrices test. Intelligent individuals may be better at decomposing problems into manageable segments and at managing a hierarchy of goals and subgoals. Duncan et al. (1996) suggest that the planning component of intelligence relates to frontal lobe function.

Another active area of cognitive correlates research relates to working memory. It is well-known that short-term memory tends to relate to intelligence, and digit span is sometimes used to assess intelligence. More recent work has attempted to discriminate different short-term retention functions. For example, Cantor, Engle and Hamilton (1991) attempt to relate verbal intelligence to Baddeley's (1986) working memory model, discussed in 3.5.2. They suggest that verbal ability may relate to both passive storage of information and to the functioning of the central executive. Other work has tested detailed models of how information processing and ability factors interrelate. This approach (structural equation modelling) integrates the cognitive correlates and psychometric approaches with attempts to discriminate causal links between factors. Kyllonen and Christal (1990) developed a model of this

**TABLE 14.1**

Contribution of the phonological loop and central executive components of working memory to different language processing activities (Gathercole & Baddeley, 1993, p. 232).

| Language activity | Phonological loop | Central executive |
|---|---|---|
| Comprehension | Used to maintain a phonological record that can be consulted during off-line language processing | Involved in processing syntactic and semantic information and storing products of processing |
| Vocabulary acquisition | Critical for the long-term learning of phonological forms of new words | Involved in interpreting the meaning of new words |
| Learning to read | Contributes to the development of a phonological recording strategy | Unknown |
| Reading familiar words | None, except when complex judgements about phonological structure are required | Unknown |
| Speech | None | Involved in planning production of the conceptual content of speech |

kind in which a working memory factor defined by a number of specific tasks strongly influenced a general intelligence factor.

## 14.3.2 Cognitive correlates of verbal skills

Research on cognitive predictors of verbal ability leads into studies of predictors of other verbal skills. Much of this work has a working memory orientation. Measures of overall capacity of working memory predict a variety of complex tasks including reasoning, playing bridge and computer programming (Daneman & Merikle, 1996). Some of these tasks have important non-verbal aspects, and working memory capacity seems to relate to g as much as it does to verbal ability. As we saw in 3.5, theorists disagree on whether working memory should be explained in terms of multiple stores and ancillary processes (Baddeley, 1986), or in terms of activation of LTM representations (Cowan, 1995). Both theoretical strands are represented in studies of individual differences.

Table 14.1 summarises Gathercole and Baddeley's (1993) review of how working memory may relate to language processing activities. As discussed in 3.5.2, the phonological loop contributes to short-term retention through subvocal rehearsal, which may in turn facilitate comprehension, vocabulary acquisition and learning to read. The majority of evidence in this field is experimental, but there is increasing interest in individual differences. Gathercole and Baddeley reviewed evidence from studies of children that performance on a nonword repetition task thought to require use of the phonological loop correlates with the development of vocabulary, especially at younger ages. Similarly, various measures related to the phonological loop are associated with individual differences in reading development, including nonword repetition, awareness of rhyme and auditory digit, word and sentence span (Bryant, MacLean, Bradley, & Crossland, 1990; Ellis, 1990). Longitudinal studies confirm that phonological processing is causally related to reading acquisition, especially in younger children (Wagner, Torgesen, Rashotte, & Hecht, 1997).

The role of the central executive in individual differences in comprehension has been investigated using rather complex working memory tasks to predict reading performance. For example, Daneman and Carpenter (1980) assessed working memory by having participants abstract words from sentences and recall them in the correct order. This measure predicted reading and listening comprehension on other tasks, and overall verbal ability. Gathercole and Baddeley (1993) caution that Table 14.1 may underestimate the involvement of the central executive in other linguistic functions, due to difficulties in investigating this somewhat vaguely-specified system empirically. Unfortunately, it has proved difficult to obtain psychometrically-acceptable measures of central executive functioning, despite its presumed neuropsychological basis. Individual differences on tasks purporting to relate to the executive are poorly correlated (Lehto, 1996).

Just and Carpenter (1992) have developed an activation model of working memory within which individual differences relate to the amount of activation available for processing and storage (see also Just, Carpenter, & Keller, 1996). Reading for comprehension requires simultaneous activation of various LTM elements which cannot, in general, be accommodated within conscious attention. Activation is seen as a limited resource. Individuals who have more available activation can activate more elements and so have better "working memory" and comprehension. This model explains why working memory predicts reading (Daneman & Carpenter, 1980). However, the equation of working memory with activation is challenged by studies of individual differences in semantic priming (Woltz, 1999). As previously discussed (2.3.1), encoding of word meanings tends to prime semantic networks to react more rapidly to subsequent stimuli with related meanings, a process often attributed to spreading activation. Larkin (1996) showed that working memory and a semantic priming measure predicted reading comprehension independently, implying that working memory capacity and activation represent distinct influences on reading.

In general, it seems that aptitude for acquiring verbal skills may reflect individual differences in a variety of processing functions. Some of these functions, such as working memory, may be quite closely related to conventional ability measures, including *g*. Other functions, such as those relating to phonological processing and to activation processes, are more distinct from general and verbal intelligence.

### 14.3.3  Cognitive components and ability

A more sophisticated approach is the analysis of cognitive components (Sternberg, 1977). This approach is based on the development of a self-contained, process-oriented model of the aspect of performance of interest, which will generalise to different paradigms, contents and tasks. Specialised sub-tasks are devised to identify individual processes or components. Estimates of parameters of the model, such as error probabilities and execution speeds for particular components, can then be correlated with external correlates such as intelligence and other psychometric tests, to indicate the locus and nature of individual differences in performance. An important implication of this approach is that individual differences in skill can be investigated both from the "inside", with respect to the component cognitive processes of a task, and from the "outside", with respect to major psychometric dimensions such as those of ability and personality. Sternberg's empirical work was based on detailed modelling of the solution of analogy and classification problems. The parameters of the models showed differing correlations with general intelligence. The componential approach has also been applied to individual differences in reading. Frederiksen (1982) identified components such as grapheme encoding, letter recognition, perception of multiletter units and so forth, which were systematically related to overall word recognition performance. These and additional component measures also predicted overall comprehension in reading.

The difficulties of the componential approach are empirical. As Brody (1992) points out, measures of the same component derived from different tasks should be highly intercorrelated. Conversely, measures of different components derived from the same task should not be correlated. In fact, Brody shows that Sternberg's own data are incompatible with these predictions. It has proved difficult to establish that components generalise across tasks, and unrelated components do tend to correlate. This latter finding may be seen as an instance of "the positive manifold"; all mental tests and measures tend to correlate positively, although correlation magnitudes may be small. Somewhat similarly, Neubauer and Bucik

(1996) addressed the hypothesis that correlations between performance speed measures reflect common content, in terms of specific verbal or numerical skills, for example, rather than general ability. Contrary to the hypothesis, substantial correlations between measures based on differing content were found, implying an ability common to tasks based on differing content. Evidently, more research on components is required, in order to fulfill the theoretical promise of the approach. In fact, cognitive correlates studies have tended to become more "componential" as the theoretical rationale for the measures used becomes more detailed (e.g. Carpenter et al., 1990).

Cognitive ability research has made important contributions, but it has two difficult hurdles still to overcome. The first concerns the limitations of correlational methods. Cognitive researchers tend to assume that if an elementary processing measure correlates with an IQ test, the process concerned contributes directly to performance of the test items. For example, RT may correlate with IQ because intelligence tests are often completed under speed conditions. However, there are a variety of other reasons why performance measures intercorrelate (Matthews & Dorn, 1995). Elementary processing functions may constrain the development of intelligence (Anderson, 1992), or there may be overlap in the genes coding for elementary and higher processing functions. The second difficulty relates to the basic limitations of an analysis of cognition in terms of information processing alone, as discussed in 1.3.3. Cognitive explanation requires supplementation with both biological and knowledge-related explanations, as indicated in 14.1.2.

## 14.4 GROUP DIFFERENCES IN ABILITY

Controversies over group differences have been part of intelligence research from the early days of IQ testing. The interpretation of differences in test scores associated with race and social class has been especially contentious. The hypothesis that such group differences may be partially genetically-based has recently been revived by Herrnstein and Murray (1994), and widely criticised (e.g. Devlin, Roeder, & Resnick, 1997). Such debates are politicised and often polemical. In this section, we look briefly at two possible sources of group differences that have attracted significant amounts of experimental, and relatively dispassionate, research: age and sex differences.

Investigation of any group difference requires several separate questions to be addressed, in a logical sequence:

1. *Is there a reliable difference in test scores?* If so, there are many possible explanations: the existence of a difference tells us little in itself.

2. *If the group difference is reliable, does it reflect competence or performance?* The group difference might reflect underlying competence: women might execute certain kinds of processing operation more efficiently than men because of differences in the cognitive architecture, for example. Alternatively, differences might be derived from performance failing to reflect underlying competence in one of the groups, due to factors such as lack of motivation, discomfort with the test environment, and so forth. In this latter case, appropriate manipulations of the test setting should produce equal levels of performance in the groups compared. Differences might also reflect bias in the test items: presumably a cognitive test based on questions about football would tend to favour men.

3. *If there is a reliable competence difference, does it reflect biological or social-cultural factors (or both)?* Group differences are often attributed to biological factors, an hypothesis that requires substantiating evidence from psychophysiological or neuro-anatomical studies. It is uncontentious that ageing leads to degradation of neural function, although questions remain over how neural degradation translates into information-processing changes. In some cases, such as sex differences, a further question may arise: do differences in brain function reflect genetic differences or environmental influences on

brain development? A biological difference does not necessarily imply genetic difference: factors such as the intra-uterine environment, nutrition and early childhood experiences may affect the brain. The alternative to a biological explanation is, broadly, a learning-based explanation. Men and women may differ in cognitive function because, to some extent, boys and girls are treated differently, exposed to different activities, and so may acquire different cognitive skills. Explanations of this kind frequently refer to social and cultural factors which may influence, sex, social class and racial differences in cognitive skill acquisition.

### 14.4.1  Age differences

Performance on a variety of tasks declines with age, especially after age 60 or so. We review this research area in detail in Chapter 16. The main point to make at this stage is that scores on intelligence tests often decline with age, but the extent of decline depends on the nature of the test (see Horn, 1998, for a review). The tests that show the strongest declines are those which tap the basic cognitive processes thought to contribute to intelligence, such as reasoning and working memory. Psychometric tests of this kind are sometimes referred to as fluid intelligence: correlations between these measures and age range from −.30 to −.70 (see Stankov, 1994). Other tests are more dependent on learned intellectual skills (crystallised intelligence) such as mechanical knowledge, and having a good vocabulary and verbal comprehension abilities. These abilities are maintained into old age, and may even improve slightly, assuming the person is not afflicted with a dementing condition such as Alzheimer's disease. Ackerman (1996) points out that other forms of knowledge such as specific occupational knowledge and "avocational" knowledge (of hobbies and leisure pursuits) also hold up well. Older adults frequently possess ample learned cognitive skills to compensate for any loss of fluid intelligence. We look in more detail at the relationship between intelligence and knowledge in 14.5.2.

Depending on the task, there are genuine age differences in some aspects of intelligence test performance. How can these be explained? Although older people may have some difficulties in handling laboratory environments, for example in dealing with time pressure, their fluid intelligence deficit is primarily one of competence in processing. As we discuss in Chapter 16, studies using information-processing tasks suggest that ageing is associated with loss of working memory, attentional impairment and slowing of elementary processing speed. Furthermore, loss of central nervous system efficiency undoubtedly explains these effects to a large extent. However, there are some unresolved explanatory issues, including generational differences in intelligence, and the information-processing basis for age differences in intelligence. Simple comparisons between older and younger groups overestimate the extent of intellectual differences because of "cohort differences" (see 16.2). As Flynn (1998) has shown, average scores on IQ tests (including "fluid" abstract reasoning tests) have been steadily rising for several decades, all over the world. This "Flynn Effect" remains mysterious, but has been variously attributed to better nutrition, better education and, as a consequence of technological change, exposure to more complex visual environments (Neisser, 1998). Its consequence for ageing research is that older adults are disadvantaged (for whatever reason) through being born early this century. Longitudinal studies show smaller age-related deficits.

The relationship between loss of intelligence and degradation of processing functions remains somewhat unclear. Nettelbeck and Rabbitt (1992) showed that age differences in intelligence test performance were closely related to age differences in a measure of basic processing speed derived from simple tasks: controlling for "mental speed" eliminated the age difference on IQ measures, and some, but not all, cognitive tasks. They conclude that loss of fluid intelligence reflects loss of information-processing speed. Stankov (1994) offers a somewhat different perspective. As discussed in 16.4, complex tasks are more age-sensitive than simple tasks, so it is possible that age differences in fluid intelligence are a consequence of the complexity of the tests. However, Stankov used statistical modelling techniques to show that age was directly related to fluid intelligence but not to processing complexity. Indeed, the dependence of age differences in performance on complexity may be a secondary consequence of age-related change in fluid intelligence.

## 14.4.2 Sex differences

Sex differences research differs from ageing research in that there has been disagreement over whether substantial, practically significant group differences in ability and cognitive performance exist at all (e.g. Hyde & Linn, 1988). There is a consensus that men and women do not differ in performance on general intelligence tests, but there may be sex differences on primary ability measures. For example, it is often said that men perform better on tests of spatial abilities, whereas women may do better on verbal tests (Maccoby & Jacklin, 1978). Received wisdom in this area is expressed by the following statement from the American Psychological Association Task Force on Intelligence, convened to respond to the issues raised by the Herrnstein and Murray (1994) book (APA Public Affairs Office, 1997):

> Although there are no important sex differences in overall intelligence test scores, substantial differences do appear for specific abilities. Males typically score higher on visual-spatial and (beginning in middle childhood) mathemetical skills; females excel on a number of verbal measures. Sex hormones are clearly related to some of these differences, but social factors presumably play a role as well.

These statements are broadly correct, but they gloss over some of the complexities of the area. First, the "cognitive patterning" of sex differences is more complex than suggested, as shown in a series of papers produced by Halpern (e.g. 1992, 1997). She points out that men reliably perform better on tasks such as requiring manipulation of "images" in visuo-spatial working memory, especially mental rotation tasks, and motor aiming tasks. However, many spatial tasks show no sex differences, or even the reverse difference. For example, McBurney, Gaulin, Devineni and Adams

(1997) showed a large female advantage for a task requiring memory for the location of items. Similarly, the superior verbal performance of women may be restricted to tasks requiring rapid access to phonological and semantic information in long-term memory, and production and comprehension of complex prose. Men may be superior on some other tasks, such as solving verbal analogies. Meta-analyses show considerable variation in the effect sizes associated with sex differences: Hyde (1981) reported that the female advantage for verbal tasks (on average) was a trivial 0.1 SD difference, whereas on spatial visualisation tasks the male advantage is typically 0.5–1 SD (e.g. Hamilton, 1995).

A second area of uncertainty is the extent to which sex differences derive from competence or performance factors. One possible performance factor may be that women lack confidence on tasks associated with male sex roles, and so underperform relative to underlying competence. Brosnan (1998a) investigated such expectancy effects on the Embedded Figures Test, which requires detection of geometric figures in complex line drawings. Men outperformed women when the task was described as a test of spatial ability, but women improved to the level of men when the task was described as a test of empathy. However, the Embedded Figures Test normally shows only modest sex differences (Halpern, 1992), and it is unclear whether results would generalise to spatial visualisation tasks which tend to show a larger advantage for men. Expectancy effects have also been investigated in sex roles research: it might be expected that individuals of both sexes possessing more masculine personality characteristics might perform better on spatial tasks. Studies have shown that sex roles may relate to spatial performance, independent of actual sex, but results tend to be complex and difficult to interpret (e.g. Hamilton, 1995). Another performance factor implicated in sex differences is strategy choice. Goldstein, Haldane and Mitchell (1990) suggested that sex differences in mental rotation might reflect sex differences in (1) emphasis on accuracy as opposed to speed, and (2) willingness to guess. Practice may also eliminate or reduce sex differences on spatial tasks (Kass, Ahlers, & Dugger,

1998). However, other studies have found only limited support for the performance hypotheses (e.g. Delgado & Prieto, 1996), and, in general, at least a part of the male advantage appears to reflect greater competence (Halpern, 1997).

Let us suppose that sex differences in competence exist, at least on some tasks. How might we explain them? As we might expect, there are both biological and social-cultural explanations. Biological factors implicated in sex differences include levels of sex hormones such as oestrogens and testosterone, which may influence both brain development in the foetus, and adult brain function (Hampson & Kimura, 1993). Cerebral lateralisation and other neuro-anatomical differences have also been identified (e.g. Ellis & Ebertz, 1998), although there is currently no detailed account of how sex differences in neural functioning translate into sex differences in information processing. There is also increasing interest in evolutionary explanations for sex differences: male advantages may contribute to better hunting performance, whereas female advantages assist with foraging and social bonding (e.g. McBurney et al., 1997), although such explanations sometimes seem a little fanciful, post hoc, and far removed from the available data. Conversely, social-cultural theorists focus on the different learning experiences and social roles to which boys and girls are exposed (e.g. Hyde, 1996). Boys are more likely to engage in activities requiring spatial processing, such as competitive ball games and computer games: Baenninger and Newcombe's (1989) meta-analysis found a small but significant correlation between spatial activity participation and spatial performance although, of course, the correlation does not necessarily indicate a direct causal link. In general, until stronger causal models have been developed, it seems to safest to follow Halpern (1992) in supposing that sex differences in test performance may reflect a variety of interacting biological and cultural influences.

## 14.4.3 Practical implications of group differences in ability

In principle, group differences are relevant to performance assessment and to training. An organisation might wish to know if its older employees will be less productive, and what remedial training might be offered. However, the overriding consideration in drawing practical conclusions from the empirical evidence is the need for caution, for both social–political and scientific reasons. Performance assessment in applied settings operates within the legal and cultural framework of the country concerned. For example, as Kanfer et al. (1995) discuss, legislation in the US in effect requires organisations to demonstrate that psychological tests are non-discriminatory and valid. Typically, women and minorities receive more legal protection than the elderly: it may be difficult to use tests known to show sex differences in selection, unless validation evidence is convincing enough to allow test use to be defended in court.

The scientific questions concern the generalisation and relevance of empirical studies of group differences to specific applied settings. For example, age differences in work performance are frequently trivial, compared with the large performance deficits shown by the elderly on certain tests and information-processing tasks (Davies et al., 1991; see 16.7). Furthermore, as discussed in 1.4, there is considerably more to job performance than performance of specific tasks. There may be advantages to employing the elderly despite loss of cognitive efficiency: there is a modest trend towards greater work motivation and commitment in older workers (Davies et al., 1991). Similarly, social behavioural differences between men and women may be of considerably more practical significance than performance differences (see Eagly, 1995). Laboratory studies also tend to downplay the extent to which group differences may be eliminated by training. For example, Brosnan (1998b) discusses evidence suggesting that females experience greater anxiety and lower self-efficacy in learning how to use computers, which he links to social sex-typing of computing as a "masculine" activity. However, when courses are structured so that males and females have equal access to computers, both sexes appear to become equally proficient and confident.

Given due caution, though, there are some respects in which group differences research may be practically useful. First, group differences in real-world performance are not always trivial; in some instances, differences are sufficiently important that they demand research directed towards counter-measures: the over-representation of young males in motor vehicle accidents is a case in point. Second, small performance differences are often irrelevant, but sometimes have surprisingly large consequences. Martell, Lane and Emrich (1996) discuss how small sex differences in performance may lead to large sex differences in likelihood of promotion, when (1) there is high competition for advancement, and (2) early career success is important for promotion. Such data are relevant to the "glass ceiling" problem encountered by women in organisations. Third, such research may be educationally significant, in showing how cultural influences may impair certain groups. If the female deficit on certain spatial tasks reflects lack of exposure to appropriate activities during childhood, schools may have a role to play in providing appropriate training (in fact, training seems to benefit both males and females: Baenninger & Newcombe, 1989). Fourth, even when group differences are biologically based, there may be training regimes which help to compensate for deficits, or tasks may redesigned to assist the disadvantaged. For example, research shows how the automatic teller machines (ATM) provided by banks may be designed for ease of use by the elderly (Rogers, Gilbert, Kristen, & Fraser, 1997).

## 14.5 INDIVIDUAL DIFFERENCES IN SKILL ACQUISITION

### 14.5.1 Individual differences in learning rate

So far, we have focused largely on correlations between ability and performance proficiency at a single point in time. However, it is important also to address individual differences in learning and aptitude. Can we use ability measures to predict how rapidly a person will learn to perform a task and acquire skills? The relationship between ability and learning has been a contentious issue since the inception of intelligence testing. Early studies tended to find only weak correlations between intelligence and learning rate (e.g.

Woodrow, 1946). Zeaman and House (1967) attribute many of these negative results to methodological weaknesses, such as unreliability of measures, restricted range of ability, and ceiling and floor effects.

There are also statistical difficulties associated with comparing the performance gains resulting from learning across groups of differing ability. Ability frequently affects performance right from the beginning of training, so that high-ability groups start with a performance advantage. Sometimes, low-ability participants may partially "catch up" high-ability participants, so that ability is negatively related to performance gain, even though high-ability participants show superior performance throughout training (Ackerman, 1987). Figure 14.3 shows some real data reported by Rabbitt (1993) which show this effect. High scorers on an intelligence test showed hardly any improvement with practice on a choice RT task, whereas low scorers on the test improved over time, but never approached the response speeds of the more able individuals. Analysis of "the amount of learning" (the gain score) alone is inadequate: the correlation between ability and performance at each stage of learning must also be assessed.

Methodologically sound studies (e.g. Fleishman & Quaintance, 1984; Snow, Kyllonen, & Marshalek, 1984) show that ability does predict learning, but the size of the correlation varies with the type of ability, stage of practice, and the nature of the criterion task. IQ test scores are unrelated to classical conditioning, but IQ does modestly predict even some relatively simple verbal learning tasks such as paired-associate learning (Zeaman & House, 1967). On the whole, correlations between g and learning increase with task complexity (Snow et al., 1984). Associative learning is frequently identified as a distinct primary ability, as shown in Fig. 14.1. Kyllonen and Tirre (1988) identified a distinct ability of this kind which predicted learning speed, retention and relearning. The ability was moderately related to general knowledge and reasoning ability. Subsequently, Kyllonen (1993) has distinguished factors related to breadth of declarative and procedural learning (cf. Chapter 7) which may

**FIG. 14.3**

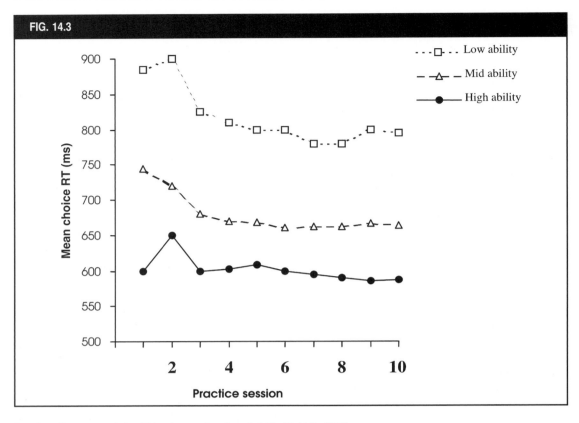

Practice effects on a choice RT task, as a function of ability (Rabbitt, 1993).

relate especially to transfer of skills, i.e. the ability to apply existing knowledge to a new task. Jensen (1980) summarises work on IQ and learning by stating that the correlation between them increases when learning is intentional, meaningful, insightful and when learning depends on mastering an interrelated sequence of elements. IQ also predicts learning of reading and other skills instilled by formal education although, as we shall see, the importance of IQ in learning such skills sometimes varies with the type of instruction (Cronbach & Snow, 1977).

Fleishman and Quaintance (1984) review studies of learning of skills with a stronger motor component. They conclude that non-motor abilities may predict performance modestly at early stages of learning, but their contribution relative to those of motor abilities decreases systematically with practice. For example, on discrimination

RT, spatial and verbal ability are initially the strongest predictors, but after extensive practice it is the motor abilities of rate of movement and motor reaction time which predict performance (Fleishman & Hempel, 1955). Similarly, on a complex coordination task, practical/mechanical knowledge was initially the strongest predictor but, after extended practice, it was superseded by rate of movement/motor RT (Fleishman & Hempel, 1955).

As with all correlational data, inferring the causal processes responsible for these relationships between ability and learning is problematic. It seems likely that ability directly affects learning of appropriate tasks. For example, Crano, Kenny and Campbell (1972) used a "cross-lag panel analysis" to show that IQ predicted future school achievement more strongly than achievement predicted IQ, to demonstrate the causal influence of $g$ (although their method has since been criticised by Rogosa, 1980). Sternberg (1985) suggests that IQ is related both to competence to deal with novel information, and to rate of proceduralisation or automatisation of knowledge. More intelligent people may have an advantage in learning unfamiliar material or tasks because of their ability to transfer pre-existing strategies to the novel situation. Studies of mentally retarded children (Ferretti & Cavalier, 1991) show that these low-IQ individuals can often be taught strategies for specific memory and problem-solving tasks, but they fail to generalise them to other, allied tasks. This failure may be attributed to poor executive control of learning, consistent with the evidence discussed previously that $g$ relates to executive function (e.g. Spilsbury, 1992). Mental retardation also seems to impair "metacognition": insight into one's own mental processes. Findings of this kind led Snow and Yalow (1982) to suggest that intelligence particularly facilitates learning when instruction is suboptimal, so that the learner has to invent new cognitive routines to overcome lack of explicitness in task instructions.

It is also probable that learning affects intelligence. A number of primary ability tests, such as those of vocabulary and mechanical knowledge, rely explicitly on prior learning, and contribute to crystallised intelligence. However, fluid intelligence is also trainable, at least to some extent (Snow, 1982). Cattell (1971) and Horn's (e.g. Horn & Noll, 1997) causal model suggests that $g_f$ is "invested" in the development of more specific, culture-bound mental skills, through learning and education. These learnt skills then comprise $g_c$. Anderson, Kline and Beasley (1980) suggested that there is a reciprocal relationship between intelligence and learning. They provide a computer simulation based on Anderson's (1983) skill theory (see Chapter 7) to demonstrate this point. Learning leads to ability in the form of new productions, but the generalisation of these productions to new situations facilitates further learning.

## 14.5.2 Abilities and skill acquisition

An issue of some practical importance is whether predictors of a skill change with practice. The selection of operational personnel on the basis of their unpractised task performance may be inefficient in selecting operators who will perform well after appropriate training and practice. We have seen already that Fleishman and Quaintance's (1984) studies of acquisition of perceptual-motor skills show a shift with practice from mental to motor abilities as the predictors of performance. Fleishman and Quaintance (1984) also claim that individual differences in performance become increasingly task-specific with practice. Meta-analysis of validity coefficients obtained in real-world studies confirms that ability tests tend to be better predictors of initial than of later performance (Hulin, Henry, & Noon, 1990). In terms of the skill models described in Chapter 7, it may be that task-specific procedures are compiled, whose efficiency is relatively weakly related to abilities. This notion has rather pessimistic implications for operator selection: prediction of final performance levels is difficult.

An alternative view of changes in ability–skill correlations has been provided by Ackerman (1987, 1988). He suggests that the apparent increase in task-specific variance found by Fleishman is an artifact of using inappropriate statistics. Re-analysis of Fleishman and Hempel's (1954, 1955) data suggests that changes in task-specific variance depend on task characteristics. According to Ackerman (1987), the task-specificity of individual differences in performance varies with the complexity of the task. In general, task-specificity tends to increase only for relatively simple tasks, such as those which are consistently mapped (see 3.3.1), or which impose a low memory load. Task-specificity decreases with practice for more complex variably-mapped and memory-loaded tasks. In other words, task-specific variance only increases with practice if performance can become more automatic in nature, such that a task-specific procedure is developed.

Ackerman (1988) also proposes a general theory of skill acquisition and ability, such that ability correlates of performance vary with both practice and task characteristics. Early in practice, formulation of new procedures to deal with the novel task is of most importance. Hence, performance is most sensitive to individual differences in general ability, $g$, and in relevant primary

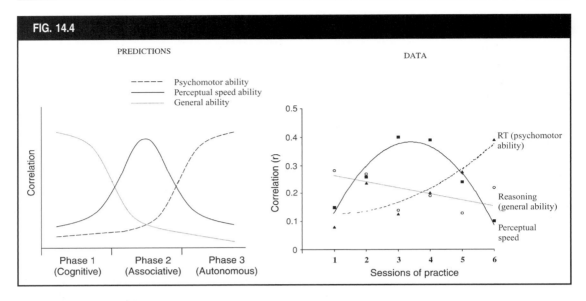

**FIG. 14.4**

Predicted and actual correlations between ability factors and performance (Ackerman, 1988).

abilities. With practice, as the person progresses from Fitts and Posner's (1967) cognitive phase to the associative phase (see 7.2.1), rate of knowledge compilation becomes more important. Hence, the role of purely mental abilities declines, even for essentially mental tasks, and an ability which Ackerman (1988) terms perceptual speed becomes progressively more important. Perceptual speed may be indexed by tasks requiring rapid consistent encoding and comparison such as letter cancellation or substituting symbols for digits according to fixed digit–symbol correspondences. If performance eventually reaches Fitts and Posner's (1967) autonomous phase, perceptual speed is replaced by psychomotor ability as the main predictor of performance. Psychomotor ability describes speed of response on tasks requiring minimal information processing, such as rapid tapping and simple reaction time. However, just as the automatisation of task performance depends on task parameters, so too do ability–performance correlations. As the task becomes less consistent or more complex, mental abilities become more predictive relative to perceptual speed and psychomotor abilities. Furthermore, mental abilities will remain predictive of performance at later stages of practice. Conversely, for a simple,

consistent task, the role of mental ability will be minor and will rapidly diminish, with a correspondingly larger role for perceptual speed and psychomotor ability.

Ackerman (1988, 1992) reports an extensive series of studies which generally support predictions from the theory. For example, several studies show that for appropriate tasks, the predictive power of perceptual speed at first increases with practice, and then decreases. Figure 14.4 shows the good correspondence between prediction and theory obtained in the study. Ackerman suggests that cognitive correlates research may overestimate the association between g and performance on simple information-processing tasks, because subjects have generally had little practice, and so are operating at the cognitive stage of skill acquisition. However, the tasks used by Ackerman (1988), such as category search and choice RT, require few motor skills, apart from speed of response. Only one of Ackerman's (1988, 1992) tasks, an air traffic control simulation, could be described as a complex skill. It is unclear, therefore, whether Ackerman's (1988) results would generalise to other tasks, such as Fleishman and Quaintance's (1984) motor skills, and to other intellectual skills such as reading and mental arithmetic. Langan-

Fox, Waycott and Galna (1997) reported limited support for predictions from Ackerman's model in a study of tracking. They found that general ability became increasingly predictive of performance at higher levels of practice.

Matthews, Jones and Chamberlain (1992) tested Ackerman's theory using a complex mail-coding task requiring skills such as keyboard use and rapid information processing. Performance on the task, after 25 hours' training, was thought to be approaching the associative stage of skill acquisition (see 7.2.1). The study also assessed various elementary cognitive tasks related to general ability and perceptual speed, and measured participants' ability level with the standard psychometric test used by the British Post Office for selection. It was reasoned that more able individuals should have progressed further from the cognitive to the associative stages of skill, due to their faster proceduralisation of performance. Hence, a measure related to general ability (digit span) should predict performance in low ability subjects, but measures related to perceptual speed (e.g. speed of 5-choice serial reaction) should relate to performance in high ability participants. In fact, all the elementary cognitive components of the task tended to be more predictive in the low ability group, but "non-cognitive" factors of extraversion and arousal were more predictive in high ability groups. Matthews et al. argue that Ackerman's model neglects the role of individual processing components, and propose an alternative explanation in terms of Norman and Shallice's (1986) schema theory. It is suggested that ability is associated with the integration of component processes into higher-order "source schemas", whose operation is sensitive to personality and arousal.

## 14.6 ABILITIES IN THE REAL WORLD

### 14.6.1 Prediction of proficiency and aptitude

Studying individual differences in performance in the field raises a variety of problems. As previously discussed, it is often hard to obtain the reliable and valid measures of performance essential for drawing meaningful conclusions from data.

There are also questions over the economic effectiveness of ability testing within a particular organisation, in terms of maximising the productivity gains obtained from the expense of testing. In personnel selection, it is important to take into account both the proportion of applicants to be hired (the selection ratio), and the proportion of applicants able to perform the job competently. Testing is most beneficial when the selection ratio is high, but there are relatively few capable applicants. More detailed analyses of utility analyses are presented by Anastasi and Urbina (1997). It is important also to decide whether ability testing is to be preferred to other validated selection methods, such as use of biographical data, testing applicants on a sample of actual work, or use of assessment centres where a variety of tests are administered over an extended time period (see Schmidt, Ones, & Hunter, 1992). Finally, there may be social and legal problems associated with testing. It is important that tests are fair to minority groups and individuals with disabilities, for example. Tests should also be seen to be fair; use of a test which seems offensive or irrelevant may cause problems in public relations and morale, even if the test is in fact valid.

There are two strategies applied to real-world performance contexts such as personnel selection (see Cronbach, 1990, for a review of this area). The first is to use a general intelligence measure. It has been known for many years that such measures predict proficiency on a variety of jobs (Schmidt & Hunter, 1998). However, not surprisingly, the validity of intelligence as a predictor of performance increases with the intellectual demands of the job (Ghiselli, 1955). The correlation between intelligence and performance (the validity coefficient) may be as high as 0.5 or so in managerial and professional occupationals, but barely larger than zero in jobs requiring manual labour (Jensen, 1980). The second approach is to use more specialised measures, such as primary ability tests, that relate to the particular demands of the job. The test is selected on the basis of an analysis of the requirements of the job, and the abilities required to fulfill them. The advantages of tailoring tests to job demands seem obvious. Surprisingly, general intelligence is often as good a predictor of occupational performance than more specialised measures (Schmidt & Hunter, 1998; Schmidt et al., 1992). However, there is continuing interest in analyses of information processing as the basis for prediction of job performance, and work of this kind is likely to contribute to better prediction of performance in jobs requiring specialised cognitive skills (Kanfer et al., 1995).

Recently, there has been much popular interest in the concept of *emotional intelligence*, the ability to understand and handle the emotions of oneself and others. However popular claims that emotional intelligence is a key ability in occupational success seem exaggerated and unsupported by evidence (Mayer, Salovey, & Caruso, 2000). There is also considerable uncertainty over whether emotional intelligence can actually be measured as a reliable and valid construct (Davies, Stankov & Roberts, 1998). Mayer et al. (2000) have obtained evidence that there is an ability dimension associated with individual differences in perceiving and understanding emotions, and in applying that emotional knowledge to real-world problems. However, the relationship between this ability and real-world criteria remains to be explored, and much of what is described as "emotional intelligence" may be better conceptualised in terms of personality traits such as emotional stability and conscientiousness (Matthews & Zeidner, in press). These traits are discussed in the next chapter.

### 14.6.2 The role of knowledge

In some respects, the aims of intelligence testing conflict with the aim of optimal prediction of occupational performance. Contemporary IQ tests try to minimise the role of specialised knowledge, so that the content of the test items is either highly abstract and unfamiliar (e.g. Raven's Matrices test) or very familiar (e.g. verbal reasoning tests). However, as discussed in Chapter 7, the most important factor in skill acquisition and expertise is simply practice and experience. The cognitive changes that take place during skill acquisition tend to reduce the processing constraints imposed by the cognitive architecture. These include learning strategies for organising task material, pattern-matching routines and

domain-specific knowledge. Studies of expert performance confirm that people who are good at their jobs have acquired much specialised knowledge (see Ericsson, 1996a). Similarly, acquisition of real-world skills presumably reflects the person's interests and learning related to the job. A person whose hobby is tinkering with cars might make a better mechanic than a person with high spatial ability but little applied knowledge. This commonsense position is not the whole story. First, people's interests may reflect their aptitudes: car enthusiasts may possess higher spatial ability to begin with. Second, in some areas at least, "trainability" may substitute for initial knowledge. A high-spatial mechanical novice might be a better long-term prospect than a low-spatial car hobbyist.

Ackerman (1996, 1999) has tried to conceptualise the role of knowledge rather more formally. His developmental theory of intelligence resembles earlier theories (e.g. Cattell, 1971) which proposed that some basic intellectual aptitude (fluid intelligence) is invested in learned intellectual skills (crystallised intelligence). He suggests that "crystallised intelligence" is too broad a construct to be very useful: intellectual skills tend to become increasingly specific as people move into adulthood. To assess knowledge, Rolfhus and Ackerman (1996) developed reliable self-report measures of knowledge in 32 domains, and Ackerman (1999) reports initial data on objective knowledge measures. Objective knowledge measures in particular seem to be substantially correlated with conventional ability tests: knowledge of science subjects relates most strongly to general intelligence, and knowledge of literature and art relates especially to verbal ability. However, knowledge also relates to personality, motivation and interest variables: all scales were significantly correlated with a questionnaire measure of "typical intellectual engagement". Evidence from other sources (see Ericsson, 1996a) suggests that interest and motivation are required for the sustained, effortful investment of initial abilities in acquiring specialised knowledge necessary to attain high levels of expertise. Ackerman has yet to relate knowledge to occupational performance measures, but the expectation is that job-relevant knowledge will add to the variance predicted by conventional ability tests.

## 14.6.3 Training issues: Aptitude × treatment interaction

We have seen that ability measures predict not only proficiency on various tasks, but also aptitude for a variety of types of learning. We can then ask whether ability–learning correlations vary with type of instruction or training. Although the correlation will generally be positive, perhaps ability influences learning more strongly under some instructional treatments than under others. A considerable research effort in education has been directed towards such aptitude × treatment interactions (ATI). Suppose that two "treatments" $T_1$ and $T_2$ (e.g. rote learning vs. self-discovery) are compared. Figure 14.5 shows some of the possible outcomes (see Snow & Yalow, 1982). In the top panel, both aptitude and treatment influence learning, but their effects are additive and there is no ATI. The advantage of $T_2$ is the same regardless of the learner's aptitude. The middle panel shows an ATI, such that $T_1$ benefits low aptitude individuals, but $T_2$ helps high aptitude individuals. The lower panel shows a different ATI: $T_2$ is generally more effective, but it particularly benefits higher aptitude individuals.

The applied goals of ATI research depend on educational and social policy. Within an egalitarian social policy, the aim may be to educate all children to a similar level of attainment. Given that high-ability children will often learn faster, the aim is then to find a treatment that benefits low-ability children more than high-ability children. Likewise, a company may need to train a mixed-ability group of learners to a fixed criterion of performance efficiency. If, as is likely, ability is related to initial level of performance, a training regime under which low-ability trainees learn as fast or faster than high-ability trainees may be the most effective. Conversely, there may be instructional treatments that are particularly advantageous for high-ability learners. Such treatments may be sought if the aim is to accelerate the learning of gifted or "hothouse" children, or if trainees in an industrial setting have been highly selected for ability.

**FIG. 14.5**

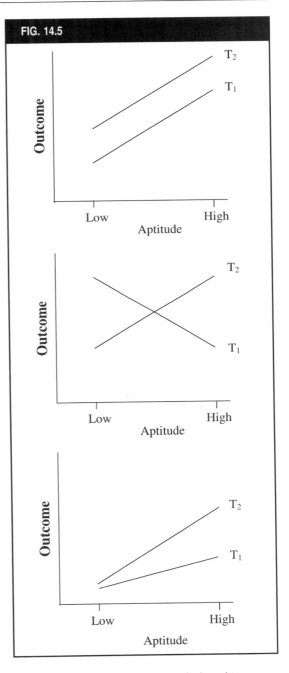

ATIs: Possible interactive effects of aptitude and two instructional treatments on learning outcome (adapted from Snow & Yalow, 1982).

Cronbach and Snow (1977) and Snow (1989) review much of the research on ATI. "Ability" in these studies generally refers to general, fluid or crystallised intelligence, or to task-relevant primary abilities. Although this research is concerned mainly with learning in education, of skills such as reading, mathematics, science and foreign language use, it is plausible that the main conclusions generalise to other skills also. Cronbach and Snow consider that evidence for ATI, of various types, is widespread, but generalisations about the nature of ATI are difficult. The kind of ATI found within similar studies often varies considerably. These inconsistencies may be attributed to methodological and analytical weaknesses, or to the sensitivity of ATI to the fine detail of instructional treatments and instructor behaviour. Cronbach and Snow also caution that distinctions between broad types of instruction, such as meaningful versus rote learning, or teacher- versus learner-centred instruction, may be over-simplistic, and not systematically related to ATI effects.

Cronbach and Snow's (1977) main substantive findings may be briefly summarised as follows. It appears that intelligence is most strongly related to learning when instruction is unstructured, so that learners must organise material themselves, and when instruction places heavy information-processing demands on learners. Specific instructions that tend to increase the ability–learning correlation include removing extraneous details, teaching through use of systematic explanations, allowing more self-direction, and increasing the pace of instruction. Conversely, when the task is simplified or broken down into steps, using methods such as programmed instruction, ability is less strongly correlated with learning.

In the great majority of studies of programmed instruction, the correlation between ability or initial test score and subsequent learning remains positive. Interactions of the form shown in the lower panel of Fig. 14.5 are much more common than those shown in the middle panel. There are a few studies (e.g. Salomon, 1974) where information presented by simplified demonstrations or simulations appears to interfere with learning in more able groups. In general, however, it is difficult to eliminate the ability–learning relationship.

Some studies have tested whether ATI effects are modified by the type of ability tested. On the whole, general ability is more strongly related to treatment outcome than primary abilities, although there may be some differences between fluid and crystallised ability (Snow, 1989). There is some evidence that learners high in verbal ability benefit from verbal instruction, but there is little evidence that high spatial ability learners benefit from greater use of symbols or diagrams. The main difficulty of ATI research is that results show "mostly A and T with not much I" (Bond & Glaser, 1979). Findings of interaction tend to be inconsistent across studies, and may not generalise across tasks and populations (Jonassen & Grabowski, 1993). Nevertheless, there is continuing interest in attempts to match the characteristics of the trainee to the training environment, and to find instructional regimes that maximise the potential of lower ability individuals (Brody, 1997).

## 14.7  CONCLUSIONS

We have seen how individual differences in performance may be characterised psychometrically, in terms of ability factors. At this level of analysis, there is good evidence for a general factor of cognitive ability, general intelligence or $g$. The information-processing underpinnings of this factor have been investigated using the methods of cognitive psychology. It turns out that $g$ is correlated with a bewildering array of processing functions, including perceptual processes, speed of reaction, working memory and executive processes. Detailed, process-oriented research is required to untangle the nexus of correlations, and to determine the causal basis for general intelligence, in terms of individual differences in cognitive architecture. A full explanation of intelligence also requires understanding of its biological bases, and its adaptive functions in the real world. $g$ is also of considerable practical importance, and is the single strongest predictor of occupational performance and aptitude for learning. However, factors other than $g$ may also be important. There appear to be additional abilities which may relate to specific processing systems. For example, individual differences in attention are often only weakly related to $g$, and there may be several distinct attentional factors. Similarly, motor skills are associated with further abilities. In occupational settings, job-related knowledge may also relate to performance, though ability and knowledge measures may be complexly interrelated. In the context of learning, several factors additional to $g$ appear to be important, such as phonological memory, and perceptual and psychomotor speed. Different abilities may predict performance at different stages of skill acquisition. At a practical level, the factors that predict speed of initial learning may differ from those that predict eventual expertise, especially if the task has consistent elements.

## FURTHER READING

Carroll (1993) provides perhaps the definitive account of dimensions of ability. Anastasi and Urbina (1997) and Cronbach (1990) review measures issues relevant to applied settings. Sternberg's (in press) edited book covers all aspects of intelligence research, with most of the chapters devoted to performance issues. Sternberg's (1985) own book provides an influential theory of intelligence. Fleishman and Quaintance's (1984) book is seen as a standard work on individual differences in motor skill learning. The Ackerman, Kyllonen and Roberts (1999) collection describes contemporary research on individual differences in learning.

# 15

# Individual differences: Personality and mood

---

## 15.1 INTRODUCTION

The previous chapter considered how performance relates to individual differences in ability. However, there is more to individual differences than ability alone. A talented individual may fail to perform effectively as a result of qualities such as laziness or distractibility, or because of temporary mood states such as fatigue and emotional agitation. Personality may influence both the style and efficiency of performance. For example, a generally impulsive person might tend to show a risky speed–accuracy tradeoff. An impulsive person might also show impaired efficiency on tasks requiring reflection and delay of response, such as solving difficult problems. Emotional reactions are also important, especially in stressful environments. Plausibly, someone who is easily upset might find it hard to maintain concentration on a task. To investigate how such characteristics relate to performance, we first require a taxonomy or classificatory scheme for distinguishing the different characteristics of interest.

The first distinction made is that between *traits* and *states*. A trait is a stable disposition affecting a variety of psychological functions, and a component of personality, whereas a state is a more transient reaction. A general tendency to become anxious is a trait, but the immediate experience of being anxious is a state (Spielberger, 1972). Traits and states may be further subdivided. Current research on personality traits is dominated by two taxonomies (see Brody & Erlichman, 1998; Matthews & Deary, 1998). Eysenck and Eysenck (1985) identify three principal personality dimensions contrasting (1) extraversion with introversion, (2) neuroticism and emotionality with emotional stability, and (3) psychoticism and toughmindedness with tender-mindedness. Questionnaires developed by Eysenck and Eysenck (1985) and their colleagues provide scores on the three basic dimensions. These scores are said to provide a good indication of the central features of the individual's personality. A rival scheme, the Big Five (Costa & McCrae, 1992; Goldberg, 1993), retains the extraversion and emotionality dimensions, but replaces psychoticism with three additional dimensions of conscientiousness, agreeableness and openness. Table 15.1 lists the characteristics associated with the Big Five, which may be assessed by various questionnaires. Taxonomies

**TABLE 15.1**

Personality characteristics associated with the Big Five.

|      | Extraversion | Emotionality | Conscientiousness | Agreeableness | Openness |
|------|------|------|------|------|------|
| High | Sociable<br>Impulsive<br>Assertive | Moody<br>Anxious<br>Unstable | Systematic<br>Meticulous<br>Efficient | Kind<br>Helpful<br>Sympathetic | Artistic<br>Creative<br>Complex |
| Low  | Quiet<br>Restrained<br>Withdrawn | Calm<br>Relaxed<br>Content | Disorganised<br>Careless<br>Lazy | Cold<br>Rude<br>Unpleasant | Simple<br>Shallow<br>Practical |

of state are less well-developed, although it is generally accepted that emotional states such as mood should be distinguished from cognitive states such as worry (Morris, Davis, & Hutchings, 1981). There are several dimensional models of mood: Matthews, Jones and Chamberlain (1990), for example, identify energy–fatigue, tension–relaxation and happiness–unhappiness as three fundamental aspects of mood.

As in ability research, we can investigate correlations between indices of performance and validated measures of personality and mood. In general, individual differences in performance are less central to personality than they are to ability, and it is harder to find reliable performance correlates. Three methodological problems occur frequently:

1. *Context-dependence.* Relationships between personality and performance are often sensitive to details of the experimental context and procedure, such as the level and type of stress reactions provoked. For example, introverted and neurotic individuals tend to perform relatively poorly in stressful and arousing environments (Eysenck & Eysenck, 1985).

2. *Task-dependence.* Effects of personality and mood vary with the information-processing demands of the task. Typically, a personality trait such as extraversion will be positively correlated with some performance measures, negatively related to other measures, and completely unrelated to others still. As in stress research generally (see 9.4), personality and

mood dimensions tend to be associated with a complex patterning of performance characteristics (Zeidner & Matthews, in press).

3. *Trait vs. state effects.* Personality traits and mood states tend to be interrelated, but they may differ in their effects on performance. In some cases, trait effects may be *mediated* by the state. According to Spielberger's (1972) anxiety theory, trait anxiety predisposes the person to state anxiety, which disrupts information processing and impairs performance. Hence, state anxiety has a more direct effect on performance than trait anxiety and, empirically, the state is often a more reliable predictor of performance impairment than the trait (Eysenck, 1982). However, as we shall see, there are other circumstances in which effects of traits cannot be reduced to states.

In this chapter, we review the most active areas of research on personality and performance. First, we discuss extraversion–introversion effects, and contrast biological and cognitive explanations for relationships between extraversion and performance. Second, we review anxiety and performance. Anxiety appears to affect not only the overall efficiency of performance, but the qualitative style of performance also, in that anxious subjects are prone to focus attention on threatening stimuli. Third, we consider how transient mood states such as energy and unhappiness relate to performance. Fourth, we review studies of personality and occupational performance, within the framework provided by the Big Five. These studies demonstrate the relevance of personality research to real-world settings, although they do not provide the insights into information processing that laboratory studies do. Finally, we attempt to link real-world and information-processing research by considering the adaptive significance of the performance correlates of personality.

## 15.2 EXTRAVERSION

Most studies of extraversion and performance are inspired by Eysenck's (1967) theory of extraversion–introversion. Eysenck sees extraversion as a rather broad personality trait, associated with a variety of narrower qualities such as impulsivity, sociability and assertiveness. Eysenck develops a psychobiological account of extraversion, which relates it to individual differences in the arousability of the ascending reticular activating system (ARAS), the foundation for the traditional arousal theory discussed in 9.3. Introverts are more easily aroused than extraverts, and so tend to have higher levels of cortical arousal. A contrasting perspective is provided by cognitive theorists who try to infer individual differences in processing from the cognitive patterning of extraversion–introversion (Matthews, 1997d; Revelle, 1993). In this section, we review the main empirical findings, and consider the adequacy of arousal theory as an explanation.

### 15.2.1 Cognitive correlates of extraversion

Studies of extraversion can be loosely divided into two types—investigation of the cognitive correlates of extraversion, and studies of how extraversion modifies the impact of stress and emotion on cognition. Reviews of these studies (Eysenck, 1982; Matthews, 1992a, 1997d; Matthews & Dorn, 1995) show that effects of extraversion depend on the type of task. There are several kinds of task on which extraverts show superior performance efficiency: dual-task performance, memory tasks involving high response competition, short-term memory tasks generally, and retrieval from memory. Eysenck (1982) suggests that extraverts typically have more processing resources available, so that they will out-perform introverts on relatively

demanding tasks. Evoked potential studies (reviewed by Stelmack & Houlihan, 1995) show smaller-amplitude P300 responses in extraverts than in introverts during performance of discrimination tasks, which may indicate that stimulus processing is less attentionally demanding for extraverts. Evoked potential studies also suggest greater sensory reactivity in introverts, consistent with their lower sensory thresholds. However, it is unclear whether extraversion relates to some general resource, or to multiple elementary processes. For example, Brebner (1998) found that the psychological refractory period (PRP: see 4.1.1) was reduced in extraverts, implying a personality effect on the response bottleneck. Extraverts are also more resistant to distraction than introverts (Eysenck 1982). Furnham and Bradley (1997) showed that pop music tended to impair reading comprehension and learning more in introverts than in extraverts. The use of verbal material may be a factor in extraverts' performance superiority in this case. Although there is only a small positive relationship between extraversion and verbal ability (Ackerman, 1996), extraverts display faster and more fluent speech production (Dewaele & Furnham, in press).

On other tasks introverts show better performance. Koelega (1992) reviewed 56 studies of extraversion and vigilance, with a total $N$ of 3,098, and concluded that introverts tend to show a superior detection rate and perceptual sensitivity. Extraverts are normally poorer than introverts at difficult problem solving (Malhotra, Malhotra, & Jerath, 1989). Tasks of this kind presumably require insight, rather than processing capacity per se. Introverts may also show superior memory over relatively long time periods (Eysenck, 1981).

Extraverts and introverts differ in choice of task strategy also. Behaviourally, extraverts are more impulsive than introverts. Some studies show that extraverts tend to respond quickly at the expense of an increased error rate (see Brebner & Cooper, 1985), but the effect on speed-accuracy tradeoff is not very reliable (e.g. Socan & Bucik, 1998). Reaction time studies discriminating "decision time" from "movement time" show that extraverts are faster in movement time only (Doucet & Stelmack, 1997), implying an effect on response execution speed rather than strategy. Studies of vigilance (Davies & Parasuraman, 1982) and recognition memory (Danzinger & Larsen, 1989) suggest that extraverts may have a lower internal criterion for responding than introverts, although the effect is not very strong or consistent (Koelega, 1992). Differences in psychomotor performance also tend to be strategic. Frith (1971), using a pursuit-rotor task, found that introverts tracked position accurately, using small, accurate movements, but misjudged velocity. In contrast, extraverts made more sweeping movements which matched velocity but were positionally inaccurate. Extraverts also benefit more from rest pauses during pursuit-rotor performance (Eysenck, 1964). Extraverts perhaps proceed by a succession of discrete episodes of responding, whereas introverts maintain smoother, more continuous responding.

The relationship between extraversion and impulsiveness merits further discussion. It is important to distinguish between impulsivity as a personality construct associated with extraversion measured by questionnaire, and impulsive behaviours measured objectively using performance tests. Because self-reports of behaviour are sometimes invalid, we cannot assume that people who appear to be impulsive on the basis of questionnaire scores are necessarily impulsive in their processing and performance. In fact, questionnaire impulsivity may relate to specific types of information processing only. Dickman and Meyer (1988) applied the additive factors method for identifying processing stages to a speeded visual comparison task. They showed that questionnaire impulsivity was associated with speed–accuracy tradeoff at an early feature comparison stage, but not at a later response execution stage. Relationships between impulsivity and certain aspects of processing may be responsible for some of the performance correlates of extraversion. Weinman (1987) presents evidence suggesting that extraverts' problem-solving may be hindered by their tendency to adopt impulsive strategies, so that processing is terminated prematurely. Humphreys and Revelle (1984) have made the stronger claim that impulsivity may, so to speak, be the "active ingredient" among the various narrow traits which relate to extraversion.

Their work shows that impulsivity is consistently a stronger predictor of performance than sociability. However, there have been difficulties in replicating this result (Amelang & Ullwer, 1991).

### 15.2.2 Extraversion and performance under stress and arousal

The typical finding of studies of personality, performance and stress is that extraverts tend to perform well under conditions of high stimulation or arousal, whereas introverts perform better under dearousing conditions (Eysenck & Eysenck, 1985; Matthews, 1992a). This result applies to a wide range of tasks, including intelligence and creativity tests, paired-associate learning and vigilance and other attentional tasks, and a wide range of stressors/arousal manipulations, including stimulant and depressant drugs, self-report arousal, noise and anxiety. Figure 15.1 shows an example (Revelle, Amaral, & Turriff, 1976). Introverts perform better on an intelligence test, when the test environment is relatively dearousing (unlimited time). However, in arousing conditions (time pressure + the stimulant drug caffeine) it is extraverts who show the performance advantage. Evidence of this kind has generally been explained by Eysenck's (1967) psychobiological theory of extraversion. The sensitivity to stimulation of a corticoreticular feedback loop is said to be negatively correlated with extraversion. Under most conditions, extraverts will then be lower in cortical arousal than introverts, an hypothesis which commands partial support from psychophysiological studies (Matthews & Gilliland, 1999; Stelmack, 1990).

The superior performance of extraverts under high arousal can then be predicted from the Yerkes-Dodson Law, the hypothesis that arousal is related to performance by an inverted U (see 9.3). It is assumed that extraverts are normally somewhat underaroused, so that extraverts need stimulation to reach the optimal level of arousal for performance (Eysenck & Eysenck, 1985). However, introverts are typically close to the optimum, so they become overaroused in stimulating testing conditions. The Yerkes-Dodson Law may also explain extraverts' superiority on relatively difficult tasks. The optimal level of arousal for

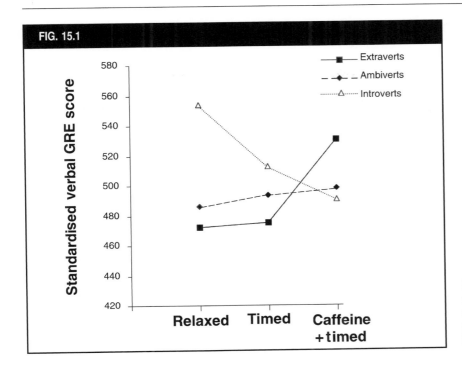

FIG. 15.1

Effects of arousal manipulations and extraversion on performance of an ability test (Revelle et al., 1976).

performance decreases as task difficulty increases: i.e. the inverted-U shifts to the left on the graph, as shown in Fig. 9.3. Hence, on difficult tasks, extraverts' normal low level of arousal is close to the optimum, but introverts are overaroused, even with no additional stimulation, so that introverts' performance is impaired relative to that of extraverts.

### 15.2.3 Extraversion and real-world performance

On the whole, data on extraversion and performance on real-world skills are consistent with the laboratory studies discussed above. Extraverts have higher motor vehicle accident rates than introverts, an effect associated with the impulsivity aspect of extraversion (Loo, 1979), and so presumably the result of impulsive driving. Extraverts are also more susceptible to deterioration in driving performance over several hours (Fagerstrom & Lisper, 1977). This appears to be the result of a progressive arousal decrease during extended driving: extraverts benefited more than introverts from the car radio being turned on. Extraverts' superiority at attentionally demand-

ing tasks may generalise to some aspects of skilled performance. Pilots failing flying training tend to be introverted (Bartram & Dale, 1982). Matthews et al. (1992) found that extraverted post office workers were faster and more accurate than introverts on a training simulation of mail sorting. Extraverts' superiority in short-term memory has been shown to generalise to memory for TV weather forecasts, in some circumstances (Gunter & Furnham, 1986).

There are various research findings showing extraversion–introversion effects on real-world learning. Introverts show superior academic attainment to extraverts beyond the age of 13 or 14 (Eysenck & Eysenck, 1985). This may be a kind of ATI effect (see 14.5.3). Introverts appear to learn better in the more structured learning environments provided in secondary and higher education (Eysenck & Eysenck, 1985). The level of stimulation provided by the learning environment may also be important. Less stimulating environments benefit introverts, who choose to avoid study locations providing external stimulation (Campbell & Hawley, 1983; Schmeck & Lockhart, 1983). Laboratory studies provide some evidence that extraverts condition better in response to reward signals, whereas introverts benefit from punishment signals (Pickering, Diaz, & Gray, 1995). Comparable findings have been reported for classroom learning of mathematics, in response to rewards and punishments delivered by the teacher (McCord & Wakefield, 1991).

### 15.2.4 Explaining performance correlates of extraversion

To summarise the empirical data, the effects of extraversion on performance are pervasive but complex. The effects of extraversion on any particular skill task depend on the balance between several different effects of extraversion on processing. Task conditions favouring extraverts appear to be routine but attention-demanding tasks of short duration, with little opportunity for impulsive strategies, and also external stress or arousal. Introverts tend to perform best under the opposite conditions.

Eysenck and Eysenck (1985) claim that arousal theory can account for a large part of the data on extraversion and performance. How valid is this claim? As discussed in 9.3.3, the Yerkes-Dodson Law has many general shortcomings as an explanation for effects of stress on performance. There are additional difficulties in applying arousal theory to extraversion data.

First, as discussed by Matthews (1992a), it has not been established that extraversion effects are directly mediated by individual differences in arousal. Extraversion may influence performance even when it is independent of concurrent arousal measures, or when arousal level is statistically controlled. Matthews and Amelang (1993) showed that the relationship between EEG alpha (an index of low cortical arousal) and performance is qualitatively different in extraverted and introverted individuals. Extraverts appear to benefit from high cortical arousal, but introverts perform best when arousal is low. Second, time of day has rather unexpected effects on the relationship between extraversion and performance. Revelle, Humphreys, Simon and Gilliland (1980) showed that in the morning caffeine improved the verbal ability test performance of extraverts (strictly, high impulsives), but impaired introverts' (low impulsives) performance, as expected. In the evening,

though, caffeine was helpful to introverts and detrimental to extraverts, implying that extraverts may actually be higher in arousal than introverts late in the day (see Fig. 15.2). Third, there appear to be multiple, independent processing functions associated with extraversion–introversion (Matthews & Dorn, 1995). As with manipulated stressors, extraversion appears to relate to a cognitive patterning of performance, which cannot be reduced to any single mechanism (see 9.4).

Cognitively-oriented researchers have tried to identify information-processing mechanisms for these various findings. Humphreys and Revelle (1984) have developed an ambitious multiple resource model of personality and stress effects in which performance is controlled by availability of two different resources: sustained information transfer (SIT), required for demanding attentional tasks, and short term memory (STM). They suggest that arousal controls a tradeoff between availability of the two types of resource: as arousal increases, SIT resource availability increases, but STM resources decrease. Extraverts (high impulsives) are less aroused than introverts in the morning, but more aroused in the evening; i.e. extraverts tend to be evening types and introverts morning types (see 13.4.2). Hence, extraverts should have a pattern of performance characterised by good STM but poor attention in the morning, but poor STM/good attention in the evening. There is some empirical support for these propositions (Revelle & Loftus, 1992), but also some failures of prediction (Matthews, 1992a).

Matthews and Dorn (1995) emphasise the diversity of effects of extraversion on performance. They claim that extraversion affects a variety of distinct information-processing functions which cannot be reduced to simple arousal mechanisms. Specifically, extraversion seems to relate to greater availability of resources for verbal tasks, use of impulsive strategies, and a greater passive short-term storage capacity. Data suggest that the characteristic interactive effect of extraversion and arousal on performance may be restricted to tasks whose performance is influenced by routine, stimulus-driven processing, such as semantic priming at short time lags. Matthews and Harley (1993) developed a connectionist model of extraversion × arousal interactions based on individual differ-

FIG. 15.2

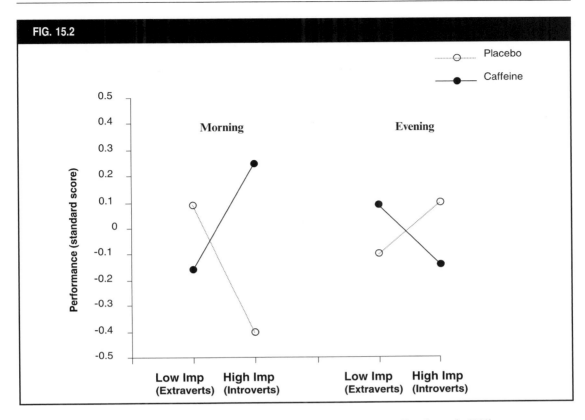

Effects of time of day, caffeine and impulsivity on performance of a verbal ability test (Revelle et al., 1980). Imp = Impulsivity.

ences in spreading activation, which provides an alternative explanation to arousal theory. In general, there are reasonable empirical grounds for predicting effects of extraversion on performance of various tasks, but difficulties of explanation remain. If it is accepted that extraversion relates to multiple processing functions, there is still the problem of explaining the overall patterning. We return to this issue in 15.6.

## 15.3 ANXIETY AND NEUROTICISM

### 15.3.1 Cognitive correlates of anxiety and depression

The second major dimension of personality is trait anxiety or neuroticism. Scales for the two constructs correlate at about 0.6–0.8, and they are often grouped together as measuring "negative affectivity", a general tendency to experience negative emotion and mood (Watson & Clark, 1984). Anxiety tends to have adverse effects on performance, but such effects are only robust on specific tasks (Eysenck, 1981). The tasks most susceptible to anxiety decrements are difficult tasks, short-term or working memory tasks, and secondary tasks in dual-task paradigms (Darke, 1988; Eysenck, 1992, 1997). Anxiety is occasionally associated with *improvements* in performance, on tasks such as easy paired-associate learning, perhaps because it has a motivating effect (Zeidner, 1998). Anxiety may also impair motor performance: Calvo and Alamo (1987) found that anxious participants are impaired on fine but not gross motor tasks. Eysenck and Calvo (1992) have proposed that anxious subjects may sometimes be able to compensate for their impairment by exerting extra effort, particularly if the effort is seen as instrumental in reducing anxiety. In other words, the efficiency of processing is more sensitive to anxiety than is the overall effectiveness of performance. For example, Weinberg (1978) found that on a ball throwing task, anxious participants achieved the same performance level as non-anxious participants, but the former used their muscular energy less efficiently. Anxiety effects on task strategy are inconsistent. Reports of both more risky (Leon & Revelle, 1985) and more cautious (Geen, 1987) speed–accuracy tradeoff in anxious individuals may be found in the literature.

There are several reports of anxiety or neuroticism impairing real-world skills such as computer data entry (Mahar, Henderson, & Deane, 1997), computer-based learning (O'Neil & Richardson, 1980), mathematics (Anton & Klisch, 1995), typewriting (Morris, Smith, Andrews, & Morris, 1975) and military flying (Bartram & Dale, 1982). There is some evidence that anxiety relates to accident susceptibility in occupational settings (Furnham, 1992). For example, Hansen (1989) performed multivariate causal modelling on data obtained from 362 chemical industry workers. One of the causal factors influencing accident risk in the model was a factor of neurotic distractibility. It is widely believed that anxiety may impair sporting performance, particularly for more complex sports (Landers & Boutcher, 1986), but evidence for this proposition is inconclusive (Tenenbaum & Bar-Eli, 1995). Self-report data suggest that management and control of anxiety may be more important for exceptional athletic performance rather than anxiety level per se (Mahoney, Gabriel, & Perkins, 1987).

Anxiety also tends to impair learning and achievement in educational settings, due to interference with attention, working memory and retrieval, although effects of anxiety may be moderated by student motivation (Boekaerts, 1995; Zeidner, 1998). Anxiety slows reading, because anxious readers have trouble with higher-level processes such as integrating information across sentences, although they seem not to have any basic deficit in low-level encoding and lexical access processes (Calvo & Carreiras, 1993). Anxious individuals may be able to compensate for reading difficulties by using compensatory strategies such as reading more slowly, using subvocal rehearsal, and backtracking in the text (Calvo et al., 1994). Tobias (1977, 1992) presents evidence that test-anxious students have particular difficulties with instructional material which lacks organisation, and which requires short- and intermediate-term memory. These data are consistent with laboratory and applied studies showing that anxiety reduces active reorganisation of material in memory (Mueller, 1992; Naveh-Benjamin et al., 1997). Hence, anxious students should perform better in more structured courses, and this is indeed the case (McKeachie, 1990; Zeidner, 1998).

Two factors that appear to moderate the relationship between anxiety and performance are the *type* of anxiety involved, and the *motivational context* in which performance takes place. As previously stated, state anxiety is often a better predictor of performance impairment than trait anxiety (Eysenck, 1982). Morris and Liebert (1970) identify distinct worry and emotionality components of anxiety, and suggest that it is worry only which is associated with poor performance. Research on test anxiety—anxiety about tests and examinations—shows that anxiety impairs performance mainly where people believe that they are being evaluated (Sarason, Sarason, & Pierce, 1995). Evaluation tends to generate cognitive interference and worry, particularly in test-anxious participants (Sarason et al., 1986). Under relaxing conditions, however, test-anxious participants may even out-perform those low in test anxiety. Geen (1985) demonstrated that even vigilance, which is not usually sensitive to effects of anxiety and neuroticism (Davies & Parasuraman, 1982), is impaired under evaluative conditions in high test-anxious participants in which the task was described as an intelligence test (see Fig. 15.3). Explicit success and feedback cues are a further motivational influence. Weiner and Schneider (1971; see also Eysenck, 1981) showed that the normal anxiety × difficulty interaction can be reversed, with anxious participants showing superior performance on a difficult task, if participants doing the difficult task were given success feedback, and participants doing the easy task failure feedback. Data of this kind indicate the

FIG. 15.3

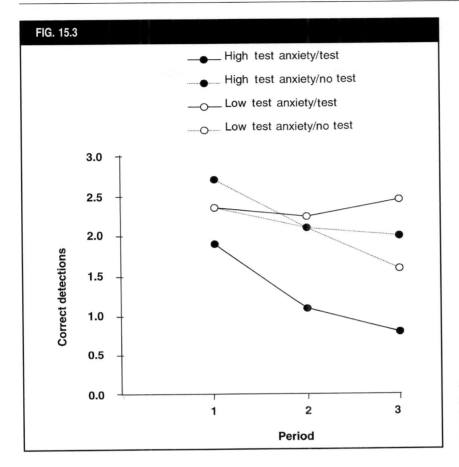

- High test anxiety/test
- High test anxiety/no test
- Low test anxiety/test
- Low test anxiety/no test

Correct detections on a vigilance task as a function of test anxiety, test instructions and task period (Geen, 1985).

importance of cognitive appraisal and attribution in anxiety. Negative expectations, poor performance and anxiety may be linked by positive feedback loops, which exert damaging effects in educational settings (Pekrun, 1992).

Other traits or states associated with worry, such as depression, may also be associated with performance deficit. Hartlage, Alloy, Vazquez and Dykman (1993) review data suggesting that depression relates specifically to a deficit in controlled processing. Performance deficit in depression may also reflect cognitive interference from intrusive thoughts (Gotlib, Roberts & Gilboa, 1996) and lack of motivation and effort (Johnson & Magaro, 1987). The role of motivation is shown most directly by data on depression and task strategy. Griffin, Dember and Warm (1986) showed

that depressed undergraduates failed to adjust their strategy to changing signal probabilities in a vigilance task, implying a degree of strategic inertia. Depression failed to influence perceptual sensitivity, implying that depressed individuals were not lacking in attentional resources, just rather passive in their approach to the task. Of course, depressed patients are more likely to suffer resource deficits than are students. However, similar strategic effects may operate in clinical depression also. Somewhat paradoxically, performance of depressed individuals may actually be facilitated by addition of a dual task (Foulds, 1952; Wells & Matthews, 1994). This result suggests that depressives have difficulties in allocating the available resources to processing, except when forced to by task demands.

## 15.3.2 Anxiety and cognitive bias

Anxious individuals show a general tendency towards making more self-related negative judgments and evaluations (Wells & Matthews, 1994). Anxious participants tend to obtain lower scores on the Cognitive Failures Questionnaire discussed in 8.5.3, i.e. rating themselves as more error-prone. Matthews and Wells (1988) suggest that self-focus of attention, i.e. being preoccupied with one's own thoughts and feelings, may lead to both anxiety and actual cognitive failure. However, given that the CFQ is a rather inconsistent predictor of objective performance, it is also possible that anxious individuals have elevated CFQ scores simply as a consequence of their negative appraisals of themselves. In other words, they have a generalised belief in inefficiency of cognitive functioning, rather than a specific awareness of objective errors (Wells & Matthews, 1994). Such beliefs are also evident in the tendency of anxious individuals to be unrealistically pessimistic about their future performance (Eysenck & Derakshan, 1997) and to show greater self-reported concerns about performance than actual problems (Calvo & Eysenck, 1998).

Why are trait-anxious individuals so negative about themselves? There are several, non-exclusive possibilities. One possibility, supported by clinical evidence, is that anxious individuals have more negative self-beliefs available in long-term memory, represented in schema-like form (Matthews et al., 2000). In addition, anxiety may bias the accessibility of negative information in memory. Studies have tested for biases in both explicit and implicit memory in controlled studies, often with the intent of comparing the two types of memory. Results are rather inconsistent, although enhanced memory for threat words in anxious individuals has been demonstrated in both paradigms (MacLeod & McLaughlin, 1995; Nugent & Mineka, 1994). Finally, processing biases may increase attention to threatening elements of events. Anxious individuals tend to interpret ambiguous stimuli negatively. Richards and French (1992) used a semantic priming paradigm to show that anxious individuals are more sensitive to the negative meanings of 'homographs' such as BEAT, words with both a threatening and non-threatening meaning. Calvo, Eysenck, and Castillo (1997) showed a similar interpretation bias in a study of reading ambiguous, potentially threatening sentences. Careful examination of the time-course of processing demonstrated that bias was introduced relatively late in processing, following lexical access.

Selective attentional bias towards negative or threatening material has been demonstrated directly, although biasing effects of anxiety on perception are rarely found (MacLeod & Mathews, 1991). Selective attention bias has been shown using several of the well-established tasks discussed in Chapter 4. One of these is the emotional Stroop test. On this task, the participant must name the ink-colours of words which typically include both threatening or emotional words, and neutral control words. Anxious participants tend to show a slowing of response when colour-naming threatening words, suggesting that their attention is drawn towards threat stimuli, possibly involuntarily (Mathews & MacLeod, 1985). Patients suffering from other emotional disorders show biases congruent with their condition: spider phobics are slowed by words such as "Web" and "Tarantula", and trauma patients by words relating to the traumatic event (Wells & Matthews, 1994). Another standard selective attention task which has been used to demonstrate bias is dichotic listening: MacLeod and Mathews (1986) demonstrated that anxious patients were distracted by threat words presented to the unattended ear, seemingly without awareness. In visual search, anxious individuals tend to be slowed when threatening distractor stimuli are present (Mathews, May, Mogg, & Eysenck, 1990). Although the most robust effects are obtained in studies of clinical patients, bias seems to be fairly consistent in studies of non-clinical trait anxious individuals, provided care is taken with methods (e.g. Richards et al., 1992). Attentional bias appears most reliably as an interactive effect of trait and state, rather than as an effect of state anxiety alone (Eysenck, 1992).

## 15.3.3 Contextualisation of anxiety: The example of driver stress

Laboratory studies of general anxiety overlook the possibility that anxiety effects on real-world tasks may be "contextualised", i.e. they reflect the person's cognitions and experience of the particular stressor concerned. A good example of contextualisation is provided by driver stress effects on performance. Accident data show that severe life events are associated with increased motor vehicle accident risk (Selzer & Vinokur, 1975). It is plausible that the worry generated by events such as bereavement and divorce interferes with attention to the road. Gulian et al. (1989) showed that people differ in their vulnerability to negative emotion while driving. They distinguished various personality dimensions related to stress vulnerability, including Dislike of Driving, an anxiety-like dimension associated with tension and unhappiness, and Aggression, a dimension related to anger and frustration. Both dimensions are correlated with high N, but they are more predictive of emotional responses to driving than the standard Eysenck personality scales (Dorn & Matthews, 1995).

Simulator studies showed that the Gulian et al. (1989) driver stress dimensions were more strongly related to performance measures than the Eysenck dimensions (Matthews et al., 1998). Dislike of Driving was associated with poorer vehicle control, whereas Aggression related to risk taking:

faster speed and overtaking despite oncoming traffic. Matthews et al. (1998) present a transactional view of driver stress based on Lazarus and Folkman's (1984) stress theory. In effect, the stressed driver has to balance competing motivations against one another. Drivers high in Dislike are concerned with what they perceive to be their own shortcomings as drivers, and so they tend to worry about themselves rather than attend to the traffic environment. Aggressive drivers appraise other drivers as hostile, and are motivated to intimidate or compete with others, impulses which conflict with safety, as shown by the association between aggression and accident involvement (Matthews, Desmond, Joyner, & Carcary, 1997; Matthews, Tsuda, Xin, & Ozeki, 1999c).

Matthews et al. (1996) tested the transactional account of Dislike of Driving against the hypothesis that high Dislike is associated with reduced resource availability. A simulator study showed that Dislike was associated with impaired vehicle control mainly when the driving task was easy, contrary to the resource hypothesis. Impairment of control (assessed as heading error) was more robust on straights than on curves, and during single-task performance as opposed to performance with a concurrent secondary task (see Fig. 15.4).

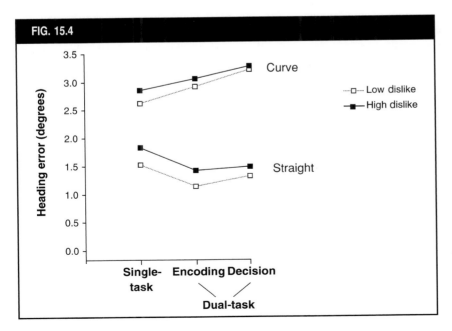

**FIG. 15.4**

Heading error as a function of task demands and Dislike of Driving, in a study of simulated driving (Matthews et al., 1996).

Matthews et al. suggest that negative emotionality related to difficulties in regulating the amount of effort applied to the task. The stress-prone driver is most vulnerable to distraction by worries when the task is appraised as relatively undemanding, and the need for active control of the task is underestimated (see Matthews, 2000b, for a review).

### 15.3.5 Theories of anxiety and performance

Arousal theory is occasionally used to explain anxiety effects but this hypothesis has not been widely accepted. Anxiety does not seem to be consistently associated with arousal (e.g. Holroyd & Appel, 1980) and, in any case, it is the cognitive rather than the physiological aspect of anxiety that relates to performance decrement (Morris et al., 1981; Mueller, 1992). At a theoretical level, the most popular view of anxiety has been that state anxiety and worry are associated with self-evaluative cognitions that divert attention away from the task (Sarason et al., 1995; Wine, 1982). Focusing attention on the self appears to be detrimental to performance even in the absence of overt anxiety (Carver, Peterson, Follansbee, & Scheier, 1983). In effect, anxious people are distracted by their own thoughts. The theoretical problem has been to determine the specific cognitive processes impaired. Several specific mechanisms have been suggested for the locus of interference between anxiety and performance: reduction in selective attention to the task (Wine, 1982), impairment of working memory (Eysenck, 1982), and reduction in on-task effort (Humphreys & Revelle, 1984). However performance studies do not distinguish unequivocally between these mechanisms, and it is possible that the impact of anxiety on performance depends on task strategy.

There has been controversy also over the processing mechanisms contributing to bias in selective attention. One hypothesis is that the mechanism is automatic, such that early, "pre-attentive" stages of processing are particularly sensitive to threat stimuli (McNally, 1995; Williams, Watts, MacLeod, & Mathews, 1988). Consistent with this view are demonstrations that emotional Stroop interference may be obtained in anxious individuals even when the word stimuli are masked so that they cannot be consciously perceived (Bradley,

Mogg, Millar, & White, 1995). A contrary view is that bias reflects a voluntary strategy of monitoring for threat stimuli (Matthews & Wells, 1999). This hypothesis explains why attentional bias is often sensitive to expectancy and contextual effects (e.g. Richards et al., 1992). Even with subliminal stimuli, bias appears to be contingent upon prior conscious identification of threat stimuli (Fox, 1996), implying a top-down influence. Matthews and Harley (1996) explore how such a mechanism might operate through connectionist models of bias on the emotional Stroop. There have been attempts also to integrate work on performance deficit and attentional bias. Eysenck's (1992) hypervigilance theory proposes that anxiety is characterised by scanning of the environment for threat, followed by focusing of attention on channels where threat stimuli are detected. Hence, anxious participants are easily distracted from the task at hand, leading to performance deficit, unless the task itself requires processing of threat stimuli. Derryberry and Reed (1997) present a cognitive neuroscience analysis of anxiety effects. Performance data suggest that anxiety relates to several distinct attentional mechanisms including focusing on fine detail, controlled by left hemisphere object processing pathways, and disengagement from locations related to threat controlled by one of the subcomponents of Posner and Raichle's (1994) anterior system, decribed in 4.3.3.

Wells and Matthews (1994) propose a model of self-referent executive function (S-REF), which relates disruption of performance to a mode of processing focused on negative self-beliefs. Excessive self-focus of processing tends to generate negative cognitions that interfere with concurrent task processing. In addition, coping strategies initiated by negative beliefs, such as active search for threat, generate attentional bias. The S-REF model also accommodates the role of contextualisation. Choice of coping strategy reflects the individual's self-beliefs and personal goals within the particular stress-provoking situation. Hence, stress-vulnerable drivers are those with maladaptive beliefs about the traffic environment, which feed into excessive worry about the self (Dislike of Driving) or hostile reactions to other drivers (Aggression).

## 15.4 MOOD STATES

Recent years have seen a surge of interest in mood states, which may be defined as relatively transient affective states lasting for perhaps minutes or hours. Factor analysis of descriptors of mood suggests that there are only two or three fundamental dimensions (Matthews, 1992b). Two dimensional models of mood (Thayer, 1989, 1996; Watson & Clark, 1992) distinguish dimensions of (1) energy or positive affect, and (2) tension or negative affect.

Matthews et al. (1990) distinguished three separate dimensions of energy–fatigue, tension–relaxation, and pleasure–displeasure. All three dimensions are probably influenced by both biological and cognitive processes, but tension and energy are both correlated with level of autonomic arousal (Matthews, 1992b). Moods may be either manipulated directly, through autosuggestion procedures such as hypnosis, or naturally occuring mood states may be measured through self-report. Three kinds of mechanism have been proposed to explain relationships between mood and performance. First, cognitive activity associated with the mood may *interfere* with task processing, as shown by the relationship between worry and performance impairment (Sarason, Sarason, & Pierce, 1995). Second, moods may be associated with the *energisation* and mobilisation of processing. Third, moods may *bias* cognition towards mood-congruent processing: inducing a happy mood may cause a rather rosy view of the world and one's place in it, for example. We have already discussed how state anxiety interferes with performance, and perhaps also with cognitive bias towards threatening stimuli. State anxiety is similar to tension, so this aspect of mood need not be considered further. In the remainder of this section, we discuss performance correlates of energy and pleasantness of mood.

### 15.4.1 Mood and performance energisation

Matthews and Davies (1998) review a series of studies of sustained attention that suggest that energy is positively correlated with attentional resource availability (see Chapter 5). In these stud-

ies, resource demands of the task were manipulated by varying task parameters such as stimulus quality and time on task. Higher pre-task energy predicted higher perceptual sensitivity only when the task made heavy demands on resources. Figure 15.5 shows an example study: here, energy seemd to enhance vigilance only when stimuli were degraded with a masking stimulus. Energy also correlates positively with performance efficiency of other demanding attentional tasks such as "controlled" visual search, but is unrelated to "automatic" search (Matthews, Davies, & Lees, 1990), which is said to require few resources (Shiffrin & Schneider, 1977). Matthews and Margetts (1991) tested energy effects on dual-task performance, varying the priorities assigned to two independent searches of a display. Results showed that the beneficial effects of high-energy were found only for high-priority task components. In other words, the extra attentional resources of high-energy subjects may only be deployed to important task elements, consistent with the view that arousal increases attentional selectivity (Eysenck, 1982). Effects of energy on working memory have been less consistent (e.g. Matthews et al., 1990), although high energy has been found to predict speed of controlled memory search (Matthews & Westerman, 1994), and performance on a working memory task combining arithmetic with recall of strings of words (Matthews et al., 1999b).

Traditional arousal theory, as expressed by the Yerkes-Dodson Law, cannot explain the results reviewed by Matthews and Davies (1998). Relationships between energy and performance, where found, were generally linear rather than conforming to an inverted-U. Instead, subjective energy seems to be associated with the cognitive energisation of attentional processes, which may be described by the attentional resource metaphor. This energy effect is comparable to that of some stimulant drugs, such as nicotine (Wesnes & Parrott, 1992) and amphetamine (Humphreys & Revelle, 1984). Possibly, subjective energy is an indication of the activity of neural activating systems. Singh, Molloy and Parasuraman (1993) showed energy effects on a more complex sustained performance task intended to simulate

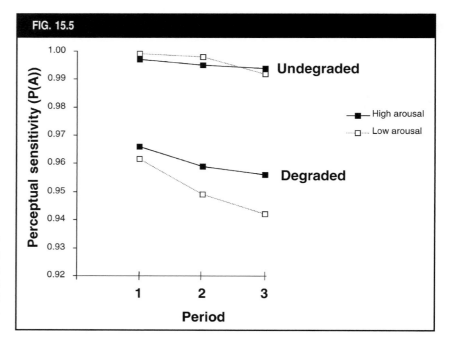

**FIG. 15.5**

Perceptual sensitivity on a vigilance task as a function of stimulus degradation, energetic arousal and task period (Matthews, Davies, & Lees, 1990).

some of the attentional demands of flying, such as tracking and system monitoring. Automation of system monitoring is thought to promote complacency. Energy appeared to facilitate detection performance when complacency was induced experimentally. Hence, energy may sometimes be associated with real-world sustained performance.

### 15.4.2  Mood-congruence and bias

In the majority of studies of mood-congruence, either mood is manipulated by suggestive techniques such as hypnosis, or severely or mildly depressed individuals are compared with controls. Mood-congruence effects are widespread in memory: unhappy individuals tend to recall more negative and less positive material in experimental studies of word lists, for example, and show similar bias in recall of autobiographical memory (see reviews by Blaney, 1986; Ucros, 1989; Mineka & Nugent, 1996). Mood-congruence in simple perceptual and attentional tasks is more difficult to demonstrate (Bower, 1987), although some instances have been reported. For example, depressed participants show slower naming of words of negative content on the Stroop test (Gotlib & McCann, 1984; Segal & Gemar, 1997)

and happy participants show more priming of positive word pairs in lexical decision (Matthews, Pitcaithly, & Mann, 1995). Pleasantness of mood appears to colour more complex perceptions and evaluations more consistently. Positive moods are associated with more positive judgements of satisfaction with life, self-efficacy and task performance, and of other people (Bower, 1981; Forgas, 1995). Conversely, negative mood seems to lead to more negative judgements, especially of the self. Depressed participants may actually be more accurate at perceiving lack of personal control of events than non-depressed controls (Alloy & Abramson, 1988). Figure 15.6 shows an example of mood-congruence (Forgas & Bower, 1987): recall of positive incidents in a story was boosted by induced positive mood, but lowered by negative mood. Recall of negative incidents showed the opposite pattern of effect.

Bower (1981) suggests that mood-congruence may be explained by a semantic network model. Mood states are associated with the activation of a network node for the emotion, from which activation spreads to the nodes for other associated concepts. The person is then primed to perceive or retrieve these mood-congruent concepts. Other

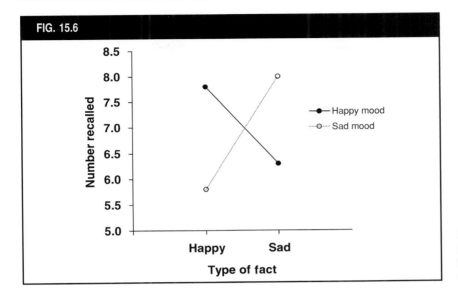

FIG. 15.6

Recall of story incidents as a function of type of fact and induced mood (Bower & Forgas, 1987).

important theoretical issues include the role of control processes in modifying spreading activation (Ingram, 1984), the role of self-related cognitions (Bower, 1987), and the possibility that pleasantness of mood primarily affects late, elaborative processing rather than early, pre-attentive processing (Williams et al., 1988). Siemer and Reisenzein (1998) showed that mood effects on evaluative judgements were found only when moods were salient to participants. They concluded that mood effects depended on a controlled inference strategy rather than on the automatic priming effects described in the original Bower (1981) theory. Unfortunately, there seem to be no empirical studies of the generalisation of mood-congruence to skilled psychomotor performance, although it is plausible that pleasure–displeasure will affect complex tasks with some emotional content.

Recent work suggests that it is simplistic to suppose moods only produce straightforward mood-congruence. Forgas (1995), in a review of studies of judgement and decision making, argued that mood effects are not restricted to the mood-priming effects described by Bower. Mood also functions as information, in that it provides the decision-maker with cues to how they should react to emotional stimuli. Processing of mood may function as an "heuristic" that allows the

person to arrive at a judgement or decision without detailed stimulus analysis. Forgas goes on to describe how the effects of mood-priming and mood-as-information on judgement may vary with task strategy. This work is too complex to review here, but one of its implications is that negative moods may have advantages to set against the performance impairments previously described. They appear to bias the person towards more thorough, systematic evaluation of information, whereas positive moods tend to lead towards simpler, more heuristic strategies.

## 15.5 PERSONALITY AND OCCUPATIONAL PERFORMANCE

### 15.5.1 Personality as a weak predictor of job performance

So far, we have reviewed studies of individual differences in performance, for the most part using objective performance indices obtained in controlled laboratory environments. There is also a large literature on personality and job performance (Kanfer et al., 1995; Matthews, 1997b). Personality tests are widely used in personnel selection in many countries. However, so too are techniques with little scientific support such as graphology—popularity does not ensure validity! In fact, correlations between personality and performance are often low and non-significant, leading some to call into question the utility of personality testing in industry (e.g. Smith & George, 1992). There are two principal reasons why the apparent small magnitude of correlations may be misleading (Tett, Jackson, & Rothstein, 1991). First, the validity and reliability of performance data in occupational studies are often lower than in laboratory studies. Use of unreliable and invalid criterion measures lowers their correlations with other factors, such as personality (Eysenck & Eysenck, 1980). Performance may be assessed through a supervisor's rating rather than through an objective measure. It may also be impractical to discriminate different components of job performance, which may be differentially related to personality. For example, an extraverted doctor might perform better at eliciting information from the patient than in completing necessary paperwork.

Second, the basis for many occupational studies is the exploratory "fishing trip", in which there is no particular reason to expect the personality measure of choice to relate to performance. Of more interest are studies that aim to test or confirm specific hypotheses based on an a priori rationale. In addition, relatively small correlations (i.e. validity coefficients) of the order of .3 or even .2 are of more practical utility than their

magnitude at first implies, especially when only a small proportion of job applicants are to be selected (see Anastasi & Urbina, 1997).

## 15.5.2 Meta-analyses of personality and job performance

Two major meta-analyses have clarified the relationship between personality and performance (Barrick & Mount, 1991; Tett et al., 1991). Both papers attempted to identify relevant studies, and to classify the personality measures used in terms of the "Big Five" dimensions listed in Table 15.1. The authors of the papers then calculated the average magnitude, or *effect size*, of the relationship between each personality dimension and various occupational criteria, including job performance. As previously mentioned, correlations between personality and occupational criteria are probably depressed for statistical reasons. Both papers attempt to correct for factors such as unreliability of measures, although there has been some debate over the correction procedures to be used (see Tett, Jackson, Rothstein, & Reddon, 1994).

Table 15.2 summarises these corrected effect sizes, expressed as correlations. Both studies report job proficiency data, but Tett et al. (1991) used a subset of studies which were "confirmatory", in that they aimed to test hypotheses specified before the study was conducted. As expected, the personality–performance correlation was generally stronger in confirmatory studies. Barrick

---

**TABLE 15.2**

Relationships between the Big Five and three occupational criteria obtained in two meta-analyses (Barrick & Mount, 1991; Tett, Jackson, & Rothstein, 1991).

|  | Job proficiency | Job proficiency (confirmatory studies) | Training proficiency |
|---|---|---|---|
| Extraversion | .10 | .16 | .26 |
| Emotionality | −.07 | −.22 | −.07 |
| Conscientiousness | .23 | .18 | .23 |
| Agreeableness | .06 | .33 | .10 |
| Openness | −.03 | .27 | .25 |

*Note:* Job and training proficiency data from Barrick and Mount (1991), job proficiency (confirmatory studies) data from Tett et al., 1991. All correlations are corrected for statistical artifact, and are based on varying subject numbers.

and Mount (1991) also reported data on training proficiency. Table 15.2 shows that correlations between E and N and performance are generally modest, although E relates more strongly to training performance than to job performance. Subsequent studies have suggested that extraversion facilitates performance in more "people-oriented" occupations such as sales (Barrick & Mount, 1991; P.T. Costa, 1996; Vinchur et al., 1998). In part, the failure to find more substantial correlations with these dimensions may result from a failure to take into account the moderating factors identified in laboratory studies. As discussed above, relationships between the two personality factors and performance are strongly dependent on the information-processing demands of the task, and on the level and nature of environmental stress. Eysenck and Calvo (1992) suggested that increased effort may compensate for the loss of processing efficiency associated with high N/trait anxiety. Consistent with this idea, Mughal, Walsh and Wilding (1996) found that anxious insurance sales personnel applied more effort through seeing more people and working more hours/month, and also closed more sales. However, high N may be associated with performance decrements in particularly stressful jobs such as police work (Cortina et al., 1992).

Conscientiousness (C) appears to be a fairly general influence on performance (P.T. Costa, 1996). Barrick and Mount (1991) divided their sample into differerent occupational groups, and showed that the correlation between C and performance was similar in each one. It is likely that C is associated with higher motivation, and performance-enhancing factors such as goal setting and commitment to achieving goals (Barrick, Mount, & Strauss, 1993). It has been suggested that C is the basis for questionnaire measures of "integrity", such as honesty, responsibility and reliability at work. Integrity tests appear to be quite successful as predictors of performance and disruptive behaviours such as absenteeism, theft and violence at work (Ones, Viswesvaran, & Schmidt, 1993). In a further meta-analysis, Hough (1992) divided conscientiousness into two narrow dimensions of Achievement and Dependability, and showed that their occupational correlates were

rather different. Achievement was more strongly related to job proficiency, but Dependability was the stronger predictor of law-abiding behaviour. As Hough discusses, there is a long-running (and unresolved) controversy over whether broad personality dimensions such as the Big Five are to be preferred to narrower, more specific dimensions such as Achievement.

The two remaining dimensions, Openness (O) and Agreeableness (A), perform better in confirmatory studies than exploratory studies, although O appears to be an acceptable predictor of training performance. This finding might be expected on the basis that one of the central characteristics of O is interest in novel experiences, but its basis in information processing is unclear. Rolfhus and Ackerman (1996) found that O related both to general intellectual engagement, and to self-reported knowledge (see 14.5.2). In Hough's (1992) review of the data, A related to superior teamwork, but lower creativity. There is evidence, too, that agreeableness is a disadvantage when the job offers a high degree of autonomy (Barrick & Mount, 1993). Perhaps the high A person cooperates well with others but lacks initiative and enterprise. An additional perspective on creativity is provided by work on Psychoticism, which relates to low agreeableness. High Psychoticism is a feature of highly-creative individuals such as artists and writers. Furthermore, high scorers on the Psychoticism scale tend to perform well on laboratory tests of "creativity", such as making unusual word associations (Eysenck, 1995). In terms of information processing, Psychoticism may relate to failures to inhibit attention to task-irrelevant stimuli (Beech & Williams, 1997).

## 15.6 PERSONALITY, PERFORMANCE AND ADAPTATION TO REAL-WORLD ENVIRONMENTS

So far, the discussion of personality has been based on a simple premise. Traits reflect stable individual differences in brain function or information processing that feed forward into performance. This is a reasonable approximation, in that, empirically, broad traits are fairly stable over periods of time as long as decades (Matthews & Deary, 1998). However, it may be too simplistic a basis for explaining how personality and performance are interrelated in the real world. People of different personality characteristics tend to have rather different kinds of experience and learning (see Furnham, 1992), which may feed back into performance. For example, perhaps extraverts' ability to perform well in arousing conditions reflects greater real-life experience of performing under high arousal. Personality differences found in occupational contexts might reflect interests and knowledge rather than basic differences in processing.

### 15.6.1  A cognitive-adaptive framework for individual differences in performance

In this section, we summarise a *cognitive-adaptive* framework for personality research (Matthews, 1997c, 1999) that attempts to explain how the individual's attempts at adapting to real-world environments may be related to their performance capabilities. A basic premise is that some correlates of personality, such as neurological correlates and aspects of the cognitive architecture, may be treated as set to fixed, or near-fixed, values by genes and early experience. Other aspects of personality are more open to modification by the person's life experiences. *Skills* refers to acquired processing routines for performing complex, real-world tasks, such as job skills. *Knowledge* refers to the various constructs associated with motivations and beliefs about how personal goals may be achieved (i.e. constructs at the knowledge level of explanation). These include knowledge of coping strategies for dealing with demanding environments, as specified by the transactional model of stress (see 9.2.2). In this context, we can treat knowledge as a broad construct that bundles together motivations, beliefs about personal efficacy and a variety of stress reactions, including emotion. (It is important to distinguish such constructs in other circumstances.) The cognitive-adaptive perspective proposes that personality relates to both skill and knowledge.[1]

Figure 15.7 shows how these different constructs may be dynamically interrelated. The individual's processing and neural functions provide the platform for skill acquisition. For example, especially in the early stages of skill acquisition, individual differences in molar performance reflects the individual molecular components from which the skill is compiled, as described by skill theory (see Chapters 7 and 14). However, adaptation reflects not only the skill but also the knowledge which determines how effectively skills are used. It is supposed that skills and knowledge tend to be mutually reinforcing, as described by Bandura's (1989) self-efficacy theory. Objective competence supports interest, beliefs in personal self-efficacy and facilitates coping with stress. Conversely, self-efficacy, motivation and effective stress management feed back into enhancement of objective skill

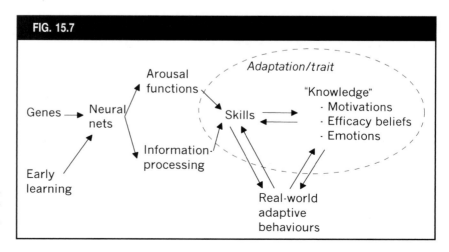

**FIG. 15.7**

A cognitive-adaptive framework for personality and ability traits (Matthews, 1997c).

through increasing willingness to practise and to expose oneself to potentially stressful situations. It is likely that skills and knowledge interact dynamically. There is some evidence that personality changes somewhat over time to reflect job characteristics but, conversely, the person may have some scope for shaping the job to match their personality (Semmer & Schallberger, 1996). For example, extraverts seem to have an aptitude for sales work (Barrick & Mount, 1993)—but sales training increases extraversion (Turnbull, 1976).

## 15.6.2 Individual differences in adaptation: Extraversion, neuroticism and intelligence

The various empirical correlates of personality can then be organised within this framework, as shown in Table 15.3. The initial basis for extraversion is provided by the processing functions that make up its cognitive patterning and, possibly, by the neural characteristics described by arousal theory. The cognitive characteristics of extraversion facilitate the acquisition of characteristically "extraverted" skills such as effectiveness in conversation (Argyle, Martin, & Crossland, 1989) handling informationally overloading environments (Matthews & Dorn, 1995), and fluency in spoken language (Dewaele & Furnham, in press). Such skills are also fostered by the knowledge-related characteristics of extraversion, such as greater social motivation and use of task-focused coping (e.g. Costa, Somerfield, & McCrae, 1996). Knowledge and skills jointly influence the adaptations favoured by extraverts, such as working in demanding jobs. Real-world performance reflects both the elementary processing characteristics of extraverts (see 15.2.3) and the knowledge brought to the the task environment. For example, Piedmont and Weinstein (1994) found that, in sales and customer service personnel, E related to supervisor ratings of interpersonal relations, task orientation ("getting things done") and coping with setbacks. Conversely, introverts' skills and interests may suit them to more reflective occupations such as being a scientist or artist. Hence, extraversion–introversion may reflect individual differences in adaptation to cognitively demanding environments, including social environments.

A similar analysis may be applied to neuroticism/trait anxiety. More anxious individuals are maladapted to overtly stressful environments, due to their impairments in working memory and/or attention under stress. They have little confidence in their abilities, and adopt coping strategies, such as worry (emotion-focused coping), that tend to interfere with performance (Wells & Matthews, 1994). However, their threat-sensitivity and concerns with personal danger may pay off when threats are covert or ambiguous. Negative mood may contribute to more careful decision making, in some circumstances (Forgas, 1995). Hence, as described in the previous section, N may relate to poor performance in stressful jobs, but better performance when circumstances favour compensatory effort, as in the Mughal et al. (1996) study. The cognitive-adaptive framework also accommodates the contextualisation of anxiety. General anxiety seems to relate to general preoccupations with personal and social competence (Matthews et al., 2000). However, people may also have concerns about particular environments in which they feel insecure. Hence, within the driving context, the "driving anxiety" scale (Dislike of Driving) discussed in 15.3.3 correlates with subjective and objective cognitive measures as we expect an anxiety measure to do. However, it is only weakly correlated with neuroticism (Matthews et al., 1997): the self-knowledge concerned is mostly specific to the driving context.

Finally, for comparison with the ability research covered in Chapter 14, Table 15.3 also shows a similar analysis for general intelligence $g$ (see Zeidner & Matthews, in press, for a detailed account). The influence of intelligence on performance probably reflects feed-forward from the cognitive architecture to a greater extent than is the case for personality traits. However, consistent with fluid-crystallised intelligence theory (Cattell, 1971), acquired intellectual skills support adaptation more directly rather than rapid processing speed or good working memory. The skills concerned may be those directed towards handling novelty, complexity and the transfer of existing knowledge to new situations (Sternberg, 1985). In addition, as discussed in 14.5.2, performance

**TABLE 15.3**

Relationships between three individual difference factors and components of the cognitive-adaptive framework (adapted from Zeidner & Matthews, in press).

|  | Intelligence | Extraversion | Anxiety/neuroticism |
|---|---|---|---|
| Neural functions | Neural efficiency?<br>Brain size/connectivity? | Cortical arousability<br>Sensitivity to reward signals? | Autonomic arousal?[1]<br>Sensitivity to punishment signals |
| Information processing | Processing speed (+)<br>Working memory (+)<br>Executive functions (+) | Dual task (+)<br>Short term memory (+)<br>Response criterion (−)<br>Vigilance (−)<br>Problem-solving (−)<br>Arousal-dependent effects | Working memory (−)<br>Attentional resources (−)<br>Judgement (negative bias)<br>Selective attention (negative bias) |
| Skills | Intellectual skills<br>— handling complexity<br>— handling novelty<br>— transfer across contexts | Conversation<br>Rapidity of action<br>Social encounters | Awareness of danger<br>Safety behaviours<br>More "substantive" decision-making[1] |
| Knowledge | Achievement motivation<br>Self-efficacy?<br>Intellectual interest | Social motivations<br>Self-efficacy<br>Positive affect<br>Task-focused coping | Self-protective motivations<br>Low self-efficacy<br>Negative affect<br>Emotion-focused coping<br>Domain-specific knowledge[2] |
| Real-world adaption | Academic and educational environments, cognitively complex jobs | High pressure occupations[3]<br>Social interaction | Covert or delayed threats[4] |

[1] Relates to state anxiety only.
[2] Knowledge referring to specific threats or environments, e.g. test situations, traffic.
[3] Introverts adapted to activities offering little external stimulation, e.g. literary and scientific work.
[4] Emotionally stable individuals adapted to overtly threatening environments.

of real-world skills may also reflect knowledge-level factors such as motivations and interests as well as basic aptitude (Ackerman, 1996, 1999).

## 15.7 CONCLUSIONS

A variety of personality and mood factors that relate to performance and information processing have been identified. The widespread use of personality assessment for selection in industry has some justification. However, expectations should not be exaggerated, given the modest values of validity coefficients, and prediction should be based on a priori hypotheses. Some personality and mood factors, especially low anxiety and high energy, are broadly beneficial. Nevertheless, as a general principle, personality and mood factors contrast with ability in that they tend to relate to a complex pattern of enhancements, deficits and qualitative differences in the style of performance, depending on the task. Like environmental stressors, personality and mood relate to cognitive patternings (see 9.4). For example, extraverts trade off superior dual-task performance and short-term memory against poor vigilance and reflective problem solving. Anxious individuals tend to show reduced attentional efficiency, but maintain awareness of threat and more thorough decision making.

The traditional level of explanation for personality and mood effects has been psychobiological, in terms of arousal theory and its extensions. However, arousal theory has the same deficiencies as in environmental stress research: weak empirical support and lack of explanatory power. Although biology is likely to play some role, cognitive explanations may often be more satisfactory. We have seen that both personality and mood constructs have been linked to individual differences in resource availability. Other relevant cognitive constructs include spreading activation, working memory and selective attention. As ever, information-processing analyses may be essential but insufficient for a full explanation. In the case of extraversion–introversion, it is hard to see why a personality trait whose central features include sociability and assertiveness should be related to a complex set of processing functions in the way it appears to be. We also discussed a cognitive-adaptive framework which attempts to link the performance correlates of traits to real-life adaptations. Extraversion may represent adaptation to demanding environments characterised by high information flow, including many social environments. Similarly, neuroticism/anxiety may be related to adaptation to disguised or delayed threats, and other personality traits may relate to other adaptive specialisations.

## FURTHER READING

Brody and Erlichman (1998) and Matthews and Deary (1998) provide a general overview of personality research. The psychobiological approach to personality is discussed by Eysenck and Eysenck (1985). Contributors to the volume edited by Matthews (1997e) apply cognitive science analyses to a variety of issues related to personality, mood and performance. Much of the work in this area has focused on anxiety and negative affect: for reviews, see Eysenck (1992), Wells and Matthews (1994), and Zeidner (1998). Dalgleish and Power's (1999) edited book provides a more general review of emotion and cognition. Furnham (1992) surveys studies of personality and work, and Zeidner and Saklofske's (1995) edited book covers various applications of both personality and intelligence research.

## NOTE

1. Note the cognitive science use of "knowledge" here differs from Ackerman's (1996) usage, discussed in 14.5.2. Roughly, our use of knowledge corresponds to Ackerman's subjectively-defined knowledge, whereas we would classify Ackerman's objective tests of knowledge as relating primarily to skill.

# 16

# Ageing and human performance

## 16.1 INTRODUCTION

It is only during the past three hundred years or so, and especially during the present century, that significant numbers of people have survived to the age of 65 and beyond. Up to the 17th century, probably about one in every 100 persons did so in Western Europe, and by the 19th century roughly one person in 25 reached this age. Currently, in the United Kingdom, around 10 million people are aged 65 and over, approximately one-sixth of the total population. Since the life expectancy at birth of women tends to be greater than that of men (currently in the UK by almost five years), the majority of elderly people are women, particularly in the population aged 75 and over. Among 80-year-olds in the UK, for example, women outnumber men by 4:1, whereas among 40-year-olds the sex ratio is approximately equal. The growth in the numbers of individuals aged 65 and over relative to the remainder of the population is expected to continue well into the 21st century.

Growing older is typically associated with declines in both physical and mental abilities, and in most people such declines become more noticeable in the late 50s or early 60s. Older people tend to exhibit reduced levels of physical activity and a decreased capacity for strenuous physical exertion (see Stones & Kozma, 1985). Their vision, hearing and other sensory capacities are likely to show signs of impairment. Older adults also tend to obtain lower scores than do younger ones on standard psychometric tests of intelligence, although the differences due to ageing are relatively small and, even at quite advanced ages, there are likely to be some individuals obtaining higher scores than the average 20-year-old (see Salthouse, 1991). In this chapter, we are principally concerned with differences between the task performance of young adults, typically men and women in their 20s and early 30s, and older adults, typically men and women aged between 50 and 90. We begin by describing some of the methodological problems associated with the investigation of age differences in human performance and continue with a brief outline of the relation between age and sensory abilities, emphasising vision and audition. We next discuss age differences in response speed, which affect performance in a wide range of task situations. We then consider the effects of ageing on performance in attention and memory tasks. The implications of age differences in laboratory task performance for possible age differences in job performance are subsequently reviewed. We conclude with a brief survey of the main interpretations of age-related decrements in the performance of laboratory tasks.

## 16.2 METHODOLOGICAL CONSIDERATIONS IN RESEARCH ON AGEING AND HUMAN PERFORMANCE

Investigations of the relation between ageing and human performance have generally employed cross-sectional designs, in which the performance of groups of older and younger adults working at the same task at more or less the same time are compared (see Columns A, E, I; B, F, J, M; C, G, K, N, P and D, H, L, O, Q, R in Table 16.1). Usually the average performance of the younger group is superior to that of the older group, though within-group differences often exceed between-group differences and become greater as age increases. Cross-sectional designs confound age effects with cohort or generational effects, broadly defined as the accumulation of life experiences and socio-cultural influences that individuals of different ages bring to the task situation as a consequence of having been born at a particular historical time. Later cohorts or generations are likely to have received more formal education, to have been exposed to more varied cognitive stimulation and to have enjoyed greater access to health care, relative to earlier ones. Since all these factors may affect task performance, it is unclear whether the performance differences normally observed in cross-sectional studies are solely due to the effects of ageing, or whether some combination of the effects of educational level, cognitive stimulation or health status also contribute to the performance differences obtained.

Other designs used in the investigation of ageing and performance, such as the longitudinal design, in which the same individuals are tested at different chronological ages (see Rows A, B, C, D; E, F, G, H; I, J, K, L; M, N, O and P, Q in Table 16.1) and the time-lag design, in which groups from different cohorts are tested at the same chronological age (see Diagonals A, F, K, O; E, J, N, Q and I, M, P, R in Table 16.1), are also unable to separate the effects of ageing from those of other variables. While longitudinal designs control cohort effects, since only one cohort is repeatedly tested, they confound age effects with time-of-measurement or cultural change effects that reflect the impact on behaviour of specific events, such as wars or economic depressions, which affect all individuals regardless of cohort membership, though not necessarily in the same way. Longitudinal designs also face the problem of selective attrition; for a variety of reasons, not all the individuals originally tested will be available for retesting, and it seems unlikely that attrition occurs randomly. Instead, it often appears that those who present themselves for testing on subsequent occasions are the most able on initial testing. Selective attrition can thus contribute to sampling bias. Time-lag designs control age effects, since all individuals are tested at the same chronological age, but confound time-of-measurement and cohort effects. Combining cross-sectional, longitudinal and time-lag designs in various ways to produce what is known as a sequential design, enables age, cohort and time-of-measurement effects to be separated, at least in principle (see Schaie, 1977), although sequential designs have seldom been used in the investigation of ageing and human performance. An example of one type of sequential design is shown in Table 16.1.

Cohort effects appear to be particularly important in the investigation of age differences in performance on standard intelligence tests, such as the Wechsler Adult Intelligence Scale (WAIS; Wechsler, 1958) or the Primary Mental Abilities Test (PMA; Thurstone & Thurstone, 1949). Controlling for cohort effects, such as educational level, markedly attenuates the frequently-observed decline in intelligence test performance with age (see, for example, Green, 1969). Moreover, while cross-sectional studies indicate that intelligence test performance deteriorates with age, the few studies employing longitudinal designs report an age-related improvement (for example, Owens, 1959, 1966), though this is probably attributable to selective attrition. Sequential studies using the PMA test suggest that age differences in intellectual performance are largely due to cohort differences up to the late 60s and only thereafter does age begin to affect test scores (for example, Schaie & Parham, 1977). However, Kausler (1982) has argued that cohort effects in studies of human

**TABLE 16.1**

Illustration of hypothetical cross-sectional and longitudinal studies showing that chronological age reflects the interaction of year of birth and year of measurement. From Kimmel (1990).

| Year born | Year measured | | | |
|---|---|---|---|---|
| | 1960 | 1970 | 1980 | 1990 |
| 1910 | (A)  50 | (B)  60 | (C)  70 | (D)  80 |
| 1920 | (E)  40 | (F)  50 | (G)  60 | (H)  70 |
| 1930 | (I)  30 | (J)  40 | (K)  50 | (L)  60 |
| 1940 | | (M)  30 | (N)  40 | (O)  50 |
| 1950 | | | (P)  30 | (Q)  40 |
| 1960 | | | | (R)  30 |

performance are likely to be minimal, if indeed they operate at all. He pointed out that data for some performance tasks, obtained under similar conditions, are available for young adults from different cohorts, in certain cases extending back to the last century. On the basis of an analysis of between-cohort comparisons, Kausler concluded that for a number of tasks, including paired-associate learning, serial learning, digit span and span of apprehension, cohort differences were negligible. It seems reasonable to assume, therefore, that cohort effects do not appreciably distort the conclusions drawn from cross-sectional studies of age differences in human performance.

## 16.3 AGE AND SENSORY PERFORMANCE

With the possible exception of pain sensitivity (see Corso, 1981), the efficiency of all the main sensory systems tends to be impaired by ageing, although age-related declines in vision and hearing are the most important, both subjectively and objectively. Loss of vision, for example, is second only to cancer as the most feared consequence of ageing (see Verrillo & Verrillo, 1985) and in the USA the incidence of legal blindness increases from around 1/1000 among individuals below the age of 21 to around 14/1000 for individuals in their late 60s (Santrock, 1992). As reviews by Fozard (1990) and Kline and Scialfa (1996) have noted, survey data indicate that older individuals

find several aspects of visual functioning to be particularly problematic for everyday activities, such as driving, reading and watching television. These include visual search and visual processing speed (for example, locating and reading a traffic sign), light sensitivity (for example, seeing objects in twilight or at night), dynamic vision (for example, assimilating information presented on a scrolling cinema or television screen) and near vision (for example, reading small print). Similarly, older people report marked age-related hearing difficulties with temporal resolution, with distinguishing speech or other sounds in the presence of background noise, with hearing high-pitched sounds and with comprehending speech, especially if it is distorted, as in a telephone conversation (Kline and Scialfa, 1996). The incidence of legal deafness in the USA is around 150/1000 for individuals aged 65 and over, and 75% of those aged 75–79 are estimated to have some type of hearing problem, compared with 19% of individuals aged 45–54 (Santrock, 1992).

### 16.3.1 Age and visual performance

Age-related changes in visual performance are partly attributable to structural changes taking place in the visual system, particularly in the eye (see Fig. 16.1). Pupil size gradually diminishes with age and the aqueous humor becomes less transparent. Both of these changes reduce the amount of light reaching the retina, by about 65% from the 20s to the late 60s, so that older people require higher ambient illumination levels to

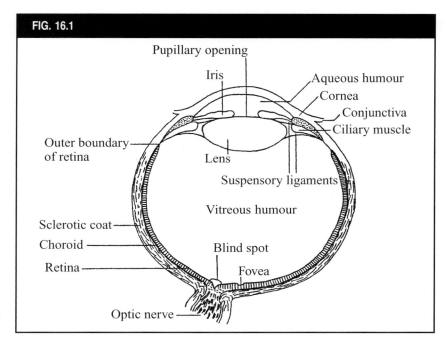

**FIG. 16.1**

Pupillary opening

Iris

Aqueous humour

Cornea

Conjunctiva

Ciliary muscle

Outer boundary
of retina

Lens

Suspensory ligaments

Vitreous humour

Sclerotic coat

Choroid

Blind spot

Retina

Fovea

Optic nerve

The structure of the
human eye.

function effectively. However, with advancing age the pupil also takes longer to respond to sudden changes in illumination levels so that, for example, at night the glare of oncoming headlights is more disruptive for older drivers than for younger ones. The difference in size between the light-adapted and dark-adapted pupil is much diminished, and in dark conditions the pupil size of older individuals is considerably smaller than that of younger individuals, resulting in impairments of nocturnal vision. The lens becomes thicker and less flexible with age and, as a result, it is more difficult to focus on objects which are in near vision, that is, relatively close to the eye. The lens also becomes more opaque with age, thus further reducing the amount of light that reaches the photoreceptors in the retina, at the rear of the eye. Visual acuity, the ability to discriminate fine detail, improves until the early 30s, then stabilises until the mid-40s. After the age of 50 or so there is a steady decline, with the greatest loss of acuity taking place after the age of 60 (see Verrillo & Verrillo, 1985). By the mid-80s, the ability to discriminate fine detail in a visual scene is only about a fifth of the peak level achieved during the late

20s to early 30s. Contrast sensitivity, the ability to detect differences in luminance, which is a strong predictor of visual performance in everyday settings, deteriorates sharply as individuals become older, particularly at intermediate and high spatial frequencies (Kline & Scheiber, 1985). Performance at tasks involving the perception of motion is also adversely affected by ageing and in consequence the mobility of older individuals may be impaired and the likelihood of falls increased (see Simoneau & Leibowitz, 1996). In contrast, depth perception and colour vision exhibit relatively modest age-related declines, although the ability to discriminate among colours in the blue-green range of the visible spectrum is adversely affected by ageing (Charness & Bosman, 1992; Kline & Scialfa, 1996).

### 16.3.2 Age and auditory performance

As noted in Chapter 10, the audible spectrum extends from 20 to 20,000 Hz, although the audible frequency range becomes constricted with age. Both cross-sectional and longitudinal studies have demonstrated that, compared to young adults in their 20s, older adults are less able to hear high frequency sounds (see Fozard, 1990). Auditory thresholds for pure tones of different frequencies, typically ranging from around 125 Hz up to 8,000 Hz, increase throughout adulthood, but the threshold increase is greater for high frequency tones than for low frequency ones, especially after the mid-50s. The rate of hearing loss is around 3 db per decade up to age 55, rising to 9 db per decade thereafter (Kline & Scialfa, 1996). Age-related hearing loss, generally termed presbycusis, is largely attributable to structural changes in the auditory system associated with ageing, such as atrophy and degeneration of the sensory receptors for hearing (the hair cells in the cochlea, see Fig. 16.2), the loss of nerve cells in the auditory pathway linking the hair cells to the auditory cortex, and the stiffening of vibrating bone structures in the cochlea (the malleus or hammer, incus or anvil and stapes or stirrup; see Fig. 16.2). Presbycusis can be exacerbated by prolonged and repeated exposure to loud noise, typically in a work setting (Verrillo & Verrillo, 1985) and, perhaps because of their greater exposure to

industrial noise, men tend to have poorer hearing sensitivity at higher frequencies than do women, a difference that increases with age. But the effects of noise should not be overestimated, since comparisons between the hearing sensitivity of men and women from low-noise occupations indicate that hearing loss occurs at a faster rate in men from around the age of 30 onwards (see Kline & Scialfa, 1996). Other factors affecting hearing loss include diets high in saturated fats, smoking, and the presence of cardiovascular disease (Verrillo & Verrillo, 1985).

Measures of hearing sensitivity for pure tones predict measures of speech perception fairly accurately (correlations range from +0.5 to +0.9) and, once age-related differences in pure tone sensitivity are controlled for, age differences in speech recognition are slight or non-existent (Kline & Scialfa, 1996). Older individuals who are hearing-impaired tend to have higher speech recognition scores than younger individuals with similar levels of hearing impairment and older listeners appear to make rather greater use of contextual

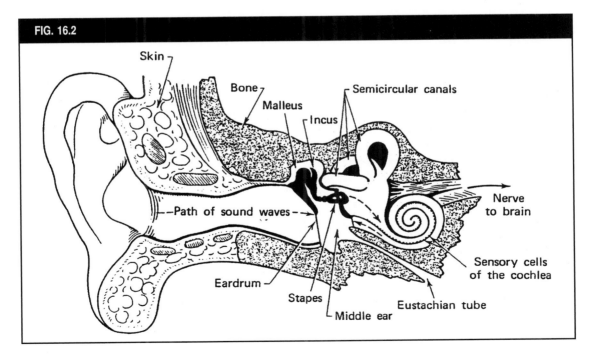

FIG. 16.2

The structure of the human ear.

cues to facilitate speech recognition than do their younger counterparts. However, the ability of older adults to comprehend speech deteriorates in noisy or reverberant environments, when the speech is interrupted or filtered and when the rate of speech presentation is increased (Verrillo & Verrillo, 1985).

A considerable amount of information is available concerning age-related changes in vision and audition and much less is known about the effects of ageing on the cutaneous system (touch), the vestibular system (balance), the gustatory system (taste) and the olfactory system (smell), although for all these systems there is some evidence of age-related performance impairments (see Verrillo & Verrillo, 1985). Sensory deficits might be expected to exert quite marked effects on the performance of older individuals in a wide variety of situations. For example, Kosnick, Sekuler and Kline (1990) noted that older drivers who had given up driving reported more visual problems than older drivers who continued to drive. In response to questions about visual problems experienced while driving, older drivers frequently mentioned difficulties with speed judgements, with cars "appearing" in the visual periphery, in reading road signs, in seeing the instrument panel and in perceiving the position of other cars through windscreen glare. Many older drivers attempt to counteract such difficulties by driving fewer miles, avoiding high-risk situations such as rush hour traffic and reducing or eliminating night driving (see Davies, Taylor, & Dorn, 1992). Moreover, the size of the useful field of view and the extent of the visual field required for the performance of a particular task, have been shown to be good predictors of accident frequency in a group of older drivers (Owsley et al., 1991). Sensory functioning also appears to be a strong predictor of intellectual performance, at least in those individuals aged 70 and over (Lindenberger & Baltes, 1994). Lindenberger and Baltes obtained measures of visual and auditory acuity from a group of 156 older individuals, with a mean age of 84.9 years and a range between 70 and 103. Intellectual performance was assessed with a battery of 14 tests measuring five cognitive abilities (speed, reasoning, memory, knowledge and fluency). Together,

visual and auditory acuity accounted for 49.2% of the total variance and 93.1% of the age-related variance in intellectual performance. Lindenberger and Baltes concluded that visual and auditory acuity may be indicators of the physiological integrity of the ageing brain. Similar findings with respect to visual acuity were reported by Salthouse, Hancock, Meinz and Hambrick (1996).

## 16.4 AGE AND RESPONSE SPEED

Response speed progressively decreases with age and age-related behavioural slowing is a major contributor to age differences in human performance (Birren & Fisher, 1995; Welford, 1977, 1985). Slowing is neither confined to tasks presented to a particular sensory modality, nor to tasks requiring a particular motor response. Similar age-related decrements have been observed in both visual and auditory simple RT tasks (Koga & Morant, 1923) and in simple RT tasks in which responses made with the finger, foot or jaw have been compared (Birren & Botwinick, 1955). Response latencies in simple reaction-time (RT) tasks increase by about 25% from the 20s to the 60s (Welford, 1977), though in absolute terms the difference is slight, usually being less than 50 msec. Correlations between measures of the speed of performance across different tasks increase with age, and factor analyses suggest that the speed of performance of older adults is characterised by a general speed factor, while that of younger adults is not (Salthouse, 1985). Attempts to localise age-related slowing at a particular processing stage, such as encoding, comparison, or response selection and execution (see Chapter 2), suggest that all processing stages are characterised by slowing and hence that slowing is not attributable to the malfunctioning of a particular stage (Salthouse & Somberg, 1982). In the light of such evidence, age-related response slowing is often thought to be general rather than specific (Birren, 1965; Birren & Fisher, 1995; Salthouse, 1985). Since age differences in the latencies of retinal or pupillary responses are small, motor reactions are usually relatively simple and highly practised, and motor times (the delay between electromyographic and mechanical responses) show minimal changes with age (Surwillo, 1968), response slowing is frequently held to result primarily from changes in the central nervous system (more specifically, in the rate of central information processing speed) rather than from changes in peripheral sensory and motor systems (Birren & Fisher, 1995). Furthermore, age differences in peripheral nerve conduction velocities and in synaptic and neuro-muscular delay have been estimated to contribute less than 5% to age differences in response speed (see Surwillo, 1968).

Age differences in the speed of performance become more pronounced as task difficulty or complexity increases, so that differences between the response times of older and younger individuals tend to be greater in choice RT tasks than in simple RT tasks. The "complexity hypothesis" suggests that absolute differences between the response times of older and younger individuals become greater as central processing demands are increased while peripheral processing demands are controlled (see Salthouse, 1985). This hypothesis has usually been tested by constructing what are now termed "Brinley plots", following a procedure introduced by Brinley (1965) in which mean RTs for older adults in a particular task are plotted against mean RTs for younger adults. Brinley reported that mean RTs for older adults were a linear function of mean RTs for younger adults, a finding that has since been repeatedly confirmed. Using Brinley plots, Cerella (1985; Cerella, Poon, & Williams, 1980) conducted a meta-analysis of younger and older adults' choice RTs, drawn from a large number of separate studies in which task complexity had been varied. This analysis revealed that across all levels of complexity, in a variety of different tasks, mean choice RTs for older adults were linearly related to mean choice RTs for younger adults, with an intercept close to zero, although slightly negative, and a slope of around 1.4. Moreover, a general slowing coefficient appeared to account for the majority of the variance in mean response latencies.

These findings, and other similar ones, have been interpreted as supporting a generalised slowing hypothesis, which suggests that increments in response times observed in older adults are proportionately identical in all tasks, regardless of their complexity. Absolute age differences in response speed are held to be greater for complex tasks than for simple ones because a greater number of component processes, each of which is assumed to take more time in older individuals, intervene between stimulus presentation and response execution (see Cerella, 1985, 1990), though different models of age-related slowing characterise the processes involved in somewhat different ways (see Myerson & Hale, 1993). But the power of Brinley plots to discriminate among models of age-related slowing has been questioned (see, for example, Fisk, Fisher, & Rogers, 1992; Sliwinski et al., 1994), and the degree to which age-related slowing varies with the type of processing required by specific tasks is the subject of some debate.

The task-specific slowing hypothesis (see Birren & Fisher, 1995) suggests that slowing in one task component process (e.g. an input process) may be independent of slowing in other task component processes (e.g. an output process) and hence that the extent of age-related slowing is related to the nature of the task being performed, perhaps because the performance of older individuals is differentially sensitive to particular task characteristics, such as information presentation rate or working memory load. Across different tasks, the ratio of mean RTs for older individuals to mean RTs for younger individuals can vary quite widely and these variations appear to be systematic rather than random, suggesting that age adversely affects the speed of performance more on some tasks than on others (see, for example, Rabbitt, 1993, 1996b). Lima, Hale and Myerson (1991), for instance, in a meta-analysis of response times in lexical decision tasks, found that the degree of slowing manifested by older individuals was not as great as would have been anticipated from age differences in response speed in the performance of non-lexical decision tasks. They argued that the lexical/non-lexical distinction was a fundamental one with respect to age-related slowing and that research should be directed at elucidating differences between the two task categories which might be critical for the ageing process.

While response slowing undoubtedly increases with age, there is some dispute about the extent to which it is general or specific. Attempts to answer the more basic question of why age-related slowing occurs at all have ranged from the psychological to the biological, although such explanations are not mutually exclusive; older individuals may well try to compensate for biologically-based changes in response speed by altering the way in which they carry out a task. For instance, older and younger individuals seem to adopt different strategies when performing both psychomotor and cognitive tasks. Typically, older people employ more cautious strategies, favouring accuracy over speed, while younger people adopt more risky strategies, favouring speed at the expense of accuracy. Rabbitt (1981) suggested that errors made during task performance provide information about whether performance is being carried out at the optimal speed and hence enable the trade-off between speed and accuracy to be adjusted appropriately. Older individuals may be less sensitive to error feedback information, so that inappropriate adjustments are made to response criteria, resulting in increases both in error rates and in response times. The adoption of a more cautious response criterion probably accounts for some proportion of response slowing (see Strayer, Wickens, & Braune, 1987) but since age differences in response speed persist when older and younger individuals are compared at exactly the same level of performance accuracy, differences among age groups in speed/accuracy trade-offs cannot provide a complete explanation of age-related slowing (Salthouse, 1985).

The hypothesis that age-related slowing has a biological basis is supported by the results of a number of studies indicating that health-related factors can affect response slowing. For example, a number of studies of response speed in healthy, active and physically fit older people, aged 50–70, indicate that such individuals not only respond much more quickly than their sedentary and less healthy age peers, but also perform at comparable levels to those achieved by physically inactive college students in their 20s, and in some cases exceed them (see Spirduso & MacRae, 1990). But younger active students still respond more quickly

than do older active individuals in both simple and choice RT tasks, though age differences are relatively small. Cardiovascular fitness can affect not only the mean RTs of older individuals, though it does not invariably do so, but also the incidence of occasional very slow response times, sometimes referred to as "blocks" (Bunce, Warr, & Cochrane, 1993). Bunce et al. found that older unfit individuals produced more "blocks" than did older fit individuals, but they interpreted this finding in terms of an inability to maintain concentration rather than as an indication of an age-related decline in response speed. The presence of cardiovascular disease is also associated with increased response slowing (Deeg, Kardaun, & Fozard, 1996; Elias et al., 1990), as is the presence of risk factors for neurological dysfunction, such as exposure to neurotoxins (Houx, Vreeling, & Jolles, 1991).

## 16.5  AGE AND ATTENTION

As noted in Chapter 3, attention can be subdivided into three main categories: first, selective attention, the ability to focus upon or select relevant and to ignore irrelevant information; second, divided attention, the ability to attend to two or more sources of information simultaneously; and third, sustained attention, the ability to maintain the focus of attention on one or more sources of information over relatively long periods of time.

### 16.5.1  Selective attention

Selective attention tasks can be divided into filtering (for example, dichotic shadowing tasks) or search tasks, involving feature or conjunction search (see Chapter 3). Older adults make more errors than do younger adults in dichotic shadowing (see Craik, 1977; Davies, Jones, & Taylor, 1984). Barr and Giambra (1990) found that age differences in shadowing efficiency persisted even when shadowing efficiency on a monaural version of the task and fluid intelligence, assessed by Raven's Progressive Matrices Test, were statistically controlled for; moreover, age differences in shadowing efficiency could not be accounted for by age differences in pure tone hearing loss. The performance of older adults is also impaired in the dichotic listening or "split-span" task (Broadbent, 1954). This task involves the rapid presentation of a short series of digit pairs, one member of the pair being presented to the left ear at the same time as the other digit is presented to the right. Listeners are then required to recall the digit pairs, sometimes being instructed as to which ear's digits should be reported first and sometimes being free to choose the order of report; the digits presented to the ear recalled first are described as the first half-set, while those presented to the ear recalled second are termed the second half-set. Recall is generally better for the first half-set than for the second, and this superiority becomes more apparent from around the age of 60 onwards (see Inglis, 1965), although age differences may also be observed in the recall of the first half-set (for example, Craik, 1965). Poorer recall of the second half-set by older adults may be due to an age-related deficit in working memory (Hasher & Zacks, 1988; Salthouse, 1990c).

Age-related decrements have also been observed in the performance of the Stroop Test (Stroop, 1935), described in 4.4.3, which can be regarded as a visual filtering task (Plude, Enns, & Brodeur, 1994). Naming incongruent colour-word stimuli on the basis of ink colour typically takes much longer than either naming colour patches or reading colour words printed in black, and this difference increases with age from the early 60s onwards (see Cohn, Dustman, & Bradford, 1984; Comalli, Wapner, & Werner, 1962). Moreover, age-related increases in response latencies to incongruent stimuli persist after effects due to response slowing have been controlled for (Spieler, Balota, & Faust, 1996), are unaffected by practice (Dulaney & Rogers, 1994), and are observed in both tachistoscopic and card-sorting versions of the task (Davies et al., 1984). However, different versions of the Stroop task appear to be differentially sensitive to the effects of ageing (Brink & McDowd, 1999; Hartley, 1993). Increased Stroop interference in older adults, frequently measured by subtracting response latencies for naming colour patches from response latencies for naming incongruent colour-word stimuli (that is, CW–C; see Jensen, 1965), tends to be positively related to institutionalisation (Comalli, Krus, & Wapner, 1965) and to the presence of organic brain syndrome (Bettner, Jarvik, & Blum, 1971) or of various biological life events that are likely to impair brain function, such as repeated exposure to general anaesthesia (Houx, Jolles, & Vreeling, 1993).

In feature search tasks the response times of both older and younger adults seem to be unaffected by display size (D'Aloisio & Klein, 1990; Plude & Doussard-Roosevelt, 1989), while in conjunction search tasks the response times of older adults increase with display size to a much greater extent than do those of younger adults (Plude & Doussard-Roosevelt, 1989; Rabbitt, 1965). In Rabbitt's study, younger (age range 17–24 years) and older (age range 65–74 years) adults sorted cards into two piles according to whether they bore the target letters A or B; each card bore in addition 0, 1, 4 or 8 distractor letters, and the target letter (A or B) might be in any one of nine locations on the card. In a second condition, the same individuals sorted cards into eight piles corresponding to the target letters A to H, again with 0, 1, 4 or 8 distractor letters accompanying the target (presentation of the two conditions was counterbalanced across participants). Rabbitt found that the effect on sorting times of an increase in the number of target letters from two to eight was much the same for the two age groups. However, the sorting times of older adults increased significantly more steeply than did those of younger adults as the number of distractors was increased, particularly in the second condition where eight target letters, rather than two, had to be located. The extent to which targets and distractors resemble one another also affects response times in visual search (Farkas & Hoyer, 1980; Scialfa, Esau, & Joffe, 1998). When targets and distractors are dissimilar, the search times of younger adults are largely unaffected, while those of older adults increase. However, when targets and distractors are similar, both older and younger adults take longer to search a display, but the increase in search times is more pronounced for older adults. Susceptibility to distractors in visual search tasks thus becomes greater with age.

## 16.5.2 Divided attention

Numerous studies have demonstrated that in dual-task situations older adults exhibit greater performance decrements than do younger ones, although there may be no age difference when each task is performed on its own. For example, when two tasks, such as an auditory monitoring task and a memory task, are performed simultaneously, older individuals are likely to exhibit significantly poorer performance on both tasks than are younger individuals, even though both age groups may perform at comparable levels on each task when presented alone. Many of the early studies of age differences in dual-task performance, reviewed by Craik (1977), used dichotic listening or "split-span" tasks (see 16.4.1), although meta-analytic procedures suggest that age differences in the performance of dichotic listening tasks are attributable to different factors than those affecting age differences in other dual-task situations (see Hartley, 1992). In dual-task situations in which dichotic listening tasks have not been employed, a key determinant of the nature and extent of age-related decrements would appear to be the complexity of the tasks involved (see McDowd & Birren, 1990).

Somberg and Salthouse (1982) examined possible age differences in the performance of visual search tasks under single- and dual-task conditions. Single-task baseline performance accuracy was equated across the two age groups and, since participants were instructed to employ different attention allocation strategies, it was possible to derive performance operating characteristics (POCs; see 5.5.1) for older and younger individuals. Surprisingly, Somberg and Salthouse found that the costs of dividing attention between the two search tasks were no greater for older than for younger adults, and the shape of the POCs was unaffected by age. They concluded that age deficits in divided attention resulted from failures to equate age groups on baseline levels of single-task performance accuracy. However, in a subsequent divided attention study, using more complex tasks involving memory for simultaneously presented letters and digits, Salthouse, Rogan and Prill (1984) reported that divided attention costs were higher for older than for younger adults,

even when single-task baseline performance was statistically controlled across age groups. Age-related decrements in divided attention performance have also been reported in other well controlled dual-task experiments using complex tasks (Korteling, 1991; Ponds, Brouwer, & Van Wolfelaar, 1988).

Task complexity, defined as the number of hypothetical component processes involved in the performance of a particular task, thus appears to be a major determinant of age differences in divided attention. The findings of McDowd and Craik (1988) provide further support for the view that age-related decrements in dual-task performance are enhanced when the tasks involved are complex rather than simple. McDowd and Craik suggested that age deficits in divided attention are likely to be observed in all dual-task situations except those in which the tasks concerned are extremely simple, highly repetitive and strongly emphasise automatic processing. They also argued that dual-task situations are more complex than single-task situations, and that it is this increase in complexity rather than the requirement to divide attention per se that produces difficulties for older adults. However, as Kramer, Larish and Strayer (1995) have pointed out, some studies of age-related differences in dual-task performance have reported larger age differences for less complex compared to more complex tasks, while others indicate that age differences in dual-task situations are selective rather than general, affecting some processes but not others.

Finally, it is worth noting that as with speeded performance, the dual-task performance of older adults can be improved by aerobic exercise, even though single-task performance is unaffected (Hawkins, Kramer, & Capaldi, 1992).

## 16.5.3 Sustained attention

As noted in Chapter 6, sustained attention or vigilance tasks require observers to monitor displays for the infrequent occurrence of targets that are difficult to discriminate from non-target or background events (see Davies & Parasuraman, 1982). Studies of adult age differences in sustained attention suggest that detection efficiency tends to decrease with age from around the late 50s/early

60s onwards, although the magnitude of the age deficit depends on the nature of the vigilance task being performed (Davies & Parasuraman, 1982; Parasuraman, 1986). For example, in one of the earliest studies of age and vigilance, men in their late 50s and early 60s and men in their 20s were observed in a 40-minute auditory vigilance task that required the detection of particular three-digit sequences. There were significant age differences in the overall level of detection efficiency, when observers were required to write down the targets as they were detected, but not when they were instructed to press a key when a target occurred, a result attributed to the additional load on short-term memory imposed by writing down the digits (see Davies & Griew, 1965). More recently, Parasuraman, Nestor and Greenwood (1989) investigated the effects of stimulus degradation on possible age differences in overall perceptual sensitivity, indexed by $d'$, and in the rate of decline of perceptual sensitivity over the course of a vigil. They tested older (mean age 69.5 years) and younger (mean age 24.9 years) adults on a visual digit-discrimination task, requiring the detection of zeros in a stream of digits. Events were presented at a rate of 15 per minute. Compared to younger adults, older adults were found to have lower levels of perceptual sensitivity, but sensitivity only declined significantly in the most degraded condition and there were no age differences in the rate of decline.

Deaton and Parasuraman (1993) conducted a series of studies examining age differences in sensory and cognitive vigilance tasks varying in event rate. The same materials, pairs of digits drawn from the set 0, 2, 3, 5, 6, and 9, were used in both the sensory and cognitive vigilance tasks. In the sensory task, observers were required to discriminate a difference in the physical size of the two digits, which were presented simultaneously. In the cognitive task a target occurred when one member of the digit pair was even and the other odd. Events were presented at rates of either 40 per minute (the high event rate condition) or 15 per minute (the low event rate condition). Sixty people participated in the experiment and were divided into three age groups: young (mean age 20.3 years), middle-aged (mean age 45.7 years)

and old (mean age 72.8 years). Sensory and cognitive vigilance tasks were found to produce different patterns of responding, with a vigilance decrement being observed in the sensory task but not in the cognitive one, and age differences in detection efficiency were obtained only in the sensory task, with the two older groups making significantly more false alarms than the younger group. But detection efficiency declined at much the same rate in both age groups. In a second experiment, identical to the first except that a middle-aged group was not included and only the fast event rate condition was used, Deaton and Parasuraman found that older adults (mean age 70.2 years) made fewer correct detections and more false alarms in both tasks than did young adults (mean age 22.5 years), although again there were no age differences in the extent of the vigilance decrement. A third experiment, identical to the second except for an increased event display time (500 ms vs. 300 ms) and a longer practice session, obtained significant age differences in correct detections, but not in false alarm rates, and once more there were no age differences in the decline in performance with time on task.

In sustained attention tasks, therefore, more often than not age differences are obtained in the overall level of detection efficiency, but virtually never in the rate at which detection efficiency declines with time at work; an exception is the study of Surwillo and Quilter (1964), although the differential age-related decline they observed may well be artefactual (see Giambra & Quilter, 1988). Usually, older adults are less efficient in sustained attention tasks than are younger ones, especially when task demands are high (Mouloua & Parasuraman, 1995). However, Tomporowski and Tinsley (1996) have reported a study in which the detection efficiency of older adults was superior to that of younger ones in a 60-minute complex cognitive vigilance task. In their first experiment, Tomporowski and Tinsley compared the performance of older adults (mean age 63.1 years) who were paid for performing the task, with the performance of two groups of younger adults, both in their early 20s, one of which was paid for participation in the study while the other was not. While perceptual sensitivity, indexed by

P(A), was comparable for older and younger adults who were paid, it was significantly higher for both paid groups than for younger adults who were unpaid. In a second study, in which the memory demands of the task were increased and no payment was made for participation, perceptual sensitivity was significantly higher for a group of older adults (mean age 67.2 years) than it was for a group of younger adults (mean age 18.9 years). Tomporowski and Tinsley attributed these somewhat surprising results to greater intrinsic motivation on the part of older individuals and to participant selection bias. Without contradicting earlier findings, their results confirm that age-related deficits are less likely to be observed in sustained attention tasks than in other task situations involving attention, and provide further support for the view that the ability to maintain attention over relatively long periods of time is not substantially affected by ageing. Physical fitness can also attenuate any age effects that may be observed (Bunce, Barraclough, & Morris, 1996).

## 16.6  AGE AND MEMORY

As noted in 3.4, several different types of memory have been distinguished, with the distinction between explicit and implicit memory being perhaps the most fundamental. Most studies of ageing and explicit memory have used verbal materials, such as word lists, but some studies have examined age differences in explicit memory for non-verbal materials, such as pictures or drawings, though age effects appear to be broadly similar for the retention of both verbal and non-verbal materials (Craik & Jennings, 1992). Implicit memory is typically assessed in the laboratory by a variety of indirect methods, including priming (for example, the effect of prior exposure of a word on its subsequent identification in fragmented or incomplete form), conditioning, or non-associative procedures, such as habituation. Researchers concerned with ageing and performance have also investigated possible age differences in short- and long-term memory (STM and LTM), and also in working memory, which is similar to the active short-term memory system hypothesised by Welford (1958) to be especially vulnerable to the effects of ageing.

Older adults refer to memory problems more than younger adults do, and in laboratory tests of memory perform less well on a variety of memory tasks. Moreover, age differences in memory performance do not appear to be due to cohort effects, since they are observed both in longitudinal studies and in cross-sectional studies in which older and younger adults are matched for educational level and for vocabulary scores (Kausler, 1985). Age-related memory impairments thus appear to be mainly attributable to the effects of ageing rather than to other possible confounding factors. Age differences in explicit memory are outlined first, followed by a brief description of the effects of ageing on implicit memory. As will be seen below, the ageing process mainly affects explicit memory, particularly long-term episodic memory, although it also impairs working memory. The effects of age on implicit memory appear to be slight, although the body of evidence relevant to ageing and implicit memory is much smaller than that concerned with ageing and explicit memory. Since age differences in forgetting rates in explicit memory tasks seem to be minimal once initial performance levels have been equated across age groups (Craik, 1977), it has been generally assumed that ageing exerts little effect upon information storage and that age differences in memory performance are more likely to result from encoding or retrieval deficits, or both.

### 16.6.1  Explicit memory

Age differences in explicit memory appear to be minimal in STM tasks but relatively substantial in both LTM and working memory tasks (Craik, 1977; Craik & Jennings, 1992). Apart from memory span, measures used to assess STM include the recency effect in the free recall of word lists (the tendency for the last few list items to be better recalled than earlier items, discussed in 3.4.1), and the Brown-Peterson task, which provides an estimate of the rate of short-term forgetting. In this task, three-digit items are presented, with a brief delay between presentation and recall which is filled by an interpolated task, usually counting backwards in threes from a specified number. Small but reliable decrements in memory span have been reported for both digits and words (Dobbs & Rule, 1989; Hayslip & Kennelly, 1982; Parkinson, 1982) and the negative correlation between age and span length has been found to be higher for words than for digits (Salthouse & Babcock, 1989). The recency effect in free recall involves both STM and LTM (Waugh & Norman, 1965) but age decrements in the recency effect have been found to be almost entirely due to impairments of LTM (Delbecq-Derousne & Beauvois, 1989). Age also appears to exert little effect either on the level of recall or the rate of forgetting in the Brown-Peterson task (Dobbs & Rule, 1989; Puckett & Stockberger, 1988). The effects of ageing on STM are thus relatively slight.

In contrast to STM, age differences in long-term or secondary episodic memory are quite marked (see Craik, 1977; Kausler, 1982; Light, 1991 for reviews) and have been reported not only for standard laboratory tasks but also for memory tasks designed to have greater ecological validity (Light, 1991). As Light noted, age differences have been found in memory for prose, for the names and faces of people, for the appearance of commonly encountered objects, such as coins and telephone dials, for activities performed relatively recently, and for the location of buildings on the major streets of a familiar town. But memory for remote events, both public and private, which older people often claim to be clearer than memory for more recent events (although such memories may seem clearer because they are highly selective, more frequently rehearsed and more likely to be embellished with the passage of time) shows similar declines from the present to the past for both older and younger adults (Craik & Jennings, 1992). Age differences in remote memory thus appear to be minimal.

Memory can be assessed not only for past events but also for actions to be carried out in the future (prospective memory), for example, remembering to take tomorrow's medication or to attend a meeting scheduled for next Tuesday afternoon. Naturalistic studies of prospective memory suggest that whether or not age differences are obtained seems to depend on the availability of environmental prompts, such as notes or lists, which depends on the extent to which individuals are able to plan ahead and provide themselves with effective memory aids (e.g. Maylor, 1990). For instance, when instructed to make a telephone call to the laboratory at various times on specified days, older adults are rather more likely to remember to do so than are younger adults, but they are also more likely to place written reminders near the telephone (Moscovitch, 1982). When Moscovitch requested older participants to refrain from using external memory aids, no age differences in prospective memory were observed. Older adults thus perform less well in prospective memory tasks when environmental prompts are lacking in salience or are absent altogether (see Dobbs & Rule, 1987; Einstein & McDaniel, 1990; Einstein, Holland, McDaniel, & Guynn, 1992; West, 1988), particularly if the task is time-based (e.g. remembering to listen to a radio programme at 8 o'clock tonight) rather than event-based (e.g. remembering to ask your brother-in-law to return a book next time you meet) (see Park et al., 1997). Low verbal ability also appears to impair prospective memory in older adults (Cherry & LeCompte, 1999).

While episodic memory tasks exhibit reliable age decrements, age differences are less likely to be observed in semantic memory tasks. Semantic memory seems to be relatively resistant to the effects of ageing, and some studies have obtained age-related improvements in tasks such as vocabulary recall or memory for factual information (e.g. Mitchell, 1989). But older adults tend to respond more slowly in a wide range of primary and secondary memory tasks (Waugh, Fozard, & Thomas, 1978) and appear to be disadvantaged when they are required to retrieve information from semantic memory at a rapid rate (e.g. Eysenck, 1975). Furthermore, older people frequently complain that they experience difficulty in accessing desired words in speaking and writing (Burke & Light, 1981) and tend to perform less efficiently when asked to retrieve a particular word in response to a dictionary definition (Bowles & Poon, 1985).

Finally, large and reliable age-related decrements in working memory have been frequently reported (see Smith, 1996; Verhaeghen, Marcoen,

& Goossens, 1993) and comparisons between performance on "passive" memory tasks, such as digit span, and on working-memory tasks indicate that age differences are minimal in the former but substantial in the latter (for example, Dobbs & Rule, 1989; Fisk & Warr, 1996). Dobbs and Rule compared the performance of individuals aged between 30 and 93 years on three memory tasks, two of them "passive" and the third a working memory task. The passive tasks were digit span (forwards and backwards) and the Brown-Peterson task. The working memory task required participants to listen to a series of random digits and then to recall either the digit just heard (the zero lag condition), the digit prior to the one just heard (the "one back" or lag one condition), or the digit two before the one just heard (the "two back" or lag two condition). Dobbs and Rule's findings for the two passive tasks are presented in Table 16.2, from which it can be seen that age differences in the performance of both tasks were slight; indeed, educational level, but not age, was found to be a significant predictor of performance in these tasks. Their results for the working memory task are shown in Fig. 16.3, in which it is apparent that performance declined markedly for the two oldest age groups tested; moreover, in this task, age *was* a reliable predictor of performance. The processing component of working memory seems to be principally responsible for the age deficit, with the storage component and the executive

component, which coordinates storage and processing, making only a negligible contribution (Salthouse & Babcock, 1991).

### 16.6.2 Implicit memory

Implicit memory tasks often involve an initial presentation of material that serves to facilitate or "prime" subsequent responding, although there may be no conscious recollection of the facilitating event (see 3.4.3). For instance, the lexical decision as to whether a letter string is a word or a non-word tends to be made more quickly if the target word has been preceded by a semantically related word (for example, doctor–nurse), an effect termed semantic priming. Semantic priming effects tend to be larger in older than in younger adults (Laver & Burke, 1993). Tasks used to investigate implicit memory include:

- perceptual identification (where participants are required to read words presented very rapidly or in degraded form)
- generating category exemplars (e.g. table) in response to category names (e.g. furniture)
- completing word stems (e.g. bec___) or word fragments (for example, _ar_d_gm)
- spelling auditorily presented words which are in fact homophones (e.g. reed vs. read), having been primed in the direction of specific spellings by a prior orienting task (Howard, 1988)
- making lexical decisions.

---

**TABLE 16.2**

Performance of different age groups on two "passive" short-term memory tasks (adapted from Dobbs & Rule, 1989, p. 501).

| Measure | Age range | | | | |
|---|---|---|---|---|---|
| | 30–39 | 40–49 | 50–59 | 60–69 | 70+ |
| **Mean recall digit span** | | | | | |
| Forwards | 7.02 | 6.48 | 6.93 | 6.29 | 6.60 |
| Backwards | 5.57 | 5.30 | 5.67 | 5.28 | 5.02 |
| **Percentage correct Brown-Peterson task** | | | | | |
| 3s retention | 87.8 | 84.2 | 85.2 | 85.8 | 80.5 |
| 6s retention | 71.2 | 69.0 | 70.0 | 71.5 | 67.0 |
| 12s retention | 63.3 | 64.3 | 66.0 | 65.2 | 56.8 |

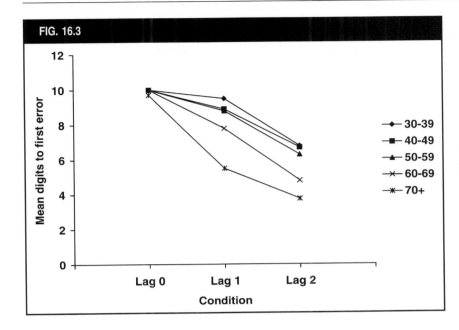

FIG. 16.3

The performance of different age groups under different lag conditions in a working memory task. From Dobbs & Rule (1989). In A.P. Smith & D.M. Jones (Eds.), Handbook of human performance. Volume 3: Trait and state. Wiley. Reprinted with permission.

Although in some studies age differences in the performance of implicit memory tasks have been obtained, with younger adults having slightly but significantly higher performance levels (Chiarello & Hoyer, 1988; Davis et al., 1990; Rose, Yesavage, Hill, & Bower, 1986), most studies of age and implicit memory have found that age differences in the performance of implicit memory tasks, if they occur at all, tend to be much smaller than those found in the performance of explicit memory tasks (Light, 1991; Smith, 1996). In a direct comparison of the effects of age on explicit and implicit memory, Light and Singh (1987) examined the performance of older and younger adults on a cued recall task (explicit memory) and on a word-stem completion task (implicit memory), using the same stems as cues. Only the instructions for the two tasks were altered, participants being instructed either to use the word stems to recall words from a list studied earlier (cued recall) or to complete the stems with any word that came to mind (word-stem completion). No age differences were observed in the performance of the word-stem completion task, but a substantial age-related decline in performance was observed in the cued recall task.

## 16.7 AGE AND JOB PERFORMANCE

Both supervisory ratings and work output records have been used in studies of the job performance of older workers, defined here, following the US Age Discrimination in Employment Act of 1967, as workers age 40 and over. Provided that certain practical and methodological difficulties can be minimised, the use of output records is clearly more satisfactory, since supervisory ratings may be subject to age bias (Davies et al., 1991). One practical difficulty is that of obtaining output record data over a long enough period to ensure their reliability, since companies may keep such data only for a limited time. A second is that of obtaining sufficient numbers of workers in the oldest age groups to ensure valid comparisons with younger workers, since the labour force participation rates of workers in their late 50s and early 60s have fallen sharply in recent years, especially among men. Third, even within the same job, younger and older workers may be differentially allocated to tasks which are more or less complex, strenuous, demanding, or even dangerous.

Moreover, when assessing age differences in the performance of a particular job, a number of selection factors may be operating that either inflate or reduce the apparent efficiency of older workers. On the one hand, less productive older workers may well be transferred to other work, sacked, or persuaded to take early retirement (Welford, 1958) while, on the other hand, more productive older workers may be promoted to supervisory positions, leaving less productive older workers behind. Furthermore, the most efficient younger workers may leave for jobs elsewhere, especially in industries where there is a high demand for labour. In all these cases, comparison of age differences in job performance is likely to be vitiated. Such comparisons are therefore more likely to be valid when turnover and internal transfer rates are low, and when checks are made on task allocation within particular jobs (Davies & Sparrow, 1985).

### 16.7.1  Output records

Although the relationship between age and job performance in studies using output records is somewhat variable, the general conclusion has been that the effects of age on job performance are negligible (Davies et al., 1991; Davies & Sparrow, 1985; Rhodes, 1983; Warr, 1994). The absence of any age-related decline in job performance is illustrated in Table 16.3, which summarises the results of two meta-analyses (McEvoy & Cascio, 1989; Waldman & Avolio, 1986) of the relation between age and productivity measures (output or production records). As Table 16.3 indicates, Waldman and Avolio obtained a modest, positive correlation (+0.27) between age and productivity, suggesting that productivity improves slightly with age, while McEvoy and Cascio obtained an even more modest correlation (+0.08), suggesting that age and productivity are essentially unrelated.

Warr (1996b) summarised the results of six studies of age and work output, standardising the scores for different age groups around those for workers aged 35–44. His summary is shown in Table 16.4, which suggests that productivity increases from the late teens to the mid-30s and then either continues to increase, levels off or

**TABLE 16.3**

Mean correlations ($r$) between age and productivity reported in two meta-analyses.

| Study | Productivity measures | |
|---|---|---|
| | $N$ | $r$ |
| Waldman & Avolio, 1986 | 2,745 | 0.27 |
| McEvoy & Cascio, 1989 | 13,184 | 0.07 |

Adapted from Davies et al., 1991, p. 168.

declines, most markedly in the group of equipment service engineers studied by Sparrow and Davies (1988). In this study, the performance of 1308 service engineers employed by a multinational office equipment company was investigated. Turnover and internal transfer rates were low, and educational levels were similar across age cohorts. In addition to age, Sparrow and Davies also examined the effects of tenure, recency of training, and job complexity, indexed by the size of the machine to be serviced and the range of functions of which it was capable. Checks were made to ensure that older and younger engineers were not differentially allocated to machines of different complexity. Two output measures were obtained: (1) quality of performance, assessed as the rate of machine performance between services compared with the national average for machines of its type, and (2) speed of performance, assessed by the time taken to service a machine. Surprisingly, although job complexity significantly affected both performance measures, in neither case did it interact significantly with age. As Fig. 16.4 indicates, age and the quality of performance were curvilinearly related, with performance peaking in the mid-30s and early 40s, and showing some decline thereafter, for services of both "simple" and "complex" machines. However, as Warr (1996b) pointed out, the decline in the quality of performance for the 45–54 age group was found only in engineers who had not recently been trained, and not in engineers who had received recent training, suggesting that training may

| TABLE 16.4 | | | | | |
|---|---|---|---|---|---|
| **Age and job performance: Examples of research findings through measures of output.** | | | | | |
| | **Under 25** | **25–34** | **35–44** | **45–54** | **55 and over** |
| 1. Skilled manufacturing operators (USA) | 77 | 85 | 100 | 106 | 106 |
| 2. Semi-skilled assembly workers (USA) | 89 | 87 | 100 | 105 | 101 |
| 3. Mail sorters (USA) | 101 | 102 | 100 | 101 | 99 |
| 4. Office workers (USA) | 92 | 99 | 100 | 99 | 98 |
| 5. Manufacturing machine operators (USA) | 96 | 100 | 100 | 97 | 94 |
| 6. Equipment service engineers (UK) | | 99 | 100 | 94 | |

*Sources:* 1. Giniger, Dispenzieri and Eisenberg, 1983; 2. Schwab and Heneman, 1977; 3. Walker, 1964; 4. Mark, 1957; 5. Kutscher and Walker, 1960; 6. Sparrow and Davies, 1988.

In A.P. Smith & D.M. Jones (Eds.), Handbook of human performance. Volume 3: Trait and state. Wiley. Reprinted with permission.

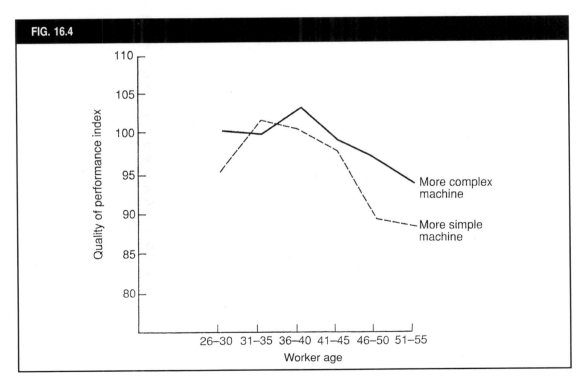

**FIG. 16.4**

The relation between worker age (as shown on the abscissa) and the quality of performance at the most simple and most complex machine complexity levels. From Sparrow & Davies (1988).

attenuate or even abolish any age-related decline in job performance. Speed of performance was affected more strongly by training and tenure than by age, although the youngest group was significantly faster than the other age groups. But for both performance measures, each main effect or interaction involving age accounted for less than 1% of the variance. The curvilinear relation between age and job performance shown in Fig. 16.4 is relatively common in studies of skilled and semi-skilled manual and technical jobs (Davies et al., 1991) but it has also been reported in studies of salespeople (Day, 1993; Kelleher & Quirk, 1973), in studies of publication output in research scientists, although the age at which performance peaks varies with the research domain, with career age usually being a more important factor than chronological age (see Simonton, 1988), and in a study of major league baseball players (Schulz, Musa, Staszewski, & Siegler, 1994).

### 16.7.2 Supervisory ratings

Ratings of job performance by supervisors or managers are less satisfactory than objective measures of output or productivity, since there tends to be unreliability across raters and over time, and ratings can be susceptible to bias on the part of the rater (Cattell & Kline, 1977). However, bias does not necessarily operate against employees who are older than their supervisors (Vecchio, 1993) and age bias may not apply exclusively to older workers (Shore & Bleicken, 1991). Table 16.5 shows the results for supervisors' ratings from the meta-analyses conducted by McEvoy and

Cascio (1989) and Waldman and Avolio (1986). As can be seen from Table 16.5, McEvoy and Cascio obtained a similar result for supervisory ratings to that obtained for productivity measures, a correlation approaching zero between age and job performance. But Waldman and Avolio obtained a modest negative correlation (−0.14), indicating that performance fell slightly with age, the opposite result to that obtained for output measures, although they also reported a small positive correlation (+0.10) between age and performance for peer ratings. Despite the possibility of age bias among raters, several studies have obtained no significant differences in the job performance ratings given to younger and older clerical and industrial workers (for example, Arvey & Muscio, 1973) and such differences are more likely to be observed in studies of managerial and professional jobs (Dalton & Thompson, 1971; Price, Thompson, & Dalton, 1975), although relatively few such studies appear to have been conducted (Salthouse & Maurer, 1996).

### 16.7.3 Age and the determinants of job performance

Findings from investigations of age and job performance using both output records and performance ratings thus indicate that performance in work situations seems to be largely unaffected by worker age, and even when age differences are observed, they are relatively small. This finding is somewhat surprising, since cognitive ability appears to be one of the best predictors of job performance (Salthouse & Maurer, 1996) and, as noted earlier, age-related decrements in cognitive functioning

---

**TABLE 16.5**

Mean correlations ($r$) between age and rating measures of performance reported in two meta-analyses.

| Study | Rating measures | | | | | |
| --- | --- | --- | --- | --- | --- | --- |
| | Supervisor | | Peer | | Non-supervisor | |
| | *N* | *r* | *N* | *r* | *N* | *r* |
| Waldman & Avolio, 1986 | 3,660 | −0.14 | 3,622 | 0.10 | — | — |
| McEvoy & Cascio, 1989 | 18,781 | 0.03 | — | — | 3,227 | −0.09 |

Ratings by supervisors, peers and non-supervisors. Adapted from Davies et al., 1991, p. 168.

can be fairly substantial. Indeed, results from a study of age and synthetic work performance conducted by Salthouse, Hambrick, Lukas and Dell (1996) suggest that more than 70% of the age-related variance in the performance of four moderately-complex synthetic work tasks performed for 25 sessions over a three-day period was shared with measures of information-processing speed obtained prior to task performance. But although cognitive ability is an important determinant of job performance, so too is job experience (Salthouse, 1990a, 1990b; Salthouse & Maurer, 1996), and experience is widely believed to protect performance from the effects of ageing (see Davies et al., 1992). It might therefore be expected that experience—usually measured by tenure, or length of service, which tends to be highly positively correlated with worker age— would counteract the effects of age-related cognitive declines on job performance. Some studies of industrial and clerical jobs have shown that when length of service is controlled for, age effects on performance disappear; conversely, when age is controlled for, the effects of experience remain (for example, Giniger, Dispenzieri, & Eisenberg, 1983). Experience can, therefore, be a stronger predictor of job performance than is age. Studies of drill-press operators (Murrell, Powesland, & Forsaith, 1962), and of simultaneous language translators (Murrell & Humphries, 1978), reported no performance differences between older and younger experienced workers, while finding that inexperienced older adults performed at lower levels than did inexperienced younger adults. However, Salthouse, Babcock, Skovronek, Mitchell and Palmon (1989) obtained age-related declines in spatial visualisation abilities in a group of experienced practising architects as well as in a group of non-architects, suggesting that experience does not invariably counteract the effects of ageing.

Experience has been thought to affect job performance in a number of ways (see Davies et al., 1991; Park, 1992; Salthouse & Maurer, 1996; Warr, 1996b for reviews). First, experience fosters job knowledge and enables the development of general job-related expertise. Second, older workers are likely to have acquired methods of coping with job demands that may tax their cognitive abilities: for example, they may place greater reliance on environmental supports in the workplace, they may make more use of written notes to reduce memory load, and they may adopt strategies for the performance of individual work tasks that "compensate" for perceived ability declines. For example, Salthouse (1984) investigated possible age differences in the performance of skilled transcription typists, obtaining an age-related deficit in choice reaction time, but no age-related decline in typing speed. Using an experimental design that enabled the number of visible "to-be-typed" characters to be controlled, Salthouse was able to demonstrate that, compared to younger typists, older typists looked further ahead in the material to be typed, relying on more extensive anticipation of forthcoming keystrokes, thereby compensating for their declining response speed. Salthouse's findings have been replicated and extended by Bosman (1993). Third, the cognitive integration of component task elements may become more efficient with experience.

Theories of skill acquisition (see Chapter 7) have proposed that skilled performance reflects a process of "compilation", with repeated use of specific items of declarative knowledge resulting in proceduralisation, so that access to such knowledge becomes "automatised". Moreover, automatic processing appears to be relatively unaffected by age (Hasher & Zacks, 1979). Further, through practice, relatively simple task elements may be subsumed into more complex higher-level operations, with the result that performance of the molar task becomes largely independent of the performance of its individual components. For instance, in a study of the effects of practice on the performance of a two-digit mental arithmetic task, Charness and Campbell (1988) found that most of the improvement with practice was due to higher-order learning, rather than an improvement in the speed with which the basic arithmetical operations were carried out. However, in a study of the performance of older and younger experienced word processing operators, Westerman et al. (1998) obtained little evidence for the involvement of compilation, though they did obtain some support for compensation processes.

Finally, if the performance of a job exacerbates perceived age-related deficiencies, then the job may simply be avoided, or eliminated, or delegated to someone else, if the worker is in a position to do so. In a series of studies of the age structure of jobs, conducted in the 1950s, it was shown that older workers tended to be found less frequently in jobs making heavy demands on skills and abilities known to decline with age than would be expected on the basis of population or company employment statistics, and that older workers tended to move to jobs in which these demands were minimised (for example, Belbin, 1953; Murrell & Griew, 1958). Griew (1959) also showed that older workers working in "young" jobs experienced higher accident rates than would be expected. Later research on the age structures of occupations, using United Kingdom census data (Smith, 1975), has strongly suggested that the age structures of occupations reflect the degree of difficulty that job demands make on particular age groups. The sensory, perceptual and cognitive demands of some jobs can pose problems for older workers, though these may be to some extent be alleviated through job redesign (for example, Griew, 1964). Nevertheless, for at least some older workers who continue to perform such jobs, age-related decrements in job performance are likely to be observed. One of the advantages conferred by experience, which may in part explain the higher levels of job satisfaction typically found among older workers (see Davies et al., 1991; Davies & Sparrow, 1985), may be the greater opportunity to match jobs and their component tasks to the individual's perceived abilities.

## 16.8 THEORIES OF AGE DIFFERENCES IN PERFORMANCE

Returning to laboratory studies, where the emphasis is on "maximal" performance, in situations designed to push participants close to their performance limits, rather than the "typical" performance of the work environment, four main conclusions can be drawn from the foregoing brief and selective summary of the effects of ageing on human performance. First, age-related performance differences are sometimes relatively large, as in complex speeded performance or working memory, and sometimes negligible, as in implicit memory tasks or sustained attention. Age-related decrements in human performance would thus seem to be selective rather than general. Second, age-related performance differences are exacerbated when task demands are high, being relatively minimal in simple task situations, but generally substantial in complex ones. Third, in most kinds of human performance, physical fitness, and perhaps other characteristics too, such as intrinsic motivation, can attenuate age-related performance differences, so that the effects of ageing are more apparent in some older adults than in others. Fourth, training can often counteract the effects of ageing on human performance. The beneficial effects of training on the performance of older individuals have been most consistently observed in psychometric tests (see Willis, 1989, for review), but similar results have been reported for tasks used in human performance research, such as divided attention tasks (for example, Kramer et al., 1995). The performance of older adults is therefore not fixed and immutable, but is capable of modification. We now consider some of the explanations that have been put forward to account for age differences in human performance, examining first the role of the brain.

### 16.8.1 Age-related performance differences and age-related changes in the brain

It has been known for some time that frontal regions of the brain tend to be most affected by the process of normal (non-pathological) ageing and the "frontal lobe hypothesis" of cognitive ageing (see West, 1996, for review) suggests that cognitive functions supported by prefrontal cortex, which are among the last to develop in childhood, are also the first to exhibit declines in late adulthood. Such declines are associated with reductions in gross brain volume from the late 50s onwards, resulting from shrinkage of cortical neurons, a loss of dendritic extensions and a decrease in the number of synapses. All these changes are particularly apparent in the frontal lobes (especially the prefrontal cortex), and in the areas with which they are principally connected (such as the basal ganglia and the thalamus), compared to other regions of the brain. In addition, age-related reductions in the rate of cerebral blood flow and in cerebral metabolism occur earlier, and are more pronounced, in the frontal lobes than they are in other brain areas. Task performance that depends upon the integrity of frontal lobe functioning should therefore be associated with larger age-related decrements than should other kinds of performance. Much evidence supports this view: age-related distractibility effects in visual search, age-related interference effects in the Stroop test, age-related prospective memory deficits, and age-related decreases in the ability to manage and coordinate dual-task performance have all been linked to age-related declines in frontal lobe functioning (see Birren & Fisher, 1995; Kramer et al., 1995; West, 1996; Woodruff-Pak, 1997). In conjunction with the hippocampus, the prefrontal cortex is also thought to be the principal brain structure subserving working memory (Woodruff-Pak, 1997).

Inhibitory processes are among the most important functions supported by the frontal lobes, and are thus especially vulnerable to the effects of ageing (see Dempster, 1992). Hasher and Zacks (1988) have advanced an inhibition hypothesis of cognitive ageing, which suggests that as age increases there is a greater weakening of inhibitory processes relative to facilitatory ones. The inhibition hypothesis predicts that the effects of age-related reductions in the efficiency of inhibitory processes should be observed in the performance of a variety of attentional and memory tasks. For example, response competition has been assumed to be the major contributor to Stroop interference (see MacLeod, 1991) and age-related increases in interference have been attributed to reductions in the efficiency of inhibitory processes, which would produce greater susceptibility to interference from irrelevant stimulus dimensions. Hasher and Zacks (1988) also argued that because inhibitory mechanisms are deficient in older individuals it becomes more difficult for them to prevent the intrusion of task-irrelevant information into working memory. Such intrusions effectively reduce the functional capacity of working memory and detract from the processing of task-relevant information. Although Hasher and Zacks's inhibition hypothesis receives support in some task situations, for example, negative priming (see Hasher, Stoltzfus, Zacks, & Rypma, 1991; McDowd & Oseas-Kreger, 1991),

in others support is more limited (Kramer, Humphrey, Larish, & Logan, 1994).

Ageing has also been assumed to affect the timing of neurobiological processes in the central nervous system (see, for example, Birren, 1974). Surwillo (1968) put forward an "internal clock hypothesis", arguing that the EEG alpha rhythm functions as an internal clock or "master timing mechanism" that coordinates neural activities and organises the timing of behaviour. He also noted that the alpha rhythm typically slows with age, from a resting level of around 11–13 Hz per second in young adulthood to a level of 8–10 Hz per second from about the age of 60 onwards (Obrist, 1965; Woodruff-Pak, 1985). Surwillo suggested that the internal clock operates at a slower rate in older individuals and that this slower rate of operation underlies age differences in response slowing. Although Surwillo reported evidence broadly consistent with the internal clock hypothesis, subsequent tests have produced mixed results (Salthouse, Wright, & Ellis, 1979). More recently, Bashore (1990, 1993) has argued that age-related changes in event-related potential (ERP) components, particularly in P300, a positive-going potential peaking approximately 300 ms after the delivery (or expected delivery) of a stimulus, could help to clarify the nature of age-related response slowing. The amplitude and, in particular, the latency of later ERP components, such as P300, are much more likely to be affected by ageing than are the amplitude and latency of earlier components, such as N100. The latency of P300 has been regarded as indexing stimulus-evaluation time. Although the brain structures responsible for generating P300 have yet to be definitively determined, depth electrode recordings and magnetic field studies indicate that the most likely candidate is the medial temporal lobe, probably including the hippocampus, a subcortical structure which is part of the limbic system (see Woodruff-Pak, 1997). Hicks and Birren (1970) reviewed evidence suggesting that a neural system centred on the extrapyramidal centres of the basal ganglia, midbrain and thalamic reticular formation was implicated in response slowing and more recent evidence indicates that changes in subcortical white matter (termed leukoaraiosis) are linked to attention and to the speed of mental processing in older individuals (for example, Ylikoski et al., 1993). In this study the presence of periventricular leukoaraiosis was quite strongly associated with declines in processing speed. White matter changes have also been linked with damage to prefrontal cortex as well as to cerebrovascular risk factors.

## 16.8.2 Psychological interpretations of age-related performance differences

Psychological interpretations of age differences in task performance have tended to associate age-ing with a reduction in processing resources, such as attentional capacity, working memory and processing speed (see, for example, Salthouse, 1988, 1992). While processing resources tend to be vaguely defined, and their mode of operation is seldom specified in any detail, resource-based explanations of age-related declines in cognitive performance have nevertheless become popular in recent years and age-related resource deficits have been invoked to explain age differences in the performance of both attention and memory tasks, such as sustained attention, cued recall, discourse recall and prose comprehension. For example, age deficits in divided attention have been explained in terms of a resource model of attentional allocation (Craik, 1977). Craik sug-gested that processing resources are required to organise the division of attention. He argued that older adults have to commit a larger share of their processing resources to the task of programming the division of attention for multiple inputs, espe-cially when these inputs are complex and demand-ing. In consequence, under conditions of divided attention, particularly if the tasks involved are complex and difficult, older adults will have fewer processing resources available for performing the specific operations required by each task. Age deficits in dual-task performance would therefore be expected, even though neither task produces an age-related performance decrement when performed alone. This explanation assumes that there is no reduction in processing resources with age. If resources diminish as age increases, a greater deficit in dual-task performance would be anticipated.

Resource theory approaches have also been adopted to explain age deficits in explicit memory. It has been suggested, for instance, that due to diminished processing resources, older adults encode information in more general, but less distinctive, less elaborated and less contextually specific ways, thus rendering the encoded event or episode less salient or memorable and hence impairing memory performance (see, for instance, Rabinowitz, Craik, & Ackerman, 1982). While the evidence in support of this view is somewhat mixed (Craik, Anderson, Kerr, & Li, 1995; Light, 1991), older adults do appear to encode contex-tual information less fully and are less likely to remember the context in which specific informa-tion was originally acquired (see Craik & Jennings, 1992). Craik (1986) has argued that remembering reflects an interaction between internal factors (existing memory schemata and self-initiated memory processes) and external factors (the stimu-lus items to be remembered and their associated contexts) and, compared to the memory perform-ance of younger adults, that of older adults relies more heavily on external factors than on internal ones. Moreover, external factors differ in the de-gree of environmental support they provide for encoding and retrieval processes. For example, when evidence of retention is required, recogni-tion memory tasks, in which the stimulus items originally presented are presented again mixed with new items, provide more environmental sup-port for retrieval than do recall tasks, in which the original items are presented only once. Several studies have demonstrated that age differences in recognition tasks are minimal while age differ-ences in recall tasks are substantial (e.g. Craik & McDowd, 1987; Rabinowitz, 1984; Schonfield & Robertson, 1966). Age differences are also greater in free recall tasks than in cued recall (for ex-ample, Craik, Byrd, & Swanson, 1987), a finding which is consistent with the environmental sup-port hypothesis. Also consistent with this hypo-thesis are the findings from prospective memory tasks that age differences are small or non-existent in tasks where external memory aids are used, but relatively substantial when such aids are not available.

To some extent, therefore, environmental sup-port and guidance seem to be able to "compensate" older adults for their relative inability to "self-initiate" effective encoding and retrieval processes in memory situations, an inability which ultimately results from the decline in the efficiency of cortical processing with age (Craik et al., 1995). The performance of tasks providing minimal environmental support is often thought to involve more "effortful" processing, and hence to require more processing resources. A reduction in processing resources may deter older adults from spontaneously adopting effective strategies when performing memory tasks, since the adoption of such strategies is in itself "effortful" and imposes greater demands upon processing resources. For example, older adults are less likely than are younger adults to use mediators in paired-associate tasks, especially imaginal mediators which promote effective learning (Canestrari, 1968). Older adults also rehearse items less frequently in free recall tasks than do younger adults (Sanders, Murphy, Schmitt, & Walsh, 1980) and are less likely to categorise or cluster items in recall.

Resource theory approaches thus seem capable of providing plausible explanations of age differences in the performance of a variety of attention and memory tasks. One difficulty with such approaches is to provide a generally-acceptable definition of processing resources, as indicated in 5.1. Another is to specify the contribution made by processing resources to age-related differences in the performance of different tasks. For instance, on the basis of results from a number of verbal reasoning and spatial ability tasks varying in task complexity, Salthouse, Mitchell, Skovronek and Babcock (1989) concluded that age-related resource reductions accounted for a relatively small proportion (perhaps only around 15–20%) of age-related performance decrements.

## 16.9 CONCLUSIONS

The process of ageing is associated with a variety of deficits, ranging from sensory impairments and response slowing to deficits in working memory

and the performance of demanding attentional tasks. Age differences in the performance of other tasks, such as short-term memory, sustained attention and implicit memory are relatively minor. Although age-related deficits on some laboratory tasks can be sizeable, impairments on real-life tasks tend to be smaller. Age differences in job performance are frequently negligible, although some cognitively demanding jobs, such as vehicle driving, may be sensitive to age effects; older drivers have a higher accident risk per mile driven. There are a variety of reasons why ageing is less maladaptive than laboratory data suggest. Older people are often able to develop strategies that can minimise performance deficits. Training and experience can also compensate for cognitive changes associated with ageing. Finally, there is a higher degree of variability in the performance of older individuals than there is in the performance of younger adults. Older people with physical health problems may exhibit marked age-related performance declines, while physically fit older people may not fall far short of many younger adults in the levels of performance they are capable of achieving.

## FURTHER READING

The book, *Aging and human performance*, edited by Charness (1985), provides the most accessible introduction to the area, while Salthouse (1991) elaborates on cognitive theories of ageing. Like its predecessors, the most recent (fourth) edition of Birren and Schaie's *Handbook of the psychology of aging* (1996) includes contributions from leading researchers in the field. Snel and Cremer's (1994) book comprises various perspectives on work and ageing, including a chapter by Warr on age and job performance. Davies et al. (1991) also provide a review of age and occupational performance. The most influential book on age and skilled performance is Welford's (1958) *Ageing and human skill*.

# Epilogue

We have seen that performance research embraces many seemingly disparate topics, ranging from sensorimotor reflexes to the social psychology of organisations. How can this diversity be integrated within a coherent disciplinary framework? We have argued throughout this book that understanding performance requires appreciation of several levels of discourse. It is a truism, though, that different types of explanation are appropriate for different problems, and coherence requires that we advance beyond this simple recognition. To integrate, we must first discriminate. We proposed in the first chapter that the three levels of explanation proposed by the "classical theory" of cognitive science provide a suitable framework for performance studies. The distinction between neural, cognitive-architectural and knowledge levels allows us to place the many aspects of performance studies within a common framework. Furthermore, although the "classical theory" of cognitive science originated in somewhat technical AI research, it may also serve to guide practice in real-world applications. In both theoretical and applied contexts, the cognitive science framework demands that we are explicit about the level of description required.

This book has attempted to present the complementary accounts of performance seen from the three perspectives, though with a primary focus on the cognitive-architectural perspective. As a conclusion, we briefly summarise the picture of the performer as viewed from each perspective. Each one has its strengths and limitations, and implications for applied psychology.

## THE BIOLOGICAL PERFORMER

Cognitive neuroscience has made great advances, and neuropsychological evidence has already made powerful contributions to cognitive theories of perception, attention, memory and action. In studies of attention, for example, studies of brain-imaging and evoked potentials suggest that the brain is capable of early selection (Luck & Girelli, 1998), and studies of neglect patients seem to favour object- over space-based selection (Driver & Halligan, 1991). Stress, of course, originated as a biological construct (Selye, 1976), but in this context, the pendulum has tended to swing from neural to cognitive explanations for performance effects. In part, disaffection with physiology derives from the problems of arousal theory, but contemporary stress research is informed by a more fine-grained understanding of discrete brain systems. In Chapter 13, for example, we saw how everyday lifestyles involve exposure to biological agents that impinge on performance.

There has been a revival, too, in biological models of individual and group differences. Nobody doubts that ageing effects reflect loss of neural function, but the notion of inherited individual differences in ability and personality has long been a source of contention. In fact, the steady accumulation of behaviour genetic findings and, increasingly, molecular genetic evidence makes it difficult to question the partial heritability of traits. Again, such evidence constrains the range of cognitive theories possible. If intelligence is partly inherited, it is unlikely to be solely an expression of cultural values or quality of education although, of course, social-cultural factors are likely to be important. The challenge has been to find the neural functions sensitive to genetic influences, and mapping the pathways from genes to proteins to neural operations remains to be accomplished. At the same time, cognitive science theory indicates the limitations of a purely neuropsychological approach. Sometimes, it seems as though biological studies fall into a crude reductionism whereby localising a function is seen as "explaining" it. PET-scanning studies tell us which brain areas are active while the person is performing a working memory task, but they do not indicate either the neural or the information-processing operations that support working memory. Psychophysiological studies of this kind are necessarily correlational. Experimental studies, for example of drug effects, have the disadvantage that it is very hard to control for cognitions and expectancies; even within the double-blind design, participants in studies form beliefs which may be confounded with manipulations (Kirsch & Weixel, 1988).

There is also the fundamental difficulty, discussed by Pylyshyn (1984), that information-processing functions are not necessarily reducible to physical processes in any straightforward way. It may not be possible to infer the rules that govern software operation by investigating the hardware. In this context, the tacit assumptions of neurological and information-processing researchers seem to differ. Neurological researchers often seem to assume that there are simple mappings between neural operations and processing codes, as explored by Gray (1982) in animal studies and Rolls (1998) in human studies of memory and emotion. Some cognitive psychological researchers are more sceptical that useful neural-level descriptions of processing are easily attained. There may not be any simple mappings between neural firings and propositional codes (Pylyshyn, 1984). Anderson (1990) suggests that there may even be problems in modelling the functional architecture of communication channels and memory structures that might map onto neural systems, advocating instead a focus on the algorithmic rules for symbol processing.

Some applications are directly related to cognitive neuropsychological research, such as rehabilitation for brain-damaged patients, and attempts to minimise the behavioural impairments consequent upon Alzheimer's disease and other degenerative illness of ageing. Very often, however, the impact of biological agents on real-world behaviours is modified by cognitive factors, such as expectancies, as discussed under the heading of stress research. Hence, biologically-based interventions in real-world problems, such as the "neuroergonomic" techniques listed in Table 1.1, must be informed in two different respects. First, intervention must be guided by the reasonably fine-grained understanding of brain functioning afforded by contemporary studies. Crude attempts to influence brain function, such as adminstration of amphetamine as a stimulant to night-workers, tend to have disadvantages which outweigh their advantages. In contrast, efforts to develop better shiftwork regimes based on understanding of circadian oscillators (see 12.4.5) are more likely to enhance performance and wellbeing without side-effects. Second, intervention should be informed by cognitive moderation of neural processing. For example, Parasuraman and Greenwood (1998) discuss evidence that persons with early Alzheimer's disease show little impairment in moving attention to a cued location, but have difficulty in disengaging attention subsequently. Hence, although the deficit has a neural origin, perhaps it may be countered by careful attention to the cues to spatial attention offered in real-world settings. Perhaps disengagement could be explicitly trained, or supplementary cues provided.

In sum, neural and cognitive approaches have much to gain from mutual communication. The combination of neuropsychological methods with those of cognitive psychology and connectionist models provides a powerful set of techniques for obtaining converging lines of evidence on at least some aspects of performance.

## THE INFORMATION-PROCESSING PERFORMER

The application of cognitive psychology to attention, memory and skill has been accepted for several decades. More recently, it has become accepted as one of several approaches to understanding stress effects and individual differences in performance. In Pylyshyn's (1984) formulation, the symbol-processing algorithm enables cognitive functioning, and the functional architecture of real-time processing operations constrains speed of processing, memory and so forth. Performance psychology is concerned especially with the constraints on processing. We have seen how capacity limits on attention and memory are a central concern of the field. Similarly, stress and individual difference research is most often focused on suboptimal performance. Task manipulations derived from cognitive theory are critical: patterns of performance are readily altered by varying attentional demands, memory loads and stimulus representation. Such factors moderate the impact of stressors, and correlations between individual difference factors and performance.

The hope of cognitive psychology is that the moderating effects of task parameters will inform understanding of the architecture. Various architectural constructs have been widely, if not universally, accepted as elements of a larger system, including a selective attention process intervening between early and later stages of processing, distinctions between codes such as phonemic and semantic codes, short-term memory stores, the response-selection bottleneck identified in PRP studies, and some controlling executive system.

The power of such constructs is that they prove to generalise beyond the specific experimental paradigms which spawned them. Baddeley's (1986) working memory construct has informed understanding of stress, mood and ageing effects on performance. Measures of working memory are substantially correlated with intelligence (Kyllonen & Chrystal, 1990), and with various real world tasks (Daneman & Merikle, 1996).

At the same time, there is a tradeoff between rigour and applicability. Pashler (1998), for example, makes a strong argument that the response bottleneck is more strongly supported by experimental evidence than is performance-limitation by a graded resource. Nevertheless it is the resource construct that has had more influence on theories of stress and individual differences, and on human factors practice. There might be various reasons for the limited impact of many processing models outside their own immediate domain of application. However, perhaps cognitive psychology has difficulty capturing generalised aspects of processing that may affect many tasks, which are often precisely those aspects relevant to applied performance studies. We have seen in this book that energetic metaphors, such as resource allocation, are central to understanding stress and individual differences, for example.

As suggested in Chapter 1, information-processing models may be necessary but insufficient. We have already discussed the contribution of cognitive neuropsychology, although there is considerable disagreement on how much weight should be given to neuropsychological evidence in constructing models of the cognitive architecture. Conversely, information-processing models are incomplete without an understanding of strategy and voluntary control of performance. Here, stress research has led the way. There is ample evidence that the effects of stressors such as noise on performance often cannot be understood without an appreciation of the operator's intentions and beliefs about what constitutes success on the task (Jones, 1984; Rabbitt, 1979). Performance research must focus not only on what the operator *can* do (i.e. within the constraints set by the architecture), but on what the operator *chooses* to do within a given context, which is a knowledge-level question.

## THE INTENTIONAL PERFORMER

Cognitive psychologists have often viewed with suspicion the issues of intentionality associated with the knowledge level of explanation. The notion of voluntary control seems to invoke an homunculus with the free will to command the programs of the mind as it chooses. The whole point of developing a computational model is to show that a given behaviour can be reproduced without reference to such dubious notions. Furthermore, constructs related to intentionality raise methodological problems. In stress research, for example, the concept of "strategy" has been abused as a post hoc "fudge factor" when results fail to conform to expectation.

Nevertheless, performance researchers cannot avoid the observation that intentions and strategies make a difference. Performance often reflects not just the psychophysical parameters of the task, but the motivations, attitudes and expectancies that the person brings to the task environment. In some contexts, it may be possible to reduce or control such factors, but the performance psychologist does not have this luxury. Strategy use is expressed in such basic findings as the speed–accuracy tradeoff and in reactions to stress and mood states. Most often, performance deficits are accompanied by attempts to implement a compensatory strategy. In practical settings, as discussed in 1.4.1, the person's goals and willingness to apply effort are often as important as their processing capabilities.

In part, such problems are addressed by modelling control structures within the cognitive architecture, i.e. by specifying specific executive processes, including the inputs that initiate executive processing and their outputs, as codes sent to other processing units. However, the thrust of Pylyshyn's (1984) and Newell's (1980) argument is that modelling of this kind does not address the issue of the personal meanings of external events which is supported by computation. For this reason, a *relational perspective* is integral to the knowledge level of explanation. For example, the transactional model of stress (see Chapter 9) sees emotions and other stress reactions (including performance change) as an expression of the relation between person and environment. Similar ideas are expressed by Neisser's (1976) concept of a perceptual-action cycle supporting dynamic interaction between the person and the stimulus field, and "ecological" approaches that seek to place performance in adaptive context (Gibson, 1979). Nevertheless, it is important to maintain computational rigour as far as possible, for example by linking "strategy" in the sense of a goal-directed intention to task strategies described computationally.

The knowledge level also links performance to wider societal and cultural concerns. The well-known "Hawthorne effect" refers to the supposed tendency of almost any workplace intervention, such as adding a few potted plants, to improve performance (Yorks & Whitsett, 1985). In fact, the power of the Hawthorne effect is often overstated, but it points to the importance of the personal meanings that workers infer, e.g. about management's concern for their wellbeing. Hancock (1997) has provided a penetrating account of the symbiotic relationship between humans and machines that discusses changing societal attitudes towards machines as technology evolves. He highlights the importance of autonomy and control as a key factor in maintaining job satisfaction. New technology is potentially dangerous in that the reallocation of operator functions from person to machine reduces the person to a tool of the machine and, ultimately, to a slave. As we saw in 8.2.1, automated systems that alter the operator's role from skilled executive to passive monitor are both stressful and prone to operator failure. Conversely, technology is potentially beneficial in allowing more intelligent allocation of functions between person and machine. Hancock (1997, pp. 136–137) suggests some tentative guidelines for making jobs more worthwhile, as listed here:

- Work should be structured to "afford" enjoyment
- The provision of autonomy and choice are critical design characteristics of all work
- Work should be paced by operators, not machines

- Interfaces should be adaptive. Both the physical workstation and the information interface should permit and promote individual customisation
- Tasks should present challenge and promote safe exploration of possible operational states
- Rote tasks with no variation are direct candidates for automation
- Tasks should be designed such that the prescribed goals of operation provide intrinsic satisfaction in their achievement
- The operator should be involved in the design of tasks and especially in how the required system functions are mapped to interface characteristics.

The operator's intentions are central to the guidelines, in that they emphasise personal choice, and some scope for pursuing personally-significant goals within the work environment. As Hancock (1997) also notes, design issues must be seen within a broader social context. He points towards the dangers of a part of the population being computer-literate, and the remainder incompetent with information technology.

## THE FUTURE OF HUMAN PERFORMANCE RESEARCH

The diversity of performance research is both a threat and a challenge. The threat is one of fractionation between sub-disciplines speaking in many tongues with little mutual comprehension. The challenge is that of developing a psychological science that is both theoretically coherent and directly applicable to practical problems. Much essential work remains to be done within each level of explanation, in understanding neural function, information processing and human motivations and adaptation. Cognitive science promotes communication between different levels of theory, and avoidance of category errors, such as confusions between neurological and symbol-manipulation models.

However, the most exciting frontiers of performance research may be located at the interfaces between levels. We have highlighted the role of connectionism in bridging the explanatory divide between neural and cognitive-architectural levels, and the strategy concept as a link between architecture and the knowledge level. Matthews (1997a) suggests that evolutionary psychology may link the neural and knowledge levels, i.e. that intentions are shaped by the neural competences provided by natural selection, as well as by social and cultural factors. The practitioner certainly has an awareness of the different levels of explanation for cognitive phenomena. Interface design, for example, requires understanding of biological ergonomics, of human processing limitations and, as indicated in Hancock's (1997) guidelines, the operator's needs for autonomy and satisfaction of personal goals.

Performance research also requires a greater understanding of the dynamic interplay between person and task, over various time periods. The traditional, discrete-trial experimental psychology study is singularly ill-suited to investigating such issues. Over short time periods, trial-to-trial feedback is evidently important in regulating speed–accuracy tradeoff (3.2.4), in skill acquisition (7.5.2) and in moderating motivational effects of performance (9.5.2). Over intervals of minutes or hours, person–task interaction is critical in the development and progression of stress reactions. As discussed in Chapter 9, task characteristics influence physiological and subjective stress responses, which in turn feed back to influence performance outcome, both through exceeding architectural limitations on processing, and through self-regulation and strategy choice. Over intervals of several months, the person's habitual style of coping with a particular environment involves a mutual shaping. The cognitions of an individual starting a new job are progressively moulded by the demands of work and the training they receive, but the person also influences job characteristics so far as is possible to meet their personal needs. Skill acquisition involves not only increased competence for performance but changing attitudes and emotions in the work context, and the growing capability to influence environmental demands. Finally, as Hancock (1997) discusses, over periods of years there is a mutual interplay between people and technology. Machines are (for the present) designed by people, but people's experiences of technology shape social attitudes, which in turn feed back into design priorities. Hancock (1997) sees the mismatch between the growth of human and machine capabilities as a powerful driver of social change. If so, human performance psychology has important contributions to make not only to task design and training, but also to personal and societal development.

# References

Ackerman, P.L. (1987). Individual differences in skill learning: An integration of psychometric and information processing perspectives. *Psychological Bulletin, 102,* 3–27.

Ackerman, P.L. (1988). Determinants of individual differences during skill acquisition: Cognitive abilities and information processing. *Journal of Experimental Psychology: General, 117,* 288–318.

Ackerman, P.L. (1992). Predicting individual differences in complex skill acquisition: Dynamics of ability determinants. *Journal of Applied Psychology, 77,* 598–614.

Ackerman, P.L. (1996). A theory of adult intellectual development: Process, personality, interests, and knowledge. *Intelligence, 22,* 227–257.

Ackerman, P.L. (1999). Traits and knowledge as determinants of learning and individual differences: Putting it all together. In P.L. Ackerman, P.C. Kyllonen & R.D. Roberts (Eds.), *Learning and individual differences: Process, trait, and content determinants.* Washington, DC: American Psychological Association.

Ackerman, P.L., Kyllonen, P.C., & Roberts, R.D. (Eds.) (1999). *Learning and individual differences: Process, trait, and content determinants.* Washington, DC: American Psychological Association.

Ackerman, P.L., Schneider, W., & Wickens, C.D. (1984). Deciding the existence of a time-sharing ability: A combined theoretical and methodological approach. *Human Factors, 26,* 71–82.

Adams, J.A. (1963). *Experimental studies of human vigilance.* U.S. Airforce Technical Document Report, No. FSD-TDR, 63–320.

Adams, J.A. (1971). A closed-loop theory of motor learning. *Journal of Motor Behavior, 3,* 111–150.

Adams, J.A. (1976). Issues for a closed-loop theory of motor learning. In G.E. Stelmach (Ed.), *Motor control: Issues and trends.* London: Academic.

Adams, M.J., Tenney, Y.J., & Pew, R.W. (1995). Situation awareness and the cognitive management of complex systems. *Human Factors, 37,* 85–104.

Ainsworth, W.A. (1985). Noise and communication. In W. Tempest (Ed.), *The noise handbook.* London: Academic.

Akerstedt, T. (1988). Sleepiness as a consequence of shift work. *Sleep, 11,* 17–34.

Aleksander, I., & Morton, H. (1993). *Neurons and symbols: The stuff that mind is made of.* London: Chapman & Hall.

Alferdinck, J.W.A.M. (1996). Traffic safety aspects of high-intensity discharge headlamps: Discomfort glare and direction indicator conspicuity. In A.G. Gale (Ed.), *Vision in vehicles V.* Amsterdam: Elsevier.

Alloy, L.B., & Abramson, L.Y. (1988). Depressive realism: Four theoretical perspectives. In L.B. Alloy (Ed.), *Cognitive processes in depression.* New York: Guilford Press.

Allport, A. (1980). Attention and performance. In G. Claxton (Ed.), *Cognitive psychology: New directions.* London: Routledge.

Allport, A. (1989). Visual attention. In M.I. Posner (Ed.), *Foundations of cognitive science.* Cambridge, MA: MIT Press.

Allport, A. (1992). Attention and control: Have we been asking the wrong questions? A critical review of twenty-five years. In D.E. Meyer & S. Kornblum

(Eds.), *Attention and Performance XIV*. Cambridge, MA: MIT Press.

Allport, D.A., Antonis, B., & Reynolds, P. (1972). On the division of attention: A disproof of the single-channel hypothesis. *Quarterly Journal of Experimental Psychology, 24*, 255–265.

Amelang, M., & Ullwer, U. (1991). Correlations between psychometric measures and psychophysiological as well as experimental variables in studies on extraversion and neuroticism. In J. Strelau & A. Angleitner (Eds.), *Explorations in temperament*. New York: Plenum.

Anastasi, A., & Urbina, S. (1997). *Psychological testing (7th Ed.)*. Englewood Cliffs, NJ: Prentice Hall.

Anderson, J. (1980). *Cognitive psychology and its implications* (pp. 225–226). New York: Freeman.

Anderson, J.R. (1982). Acquisition of cognitive skill. *Psychological Review, 89*, 369–406.

Anderson, J.R. (1983). *The architecture of cognition*. Hillsdale, NJ: Lawrence Erlbaum Associates Inc.

Anderson, J.R. (1987). Skill acquisition: Compilation of weak-method problem situations. *Psychological Review, 94*, 192–210.

Anderson, J.R. (1990). *The adaptive character of thought*. Hillsdale, NJ: Lawrence Erlbaum Associates Inc.

Anderson, J.R. (1993). *Rules of the mind*. Hillsdale, NJ: Lawrence Erlbaum Associates Inc.

Anderson, J.R. (1995). *Cognitive psychology*. New York: Freeman.

Anderson, J.R., & Bower, G.H. (1973). *Human associative memory*. Washington, DC: V.H. Winston & Sons.

Anderson, J.R., Kline, P.J., & Beasley, C.M., Jr. (1980). Complex learning processes. In R.E. Snow, P.-A. Federico & W.E. Montague (Eds.), *Aptitude, learning and instruction: Vol. 2 Cognitive process analyses of learning and problem-solving*. Hillsdale, NJ: Erlbaum.

Anderson, J.R., & Reder, L.M. (1979). An elaborative processing explanation of levels of processing. In L.S. Cermak & F.I.M. Craik (Eds.), *Levels of processing in human memory*. Hillsdale, NJ: Lawrence Erlbaum Associates Inc.

Anderson, K.J. (1990). Arousal and the inverted-U hypothesis: A critique of Neiss's "Reconceptualizing arousal". *Psychological Bulletin, 107*, 96–100.

Anderson, M. (1992). *Intelligence and development: A cognitive theory*. Oxford: Blackwell.

Anderson, N., & Herriot, P. (Eds.) (1997). *International handbook of selection and appraisal (2nd ed.)*. London: John Wiley & Sons Ltd.

Anderson, S.J., & Holliday, I.E. (1995). Night driving: Effects of glare from vehicle headlights on motion perception. *Ophthalmic and Physiological Optics, 15*, 545–551.

Annett, J. (1982). Action, language and imagination. In L. Wankel & R.B. Wilberg (Eds.), *Psychology of sport and motor behavior* (pp. 271–281). Edmonton, Canada: University of Alberta.

Annett, J. (1991). Skill acquisition. In J.E. Morrison (Ed.), *Training for performance* (pp. 13–51). Chichester, UK: John Wiley.

Annett, J. (1993). The learning of motor skills: Sports science and ergonomics perspectives. *Ergonomics, 37*, 5–16.

Annett, J., & Kay, H. (1956). Skilled performance. *Occupational Psychology, 30*, 112–117.

Angus, R.G., Heslegrave, R.J., & Myles, W.S. (1985). Effects of prolonged sleep deprivation, with and without chronic physical exercise, on mood and performance. *Psychophysiology, 22*, 276–282.

Anton, W.D., & Klisch, M.C. (1995). Perspectives on mathematics anxiety and test anxiety. In C.D. Spielberger & P.R. Vagg (Eds.), *Test anxiety: Theory, assessment, and treatment*. Washington, DC: Taylor & Francis.

APA Public Affairs Office (1997). *Intelligence: Knowns and unknowns*. Washington, DC: American Psychological Association.

Arbous, A.G., & Kerrich, J.E. (1951). Accident statistics and the concept of accident proneness. *Biometrics, 7*, 340–429.

Aretz, A.J., Johannsen, C., & Obser, K. (1996). An empirical validation of subjective workload ratings. In *Proceedings of the Human Factors and Ergonomics Society 40th Annual Meeting*. Santa Monica, CA: HF&ES.

Argyle, M., Martin, M., & Crossland, J. (1989). Happiness as a function of personality and social encounters. In J.P. Forgas & J.M. Innes (Eds.), *Recent advances in social psychology: An international perspective*. North Holland: Elsevier.

Arthur, W., Jr., Barrett, G.V., & Alexander, R.A. (1991). Prediction of vehicular accident involvement: A meta-analysis. *Human Performance, 4*, 89–105.

Arthur, W., Jr., Barrett, G.V., & Doverspike, D. (1990). Validation of an information-processing-based test battery for the prediction of handling accidents among petroleum transport drivers. *Journal of Applied Psychology, 75*, 621–628.

Arthur, W., Jr., & Doverspike, D. (1992). Locus of control and auditory selective attention as predictors of driving accident involvement: A comparative longitudinal investigation. *Journal of Safety Research, 23,* 73–80.

Arthur, W., Jr., & Graziano, W.G. (1996). The five-factor model: Conscientiousness and driving accident involvement. *Journal of Personality, 64,* 593–618.

Arvey, R.D., & Muscio, S.J. (1973). Test discrimination, job performance, and age. *Industrial Gerontology, 16,* 2–29.

Ashby, W.R. (1956). *An introduction to cybernetics.* London: Chapman & Hall.

Asso, D. (1987). Cyclical variations. In M.A. Baker (Ed.), *Sex differences in human performance.* Chichester: John Wiley & Sons Ltd.

Astley, R.W., & Fox, J.G. (1975). The analysis of an inspection task in the rubber industry. In C.G. Drury & J.G. Fox (Eds.), *Human reliability in quality control.* London: Taylor & Francis.

Atkinson, J.W. (1974). Strength of motivation and efficiency of performance. In J.W. Atkinson & J.O. Rayner (Eds.), *Motivation and achievement.* Washington, DC: Winston.

Atkinson, R.C., & Shiffrin, R.M. (1968). Human memory: A proposed system and its control processes. In K. Spence & J. Spence (Eds.), *The psychology of learning and motivation (Vol. 2).* New York: Academic.

Babkoff, H., Caspy, T., & Mikulincer, M. (1991). Subjective sleepiness ratings: The effects of sleep deprivation, circadian rhythmicity and cognitive performance. *Sleep, 14,* 534–539.

Babkoff, H., Mikulincer, M., Caspy, T., & Kempinski, D. (1988). The topology of performance curves during 72 hours of sleep loss: A memory and search task. *Quarterly Journal of Experimental Psychology: Human Experimental Psychology, 40A,* 737–756.

Baddeley, A.D. (1986). *Working memory.* Oxford: Oxford University Press.

Baddeley, A.D. (1990). *Human memory: Theory and practice.* Boston, MA: Allyn & Bacon, Inc.

Baddeley, A.D. (1993). Working memory or working attention? In A.D. Baddeley & L. Weiskrantz, (Eds.), *Attention: Selection, awareness, and control: A tribute to Donald Broadbent.* Oxford: Oxford University Press.

Baddeley, A.D. (1996). Exploring the central executive. *Quarterly Journal of Experimental Psychology: Human Experimental Psychology, 49A,* 5–28.

Baddeley, A.D. (1997). *Human memory: Theory and practice.* Hove, UK: Psychology Press.

Baddeley, A.D., & Colquhoun, W.P. (1969). Signal probability and vigilance: A reappraisal of the "signal rate" effect. *British Journal of Psychology, 60,* 165–178.

Baddeley, A.D., & Della Sala, S. (1998). Working memory and executive control. In A.C. Roberts & T.W. Robbins (Eds.), *The prefrontal cortex: Executive and cognitive functions.* New York: Oxford University Press.

Baddeley, A.D., & Hitch, G. (1974). Working memory. In G. Bower (Ed.), *Recent advances in learning and motivation.* New York: Academic.

Baddeley, A.D., & Hitch, G. (1977). Recency re-examined. In S. Dornic (Ed.), *Attention and performance VI.* Hillsdale, NJ: Lawrence Erlbaum Associates Inc.

Baddeley, A.D., & Weiskrantz, L. (Eds.) (1993). *Attention: Selection, awareness, and control: A tribute to Donald Broadbent.* Oxford: Oxford University Press.

Baenninger, M., & Newcombe, N. (1989). The role of experience in spatial test performance: A meta-analysis. *Sex Roles, 20,* 327–344.

Bahrick, H.P., & Shelly, C. (1958). Time sharing as an index of automatization. *Journal of Experimental Psychology, 56,* 288–293.

Bainbridge, L. (1978). Forgotten alternatives in skill and workload. *Ergonomics, 21,* 169–185.

Bakan, P. (1959). Extroversion-introversion and improvement in an auditory vigilance task. *British Journal of Psychology, 50,* 325–332.

Baker, C.H. (1959). Towards a theory of vigilance. *Canadian Journal of Psychology, 13,* 35–42.

Baker, C.H. (1962). On temporal extrapolation. *Canadian Journal of Psychology, 16,* 37–41.

Baker, C.H. (1963a). Signal duration as a factor in vigilance tasks. *Science, 141,* 1296–1297.

Baker, C.H. (1963b). Further toward a theory of vigilance. In D.N. Buckner & J.J. McGrath (Eds.), *Vigilance: A symposium.* New York: McGraw Hill.

Baker, M.A., & Holding, D.H. (1993). The effects of noise and speech on cognitive task performance. *Journal of General Psychology, 120,* 339–355.

Bakkevig, M.K., & Nielsen, R. (1994). Impact of wet underwear on thermoregulatory responses and thermal comfort in the cold. *Ergonomics, 37,* 1375–1389.

Banderet, L.E., & Burse, R.L. (1991). Effects of high terrestrial altitude on military performance. In R. Gal & A.D. Mangelsdorff (Eds.), *Handbook of military psychology.* Chichester: John Wiley & Sons Ltd.

Bandura, A. (1986). *Social foundations of thought and action: A social cognitive theory.* Englewood Cliffs, NJ: Prentice-Hall.

Bandura, A. (1989). Human agency in social cognitive theory. *American Psychologist, 44,* 1175–1184.

Banich, M.T. (1998). The missing link: The role of interhemispheric interaction in attentional processing. *Brain and Cognition, 36*, 128–157.

Banquet, J.P, Gaussier, P., Dreher, J.C., Joulain, C., Revel, A., & Günther, W. (1997). Space-time, order, and hierarchy in fronto-hippocampal system: A neural basis for personality. In G. Matthews (Ed.), *Cognitive science perspectives on personality and emotion*. Amsterdam: Elsevier.

Bargh, J.A. (1992). The ecology of automaticity: Toward establishing the conditions needed to produce automatic processing effects. *American Journal of Psychology, 105*, 181–199.

Barr, R.A., & Giambra, L.W. (1990). Age-related decrement in auditory selective attention. *Psychology and Aging, 5*, 597–599.

Barrick, M.R., & Mount, M.K. (1991). The Big Five personality dimensions and job performance: A meta-analysis. *Personnel Psychology, 44*, 1–26.

Barrick, M.R., & Mount, M.K. (1993). Autonomy as a moderator of the relationships between the Big Five personality dimensions and job performance. *Journal of Applied Psychology, 78*, 111–118.

Barrick, M.R., Mount, M.K., & Strauss, J.P. (1993). Conscientiousness and performance of sales representatives: Test of the mediating effects of goal setting. *Journal of Applied Psychology, 78*, 715–722.

Bartlett, F.C. (1932). *Remembering: A study in experimental and social psychology*. Cambridge: Cambridge University Press.

Bartlett, F.C. (1943). Fatigue following highly skilled work. *Proceedings of the Royal Society (B), 131*, 147–257.

Bartley, S. H., & Chute, E. (1947). *Fatigue and impairment in man*. New York: McGraw-Hill.

Bartram, D., & Dale, H. (1982). The Eysenck Personality Inventory as a selection test for military pilots. *Journal of Occupational Psychology, 55*, 287–296.

Bashore, T.R. (1990). Age-related changes in mental processing revealed by analyses of event-related brain potentials. In J.W. Rohrbaugh & R. Parasuraman (Eds.), *Event-related brain potentials: Basic issues and applications*. New York: Oxford University Press.

Bashore, T.R. (1993). Differential effects of aging on the neuro-cognitive functions subserving speeded mental processing. In J. Cerella, J.M. Rybash, W.J. Hoyer & M.L. Commons (Eds.), *Adult information processing: Limits on loss*. San Diego, CA: Academic.

Baumeister, R.F. (1984). Choking under pressure: Self-consciousness and paradoxical effects of incentives on skillful performance. *Journal of Personality and Social Psychology, 46*, 610–620.

Baylis, G.C., & Driver, J. (1993). Visual attention and objects: Evidence for hierarchical coding of location. *Journal of Experimental Psychology: Human Perception and Performance, 19*, 451–470.

Beatty, J. (1982). Task-evoked pupillary responses, processing load, and the structure of processing resources. *Psychological Bulletin, 91*, 276–292.

Beatty, J. (1986). Computation, control and energetics: A biological perspective. In G.R.J Hockey, A.W.K Gaillard & M.G.H. Coles (Eds.), *Energetics and human information processing*. Dordrecht: Martinus Nijhoff.

Becker, A.B., Warm, J.S., Dember, W.N., & Hancock, P.A. (1995). Effects of jet engine noise and performance feedback on perceived workload in a monitoring task. *International Journal of Aviation Psychology, 5*, 49–62.

Becker, A.B., Warm, J.S., Dember, W.N., & Howe, S. (1994). Specific and non-specific transfer effects in training for vigilance. In M. Mouloua & R. Parasuraman (Eds.), *Human performance in automated systems: Current research and trends*. Mahwah, NJ: Lawrence Erlbaum Associates Inc.

Beech, A., & Williams, L. (1997). Investigating cognitive processes in schizotypal personality and schizophrenia. In G. Matthews (Ed.), *Cognitive science perspectives on personality and emotion*. Amsterdam: Elsevier.

Beh, H.C., Connelly, N., & Charles, M. (1997). Effect of noise stress on chronic fatigue syndrome patients. *Journal of Nervous and Mental Disease, 185*, 55–58.

Belbin, R.M. (1953). Difficulties of older people in industry. *Occupational Psychology, 27*, 177–190.

Bell, P.A. (1978). Effects of noise and heat stress on primary and subsidiary task performance. *Human Factors, 20*, 749.

Bellenkes, A.H., Wickens, C.D., & Kramer, A.F. (1997). Visual scanning and pilot expertise: The role of attentional flexibility and mental model development. *Aviation, Space, and Environmental Medicine, 68*, 569–579.

Benignus, V.A., Otto, D.A., & Knelson, J.H. (1975). Effect of low frequency random noises on performance of a numeric monitoring task. *Perceptual and Motor Skills, 40*, 231–239.

Bennett, K.B., & Flach, J.M. (1992). Graphical displays: Implications for divided attention, focused attention, and problem solving. *Human Factors, 34*, 513–533.

Benton, D. (1995). Do low cholesterol levels slow mental processing? *Psychosomatic Medicine, 57*, 50–53.

Benton, D., & Owens, D.S. (1993). Blood glucose and human memory. *Psychopharmacology, 113*, 83–88.

Berlyne, D.E., Borsa, D.M., Hamacher, J.H., & Koenig, I.D.V. (1966). Paired-associate learning and the timing of arousal. *Journal of Experimental Psychology, 72*, 1–6.

Berrien, F.K. (1946). The effects of noise. *Psychological Bulletin, 43*, 141–161.

Berry, D.C., & Broadbent, D.E. (1988). Interactive tasks and the implicit-explicit distinction. *British Journal of Psychology, 79*, 251–272.

Bertelson, P., & Joffe, R. (1963). Blockings in prolonged serial responding. *Ergonomics, 6*, 109–116.

Bettner, L.G., Jarvik, L.F., & Blum, J.E. (1971). Stroop color-word test, nonpsychotic organic brain syndrome, and chromosome loss in aged twins. *Journal of Gerontology, 26*, 458–469.

Biederman, I. (1995). Visual object recognition. In S. Kosslyn & D.N. Osherson (Eds.), *Visual cognition: An invitation to cognitive science (Vol. 2) (2nd ed.)*. Cambridge, MA: MIT Press.

Billings, M.L. (1914). The duration of attention. *Psychological Review, 21*, 121–135.

Bills, A.G. (1934). *Human experimental psychology*. New York: Longman-Green.

Binet, A. (1903). *L'étude experimentale de l'intelligence*. Paris: Schleicher et Frenes.

Birren, J.E. (1965). Age changes in speed of behavior: Its central nature and physiological correlates. In A.T. Welford & J.E. Birren (Eds.), *Behavior, aging and the nervous system*. Springfield, IL: Charles C. Thomas.

Birren, J.E. (1974). Translations in gerontology—from lab to life: Psychophysiology and speed of response. *American Psychologist, 29*, 808–815.

Birren, J.E., & Botwinick, J. (1955). Age differences in finger, jaw, and foot reaction time to auditory stimuli. *Journal of Gerontology, 10*, 429–432.

Birren, J.E., & Fisher, L.M. (1995). Aging and speed of behavior: Possible consequences for psychological functioning. *Annual Review of Psychology, 46*, 329–353.

Birren, J.E., & Schaie, K.W. (Eds.) (1977). *Handbook of the psychology of aging*. New York: Van Nostrand Reinhold.

Birren, J.E., & Schaie, K.W. (Eds.). (1985). *Handbook of the psychology of aging (2nd ed.)*. New York: Van Nostrand Reinhold.

Birren, J.E., & Schaie, K.W. (Eds.) (1992). *Handbook of the psychology of aging (3rd ed.)*. San Diego, CA: Academic Press.

Birren, J.E., & Schaie, K.W. (Eds.) (1996). *Handbook of the psychology of aging (4th ed.)*. San Diego, CA: Academic Press.

Bjork, E.L., & Bjork, R.A. (Eds.) (1996). *Memory*. San Diego, CA: Academic Press.

Blackburn, J.M. (1936). *Acquisition of skill: An analysis of learning curves*. Industrial Health Research Board Report No. 73. London: HMSO.

Blackman, J.D., Towle, V.L., Lewis, G.F., Spire, J.P., & Polonsky, K.S. (1990). Hypoglycaemic thresholds for cognitive dysfunction in humans. *Diabetes, 39*, 828–835.

Blair, W.C., & Kaufman, M. (1959). Command control: I Multiple display monitoring. II Control-display spatial arrangement. *Electric Boat Technical Report, No. SPD-59-082*.

Blake, M.J.F. (1967). Time of day effects on performance in a range of tasks. *Psychonomic Science, 9*, 349–350.

Blaney, P.H. (1986). Affect and memory: A review. *Psychological Bulletin, 99*, 229–246.

Blockey, P.N., & Hartley, L.R. (1995). Aberrant driver behaviour: Errors and violations. *Ergonomics, 38*, 1759–1771.

Blumberg, M., & Pringle, C.D. (1982). The missing opportunity in organizational research: Some implications for a theory of work performance. *Academy of Management Review, 7*, 560–569.

Bobko N., Karpenko A., Gerasimov A., & Chernyuk V. (1998). The mental performance of shiftworkers in nuclear and heat power plants of Ukraine. *International Journal of Industrial Ergonomics, 21*, 333–340.

Boekaerts, M. (1995). The interface between intelligence and personality as determinants of classroom learning. In D. Saklofske & M.S. Zeidner (Eds.), *International handbook of personality and intelligence*. New York: Plenum.

Boggs, D.H., & Simon, J.R. (1968). Differential effect of noise on tasks of varying complexity. *Journal of Applied Psychology, 52*, 148–153.

Boles, D.B., & Law, M.B. (1998). A simultaneous task comparison of differentiated and undifferentiated hemispheric resource theories. *Journal of Experimental Psychology: Human Perception and Performance, 24:1*, 204–215.

Bond, L., & Glaser, R. (1979). ATI but mostly A and T with not much I. *Applied Psychological Measurement, 3*, 137–140.

Bonnet, M.H., Johnson, L.C., & Webb, W.B. (1978). The reliability of arousal threshold during sleep. *Psychophysiology, 15*, 412–416.

Bonnet, M.H., & Rosa, R.R. (1987). Sleep and performance in young adults and older normals and insomniacs during acute sleep loss and recovery. *Biological Psychology, 25*, 153–172.

Bootsma, R.J., & van Wieringen, P.C.W. (1990). Timing an attacking forehand drive in table tennis. *Journal of Experimental Psychology: Human Perception and Performance, 16*, 21–29.

Borbely, A.A., & Tobler, I. (1989). Endogenous sleep-promoting substances and sleep regulation. *Physiological Reviews, 69*, 605–670.

Bosman, E.A. (1993). Age-related differences in the motoric aspects of transcription typing skill. *Psychology and Aging, 8*, 87–102.

Boulter, L.R., & Adams, J.A. (1963). Vigilance decrement, the expectancy hypothesis and inter-signal interval. *Canadian Journal of Psychology, 17*, 201–209.

Bovair, S., Kieras, D.E., & Polson, P.G. (1990). The acquisition and performance of text-editing skill: A cognitive complexity analysis. *Human–Computer Interaction, 5*, 1–48.

Bower, G.H. (1981). Mood and memory. *American Psychologist, 36*, 129–148.

Bower, G.H. (1987). Commentary on mood and memory. *Behaviour Research and Therapy, 25*, 443–455.

Bowles, N.L., & Poon, L.W. (1985). Aging and retrieval of words in semantic memory. *Journal of Gerontology, 40*, 71–77.

Boyle, A.J. (1980). "Found experiments" in accident research: Report of a study of accident rates and implications for future research. *Journal of Occupational Psychology, 53*, 53–64.

Bradley, B.P., Mogg, K., Millar, N., & White, J. (1995). Selective processing of negative information: Effects of clinical anxiety, concurrent depression, and awareness. *Journal of Abnormal Psychology, 104*, 532–536.

Braun, J. (1998). Divided attention: Narrowing the gap between brain and behavior. In R. Parasuraman (Ed.), *The attentive brain*. Boston: MIT Press.

Braune, R., & Wickens, C.D. (1986). Time-sharing revisited: Test of a componential model for the assessment of individual differences. *Ergonomics, 29*, 1399–1414.

Brebner, J. (1998). Extraversion and the psychological refractory period. *Personality and Individual Differences, 25*, 543–551.

Brebner, J., & Cooper, C. (1985). A proposed unified model of extraversion. In J.T. Spence & C.E. Izard (Eds.), *Motivation, emotion and personality*. Amsterdam: North-Holland.

Brener, J. (1986). Behavioural efficiency: A biological link between informational and energetic processes. In G.R.J. Hockey, A.W.K. Gaillard & M.G.H. Coles (Eds.), *Energetics and human information processing*. Dordrecht: Martinus Nijhoff.

Brewer, N., & Sandow, B. (1980). Alcohol effects on driver performance under conditions of divided attention. *Ergonomics, 23*, 185–190.

Brewer, N., & Smith, G.A. (1984). How normal and retarded individuals monitor and regulate speed and accuracy of responding in serial choice tasks. *Journal of Experimental Psychology: General, 113*, 71–93.

Brink, J.M., & McDowd, J.M. (1999). Aging and selective attention: An issue of complexity or multiple mechanisms. *Journals of Gerontology, 54B*, P30–P33.

Brinley, J.F. (1965). Cognitive sets, speed and accuracy of performance in the elderly. In A.T. Welford & J.E. Birren (Eds.), *Behavior, aging and the nervous system*. Springfield, IL: Charles C. Thomas.

Broadbent, D.E. (1950). *The twenty dials test under quiet conditions*. Medical Research Council Applied Psychology Unit Report, No. 130/50.

Broadbent, D.E. (1952a). Listening to one of two synchronous messages. *Journal of Experimental Psychology, 44*, 51–55.

Broadbent, D.E. (1952b). Failures of attention in selective listening. *Journal of Experimental Psychology, 44*, 428–433.

Broadbent, D.E. (1954). The role of auditory localization in attention and memory span. *Journal of Experimental Psychology, 47*, 191–196.

Broadbent, D.E. (1955). Variations in performance arising from continuous work. In *Proceedings of Conference on Individual Efficiency in Industry*. Cambridge: Medical Research Council.

Broadbent, D.E. (1958). *Perception and communication*. London: Pergamon Press.

Broadbent, D.E. (1963a). Some recent research from the Applied Psychology Research Unit. In D.N. Buckner & J.J. McGrath (Eds.), *Vigilance: A symposium*. New York: McGraw Hill.

Broadbent, D.E. (1963b). Differences and interactions between stresses. *Quarterly Journal of Experimental Psychology, 15*, 205–211.

Broadbent, D.E. (1971). *Decision and stress*. London: Academic Press.

Broadbent, D.E. (1977). Levels, hierarchies, and the locus of control. *Quarterly Journal of Experimental Psychology, 29*, 181–201.

Broadbent, D.E. (1982). Task combination and selective intake of information. *Acta Psychologica, 50*, 253–290.

Broadbent, D.E., Broadbent, M.H., & Jones, J.L. (1986). Performance correlates of self-reported cognitive failure and of obsessionality. *British Journal of Clinical Psychology, 25*, 285–299.

Broadbent, D.E., Cooper, P.F., Fitzgerald, P., & Parkes, K.R. (1982). The Cognitive Failures Questionnaire (CFQ) and its correlates. *British Journal of Clinical Psychology, 21*, 1–16.

Broadbent, D.E., & Gregory, M. (1963). Vigilance considered as a statistical decision. *British Journal of Psychology, 54*, 309–323.

Broadbent, D.E., & Little, E.A.J. (1960). Effects of noise reduction in a work situation. *Occupational Psychology, 34*, 133–140.

Broadhurst, P.L. (1957). Emotionality and the Yerkes-Dodson Law. *Journal of Experimental Psychology, 54*, 345–352.

Brody, N. (1992). *Intelligence (2nd ed.)*. New York: Academic Press.

Brody, N. (1997). Intelligence, schooling, and society. *American Psychologist, 52*, 1046–1050.

Brody, N., & Erlichman, H. (1998). *Personality psychology: The science of individuality*. Upper Saddle River, NJ: Prentice Hall.

Bronzaft, A.L., & McCarthy, D.P. (1975). The effects of elevated train noise on reading ability. *Environment and Behavior, 7*, 517–527.

Brooke, S., & Ellis, H. (1992). Cold. In A.P. Smith & D.M. Jones (Eds.), *Handbook of human performance. Vol. 1: The physical environment*. London: Academic Press.

Brookhuis, K.A., & De Waard, D. (1993). The use of psychophysiology to assess driver status. *Ergonomics, 39*, 1099–1110.

Brookings, J.B. (1990). A confirmatory factor analytic study of time-sharing performance and cognitive abilities. *Intelligence, 14*, 43–59.

Brosnan, M.J. (1998a). The implications for academic attainment of perceived gender-appropriateness upon spatial task performance. *British Journal of Educational Psychology, 68*, 203–215.

Brosnan, M.J. (1998b). *Technophobia: The psychological impact of information technology*. London: Routledge.

Brown, G.D.A., Hulme, C., & Dalloz, P. (1996). Modelling human memory: Connectionism and convolution. *British Journal of Mathematical and Statistical Psychology, 49*, 1–24.

Brown, I.D. (1994). Driver fatigue. *Human Factors, 36*, 298–314.

Brown, I.D., Tickner, A.H., & Simmonds, D.C.V. (1970). Effect of prolonged driving on overtaking criteria. *Ergonomics, 13*, 239–242.

Bryant, P.E., MacLean, M., Bradley, L.L., & Crossland, J. (1990). Rhyme and alliteration, phoneme detection, and learning to read. *Developmental Psychology, 26*, 429–438.

Bunce, D.J., Barraclough, A., & Morris, I. (1996). The moderating influence of physical fitness on age gradients in vigilance and serial choice responding. *Psychology and Aging, 11*, 671–682.

Bunce, D.J., Warr, P.B., & Cochrane, T. (1993). Blocks in choice responding as a function of age and physical fitness. *Psychology and Aging, 8*, 26–33.

Bundesen, C., & Shibuya, H. (Eds.) (1995). *Visual selective attention: A special issue of Visual Cognition*. Hove, UK: Lawrence Erlbaum Associates Ltd.

Bungener, C., le Houezec, J., Pierson, A., & Jouvent, R. (1996). Cognitive and emotional deficits in early stages of HIV infection: An event-related potentials study. *Progress in Neuro-Psychopharmacology and Biological Psychiatry, 20*, 1303–1314.

Burke, D.M., & Light, L.L. (1981). Memory and aging: The role of retrieval processes. *Psychological Bulletin, 90*, 513–546.

Bushnell, P.J. (1998). Behavioral approaches to the assessment of attention in animals. *Psychopharmacology, 138*, 231–259.

Caldwell, J.A., Jr., & Ramspott, S. (1998). Effects of task duration on sensitivity to sleep deprivation using the multi-attribute task battery. *Behavior Research Methods, Instruments and Computers, 30*, 651–660.

Caldwell, J.L., & Caldwell, J.A., Jr. (1997). An in-flight investigation of the efficacy of dextroamphetamine for sustaining helicopter pilot performance. *Aviation, Space, and Environmental Medicine, 68*, 1073–1080.

Caldwell, J.L., Caldwell, J.A., Jr., & Salter, C.A. (1997). Effects of chemical protective clothing and heat stress on army helicopter pilot performance. *Military Psychology, 9*, 315–328.

Calvo, M.G., & Alamo, L. (1987). Test anxiety and motor performance: The role of muscular and attentional demands. *International Journal of Psychology, 22*, 165–178.

Calvo, M.G., & Carreiras, M. (1993). Selective influence of test anxiety on reading processes. *British Journal of Psychology, 84*, 375–388.

Calvo, M.G., & Eysenck, M.W. (1998). Cognitive bias to internal sources of information in anxiety. *International Journal of Psychology, 33*, 287–299.

Calvo, M.G., Eysenck, M.W., & Castillo, M.D. (1997). Interpretation bias in test anxiety: The time course of predictive inferences. *Cognition and Emotion, 11*, 43–63.

Calvo, M.G., Eysenck, M.W., Ramos, P.M., & Jimenez, A. (1994). Compensatory reading strategies in test anxiety. *Anxiety, Stress and Coping: An International Journal, 7*, 99–116.

Cameron, C. (1975). Accident proneness. *Accident Analysis and Prevention, 7*, 49–53.

Campbell, J.B., & Hawley, C.W. (1983). Study habits and Eysenck's theory of extroversion-introversion. *Journal of Research in Personality, 16*, 139–146.

Campbell, J.P., McCloy, R.A., Oppler, S.H., & Sager, C.E. (1993). A theory of performance. In N. Schmitt & W.C. Borman (Eds.), *Frontiers in industrial and organizational psychology: Personnel selection.* San Francisco: Jossey-Bass.

Campbell, S.S. (1992). Effects of sleep and circadian rhythms on performance. In A.P. Smith & D.M. Jones (Eds.), *Handbook of human performance Vol. 3: State and trait.* London: Academic.

Canestrari, R.E., Jr. (1968). Age changes in acquisition. In G.A. Talland (Ed.), *Human aging and behavior: Recent advances in research and theory.* New York: Academic Press.

Cannon, W.B. (1927). The James-Lange theory of emotions: A critical examination and an alternative theory. *American Journal of Psychology, 39*, 106–124.

Cantor, J., Engle, R.W., & Hamilton, J. (1991). Short-term memory, working memory, and verbal abilities: How do they relate? *Intelligence, 15*, 229–246.

Cappell, H. (1987). Alcohol and tension reduction: What's new? In E. Gottheil & K.A. Druley (Eds.), *Stress and addiction.* New York: Brunner/Mazel.

Card, S.K., Moran, T.P., & Newell, A. (1983). *The psychology of human–computer interaction.* Hillsdale, NJ: Lawrence Erlbaum Associates Inc.

Carlson, L.D. (1961). *Human performance under different thermal loads (Tech. Rep. No. 61–43).* Brooks AFB, TX: USAF Aerospace Medical Center, School of Aviation Medicine.

Carpenter, P.A., Just, M.A., & Schell, P. (1990). What one intelligence test measures: A theoretical account of the processing in the Raven Progressive Matrices Test. *Psychological Review, 97*, 404–431.

Carroll, J.B. (1993). *Human cognitive abilities: A survey of factor-analytic studies.* New York: Cambridge University Press.

Carskadon, M.A., & Roth, T. (1991). Sleep restriction. In T.H. Monk (Ed.), *Sleep, sleepiness and performance.* New York: John Wiley & Sons Inc.

Carver, C.S., Peterson, L.M., Follansbee, D.J., & Scheier, M.F. (1983). Effects of self-directed attention and resistance among persons high and low in test-anxiety. *Cognitive Therapy and Research, 7*, 333–354.

Carver, C.S., & Scheier, M.F. (1990). Origins and functions of positive and negative affects: A control-process view. *Psychological Review, 97*, 19–35.

Cattell, R.B. (1971). *Abilities: Their structure, growth and action.* Boston: Houghton Mifflin.

Cattell, R.B., & Kline, P. (1977). *The scientific analysis of personality and motivation.* New York: Academic Press.

Cattell, R.B., Eber, H.W., & Tatsuoka, M.M. (1970). *Handbook for the Sixteen Personality Factor Questionnaire.* Champaign, IL: IPAT.

Cave, K.R., & Wolfe, J.M. (1990). Modeling the role of parallel processing in visual search. *Cognitive Psychology, 22*, 225–271.

Cerella, J. (1985). Information processing rates in the elderly. *Psychological Bulletin, 98*, 67–83.

Cerella, J. (1990). Aging and information processing rate. In J.E. Birren & K.W. Schaie (Eds.), *Handbook of the psychology of aging, 3rd edition.* San Diego, CA: Academic Press.

Cerella, J., Poon, L.W., & Williams D.M. (1980). Age and the complexity hypothesis. In L.W. Poon & K.W. Schaie (Eds.), *Aging in the1980s: Psychological issues.* Washington, DC: American Psychological Association.

Cervone, D. (1989). Effects of envisioning future activities on self-efficacy judgments and motivation: An availability heuristic interpretation. *Cognitive Therapy and Research, 13*, 247–261.

Charness, N. (Ed.) (1985). *Aging and human performance.* Chichester: John Wiley & Sons Ltd.

Charness, N., & Bosman, E.A. (1992). Human factors and age. In F.I.M. Craik & T.A. Salthouse (Eds.), *The handbook of aging and cognition.* Hillsdale, NJ: Erlbaum.

Charness, N., & Campbell, J.I.D. (1988). Acquiring skill at mental calculation in adulthood: A task decomposition. *Journal of Experimental Psychology: General, 117*, 115–129.

Chase, W.G., & Ericsson, K.A. (1982). Skill and working memory. In G.H. Bower (Ed.), *The psychology of learning and motivation (Vol. 16).* New York: Academic Press.

Chase, W.G., & Simon, H.A. (1973). The mind's eye in chess. In W.G. Chase (Ed.), *Visual information processing.* New York: Academic Press.

Cherns, A.B. (1962). Accidents at work. In A.T. Welford, M. Argyle, D.V. Glass, & J.W. Morris (Eds.), *Society: Problems and methods of study.* London: Routledge & Kegan Paul.

Cherry, E.C. (1953). Some experiments on the recognition of speech, with one and with two ears. *Journal of the Acoustical Society of America, 25*, 975–979.

Cherry, K.E., & Lecompte, D.C. (1999). Age and individual differences influence prospective memory. *Psychology and Aging, 14*, 60–76.

Chi, M.T.H., Feltovich, P.J., & Glaser, R. (1981). Categorization and representation of physics problems by experts and novices. *Cognitive Science, 5*, 121–152.

Chi, C-F., & Lin, F-T. (1998). A comparison of seven visual fatigue assessment techniques in three data-acquisition VDT tasks. *Human Factors, 1998*, 577–590.

Chiarello, C., & Hoyer, W.J. (1988). Adult age differences in implicit and explicit memory: Time course and encoding effects. *Psychology and Aging, 3*, 358–366.

Chiles, W. (1955). *Experimental studies of prolonged wakefulness.* USAF Wright Air Development Center (Tech. Report no. 55–395).

Chomsky, N. (1965). *Aspects of a theory of syntax.* Cambridge, MA: MIT Press.

Christensen, L. (1993). Effects of eating behavior on mood: A review of the literature. *International Journal of Eating Disorders, 14*, 171–183.

Christie, M.J., & McBrearty, E.M. (1979). Psychophysiological investigations of post lunch state in male and female subjects. *Ergonomics, 22*, 307–323.

Clark, H.H., & Chase, W.G. (1972). On the process of comparing sentences against pictures. *Cognitive Psychology, 3*, 472–517.

Claypoole, K.H., Townes, B.D., Collier, A.C., Marra, C., Longstreth, W.T., Cohen, W., Coombs, R.W., Goldstein, D., Sanchez, P., & Handsfield, H.H. (1993). Cognitive risk factors and neuropsychological performance in HIV infection. *International Journal of Neuroscience, 70*, 13–27.

Cohen, A. (1974). Industrial noise and medical, absence, and accident record data on exposed workers. In D.M. Ward (Ed.), *Proceedings of the International Congress on Noise as a Public Health Problem.* Washington, DC: US Environmental Protection Agency.

Cohen, A. (1976). The influence of a company hearing conservation program on extra-auditory problems in workers. *Journal of Safety Research, 8*, 146–162.

Cohen, J.D., Dunbar, K., & McClelland, J.L. (1990). On the control of automatic processes: A parallel distributed processing account of the Stroop effect. *Psychological Review, 97*, 332–361.

Cohen, J.D., & Servan-Schreiber, D. (1992). Context, cortex, and dopamine: A connectionist approach to behavior and biology in schizophrenia. *Psychological Review, 99*, 45–77.

Cohen, J.D., Servan-Schreiber, D., & McClelland, J.L. (1992). A parallel distributed approach to automaticity. *American Journal of Psychology, 105*, 239–269.

Cohen, R.A. (1993). *The neuropsychology of attention.* New York: Plenum.

Cohen, S. (1980). After effects of stress on human performance and social behavior: A review of research and theory. *Psychological Bulletin, 88*, 82–108.

Cohen, S., Evans, G.W., Krantz, D.S., & Stokols, D. (1980). Physiological, motivational and cognitive effects of aircraft noise on children: Moving from the laboratory to the field. *American Psychologist, 35*, 231–243.

Cohen, S., Glass, D.C., & Singer, J.E. (1973). Apartment noise, auditory discrimination, and reading ability in children. *Journal of Experimental Social Psychology, 9*, 407–442.

Cohen, S., & Spacapan, S. (1978). The aftereffects of stress: An attentional interpretation. *Environmental Psychology and Nonverbal Behavior, 3*, 43–57.

Cohn, N.B., Dustman, R.E., & Bradford, D.C. (1984). Age-related decrements in Stroop Color Test performance. *Journal of Clinical Psychology, 40*, 1244–1250.

Coles, M.G.H., Gratton, G., Bashore, T.R., Eriksen, C.W., & Donchin E. (1985). A psychophysiological investigation of the continuous flow model of human information processing. *Journal of Experimental Psychology: Human Perception and Performance, 11*, 529–553.

Collins, A.M., & Loftus, E.F. (1975). A spreading-activation theory of semantic processing. *Psychological Review, 82*, 407–428.

Collins, A.M., & Quillian, M.R. (1969). Retrieval time from semantic memory. *Journal of Verbal Learning and Verbal Behavior, 8*, 240–247.

Collins W.E., & Chiles, W.D. (1980). Laboratory performance during acute alcohol intoxication and hangover. *Human Factors, 22*, 445–462.

Colquhoun, W.P. (1962). Effects of a small dose of alcohol and certain other factors on the performance of a vigilance task. *Bulletin du C.E.R.P., 11*, 27–44.

Colquhoun, W.P. (1967). Sonar target detection as a decision process. *Journal of Applied Psychology, 51*, 187–190.

Colquhoun, W.P. (1971). Circadian variations in mental efficiency. In W.P. Colquhoun (Ed.), *Biological rhythms and human performance*. London: Academic Press.

Colquhoun, W.P., & Baddeley, A.D. (1964). Role of pretest expectancy in vigilance decrement. *Journal of Experimental Psychology, 68*, 156–160.

Colquhoun, W.P., & Baddeley, A.D. (1967). Influence of signal probability during pretraining on vigilance decrement. *Journal of Experimental Psychology, 73*, 153–155.

Comalli, P.E., Jr., Krus, D.M., & Wapner, S. (1965). Cognitive functioning in two groups of aged: One institutionalized, the other living in the community. *Journal of Gerontology, 20*, 9–13.

Comalli, P.E., Jr., Wapner, S., & Werner, H. (1962). Interference effects of Stroop color-word test in childhood, adulthood and aging. *Journal of Genetic Psychology, 100*, 47–53.

Comrey, A.L., & Lee, H.B. (1992). *A first course in factor analysis (2nd ed.)*. Hillsdale, NJ: Lawrence Erlbaum Associates Inc.

Condry, J. (1977). Enemies of exploration: Self-initiated versus other-initiated learning. *Journal of Personality and Social Psychology, 35*, 459–477.

Conrad, R. (1964). Acoustic confusion in immediate memory. *British Journal of Psychology, 55*, 75–84.

Coren, S., & Halpern, D.F. (1991). Left handedness: A marker for decreased survival fitness. *Psychological Bulletin, 90*–106.

Corr, P.J., Pickering, A.D., & Gray, J.A. (1995a). Personality and reinforcement in associative and instrumental learning. *Personality and Individual Differences, 19*, 47–72.

Corr, P.J., Pickering, A.D., & Gray, J.A. (1995b). Sociability/impulsivity and caffeine-induced arousal: Critical flicker/fusion frequency and procedural learning. *Personality and Individual Differences, 18*, 713–730.

Corso, J.F. (1980). Age correction factor in noise-induced hearing loss: A quantitative model. *Audiology, 19*, 221–232.

Corso, J.F. (1981). *Aging sensory systems and perception*. New York: Greenwood.

Corteen, R.S., & Wood, B. (1972). Autonomic responses to shock-associated words in an unattended channel. *Journal of Experimental Psychology, 94*, 308–313.

Corteen, R.S., & Dunn, D. (1973). Shock associated words in a nonattended message. A test for momentary awareness. *Journal of Experimental Psychology, 102*, 1143–1114.

Cortina, J.M., Doherty, M.L., Schmitt, N., Kaufman, G., & Smith, R.G. (1992). The "Big Five" personality factors in the IPI and MMPI: Predictors of police performance. *Personnel Psychology, 45*, 119–140.

Costa, G. (1996). The impact of shift and night work on health. *Applied Ergonomics, 27*, 9–16.

Costa, P.T., Jr. (1996). Work and personality: Use of the NEO-PI-R in industrial/organisational psychology. *Applied Psychology: An International Journal, 45*, 225–241.

Costa, P.T., Jr., & McCrae, R.R. (1992). Four ways five factors are basic. *Personality and Individual Differences, 13*, 653–665.

Costa, P.T., Jr., Somerfield, M.R., & McCrae, R.R. (1996). Personality and coping: A reconceptualization. In M. Zeidner & N.S. Endler (Eds.), *Handbook of coping: Theory, research, applications*. New York: John Wiley & Sons Inc.

Cowan, N. (1988). Evolving conceptions of memory storage, selective attention, and their mutual constraints within the human information-processing system. *Psychological Bulletin, 104*, 163–191.

Cowan, N. (1995). *Attention and memory: An integrated framework*. New York: Oxford University Press.

Cox, T., & Ferguson, E. (1991). Individual differences, stress and coping. In C.L. Cooper & R. Payne (Eds.), *Personality and stress: Individual differences in the coping process*. Chichester: Wiley.

Craig, A. (1978). Is the vigilance decrement simply a response adjustment towards probability matching? *Human Factors, 20*, 441–446.

Craig, A. (1983). Vigilance and inspection. *Studia Psychologica, 25*, 259–270.

Craig, A. (1986). Acute effects of meals on perceptual and cognitive efficiency. *Nutrition Reviews Supplement, 44*, 163–171.

Craig, A. (1987). Signal detection theory and probability matching apply to vigilance. *Human Factors, 29*, 645–652.

Craig, A. (1988). Decision processes in vigilance. In H.E. Ross (Ed.), *Fechner Day '88*. Stirling: International Society for Psychophysics.

Craig, A., Baer, K., & Diekmann, A. (1981). The effects of lunch on sensory-perceptual functioning in man. *International Archives of Occupational and Environmental Health, 49*, 105–114.

Craig, A., & Colquhoun, W.P. (1975). Vigilance: A review. In C.G. Drury & J.G. Fox (Eds.), *Human reliability in quality control*. London: Taylor & Francis.

Craig, A., & Cooper, R.E. (1992). Symptoms of acute and chronic fatigue. In A.P. Smith & D.M. Jones (Eds.), *Handbook of human performance. Vol. 3: Trait and state.* London: Academic Press.

Craig, A., & Davies, D.R. (1991). Vigilance: Sustained visual monitoring and attention. In J.A.J. Roufs (Ed.), *The man–machine interface, Vol. 15 of Vision and visual dysfunction* (General Ed., J.R. Cronly-Dillon). Basingstoke: Macmillan.

Craig, A., Davies, D.R., & Matthews, G. (1987). Diurnal variation, task characteristics and vigilance performance. *Human Factors, 29*, 675–684.

Craik, F.I.M. (1965). The nature of the age decrement in dichotic listening tasks. *Quarterly Journal of Experimental Psychology, 17*, 227–240.

Craik, F.I.M. (1977). Age differences in human memory. In J.E. Birren & K.W. Schaie (Eds.), *Handbook of the psychology of aging.* New York: Van Nostrand Reinhold.

Craik, F.I.M. (1986). A functional account of age differences in memory. In F. Klix & H. Hagendorf (Eds.), *Human memory and cognitive capabilities: Mechanisms and performances.* Amsterdam: Elsevier.

Craik, F.I.M., Anderson, N.D., Kerr, S.A., & Li, K.Z.H. (1995). Memory changes in normal aging. In A.D. Baddeley & B.A. Wilson (Eds.), *Handbook of memory disorders.* Chichester: John Wiley & Sons Ltd.

Craik, F.I.M., Byrd, M., & Swanson, J.M. (1987). Patterns of memory loss in three elderly samples. *Psychology and Aging, 2*, 79–86.

Craik, F.I.M., & Jennings, J.M. (1992). Human memory. In F.I.M. Craik & T.A. Salthouse (Eds.), *The handbook of aging and cognition.* Hillsdale, NJ: Lawrence Erlbaum Associates Inc.

Craik, F.I.M., & Lockhart, R.S. (1972). Levels of processing: A framework for memory research. *Journal of Verbal Learning and Verbal Behavior, 11*, 671–684.

Craik, F.I.M., & McDowd, J.M. (1987). Age differences in recall and recognition. *Journal of Experimental Psychology: Learning, Memory and Cognition, 13*, 474–479.

Craik, K.J.W. (1948). Theory of the human operator in control systems. II. Man as an element in a control system. *British Journal of Psychology, 39*, 142–148.

Crano, W.D., Kenny, D.A., & Campbell, D.T. (1972). Does intelligence cause achievement?: A cross-lagged panel analysis. *Journal of Educational Psychology , 63*, 258–275.

Cresswell, W.L., & Froggatt, P. (1963). *The causation of bus driver accidents.* Oxford: Oxford University Press.

Cronbach, L.J. (1990). *Essentials of psychological testing (5th ed.).* New York: Addison-Wesley.

Cronbach, L.J., & Snow, R.E. (1977). *Aptitudes and instructional methods: A handbook for research on interactions.* New York: Irvington.

Crossman, E.R.F.W. (1959). A theory of the acquisition of speed skill. *Ergonomics, 2*, 153–166.

Curran, T., & Keele, S.W. (1993). Attentional and nonattentional forms of sequence learning. *Journal of Experimental Psychology: Learning, Memory, and Cognition, 19*, 189–202.

Daee, S., & Wilding, J.M. (1977). Effects of high intensity white noise on short-term memory for position in a list and sequence. *British Journal of Psychology, 68*, 335–349.

Dalgleish, T., & Power, M. (Eds.) (1999) *Handbook of cognition and emotion.* New York: John Wiley & Sons Inc.

D'Aloisio, A., & Klein, R.M. (1990). Aging and the deployment of visual attention. In J.T. Enns (Ed.), *The development of attention: Research and theory.* Amsterdam: North Holland.

Dalrymple-Alford, E.C., & Budayr, B. (1966). Examination of some aspects of the Stroop color-word test. *Perceptual & Motor Skills, 23*, 1211–1214.

Dalton, G.W., & Thompson, P.H. (1971). Accelerating obsolescence of older engineers. *Harvard Business Review, 49*, 57–68.

Daly, J.W. (1993). Mechanism of action of caffeine. In S. Garattini (Ed.), *Caffeine, coffee and health.* New York: Raven Press.

Damos, D.L. (Ed.) (1991). *Multiple-task performance.* London: Taylor & Francis.

Damos, D.L. (1993). Using meta-analysis to compare the predictive validity of single- and multiple-task measures of flight performance. *Human Factors, 35*, 615–628.

Daneman, M., & Carpenter, P.A. (1980). Individual differences in working memory and reading. *Journal of Verbal Learning and Verbal Behavior, 19*, 450–466.

Daneman, M., & Merikle, P.M. (1996). Working memory and language comprehension: A meta-analysis. *Psychonomic Bulletin and Review, 3*, 422–433.

Danzinger, P.R., & Larsen, J.D. (1989). Personality dimensions and memory as measured by signal detection. *Personality and Individual Differences, 10*, 809–812.

Darke, S. (1988). Anxiety and working memory capacity. *Cognition and Emotion, 2,* 145–154.

Daugherty, S.A., Henry, B.E., Peterson, D.L., Swarts, R.L., Bastien, S., & Thomas, R.S. (1991). Chronic fagitue syndrome in Northern Nevada. *Reviews of Infectious Diseases, 13,* 39–44.

Davidson, L.M., Hagmann, J., & Baum, A. (1990). An exploration of a possible physiological explanation for stressor after-effects. *Journal of Applied Social Psychology, 20,* 869–880.

Davies, A.D.M., & Davies, D.R. (1975). The effects of noise and time of day upon age differences in performance at two checking tasks. *Ergonomics, 18,* 321–336.

Davies, D.R. (1968a). Physiological and psychological effects of exposure to high intensity noise. *Applied Acoustics, 1,* 215–233.

Davies, D.R. (1968b). Age differences in paced inspection tasks. In G.A. Talland (Ed.), *Human aging and behavior: Recent advances in research and theory.* New York: Academic Press.

Davies, D.R. (1976). Noise and the autonomic nervous system. In G. Rossi & M. Vigone (Eds.), *Man and noise.* Turin: Minerva Medica.

Davies, D.R. (1985). Individual and group differences in sustained attention. In S. Folkard & T.H. Monk (Eds.), *Hours of work: Temporal factors in work-scheduling.* Chichester: John Wiley & Sons Ltd.

Davies, D.R., & Griew, S. (1965). Age and vigilance. In A.T. Welford & J.E. Birren (Eds.), *Behavior, aging and the nervous system.* Springfield, ILL: Charles C. Thomas.

Davies, D.R., & Hockey, G.R.J. (1966). The effects of noise and doubling the signal frequency on individual differences in visual vigilance performance. *British Journal of Psychology, 57,* 381–389.

Davies, D.R., Hockey, G.R.J., & Taylor, A. (1969). Varied auditory stimulation, temperament differences, and vigilance performance. *British Journal of Psychology, 64,* 383–389.

Davies, D.R., & Jones, D.M. (1975). The effects of noise and incentives upon attention in short-term memory. *British Journal of Psychology, 66,* 61–68.

Davies, D.R., & Jones, D.M. (1982). Hearing and noise. In W.T. Singleton (Ed.), *The body at work.* Cambridge: Cambridge University Press.

Davies, D.R., & Jones, D.M. (1985). Noise and efficiency. In W. Temple (Ed.), *The noise handbook.* London: Academic Press.

Davies, D.R., Jones, D.M., & Taylor, A. (1984). Selective and sustained attention: Individual and group differences. In R. Parasuraman & D.R. Davies (Eds.), *Varieties of attention.* New York: Academic Press.

Davies, D.R., & Krkovic, A. (1965). Skin conductance, alpha-activity, and vigilance. *American Journal of Psychology, 78,* 304–306.

Davies, D.R., Lang, L., & Shackleton, V.J. (1973). The effects of music and task difficulty on performance at a visual vigilance task. *British Journal of Psychology, 64,* 383–389.

Davies, D.R., Matthews, G., & Westerman, S.J. (submitted). Self-report arousal and dual-task vigilance performance.

Davies, D.R., Matthews, G., & Wong, C.S.K. (1991). Age and work behaviour. In C.L. Cooper & I.T. Robertson (Eds.), *International review of industrial and organizational psychology* (Vol. 6). Chichester: John Wiley & Sons Ltd.

Davies, D.R., & Parasuraman, R. (1977). Cortical evoked potentials and vigilance: A decision theory analysis. In R.R. Mackie (Ed.), *Vigilance: Theory, operational performance, and physiological characteristics.* New York: Plenum Press.

Davies, D.R., & Parasuraman, R. (1982). *The psychology of vigilance.* London: Academic Press.

Davies, D.R., Shackleton, V.J., & Parasuraman, R. (1983). Monotony and boredom. In G.R.J. Hockey (Ed.), *Stress and fatigue in human performance.* Chichester: John Wiley & Sons Ltd.

Davies, D.R., & Sparrow, P.R. (1985). Age and work behaviour. In N. Charness (Ed.), *Aging and human performance.* Chichester: Wiley.

Davies, D.R., Taylor, A., & Dorn, L. (1992). Aging and human performance. In A.P. Smith & D.M. Jones (Eds.), *Handbook of human performance, Vol. 3: Trait and state.* Chichester: Wiley.

Davies, M., Stankov, L., Roberts, R.D. (1998). Emotional intelligence: In search of an elusive construct. *Journal of Personality and Social Psychology, 75,* 989–1015.

Davis, D.R. (1958). Human errors in transport accidents. *Ergonomics, 1,* 24–33.

Davis, D.R. (1966). Railway signals passed at danger: The drivers, circumstances and psychological processes. *Ergonomics, 9,* 211–222.

Davis, H.P., Cohen, A., Gandy, M., Colombo, P., VanDusseldorp, C., Simolke, R., & Romano, N. (1990). Lexical priming deficits as a function of age. *Behavioral Neuroscience, 104,* 288–297.

Davis, Z.T. (1987). Effects of time-of-day of instruction on beginning reading-achievement. *Journal of Educational Research, 80,* 138–140.

Dawson, D., Encel, N., & Lushington, K. (1995). Improving adaptation to simulated night shift: Timed exposure to bright light versus daytime melatonin administration. *Sleep, 18,* 11–21.

Dawson, D., & Reid, K. (1997). Fatigue, alcohol and performance impairment. *Nature, 388,* 235.

Dawson, M.E., & Schell, A.M. (1982). Electrodermal responses to attended and nonattended significant stimuli during dichotic listening. *Journal of Experimental Psychology: Human Perception and Performance, 8,* 315–324.

Day, N.E. (1993). Performance in salespeople: The impact of age. *Journal of Managerial Issues, 5,* 254–273.

Deary, I.J. (1992). Diabetes, hypoglycaemia and cognitive performance. In A.P. Smith & D.M. Jones (Eds.), *Handbook of human performance. Vol. 2: Health and performance.* London: Academic Press.

Deary, I.J. (1995). Intelligence, personality, and severe hypoglycemia in diabetes. In D.H. Saklofske & M. Zeidner (Eds.), *International handbook of personality and intelligence.* New York: Plenum.

Deary I.J., & Caryl P.G. (1997). Neuroscience and human intelligence differences. *Trends in Neurosciences, 20,* 365–371.

Deaton, J.E., & Parasuraman, R. (1993). Sensory and cognitive vigilance: Effects of age on performance and cognitive workload. *Human Performance, 6,* 71–97.

Deci, E.L. (1975). *Intrinsic motivation.* New York: Plenum Press.

Deci, E.L., & Ryan, R.M. (1985). *Intrinsic motivation and self-determination in human behavior.* New York: Plenum.

Deeg, D.J.H., Kardaun, J.W.P.F., & Fozard, J.L. (1996). Health, behavior, and aging. In J.E. Birren & K.W. Schaie (Eds.), *Handbook of the psychology of aging, 3rd edition.* San Diego, CA: Academic Press.

Deese, J. (1955). Some problems in the theory of vigilance. *Psychological Review, 62,* 359–368.

de Groot, A.D. (1965). *Thought and choice in chess.* The Hague: Mouton.

Delbecq-Derousne, J., & Beauvois, M-F. (1989). Memory processes and aging: A defect of automatic rather than controlled processes? *Archives of Gerontology and Geriatrics, Supplement 1,* 121–150.

Delgado, A.R., & Prieto, G. (1996). Sex differences in visuospatial ability: Do performance factors play such an important role? *Memory and Cognition, 24,* 504–510.

DeLuca, J., Johnson, S.K., Ellis, S.P., & Natelson, B.H. (1997). Cognitive functioning is impaired in patients with chronic fatigue syndrome devoid of psychiatric disease. *Journal of Neurology, Neurosurgery and Psychiatry, 62,* 151–155.

Dember, W.N., & Warm, J.S. (1979). *The psychology of perception.* New York: Holt, Rinehart & Winston.

Dement, W.C. (1974). *Some must watch while some must sleep.* San Francisco: Freeman.

Dempster, F.N. (1992). The rise and fall of the inhibitory mechanism: Towards a unified theory of cognitive development and aging. *Developmental Review, 12,* 45–75.

Derryberry, D., & Reed, M.A. (1997). Motivational and attentional components of personality. In G. Matthews (Ed.), *Cognitive science perspectives on personality and emotion.* Amsterdam: Elsevier Science.

Desimone, R., & Duncan, J. (1995). Neural mechanisms of selective visual attention. *Annual Review of Neuroscience, 18,* 193–222.

Desmond, P.A. (1997). *Fatigue and stress in driving performance.* Unpublished doctoral dissertation, University of Dundee.

Desmond, P.A., & Matthews, G. (1997). Implications of task-induced fatigue effects for in-vehicle countermeasures to driver fatigue. *Accident Analysis and Prevention, 29,* 513–523.

D'Esposito, M., Detre, J.A., Alsop, D.C., Shin, R.K., Atlas, S., & Grossman, M. (1995). The neural basis of the central executive of working memory. *Nature, 378,* 279–281.

Dessouky, M.I., Moray, N., & Kijowski, B. (1995). Taxonomy of scheduling systems as a basis for the study of strategic behavior. *Human Factors, 37,* 443–472.

Deutsch, J.A., & Deutsch, D. (1963). Attention: Some theoretical considerations. *Psychological Review, 70,* 80–90.

Devlin, B., Roeder, K., & Resnick, D.P. (Eds.) (1997). *Intelligence, genes, and success: Scientists respond to The Bell Curve.* New York: Springer.

Dewaele, J-M., & Furnham, A. (in press). Extraversion: The unloved variable in applied linguistic research. *Language Learning.*

Dickman, S.J., & Meyer, D.E. (1988). Impulsivity and speed-accuracy tradeoffs in information processing. *Journal of Personality and Social Psychology, 54,* 274–290.

Dienes, Z., & Berry, D. (1997). Implicit learning: Below the subjective threshold. *Psychonomic Bulletin and Review, 4,* 3–23.

Dinges, D.F., Pack, F., Williams, K., Gillen, K.A., Powell, J.W., Ott, G.E., Aptowicz, C., & Pack, A.I. (1997). Cumulative sleepiness, mood disturbance and psychomotor vigilance performance decrements during a week of sleep restricted to 4–5 hours per night. *Sleep, 20*, 267–277.

Dobbs, A.R., & Rule, B.G. (1987). Prospective memory and self-reports of memory abilities in older adults. *Canadian Journal of Psychology, 41*, 209–212.

Dobbs, A.R., & Rule, B.G. (1989). Adult age differences in working memory. *Psychology and Aging, 4*, 500–503.

Donders, F. (1868/1969). On the speed of mental processes. In W.G. Koster (Ed. and trans.) *Attention and performance II*. Amsterdam: North-Holland.

Donnerstein, E., & Wilson, D.W. (1976). Effects of noise and perceived control on ongoing and subsequent aggressive behavior. *Journal of Personality and Social Psychology, 34*, 774–781.

Dorn, L., & Matthews, G. (1995). Prediction of mood and risk appraisals from trait measures: Two studies of simulated driving. *European Journal of Personality, 9*, 25–42.

Dornic, S. (1975). Some studies on the retention of order information. In P.M.A. Rabbitt & S. Dornic (Eds.), *Attention and performance, V*. London: Academic Press.

Dornic, S., & Ekehammar, B. (1990). Extraversion, neuroticism, and noise sensitivity. *Personality and Individual Differences, 11*, 989–992.

Doucet, C., & Stelmack, R.M. (1997). Movement time differentiates extraverts from introverts. *Personality and Individual Differences, 23*, 775–786.

Drew, G.C. (1940). *An experimental study of mental fatigue*. Flying Personnel Research Committee Report 227. [Reprinted in E.J. Dearnaley & P.B. Warr (1979), *Aircrew stress in wartime operations*. New York and London: Academic Press].

Drewnowski, A., & Healy, A.F. (1977). Detection errors on "the" and "and": Evidence for reading units larger than the word. *Memory and Cognition, 5*, 636–647.

Driver, J., & Halligan, P.W. (1991). Can visual neglect operate in object-centered co-ordinates? An affirmative single-case study. *Cognitive Neuropsychology, 8*, 475–496.

Duffy, E. (1962). *Activation and behavior*. New York: John Wiley & Sons Inc.

Dugas Garcia, K.D., & Wierwille, W.W. (1985). Effect of glare on performance of a VDT reading-comprehension task. *Human Factors, 27*, 163–173.

Dulaney, C.L., & Rogers, W.A. (1994). Mechanisms underlying reduction in Stroop interference with practice for young and old adults. *Journal of Experimental Psychology: Learning, Memory and Cognition, 20*, 470–484.

Duncan, J. (1979). Divided attention: The whole is more than the sum of its parts. *Journal of Experimental Psychology: Human Perception and Performance, 11*, 583–597.

Duncan, J. (1980). The locus of interference in the perception of simultaneous stimuli. *Psychological Review, 87*, 272–300.

Duncan, J. (1984). Selective attention and the organization of visual information. *Journal of Experimental Psychology: General, 113*, 501–517.

Duncan, J. (1996). Cooperating brain systems in selective perception and action. In T. Inui & J.L. McClelland (Eds.), *Attention and Performance 16: Information integration in perception and communication*. Cambridge, MA: MIT Press.

Duncan, J., Emslie, H., Williams, P., Johnson, R., & Freer, C. (1996). Intelligence and the frontal lobe: The organization of goal-directed behavior. *Cognitive Psychology, 30*, 257–303.

Duncan, J., & Humphreys, G. (1989). Visual search and stimulus similarity. *Psychological Review, 96*, 433–458.

Duncan, J., & Humphreys, G. (1992). Beyond the search surface: Visual search and attentional engagement. *Journal of Experimental Psychology: Human Perception and Performance, 18*, 578–588.

Dusek, E.R. (1957) Effect of temperature on mental performance. In *Protection and functioning of the head in cold climates*. Washington, DC: National Academic Science Natural Resource Council.

Dutta, A., & Proctor, R.W. (1992). Persistence of stimulus–response compatibility effects with extended practice. *Journal of Experimental Psychology: Learning, Memory, and Cognition, 18*, 801–809.

Eagly, A.H. (1995). The science and politics of comparing women and men. *American Psychologist, 50*, 145–158.

Easterbrook, J.A. (1959) The effect of emotion on cue utilization and the organization of behavior. *Psychological Review, 66*, 183–201.

Edkins, G.D., & Pollock, C.M. (1997). The influence of sustained attention on railway accidents. *Accident Analysis and Prevention, 29*, 533–539.

Egan, J., Carterette, E., & Thwing, E. (1954). Some factors affecting multichannel listening. *Journal of the Acoustical Society of America, 26*, 774–782.

Egan, J.P., Greenberg, G.Z., & Schulman, A.J. (1961). Operating characteristics, signal detectability, and the method of free response. *Journal of the Acoustical Society of America, 33*, 993–1007.

Egan, V., & Deary, I.J. (1992) Are specific inspection time strategies prevented by concurrent tasks? *Intelligence, 16,* 151–168.

Egan, V., & Goodwin, G. (1992) HIV and AIDS. In A.P. Smith & D.M. Jones (Eds.), *Handbook of human performance. Vol. 2: Health and performance.* London: Academic Press.

Eggemeier, F.T., Crabtree, M.S., & LaPointe, P.A. (1983). The effect of delayed report on subjective ratings of mental workload. *Proceedings of the Human Factors Society Twenty-Seventh Annual Meeting.* Santa Monica, CA: Human Factors Society.

Einstein, G.O., Holland, L.J., McDaniel, M.A., & Guynn, M.J. (1992). Age-related deficits in prospective memory: The influence of task complexity. *Psychology and Aging, 7,* 471–478.

Einstein, G.O., & McDaniel, M.A. (1990). Normal aging and prospective memory. *Journal of Experimental Psychology: Learning, Memory and Cognition, 16,* 717–726.

Elias, M.F., Elias, J.W., & Elias, P.K. (1990). Biological and health influences on behavior. In J.E. Birren, & K.W. Schaie, (Eds.), *Handbook of the psychology of aging (3rd ed.).* San Diego, CA: Academic Press.

Elias, M.F., Elias, P.K., Cobb, J., D'Agostino, R.B., White, L.R., & Wolf, P.A. (1995). In J.E. Dimsdale & A. Baum (Eds.), *Quality of life in behavioral medicine research.* Hillsdale, NJ: Lawrence Erlbaum Associates Inc.

Elithorn, A., & Lawrence, C. (1955). Central inhibition —some refractory observations. *Quarterly Journal of Experimental Psychology, 7,* 116–127.

Ellis, A.W. (1993). *Reading, writing and dyslexia: A cognitive analysis (2nd ed.).* Hove, UK: Lawrence Erlbaum Associates Ltd.

Ellis, H.D. (1982). The effects of cold on performance of serial choice reaction time and various discrete tasks. *Human Factors, 24,* 589–598.

Ellis, H.D., Wilcock, S.E., & Zaman, S.A. (1985). Cold and performance: The effects of information load, analgesics and the rate of cooling. *Aviation, Space, and Environmental Medicine, 56,* 233–237.

Ellis, L., & Ebertz, L. (Eds.) (1998). *Males, females, and behavior: Toward biological understanding.* Westport, CT: Praeger Publishers/Greenwood Publishing Group.

Ellis, N. (1990). Reading, phonological skills and short-term memory: Interactive tributaries of development. *Journal of Research in Reading, 13,* 107–122.

Elsass, P., Mellerup, E.T., Rafaelsen, O.J., & Theilgaard, A. (1981). Effect of lithium on reaction time: A study of diurnal variations. *Psychopharmacology, 72,* 279–282.

Enander, A.E. (1987). Effects of moderate cold on performance of psychomotor and cognitive tasks. *Ergonomics, 30,* 1431–1445.

Enander, A.E., & Hygge, S. (1990). Thermal stress and human performance. *Scandinavian Journal of Work, Environment and Health, 16 (Suppl. 1),* 44–50.

Endler, N., & Parker, J. (1990). Multi-dimensional assessment of coping: A critical review. *Journal of Personality and Social Psychology, 58,* 844–854.

Endsley, M.R. (1995a). Towards a theory of situation awareness in dynamic systems. *Human Factors, 37,* 31–64.

Endsley, M.R. (1995b). Measurement of situation awareness in dynamic systems. *Human Factors, 37,* 65–84.

Endsley, M.R. (1996). Automation and situation awareness. In R. Parasuraman & M. Mouloua (Eds.), *Automation and human performance: Theory and applications.* Mahwah, NJ: Erlbaum.

Endsley, M.R., & Kiris, E.O. (1995). The out-of-the-loop performance problem and level of control in automation. *Human Factors, 37,* 381–394.

Ericsson, K.A. (1996a). The acquisition of expert performance: An introduction to some of the issues. In K.A. Ericsson (Ed.), *The road to excellence: The acquisition of expert performance in the arts and sciences, sports, and games.* Mahwah, NJ: Lawrence Erlbaum Associates Inc.

Ericsson, K.A. (Ed.) (1996b). *The road to excellence: The acquisition of expert performance in the arts and sciences, sports, and games.* Mahwah, NJ: Lawrence Erlbaum Associates Inc.

Ericsson, K.A., & Charness, N. (1994). Expert performance: Its structure and acquisition. *American Psychologist, 49,* 725–747.

Eriksen, C.W. (1995). The flankers task and response competition: A useful tool for investigating a variety of cognitive problems. *Visual Cognition, 2,* 101–118.

Eriksen, C.W., & Collins, J.F. (1969). Visual perceptual rate under two conditions of search. *Journal of Experimental Psychology, 80,* 489–492.

Eriksen, C.W., & Eriksen, B.A. (1979). Target redundancy in visual search: Do repetitions of the target within the display impair processing? *Perception and Psychophysics, 26,* 195–205.

Eriksen, C.W., & Hoffman, J.E. (1973). The extent of processing of noise elements during selective encoding from visual displays. *Perception and Psychophysics, 14,* 155–160.

Eriksen, C.W., & Yeh, Y-Y. (1985). Allocation of attention in the visual field. *Journal of Experimental Psychology: Human Perception and Performance, 11,* 583–597.

Estes, W.K. (1991). Cognitive architectures from the standpoint of an experimental psychologist. *Annual Review of Psychology, 42,* 1–28.

European Foundation for the Improvement of Living and Working Conditions (1996). *Working conditions in the European Union.* Dublin: European Foundation for the Improvement of Living and Working Conditions.

Eysenck, H.J. (1964). Involuntary rest pauses in tapping as a function of drive and personality. *Perceptual and Motor Skills, 18,* 173–174.

Eysenck, H.J. (1967). *The biological basis of personality.* Springfield, IL: Thomas.

Eysenck, H.J. (1995). Creativity as a product of intelligence and personality. In D.H. Saklofske & M. Zeidner (Eds.), *International handbook of personality and intelligence.* New York: Plenum Press.

Eysenck, H.J., & Eysenck, M.W. (1985). *Personality and individual differences: A natural science approach.* New York: Plenum Press.

Eysenck, M.W. (1975). Retrieval from semantic memory as a function of age. *Journal of Gerontology, 30,* 174–180.

Eysenck, M.W. (1975). Effects of noise, activation level, and response dominance on retrieval from semantic memory. *Journal of Experimental Psychology, 104,* 143–148.

Eysenck, M.W. (1981). Learning, memory and personality. In H.J. Eysenck (Ed.), *A model for personality.* Berlin: Springer.

Eysenck, M.W. (1982). *Attention and arousal: Cognition and performance.* New York: Springer.

Eysenck, M.W. (1983) Incentives. In G.R.J. Hockey, (Ed.), *Stress and fatigue in human performance.* Chichester: Wiley.

Eysenck, M.W. (1989). Individual differences in vigilance performance. In A. Coblentz (Ed.), *Vigilance and performance in automatized systems.* Dordrecht, Netherlands: Kluwer Academic Publishers.

Eysenck, M.W. (1992) *Anxiety: The cognitive perspective.* Hove, UK: Lawrence Erlbaum Associates Ltd.

Eysenck, M.W. (1997). *Anxiety and cognition: A unified theory.* Hove, UK: Psychology Press.

Eysenck, M.W., & Calvo, M.G. (1992). Anxiety and performance: The processing efficiency theory. *Cognition and Emotion, 6,* 409–434.

Eysenck, M.W., & Derakshan, N. (1997). Cognitive biases for future negative events as a function of trait anxiety and social desirability. *Personality and Individual Differences, 22,* 597–605.

Eysenck, M.W., & Eysenck, H.J. (1980) Mischel and the concept of personality. *British Journal of Psychology, 71,* 191–204.

Eysenck, M.W., & Folkard, S. (1980). Personality, time of day, and caffeine: Some theoretical and conceptual problems in Revelle et al. *Journal of Experimental Psychology: General, 109,* 32–41.

Eysenck, M.W., & Keane, M.T. (1995). *Cognitive psychology: A student's handbook (3rd. ed).* Hove, UK: Lawrence Erlbaum Associates Ltd.

Fagerstrom, K.O., & Lisper, H.O. (1977). Effects of listening to car radio, experience, and personality of the driver on subsidiary reaction time and heart rate in a long-term driving task. In R.R. Mackie (Ed.), *Vigilance: Theory, operational performance, and physiological characteristics.* New York: Plenum Press.

Fahrenberg, J. (1987). Concepts of activation and arousal in the theory of emotionality (neuroticism): A multivariate conception. In J. Strelau & H.J. Eysenck (Eds.), *Personality dimensions and arousal.* New York: Plenum Press.

Fairclough, S.H., & Graham, R. (1999). Monitoring driver impairment due to sleep deprivation or alcohol. In M. Scerbo (Ed.), *Automation technology and human performance: Current research and trends.* Hillsdale, NJ: Lawrence Erlbaum Associates Inc.

Fairclough, S.H., & Ward, N.J. (1996). A protocol for the assessment of subjective sleepiness. In E. Carbonell Vaya & J.A. Rothengatter, (Eds.), *Traffic and transport psychology: Theory and application.* Amsterdam: Pergamon.

Farkas, M.S., & Hoyer, W.J. (1980). Processing consequences of perceptual grouping in selective attention. *Journal of Gerontology, 35,* 207–216.

Farmer, E.W. (1992). Ionization. In A.P. Smith & D.M. Jones (Eds.), *Handbook of human performance. Vol. 1: The physical environment.* London: Academic Press.

Fedio, P., & Mirsky, A.F. (1969). Selective intellectual deficits in children with temporal lobe or centrencephalic epilepsy. *Neuropsychologia, 7,* 287–300.

Felleman, D., & Van Essen, D. (1991). Distributed hierarchical processing in the primate cerebral cortex. *Cerebral Cortex, 1,* 1–47.

Feltz, D.L., & Mugno, D.A. (1983). A replication of the path analysis of the causal elements in Bandura's theory of self-efficacy and the influence of autonomic perception. *Journal of Sport Psychology, 5,* 263–277.

Ferretti, R.P., & Cavalier, A.R. (1991). Constraints on the problem solving of persons with mental retardation. *International Review of Research in Mental Retardation, 17*, 153–192.

Feyer, A-M., Williamson, A.M., & Cairns, D.R. (1997). The involvement of human behaviour in occupational accidents: Errors in context. *Safety Science, 25*, 55–65.

Fillmore, M.T., & Vogel-Sprott, M. (1994). Psychomotor performance under alcohol and under caffeine: Expectancy and pharmacological effects. *Experimental and Clinical Psychopharmacology, 2*, 319–327.

Fine, B.J., & Kobrick, J.L. (1978). Effects of altitude and heat on complex cognitive tasks. *Human Factors, 20*, 115–122.

Fine, B.J., & Kobrick, J.L. (1987). Effect of heat and chemical protective clothing on cognitive performance. *Aviation, Space, and Environmental Medicine, 58*, 149–154.

Finkelmann, J.M., & Glass, D.C. (1970). Reappraisal of the relationship between noise and performance by means of a subsidiary task measure. *Journal of Applied Psychology, 54*, 211–213.

Finnigan, F., & Hammersley, R. (1992). The effects of alcohol on performance. In A.P. Smith & D.M. Jones (Eds.), *Handbook of human performance. Vol. 2: Health and performance*. London: Academic Press.

Finnigan, F., Hammersley, R., & Millar, K. (1998). Effects of meal composition on blood alcohol level, psychomotor performance and subjective state after ingestion of alcohol. *Appetite, 31*, 361–375.

Fisher, S. (1984a). *Stress and the perception of control*. Hillsdale, NJ: Lawrence Erlbaum Associates Inc.

Fisher, S. (1984b). The microstructure of attentional deployment on a dual task in loud noise. *Canadian Journal of Psychology, 38*, 561–578.

Fisher, S. (1986). *Stress and strategy*. Hillsdale, NJ: Lawrence Erlbaum Associates Inc.

Fisk, A.D., & Schneider, W.W. (1981). Control and automatic processing in tasks requiring sustained attention: A new approach to vigilance. *Human Factors, 23*, 737–750.

Fisk, A.D., & Schneider, W.W. (1983). Category and word search: Generalizing search principles to complex processing. *Journal of Experimental Psychology: Learning, Memory and Cognition, 9*, 177–195.

Fisk, A.D., Fisher, D.L., & Rogers, W.A. (1992). General slowing alone cannot explain age-related search effects: A reply to Cerella (1991). *Journal of Experimental Psychology: General, 121*, 73–78.

Fisk, J.E., & Warr, P.B. (1996). Age and working memory: The role of perceptual speed, the central executive, and the phonological loop. *Psychology and Aging, 11*, 316–323.

Fitts, P.M. (1954). The information capacity for the human motor system in controlling the amplitude of movement. *Journal of Experimental Psychology, 47*, 381–391.

Fitts, P.M. (1962). Factors in complex skill training. In R. Glaser (Ed.), *Training research and education*. Pittsburgh, PA: University of Pittsburgh Press. [Reprinted, 1990. In M. Venturino (Ed.), *Selected readings in human factors* (pp. 275–296). Santa Monica, CA: Human Factors Society.]

Fitts, P.M. (1964). Perceptual-motor skill learning. In A.W. Melton (Ed.), *Categories of human learning* (pp. 243–285). New York: Academic Press.

Fitts, P.M., & Posner, M.I. (1967). *Human performance*. Belmont, CA: Wadsworth.

Flach, J.M. (1995). Situation awareness: Proceed with caution. *Human Factors, 37*, 149–157.

Fleishman, E.A., & Hempel, W.E., Jr. (1954). Changes in factor structure of a complex psychomotor test as a function of practice. *Psychometrika, 19*, 239–252.

Fleishman, E.A., & Hempel, W.E., Jr. (1955). The relation between abilities and improvement with practice in a visual discrimination reaction task. *Journal of Experimental Psychology, 49*, 301–312.

Fleishman, E.A., & Quaintance, M.K. (1984). *Taxonomies of human performance*. New York: Academic Press.

Flynn, J.R. (1998). IQ gains over time: Toward finding the causes. In U. Neisser (Ed), *The rising curve: Long-term gains in IQ and related measures*. Washington, DC: American Psychological Association.

Fodor, J.A., & Pylyshyn, Z.W. (1988). Connectionism and cognitive architecture: A critical analysis. *Cognition, 28*, 3–71.

Folkard, S. (1975). Diurnal variation in logical reasoning. *British Journal of Psychology, 66*, 1–8.

Folkard, S. (1979). Changes in immediate memory strategy under induced muscle tension and with time of day. *Quarterly Journal of Experimental Psychology, 31*, 621–633.

Folkard, S. (1983). Diurnal variation in human performance. In G.R.J. Hockey, (Ed.), *Stress and fatigue in human performance*. Chichester: John Wiley & Sons Ltd.

Folkard, S. (1996). Body rhythms and shiftwork. In P. Warr (Ed.), *Psychology at work*. London: Penguin.

Folkard, S. (1997). Black times: Temporal determinants of transport safety. *Accident Analysis and Prevention, 29*, 417–430.

Folkard, S., Hume, K.I., Minors, D.S., Waterhouse, J.M., & Watson, F.L. (1985). Independence of the circadian rhythm in alertness from the sleep/wake cycle. *Nature, 313*, 678–679.

Folkard, S., & Monk, T.H. (1980). Circadian rhythms in human memory. *British Journal of Psychology, 71*, 295–307.

Folkard, S., Wever, R.A., & Wildgruber, C.M. (1983). Multi-oscillatory control of circadian-rhythms in human performance. *Nature, 305*, 223–226.

Forgas, J.P. (1995). Mood and judgement: The affect infusion model (AIM). *Psychological Bulletin, 117*, 39–66.

Forgas, J.P., & Bower, G.H. (1987) Affect in social and personal judgements. In K. Fiedler & J. Forgas (Eds.), *Affect, cognition and social behavior: New evidence and integrative attempts*. Lewiston, NY: Hogrefe.

Foulds, G.A. (1952). Temperamental differences in maze performance II: The effect of distraction and of electroconvulsive therapy on psychomotor retardation. *British Journal of Psychiatry, 43*, 33–41.

Fowler, C.J., & Wilding, J. (1979). Differential effects of noise and incentives on learning. *British Journal of Psychology, 70*, 149–153.

Fox, E. (1995). Negative priming from ignored distractors in visual selection: A review. *Psychonomic Bulletin and Review, 2*, 145–173.

Fox, E. (1996) Selective processing of threatening words in anxiety: The role of awareness. *Cognition and Emotion, 10*, 449–480.

Fozard, J.L. (1990). Vision and hearing in aging. In J.E. Birren & K.W. Schaie (Eds.), *Handbook of the psychology of aging* (3rd ed.). San Diego, CA: Academic.

Fracker, M.L., & Wickens, C.D. (1989). Resources, confusions, and compatibility in dual-axis tracking displays, controls, and dynamics. *Journal of Experimental Psychology: Human Perception and Performance, 15*, 80–96.

Frankenhaeuser, M. (1986). A psychobiological framework for research. In M.H. Appley & R. Trumbull (Eds.), *Dynamics of stress: Physiological, psychological and social perspectives*. New York: Plenum Press.

Freeman, G.L., & Hovland, C.I. (1934). Diurnal variations in performance and other related physiological processes. *Psychological Bulletin, 31*, 777–799.

Frederiksen, J.R. (1982). A componential theory of reading skills and their interactions. In R.J. Sternberg (Ed.), *Advances in the psychology of human intelligence (Vol. 1)*. Hillsdale, NJ: Lawrence Erlbaum Associates Inc.

French, J.R.P., Jr., Caplan, R.D., & Harrison, R.V. (1982). *The mechanisms of job stress and strain*. New York: John Wiley & Sons Inc.

Frewer, L.J., & Lader, M. (1991). The effects of caffeine on two computerized tests of attention and vigilance. *Human Psychopharmacology Clinical and Experimental, 6*, 119–128.

Friedman, A., Polson, M.C., & Dafoe, C.G. (1988). Dividing attention between the hands and the head: Performance trade-offs between rapid finger tapping and verbal memory. *Journal of Experimental Psychology: Human Perception and Performance, 14*, 60–68.

Friedman, A., Polson, M.C., Dafoe, C.G., & Gaskill, S.J. (1982). Dividing attention within and between hemispheres: Testing a multiple resources approach to limited-capacity information processing. *Journal of Experimental Psychology: Human Perception and Performance, 8*, 625–650.

Frith, C.D. (1971). Strategies in rotary pursuit tracking. *British Journal of Psychology, 62*, 187–197.

Fuller, R. (1990). Learning to make errors: Evidence from a driving task simulation. *Ergonomics, 33*, 1241–1250.

Furnham, A. (1992). *Personality at work: The role of individual differences in the workplace*. London: Routledge.

Furnham, A., & Bradley, A. (1997). Music while you work: The differential distraction of background music on the cognitive test performance of introverts and extroverts. *Applied Cognitive Psychology, 11*, 445–455.

Furnham, A., & Saipe, J. (1993). Personality correlates of convicted drivers. *Personality and Individual Differences, 14*, 329–336.

Gaba, D.M., & Howard, S.K. (1995). Situation awareness in anesthesiology. *Human Factors, 37*, 20–31.

Gafafer, W.M. (1964). *Occupational diseases: A guide to their recognition*. Washington, DC: US Department of Health, Education and Welfare, USGPO.

Gale, A. (1977). Some EEG correlates of sustained attention. In R.R. Mackie (Ed.), *Vigilance: Theory, operational performance, and physiological correlates*. New York: Plenum Press.

Galinsky, T.L., Rosa, R., Warm, J.S., & Dember, W.N. (1993). Psychophysical determinants of stress in sustained attention. *Human Factors, 35*, 603–614.

Galinsky, T.L., Warm, J.S., Dember, W.N., Weiler, E.M., & Scerbo, M.W. (1990). Sensory alternation and vigilance performance: The role of pathway inhibition. *Human Factors, 32*, 717–728.

Gardner, H. (1987). *The mind's new science: A history of cognitive revolution*. New York: HarperCollins.

Gardner, H., Kornhaber, M.L., & Wake, W.K. (1996). *Intelligence: Multiple perspectives*. Fort Worth, TX: Harcourt Brace College Publishers.

Gathercole, S.E., & Baddeley, A.D. (1993). *Working memory and language*. Hillsdale, NJ: Lawrence Erlbaum Associates Inc.

Gawron, V.J. (1982). Performance effects of noise intensity, psychological set, and task type and complexity. *Human Factors, 24*, 225–243.

Geen, R.G. (1984). Preferred stimulation levels in introverts and extraverts: Effects on arousal and performance. *Journal of Personality and Social Psychology, 46*, 1303–1312.

Geen, R.G. (1985). Test anxiety and visual vigilance. *Journal of Personality and Social Psychology, 49*, 963–970.

Geen, R.G. (1987). Test anxiety and behavioral avoidance. *Journal of Research in Personality, 21*, 481–488.

Geen, R.G. (1995). *Human motivation: A social psychological approach*. Pacific Grove, CA: Brooks/Cole Pub. Co.

Geen, R.G., McCown, E.J., & Broyles, J.W. (1985). Effects of noise on sensitivity of introverts and extraverts to signals in a vigilance task. *Personality and Individual Differences, 6*, 237–241.

Gerbert, K., & Kemmler, R. (1986). The causes of causes: Determinants and background variables of human factors incidents and accidents. *Ergonomics, 29*, 1439–1453.

Ghiselli, E.E. (1966). *The validity of occupational aptitude tests*. New York: John Wiley & Sons Inc.

Giambra, L.W., & Quilter, R.E. (1988). Sustained attention in adulthood: A unique, large-sample, longitudinal and multi-cohort analysis using the Mackworth Clock-test. *Psychology and Aging, 3*, 75–83.

Gibson, J.J. (1979) *The ecological approach to visual perception*. Boston: Houghton Mifflin.

Gillberg, M., Kecklund, G., Axelsson, J., & Akerstedt, T. (1996). The effects of a short daytime nap after restricted night sleep. *Sleep, 19*, 570–575.

Giniger, B., Dispenzieri, A., & Eisenberg, J. (1983). Age, experience and performance on speed and skill jobs in an applied setting. *Journal of Applied Psychology, 68*, 469–475.

Glass, D.C., & Singer, J.E. (1972). *Urban stress: Experiments on noise and social stressors*. New York: Academic.

Glendon, A.I., McKenna, S.P., Hunt, K., & Blaylock, S.S. (1988).Variables affecting cardiopulmonary resuscitation skill decay. *Journal of Occupational Psychology, 61*, 243–55.

Goldberg, L.R. (1993). The structure of phenotypic personality traits. *American Psychologist, 48*, 26–34.

Goldstein, D., Haldane, D., & Mitchell, C. (1990). Sex differences in visual-spatial ability: The role of performance factors. *Memory and Cognition, 18*, 546–550.

Goldstein, P.C., Rosenbaum, G., & Taylor, M.J. (1997). Assessment of differential attention mechanisms in seizure disorders and schizophrenia. *Neuropsychology, 11*, 309–317.

Goolkasian, P., & Edwards, D.C. (1977). The effect of loud noise on the psychological refractory period. *Bulletin of the Psychonomic Society, 9*, 139–141.

Gopher, D. (1996). Attention control: Explorations of the work of an executive controller. *Cognitive Brain Research, 5*, 23–38.

Gotlib, I.H., & McCann, C.D. (1984). Construct accessibility and depression: An examination of cognitive and affective factors. *Journal of Personality and Social Psychology, 47*, 427–439.

Gotlib, I.H., Roberts, J.E., & Gilboa, E. (1996). Cognitive interference in depression. In I.G. Sarason & G.R. Pierce (Eds.), *Cognitive interference: Theories, methods, and findings*. Mahwah, NJ: Lawrence Erlbaum Associates Inc.

Gould, J.D., & Grischkowsky, N.L. (1986). Does visual angle of a line of characters affect reading speed? *Human Factors, 28*, 165–173.

Graf, P., Squire, L.R., & Mandler, G. (1984). The information that amnesic patients do not forget. *Journal of Experimental Psychology: Learning, Memory, and Cognition, 10*, 164–178.

Grainger, J., & Jacobs, A.M. (1994). A dual read-out model of word context effects in letter perception: Further investigations of the word superiority effect. *Journal of Experimental Psychology: Human Perception and Performance, 20*, 1158–1176.

Grandjean, E. (1987). Design in VDT workstations. In G. Salvendy (Ed.), *Handbook of human factors*. New York: John Wiley & Sons Inc.

Gray, J.A. (1982) *The neuropsychology of anxiety: An enquiry into the functions of the septo-hippocampal system*. Oxford: Oxford University Press.

Gray, J.A. (1987). *The psychology of fear and stress (2nd ed.)*. Cambridge: Cambridge University Press.

Gray, J.A., & Wedderburn, A.A. (1960). Grouping strategies with simultaneous stimuli. *Quarterly Journal of Experimental Psychology, 12*, 180–184.

Green, R.F. (1969). Age–intelligence relationship between ages sixteen and sixty-four: A rising trend. *Developmental Psychology, 1*, 618–627.

Green, D.M., & Swets, J.A. (1966). *Signal detection theory and psychophysics*. New York: John Wiley & Sons Inc.

Green, M.W., Elliman, N.A., & Rogers, P.J. (1997). The effects of food deprivation and incentive motivation on blood glucose levels and cognitive function. *Psychopharmacology, 134*, 88–94.

Greenwood, M., & Woods, H.M. (1919). The incidence of industrial accidents upon individuals with special reference to multiple accidents. *Industrial Health Research Board Report No.4*. London: HMSO.

Grether, W.R. (1973). Human performance at elevated environmental temperature. *Aerospace Medicine, 44*, 747–755.

Griew, S. (1959). A study of accidents in relation to occupation and age. *Ergonomics, 2*, 17–23.

Griew, S. (1964). *Job re-design for older workers*. Paris: OECD.

Griffin, J.A., Dember, W.N., & Warm, J.S. (1986) Effects of depression on expectancy in sustained attention. *Motivation and Emotion, 10*, 195–205.

Griffin, M.J. (1992).Vibration. In A.P. Smith & D.M. Jones (Eds.), *Handbook of human performance. Vol. 1: The physical environment*. London: Academic Press.

Griffin, M.J. (1997). Vibration and motion. In G. Salvendy (Ed.), *Handbook of human factors and ergonomics*. New York: John Wiley & Sons Inc.

Griffin-Fouco, M., & Ghertman, F. (1987). Data collection on human factors. In J. Rasmussen, K. Duncan & J. Leplat (Eds.), *New technology and human error*. Chichester: John Wiley & Sons Ltd.

Grobe, J.E., Perkins, K.A., Goettler-Good, J., & Wilson, A. (1998). Importance of environmental distractors in the effects of nicotine on short-term memory. *Experimental and Clinical Psychopharmacology, 6*, 209–216.

Groves, P.M., & Thompson, R.F. (1970). Habituation: A dual process theory. *Psychological Review, 77*, 419–450.

Grubb, P.L., Miller, L.C., Nelson, W.T., Warm, J.S., Dember, W.N., & Davies, D.R. (1994). Cognitive failure and perceived workload in vigilance performance. In M. Mouloua & R. Parasuraman (Eds.), *Human performance in automated systems: Current research and trends*. Hillsdale, NJ: Lawrence Erlbaum Associates Inc.

Grudin, J. (1983). Non-hierarchic specification of components in transcription typewriting. *Acta Psychologica, 54*, 249–262.

Guion, R.M. (1997) Criterion measures and the criterion dilemma. In N. Anderson, & P. Herriot (Eds.), *International handbook of selection and appraisal (2nd ed.)*. London: John Wiley & Sons Ltd.

Gugerty, L.J. (1997). Situation awareness during driving: Explicit and implicit knowledge in dynamic spatial memory. *Journal of Experimental Psychology: Applied, 3*, 42–66.

Gulian, E., & Thomas, J.R. (1986). The effects of noise, cognitive set and gender on mental arithmetic performance. *British Journal of Psychology, 77*, 503–511.

Gulian, E., Matthews, G., Glendon, A.I., Davies, D.R., & Debney, L.M. (1989). Dimensions of driver stress. *Ergonomics, 32*, 585–602.

Gunter, B., & Furnham, A. (1986). Sex and personality differences in recall of violent and non-violent news from three presentation modalities. *Personality and Individual Differences, 6*, 829–838.

Guralnick, M. (1972). Observing responses and decision processes in vigilance. *Journal of Experimental Psychology, 93*, 239–244.

Gustafsson, C., Gennser, M., Oernhagen, H., & Derefeldt, G. (1997). Effects of normobaric hypoxic confinement on visual and motor performance. *Aviation, Space, Environmental Medicine, 68*, 985–992.

Haernqvist, K., Gustafsson, J.-E., Muthen, B.O., & Nelson, G. (1994). Hierarchical models of ability at individual and class levels. *Intelligence, 18*, 165–187.

Haga, S. (1984). An experimental study of signal vigilance errors in train driving. *Ergonomics, 27*, 755–765.

Hagman, J.D., & Rose, A.M. (1983). Retention of military tasks: A review. *Human Factors, 25*, 199–213.

Haider, M., Spong, P., & Lindsley, D.B. (1964). Attention, vigilance and cortical evoked potentials in humans. *Science, 145*, 180–182.

Hale, A., & Glendon, A.I. (1987). *Individual behaviour in the control of danger*. Amsterdam: Elsevier.

Hall, S., & Smith, A.P. (1996). Investigation of the effects and aftereffects of naturally occurring upper respiratory tract illnesses on mood and performance. *Physiology and Behavior, 59*, 569–577.

Halpern, D.F. (1992). *Sex differences in cognitive abilities (2nd ed.)*. Hillsdale, NJ: Lawrence Erlbaum Associates Inc.

Halpern, D.F. (1997). Sex differences in intelligence—Implications for education. *American Psychologist, 52*, 1091–1102.

Hamilton, C.J. (1995). Beyond sex differences in visuospatial processing: The impact of gender trait possession. *British Journal of Psychology, 86*, 1–20.

Hampson, E., & Kimura, D. (1993). Neural and hormonal mechanisms mediating sex differences in cognition. In P.A. Vernon (Ed.), *Biological approaches to the study of human intelligence.* Norwood, NJ: Ablex.

Hampson, S.E. (1988). *The construction of personality (2nd ed.).* London: Routledge.

Hancock, P.A. (1983). The effect of an induced selective increase in head temperature upon performance of a simple mental task. *Human Factors, 25,* 441–448.

Hancock, P.A. (1986). Sustained attention under thermal stress. *Psychological Bulletin, 99,* 263–281.

Hancock, P.A. (1997). *Essays on the future of man-machine systems.* Minneapolis: Peter Hancock.

Hancock, P.A., & Desmond, P.A. (Eds.) (2000). *Stress, workload and fatigue.* Hillsdale, NJ: Lawrence Erlbaum Associates Inc.

Hancock, P.A., & Pierce, J.O. (1985). Combined effects of heat and noise on human performance: A review. *American Industrial Hygiene Association Journal, 46,* 555–566.

Hancock, P.A., & Warm, J.S. (1989). A dynamic model of stress and sustained attention. *Human Factors, 31,* 519–537.

Hansen, C.P. (1988). Personality correlates of the accident involved employee. *Journal of Business and Psychology, 2,* 346–365.

Hansen, C.P. (1989). A causal model of the relationship among accidents, biodata, personality, and cognitive factors. *Journal of Applied Psychology, 74,* 81–90.

Harackiewicz, J.M., & Manderlink, G. (1984). A process analysis of the effects of performance: Contingent rewards on intrinsic motivation. *Journal of Experimental Social Psychology, 20,* 531–551.

Hardy, D.J., & Parasuraman, R. (1997). Cognition and flight performance in older pilots. *Journal of Experimental Psychology: Applied, 3,* 313–348.

Harris, D.H. (1968). Effect of defect rate on inspector accuracy. *Journal of Applied Psychology, 52,* 377–379.

Harris, L.J. (1993). Do left-handers die sooner than right-handers? Commentary on Coren and Halpern's (1991) "Left-handedness: A marker for decreased survival fitness". *Psychological Bulletin, 109,* 90–106.

Hart, S.G., & Staveland, L.E. (1988). Development of NASA-TLX (Task Load Index): Results of empirical and theoretical research. In P.A. Hancock & N. Meshkati (Eds.), *Human mental workload.* Amsterdam: Elsevier.

Hartlage, S., Alloy, L.B., Vazquez, C., & Dykman, B. (1993) Automatic and effortful processing in depression. *Psychological Bulletin, 113,* 247–278.

Hartley, A.A. (1992). Attention. In F.I.M. Craik & T.A. Salthouse (Eds.), *The handbook of aging and cognition.* Hillsdale, NJ: Lawrence Erlbaum Associates Inc.

Hartley, A.A. (1993). Evidence for the selective preservation of spatial selective attention in old age. *Psychology and Aging, 8,* 371–379.

Hartley, L.R. (1992). Prescribed psychotropic drugs: The major and minor tranquillizers. In A.P. Smith & D.M. Jones (Eds.), *Handbook of human performance. Vol. 2: Health and performance.* London: Academic Press.

Hartley, L.R., Morrison, D., & Arnold, P. (1989). Stress and skill. In A.M. Colley & J.R. Beech (Eds.), *Acquisition and performance of cognitive skills* (pp. 265–300). Chichester, UK: John Wiley.

Hasher, L., Stolzfus, E.R., Zacks, R.T., & Rypma, B. (1991). Age and inhibition. *Journal of Experimental Psychology: Learning, Memory and Cognition, 17,* 163–169.

Hasher, L., & Zacks, R.T. (1979). Automatic and effortful processes in memory. *Journal of Experimental Psychology: General, 108,* 356–388.

Hasher, L., & Zacks, R.T. (1988). Working memory, comprehension, and aging. A review and a new view. In G.H. Bower (Ed.), *The psychology of learning and motivation: Advances in research and theory, Vol. 22.* San Diego, CA: Academic Press.

Hatano, G., Miyake, Y., & Binks, M.G. (1977). Performance of expert abacus operators. *Cognition, 5,* 47–55.

Haworth, N.L. (1996). Feasibility of development of a driver fatigue warning system for trucks. In *Proceedings of the Second International Conference on Driver Impairment, Fatigue and Driving Simulation.* Applecross, Western Australia: Promaco Conventions.

Hay, B. (1975). International legislation on external industrial noise. *Applied Acoustics, 8,* 133–148.

Hawkins, H.L., Kramer, A.F., & Capaldi, D. (1992). Aging, exercise and attention. *Psychology and Aging, 7,* 643–653.

Hayslip, B., & Kennelly, K. (1982). Short-term memory and crystallized-fluid intelligence in adulthood *Research on Aging, 4,* 314–332.

Head, H. (1923). The conception of nervous and mental energy. II. Vigilance: A physiological state of the nervous system. *British Journal of Psychology, 14,* 126–147.

Healy, A.F. (1994). Letter detection: A window to unitization and other cognitive processes in reading text. *Psychonomic Bulletin & Review, 1*, 333–344.

Hebb, D.O. (1949). *The organization of behavior.* New York: John Wiley & Sons Inc.

Heckhausen, H., & Beckmann, J. (1990). Intentional action and action slips. *Psychological Review, 97*, 36–48.

Hedge, A., Sims, W.R., & Becker, F.D. (1995). Effects of lensed-indirect and parabolic lighting on the satisfaction, visual health, and productivity of office workers. *Ergonomics, 38*, 260–280.

Heneman, R.L. (1986) The relationship between supervisory ratings and results-oriented measures of performance: A meta-analysis. *Personnel Psychology, 39*, 811–926.

Herrman, D.J. (1982). Know thy memory: The use of questionnaires to assess and study memory. *Psychological Bulletin, 92*, 434–452.

Herrnstein, R.J., & Murray, C.A. (1994). *The bell curve: Intelligence and class structure in American life.* New York: Free Press.

Hetu, R., Truchon-Gagnon, C., & Bilodeau, S. (1990). Problems of noise in school settings: A review of literature and the results of an exploratory study. *Journal of Speech, Language, Pathology, and Audiology, 14*, 31–39.

Heuer, H. (1985). Some points of contact between models of central capacity and factor-analytic models. *Acta Psychologica, 60*, 135–156.

Heuer, H. (1996). Dual-task performance. In O. Neumann & A.F. Sanders (Eds.), *Handbook of perception and action. Vol. 3. Attention.* London: Academic Press.

Heuer, H., Spijkers, W., Kiesswetter, E., & Schmidtke, V. (1998). Effects of sleep loss, time of day, and extended mental work on implicit and explicit learning of sequences. *Journal of Experimental Psychology: Applied, 4*, 139–162.

Hex, J.R. (1988). Measuring mental workload: Problems, progress, and promises. In P.A. Hancock & N. Meshkati (Eds.), *Human mental workload.* North Holland: Elsevier.

Hick, W.G. (1952). On the rate of gain of information. *Quarterly Journal of Experimental Psychology, 4*, 11–26.

Hicks, L.H., & Birren, J.E. (1970). Aging, brain damage, and psychomotor slowing. *Psychological Bulletin, 74*, 377–396.

Hildebrandt, G., Rohmert, W., & Rutenfranz, J. (1975a). 12 and 24 hour rhythms in error frequency of locomotive drivers and the influence of tiredness. *International Journal of Chronobiology, 2*, 175–180.

Hildebrandt, G., Rohmert, W., & Rutenfranz, J. (1975b). The influence of fatigue and rest period on the circadian variation of error frequency in shift workers (engine drivers). In P. Colquhoun, S. Folkard, P. Knauth & J. Rutenfranz (Eds.), *Experimental studies of shiftwork.* Opladen: Westdeutscher Verlag.

Hillyard, S.A., & Hansen, J.C. (1986). Attention: Electrophysiological approaches. In M.G.H. Coles, E. Donchin, & S.W. Porges (Eds.), *Psychophysiology: Systems, processes and approaches.* New York: Guilford Press.

Hillyard, S.A., Hink, R.F., Schwent, V.L., & Picton, T.W. (1973). Electrical signs of selective attention in the human brain. *Science, 182*, 177–179.

Hindmarch, I. (1982). Critical flicker fusion (CFF): The effects of psychotropic compounds. *Pharmacopsychiatrica, 15 (Supplement 1)*, 44–48.

Hinkin, C.H., van Gorp, W.G., Satz, P., Marcotte, T., Durvasula, R.S., Wood, S., Campbell, L., & Baluda, M.R. (1996). Actual versus self-reported cognitive dysfunction in HIV-1 infection: Memory-metamemory dissociations. *Journal of Clinical and Experimental Neuropsychology, 18*, 431–443.

Hirst, W., Spelke, E.S., Reaves, C.C., Caharack, G., & Neisser, U. (1980). Dividing attention without alternation or automaticity. *Journal of Experimental Psychology: General, 109*, 98–117.

Hirst, W. (1986). Aspects of divided and selective attention. In J. LeDoux & W. Hirst (Eds.), *Mind and brain.* New York: Cambridge University Press.

Hirst, W., & Kalmar, D. (1987). Characterising attentional resources. *Journal of Experimental Psychology: General*, 116, 68–81.

Hoagland, H. (1933). The physiological control of judements of duration: Evidence for a chemical clock. *Journal of General Psychology, 9*, 267–287.

Hockey, G.R.J. (1970a). Signal probability and spatial location as possible bases for increased selectivity in noise. *Quarterly Journal of Experimental Psychology, 2*, 37–42.

Hockey, G.R.J. (1970b) Change in attention allocation in a multi-component task under loss of sleep. *British Journal of Psychology, 61*, 473–480.

Hockey, G.R.J. (Ed.) (1983). *Stress and human performance.* Chichester, UK: John Wiley.

Hockey, G.R.J. (1984). Varieties of attentional state: The effects of the environment. In R. Parasuraman & D.R. Davies (Eds.), *Varieties of attention.* New York: Academic Press.

Hockey, G.R.J. (1986). A state control theory of adaptation to stress and individual differences in stress management. In G.R.J. Hockey, A.W.K. Gaillard, & M.G.H. Coles (Eds.), *Energetics and human information processing.* Dordrecht: Martinus Nijhoff.

Hockey, G.R.J. (1997). Compensatory control in the regulation of human performance under stress and high workload: A cognitive-energetical framework. *Biological Psychology, 45*, 73–93.

Hockey, G.R.J., Gaillard, A.W.K., & Coles, M.G.H. (Eds.) (1986). *Energetics and human information processing.* Dordrecht: Martinus Nijhoff.

Hockey, G.R.J., & Hamilton, P. (1970). Arousal and information selection in short-term memory. *Nature, 226*, 866–867.

Hockey, G.R.J., & Hamilton, P. (1983). The cognitive patterning of stress states. In G.R.J. Hockey (Ed.), *Stress and human performance.* Chichester: John Wiley & Sons Ltd.

Hockey, G.R.J., Maclean, A., & Hamilton, P. (1981). State changes and the temporal patterning of component resources. In J. Long & A. Baddeley (Eds.), *Attention and performance IX.* Hillsdale, NJ: Laurence Erlbaum Associates Inc.

Hockey, G.R.J., Wastell, D.G., & Sauer, J. (1998). Effects of sleep deprivation and user interface on complex performance: A multilevel analysis of compensatory control. *Human Factors, 40*, 233–253.

Hoeksema-van Orden, C.Y.D., Gaillard, A.W.K., & Buunk, B.P. (1998). Social loafing under fatigue. *Journal of Personality and Social Psychology, 75*, 1179–1190.

Hoffman, R.G., Speelman, D.J., Hinnen, D.A., Conley, K.L., Guthrie, R.A., & Knapp, R.K. (1989). Changes in cortical functioning with acute hypoglycaemia and hyperglycaemia in Type 1 diabetes. *Diabetes, 34*, 949–957.

Hoffman, R.R. (1997). American cognitive psychology. In W.G. Bringmann, H.E. Luck, R. Miller, & C. Early (Eds.), *A pictorial history of psychology.* Carol Stream, IL: Quintessence Books.

Hogg, N., Folleso, K., Strand-Volden, F., & Torralba, B. (1995). Development of a situation awareness measure to evaluate advanced alarm systems in nuclear power plant control rooms. *Ergonomics, 38*, 2394–2413.

Hohnsbein, J., Piekarski, C., & Kampmann, B. (1983). Influence of high ambient temperature and humidity on visual sensitivity. *Ergonomics, 26*, 905–911.

Hohnsbein, J., Piekarski, C., Kampman, B., & Noack, T. (1984). Effects of heat on visual acuity. *Ergonomics, 27*, 1239–1246.

Holding, D.H. (1983). Fatigue. In G.R.J. Hockey (Ed.), *Stress and fatigue in human performance.* Chichester: John Wiley & Sons Ltd.

Holding, D.H. (Ed.) (1989). *Human skills.* Chichester: John Wiley & Sons Ltd.

Holding, Dennis H. (1992). Theories of chess skill. *Psychological Research, 54*, 10–16.

Holender, D. (1986). Semantic activation without conscious identification in dichotic listening, parafoveal vision, and visual masking: A survey and appraisal. *Behavioral and Brain Sciences, 9*, 1–66.

Holland, C.A., & Rabbitt, P.M.A. (1991). Social and psychological gerontology: The course and causes of cognitive change with advancing age. *Reviews in Clinical Gerontology, 1*, 81–96.

Holroyd, K.A., & Appel, M.A. (1980). Test anxiety and physiological responding. In I.G. Sarason (Ed.), *Test anxiety: Theory, research and applications.* Hillsdale, NJ: Laurence Erlbaum Associates Inc.

Holt, W.R., & Brainerd, E.C. (1976). Selective hyperthermia and reaction time. *Perceptual and Motor Skills, 43*, 375–382.

Hogervorst, E., Riedel, W., Jeukendrup, A., & Jolles, J. (1996). Cognitive performance after strenuous physical exercise. *Perceptual and Motor Skills, 83*, 479–488.

Horn, J.L. (1998). A basis for research on age differences in cognitive capabilities. In J.J. McArdle & R.W. Woodcock (Eds.), *Human cognitive abilities in theory and practice.* Mahwah, NJ: Lawrence Erlbaum Associates Inc.

Horn, J.L., & Noll, J. (1997). Human cognitive capabilities: Gf-Gc theory. In D.P. Flanagan & J.L. Genshaft (Eds.), *Contemporary intellectual assessment: Theories, tests, and issues.* New York: Guilford Press.

Horne, J.A. (1988). Sleep loss and "divergent" thinking ability. *Sleep, 11*, 528–536.

Horne, J.A., Anderson, N.R., & Wilkinson, R.T. (1983). Effects of sleep deprivation on signal detection measures of vigilance: Implications for sleep function. *Sleep, 6*, 347–358.

Horne, J.A., & Pettitt, A.N. (1985). High incentive effects on vigilance performance during 72 hours of total sleep deprivation. *Acta Psychologica, 58*, 123–139.

Horvath, M., Frantik, E., Kopriva, K., & Meissner, J. (1975). EEG theta activity increase coinciding with performance decrement in a monotonous task. *Activitas Nervosa Superior, 18*, 207–210.

Horvath, S.M., & Drechsler-Parks, D.M. (1992). Air pollution and behavior. In A.P. Smith & D.M. Jones (Eds.), *Handbook of human performance. Vol. 1: The physical environment.* London: Academic Press.

Hough, L.M. (1992). The "Big Five" personality variables—construct confusion: Description versus prediction. *Human Performance, 5*, 139–155.

Houghton, G., & Tipper, S.P. (1994). A model of inhibitory mechanisms in selective attention. In D. Dagenbach & T.H. Carr (Eds.), *Inhibitory processes in attention, memory, and language*. San Diego, CA: Academic Press.

Houghton, G., & Tipper, S.P. (1998). A model of selective attention as a mechanism of cognitive control. In J.E. Grainger & A.M. Jacobs (Eds.), *Localist connectionist approaches to human cognition*. Mahwah, NJ: Lawrence Erlbaum Associates Inc.

Houx, P.J., Jolles, J.W., & Vreeling, F.W. (1993). Stroop interference: Aging effects assessed with the Stroop Color-Word Test. *Experimental Aging Research, 19*, 209–224.

Houx, P.J., Vreeling, F.W., & Jolles, J. (1991). Rigorous health screening reduces age effect on memory scanning task. *Brain and Cognition, 15*, 246–260.

Howard, D.V. (1988). Implicit and explicit assessment of cognitive aging. In M.L. Howe & C.J. Brainerd (Eds.), *Cognitive development in adulthood*. New York: Springer-Verlag.

Howland, D. (1958). *An investigation of the performance of the human monitor*. U.S. Airforce, Wright Air Development Center Technical Report (No. 57–431).

Hsu, S.H. (1991). Human errors in maintenance. In M. Kuchashiro & E.D. Megaw (Eds.), *Human work: Solutions to problems in occupational health and safety*. London: Taylor & Francis.

Hulin, C.L., Henry, R.A., & Noon, S.Z. (1990). Adding a dimension: Time as a factor in the generalizability of predictive relationships. *Psychological Bulletin, 107*, 328–340.

Hultsch, D.F., Hammer, M., & Small, B.J. (1993). Age differences in cognitive performance in later life: Relationships to self-reported health and activity life style. *Journal of Gerontology, 48*, 1–11.

Humphreys, G.W., & Bruce, V. (1989). *Visual cognition: Computational, experimental, and neuropsychological perspectives*. Hove, UK: Lawrence Erlbaum Association Ltd.

Humphreys, G.W., & Mueller, H.J. (1993). SEarch via Recursive Rejection (SERR): A connectionist model of visual search. *Cognitive Psychology, 25*, 43–110.

Humphreys, M.S., & Revelle, W. (1984). Personality, motivation and performance: A theory of the relationship between individual differences and information processing. *Psychological Review, 91*, 153–184.

Hunt, E. (1978). Mechanics of verbal ability. *Psychological Review, 85*, 109–130.

Hunt, E., & MacLeod, C.M. (1977). The sentence-verification paradigm: A case study of two conflicting approaches to individual differences. In R.J. Sternberg & D.K. Detterman (Eds.), *Human intelligence: Perspectives on its theory and measurement*. Norwood, NJ: Ablex.

Hyde, J.S. (1981). How large are cognitive gender differences? A meta-analysis using $\omega^2$ and $d'$. *American Psychologist, 36*, 892–901.

Hyde, J.S. (1996). *Half the human experience: The psychology of women (5th ed.)*. Lexington, MA: D.C. Heath.

Hyde, J.S., & Linn, M.C. (1988). Gender differences in verbal ability: A meta-analysis. *Psychological Bulletin, 104*, 53–69.

Hygge, S. (1991). The interaction of noise and mild heat on cognitive performance and serial reaction time. *Environment International, 17*, 229–234.

Hygge, S. (1992). Heat and performance. In A.P. Smith & D.M. Jones (Eds.), *Handbook of human performance. Vol. 1: The physical environment*. London: Academic Press.

Hyman, R. (1953). Stimulus information as a determinant of reaction time. *Journal of Experimental Psychology, 45*, 188–196.

Iampietro, P.F., Melton, C.E., Higgins, E.A., Vaughan, J.A., Hoffman, S.M., Funkhouser, G.E., & Saldivar, J.T. (1972). High temperature and performance in a flight task simulator. *Aerospace Medicine, 43*, 1215–1218.

Idzikowski, C. (1984). Sleep and memory. *British Journal of Psychology, 75*, 439–449.

Idzikowski, C.F.J., & Baddeley, A.D. (1983). Fear and performance in dangerous environments. In G.R.J. Hockey (Ed.), *Stress and fatigue in human performance*. Chichester: Wiley.

Inglis, J. (1965). Immediate memory, age and brain function. In A.T. Welford & J.E. Birren (Eds.), *Behavior, aging and the nervous system*. Springfield, IL: Charles C.Thomas.

Ingram, R.E. (1984). Toward an information-processing analysis of depression. *Cognitive Therapy and Research, 8*, 443–478.

International Labour Organization (1996). Tackling sources of stress in high-risk groups. *World Of Work, 18*, 13–16. Geneva: ILO.

Jagust, W.J., Eberling, J.L., Reed, B.R., & Mathis, C.A. (1997). Clinical studies of cerebral blood flow in Alzheimer's disease. In J.C. de la Torre & V. Hachinski (Eds.), *Cerebrovascular pathology in Alzheimer's disease*. New York: New York Academy of Sciences.

James, W. (1890). *Principles of psychology*. New York: Holt.

Jarvis, M.J. (1993). Does caffeine intake enhance absolute levels of cognitive performance? *Psychopharmacology, 110*, 45–52.

Jennings, J.R., & Coles, M.G.H. (Eds.) (1991). *Handbook of cognitive psychophysiology: Central and autonomic nervous system*. Chichester: John Wiley & Sons Ltd.

Jensen, A.R. (1965). Scoring the Stroop Test. *Acta Psychologica, 29*, 398–408.

Jensen, A.R. (1980). *Bias in mental testing*. New York: Free Press.

Jensen, A.R. (1987). Individual differences in the Hick paradigm. In P. Vernon (Ed.), *Speed of information processing and intelligence*. Norwood, NJ: Ablex.

Jensen, A.R. (1998). *The g factor: The science of mental ability*. Westport, CT: Praeger Publishers/ Greenwood Publishing Group, Inc.

Jerison, H.J. (1959). *Experiments on vigilance: V. The empirical model for human vigilance*. US Airforce, Wright Air Development Center Technical Report (No. 58–526).

Jerison, H.J. (1970). Vigilance, discrimination and attention. In D.I. Mostofsky (Ed.), *Attention: Contemporary theory and analysis*. New York: Appleton-Century Crofts.

Jerison, H.J. (1977). Vigilance: Biology, psychology, theory and practice. In R.R. Mackie (Ed.), *Vigilance: Theory, operational performance and physiological correlates*. New York: Plenum Press.

Jerison, H.J., & Pickett, R.M. (1964). Vigilance: The importance of the elicited observing rate. *Science, 143*, 970–971.

Jerison, H.J., & Wallis, R.A. (1957). *Experiments on vigilance: II. One-clock and three-clock monitoring*. US Airforce, Wright Air Development Center Technical Report (No. 57–206).

Johansson, G. (1973). Visual perception of biological motion and a model for its analysis. *Perception and Psychophysics, 14*, 201–211.

Johansson, G., & Aronsson, G. (1984). Stress reactions in computerized administrative work. *Journal of Occupational Behavior, 5*, 159–181.

Johnson, L.C. (1982). Sleep deprivation and performance. In W.B. Webb (Ed.), *Biological rhythms, sleep, and performance*. Chichester: John Wiley & Sons Ltd.

Johnson, M.H., & Magaro, P.A. (1987). Effects of mood and severity on memory processes in depression and mania. *Psychological Bulletin, 101*, 28–40.

Johnson, P. (1982). The functional equivalence of imagery and movement. *Quarterly Journal of Experimental Psychology, 34A*, 349–365.

Johnston, M.K., Hashtroudi, S., & Lindsay, S. (1993). Source monitoring. *Psychological Bulletin, 114*, 3–28.

Johnston, W.A., & Dark, V.J. (1986). Selective attention. *Annual Review of Psychology, 37*, 43–75.

Johnston, W.A., & Heinz, S.P. (1978). Flexibility and capacity demands of attention. *Journal of Experimental Psychology: General, 107*, 420–435.

Jonassen, D.H., & Grabowski, B.L. (1993). *Handbook of individual differences: Learning and instruction*. Hillsdale, NJ: Laurence Erlbaum Associates Inc.

Jones, D.G., & Endsley, M.R. (1995). Sources of situation awareness errors in aviation. *Aviation, Space and Environmental Medicine, 67*, 507–512.

Jones, D.M. (1983). Loud noise and levels of control: A study of serial reaction. In B. Berglund & T. Lindvall (Eds.), *Proceedings of the Fourth International Congress on Noise as a Public Health Problem*. Stockholm: Swedish Council for Building Research.

Jones, D.M. (1984). Performance effects. In D.M. Jones & A.J. Chapman (Eds.), *Noise and society*. Chichester: John Wiley & Sons Ltd.

Jones, D.M. (1993). Objects, streams, and threads of auditory attention. In A.D. Baddeley & L. Weiskrantz (Eds.), *Attention: selection, awareness, and control: A tribute to Donald Broadbent*. Oxford: Oxford University Press.

Jones, D.M. (1994). Disruption of memory for lip-read lists by irrelevant speech: Further support for the changing state hypothesis. *Quarterly Journal of Experimental Psychology, 47A*, 143–160.

Jones, D.M., & Broadbent, D.E. (1987). Noise. In G. Salvendy (Ed.), *Handbook of human factors*. New York: John Wiley & Sons Inc.

Jones, D.M., Auburn, T.C., & Chapman, A.J. (1982). Perceived control in continuous loud noise. *Current Psychological Research, 2*, 111–122.

Jones, D.M., & Chapman, A.J. (Eds.) (1984). *Noise and society*. Chichester, UK: John Wiley.

Jones, D.M., & Davies, D.R. (1984). Individual and group differences in the response to noise. In D.M. Jones & A.J. Chapman (Eds.), *Noise and society* Chichester, UK: John Wiley & Sons Ltd.

Jones, D.M., Farrand, P., Stuart, G., & Morris, N. (1995). Functional equivalence of verbal and spatial information in serial short-term memory. *Journal of Experimental Psychology: Learning, Memory, and Cognition, 21*, 1008–1018.

Jones, D.M., & Macken, W.J. (1995). Phonological similarity in the irrelevant speech effect: Within- or between-stream similarity? *Journal of Experimental Psychology: Learning, Memory and Cognition, 21*, 103–115.

Jones, D.M., Miles, C., & Page, J. (1990). Disruption of reading by irrelevant speech: Effects of attention, arousal, or memory? *Applied Cognitive Psychology, 4*, 89–108.

Jones, D.M., & Morris, N. (1992). Irrelevant speech and cognition. In D.M. Jones & A.P. Smith (Eds.), *Handbook of human performance, Vol. 1, The physical environment*. London: Academic Press.

Jones, D.M., Smith, A.P., & Broadbent, D.E. (1979). Effects of moderate intensity noise on the Bakan vigilance task. *Journal of Applied Psychology, 64*, 627–634.

Jonides, J., & Smith, E.E. (1997). The architecture of working memory. In M.D. Rugg (Ed.), *Cognitive neuroscience*. Cambridge, MA: MIT Press.

Joyce, E., Blumenthal, S., & Wessely, S. (1996). Memory, attention, and executive function in chronic fatigue syndrome. *Journal of Neurology, Neurosurgery and Psychiatry, 60*, 495–503.

Just, M.A., & Carpenter, P.A. (1992). A capacity theory of comprehension: Individual differences in working memory. *Psychological Review, 99*, 122–149.

Just, M.A., Carpenter, P.A., & Keller, T.A. (1996). The capacity theory of comprehension: New frontiers of evidence and arguments. *Psychological Review, 103*, 773–780.

Kahneman, D. (1973). *Attention and effort*. Englewood Cliffs, NJ: Prentice Hall.

Kahneman, D., Ben-Ishai, R., & Lotan, M. (1973). Relation of a test of attention to road accidents. *Journal of Applied Psychology, 58*, 113–115.

Kahneman, D., & Treisman, A.M. (1984). Changing views of attention and automaticity. In R. Parasuraman & D.R. Davies (Eds.), *Varieties of attention*. San Diego, CA: Academic Press.

Kanfer, R. (1994). Work motivation: New directions in theory and research. In C.L. Cooper & I.T. Robertson (Eds.), *Key reviews in managerial psychology: Concepts and research for practice*. Chichester, UK: John Wiley.

Kanfer, F.H., & Stevenson, M.K. (1985) The effects of self-regulation on concurrent cognitive processing. *Cognitive Therapy and Research, 9*, 667–684.

Kanfer, R., & Ackerman, P.L. (1989). Motivation and cognitive abilities: An integrative/aptitude treatment interaction approach to skill acquisition. *Journal of Applied Psychology, 74*, 657–690.

Kanfer, R., Ackerman, P.L., Murtha, T.C., Dugdale, B., & Nelson, L. (1994). Goal-setting, conditions of practice, and task-performance—a resource-allocation perspective. *Journal of Applied Psychology, 79*, 826–835.

Kanfer, R., Ackerman, P.L., Murtha, T., & Goff, M. (1995). Personality and intelligence in industrial and organizational psychology. In D.H. Saklofske & M. Zeidner (Eds.), *International handbook of personality and intelligence*. New York: Plenum Press.

Karasek, R., & Theorell, T. (1989). *Healthy work: Stress, productivity, and the reconstruction of working life*. New York: Basic Books.

Kass, S.J., Ahlers, R.H., & Dugger, M. (1998). Eliminating gender differences through practice in an applied visual spatial task. *Human Performance, 11*, 337–349.

Kausler, D.H. (1982). *Experimental psychology and human aging*. New York: John Wiley & Sons Inc.

Kausler, D.H. (1985). Episodic memory: Memorizing performance. In N. Charness (Ed.), *Aging and human performance*. Chichester: John Wiley & Sons Ltd.

Keele, S.W. (1968). Movement control in skilled motor performance. *Psychological Bulletin, 70*, 387–403.

Keele, S.W. (1986). Motor control. In K.R. Boff & L. Kaufman (Eds.), *Handbook of perception and human performance. Vol. II: Cognitive processes and performance* (pp. 1–60). New York: John Wiley.

Keele, S.W., & Hawkins, H.L. (1982). Explorations of individual differences relevant to high level skill. *Journal of Motor Behavior, 14*, 3–23.

Keele, S.W., & Summers, J.J. (1976). The structure of motor programs. In G.E. Stelmach (Ed.), *Motor control: Issues and trends*. New York: Academic Press.

Kelleher, C.H., & Quirk, D.A. (1973). Age, functional capacity and work: An annotated bibliography. *Industrial Gerontology, 19*, 80–98.

Kelso, J.A.S. (1995). *Dynamic patterns: The self-organization of brain and behavior*. Cambridge, MA: MIT Press.

Kerr, J.S., & Hindmarch, I. (1998). The effects of alcohol alone or in combination with other drugs on information processing, task performance and subjective responses. *Human Psychopharmacology Clinical and Experimental, 13*, 1–9.

Kerr, J.S., Sherwood, N., & Hindmarch, I. (1991). Separate and combined effects of the social drugs on psychomotor performance. *Psychopharmacology, 104*, 113–119.

Kerr, W.A. (1950). Accident proneness of factory departments. *Journal of Applied Psychology, 34*, 167–170.

Kieras, D., & Polson, P.G. (1985). An approach to the formal analysis of user complexity. *International Journal of Man-Machine Studies, 22*, 365–394.

Kimmel, D.C. (1990). *Adulthood and aging: An interdisciplinary, developmental view.* New York: John Wiley.

Kinsbourne, M., & Hicks, R.E. (1978). Functional cerebral space: A model for overflow, transfer and interference effects in human performance: A tutorial review. In J. Requin (Ed.), *Attention and performance VII.* Hillsdale, NJ: Laurence Erlbaum Associates Inc.

Kirsch, I., & Weixel, L.J. (1988). Double-blind versus deceptive administration of a placebo. *Behavioral Neuroscience, 102*, 319–323.

Kirsner, K., Speelman, C., Maybery, M., O'Brien-Malone, A., Anderson, M., & MacLeod, C. (Eds.) (1998). *Implicit and explicit mental processes.* Mahwah, NJ: Lawrence Erlbaum Associates Inc.

Kitayama, S. (1997). Affective influence in perception: Some implications of the amplification model. In G. Matthews (Ed.), *Cognitive science perspectives on personality and emotion.* Amsterdam: Elsevier.

Klein, K.E., Wegmann, H.M., & Hunt, B.I. (1972). Desynchronization of body temperature and performance circadian rhythm as a result of outgoing and homegoing transmeridian flights. *Aerospace Medicine, 43*, 119–132.

Kleiss, J.A., & Lane, D.M. (1986). Locus and persistence of capacity limitations in visual information processing. *Journal of Experimental Psychology: Human Perception and Performance, 12*, 200–210.

Kleitman, N. (1963). *Sleep and wakefulness (2nd ed.).* Chicago: University of Chicago Press.

Kline, D.W., & Scheiber, F. (1985). Vision and aging. In J.E. Birren & K.W. Schaie (Eds.), *Handbook of the psychology of aging (2nd ed.).* New York: Van Nostrand Reinhold.

Kline, D.W., & Scialfa, C.T. (1996). Visual and auditory aging. In J.E. Birren & K.W. Schaie (Eds.), *Handbook of the psychology of aging (4th ed.).* San Diego, CA: Academic Press.

Kline, P. (1994). *An easy guide to factor analysis.* London: Routledge.

Kluger, A.N., & DeNisi, A. (1996). The effects of feedback interventions on performance: A historical review, a meta-analysis, and a preliminary feedback intervention theory. *Psychological Bulletin, 119*, 254–284.

Knez, I. (1995). Effects of indoor lighting on mood and cognition. *Journal of Environmental Psychology, 15*, 39–51.

Knez, I., & Enmarker, I. (1998). Effects of office lighting on mood and cognitive performance and a gender effect in work-related judgment. *Environment and Behavior, 30*, 553–567.

Knowles, W.B. (1963). Operator loading tasks. *Human Factors, 5*, 155–161.

Koch, R. (1993). *Die Psychologische Refräktarperiode [The Psychological Refractory Period].* Unpublished doctoral dissertation, Ludwig-Maximilian University, Munich.

Koelega, H.S. (1992). Extraversion and vigilance performance: 30 years of inconsistencies. *Psychological Bulletin, 112*, 239–258.

Koelega, H.S., & Brinkman, J.A. (1986). Noise and vigilance: An evaluative review. *Human Factors, 28*, 465–481.

Koelega, H.S., Verbaten, M.N., Van Leeuwen, T.H., Kenemans, J.L., Kemner, C., & Sjouw, W. (1992). Time effects on event-related potentials and vigilance performance. *Biological Psychology, 34*, 59–86.

Koga, Y., & Morant, G.M. (1923). On the degree of association between reaction times in the case of different senses. *Biometrika, 15*, 346–372.

Kohn, P.M. (1996). On coping adaptively with daily hassles. In M. Zeidner & N.S. Endler (Eds.), *Handbook of coping: Theory, research, application.* New York: John Wiley & Sons Inc.

Korteling, J-E. (1991). Effects of skill integration and perceptual competition on age-related differences in dual-task performance. *Human Factors, 33*, 35–44.

Koslowsky, M., & Babkoff, H. (1992). Meta-analysis of the relationship between total sleep deprivation and performance. *Chronobiology International, 9*, 132–136.

Kosnick, W.D., Sekuler, P., & Kline, D.W. (1990). Self-reported visual problems of older drivers. *Human Factors, 32*, 95–108.

Kozena, L., Frantik, E., & Dvorak, J. (1996). Vigilance enhanced by psychophysiological means: Comparison of several methods. *Homeostasis in Health and Disease, 37*, 256–260.

Kramer, A.F. (1991). Physiological metrics of mental workload: A review of recent progress. In D.L. Damos (Ed.), *Multiple-task performance.* London: Taylor & Francis.

Kramer, A.F., & Coles, M.G.H. (Eds.) (1996). *Converging operations in the study of visual selective attention.* Washington, DC: American Psychological Association.

Kramer, A.F., Larish, J.F., & Strayer, D.L. (1995). Training for attentional control in dual-task settings: A comparison of young and old adults. *Journal of Experimental Psychology: Applied, 1,* 50–76.

Kramer, A.F., Humphrey, D.G., Larish, J.F., & Logan, G.D. (1994). Age and inhibition: Beyond a unitary view of inhibitory processing in attention. *Psychology and Aging, 9,* 491–512.

Kramer, A.F., Schneider, W., Fisk, A., & Donchin, E. (1986). The effects of practice and task structure on components of the vent-related brain potential. *Psychophysiology, 23,* 33–47.

Kramer, A.F., & Watson, S.E. (1996). Object-based visual selection and the principle of uniform connectedness. In A.F. Kramer & M.G.H. Coles (Eds.), *Converging operations in the study of visual selective attention.* Washington, DC: American Psychological Association.

Kranzler, J.H., & Jensen, A.R. (1989). Inspection time and intelligence: A meta-analysis. *Intelligence, 13,* 329–347.

Krueger, G.P. (1989). Sustained work, fatigue, sleep loss and performance: A review of the issues. *Work and Stress, 3,* 129–141.

Krulewitz, J., Warm, J.S., & Wohl, T.H. (1975). Effects of shifts in the rate of repetitive stimulation on sustained attention. *Perception and Psychophysics, 18,* 245–249.

Kryter, K.D. (1950). The effects of noise on man. *Journal of Speech and Hearing Disorders, Monograph Supplement, No. I.*

Kryter, K.D. (1994). *The handbook of hearing and the effects of noise: Physiology, psychology, and public health.* San Diego, CA: Academic Press.

Kueller, R., & Laike, T. (1998). The impact of flicker from fluorescent lighting on well-being, performance and physiological arousal. *Ergonomics, 41,* 433–447.

Kutscher, R.E., & Walker, J.F. (1960). Comparative job performance of office workers by age. *Monthly Labor Review, 83,* 39–43.

Kyllonen, P.C. (1993). Aptitude testing inspired by information processing: A test of the four-sources model. *Journal of General Psychology, 120,* 375–405.

Kyllonen, P.C., & Chrystal, R.E. (1990). Reasoning ability is (little more than) working-memory capacity? *Intelligence, 14,* 389–433.

Kyllonen, P.C., & Tirre, W.C. (1988). Individual differences in associative learning and forgetting. *Intelligence, 12,* 393–421.

Laberg, J.C., & Löberg, T. (1989). Expectancy and tolerance: A study of acute alcohol intoxication using the balanced placebo design. *Journal of Studies on Acute Alcohol, 50,* 448–455.

LaBerge, D. (1983). Spatial extent of attention to letters and words. *Journal of Experimental Psychology: Human Perception and Performance, 9,* 371–379.

Lacey, J.I. (1967). Somatic response patterning and stress: Some revisions of activation theory. In M.H. Appley & R. Trumbull (Eds.), *Psychological stress.* New York: Meredith.

Lachman, R., Lachman, J.L., & Butterfield, E.C. (1979). *Cognitive psychology and information processing: An introduction.* Hillsdale, NJ: Laurence Erlbaum Associates Inc.

Lahtela, N., Niemi, P., Kuusela, V., & Hypen, K. (1986). Noise and visual choice-reaction time: A large-scale population survey. *Scandinavian Journal of Psychology, 27,* 52–57.

Laird, J.E., Newell, A., & Rosenbloom, P.S. (1987). SOAR: An architecture for general intelligence. *Artificial Intelligence, 33,* 1–64.

Landauer, A.A., & Howat, P. (1983). Low and moderate alcohol doses, psychomotor performance and perceived drowsiness. *Ergonomics, 26,* 647–657.

Landers, D.M., & Boutcher, S.H. (1986). Arousal-performance relationships. In J.M. Williams (Ed.), *Applied sport psychology: Personal growth to peak performance.* Palo Alto, CA: Mayfield.

Langan-Fox, J., Waycott, J., & Galna, C. (1997). Ability–performance relations during skill acquisition. *Australian Psychologist, 32,* 153–158.

Langdon, F.J. (1985). Noise annoyance. In W. Tempest (Ed.), *The noise handbook.* London: Academic Press.

Lardent, C.L. (1991). Pilots who crash: Personality constructs underlying accident prone behaviour of fighter pilots. *Multivariate Experimental Clinical Research, 10,* 1–25.

Larkin, A.A. (1996). *Semantic priming and working memory capacity: A test of distinctive roles in reading comprehension.* Unpublished doctoral dissertation, University of Utah.

Larson, G.E., Alderton, D.L., Neideffer, M., & Underhill, E. (1997). Further evidence on dimensionality and correlates of the Cognitive Failures Questionnaire. *British Journal of Psychology, 88,* 29–38.

Larson, G.E., & Merritt, C.R. (1991). Can accidents be predicted? An empirical test of the Cognitive Failures Questionnaire. *Applied Psychology: An International Review, 40,* 37–45.

Lashley, K.S. (1917). The accuracy of movement in the absence of excitation from the moving organ. *American Journal of Psychology, 43,* 169–194.

Lashley, K.S. (1942). The problem of cerebral organization in vision. In J. Cattell (Ed.), *Biological symposia. Vol. VII. Visual mechanisms.* Lancaster, PA: Jaques Cattell Press.

Latham, G.P., & Locke, E.A. (1991). Self-regulation through goal setting. *Organizational Behavior and Human Decision Processes, 50,* 212–247.

Laver, G.D., & Burke, D.M. (1993). Why do semantic priming effects increase in old age? A meta-analysis. *Psychology and Aging, 8,* 34–43.

Lavie, N. (1995). Perceptual load as a necessary condition for selective attention. *Journal of Experimental Psychology: Human Perception and Perormance, 21,* 451–468.

Lavie, N., & Driver, J. (1996). On the spatial extent of attention in object-based visual selection. *Perception and Psychophysics, 58,* 1238–1251.

Lawson, E.A. (1966). Decisions concerning the rejected channel. *Quarterly Journal of Experimental Psychology, 18,* 260–265.

Lawton, R., & Parker, R. (1998). Individual differences in accident liability: A review and integrative approach. *Human Factors, 40,* 655–671.

Lazarus, R.S. (1991). *Emotion and adaptation.* Oxford: OUP.

Lazarus, R.S., & Folkman, S. (1984). *Stress, appraisal and coping.* New York: Springer.

Leahey, T.H. (1997). *A history of psychology: Main currents in psychological thought.* Upper Saddle River, NJ: Prentice Hall.

Leary, D.E. (1990). Psyche's muse: The role of metaphor in the history of psychology. In D.E. Leary (Ed.), *Metaphors in the history of psychology.* Cambridge: Cambridge University Press.

LeCompte, D.C. (1994). Extending the irrelevant speech effect beyond serial recall. *Journal of Experimental Psychology: Learning, Memory and Cognition, 20,* 1396–1408.

LeDoux, J.E. (1996). *The emotional brain: The mysterious underpinnings of emotional life.* New York: Simon & Schuster.

Lehto, J. (1996). Are executive function tests dependent on working memory capacity? *Quarterly Journal of Experimental Psychology: Human Experimental Psychology, 49A,* 29–50.

Lenne, M.G., Triggs, T.J., & Redman, J.R. (1998). Interactive effects of sleep deprivation, time of day, and driving experience on a driving task. *Sleep, 21,* 38–44.

Leon, M.R., & Revelle, W. (1985). The effect of anxiety on analogical reasoning: A test of three theoretical models. *Journal of Personality and Social Psychology, 49,* 1302–1315.

Levy-Leboyer, C. (1989). Noise effects on two industrial tasks. *Work and Stress, 3,* 315–322.

Lieberman, H.R. (1992). Caffeine. In A.P. Smith & D.M. Jones (Eds.), *Handbook of human performance. Vol. 2: Health and performance.* London: Academic Press.

Liederman, J. (1998). The dynamics of interhemispheric collaboration and hemispheric control. *Brain and Cognition, 36,* 193–208.

Light, L.L. (1991). Memory and aging: Four hypotheses in search of data. *Annual Review of Psychology, 42,* 333–376.

Light, L.L., & Singh, A. (1987). Implicit and explicit memory in younger and older adults. *Journal of Experimental Psychology: Learning, Memory and Cognition, 13,* 531–541.

Lima, S.D., Hale, S., & Myerson, J. (1991). How general is general slowing? Evidence from the lexical domain. *Psychology and Aging, 6,* 416–425.

Lindeis, A-E., Nathoo, A., & Fowler, B. (1996). An AFM investigation of the effects of acute hypoxia on mental rotation. *Ergonomics, 39,* 278–284.

Lindenberger, U., & Baltes, P.B. (1994). Sensory functioning and intelligence in old age. *Psychology and Aging, 9,* 339–355.

Lindner, H., & Kropf, S. (1993). Asthenopic complaints associated with fluorescent lamp illumination (FLI): The role of individual disposition. *Lighting Research Technology, 25,* 59–69.

Lindsay, P.H., & Norman, D.A. (1977). *Human information processing.* New York: Academic Press.

Lisper, H-O., & Eriksson, B. (1980). Effects of the length of a rest break and food intake on subsidiary reaction time performance in an 8-hour driving task. *Journal of Applied Psychology, 65,* 117–122.

Llorente, A.M., Miller, E.N., D'Elia, L.F., Selnes, O., Wesch, A., Becker, J.T., & Satz, P. (1998). Slowed information processing in HIV-1 disease. *Journal of Clinical and Experimental Neuropsychology, 20,* 60–72.

Loeb, M., & Binford, J.R. (1970). Examination of some factors influencing performance on an auditory monitoring task with one signal per session. *Journal of Experimental Psychology, 83,* 40–44.

Loeb, M., Holding, D.H., & Baker, M.A. (1982). Noise stress and circadian arousal in self-paced computation. *Motivation and Emotion, 6,* 43–48.

Loewen, L.J., & Suedfeld, P. (1992). Cognitive and arousal effects of masking office noise. *Environment and Behavior, 24,* 381–395.

Logan, G.D. (1985). Executive control of thought and action. *Acta Psychologica, 60,* 193–210.

Logan, G.D. (1988). Towards an instance theory of automatization. *Psychological Review, 95,* 492–527.

Logan, G.D. (1992). Attention and preattention in theories of automaticity. *American Journal of Psychology, 105*, 317–339.

Logan, G.D., & Compton, B.J. (1998). Attention and automaticity. In R.D. Wright (Ed.), *Visual attention*. New York: Oxford University Press.

Logie, R.H. (1995). *Visuo-spatial working memory*. Hove, UK: Lawrence Erlbaum Associates Ltd.

Logie, R.H., & Gilhooly, K.J. (1998). *Working memory and thinking*. Hove, UK: Psychology Press.

Loke, W.H. (1988). Effects of caffeine on mood and memory. *Physiology and Behavior, 44*, 367–372.

Loo, R. (1979). Role of primary personality factors in the perception of traffic signs and driver violations and accidents. *Accident Analysis and Prevention, 11*, 125–127.

Lorist, M.M., & Snel, J. (1997). Caffeine effects on perceptual and motor processes. *Electroencephalography and Clinical Neurophysiology, 102*, 401–413.

Lorist, M.M., Snel, J., & Kok, A. (1994). Influence of caffeine on information processing stages in well rested and fatigued subjects. *Psychopharmacology, 113*, 411–421.

Losier, B.J., McGrath, P.J., & Klein, R.M. (1996). Error patterns of the Continuous Performance Test in non-medicated and medicated samples of children with and without ADHD: A meta-analytic review. *Journal of Child Psychology and Psychiatry and Allied Disciplines, 37*, 971–987.

Lucas, D. (1992). Understanding the human factor in disasters. *Interdisciplinary Science Reviews, 17*, 184–190.

Luck, S.J. (1998). Neurophysiology of selective attention. In H. Pashler (Ed.), *Attention*. Hove, UK: Psychology Press.

Luck, S.J., Fan, S., & Hillyard, S.A. (1993). Attention-related modulation of sensory-evoked brain activity in a visual search task. *Journal of Cognitive Neuroscience, 5*, 188–195.

Luck, S.J., & Girelli, M. (1998). Electrophysiological approaches to the study of selective attention in the human brain. In R. Parasuraman (Ed.), *The attentive brain*. Cambridge, MA: MIT Press.

Luna, T.D. (1997). Air traffic controller shiftwork: What are the implications for aviation safety? A review. *Aviation, Space, and Environmental Medicine, 68*, 69–79.

Maccoby, E.E., & Jacklin, C.N. (1978). *The psychology of sex differences*. Stanford, CA: Stanford University Press.

MacKay, D.G. (1973). Aspects of the theory of comprehension, memory, and attention. *Quarterly Journal of Experimental Psychology, 25*, 22–40.

Mackie, R.R. (1987). Vigilance research: Are we ready for countermeasures? *Human Factors, 29*, 707–723.

Mackie, R.R., & Miller, J.C. (1978). *Effects of hours of service, regularity of schedules and cargo loading on truck and bus driver fatigue*. Technical Report 1765-F, Human Factors Research Incorporated, Santa Barbara Research Park, Goleta, CA.

Mackie, R.R., & O'Hanlon, J.F. (1977). A study of the combined effects of extended driving and heat stress on driver arousal and performance. In R.R. Mackie (Ed.), *Vigilance: Theory, operational performance and physiological correlates*. New York: Plenum Press.

Mackworth, J.F. (1968). Vigilance, arousal, and habituation. *Psychological Review, 75*, 308–322.

Mackworth, J.F. (1969). *Vigilance and habituation*. Harmondsworth: Penguin.

Mackworth, N.H. (1946). Effects of heat on wireless telegraphy operators' hearing and recording Morse messages. *British Journal of Industrial Medicine, 3*, 143–158.

Mackworth, N.H. (1948). The breakdown of vigilance during prolonged visual search. *Quarterly Journal of Experimental Psychology, 1*, 6–21.

Mackworth, N.H. (1950). Researches on the measurement of human performance. *Medical Research Council Special Report Series 268*. London: HMSO.

Mackworth, N.H. (1957). Some factors affecting vigilance. *Advancement of Science, 53*, 389–393.

MacLeod, C. (1991). Half a century of research on the Stroop effect: An integrative review. *Psychological Bulletin, 109*, 163–203.

MacLeod, C., & Mathews, A. (1986). Discrimination of threat cues without awareness in anxiety states. *Journal of Abnormal Psychology, 95*, 131–138.

MacLeod, C., & Mathews, A. (1991). Cognitive-experimental approaches to the emotional disorders. In P.R. Martin (Ed.), *Handbook of behaviour therapy and psychological science: An integrative approach*. Oxford: Pergamon.

MacLeod, C., & McLaughlin, K. (1995). Implicit and explicit memory bias in anxiety: A conceptual replication. *Behaviour Research and Therapy, 33*, 1–14.

MacLeod, C.M., Hunt, E.B., & Mathews, N.N. (1978). Individual differences in the verification of sentence-picture relationships. *Journal of Verbal Learning and Verbal Behavior, 17*, 493–507.

MacMillan, N.A., & Creelman, C.D. (1991). *Detection theory: A user's guide*. New York: Cambridge University Press.

MacMillan, N.A., & Creelman, C.D. (1996). Triangles in ROC space: History and theory of "nonparametric" measures of sensitivity and response bias. *Psychonomic Bulletin and Review, 3,* 164–170.

Mahar, D., Henderson, R., & Deane, F. (1997). The effects of computer anxiety, state anxiety, and computer experience on users' performance of computer based tasks. *Personality and Individual Differences, 22,* 683–692.

Mahoney, M.J., Gabriel, T.J., & Perkins, T.S. (1987). Psychological skills and exceptional athletic performance. *The Sport Psychologist, 1,* 181–199.

Mairiaux, P., & Malchaire, J. (1995). Comparison and validation of heat stress indices in experimental studies. *Ergonomics, 38,* 58–72.

Makeig, S., & Inlow, M. (1993). Lapses in alertness: Coherence of fluctuations in performance and EEG spectrum. *Electroencephalography and Clinical Neurophysiology, 86,* 23–25.

Malhotra, L., Malhotra, L., & Jerath, J. (1989) Speed and accuracy in learning as a function of personality. *Journal of Personality and Clinical Studies, 5,* 5–8.

Mangun, G.R., Hillyard, S.A., & Luck, S.J. (1993). Electrocortical substrates of visual selective attention. In D. Meyer & S. Kornblum (Eds.), *Attention & performance XIV*. Cambridge, MA: MIT Press.

Marcuse, H. (1955). *Eros and civilization: A philosophical inquiry into Freud*. Boston: Beacon Press.

Marill, T. (1957). The psychological refractory phase. *British Journal of Psychology, 48,* 93–97.

Mark, J.A. (1957). Comparative job performance by age. *Monthly Labor Review, 80,* 1467–1471.

Marrocco, R.T., & Davidson, M.C. (1998). Neurochemistry of attention. In R. Parasuraman (Ed.), *The attentive brain*. Cambridge, MA: MIT Press.

Marshall, G.D., & Zimbardo, P.G. (1979). Affective consequences of inadequately explained physiological arousal. *Journal of Personality and Social Psychology, 37,* 970–988.

Marshall, P.S., Forstot, M., Callies, A., Peterson, P.K., & Schenck, C.H. (1997). Cognitive slowing and working memory difficulties in chronic fatigue syndrome. *Psychosomatic Medicine, 59,* 58–66.

Martell, R.F., Lane, D.M., & Emrich, C. (1996). Male-female differences: A computer simulation. *American Psychologist, 51,* 157–158.

Martin, E.M., Pitrak, D.L., Robertson, L.C., Novak, R.M., Mullane, K.M., & Pursell, K.J. (1995). Global-local analysis in HIV-1 infection. *Neuropsychology, 9,* 102–109.

Martin, M., & Jones, G.V. (1984). Cognitive failures in everyday life. In J.E. Harris & P.E. Morris (Eds.), *Everyday memory, actions, and absent-mindedness*. London: Academic Press.

Martindale, C. (1991). *Cognitive psychology: A neural-network approach*. Pacific Grove, CA: Brooks/Cole.

Massaro, D.W., & Loftus, G.R. (1996). Sensory and perceptual storage: Data and theory. In E.L. Bjork & R.A. Bjork (Eds.), *Memory*. San Diego, CA: Academic Press.

Maslach, C., & Jackson, S.E. (1981). The measurement of experienced burnout. *Journal of Occupational Behavior, 2,* 99–113.

Massaro, D.W., & Cowan, N. (1993). Information processing models: Microscopes of the mind. *Annual Review of Psychology, 44,* 383–425.

Mathews, A., & MacLeod, C. (1985) Selective processing of threat cues in anxiety states. *Behaviour Research and Therapy, 23,* 563–569.

Mathews, A., May, J., Mogg, K., & Eysenck, M.W. (1990). Attentional bias in anxiety: Selective search or defective filtering? *Journal of Abnormal Psychology, 98,* 131–138.

Matthews, G. (1985). The effects of extraversion and arousal on intelligence test performance. *British Journal of Psychology, 76,* 479–493.

Matthews, G. (1988). Morningness-eveningness as a dimension of personality: Trait, state and psychophysiological correlates. *European Journal of Personality, 2,* 277–293.

Matthews, G. (1992a). Extraversion. In A.P. Smith & D.M. Jones (Eds.), *Handbook of human performance. Vol. 3: State and trait*. London: Academic Press.

Matthews, G. (1992b). Mood. In A.P. Smith & D.M. Jones (Eds.), *Handbook of human performance. Vol. 3: State and trait*. London: Academic Press.

Matthews, G. (1996). Signal probability effects on high-workload vigilance tasks. *Psychonomic Bulletin and Review, 3,* 339–343.

Matthews, G. (1997a). An introduction to the cognitive science of personality and emotion. In G. Matthews (Ed.), *Cognitive science perspectives on personality and emotion*. Amsterdam: Elsevier.

Matthews, G. (1997b). The Big Five as a framework for personality assessment. In N. Anderson & P. Herriot (Eds.), *International handbook of selection and appraisal (2nd ed.)*. London: Wiley.

Matthews, G. (1997c). Intelligence, personality and information-processing: An adaptive perspective. In W. Tomic & J. Kingsma (Eds.), *Advances in cognition and educational practice. Vol. 4: Reflections on the concept of intelligence*. Greenwich, CT: JAI Press.

Matthews, G. (1997d). Extraversion, emotion and performance: A cognitive-adaptive model. In G. Matthews (Ed.), *Cognitive science perspectives on personality and emotion*. Amsterdam: Elsevier.

Matthews, G. (Ed.) (1997e). *Cognitive science perspectives on personality and emotion*. Amsterdam: Elsevier Science.

Matthews, G. (1999). Personality and skill: A cognitive-adaptive framework. In P.L. Ackerman, P.C. Kyllonen & R.D. Roberts (Eds.), *The future of learning and individual differences research: Processes, traits, and content*. Washington, DC: American Psychological Association.

Matthews, G. (2000a). Levels of transaction: A cognitive science framework for operator stress. In P.A. Hancock & P.A. Desmond (Eds.), *Stress, workload and fatigue*. Mahwah, NJ: Lawrence Erlbaum Associates Inc.

Matthews, G. (2000b). A transactional model of driver stress. In P.A. Hancock & P.A. Desmond (Eds.), *Stress, workload and fatigue*. Mahwah, NJ: Lawrence Erlbaum Associates Inc.

Matthews, G., & Amelang, M. (1993). Extraversion, arousal theory and performance: A study of individual differences in the EEG. *Personality and Individual Differences, 14*, 347–364.

Matthews, G., & Campbell, S.E. (1998). Task-induced stress and individual differences in coping. In *Proceedings of the Human Factors and Ergonomics Society 42nd Annual Meeting*. Santa Monica, CA: Human Factors and Ergonomics Society.

Matthews, G., Campbell, S.E., Desmond, P.A., Huggins, J., Falconer, S., & Joyner, L.A. (1999a). Assessment of task-induced state change: Stress, fatigue and workload components. In M. Scerbo (Ed.), *Automation technology and human performance: Current research and trends*. Hillsdale, NJ: Lawrence Erlbaum Associates Inc.

Matthews, G., Coyle, K., & Craig, A. (1990) Multiple factors of cognitive failure and their relationships with stress vulnerability. *Journal of Psychopathology and Behavioral Assessment, 12*, 49–64.

Matthews, G., & Davies, D.R. (1998). Arousal and vigilance: The role of task demands. In R.R. Hoffman, M.F. Sherrick & J.S. Warm (Eds.), *Viewing psychology as a whole: The integrative science of William N. Dember*. Washington, DC: APA.

Matthews, G., Davies, D.R., & Holley, P.J. (1990). Extraversion, arousal, and visual sustained attention: The role of resource availability. *Personality and Individual Differences, 11*, 1159–1173.

Matthews, G., Davies, D.R., & Holley, P.J. (1993). Cognitive predictors of vigilance. *Human Factors, 35*, 3–24.

Matthews, G., Davies, D.R., & Lees, J.L. (1990). Arousal, extraversion, and individual differences in resource availability. *Journal of Personality and Social Psychology, 59*, 150–168.

Matthews, G., & Deary, I. (1998). *Personality traits*. Cambridge: Cambridge University Press.

Matthews, G., & Desmond, P.A. (1998). Personality and multiple dimensions of task-induced fatigue: A study of simulated driving. *Personality and Individual Differences, 25*, 443–458.

Matthews, G., Desmond, P.A., Joyner, L.A., & Carcary, B. (1997). A comprehensive questionnaire measure of driver stress and affect. In C. Carbonell Vaya & J.A. Rothengatter (Eds.), *Traffic and transport psychology: Theory and application*. Amsterdam: Pergamon.

Matthews, G., & Dorn, L. (1995). Personality and intelligence: Cognitive and attentional processes. In D.H. Saklofske & M. Zeidner (Eds.), *International handbook of personality and intelligence*. New York: Plenum Press.

Matthews, G., Dorn, L., & Glendon, A.I. (1991). Personality correlates of driver stress. *Personality and Individual Differences, 12*, 535–549.

Matthews, G., Dorn, L., Hoyes, T.W., Davies, D.R., Glendon, A.I., & Taylor, R.G. (1998). Driver stress and performance on a driving simulator. *Human Factors, 40*, 136–149.

Matthews, G., & Gilliland, K. (1999). The personality theories of H.J. Eysenck and J.A. Gray: A comparative review. *Personality and Individual Differences, 26*, 583–626.

Matthews, G., & Harley, T.A. (1993). Effects of extraversion and self-report arousal on semantic priming: A connectionist approach. *Journal of Personality and Social Psychology, 65*, 735–756.

Matthews, G., & Harley, T.A. (1996). Connectionist models of emotional distress and attentional bias. *Cognition and Emotion, 10*, 561–600.

Matthews, G., Jones, D.M., & Chamberlain, A.G. (1990). Refining the measurement of mood: The UWIST Mood Adjective Checklist. *British Journal of Psychology, 81*, 17–42.

Matthews, G., Jones, D.M., & Chamberlain, A.G. (1992). Predictors of individual differences in mail coding skills, and their variation with ability level. *Journal of Applied Psychology, 77*, 406–418.

Matthews, G., Joyner, L., Gilliland, K., Campbell, S.E., & Huggins, J., & Falconer, S. (1999b). Validation of a comprehensive stress state questionnaire: Towards a state "Big Three"? In I. Mervielde, I.J. Deary, F. De Fruyt & F. Ostendorf (Eds.), *Personality psychology in Europe (Vol. 7)*. Tilburg: Tilburg University Press.

Matthews, G., & Margetts, I. (1991). Self-report arousal and divided attention: A study of performance operating characteristics. *Human Performance, 4*, 107–125.

Matthews, G., Pitcaithly, D., & Mann, R.L.E. (1995). Mood, neuroticism and the encoding of affective words. *Cognitive Therapy and Research, 19*, 563–587.

Matthews, G., Schwean, V.L., Campbell, S.E., Saklofske, D.H., & Mohamed A.A.R. (2000). Personality, self-regulation and adaptation: A cognitive-social framework. In M. Boekarts, P.R. Pintrich & M. Zeidner (Eds.), *Handbook of self-regulation*. New York: Academic Press.

Matthews, G., Sparkes, T.J., & Bygrave, H.M. (1996). Stress, attentional overload and simulated driving performance. *Human Performance, 9*, 77–101.

Matthews, G., Tsuda, A., Xin, G. & Ozeki, Y. (1999c). Individual differences in driver stress vulnerability in a Japanese sample. *Ergonomics, 42*, 401–415.

Matthews, G., & Wells, A. (1996). Attentional processes, coping strategies and clinical intervention. In M. Zeidner & N.S. Endler (Eds.), *Handbook of coping: Theory, research, applications*. New York: John Wiley & Sons Inc.

Matthews, G., & Wells, A. (1988). Relationships between anxiety, self-consciousness and cognitive failures. *Cognition and Emotion, 2*, 123–132.

Matthews, G., & Wells, A. (1999). The cognitive science of attention and emotion. In T. Dalgleish & M. Power (Eds.), *Handbook of cognition and emotion*. New York: John Wiley & Sons Inc.

Matthews, G., & Westerman, S.J. (1994). Energy and tension as predictors of controlled visual and memory search. *Personality and Individual Differences, 17*, 617–626.

Matthews, G., & Zeidner, M. (in press). Emotional intelligence, adaptation to stressful encounters and health outcomes. In J.D.A. Parker & R. Bar-On (Eds.), *Handbook of emotional intelligence*. San Francisco: Jossey-Bass.

Maycock, G. (1997). Sleepiness and driving: The experience of UK car drivers. *Accident Analysis and Prevention, 29*, 453–462.

Mayer, R.E., & Treat, J.R. (1977). Psychological, social, and cognitive characteristics of high risk drivers: A pilot study. *Accident Analysis and Prevention, 9*, 1–8.

Mayer, J.D., Salovey, P., & Caruso, D. (2000). Models of emotional intelligence. In R.J. Sternberg (Ed.), *Handbook of human intelligence (2nd ed.)*. New York: Cambridge University Press.

Maylor, E.A. (1985). Facilitatory and inhibitory components of orienting in visual space. In M.I. Posner & O.S. Marin (Eds.), *Attention and performance XI*. Hillsdale, NJ: Lawrence Erlbaum Associates Inc.

Maylor, E.A. (1990). Age and prospective memory. *Quarterly Journal of Experimental Psychogy: Human Experimental Psychology, 42*, 471–493.

Maylor, E.A., & Rabbitt, P.M.A. (1988). Amount of practice and degree of attentional control have no influence on the adverse effect of alcohol in word categorization and visual search tasks. *Perception and Psychophysics, 44*, 117–126.

Maylor, E.A., & Rabbitt, P.M.A. (1993). Alcohol, reaction time and memory: A meta-analysis. *British Journal of Psychology, 84*, 301–317.

Maylor, E.A., Rabbitt, P.M.A., James, G.H., & Kerr, S.A. (1990). Comparing the effects of alcohol and intelligence on text recall and recognition. *British Journal of Psychology, 81*, 299–313.

Maylor, E.A., Rabbitt, P.M.A., Sahgal, A., & Wright, C. (1987). Effects of alcohol on speed and accuracy in choice reaction time and visual search. *Acta Psychologica, 65*, 147–163.

Maxfield, L. (1997). Attention and semantic priming: A review of prime task effects. *Consciousness and Cognition: An International Journal, 6*, 204–218.

McBurney, D.H., Gaulin, S.J.C., Devineni, T., & Adams, C. (1997). Superior spatial memory of women: Stronger evidence for the gathering hypothesis. *Evolution and Human Behavior, 18*, 165–174.

McCarthy, D., Coban, R., Legg, S., & Faris, J. (1995). Effects of mild hypoxia on perceptual-motor performance: A signal-detection approach. *Ergonomics, 39*, 1979–1992.

McClelland, D.C. (1961). *The achieving society*. Princeton, NJ: Van Nostrand.

McClelland, J.L., & Rumelhart, D.E. (1981). An interactive activation model of context effects in letter perception: Part 1. An account of basic findings. *Psychological Review, 88*, 375–407.

McCord, R.R., & Wakefield, J.A. (1981). Arithmetic achievement as a function of introversion-extraversion and teacher presented reward and punishment. *Personality and Individual Differences, 2*, 145–152.

McCormack, P.D. (1962). A two-factor theory of vigilance. *British Journal of Psychology, 53*, 357–363.

McCrae, R.R., & Costa, P.T. (1987). Validation of the five-factor model of personality across instruments and observers. *Journal of Personality and Social Psychology, 52*, 81–90.

McDonald, N. (1984). *Fatigue, safety and the truck driver*. London: Taylor & Francis.

McDowd, J.M., & Birren, J.E. (1990). Aging and attentional processes. In J.E. Birren & K.W. Schaie (Eds.), *Handbook of the psychology of aging (3rd edition)*. San Diego, CA: Academic Press.

McDowd, J.M., & Craik, F.I.M. (1988). Effects of aging and task difficulty on divided attention performance. *Journal of Experimental Psychology: Human Perception and Performance, 14*, 267–280.

McDowd, J.M., & Oseas-Kreger, D.M. (1991). Aging, inhibitory processes, and negative priming. *Journal of Gerontology, 46*, 340–345.

McEvoy, G.M., & Cascio, W.F. (1989). Cumulative evidence of the relationship between employee age and job performance. *Journal of Applied Psychology, 74*, 11–17.

McGaughy, J., & Sarter, M. (1995). Behavioral vigilance in rats: Task validation and effects of age, amphetamine, and benzodiazepine receptor ligands. *Psychopharmacology, 11*, 340–357.

McGrath, J.J. (1963). Irrelevant stimulation and vigilance performance. In D.N. Buckner & J.J. McGrath (Eds.), *Vigilance: A symposium*. New York: McGraw Hill.

McGrath, J.J., & O'Hanlon, J.A. (1967). Temporal orientation and vigilance performance. In A.F. Sanders (Ed.), *Attention and performance: I*. Amsterdam: North Holland.

McKeachie, W.J. (1990). Learning, thinking, and Thorndike. *Educational Psychologist, 25*, 127–141.

McKenna, F. (1983). Accident proneness: A conceptual analysis. *Accident Analysis and Prevention, 15*, 65–71.

McLeod, P. (1977). A dual task response modality effect: Support for multiprocessor models of attention. *Quarterly Journal of Experimental Psychology, 29*, 651–667.

McLeod, P., Plunkett, K., & Rolls, E.T. (1998). *Introduction to connectionist modelling of cognitive processes*. Oxford: Oxford University Press.

McLeod, R.W., & Griffin, M.J. (1995). Mechanisms of vibration-induced interference with manual control performance. *Ergonomics, 38*, 1431–1444.

McMillen, D.L., & Wells-Parker, E. (1987). The effect of alcohol consumption on risk-taking while driving. *Addictive Behaviors, 12*, 241–247.

McNally, R.J. (1995). Automaticity and the anxiety disorders. *Behaviour Research and Therapy, 33*, 747–754.

McNicol, D. (1972). *A primer of signal detection theory*. London: Allen & Unwin.

Mech, E.V. (1953). Factors affecting routine performance under noise: 1. The influence of set. *Journal of Psychology, 35*, 283–298.

Meese, G.B., Lewis, M.I., Wyon, D.P., & Kok, R. (1984). A laboratory study of the effects of moderate thermal stress on the performance of factory workers. *Ergonomics, 27*, 19–43.

Megaw, E. (1992). The visual environment. In A.P. Smith & D.M. Jones (Eds.), *Handbook of human performance. Vol. 1: The physical environment*. London: Academic Press.

Meister, D. (1989). *Conceptual aspects of human factors*. Baltimore: Johns Hopkins University Press.

Mertens, H.W., & Collins, W.E. (1986). The effects of age, sleep deprivation, and altitude on complex performance. *Human Factors, 28*, 541–551.

Meyer, D.E., & Kieras, D.E. (1997a). A computational theory of executive cognitive processes and multiple-task performance: I. Basic mechanisms. *Psychological Review, 104*, 3–65.

Meyer, D.E., & Kieras, D.E. (1997b). A computational theory of executive cognitive processes and multiple-task performance: II. Accounts of psychological refractory-period phenomena. *Psychological Review, 104*, 749–791.

Meyer, D.E., & Schvaneveldt, R.W. (1972). Facilitation in recognizing pairs of words: Evidence of a dependence between retrieval operations. *Journal of Experimental Psychology, 90*, 227–234.

Meyer, J.P., & Rapp, R. (1995). Survey of heat stress in industry. *Ergonomics, 38*, 38–46.

Michiels, V., Cluydts, R., & Fischler, B. (1998). Attention and verbal learning in patients with Chronic Fatigue Syndrome. *Journal of the International Neuropsychological Society, 4*, 456–466.

Michiels, V., Cluydts, R., Fischler, B., & Hoffmann, G. (1996). Cognitive functioning in patients with chronic fatigue syndrome. *Journal of Clinical and Experimental Neuropsychology, 18*, 666–677.

Mihal, W.L., & Barrett, G.V. (1976). Individual differences in perceptual information processing and their relation to automobile accident involvement. *Journal of Applied Psychology, 61*, 229–233.

Miles, C., Auburn, T.C., & Jones, D.M. (1984). Effects of loud noise and signal probability on visual vigilance. *Ergonomics, 27*, 855–862.

Miller, D., & Riccio, M. (1990). Non-organic psychiatric and psychosocial syndromes associated with HIV-1 infection and disease. *AIDS, 4,* 381–388.

Miller, D.P., & Swain, A.D. (1987). Human error and human reliability. In G. Salvendy (Ed.), *Handbook of human factors.* New York: John Wiley & Sons Inc.

Miller, G.A. (1956). The magical number seven, plus or minus two: Some limits on our capacity for processing information. *Psychological Review, 63,* 81–97.

Miller, G.A., Galanter, E., & Pribram, K.H. (1960). *Plans and the structure of behavior.* New York: Holt, Rinehart and Winston.

Miller, G.A. (1965). Some preliminaries to psycholinguistics. *American Psychologist, 20,* 15–20.

Miller, G.A. (1985). Trends and debates in cognitive psychology. In A.M. Aitkenhead & J.M. Slack (Eds.), *Issues in cognitive modelling.* Hillsdale, NJ: Lawrence Erlbaum Associates Inc.

Miller, J. (1988). Discrete and continuous models of human information processing. *Acta Psychologica, 67,* 191–257.

Milliken, B., Joordens, S., Merikle, P.M., & Seifert, A.E. (1998). Selective attention: A reevaluation of the implications of negative priming. *Psychological Review, 105, 2,* 203–229.

Mineka, S., & Nugent, K. (1995). Mood-congruent memory biases in anxiety and depression. In D.L. Schacter (Ed.), *Memory distortions: How minds, brains, and societies reconstruct the past.* Cambridge, MA: Harvard University Press.

Mitchell, D.B. (1989). How many memory systems? Evidence from aging. *Journal of Experimental Psychology: Learning, Memory and Cognition, 15,* 31–49.

Mitler, M.M., Miller, J.C., Lipsitz, J.J., Walsh, J.K., & Wylie, C.D. (1997). The sleep of long-haul truck drivers. *New England Journal of Medicine, 337,* 755–761.

Mitrakou, A., Ryan, C., Veneman, T., Mokan, M., Jenssen, T., Kiss, I., Durrant, J., Cryer, P., & Gerich, J. (1991). Hierarchy of glycaemic thresholds for counterregulatory hormone secretion, symptoms and cerebral dysfunction. *American Journal of Physiology (Endocrinology and Metabolism), 23,* E67–E74.

Mogford, R.H. (1997). Mental models and situation awareness in air traffic control. *International Journal of Aviation Psychology, 7,* 331–341.

Molloy, R., & Parasuraman, R. (1996). Monitoring of an automated system for a single failure: Vigilance and task complexity effects. *Human Factors, 38,* 311–332.

Monk, T.H. (1979). Temporal effects in visual search. In J.N. Clare & M.A. Sinclair (Eds.), *Search and the human observer.* London: Taylor & Francis.

Monk, T.H. (1994). Circadian rhythms in subjective activation, mood, and performance efficiency. In M.H. Kryger, T. Roth & W.C. Dement (Eds.), *Principles and practice of sleep medicine.* Philadelphia: Saunders.

Monk, T.H., & Carrier, J. (1997). Speed of mental processing in the middle of the night. *Sleep, 20,* 399–401.

Monk, T.H., & Folkard, S. (1983). Circadian rhythms and shiftwork. In G.R.J. Hockey (Ed.), *Stress and fatigue in human performance.* Chichester: Wiley.

Monk, T.H., & Folkard, S. (1985). Shiftwork and performance. In S. Folkard & T.H. Monk (Eds.), *Hours of work: Temporal factors in work scheduling.* Chichester: John Wiley & Sons Ltd.

Monk, T.H., Knauth, P., Folkard, S., & Rutenfranz, J. (1978). Memory based performance measures in studies of shiftwork. *Ergonomics, 21,* 819–826.

Monk, T.H., & Leng, V.C. (1982). Time of day effects in simple repetitive tasks: Some possible mechanisms. *Acta Psychologica, 51,* 207–221.

Moray, N. (1959). Attention in dichotic listening: Affective cues and the influence of instructions. *Quarterly Journal of Experimental Psychology, 11,* 56–60.

Moray, N. (1967). Where is capacity limited? A survey and a model. *Acta Psychologica, 27,* 84–92.

Moray, N. (1986). Monitoring behavior and supervisory control. In K.R. Boff & L. Kaufman (Eds.), *Handbook of perception and human performance. Vol. 2: Cognitive processes and performance.* New York: John Wiley & Sons Ltd.

Moray, N., Haudegond, S., & Delange, M. (1999). An absence of vigilance decrement for complex signals in fault detection. In M.A. Hanson, E.J. Lovesey & S.A. Robertson (Eds.), *Contemporary ergonomics 1999.* Proceedings of the 50th Annual Conference of the Ergonomics Society.

Morris, L.W., Davis, M.A., & Hutchings, C.H. (1981). Cognitive and emotional components of anxiety: Literature review and a revised worry-emotionality scale. *Journal of Educational Psychology, 73,* 541–555.

Morris, L.W., & Liebert, R.M. (1970). Relationship of cognitive and emotional components of test anxiety to physiological arousal and academic performance. *Journal of Consulting and Clinical Psychology, 35,* 332–337.

Morris, L.W., Smith, L.R., Andrews, E.S., & Morris, N.C. (1975). The relationship of emotionality and worry components of anxiety to motor skills performance. *Journal of Motor Behavior, 7,* 121–130.

Morris, N., & Jones, D.M. (1990). Habituation to irrelevant speech: Effects on a visual short-term memory task. *Perception and Psychophysics, 47,* 291–297.

Morris, T.L., & Miller, J.C. (1996). Electrooculographic and performance indices of fatigue during simulated flight. *Biological Psychology, 42,* 343–360.

Moscovitch, M. (1982). A neuropsychological approach to perception and memory in normal and pathological aging. In F.I.M. Craik & S. Trehub (Eds.), *Aging and cognitive processes.* New York: Plenum Press.

Mouloua, M., & Parasuraman, R. (1995). Aging and cognitive vigilance: Effects of spatial uncertainty and event rate. *Experimental Aging Research, 21,* 17–32.

Muehlbach, M.J., & Walsh, J.K. (1995). The effects of caffeine on simulated night-shift work and subsequent daytime sleep. *Sleep, 18,* 22–29.

Mueller, J.H. (1992). Anxiety and performance. In A.P. Smith & D.M. Jones (Eds.), *Handbook of human performance. Vol. 3: State and trait.* London: Academic Press.

Mueller, C.W., Lisman, S.A., & Spear, N.E. (1983). Alcohol enhancement of human memory: Tests of consolidation and interference hypotheses. *Psychopharmacology, 80,* 226–230.

Mughal, S., Walsh, J., & Wilding, J. (1996). Stress and work performance: The role of trait anxiety. *Personality and Individual Differences, 20,* 685–691.

Muir, B.M. (1994). Trust in automation: Part I. Theoretical issues in the study of trust and human intervention in automated systems. *Ergonomics, 37,* 1905–1922.

Mulder, G. (1986). The concept and measurement of mental effort. In G.R.J. Hockey, A.W.K. Gaillard & M.G.H. Coles (Eds.), *Energetics and human information processing.* Dordrecht: Martinus Nijhoff.

Munro, L.L., Dawson, M.E., Schell, A.M., & Sakai, L.M. (1987). Electrodermal lability and rapid vigilance decrement in a degraded stimulus continuous performance task. *Journal of Psychophysiology, 1,* 249–257.

Murray, H. (1938). *Explorations in personality.* Oxford: Oxford University Press.

Murrell, K.F.H., & Griew, S. (1958). Age structure in the engineering industry: A study of regional effects. *Occupational Psychology, 32,* 1–13.

Murrell, K.F.H., & Humphries, S. (1978). Age, experience, and short-term memory. In M.M. Gruneberg, P.E. Morris & R.N. Sykes (Eds.), *Practical aspects of memory.* London: Academic Press.

Murrell, K.F.H., Powesland, P.F., & Forsaith, B. (1962). A study of pillar-drilling in relation to age. *Occupational Psychology, 36,* 45–52.

Myerson, J., & Hale, S. (1993). General slowing and age invariance in cognitive processing: The other side of the coin. In J. Cerella, J.M. Rybash, W.J. Hoyer & M.L. Commons (Eds.), *Adult information processing: Limits on loss.* San Diego, CA: Academic Press.

Näätänen, R. (1973). The inverted-U relationship between activation and performance: A critical review. In S. Kornblum (Ed.), *Attention and performance IV.* New York: Academic Press.

Nagel, D.C. (1988). Human error in aviation operations. In E.L. Wiener & D.C. Nagel (Eds.), *Human factors in aviation.* San Diego, CA: Academic Press.

Nakayama, K., & Joseph, J.S. (1998). Attention, pattern recognition, and pop-out in visual search. In R. Parasuraman (Ed.), *The attentive brain.* Cambridge, MA: MIT Press.

Natale, V., & Lorenzetti, R. (1997). Influences of morningness–eveningness and time of day on narrative comprehension. *Personality and Individual Differences, 23,* 685–690.

Naveh-Benjamin, M., Lavi, H., McKeachie, W.J., & Lin, Y-G. (1997). Individual differences in students' retention of knowledge and conceptual structures learned in university and high school courses: The case of test anxiety. *Applied Cognitive Psychology, 11,* 507–526.

Naveteur, J., & Freixa-i-Baque, E. (1987). Individual differences in electrodermal activity as a function of subject's anxiety. *Personality and Individual Differences, 8,* 615–626.

Navia, B.A., Cho, E.S., Petito, C.K., & Price, R.W. (1986). The AIDS dementia complex II: Neuropathology. *Annals of Neurology, 19,* 525–535.

Navon, D. (1984). Resources: A theoretical soupstone. *Psychological Review, 91,* 216–234.

Navon, D. (1991). Testing a queue hypothesis for the processing of global and local information. *Journal of Experimental Psychology: General, 120,* 173–189.

Navon, D., & Gopher, D. (1979). On the economy of the human-processing system. *Psychological Review, 86,* 214–255.

Navon, D., & Miller, J. (1987). The role of outcome conflict in dual-task interference. *Journal of Experimental Psychology: Human Perception and Performance, 13,* 435–448.

Neely, J.H. (1991). Semantic priming effects in visual word recognition: A selective review of current findings and theories. In D.E. Besner & G.

Humphreys (Eds.), *Basic processes in reading.* Hillsdale, NJ: Erlbaum.

Nehlig, A., Daval, J-L., & Debry, G. (1992). Caffeine and the central nervous system: Mechanisms of action, biochemical, metabolic and psychostimulant effects. *Brain Research Reviews, 17,* 139–169.

Neill, W.T. (1977). Inhibitory and facilitatory processes in selective attention. *Journal of Experimental Psychology: Human Perception and Performance, 3,* 444–450.

Neill, W.T., Valdes, L.A., Terry, K.M., & Gorfein, D.S. (1992). Persistence of negative priming: II. Evidence for episodic trace retrieval. *Journal of Experimental Psychology: Learning, Memory and Cognition, 18,* 993–1000.

Neiss, R. (1988). Reconceptualizing arousal: Psychobiological states in motor performance. *Psychological Bulletin, 103,* 345–366.

Neisser, U. (1967). *Cognitive psychology.* New York: Appleton.

Neisser, U. (1976). *Cognition and reality.* San Francisco: Freeman.

Neisser, U. (Ed.) (1998). *The rising curve: Long-term gains in IQ and related measures.* Washington, DC: American Psychological Association.

Neisser, U., & Becklen, R. (1975). Selective looking: Attending to visually specified events. *Cognitive Psychology, 7,* 480–494.

Nelson, T.M. (1997). Fatigue, mindset and ecology in the hazard dominant environment. *Accident Analysis and Prevention, 29,* 409–415.

Nesthus, T.E., Rush, L.L., & Wreggit, S.S. (1997). *Effects of mild hypoxia on pilot performances at general aviation altitudes.* Oklahoma City: FAA Office of Aviation Medicine Report, FAA-AM-97-091.

Nestor, P.G., Faux, S., McCarley, R.W., Shenton, M.E., & Sands, S.F. (1990). Measurement of visual sustained attention in schizophrenia using signal detection analysis and a newly developed computerized CPT. *Schizophrenia Research, 3,* 329–332.

Nettelbeck, T., & Rabbitt, P.M.A. (1992). Aging, cognitive performance, and mental speed. *Intelligence, 16,* 189–205.

Netter, P., Hennig, J., Huwe, S., & Olbrich, R. (1998). Personality related effects of nicotine, mode of application, and expectancies on performance, emotional states, and desire for smoking. *Psychopharmacology, 135,* 52–62.

Neubauer, A.C. (1997). The mental speed approach to the assessment of intelligence. In W. Tomic & J. Kingsma (Eds.), *Advances in cognition and educational practice. Vol. 4: Reflections on the concept of intelligence.* Greenwich, CT: JAI Press.

Neubauer, A.C., & Bucik, V. (1996). The mental speed–IQ relationship: Unitary or modular? *Intelligence, 22,* 23–48.

Neumann, O. (1996). Theories of attention. In O. Neumann & A.F. Sanders (Eds.), *Handbook of perception and action. Vol. 3: Attention* (pp. 389–446). London: Academic Press.

Neves, D.M., & Anderson, J.R. (1981). Knowledge compilation: Mechanisms for the automatization of cognitive skills. In J.R. Anderson (Ed.), *Cognitive skills and their acquisition.* Hillsdale, NJ: Lawrence Erlbaum Associates Inc.

Newell, A. (1982). The knowledge level. *Artificial Intelligence, 18,* 87–127.

Newell, A. (1990). *Unified theories of cognition.* Cambridge, MA: Harvard University Press.

Newell, A., & Rosenbloom, P.S. (1981). Mechanisms of skill acquisition and the law of practice. In J.R. Anderson (Ed.), *Cognitive skills and their acquisition.* Hillsdale, NJ: Lawrence Erlbaum Associates Inc.

Newell, A., & Simon, H.A. (1972). *Human problem solving.* Englewood Cliffs, NJ: Prentice-Hall.

Nickerson, R.S., & Adams, M.J. (1979). Long-term memory for a common object. *Cognitive Psychology, 11,* 287–307.

Nielsen, J. (1993). *Usability engineering.* London: Academic Press.

Nisbett, R.E., & Wilson, T.D. (1977). Telling more than we can know: Verbal reports on mental processes. *Psychological Review, 84,* 231–259.

Norman, D.A. (1968). Toward a theory of memory and attention. *Psychological Review, 75,* 522–536.

Norman, D.A. (1969). Memory while shadowing. *Quarterly Journal of Experimental Psychology, 21,* 85–93.

Norman, D.A. (1981). Categorization of action slips. *Psychological Review, 88,* 1–15.

Norman, D.A. (1988). *The psychology of everyday things.* New York: Basic Books.

Norman, D.A., & Bobrow, D.B. (1975). On data-limited and resource-limited processes. *Cognitive Psychology, 7,* 44–64.

Norman, D.A., & Shallice, T. (1986). Attention to action: Willed and automatic control of behaviour. In R.J. Davidson, G.E. Schwartz & D. Shapiro (Eds.), *Consciousness and self-regulation: Advances in research (Vol. 4).* New York: Plenum.

North, R.A., & Gopher, D. (1976). Measures of attention as predictors of flight performance. *Human Factors, 18,* 1–14.

Noweir, M.H. (1984). Noise exposure as related to productivity, disciplinary actions, absenteeism, and accidents among textile workers. *Journal of Safety Research, 15,* 163–174.

Nuechterlein, K., Parasuraman, R., & Jiang, Q. (1983). Visual sustained attention: Image degradation produces rapid sensitivity decrement over time. *Science, 20*, 327–329.

Nugent, K., & Mineka, S. (1994). The effect of high and low trait anxiety on implicit and explicit memory tasks. *Cognition and Emotion, 8*, 147–163.

Nurmi, J-E., & von Wright, J. (1983). Interactive effects of noise, neuroticism and state-anxiety in the learning and recall of a textbook passage. *Human Learning, 2*, 119–125.

Oakhill, J. (1986). Effects of time of day on the integration of information in text. *British Journal of Psychology, 77*, 481–488.

Oatley, K., & Johnson-Laird, P. (1987). Towards a cognitive theory of emotions. *Cognition and Emotion, 1*, 29–50.

Obrist, W.D. (1965). Electroencephalographic approach to age changes in response speed. In A.T. Welford & J.E. Birren (Eds.), *Behavior, aging, and the nervous system*. Springfield, IL: Charles C. Thomas.

O'Connor, K. (1985). A model of situational preference amongst smokers. *Personality and Individual Differences, 6*, 151–160.

O'Donnell, R.D., & Eggemeier, F.T. (1986). Workload assessment methodology. In K.R. Boff, L. Kaufman, & J.P. Thomas (Eds.), *Handbook of human performance. Vol. 2. Cognitive processes and performance.* Chichester: John Wiley & Sons Ltd.

O'Hanlon, J.A., & Beatty, J. (1977). Concurrence of electroencephalographic and performance changes during a simulated radar watch and some implications for the arousal theory of vigilance. In R.R. Mackie (Ed.), *Vigilance: Theory, operational performance, and physiological correlates*. New York: Plenum.

O'Hanlon, J.G., & Griffin, M.J. (1971). *Some effects of the vibration of reading material upon visual performance. Technical Report No. 49*, Institute of Science and Vibration Research, University of Southampton.

O'Hare, D. (1997). Cognitive ability determinants of elite pilot performance. *Human Factors, 39*, 540–552.

O'Hare, D., Wiggins, M., Batt, R., & Morrison, D. (1994). Cognitive failure analysis for aircraft accident investigation. *Ergonomics, 37*, 1855–1869.

O'Neil, H.F., Jr., & Richardson, F.C. (1980). Test anxiety and computer-based learning environments. In I.G. Sarason (Ed.), *Test anxiety: Theory, research and applications*. Hillsdale, NJ: Lawrence Erlbaum Associates Inc.

Ones, D.S., Viswesvaran, C., & Schmidt, F.L. (1993) Comprehensive meta-analysis of integrity test validities: Findings and implications for personnel selection and theories of job performance [Monograph]. *Journal of Applied Psychology, 78*, 679–703.

Owens, D.S., & Benton, D. (1994). The impact of raising blood glucose on reaction time. *Neuropsychobiology, 30*, 106–113.

Owens, W.A. (1959). Is age kinder to the initially more able? *Journal of Gerontology, 14*, 334–337.

Owens, W.A. (1966). Age and mental abilities: A second adult follow-up. *Journal of Educational Psychology, 57*, 311–325.

Owsley, C., Ball, K., Sloane, M.E., Roenker, D.L., & Bruni, J.R. (1991). Visual/cognitive correlates of vehicle accidents in older drivers. *Psychology and Aging, 6*, 403–415.

Paap, K.R., & Ogden, W.G. (1981). Letter encoding is an obligatory but capacity-demanding operation. *Journal of Experimental Psychology: Human Perception and Performance, 7*, 518–528.

Pachella, R.G. (1974). The interpretation of reaction time in information processing research. In B. Kantowitz (Ed.), *Human information processing: Tutorials in performance and cognition*. Hillsdale, NJ: Lawrence Erlbaum Associates Inc.

Paivio, A. (1969). Mental imagery in associative learning and memory. *Psychological Review, 76*, 241–263.

Palmer, S.E. (1975). The effects of contextual scenes on the identification of objects. *Memory and Cognition, 3*, 519–526.

Parasuraman, R. (1979). Memory load and event rate control sensitivity decrements in sustained attention. *Science, 205*, 924–927.

Parasuraman, R. (1984). The psychobiology of sustained attention. In J.S. Warm (Ed.), *Sustained attention and human performance*. Chichester: John Wiley & Sons Ltd.

Parasuraman, R. (1985). Sustained attention: A multifactorial approach. In M. Posner & O.S.M. Marin (Eds.), *Attention and performance XI*. Hillsdale, NJ: Lawrence Erlbaum Associates Inc.

Parasuraman, R. (1986). Vigilance, monitoring, and search. In K.R. Boff, L. Kaufman & J.P. Thomas (Eds.), *Handbook of perception and human performance, Vol. 2: Cognitive processes and performance*. New York: John Wiley & Sons Inc.

Parasuraman, R. (1990). Event-related brain potentials and human factors research. In J.W. Rohrbaugh, R. Parasuraman & R. Johnson (Eds.), *Event-related potentials: Basic issues and applications*. New York: Oxford University Press.

Parasuraman, R. (1998a). The attentive brain: Issues and prospects. In R. Parasuraman (Ed.), *The attentive brain*. Cambridge, MA: MIT Press.

Parasuraman, R. (1998b). *Neuroergonomics: The study of brain and behavior at work*. Website at http://www.acad.cua.edu/as/psy/csl/neuroerg.htm.

Parasuraman, R., & Davies, D.R. (1976). Decision theory analysis of response latencies in vigilance. *Journal of Experimental Psychology: Human Perception and Performance, 2*, 578–590.

Parasuraman, R., & Davies, D.R. (1977). A taxonomic analysis of vigilance performance. In R.R. Mackie (Ed.), *Vigilance: Theory, operational performance, and physiological correlates*. New York: Plenum Press.

Parasuraman, R., & Davies, D.R. (1984) (Eds.), *Varieties of attention*. San Diego, CA: Academic Press.

Parasuraman, R., & Greenwood, P.M. (1998). Selective attention in aging and dementia. In R. Parasuraman (Ed.), *The attentive brain*. Cambridge, MA: MIT Press.

Parasuraman, R., & Molloy, R. (1996). Monitoring an automated system for a single failure: Vigilance and task complexity effects. *Human Factors, 38*, 311–322.

Parasuraman, R., & Mouloua, M. (1987). Interaction of signal discriminability and task type in vigilance decrement. *Perception and Psychophysics, 41*, 17–22.

Parasuraman, R., & Mouloua, M. (Eds.) (1996). *Automation and human performance: Theory and applications*. Mahwah, NJ: Lawrence Erlbaum Associates Inc.

Parasuraman, R., Mutter, S.A., & Molloy, R. (1991). Sustained attention following mild closed head injury. *Journal of Clinical and Experimental Neuropsychology, 13*, 789–811.

Parasuraman, R., & Nestor, P.G. (1991). Attention and driving skills in aging and Alzheimer's disease. *Human Factors, 33*, 539–557.

Parasuraman, R., & Riley, V. (1997). Humans and automation: Use, misuse, disuse, abuse. *Human Factors, 39*, 230–253.

Parasuraman, R., Nestor, P., & Greenwood, P. (1989). Sustained attention capacity in younger and older adults. *Psychology and Aging, 4*, 339–345.

Parasuraman, R., Warm, J.S., & Dember, W.N. (1987). Vigilance: Taxonomy and utility. In L.S. Mark, J.S. Warm & R.L. Huston (Eds.), *Ergonomics and human factors: Recent research*. New York: Springer Verlag.

Parasuraman, R., Warm, J.S., & See, J.E. (1998). Brain systems of vigilance. In R. Parasuraman (Ed.), *The attentive brain*. Boston: MIT Press.

Park, D.C. (1992). Applied cognitive aging research. In F.I.M. Craik & T.A. Salthouse (Eds.), *The handbook of aging and cognition*. Hillsdale, NJ: Lawrence Erlbaum Associates Inc.

Park, D.C., Herzog, C., Kidder, D.P., Morrell, R.W., & Mayhorn, C.B. (1997). Effect of age on event-based and time-based prospective memory. *Psychology and Aging, 12*, 314–327.

Parker, D., Reason, J.T., Manstead, A.S.R., & Stradling, S.G. (1995). Driving errors, driving violations, and accident involvement. *Ergonomics, 38*, 1036–1048.

Parkin, C., Fairweather, D.B., Shamsi, Z., Stanley, N., & Hindmarch, I. (1998). The effects of cigarette smoking on overnight performance. *Psychopharmacology, 136*, 172–178.

Parkinson, S. (1982). Performance deficits in short-term memory tasks: A comparison of amnesic Korsakoff patients and the aged. In L.S. Cermak (Ed.), *Human memory and amnesia*. Hillsdale, NJ: Lawrence Erlbaum Associates Inc.

Pashler, H. (1994). Dual-task interference in simple tasks: Data and theory. *Psychological Bulletin, 116*, 220–244.

Pashler, H. (1998a). *The psychology of attention*. Cambridge, MA: MIT Press.

Pashler, H. (Ed.) (1998b). *Attention*. Hove, UK: Psychology Press.

Pashler, H., & Johnston, J.C. (1998). Attentional limitations in dual-task performance. In H. Pashler (Ed.), *Attention*. Hove, UK: Psychology Press.

Pashler, H., & O'Brien, S. (1993). Dual-task interference and the cerebral hemispheres. *Journal of Experimental Psychology: Human Perception and Performance, 19*, 315–330.

Patil, P.G., Apfelbaum, J.L., & Zacny, J.P. (1995). Effects of a cold-water stressor on psychomotor and cognitive functioning in humans. *Physiology and Behavior, 58*, 1281–1286.

Patrick, J. (1992). *Training: Research and practice*. New York: Academic.

Pavlov, I. (1927). *Conditioned reflexes* (translated by G.V. Anrep). London: Oxford University Press.

Payne, S., Squibb, H.R., & Howes, A. (1990). The nature of device models: The yoked state space hypothesis and some experiments with text editors. *Human–Computer Interaction, 5*, 415–444.

Pearlman, C.A. (1982). Sleep structure variation and performance. In W.B. Webb (Ed.), *Biological rhythms, sleep, and performance.* Chichester: John Wiley & Sons Ltd.

Pekrun, R. (1992). Expectancy-value theory of anxiety: Overview and implications. In D.G. Forgays, T. Sosnowski & K. Wrzesniewski (Eds.), *Anxiety: Recent developments in cognitive, psychophysiological, and health research.* Washington, DC: Hemisphere Publishing Corp.

Pellegrino, J.W., & Kail, R., Jr. (1982). Process analyses of spatial aptitude. In R.J. Sternberg (Ed.), *Advances in the psychology of human intelligence (Vol. 1).* Hillsdale, NJ: Lawrence Erlbaum Associates Inc.

Pellegrino, J.W., & Mumaw, R.J. (1980). *Multicomponent models of spatial ability.* Unpublished manuscript, University of California at Santa Barbara.

Penn, P.E., & Bootzin, R.R. (1990). Behavioural techniques for enhancing alertness and performance in shift work. *Work and Stress, 4,* 213–226.

Pepler, R.D., & Warner, R.E. (1968). Temperature and learning: An experimental study. *ASHRAE Transactions, 74,* 211–219.

Percival, L., & Loeb, M. (1980). Influence of noise characteristics on behavioral aftereffects. *Human Factors, 22,* 341–352.

Peterson, C., & Seligman, M.E.P. (1984). Causal explanations as a risk factor for depression: Theory and evidence. *Psychological Review, 91,* 347–374.

Petrie, K.J., & Dawson, A.G. (1997). Symptoms of fatigue and coping strategies in international pilots. *International Journal of Aviation Psychology, 7,* 251–258.

Petros, T.V., Beckwith, B.E., & Anderson, M. (1990). Individual differences in the effects of time of day and passage difficulty on prose memory in adults. *British Journal of Psychology, 81,* 63–72.

Pew, R.W. (1966). Acquisition of hierarchical control over the temporal organization of a skill. *Journal of Experimental Psychology, 71,* 764–771.

Pew, R.W. (1974). Levels of analysis in motor control. *Brain Research, 71,* 393–400.

Phaf, R.H., Van der Heijden, A.H.C., & Hudson, P.T.W. (1990). SLAM: A connectionist model for attention in visual selection tasks. *Cognitive Psychology, 22,* 273–341.

Phillips-Bute, B.G., & Lane, J.D. (1997). Caffeine withdrawal symptoms following brief caffeine deprivation. *Physiology and Behavior, 63,* 35–39.

Pickering, A.D., Díaz, A., & Gray, J.A. (1995). Personality and reinforcement: An exploration using a maze-learning task. *Personality and Individual Differences, 18,* 541–558.

Pidgeon, N.F. (1991). Safety culture and risk management in organizations. *Journal of Cross-cultural Psychology, 22,* 129–140.

Piedmont, R.L., & Weinstein, H.P. (1994). Predicting supervisor ratings of job performance using the NEO Personality Inventory. *Journal of Psychology, 128,* 255–265.

Pigache, A.M. (1996). Auditory sustained attention in schizophrenia. A comparison of the Continuous Performance Test and the Pigache Attention Task. *Psychiatry Research, 60,* 158–168.

Pilcher, J.J., & Huffcutt, A.J. (1996). Effects of sleep deprivation on performance: A meta-analysis. *Sleep, 19,* 318–326.

Pinker, S. (1994). *The language instinct.* New York: W. Morrow and Co.

Plunkett, K., & Marchman, V. (1993). From rote learning to system building: Acquiring verb morphology in children and connectionist nets. *Cognition, 48,* 21–69.

Plude, D.J., & Doussard-Roosevelt, J.A. (1989). Aging, selective attention, and feature integration. *Psychology and Aging, 4,* 98–105.

Plude, D.J., Enns, J.T., & Brodeur, D. (1994). The development of selective attention: A life span overview. *Acta Psychologica, 86,* 227–272.

Plunkett, K., & Marchman, V. (1993). From rote learning to system building: Acquiring verb morphology in children and connectionist nets. *Cognition, 48,* 21–69.

Plunkett, K., & Marchman, V. (1996). Learning from a connectionist model of the acquisition of the English past tense. *Cognition, 61,* 299–308.

Pollatsek, A., & Rayner, K. (1989). Reading. In M.I. Posner (Ed.), *Foundations of cognitive science.* Cambridge, MA: MIT Press.

Pollina, L.K., Greene, A.L., Tunick, R.H., & Puckett, J.M. (1992). Dimensions of everyday memory in young adulthood. *British Journal of Psychology, 83,* 305–321.

Polson, M.C., & Friedman, A. (1988). Task-sharing within and between hemispheres: A multiple-resources approach. *Human Factors, 30,* 633–643.

Polzella, D.J. (1975). Effects of sleep deprivation on short-term recognition memory. *Journal of Experimental Psychology: Human Learning and Memory, 1,* 194–200.

Ponds, R.M., Brouwer, W.H., & Van Wolfelaar, P.C. (1988). Age differences in divided attention in a simulated driving task. *Journal of Gerontology, 43,* 151–156.

Popper, K.R. (1959). *The logic of scientific discovery.* London: Hutchinson.

Porter, C.S. (1989). Accident proneness: A review of the concept. In D.J. Oborne (Ed.), *International reviews of ergonomics: Current trends in human factors research and practices, Vol. 2*. London: Taylor & Francis.

Porter, C.S., & Corlett, E.N. (1989). Performance differences of individuals classified by questionnaire as accident prone or non-accident prone. *Ergonomics, 32*, 317–333.

Posner, M.I. (1978). *Chronometric explorations of mind*. Hillsdale, NJ: Lawrence Erlbaum Associates Inc.

Posner, M.I. (1986). *Chronometric explorations of mind*. The third Paul M. Fitts lectures delivered at the University of Michigan, September 1976. New York: Oxford University Press.

Posner, M.I. (Ed.) (1989). *Foundations of cognitive science*. Cambridge, MA: MIT Press.

Posner, M.I., & Boies, S.J. (1971). Components of attention. *Psychological Review, 78*, 391–408.

Posner, M.I., & DiGirolamo, G. (1998). Executive attention: Conflict, target detection, and cognitive control. In R. Parasuraman (Ed.), *The attentive brain*. Boston, MA: MIT Press.

Posner, M.I., & Tudela, P. (1997). Imaging resources. *Biological Psychology, 45*, 95–107.

Posner, M.I., Inhoff, A.W., Friedrich, F.J., & Cohen, A. (1987). Isolating attentional systems: A cognitive-anatomical analysis. *Psychobiology, 15*, 107–121.

Posner, M.I., & Raichle, M.E. (1997). *Images of mind*. New York: Scientific American Library.

Posner, M.I., & Rothbart, M.K. (1991). Attentional mechanisms and conscious experience. In D. Milner & M. Rugg (Eds.), *The neuropsychology of consciousness*. San Diego, CA: Academic Press.

Posner, M.I., & Snyder, C.R.R. (1975): Attention and cognitive control. In R.L. Solso (Ed.), *Information processing and cognition: The Loyola Symposium*. Hillsdale, NJ: Lawrence Erlbaum Associates Inc.

Poulton, E.C. (1953). Two-channel listening. *Journal of Experimental Psychology, 46*, 91–96.

Poulton, E.C. (1970). *Environment and human efficiency*. Springfield, IL: Thomas.

Poulton, E.C. (1977). Arousing stresses increase vigilance. In R.R. Mackie (Ed.), *Vigilance: Theory, operational performance and physiological correlates*. New York: Plenum Press.

Poulton, E.C. (1978). Continuous noise masks auditory feedback and inner speech. *Psychological Bulletin, 84*, 977–1001.

Poulton, E.C. (1979). Composite model for human performance in continuous noise. *Psychological Review, 86*, 361–375.

Poulton, E.C., & Edwards, R.S. (1974). Interactions and range effects in experiments on pairs of stresses: Mild heat and low frequency noise. *Journal of Experimental Psychology, 102*, 621–628.

Poulton, E.C., Hitchings, N.B., & Brooke, R.B. (1965). Effect of cold and rain upon the vigilance of lookouts. *Ergonomics, 8*, 163–168.

Pressman, M.R., & Orr, W.C. (Eds.) (1997). *Understanding sleep: The evaluation and treatment of sleep disorders*. Washington, DC: American Psychological Association.

Price, J.L., Thompson, P.H., & Dalton, G.W. (1975). A longitudinal study of technological obsolescence. *Research Management*, November.

Price, R.W., & Brew, B.J. (1988). The AIDS dementia complex. *Journal of Infectious Diseases, 158*, 1079–1083.

Proctor, R.W., & Dutta, A. (1995). *Skill acquisition and human performance*. Thousand Oaks, CA: Sage.

Proctor, R.W., & van Zandt, T. (1994). *Human factors in simple and complex systems*. Boston: Allyn & Bacon.

Puckett, J.M., & Stockberger, D.W. (1988). Absence of age-related proneness to short-term retroactive interference in the absence of rehearsal. *Psychology and Aging, 3*, 342–347.

Pylyshyn, Z.W. (1984). *Computation and cognition: Toward a foundation for cognitive science*. Cambridge, MA: MIT Press.

Pylyshyn, Z.W. (1989). Symbolic architectures for cognition. In M.I. Posner (Ed.), *Foundations of cognitive science*. Cambridge, MA: MIT Press.

Quant, J.R. (1992). The effect of sleep deprivation and sustained military operations on near visual performance. *Aviation, Space, and Environmental Medicine, 63*, 172–176.

Quinlan, P.T. (1991). *Connectionism and psychology: A psychological perspective on new connectionist research*. Chicago: University of Chicago Press.

Rabbitt, P.M.A. (1965). An age decrement in the ability to ignore irrelevant information. *Journal of Gerontology, 20*, 233–238.

Rabbitt, P.M.A. (1966). Errors and error correction in choice response tasks. *Journal of Experimental Psychology, 71*, 264–272.

Rabbitt, P.M.A. (1978). Detection of errors by skilled typists. *Ergonomics, 21*, 945–958.

Rabbitt, P.M.A. (1979). How young and old subjects monitor and control processes for accuracy and speed. *British Journal of Psychology, 70*, 305–311.

Rabbitt, P.M.A. (1981). Cognitive psychology needs models for changes in performance with old age. In J. Long & A.D. Baddeley (Eds.), *Attention and performance IX*. Hillsdale, NJ: Lawrence Erlbaum Associates Inc.

Rabbitt, P.M.A. (1989). Sequential reactions. In D. Holding (Ed.), *Human skills*. Chichester: John Wiley & Sons Ltd.

Rabbitt, P.M.A. (1993). Does it all go together when it goes? *Quarterly Journal of Experimental Psychology: Human Experimental Psychology, 46A*, 385–434.

Rabbitt, P.M.A. (1996a). Do individual differences in speed reflect "global" or "local" differences in mental abilities. *Intelligence, 22*, 69–88.

Rabbitt, P.M.A. (1996b). Speed of processing and ageing. In R.T. Woods (Ed.), *Handbook of the clinical psychology of ageing*. Chichester: Wiley.

Rabbitt, P.M.A., & Abson, V. (1990). "Lost and found": Some logical and methodological limitations of self-report questionnaires as tools to study cognitive ageing. *British Journal of Psychology, 81*, 1–16.

Rabbitt, P.M.A., & Banerji, N. (1989). How does very prolonged practice improve decision speed? *Journal of Experimental Psychology: General, 118*, 338–345.

Rabbitt, P.M.A., Cumming, G., & Vyas, S.M. (1978). Some errors of perceptual analysis in visual search can be detected and corrected. *Quarterly Journal of Experimental Psychology, 30*, 319–332.

Rabbitt, P.M.A., & Maylor, E.A. (1991). Investigating models of human performance. *British Journal of Psychology, 82*, 259–290.

Rabbitt, P.M.A., & Vyas, S.M. (1970). An elementary preliminary taxonomy for some errors in laboratory choice RT tasks. *Acta Psychologica, 33*, 56–76.

Rabinowitz, J.C. (1984). Aging and recognition failure. *Journal of Gerontology, 39*, 65–71.

Rabinowitz, J.C., Craik, F.I.M., & Ackerman, B.P. (1982). A processing resource account of age differences in recall. *Canadian Journal of Psychology, 36*, 325–344.

Ramsey, J.D. (1983). Heat and cold. In G.R.J. Hockey (Ed.), *Stress and fatigue in human performance*. Chichester: Wiley.

Ramsey, J.D. (1995). Task performance in heat: A review. *Ergonomics, 38*, 154–165.

Ramsey, J.D., & Morrissey, S.J. (1978). Isodecrement curves for task performance in hot environments. *Applied Ergonomics, 9*, 66–72.

Rasmussen, J. (1983). Skills, rules, and knowledge: Signals, signs, and symbols and other distinctions in human performance models. *IEEE Transactions on Systems, Man, and Cybernetics, SMC-13*, 257–266.

Rasmussen, J. (1986). *Information processing and human–machine interaction*. Amsterdam: North-Holland.

Razmjou, S., & Kjellberg, A. (1992). Sustained attention and serial responding in heat: Mental effort in the control of performance. *Aviation, Space, and Environmental Medicine, 63*, 594–601.

Reardon, M.J., Fraser, E.B., & Omer, J.M. (1998). Flight performance effects of thermal stress and two aviator uniforms in a UH-60 helicopter simulator. *Aviation, Space, and Environmental Medicine, 69*, 569–576.

Reason, J.T. (1984). Lapses of attention in everyday life. In R. Parasuraman & D.R. Davies (Eds.), *Varieties of attention*. San Diego, CA: Academic Press.

Reason, J.T. (1988). Stress and cognitive failure. In S. Fisher & J.T. Reason (Eds.), *Handbook of life stress, cognition, and health*. Chichester: John Wiley & Sons Ltd.

Reason, J.T. (1990). *Human error*. Cambridge: Cambridge University Press.

Reason, J.T. (1995). A systems approach to organizational error. *Ergonomics, 38*, 1708–1721.

Reason, J.T., Manstead, A.S.R., Stradling, S.G., Baxter, J., & Campbell, K. (1990). Errors and violations on the roads: A real distinction. *Ergonomics, 33*, 1315–1332.

Reber, A.S. (1989). Implicit learning and tacit knowledge. *Journal of Experimental Psychology: General, 118*, 219–235.

Redelmeier, D.A., & Tibshirani, R.J. (1997). Association between cellular-telephone calls and motor vehicle collisions. *The New England Journal of Medicine, 336*, 453–458.

Redfern, P., Minors, D., & Waterhouse, J. (1994). Circadian rhythms, jet lag, and chronobiotics: An overview. *Chronobiology International, 11*, 253–265.

Regina, E.G., Smith, G.M., Keiper, C.G., & McKelvey, R.K. (1974). Effects of caffeine on alertness in simulated automobile driving. *Journal of Applied Psychology, 59*, 483–489.

Reicher, G. (1969). Perceptual recognition as a function of meaningfulness of stimulus material. *Journal of Experimental Psychology, 81*, 275–280.

Reinberg, A., Andlauer, P., Deprins, J., Malbecq, W., Vieux, N., & Bourdeleau, P. (1984). Desynchronization of the oral-temperature circadian-rhythm and intolerance to shift work. *Nature, 308*, 272–274.

Reisberg, D. (1997). *Cognition: Exploring the science of the mind*. New York: W.W. Norton.

Revelle, W. (1993). Individual differences in personality and motivation: "Non-cognitive" determinants of cognitive performance. In A.D. Baddeley & L. Weiskrantz (Eds.), *Attention: Selection, awareness and control*. Oxford: Oxford University Press.

Revelle, W., Amaral, P., & Turriff, S. (1976). Introversion/extraversion, time stress, and caffeine: Effect on verbal performance. *Science, 192*, 149–150.

Revelle, W., Humphreys, M.S., Simon, L., & Gilliland, K. (1980). The interactive effect of personality, time of day and caffeine: A test of the arousal model. *Journal of Experimental Psychology: General, 109*, 1–31.

Revelle, W., & Loftus, D.A. (1992). The implications of arousal effects for the study of affect and memory. In S-A. Christianson (Ed.), *The handbook of emotion and memory: Research and theory*. Hillsdale, NJ: Lawrence Erlbaum Associates Inc.

Rhodes, S.R. (1983). Age-related differences in work attitudes and behavior: A review and conceptual analysis. *Psychological Bulletin, 93*, 328–367.

Ribot, E., Roll, J.P., & Gauthier, G.M. (1986). Comparative effects of whole-body vibration on sensorimotor performance achieved with a mini-stick and a macro-stick in force and position control modes. *Aviation, Space, and Environmental Medicine, 57*, 792–799.

Richards, A., & French, C.C. (1992). An anxiety-related bias in semantic activation when processing threat/neutral homographs. *Quarterly Journal of Experimental Psychology, 40A*, 503–528.

Richards, A., French, C.C., Johnson, W., Naparstek, J., & Williams, J. (1992). Effects of mood manipulation and anxiety on performance of an emotional Stroop task. *British Journal of Psychology, 83*, 479–491.

Roache, J.D., & Griffiths, R.R. (1987). Interactions of diazepam and caffeine: Behavioral and subjective dose effects in humans. *Pharmacology, Biochemistry and Behavior, 26*, 801–812.

Robbins, T.W. (1986). Psychopharmacological and neurobiological aspects of the energetics of information processing. In G.R.J. Hockey, A.W.K. Gaillard & M.G.H. Coles (Eds.), *Energetics and human information processing*. Dordrecht: Martinus Nijhoff.

Robbins, T.W. (1997). Arousal systems and attentional processes. *Biological Psychology, 45*, 57–71.

Robbins, T.W. (1998). Arousal and attention: Psychopharmacological and neuropsychological studies in experimental animals. In R. Parasuraman (Ed.), *The attentive brain*. Cambridge, MA: MIT Press.

Robbins, T.W., & Everitt, B.J. (1982). Functional studies of the central catecholamines. In J.R. Smythies & R.J. Bradley (Eds.), *International review of neurobiology (Vol. 23)*. New York: Academic Press.

Roberts, R.D., Beh, H.C., & Stankov, L. (1988). Hick's law, competing task performance, and intelligence. *Intelligence, 12*, 101–120.

Roberts, S., & Sternberg, S. (1993). The meaning of additive reaction-time effects: Tests of three alternatives. In D.E. Meyer & S. Kornblum (Eds.), *Attention and performance 14: Synergies in experimental psychology, artificial intelligence, and cognitive neuroscience*. Cambridge, MA: MIT Press.

Robertson, I.H., Manly, T., Andrade, J., Baddeley, B.T., & Yiend, J. (1997). "Oops!": Performance correlates of everyday attentional failures in traumatic brain injured and normal subjects. *Neuropsychologia, 35*, 747–758.

Robertson I.H., Tegner, R., Tham, K., Lo, A., & Nimmo-Smith, I. (1995). Sustained attention training for unilateral neglect: Theoretical and rehabilitation implications. *Journal of Clinical and Experimental Neuropsychology, 17*, 416–430.

Roelfsema, P.R., Lamme, V.A.F., & Spekreijse, H. (1998). Object-based attention in the primary visual cortex of the macaque monkey. *Nature, 395*, 376–381.

Rogers, W.A., Gilbert, D., Kristen, C., & Fraser, E. (1997). An analysis of automatic teller machine usage by older adults: A structured interview approach. *Applied Ergonomics, 28*, 173–180.

Rogosa, D. (1980). A critique of cross-lagged correlation. *Psychological Bulletin, 88*, 245–258.

Rohrbaugh, J.W., Stapleton, J.M., Parasuraman, R., Zubovic, E.A., Frowein, H.W., Varner, J.L., Adinoff, B., Lane E.A., Eckardt, M.J., & Linnoila, M. (1987). Dose-related effects of ethanol on visual sustained attention and event-related potentials. *Alcohol, 4*, 293–300.

Rohsenow, D.J., & Marlatt, G.A. (1981). The balanced placebo design: Methodological considerations. *Addictive Behaviors, 6*, 107–122.

Rolfe, J. (1996). Craik and the Cambridge Cockpit. *The Psychologist, 9*, 69–71.

Rolfhus, E.L., & Ackerman, P.L. (1996). Self-report knowledge: At the crossroads of ability, interest, and personality. *Journal of Educational Psychology, 88*, 174–188.

Rolls, E.T. (1999). *The brain and emotion*. Oxford, UK: Oxford University Press.

Rosch, E. (1973). On the internal structure of perceptual and semantic categories. In T.E. Moore (Ed.),

*Cognitive development and the acquisition of language*. New York: Academic Press.

Rose, T.L., Yesavage, J.A., Hill, R.D., & Bower, G.H. (1986). Priming effects and recognition memory in young and elderly adults. *Experimental Aging Research, 12*, 31–37.

Rosler, F., Heil, M., & Roder, B. (1997). Slow negative brain potentials as reflections of specific modular resources of cognition. *Biological Psychology, 45*, 109–141.

Ross, D.F., & Pihl, R.O. (1988). Alcohol, self-focus, and complex reaction-time performance. *Journal of Studies on Alcohol, 49*, 115–125.

Rosvold, H.E., Mirsky, A.F., Sarason, I., Bransome, E.D., & Beck, L.N. (1956). A continuous performance test of brain damage. *Journal of Consulting Psychology, 20*, 343–350.

Rotter, J.T. (1966). Generalized expectancies for internal versus external control of reinforcement. *Psychological Monographs, 80* (1, Whole No. 609).

Rumelhart, D.E., & Norman, D.A. (1982). Simulating a skilled typist: A study of skilled cognitive-motor performance. *Cognitive Science, 6*, 1–36.

Rusted, J.M., & Warburton, D.M. (1995). Nicotinic receptors and information processing. In T.W. Stone (Ed.), *CNS neurotransmitters and neuromodulators: Acetylcholine*. Boca Raton, FL: CRC Press.

Rutenfranz, J., Aschoff, J., & Mann, H. (1972). The effects of a cumulative sleep deficit, duration of preceding sleep period and body temperature on multiple choice reaction time. In W.P. Colquhoun (Ed.), *Aspects of human efficiency: Diurnal rhythm and loss of sleep*. London: English Universities Press.

Ryman, D.H., Naitoh, P., & Englund, C.E. (1989). Perceived exertion under conditions of sustained work and sleep loss. *Work and Stress, 3*, 57–68.

Sack, S.A., & Rice, C.E. (1974). Selectivity, resistance to distraction and shifting as three attentional factors. *Psychological Reports, 34*, 1003–1012.

Sahakian, B.J., Elliott, R., Low, N., & Mehta, M. (1995). Neuropsychological deficits in tests of executive function in asymptomatic and symptomatic HIV-1 seropositive men. *Psychological Medicine, 25*, 1233–1246.

Saklofske, D.H., & Zeidner, M. (Eds.). (1995). *International handbook of personality and intelligence*. New York: Plenum.

Salminen, S., & Tallberg, T. (1996). Human errors in fatal and serious occupational accidents in Finland. *Ergonomics, 39*, 980–988.

Salmoni, A.W., Schmidt, R.A., & Walter, C.B. (1984). Knowledge of results and motor learning: A review and critical reappraisal. *Psychological Bulletin, 95*, 355–386.

Salomon, G. (1974). Internalization of filmic schematic operations in interaction with learners' aptitudes. *Journal of Educational Psychology, 66*, 499–511.

Salthouse, T.A. (1984). Effects of age and skill in typing. *Journal of Experimental Psychology: General, 113*, 345–371.

Salthouse, T.A. (1985). Speed of behavior and its implications for cognition. In J.E. Birren & K.W. Schaie (Eds.), *Handbook of the psychology of aging (2nd ed.)*. New York: Van Nostrand Reinhold.

Salthouse, T.A. (1986). Perceptual, cognitive, and motoric aspects of transcription typing. *Psychological Bulletin, 99*, 303–319.

Salthouse, T.A. (1988). Resource interpretations of cognitive aging. *Developmental Review, 8*, 238–272.

Salthouse, T.A. (1990a). Influence of experience on age differences in cognitive functioning. *Human Factors, 32*, 551–569.

Salthouse, T.A. (1990b). Cognitive competence and expertise in aging. In J.E. Birren & K.W. Schaie (Eds.), *Handbook of the psychology of aging (3rd ed.)*. San Diego, CA: Academic.

Salthouse, T.A. (1990c). Working memory as a cognitive resource in cognitive aging. *Developmental Review, 10*, 101–124.

Salthouse, T.A. (1991). *Theoretical perspectives on cognitive aging*. Hillsdale, NJ: Lawrence Erlbaum Associates Inc.

Salthouse, T.A. (1992). Influence of processing speed on adult age differences in working memory. *Acta Psychologica, 79*, 155–170.

Salthouse, T.A., & Babcock, R.L. (1991). Decomposing adult age differences in working memory. *Developmental Psychology, 27*, 763–776.

Salthouse, T.A., & Babcock, R.L. (1991). Decomposing adult age differences in working memory. *Developmental Psychology, 27*, 763–776.

Salthouse, T.A., Babcock, R.L., Skovronek, E., Mitchell, D.R.D., & Palmon, R. (1989). Age and experience effects in spatial visualization. *Developmental Psychology, 26*, 128–136.

Salthouse, T.A., Hambrick, D.Z., Lukas, K.E., & Dell, T.C. (1996). Determinants of adult age differences on synthetic work performance. *Journal of Experimental Psychology: Applied, 2*, 305–329.

Salthouse, T.A., Hancock, H.E., Meinz, E.J., & Hambrick, D.Z. (1996). Interrelations of age, visual acuity, and cognitive functioning. *Journal of Gerontology, 51B*, P317–P330.

Salthouse, T.A., & Maurer, T.J. (1996). Aging, job performance, and career development. In J.E. Birren & K.W. Schaie (Eds.), *Handbook of the psychology of aging* (4th ed.). San Diego, CA: Academic.

Salthouse, T.A., Mitchell, D.R.D., Skovronek, E., & Babcock, R.L. (1989). Effects of adult age and working memory on reasoning and spatial abilities. *Journal of Experimental Psychology: Learning, Memory and Cognition, 15*, 507–516.

Salthouse, T.A., Rogan, J.D., & Prill, K.A. (1984). Division of attention: Age differences on a visually presented memory task. *Memory and Cognition, 12*, 613–620.

Salthouse, T.A., & Somberg, B.L. (1982). Isolating the age deficit in speeded performance. *Journal of Gerontology, 37*, 59–63.

Salthouse, T.A., Wright, R., & Ellis, C.L. (1979). Adult age and the rate of an internal clock. *Journal of Gerontology, 34*, 53–57.

Samuel, A. (1996). Phoneme restoration. *Language & Cognitive Processes, 11*, 647–653.

Sanders, A.F. (1983). Towards a model of stress and human performance. *Acta Psychologica, 53*, 61–97.

Sanders, A.F. (1990). Issues and trends in the debate on discrete versus continuous processing of information. *Acta Psychologica, 74*, 123–167.

Sanders, A.F. (1997). A summary of resource theories from a behavioral perspective. *Biological Psychology, 45*, 5–18.

Sanders, A.F., & Reitsma, W.D. (1982). Lack of sleep and covert orienting of attention. *Acta Psychologica, 52*, 137–145.

Sanders, M.S., & McCormick, E.J. (1993). *Human factors in engineering and design (7th ed.)*. New York: McGraw-Hill.

Sanders, R.E., Murphy, M.D., Schmitt, F.A., & Walsh, K.K. (1980). Age differences in free recall rehearsal strategies. *Journal of Gerontology, 35*, 550–558.

Sanderson, P.M. (1989). The human planning and scheduling role in advanced manufacturing systems: An emerging human factors domain. *Human Factors, 31*, 635–666.

Santrock, J.W. (1992). *Life-span development (4th ed.)*. Dubuque, IA: Wm. C. Brown.

Sarason, I.G. (1989). Anxiety, self-preoccupation and attention. *Anxiety Research, 1*, 3–7.

Sarason, I.G., Sarason, B.R., Keefe, D.E., Hayes, B.E., & Shearin, E.N. (1986) Cognitive interference: Situational determinants and traitlike characteristics. *Journal of Personality and Social Psychology, 31*, 215–226.

Sarason, I.G., Sarason, B.R., & Pierce, G.R. (1990). Anxiety, cognitive interference, and performance. *Journal of Social Behavior and Personality, 5*, 1–18.

Sarason, I.G., Sarason, B.R., & Pierce, G.R. (1995) Cognitive interference: At the intelligence-personality crossroads. In D.H. Saklofske & M. Zeidner (Eds.), *International handbook of personality and intelligence*. New York: Plenum Press.

Sarter, M., & Bruno, J.P. (1997). Cognitive functions of cortical acetylcholine: Toward a unifying hypothesis. *Brain Research Reviews, 23*, 28–46.

Sarter, N.B., & Woods, D.D. (1991). Situation awareness: A critical but ill-defined concept. *International Journal of Aviation Psychology, 1*, 45–57.

Sarter, N.B., & Woods, D.D. (1995). How in the world did we ever get into that mode? Mode error and awareness in supervisory control. *Human Factors, 37*, 5–19.

Sawin, D., & Scerbo, M.W. (1995). Effects of instruction type and boredom proneness in vigilance: Implications for boredom and workload. *Human Factors, 37*, 752–765.

Scerbo, M.W. (1998). What's so boring about vigilance? In R.R. Hoffman, M.F. Sherrick & J.S. Warm (Eds.), *Viewing psychology as a whole: The integrative science of William N. Dember*. Washington, DC: American Psychological Association.

Schachter, S., & Singer, J.E. (1962). Cognitive, social and physiological determinants of emotional state. *Psychological Review, 69*, 379–399.

Schacter, D.L. (1987). Implicit memory: History and current status. *Journal of Experimental Psychology: Learning, Memory and Cognition, 13*, 501–518.

Schacter, D.L. (1993). Neuropsychological evidence for a consciousness system. In A.I. Goldman (Ed.), *Readings in philosophy and cognitive science*. Cambridge, MA: MIT Press.

Schaie, K.W. (1977). Quasi-experimental designs in the psychology of aging. In J.E. Birren & K.W. Schaie (Eds.), *Handbook of the psychology of aging*. New York: Van Nostrand Reinhold.

Schaie, K.W., & Parham, I.A. (1977). Cohort-sequential analyses of adult intellectual development. *Developmental Psychology, 13*, 649–653.

Schank, R.C., & Abelson, R. (1977). *Scripts, plans, goals, and understanding*. Hillsdale, NJ: Lawrence Erlbaum Associates Inc.

Schmeck, R.R., & Lockhart, D. (1983). Introverts and extraverts require different learning environments. *Educational Leader, 40*, 54.

Schmidt, F.L., & Hunter, J.E. (1998). The validity and utility of selection methods in personnel psychology:

Practical and theoretical implications of 85 years of research findings. *Psychological Bulletin, 124*, 262–274.

Schmidt, F.L., Ones, D.S., & Hunter, J.E. (1992). Personnel selection. *Annual Review of Psychology, 43*, 627–670.

Schmidt, R.A. (1975). A schema theory of discrete motor skill learning. *Psychological Review, 82*, 225–260.

Schmidt, R.A. (1976). The schema as a solution to some persistent problems in motor learning theory. In G.E. Stelmach (Ed.), *Motor control: Issues and trends*. New York: Academic Press.

Schmidt, R.A. (1982). *Motor control and learning: A behavioral emphasis*. Champaign, IL: Human Kinetics.

Schmidt, R.A., & Lee, T.D. (1999). *Motor control and learning (3rd ed.)*. Champaign, IL: Human Kinetics.

Schneider, W. (1985). Training high performance skills: Fallacies and guidelines. *Human Factors, 27*, 285–300.

Schneider, W., & Detweiler, M. (1989). The role of practice in dual-task performance: Toward workload modeling in a connectionist/control architecture. *Human Factors, 30*, 539–566.

Schneider, W., & Fisk, A.D. (1982). Concurrent automatic and controlled visual search: Can processing occur without resource cost? *Journal of Experimental Psychology: Learning, Memory and Cognition, 8*, 261–278.

Schneider, W., & Shiffrin, R.M. (1977). Controlled and automatic human information processing: I. Detection, search and attention. *Psychological Review, 84*, 1–66.

Schneider, W.X. (1995). VAM: A neuro-cognitive model for visual attention control of segmentation, object recognition and space-based motor action. *Visual Cognition, 2*, 331–375.

Schonfield, D., & Robertson, B. (1966). Memory storage and aging. *Canadian Journal of Psychology, 20*, 228–236.

Schooler, J.W., Ohlsson, S., & Brooks, K. (1993). Thoughts beyond words: When language overshadows insight. *Journal of Experimental Psychology: General, 122*, 166–183.

Schultz, R., Musa, D., Staszewski, J., & Siegler, R.S. (1994). The relationship between age and major league baseball performance: Implications for development. *Psychology and Aging, 9*, 274–286.

Schumann, J., Flannagan, M.J., Sivak, M., & Traube, E.C. (1997). Daytime veiling glare and driver visual performance: Influence of windshield rake angle and dashboard reflectance. *Journal of Safety Research, 28*, 133–146.

Schwab, D.P., & Heneman, H.G. (1977). Effects of age and experience on productivity. *Industrial Gerontology, 4*, 113–117.

Schweickert, R., & Mounts, J. (1998). Additive effects of factors on reaction time and evoked potentials in continuous-flow models. In C.E. Dowling & F.S. Roberts (Eds.), *Recent progress in mathematical psychology: Psychophysics, knowledge, representation, cognition, and measurement*. Mahwah, NJ: Lawrence Erlbaum Associates Inc.

Scialfa, C.T., Esau, S.P., & Joffe, K.M. (1998). Age, target-distractor similarity, and visual search. *Experimental Aging Research, 24*, 337–358.

Scott, A.J. (1994). Chronobiological considerations in shiftworker sleep and performance and shiftwork scheduling. *Human Performance, 7*, 207–233.

Sears, R.L. (1986). *A new look at accident contributions and the implications of operational and training procedures*. Unpublished report. Boeing Commercial Aircraft Company.

See, J.E., Howe, S.R., Warm, J.S., & Dember, W.N. (1995). Meta-analysis of the sensitivity decrement in vigilance. *Psychological Bulletin, 117*, 230–249.

See, J.E., Warm, J.S., & Dember, W.N. (1997). Vigilance and signal detection theory: An empirical evaluation of five measures of response bias. *Human Factors, 39*, 14–29.

Segal, Z.V., & Gemar, M. (1997). Changes in cognitive organisation for negative self-referent material following cognitive behaviour therapy for depression: A primed Stroop study. *Cognition and Emotion, 11*, 501–516.

Seidman, L.J., Biederman, J., Weber, W., Hatch, M., & Faraone, S.V. (1998). Neuropsychological function in adults with attention-deficit hyperactivity disorder. *Biological Psychiatry, 44*, 260–268.

Selfridge, O.G. (1955). Pattern recognition and modern computers. *Proceedings of the Western Joint Computer Conference*. New York: Institute of Electrical and Electronics Engineers.

Seligman, M.E.P. (1975). *Helplessness: On development, depression and death*. San Francisco: Freeman.

Selnes, O.A., Galai, N., Bacellar, H., Miller, E.N., Becker, J.T., Wesch, J., Vangorp, W., & MCarthur, J.C. (1995). Cognitive performance after progression to AIDS: A longitudinal study from the Multicenter AIDS Cohort Study. *Neurology, 45*, 267–275.

Selye, H. (1976). *The stress of life*. New York: McGraw-Hill.

Selzer, M.L., & Vinokur, A. (1975). Role of life events in accident causation. *Mental Health and Society, 2*, 36–54.

Semmer, N., & Schallberger, U. (1996). Selection, socialisation, and mutual adaptation: Resolving discrepancies between people and work. *Applied Psychology: An International Journal, 45*, 263–288.

Senders, J.W., & Moray, N. (1991). *Human error: Cause, prediction and reduction*. Hillsdale, NJ: Lawrence Erlbaum Associates Inc.

Shaikh, G.H. (1999). Occupational noise exposure limits for developing countries. *Applied Acoustics, 57*, 89–92.

Shallice, T. (1988). *From neuropsychology to mental structure*. Cambridge: Cambridge University Press.

Shallice, T., & Burgess, P. (1993). Supervisory control of action and thought selection. In A.D. Baddeley & L. Weiskrantz (Eds.), *Attention: Selection, awareness, and control: a tribute to Donald Broadbent*. Oxford: Oxford University Press.

Shanks, D.R., & St. John, M.F. (1994). Characteristics of dissociable human learning systems. *Behavioral and Brain Sciences, 117*, 367–447.

Shannon, C.E., & Weaver, W. (1949). *The mathematical theory of communications*. Urbana, IL: University of Illinois Press.

Shapiro, D.C. (1977). A preliminary attempt to determine the duration of a motor program. In D.M. Landers & R.W. Christina (Eds.), *Psychology of motor behavior and sport—1976*. Champaign, IL: Human Kinetics.

Shappell, S.A., & Wiegmann, D.A. (1997). A human error approach to accident investigation: The taxonomy of unsafe operations. *International Journal of Aviation Psychology, 7*, 269–291.

Shaw, L., & Sichel, H.S. (1971). *Accident proneness*. Oxford: Pergamon.

Sherrod, D.R., & Downs, R. (1974). Environmental determinants of altruism: The effects of stimulus overload and perceived control on helping. *Journal of Experimental Social Psychology, 10*, 468–479.

Sherwood, S.L. (Ed.) (1966). *The nature of psychology. A selection of papers, essays, and other writings by the late Kenneth J.W. Craik*. Cambridge: Cambridge University Press.

Sherwood, N. (1995). Effects of cigarette smoking on performance in a simulated driving task. *Neuropsychobiology, 32*, 161–165.

Sherwood, N., & Griffin, M.J. (1990). Effects of whole-body vibration on short-term memory. *Aviation, Space, and Environmental Medicine, 61*, 1092–1097.

Shiffrin, R.M. (1997). Attention, automatism, and consciousness. In J.D. Cohen & J.W. Schooler (Eds.), *Scientific approaches to consciousness*. Mahwah, NJ: Lawrence Erlbaum Associates Inc.

Shiffrin, R.M., & Schneider, W. (1977). Controlled and automatic human information processing: II. Perceptual learning, automatic attending and a general theory. *Psychological Review, 84*, 127–190.

Shingledecker, C.A., & Holding, D.H. (1974). Risk and effort measures of fatigue. *Journal of Motor Behaviour, 6*, 17–25.

Shinar, D. (1978). *Psychology on the road: The human factor in traffic safety*. New York: John Wiley & Sons Inc.

Shore, L.M., & Bleicken, L.M. (1991). Effects of supervisor age and subordinate age on rating congruence. *Human Relations, 44*, 1093–1105.

Siering, G.D., & Stone, L.W. (1986). In search of a time-sharing ability in zero input tracking analyzer scores. *Aviation, Space and Environmental Medicine, 57*, 1194–1197.

Simon, H.A., & Gilmartin, K. (1973). A simulation of memory for chess positions. *Cognitive Psychology, 5*, 29–46.

Siemer, M., & Reisenzein, R. (1998). Effects of mood on evaluative judgements: Influence of reduced processing capacity and mood salience. *Cognition and Emotion, 12*, 783–805.

Simoneau, G.G., & Leibowitz, H.W. (1996). Posture, gait, and falls. In J.E. Birren & K.W. Schaie (Eds.), *Handbook of the psychology of aging (4th ed.)*. San Diego, CA: Academic.

Simonton, D. (1988). Age and outstanding achievement: What do we know after a century of research? *Psychological Bulletin, 104*, 251–267.

Singh, I.L., Molloy, R., & Parasuraman, R. (1993). Individual differences in monitoring failures of automation. *Journal of General Psychology, 120*, 357–373.

Sliwinski, M., Buschke, H., Kulansky, G., Senior, G., & Scarisbrick, J. (1994). Proportional slowing and addition speed in old and young adults. *Psychology and Aging, 9*, 72–80.

Smid, H.G.O.M., Truemper, B.G., Pottag, G., Wagner, K., Lobmann, R., Scheich, H., Lehnert, H., & Heinze, H.-J. (1997). Differentiation of hypoglycaemia induced cognitive impairments: An electrophysiological approach. *Brain, 120*, 1041–1056.

Smiley, A.M. (1990). The Hinton train disaster. *Accident Analysis and Prevention, 22*, 443–445.

Smith, A.D. (1996). Memory. In J.E. Birren & K.W. Schaie (Eds.), *Handbook of the psychology of aging (4th ed.)*. San Diego, CA: Academic.

Smith, A.P. (1982). The effects of noise and task priority on recall of order and location. *Acta Psychologica, 51*, 245–255.

Smith, A.P. (1989). A review of the effects of noise on human performance. *Scandinavian Journal of Psychology, 30*, 185–206.

Smith, A.P. (1992a). Time of day and performance. In A.P. Smith & D.M. Jones (Eds.), *Handbook of human performance. Vol. 3: State and trait.* London: Academic Press.

Smith, A.P. (1992b). Colds, influenza and performance. In A.P. Smith & D.M. Jones (Eds.), *Handbook of human performance. Vol. 2: Health and performance.* London: Academic Press.

Smith, A.P., (1992c). Chronic fatigue syndrome and performance. In A.P. Smith & D.M. Jones (Eds.), *Handbook of human performance. Vol. 2: Health and performance.* London: Academic Press.

Smith, A.P., & Jones, D.M. (Eds.) (1992a). *Handbook of human performance* (3 vols.). London: Academic Press.

Smith, A.P. & Jones, D.M. (1992b). Noise and performance. In A.P. Smith & D.M. Jones (Eds.), *Handbook of human performance. Vol. 1: The physical environment.* London: Academic Press.

Smith, A.P., Jones, D.M., & Broadbent, D.E. (1981). The effects of noise on recall of categorized lists. *British Journal of Psychology, 72*, 299–316.

Smith, A.P., & Kendrick, A.M. (1992). Meals and performance. In A.P. Smith & D.M. Jones (Eds.), *Handbook of human performance. Vol. 2: Health and performance.* London: Academic Press.

Smith, A.P., Maben, A., & Brockman, P. (1994). Effects of evening meals and caffeine on cognitive performance, mood and cardiovascular functioning. *Appetite, 22*, 57–65.

Smith, A.P., & Miles, C. (1986). The effects of lunch on cognitive vigilance tasks. *Ergonomics, 29*, 1251–1261.

Smith, A.P., & Miles, C. (1987). Sex differences in the effects of noise and nightwork on performance. *Work and Stress, 1*, 333–339.

Smith, A.P., Rusted, J.M., Eaton-Williams, P., Savory, M., & Leathwood, P. (1990). Effects of caffeine given before and after lunch on sustained attention. *Neuropsychobiology, 23*, 160–163.

Smith, A.P., Thomas, M., Perry, K., & Whitney, H. (1997). Caffeine and the common cold. *Journal of Psychopharmacology, 11*, 319–324.

Smith, A.P., Tyrrell, D.A., Coyle, K., & Willman, J.S. (1987). Selective effects of minor illnesses on human performance. *British Journal of Psychology, 78*, 183–188.

Smith, C., Spelten, E., & Norman, P. (1995). Shiftwork locus of control: Scale development. *Work and Stress, 9*, 219–226.

Smith, C.S., Reilly, C., & Midkiff, K. (1989). Evaluation of three circadian rhythm questionnaires with suggestions for an improved measure of morningness. *Journal of Applied Psychology, 74*, 728–738.

Smith, J.M. (1975). Occupations classified by their age structure. *Industrial Gerontology, 2*, 209–215.

Smith, L., Folkard, S., & Poole, C.J.M. (1994). Increased injuries on night shift. *Lancet, 344* (No. 8930), 1137–1139.

Smith, M., & George, D. (1992). Selection methods. In C.L. Cooper & I.T. Robertson (Eds.), *International review of industrial and organizational psychology (Vol. 7)*. Chichester: John Wiley & Sons Ltd.

Smolensky, P. (1988). On the proper treatment of connectionism. *Behavioral and Brain Sciences, 11*, 1–74.

Snel, J., & Cremer, R. (Eds.) (1994). *Work and aging: A European perspective*. London: Taylor & Francis.

Snel, J., & Lorist, M.M. (Eds.) (1998). *Nicotine, caffeine and social drinking: Behaviour and brain function*. Amsterdam: Harwood Academic Publishers.

Snow, R.E. (1989). Aptitude-treatment interaction as a framework for research on individual differences in learning. In P.L. Ackerman, R.J. Sternberg & R. Glaser (Eds.), *Learning and individual differences: Advances in theory and research*. New York: Freeman.

Snow, R.E., Kyllonen, P.C., & Marshalek, B. (1984). The topography of ability and learning correlations. In R.J. Sternberg (Ed.), *Advances in the psychology of human intelligence (Vol. 2)*. Hillsdale, NJ: Lawrence Erlbaum Associates Inc.

Snow, R.E., & Yalow, E. (1982). Education and intelligence. In R.J. Sternberg (Ed.), *Handbook of human intelligence*. Cambridge: Cambridge University Press.

Snyder, F.R., & Henningfield, J.E. (1989). Effects of nicotine administration following 12 h of tobacco deprivation: Assessment on computerized performance tasks. *Psychopharmacology, 97*, 17–22.

Socan, G., & Bucik, V. (1998). Relationship between speed of information-processing and two major personality dimensions—extraversion and neuroticism. *Personality and Individual Differences, 25*, 35–48.

Solso, R.L. (1991). *Cognitive psychology (3rd ed.)*. Boston: Allyn & Bacon.

Somberg, B.L. & Salthouse, T.A. (1982). Divided attention abilities in young and old adults. *Journal of Experimental Psychology: Human Perception and Performance, 8*, 651–663.

Sorenson, D.J., Martin, E.M., & Robertson, L.C. (1994). Visual attention in HIV-1 infection. *Neuropsychology, 8*, 424–432.

Sostek, A.J. (1978). Effects of electrodermal lability and payoff instructions on vigilance performance. *Psychophysiology, 15*, 561–568.

Sparrow, P.R., & Davies, D.R. (1988). Effects of age, tenure, training, and job complexity on technical performance. *Psychology and Aging, 3*, 307–314.

Spearman, C. (1923). *The nature of "intelligence" and the principles of cognition.* London: Macmillan.

Spearman, C. (1927). *The abilities of man: Their nature and measurement.* London: Macmillan.

Speelman, C., & Maybery, M. (1998). Automaticity and skill acquisition. In K. Kirsner, C. Speelman, M. Maybery, A. O'Brien-Malone, M. Anderson & C. MacLeod (Eds.), *Implicit and explicit mental processes.* Mahwah, NJ: Lawrence Erlbaum Associates Inc.

Sperling, G. (1960). The information available in brief visual presentations. *Psychological Monographs: General and Applied, 74*, Whole No. 498, 1–29.

Spielberger, C.D. (1972). Anxiety as an emotional state. In C.D. Spielberger (Ed.), *Anxiety: Current trends in theory and research (Vol. 1).* London: Academic Press.

Spieler, D.H., Balota, D.A., & Faust, M.E. (1996). Stroop performance in healthy younger and older adults and in individuals with dementia of the Alzheimer's type. *Journal of Experimental Psychology: Human Perception and Performance, 2*, 461–479.

Spilsbury, G.A. (1992). Complexity as a reflection of the dimensionality of a task. *Intelligence, 16*, 31–45.

Spirduso, W.W., & MacRae, P.G. (1990). Motor performance and aging. In J.E. Birren & K.W. Schaie (Eds.), *Handbook of the psychology of aging, 3rd edition.* San Diego, CA: Academic.

Spring, B., Chiodo, J., & Bowen, D.J. (1987). Carbohydrates, tryptophan, and behavior: A methodological review. *Psychological Bulletin, 102*, 234–256.

Spurgeon, A., & Harrington, J.M. (1989). Work performance and health of junior hospital doctors—a review of the literature. *Work and Stress, 3*, 117–128.

Stammers, R.B. (1979). The man-machine interface. *Physics in Technology, 10*, 118–123.

Stammers, R.B. (1996). Training and the acquisition of knowledge and skill. In P.B. Warr (Ed.), *Psychology at work* (4th ed.). London: Penguin.

Stammers, R.B., & Patrick, J. (1975). *The psychology of training.* London: Methuen.

Stankov, L. (1988). Aging, attention, and intelligence. *Psychology and Aging, 3*, 59–74.

Stankov, L. (1991). The effects of training and practice on human abilities. In H.A.H. Rowe (Ed.). *Reconceptualization and measurement.* Hillsdale, NJ: Lawrence Erlbaum Associates Inc.

Stankov, L. (1994). The complexity effect phenomenon is an epiphenomenon of age-related fluid intelligence decline. *Personality and Individual Differences, 16*, 265–288.

Stankov, L., & Roberts, R.D. (1997). Mental speed is not the "basic" process of intelligence. *Personality and Individual Differences, 22*, 69–84.

Stansfeld, S.A. (1992). Noise, noise sensitivity, and psychiatric disorder: Epidemiological and psychophysiological studies. *Psychological Medicine*, Monograph Supplement No. 22.

Stanton, N. (1996). Engineering psychology: Another science of common sense? *The Psychologist, 9*, 300–303.

Stark, M.E., Grafman, J., & Fertig, E. (1997). A restricted "spotlight" of attention in visual object recognition. *Neuropsychologia, 35*, 1233–1249.

Stelmack, R.M. (1990). Biological bases of extraversion: Psychophysiological evidence. *Journal of Personality, 58*, 293–311.

Stelmack, R.M., & Houlihan, M. (1995). Event-related potentials, personality, and intelligence: Concepts, issues, and evidence. In D.H. Saklofske & M. Zeidner (Eds.), *International handbook of personality and intelligence.* New York: Plenum Press.

Steptoe, A. (1991). Psychological coping, individual differences and physiological stress responses. In C.L. Cooper & R. Payne (Eds.), *Personality and stress: Individual differences in the coping process.* Chichester: John Wiley & Sons Ltd.

Stern, R.A., Silva, S.G., Chaisson, N., & Evans, D.L. (1996). Influence of cognitive reserve on neuropsychological functioning in asymptomatic human immunodeficiency virus-1 infection. *Archives of Neurology, 53*, 148–153.

Stern, Y., Liu, X., Marder, K., Todak, G., Sano, M., Ehrhardt, A., & Gorman, J. (1995). Neuropsychological changes in a prospectively followed cohort of homosexual and bisexual men with and without HIV infection. *Neurology, 45*, 467–472.

Sternberg, R.J. (1977). *Intelligence, information processing and analogical reasoning: The componential analysis of human abilities.* Hillsdale, NJ: Lawrence Erlbaum Associates Inc.

Sternberg, R.J. (1985). *Beyond IQ: A triarchic theory of intelligence.* New York: Cambridge University Press.

Sternberg, R.J. (Ed.) (in press). *Handbook of human intelligence (2nd ed.)*. Cambridge: Cambridge University Press.

Sternberg, S. (1969). The discovery of processing stages: Extensions of Donders' method. In W.G. Koster (Ed.), *Attention and performance II*. Amsterdam: Elsevier.

Stewart, K.T., Hayes, B.C., & Eastman, C.I. (1995). Light treatment for NASA shiftworkers. *Chronobiology International, 12*, 141–151.

Stillings, N.A, Weisler, S.E., Chase, C.H., Feinstein, M.H., Garfield, J.L., & Rissland, E.L. (1995). *Cognitive science: An introduction (2nd ed.)*. Cambridge, MA: MIT Press.

Stokes, A.F., Belger, A., Banich, M.T., & Bernadine, E. (1994). Effects of alcohol and chronic aspartame ingestion upon performance in aviation relevant cognitive tasks. *Aviation, Space, and Environmental Medicine, 65*, 7–15.

Stokes, A.F., & Kite, K. (1994). *Flight stress: Stress, fatigue and performance in aviation*. Aldershot: Avebury Aviation.

Stollery, B. (1992a). Organic solvents. In A.P. Smith & D.M. Jones (Eds.), *Handbook of human performance. Vol. 1: The physical environment*. London: Academic Press.

Stollery, B. (1992b). Electrical fields. In A.P. Smith & D.M. Jones (Eds.), *Handbook of human performance. Vol. 1: The physical environment*. London: Academic Press.

Stones, M.J., & Kozma, A. (1985). Physical performance. In N. Charness (Ed.), *Aging and human performance*. Chichester: John Wiley & Sons Ltd.

Stout, J.C., Salmon, D.P., Butters, N., Taylor, M., Peavy, G., Heindel, W.C., Delis, D.C., Ryan, L., Atkinson, J.H., Chandler, J.L., Grant, I., Velin, R.A., Oldfield, E.C., Wallace, M.R., Malone, J., McCutchan, J.A., Spector, S.A., Thal, L., Heaton, R.K., Hesselink, J., Jernigan, T., Wiley, C.A., Olshen, R., Abramson, I., Dupont, R., Patterson, T., Zisook, S., Jeste, D., Sieberg, H., & Weinrich, J.D. (1995). Decline in working memory associated with HIV infection. *Psychological Medicine, 25*, 1221–1232.

Strayer, D.L., Wickens, C.D., & Braune, R. (1987). Adult age differences in the speed and capacity of information processing: 2. An electrophysiological approach. *Psychology and Aging, 2*, 99–110.

Stroop, J.R. (1935). Studies of interference in serial verbal reactions. *Journal of Experimental Psychology, 18*, 643–662.

Styles, E.A. (1997). *The psychology of attention*. Hove, UK: Psychology Press.

Sullivan, L., & Stankov, L. (1990). Shadowing and target detection as a function of age: Implications for the role of processing resources in competing tasks and in general intelligence. *Australian Journal of Psychology, 42*, 173–186.

Summers, J.J. (1989). Motor programs. In D. Holding (Ed.), *Human skills (2nd ed.)*. Chichester: John Wiley & Sons Ltd.

Sundstrom, E., Town, J.P., Rice, R.W., & Osborn, D.P. (1994). Office noise, satisfaction, and performance. *Environment and Behavior, 26*, 195–222.

Super, D.E., & Crites, J.O. (1962). *Appraising vocational fitness*. New York: Harper.

Surwillo, W.W. (1968). Timing of behavior in senescence and the role of the central nervous system. In G.A. Talland (Ed.), *Human aging and behavior: Recent advances in research and theory*. New York: Academic.

Surwillo, W.W., & Quilter, R.E. (1964). Vigilance, age, and response time. *American Journal of Psychology, 77*, 614–620.

Suzuki, S., & Cavanagh, P. (1995). Facial organization blocks access to low-level features: An object inferiority effect. *Journal of Experimental Psychology: Human Perception and Performance, 21*, 901–913.

Swain, A.D., & Guttman, H.E. (1983). *Handbook on human reliability analysis with emphasis on nuclear power plant applications*. Sandia National Laboratories, NM: NUREG/CR 1278, US-NRC.

Swets, J.A. (1977). Signal detection theory applied to vigilance. In R.R. Mackie (Ed.), *Vigilance: Theory, operational performance, and physiological correlates*. New York: Plenum Press.

Swets, J.A. (1984). Mathematical models of attention. In R. Parasuraman & D.R. Davies (Eds.), *Varieties of attention*. San Diego, CA: Academic Press.

Tanner, W.P., & Swets, J.A. (1954). A decision-making theory of visual detection. *Psychological Review, 61*, 401–409.

Tattersall, A.J. (1992). Visual display units. In A.P. Smith & D.M. Jones (Eds.), *Handbook of human performance. Vol. 1: The physical environment*. London: Academic Press.

Taub, J.M., & Berger, R.J. (1976). The effects of changing the phase and duration of sleep. *Journal of Experimental Psychology: Human Perception & Performance, 2*, 30–41.

Teichner, W.H. (1958). Reaction time in the cold. *Journal of Applied Psychology, 42*, 54–59.

Teichner, W.H. (1974). The detection of a simple visual signal as a function of time on watch. *Human Factors, 16*, 339–353.

Telford, C.W. (1931). The refractory phase of voluntary and associative responses. *Journal of Experimental Psychology, 14*, 1–36.

Tempest, W. (1985). Noise measurement. In W. Tempest (Ed.), *The noise handbook.* London: Academic Press.

Temple, J.G., Warm, J.S., Dember, W.N., Jones, K.S., LaGrange, C.M., & Matthews, G. (in press). The effects of signal salience and caffeine on performance, workload and stress in an abbreviated vigilance task. *Human Factors.*

Tenenbaum, G., & Bar-Eli, M. (1995). Personality and intellectual capabilities in sport psychology. In D.H. Saklofske & M. Zeidner, M. (Eds.), *International handbook of personality and intelligence.* New York: Plenum Press.

Testu, F. (1986). Diurnal variations of performance and information processing. *Chronobiologia, 13*, 319–326.

Tett, R.P., Jackson, D.N., & Rothstein, M. (1991). Personality measures as predictors of job performance: A meta-analytic review. *Personnel Psychology, 44*, 703–742.

Tett, R.P., Jackson, D.N., Rothstein, M., & Reddon, J.R. (1994). Meta-analysis of personality–job performance relations: A reply to Ones, Mount, Barrick, and Hunter (1994). *Personnel Psychology, 47*, 157–172.

Thayer, R.E. (1987). Energy, tiredness, and tension effects of a sugar snack versus moderate exercise. *Journal of Personality and Social Psychology, 52*, 119–125.

Thayer, R.E. (1989). *The biopsychology of mood and arousal.* Oxford: Oxford University Press.

Thayer, R.E. (1996). *The origin of everyday moods.* New York: Oxford University Press.

Theologus, G.C., Wheaton, G.R., & Fleishman, E.A. (1974). Effects of intermittent moderate intensity noise stress on human performance. *Journal of Applied Psychology, 59*, 539–547.

Thurstone, L.L., & Thurstone, T.G. (1949). *Examiner manual for the Primary Mental Abilities Test (Form 11–17).* Chicago: Science Research Associates.

Tiersky, L.A., Johnson, S.K., Lange, G., Natelson, B.H., Benjamin, H., & DeLuca, J. (1997). Neuropsychology of chronic fatigue syndrome: A critical review. *Journal of Clinical and Experimental Neuropsychology, 19*, 560–586.

Tilley, A., & Brown, S. (1992). Sleep deprivation. In A.P. Smith & D.M. Jones (Eds.), *Handbook of human performance. Vol. 3: Trait and state.* New York: Academic Press.

Tilley, A., & Warren, P. (1983). Retrieval from semantic memory at different times of day. *Journal of Experimental Psychology: Learning, Memory and Cognition, 9*, 718–724.

Tilley, A.J., & Empson, J.A. (1978). REM sleep and memory consolidation. *Biological Psychology, 6*, 293–300.

Tinbergen, N. (1953). *The herring gull's world: A study of the social behaviour of birds.* London: Collins.

Tipper, S.P. (1985). The negative priming effect: Inhibitory priming by ignored objects. *Quarterly Journal of Experimental Psychology: Human Experimental Psychology, 37A*, 571–590.

Tipper, S.P., & Cranston, M. (1985). Selective attention and priming: Inhibitory and facilitatory effects. *Quarterly Journal of Experimental Psychology, 37A*, 591–611.

Tipper, S.P., Lortie, C., & Baylis, G.C. (1992). Selective reaching: Evidence for action-centered attention. *Journal of Experimental Psychology: Human Perception and Performance, 18*, 891–905.

Tipper, S.P., & Weaver, B. (1998). The medium of attention: Object-based, location-centered, or scene-based? In R.D. Wright (Ed.), *Visual attention.* New York: Oxford University Press.

Tipper, S.P., Weaver, B., & Houghton, G. (1994). Behavioural goals deteremine inhibitory mechanisms of selective attention. *Quarterly Journal of Experimental Psychology, 47A*, 809–840.

Titchener, E.B. (1910). *A text-book of psychology.* New York: MacMillan.

Tobias, S. (1977). Anxiety-treatment interactions: A review of research. In J.E. Sieber, H.F. O'Neil, Jr. & S. Tobias (Eds.), *Anxiety, learning and instruction.* Hillsdale, NJ: Lawrence Erlbaum Associates Inc.

Tobias, S. (1992). The impact of test anxiety on cognition in school learning. In K.A. Hagtvet & B.T. Johnsen (Eds.), *Advances in test anxiety research (Vol. 7).* Lisse, The Netherlands: Swets & Zeitlinger.

Tomporowski, P.D., & Ellis, N.R. (1986). Effects of exercise on cognitive processes: A review. *Psychological Bulletin, 99*, 338–346.

Tomporowski, P.D., & Tinsley, V.F. (1996). Effects of memory demand and motivation on sustained attention in young and older adults. *American Journal of Psychology, 109*, 187–204.

Toni, I., Krams, M., Turner, R., & Passingham, R.E. (1998). The time course of changes during motor sequence learning: A whole brain fMRI study. *Neuroimage, 8*, 50–61.

Townsend, J.T., & Ashby, F.G. (1983). *The stochastic modelling of elementary psychological processes.* Cambridge: Cambridge University Press.

Treisman, A.M. (1960). Contextual cues in selective listening. *Quarterly Journal of Experimental Psychology, 12,* 242–248.

Treisman, A.M. (1964). Selective attention in man. *British Medical Bulletin, 20,* 12–16.

Treisman, A.M. (1988). Features and objects: The fourteenth Bartlett memorial lecture. *Quarterly Journal of Experimental Psychology, 40A,* 201–237.

Treisman, A.M. (1993). The perception of features and objects. In A.D. Baddeley & L. Weiskrantz (Eds.), *Attention: selection, awareness, and control: A tribute to Donald Broadbent.* Oxford: Oxford University Press.

Treisman, A.M. (1998). The perception of features and objects. In R.D. Wright (Ed.), *Visual attention.* New York: Oxford University Press.

Treisman, A.M., & Gelade, G. (1980). A feature-integration theory of attention. *Cognitive Psychology, 12,* 97–136.

Treisman, A. & Riley, J.G.A. (1969). Is selective attention selective perception or selective response? A further test. *Journal of Experimental Psychology, 79,* 27–34.

Trimpop, R., & Kircaldy, B. (1997). Personality predictors of driving accidents. *Personality and Individual Differences, 23,* 147–152.

Trope, Y. (1975). Seeking information about one's ability as a determinant of choice among tasks. *Journal of Personality and Social Psychology, 32,* 1004–1013.

Tsuda A., Haraguchi, M., Ozeki, Y., Kurasaki, N., & Tsuda, S. (1993). Animal model of "karoushi" (death from overwork): Characteristics of rats exposed to activity-stress. In *Proceedings of the 1993 International Congress of Health Psychology.* Tokyo: ICHP.

Tulving, E. (1966). Subjective organization and effects of repetition in multi-trial free-recall learning. *Journal of Verbal Learning and Verbal Behavior, 5,* 193–197.

Tulving, E. (1993). What is episodic memory? *Current Directions in Psychological Science, 2,* 67–70.

Turnbull, A. (1976) Selling and the salesman: Prediction of success and personality change. *Psychological Reports, 38,* 1175–1180.

Turner, C., & Spilich, G.J. (1997). Research into smoking or nicotine and human cognitive performance: Does the source of funding make a difference? *Addiction, 92,* 1423–1426.

Ucros, C.G. (1989) Mood state-dependent memory: A meta-analysis. *Cognition and Emotion, 3,* 139–167.

Van Cott, H. (1994). Human errors: Their causes and reductions. In M.S. Bogner (Ed.), *Human error in medicine.* Hillsdale, NJ: Lawrence Erlbaum Associates Ltd.

Van der Heijden, A.H.C. (1992). *Selective attention in vision.* London: Routledge.

Vanderwolf, C.H., & Robinson, T.E. (1981). Reticulo-cortical activity and behavior: A critique of the arousal theory and a new synthesis. *The Behavioral and Brain Sciences, 4,* 459–514.

Van Orden, K.F., Benoit, S.L., & Osga, G.A. (1996). Effects of cold air stress on the performance of a command and control task. *Human Factors, 38,* 130–141.

Van Reekum, C.M., & Scherer, K.R. (1997). Levels of processing in emotion-antecedent appraisal. In G. Matthews (Ed.), *Cognitive science perspectives on personality and emotion.* Amsterdam: Elsevier.

Van Servellen, G., Sarna, L., Padilla, G., & Brecht, M.-L. (1996). Emotional distress in men with life-threatening illness. *International Journal of Nursing Studies, 33,* 551–565.

Van Vliet, C., Swaen, G.M.H., Volovics, A., Slangen, J.J.M., Meijers, J.M.M., de Boorder, T., & Sturmans, F. (1989). Exposure-outcome relationships between organic solvent exposure and neuropsychiatric disorders: Results from a Dutch case-control study. *American Journal of Industrial Medicine, 16,* 707–718.

Van Voorhis, S.T., & Hillyard, S.A. (1977). Visual evoked potentials and selective attention to points in space. *Perception and Psychophysics, 22,* 54–62.

Varney, N.R., Kubu, C.S., & Morrow, L.A. (1998). Dichotic listening performances of patients with chronic exposure to organic solvents. *Clinical Neuropsychologist, 12,* 107–112.

Vecchio, R.P. (1993). The impact of differences in subordinate and supervisor age on attitudes and performance. *Psychology and Aging, 8,* 112–119.

Veeninga, A., & Kraaimaat, F.W. (1995). Causal attributions in premenstrual syndrome. *Psychology and Health, 10,* 219–228.

Veitch, J.A. (1997). Revisiting the performance and mood effects of information about lighting and fluorescent lamp type. *Journal of Environmental Psychology, 17,* 253–262.

Verhaeghen, P., Marcoen, A., & Goossens, L. (1993). Facts and fiction about memory aging: A quantitative integration of research findings. *Journal of Gerontology, 48B,* P157–P171.

Vernon, H.M. (1918). *An investigation of the factors concerned in the causation of industrial accidents.* Memo No. 21, Health of Munitions Workers Committee, London.

Verrillo, R.T., & Verrillo, V. (1985). Sensory and perceptual performance. In N. Charness (Ed.), *Aging and human performance*. Chichester: John Wiley & Sons Ltd.

Vickers, D., & Leary, J. (1983). Criterion control in signal detection. *Human Factors, 25*, 283–296.

Vickers, D., Leary, J., & Barnes, P. (1977). Adaptation to decreasing signal probability. In R.R. Mackie (Ed.), *Vigilance: Theory, operational performance, and physiological correlates*. New York: Plenum Press.

Vinchur, A.J., Schippmann, J.S., Switzer, F.S. III, & Roth, P.L. (1998). A meta-analytic review of predictors of job performance for salespeople. *Journal of Applied Psychology, 83*, 586–597.

Vollmer-Conna, U., Wakefield, D., Lloyd, A., Hickie, I., Lemon, J., Bird, K.D., & Westbrook, R.F. (1997). Cognitive deficits in patients suffering from chronic fatigue syndrome, acute infective illness or depression. *British Journal of Psychiatry, 171*, 377–381.

Von Wright, J., & Vauras, M. (1980). Interactive effects of noise and neuroticism on recall from semantic memory. *Scandinavian Journal of Psychology, 21*, 97–101.

Wagner, R.K., Torgesen, J.K., Rashotte, C.A., & Hecht, S.A. (1997). Changing relations between phonological processing abilities and word-level reading as children develop from beginning to skilled readers: A 5-year longitudinal study. *Developmental Psychology, 33*, 468–479.

Waldman, D.A., & Avolio, B.J. (1986). A meta-analysis of age differences in job performance. *Journal of Applied Psychology, 71*, 33–38.

Walker, J.F. (1964). The job performance of federal mail sorters by age. *Monthly Labor Review, 87*, 296–301.

Waller, D., & Levander, S.E. (1980). Smoking and vigilance: The effects of tobacco smoking on CFF as related to personality and smoking habits. *Psychopharmacology, 70*, 131–136.

Warburton, D.M. (1979). Physiological aspects of information processing and stress. In V. Hamilton & D.M. Warburton (Eds.), *Human stress and cognition: An information processing approach*. Chichester: John Wiley & Sons Ltd.

Warburton, D.M., & Arnall, C. (1994). Improvements in performance without nicotine withdrawal. *Psychopharmacology, 115*, 539–542.

Warburton, D.M., & Wesnes, K. (1979). The role of electrocortical arousal in the smoking habit. In A. Remond & C. Izard (Eds.), *Electrophysiological effects of nicotine*. Amsterdam: Elsevier.

Warm, J.S. (1984). An introduction to vigilance. In J.S. Warm (Ed.), *Sustained attention in human performance*. Chichester: John Wiley & Sons Ltd.

Warm, J.S. (1993). Vigilance and target detection. In B.M. Huey & C.D. Wickens (Eds.), *Workload transition: Implications for individual and team performance*. Washington, DC: National Academy Press.

Warm, J.S., & Dember, W.N. (1998). Tests of vigilance taxonomy. In R.R. Hoffman, M.F. Sherrick & J.S. Warm (Eds.), *Viewing psychology as a whole: The integrative science of William N. Dember*. Washington, DC: American Psychological Association.

Warm, J.S., Dember, W.N., & Hancock, P.A. (1996). Vigilance and workload in automated systems. In R. Parasuraman & M. Mouloua (Eds.), *Automation and human performance: Theory and applications*. Mahwah, NJ: Lawrence Erlbaum Associates Inc.

Warr, P.B. (1994). Age and employment. In H.C. Triandis, M.D. Dunnette & L.M. Hough (Eds.), *Handbook of industrial and organizational psychology (2nd ed.)*. Palo Alto, CA: Consulting Psychologists Press.

Warr, P.B (Ed.) (1996a). *Psychology at work (4th ed.)*. London: Penguin.

Warr, P.B. (1996b). Younger and older workers. In P.B. Warr (Ed.), *Psychology at work (4th ed.)*. London: Penguin.

Warren, R.M. (1970). Perceptual restorations of missing speech sounds. *Science, 167*, 392–393.

Watson, D., & Clark, L.A. (1984). Negative affectivity: The disposition to experience aversive emotional states. *Psychological Bulletin, 96*, 465–490.

Watson, D., & Clark, L.A. (1992). On traits and temperament: General and specific factors of emotional experience and their relation to the five-factor model. *Journal of Personality, 60*, 441–476.

Waugh, N.C., Fozard, J.L., & Thomas, J.C. (1978). Age-related differences in serial binary classification. *Experimental Aging Research, 4*, 433–441.

Waugh, N.C., & Norman, D.A. (1965). Primary memory. *Psychological Review, 72*, 89–104.

Webb, W.B. (1979). Theories of sleep function and some clinical applications. In R. Drucker-Colin, M. Shkurovich & M.B. Sterman (Eds.), *The function of sleep*. New York: Academic Press.

Webb, W.B. (1982a). Sleep and biological rhythms. In W.B. Webb (Ed.), *Biological rhythms, sleep, and performance*. Chichester: John Wiley & Sons Ltd.

Webb, W.B. (Ed.) (1982b). *Biological rhythms, sleep, and performance*. Chichester: John Wiley & Sons Ltd.

Wechsler, D. (1958). *Measurement of adult intelligence*. Baltimore, MD: Williams & Wilkins.

Weinberg, R.S. (1978). The effects of success and failure on the patterning of neuromuscular energy. *Journal of Motor Behavior, 8*, 219–224.

Weiner, B. (1985). An attributional theory of achievement motivation and emotion. *Psychological Review, 92,* 548–573.

Weiner, B. (1992). *Human motivation: Metaphors, theories, and research.* Newbury Park, CA: Sage.

Weiner, B., & Schneider, K. (1971). Drive versus cognitive theory: A reply to Boor and Harmon. *Journal of Personality and Social Psychology, 18,* 258–262.

Weinman, J. (1987). Non-cognitive determinants of perceptual problem-solving strategies. *Personality and Individual Differences, 8,* 53–58.

Welford, A.T. (1952). The "psychological refractory period" and the timing of high-speed performance—a review and a theory. *British Journal of Psychology, 43,* 2–19.

Welford, A.T. (1958). *Ageing and human skill.* London: Oxford University Press.

Welford, A.T. (1968). *Fundamentals of skill.* London: Methuen.

Welford, A.T. (1976). *Skilled performance: Perception and motor skills.* Scott Foresman.

Welford, A.T. (1977). Motor performance. In J.E. Birren & K.W. Schaie (Eds.), *Handbook of the psychology of aging.* New York: Van Nostrand Reinhold.

Welford, A.T. (1980). The single-channel hypothesis. In A.T. Welford (Ed.), *Reaction times.* London: Academic Press.

Welford, A.T. (1985). Changes of performance with age: An overview. In N. Charness (Ed.), *Aging and human performance.* Chichester: John Wiley & Sons Ltd.

Welford, A.T., Brown, R.A., & Gabb, J.E. (1950). Two experiments on fatigue as affecting skilled performance in civilian aircrew. *British Journal of Psychology, 40,* 195–211.

Wells, A., & Matthews, G. (1994). *Attention and emotion: A clinical perspective.* Hove, UK: Lawrence Erlbaum Associates Ltd.

Wesnes, K., & Parrott, A.C. (1992). Smoking, nicotine and human performance. In A.P. Smith & D.M. Jones (Eds.), *Handbook of human performance. Vol. 2: Health and performance.* London: Academic Press.

Wesnes, K., & Revell, A. (1984). The separate and combined effects of scopolamine and nicotine on human information processing. *Psychopharmacology, 84,* 5–11.

Wesnes, K., & Warburton, D.M. (1983). Nicotine, smoking and human performance. *Pharmacology and Therapeutics, 21,* 189–208.

Wesnes, K., Warburton, D.M., & Matz, B. (1983). Effects of nicotine on stimulus sensitivity and response bias in a visual vigilance task. *Neuropsychobiology, 9,* 41–44.

West, R.L. (1988). Prospective memory and aging. In M.M. Gruneberg, P.E. Morris & R.N. Sykes (Eds.), *Practical aspects of memory: Current research and issues, Vol. 2.* Chichester: John Wiley & Sons Ltd.

West, R.L. (1996). An application of prefrontal cortex function theory to cognitive aging. *Psychological Bulletin, 120,* 272–292.

West, R., French, D., Kemp, R., & Elander, J. (1993). Direct observation of driving, self-reports of driver behaviour, and accident involvement. *Ergonomics, 36,* 557–567.

Westerman, S.J., Davies, D.R., Glendon, A.I., Stammers, R.B., & Matthews, G. (1998). Ageing and word processing competence: Compensation or compilation? *British Journal of Psychology, 89,* 579–597.

Weston, H.C., & Adams, S. (1932). *The effects of noise on the performance of weavers. Medical Research Council Industrial Health Research Board Report, No. 65.* London: HMSO.

Weston, H.C., & Adams, S. (1935). *The performance of weavers under varying conditions of noise. Medical Research Council Industrial Health Research Board Report, No. 70.* London: HMSO.

Wever, E.G. (1949). *Theory of hearing.* New York: Wiley.

Wever, R.A. (1979). *The circadian system of man: Results of experiments under temporal isolation.* New York: Springer.

Wever, R.A. (1985). Man in temporal isolation: Basic principles of the circadian system. In S. Folkard & T. Monk (Eds.), *Hours of work: Temporal factors in work scheduling.* London: John Wiley & Sons Ltd.

White, D.A., Taylor, M.J., Butters, N., Mack, C., Salmon, D.P., Peavy, G., Ryan, L., Heaton, R.K., Atkinson, J.H., Chandler, J.L., Grant, I., Kelly, M., Wallace, M.R., McCutchan, J.A., Spector, S.A., Thal, L., Hesselink, J., Jernigan, T., Masliah, E., Wiley, C.A., Abramson, I., Dupont, R., Patterson, T., Zisook, S., Jeste, D., Sieburg, H., & Weinrich, J.D. (1997). Memory for verbal information in individuals with HIV-associated dementia complex. *Journal of Clinical and Experimental Neuropsychology, 19,* 357–366.

White, J.M. (1994). Behavioral effects of caffeine coadministered with nicotine, benzodiazepines and alcohol. *Pharmacopsychoecologia, 7,* 119–126.

White, R.W. (1959). Motivation reconsidered: The concept of competence. *Psychological Review, 66,* 297–333.

Wickens, C.D. (1980). The structure of attentional resources. In R. Nickerson (Ed.), *Attention and performance VIII*. Hillsdale, NJ: Lawrence Erlbaum Associates Inc.

Wickens, C.D. (1984a). *Engineering psychology and human performance*. New York: Harper Collins.

Wickens, C.D. (1984b). Processing resources in attention. In R. Parasuraman & D.R. Davies (Eds.), *Varieties of attention*. San Diego, CA: Academic Press.

Wickens, C.D. (1991). Processing resources and attention. In D.L. Damos (Ed.), *Multiple-task performance*. London: Taylor & Francis.

Wickens, C.D. (1992). *Engineering psychology and human performance (2nd. ed.)*. New York: Harper Collins.

Wickens, C.D., & Flach, J.M. (1988). Information processing. In E.L. Wiener & D.C. Nagel (Eds.), *Human factors in aviation*. San Diego, CA: Academic Press.

Wickens, C.D., & Liu, Y. (1988). Codes and modalities in multiple resources: A success and a qualification. *Human Factors, 30*, 599–616.

Wiegmann, D., & Shappell, S. (1997). Human factors analysis of postaccident data: Applying theoretical taxonomies of human error. *International Journal of Aviation Psychology, 7*, 67–81.

Wiener, E.L. (1985). Beyond the sterile cockpit. *Human Factors, 27*, 75–90.

Wiener, E.L. (1989). *Human factors of advanced technology ("glass cockpit") transport aircraft (Rep. 177528)*. Moffett Field, CA: NASA Ames Research Center.

Wiener, E.L., & Curry, R.E. (1980). Flight-deck automation. Promises and problems. *Ergonomics, 23*, 995–1011.

Wilding, J.M., & Mohindra, N. (1980). Effects of subvocal suppression, articulating aloud and noise on sequence recall. *British Journal of Psychology, 71*, 247–261.

Wilding, J.M., Mohindra, N., & Breen-Lewis, K. (1982). Noise effects in free recall with different orienting tasks. *British Journal of Psychology, 73*, 479–486.

Wilkins, A.J. (1995). *Visual stress*. Oxford: Oxford University Press.

Wilkinson, R.T. (1960). The effect of lack of sleep on visual watchkeeping. *Quarterly Journal of Experimental Psychology, 12*, 36–40.

Wilkinson, R.T. (1961). Comparison of paced, unpaced, irregular and continuous displays in watchkeeping. *Ergonomics, 4*, 259–267.

Wilkinson, R.T. (1962). Muscle tension during mental work under sleep deprivation. *Journal of Experimental Psychology, 64*, 565–571.

Wilkinson, R.T. (1963). Interaction of noise with knowledge of results and sleep deprivation. *Journal of Experimental Psychology, 66*, 332–337.

Wilkinson, R.T. (1964). Effects of up to 60 hours sleep deprivation on different types of work. *Ergonomics, 7*, 175–186.

Wilkinson, R.T., Edwards, R.S., & Haines, E. (1966). Performance following a night of reduced sleep. *Psychonomic Science, 5*, 471–472.

Wilkinson, R.T., Fox, R.H., Goldsmith, R., Hampton, I.F.G., & Lewis, H.E. (1964). Psychological and physiological responses to raised body temperature. *Journal of Applied Psychology, 19*, 287–291.

Wilkinson, R.T., Morlock, H.C., & Williams, H.L. (1966). Evoked cortical response during vigilance. *Psychonomic Science, 4*, 221–222.

Williams, H.L., Lubin, A., & Goodnow, J.J. (1959). Impaired performance with acute sleep loss. *Psychological Monographs, 73* (14, Whole No. 484).

Williams, J.M.G., Watts, F.N., MacLeod, C., & Mathews, A. (1988). *Cognitive psychology and emotional disorders*. Chichester: John Wiley & Sons Ltd.

Williamson, A.M., & Feyer, A.-M. (1990). Behavioural epidemiology as a tool for accident research. *Journal of Occupational Accidents, 12*, 207–222.

Williges, R.C. (1969). Within session criterion changes compared to an ideal observer criterion in a visual monitoring task. *Journal of Experimental Psychology, 81*, 61–66.

Williges, R.C. (1973). Manipulating the response criterion in visual monitoring. *Human Factors, 15*, 179–185.

Willis, S.L. (1989). Improvement with cognitive training: Which old dogs learn what tricks? In L.W. Poon, D.C. Rubin & B.A. Wilson (Eds.), *Everyday cognition in adulthood and late life*. Cambridge: Cambridge University Press.

Wilson, J.R., & Rutherford, A. (1989). Mental models: Theory and application in human factors. *Human Factors, 31*, 617–634.

Wine, J.D. (1982). Evaluation anxiety: A cognitive-attentional construct. In H.W. Krohne & L. Laux (Eds.), *Achievement, stress and anxiety*. Washington, DC: Hemisphere.

Winstein, C.J., & Schmidt, R.A. (1989). Sensorimotor feedback. In D. Holding (Ed.), *Human skills (2nd ed.)*. Chichester: Wiley.

Winton, W.M. (1990). Jamesian aspects of misattribution research. *Personality and Social Psychology Bulletin, 16*, 652–664.

Wirthlin Worldwide (1999). Americans on the job. Part 2: Rebuilding the employer/employee relationship.

*The Wirthlin Report, 9,* 1–4. McLean, VA: Wirthlin Worldwide.

Woldorff, M.G., Hansen, J.C., & Hillyard, S.A. (1987). Evidence for effects of selective attention to the midlatency range of the human auditory event related potential. In R. Johnson, J.W. Rohrbaugh & R. Parasuraman (Eds.), *Current trends in event-related brain potential research.* London: Elsevier.

Woldorff, M.G. & Hillyard, S.A. (1991). Modulation of early auditory processing during selective listening to rapidly presented tones. *Electroencephalography and Clinical Neurophysiology, 79,* 170–191.

Wolfe, J.M. (1994). Guided search 2.0: A revised model of visual search. *Psychonomic Bulletin and Review, 1,* 202–238.

Wolfe, J.M. (1998). Visual search. In H. Pashler (Ed.), *Attention.* Hove, UK: Psychology Press.

Woltz, Dan, J. (1999). Individual differences in priming: The roles of implicit facilitation from prior processing. In P.L. Ackerman, P.C. Kyllonen & R.D. Roberts (Eds.), *Learning and individual differences: Process, trait, and content determinants.* Washington, DC: American Psychological Association.

Wood, N.L., & Cowan, N. (1995). The cocktail-party phenomenon revisited: Attention and memory in the classic selective listening procedure of Cherry (1953). *Journal of Experimental Psychology: General, 124,* 243–262.

Woodrow, H. (1946). The ability to learn. *Psychological Review, 53,* 147–158.

Woods, D.D. (1984). Visual momentum: A concept to improve the cognitive coupling of person and computer. *International Journal of Man-Machine Studies, 21,* 229–244.

Woodruff-Pak, D. (1985). Arousal, sleep, and aging. In J.E. Birren & K.W. Schaie (Eds.), *Handbook of the psychology of aging (2nd ed.).* New York: Van Nostrand Reinhold.

Woodruff-Pak, D. (1997). *The neuropsychology of aging.* Oxford: Blackwell.

Woods, S.C. (1991). The eating paradox: How we tolerate food. *Psychological Review, 98,* 488–505.

Wright, R.D. (Ed.) (1998). *Visual attention.* New York: Oxford University Press.

Wright, L.L., & Elias, J.W. (1979). Age differences in the effects of perceptual noise. *Journal of Gerontology, 34,* 704–708.

Wyatt, S., & Langdon, J.N. (1932). Inspection processes in industry. *Medical Research Council Industrial Health Research Board Report, No. 63.* London: HMSO.

Wyon, D.P. (1970). Studies of children under imposed noise and heat stress. *Ergonomics, 13,* 598–612.

Wyon, D.P., Wyon, I., & Norin, F. (1996). Effects of moderate heat stress on driver vigilance in a moving vehicle. *Ergonomics, 39,* 61–75.

Yantis, S. (1998). Control of visual attention. In H. Pashler (Ed.), *Attention.* Hove, UK: Psychology Press.

Yantis, S., & Jonides, J. (1990). Abrupt visual onsets and selective attention: Voluntary versus automatic allocation. *Journal of Experimental Psychology: Human Perception and Performance, 16,* 121–134.

Yee, L.P., Laden, B., & Hunt, E. (1994). The coordination of compensatory tracking and anticipatory timing tasks. *Intelligence, 18,* 259–287.

Yeh, Y., & Wickens, C.D. (1988). Dissociation of performance and subjective measures of workload. *Human Factors, 30,* 111–120.

Yerkes, R.M., and Dodson, J.D. (1908). The relation of strength of stimulus to rapidity of habit-formation. *Journal of Comparative Neurology and Psychology, 18,* 459–482.

Ylikoski, R., Ylikoski, A., Erkinjuntti, T., Sulkava, R., Raininko, R., & Tilvis, R. (1993). White matter changes in healthy elderly persons correlate with attention and speed of mental processing. *Archives of Neurology, 50,* 818–824.

Yorks, L., & Whitsett, D.A. (1985). Hawthorne, Topeka, and the issue of science versus advocacy in organizational behavior. *Academy of Management Review, 10,* 21–30.

Yoshitake, H. (1978). Three characteristic patterns of subjective fatigue symptoms. *Ergonomics, 21,* 231–233.

Young, J.A., & Pihl, R.O. (1982). Alcohol consumption and response in men social drinkers. *Journal of Studies on Alcohol, 43,* 334–351.

Zanone, P.G., & Kelso, J.A.S. (1992). Evolution of behavioral attractors with learning: Nonequilibrium phase transitions. *Journal of Experimental Psychology: Human Perception and Performance, 18,* 403–421.

Zeaman, D., & House, B.J. (1967). The relation of IQ and learning. In R.M. Gagné (Ed.), *Learning and individual differences.* Columbus, OH: Merrill.

Zeidner, M. (1998). *Test anxiety: The state of the art.* New York: Plenum Press.

Zeidner, M., & Matthews, G. (in press). Personality and intelligence. In R.J. Sternberg (Ed.), *Handbook of intelligence (2nd ed.).* Cambridge: Cambridge University Press.

Zuckerman, M. (1991). *Psychobiology of personality.* Cambridge: Cambridge University Press.

# Author index

# Subject index